The International Lesson Annual
1994–95
September–August

THE INTERNATIONAL LESSON ANNUAL

1994–95

September–August

A Comprehensive Commentary on
The International Sunday School Lessons
Uniform Series

Edited by
William H. Willimon
and
Patricia P. Willimon

Lesson Analysis by
GAYLE CARLTON FELTON
WILLIAM H. WILLIMON
PAT McGEACHY
DAVID NEIL MOSSER

ABINGDON PRESS
Nashville

THE INTERNATIONAL LESSON ANNUAL—1994–95

Copyright © 1994 by Abingdon Press

This book is printed on recycled acid-free paper.

ISBN 0-687-19158-0

Library of Congress ISSN 0074-6770

Unless otherwise noted, scripture quotations are from the New Revised Standard Version Bible, Copyright © 1989 by the Division of Christian Education of the National Council of the Churches of Christ in the USA. Used by permission. Those marked RSV are from the Revised Standard Version of the Bible, copyright © 1946, 1952, 1971 by the Division of Christian Education of the National Council of Churches of Christ in the USA. Used by permission. Those marked NEB are from *The New English Bible.* © The Delegates of the Oxford University Press and The Syndics of the Cambridge University Press 1961, 1970. Reprinted by permission. Those marked KJV are from the King James Version of the Bible.

"Spiritual Enrichment Article" on pp. 40-44 adapted from William H. Willimon, "Pastors as Teachers," from *Rethinking Christian Education,* edited by David S. Schuller, Copyright © 1993. Used by permission of Chalice Press.

"Spiritual Enrichment Article" on pp. 128-30, "The First Christmas Pageant," by William H. Willimon. Copyright © 1978 Christian Century Foundation. Reprinted by permission from the December 20, 1978, issue of *The Christian Century.*

"Spiritual Enrichment Article" on pp. 153-56 excerpted from *Shaped by the Bible* by William H. Willimon. Copyright © 1990 by Abingdon Press. Used by permission.

"Spiritual Enrichment Article" on pp. 308-12 reprinted from *Preaching from the Old Testament,* Elizabeth Achtemeier. Copyright © 1989 by Elizabeth Achtemeier. Used by permission of Westminster/John Knox Press.

94 95 96 97 98 99 00 01 02 03 — 10 9 8 7 6 5 4 3 2 1

MANUFACTURED IN THE UNITED STATES OF AMERICA

Editors' Preface

The Uniform Lessons began in Indianapolis in 1872 as an experiment in ecumenical Christian cooperation. The dream of the organizers was to institute a worldwide method of Bible study that could be shared by all churches. We are now well into the second century of this experiment. In many places over the face of the earth, certainly among the churches of North America, Christians are studying the International Lesson. With so many divisions among Christians, it is good that many of us can join hands in the careful study of the Bible.

Those who devised the Uniform Lessons in 1872 could not have imagined all the changes that have taken place in our world since then. Yet, surely they would have believed, despite the world's changes, that the Bible would continue to speak to the world. Sometimes the Bible is spoken of as God's unchanging word. True, the Bible's message is eternal. Yet, through the inspiration and enlivening of the Holy Spirit, the message of the Bible is still capable of speaking to us in our day throughout all the changes of time and circumstance.

Through close, detailed, applied study of small portions of scripture, the International Lesson offers adult Christians the opportunity to listen to the biblical text in all of its particularity and promise. During this year's lessons, we will have the opportunity to listen to the testimony of people of faith as ancient as those of Joshua and Judges, as well as more recent writings such as Matthew's Gospel. The promise is that, if we will conscientiously listen to their message, we shall receive a lively word for our lives today.

A teacher wrote to us telling us that, although she was well over sixty, she taught a class of young adults in their twenties. The class was formed of young adults who had no church background and knew very little about scripture, but who wanted to learn more. Most of them had come to the church after their teenage years, looking for direction and purpose in their lives. At their request, she agreed to lead them in a study of the International Lesson, using the *Annual* as their guide. She wrote to us, telling us how this had been a spiritually enriching experience, not only for them, but also for her. We wish her well during their study in 1994–95.

We also wish you well. Through your work with the material in *The International Lesson Annual*, you are opening up the riches of the Bible for a new generation of Christians, continuing a century-long tradition of Bible study. Have a good year.

William H. Willimon and Patricia P. Willimon,
Editors

Contents

FIRST QUARTER

From the Conquest to the Kingdom

UNIT I: THE CONQUEST OF THE LAND
(September 4–25)

LESSON   PAGE

Introduction 11

1.   Spying Out Jericho 11
     September 4—*Joshua 1–2*

2.   Acting on Faith 19
     September 11—*Joshua 3–4*

3.   Winning the Battle 26
     September 18—*Joshua 6*

4.   Choosing to Serve God 33
     September 25—*Joshua 24*

     Spiritual Enrichment Article: Why Your Adult Class Is Important
     William H. Willimon 40

UNIT II: THE RULE OF THE JUDGES
(October 2–9)

Introduction 45

5.   Israel's Tragic Pattern of Life 45
     October 2—*Judges 2:6–3:6*

6.   Deliverance by God's Hand 52
     October 9—*Judges 6:1–8:21*

UNIT III: THE BEGINNING OF THE KINGDOM
(October 16–30)

Introduction 60

7.   Israel Demands a King 60
     October 16—*1 Samuel 7:15–8:22; 12:19-25*

8.   Saul's Opportunity as King 68
     October 23—*1 Samuel 9:15–10:1a, 20-24*

9.   King Saul Disobeys God 75
     October 30—*1 Samuel 13*

UNIT IV: THE KINGDOM UNDER DAVID AND SOLOMON
(November 6–27)

Introduction 82

10.   David Claims God's Promise 83
     November 6—*2 Samuel 7*

11.   David Sins Against God 90
     November 13—*2 Samuel 11:1–12:19*

12.   Solomon's Glorious Reign 97
     November 20—*1 Kings 9:1-9; 10:1-24*

13.   Solomon Turns from God 105
     November 27—*1 Kings 11*

SECOND QUARTER

Jesus the Fulfillment

UNIT I: JESUS AND JOHN: SETTING THE SCENE
(December 4–11)

LESSON   PAGE

Introduction 113
1.   Prepare for a New Life 113
           December 4—*Matthew 3*
2.   Hold On to Your Faith 121
           December 11—*Matthew 11:2-15*
     Spiritual Enrichment Article: The First Christmas Pageant
     William H. Willimon 128

UNIT II: EMMANUEL: GOD WITH US
(December 18–25)

Introduction 131
3.   Jesus Is Born..131
           December 18—*Matthew 1*
4.   God's Great Gift..139
           December 25—*Matthew 2*

UNIT III: JESUS, THE SON OF DAVID
(January 1–29)

Introduction 146
5.   Deliverance and Forgiveness 146
           January 1—*Matthew 8:1–9:8*
     Spiritual Enrichment Article: The Bible as the Church's Book
     William H. Willimon 153
6.   A Leader Who Serves 156
           January 8—*Matthew 12*
7.   Persistent Faith 163
           January 15—*Matthew 15:1-31*
8.   Challenged to Hear 170
           January 22—*Matthew 17:1-23*
9.   Welcome the Savior..178
           January 29—*Matthew 20:17–21:17*

UNIT IV: JESUS CHRIST: VICTOR OVER SIN AND DEATH
(February 5–26)

Introduction 185
10.   Celebrating the Covenant...185
           February 5—*Matthew 26:17-35*
11.   Experiencing Rejection...192
           February 12—*Matthew 26:36-68*
12.   Suffering for Others 199
           February 19—*Matthew 27:1-61*
13.   Follow the Leader...206
           February 26—*Matthew 27:62–28:20*

Christian Living in Community

UNIT I: RESPONDING TO CHALLENGES OF LIFE IN COMMUNITY
(March 5–26)

LESSON   PAGE

Introduction 214

1. Speaking Spiritual Truth...215
   March 5—*1 Corinthians 1:18–2:16*

2. Faithfulness in Difficult Times...222
   March 12—*1 Corinthians 4:1-2, 6-16*

3. Resisting Temptation 229
   March 19—*1 Corinthians 10:1-17*

4. Dealing with Differences...236
   March 26—*2 Corinthians 12–13*

UNIT II: NURTURING THE LIFE OF THE COMMUNITY
(April 2–23)

Introduction 244

5. Building Up the Body 244
   April 2—*1 Corinthians 12*

6. Growing Through Worship 252
   April 9—*1 Corinthians 14:1-33a*

7. Becoming a Resurrection People...259
   April 16—*Luke 24:1-11; 1 Corinthians 15*

8. Exercising Christian Freedom 265
   April 23—*1 Corinthians 8*

UNIT III: MINISTERING AS A CHRISTIAN COMMUNITY
(April 30–May 28)

Introduction 272

9. Sharing One Another's Pain..272
   April 30—*2 Corinthians 1:1-14*

10. Committed to Serve..279
    May 7—*1 Corinthians 9*

11. Motivated by Christ's Love...287
    May 14—*2 Corinthians 5*

12. Ministry Through Giving 293
    May 21—*2 Corinthians 8–9*

13. Serving with Love 301
    May 28—*1 Corinthians 13*

Spiritual Enrichment Article: Why the Old Testament Is Necessary
for the Church
Elizabeth Achtemeier..308

A Nation Turns to God

UNIT I: THE PRICE OF POWER
(June 4–25)

LESSON		PAGE
	Introduction	313
1.	When Power Is Misused	314
	June 4—*1 Kings 11:26–12:24*	
2.	Whom Will You Follow?	321
	June 11—*1 Kings 18:30-39*	
3.	Justice Corrupted	328
	June 18—*1 Kings 21:1-4, 15-20*	
4.	Sharing the Good News	335
	June 25—*2 Kings 7:1-9*	

UNIT II: THE APPROACHING JUDGMENT
(July 2–30)

	Introduction	343
5.	Condemning for National Wrongs	344
	July 2—*Amos 2:4-8; 3:1-2*	
6.	Working for Justice and Righteousness	351
	July 9—*Amos 4:4-5; 5:18-24*	
7.	Demonstrating Undeserved Love	358
	July 16—*Hosea 1:2-9; 3:1-5*	
8.	Experiencing Undeserved Love	366
	July 23—*Hosea 11:1-9*	
9.	Beware of Greed	373
	July 30—*Micah 3:5-12*	

UNIT III: THE JUDGMENT ARRIVES
(August 6–27)

	Introduction	380
10.	Responding to God's Call	381
	August 6—*Isaiah 6:1-8; 1:14-17*	
11.	Only God Can Protect	389
	August 13—*Isaiah 7:2-6, 10-17*	
12.	Fair Warning	396
	August 20—*Isaiah 5:8-12, 18-23*	
13.	Disobedience Brings Destruction	403
	August 27—*2 Kings 17:6-14*	

FIRST QUARTER

FROM THE CONQUEST TO THE KINGDOM

Gayle Carlton Felton

UNIT I: THE CONQUEST OF THE LAND

FOUR LESSONS   SEPTEMBER 4–25

The lessons for this quarter of study focus on selected passages from the Old Testament books of Joshua, Judges, 1 and 2 Samuel, and 1 Kings. They provide an overview of the important period in the history of Israel from the conquest and settlement of the promised land of Canaan through the reign of Israel's third king, Solomon.

Unit I picks up the historical account after the death of Moses, who had led the Israelites out of slavery in Egypt and through the decades of wilderness wandering. Israel is encamped just across the Jordan River from the land of promise. In Lesson 1, Joshua, Moses' successor, sends spies into Jericho to gather information to be utilized in the invasion. Through the help of the prostitute Rahab, their mission is successful. The last barrier to the land, the Jordan River, is crossed in Lesson 2 by the miraculous intervention of God. In Lesson 3, the first great victory is won in the capture of the city of Jericho. The faith in God's power that the people display here will lead them on to further victories. At the end of the book, the conquest of the land is largely completed. The final lesson of the series looks at the highly significant event of covenant-making, which occurred at Shechem. Israel constituted itself as a tribal confederacy that would be a covenant community under the kingship of Yahweh.

The emphasis throughout the unit is on the mighty acts of God in Israel's history that were the basis of the covenant. The people are called to respond to these actions, to live in faithful obedience to God.

LESSON 1   SEPTEMBER 4

Spying Out Jericho

Background Scripture: Joshua 1–2

The Main Question

The story is told of a man who prayed to God that he might be enabled to win a lottery so as to use the proceeds to provide for the needs of his family. He petitioned God frequently and ardently in this cause. Finally, God spoke to him saying, "Charlie, if you want to win the lottery so badly, at least go out

11

and buy a ticket!" Whatever we might think of the ethical question of lotteries, the point of this story is clear. If we want and expect God to do things for us, there may be certain decisions, actions, and preparations that we must undertake on our own behalf. It is not so much that God denies us those blessings that we seek until we act; it is rather that we must position ourselves in such a way as to be ready and able to receive from God.

The scripture story that is the focus of today's lesson offers examples of this truth. God had long promised possession of the land of Canaan to the Israelites. After the death of Moses, God told Joshua, the new leader, that the time for taking the land had finally come. But rather than thoughtlessly presume on the promises of God, Joshua made careful preparations. He sent two spies into the land to bring back information on which his plans would be based. These spies were able to accomplish their mission through the help of Rahab, a woman of Canaan who recognized and sided with the cause of God and God's people. Rahab is identified as a prostitute—a person whose lifestyle raises grave moral problems for us. Yet, she is the heroine of this story—one through whom God works.

What can we learn from this dramatic historical episode about how God acts, about how God evaluates people, about what God expects of us?

Selected Scripture

King James Version

New Revised Standard Version

Joshua 2:1, 8-14, 22-24

1 And Joshua the son of Nun sent out of Shittim two men to spy secretly, saying, Go view the land, even Jericho. And they went, and came into an harlot's house, named Rahab, and lodged there.

8 And before they were laid down, she came up unto them upon the roof;

9 And she said unto the men, I know that the LORD hath given you the land, and that your terror is fallen upon us, and that all the inhabitants of the land faint because of you.

10 For we have heard how the LORD dried up the water of the Red sea for you, when ye came out of Egypt; and what ye did unto the two kings of the Amorites, that *were* on the other side Jordan, Sihon and Og, whom ye utterly destroyed.

11 And as soon as we had heard *these things,* our hearts did melt, neither did there remain any more courage in any man, because of you: for the LORD your God, he *is* God in

Joshua 2:1, 8-14, 22-24

1 Then Joshua son of Nun sent two men secretly from Shittim as spies, saying, "Go view the land, especially Jericho." So they went, and entered the house of a prostitute whose name was Rahab, and spent the night there.

8 Before they went to sleep, she came up to them on the roof 9 and said to the men: "I know that the LORD has given you the land, and that dread of you has fallen on us, and that all the inhabitants of the land melt in fear before you. 10 For we have heard how the LORD dried up the water of the Red Sea before you when you came out of Egypt, and what you did to the two kings of the Amorites that were beyond the Jordan, to Sihon and Og, whom you utterly destroyed. 11 As soon as we heard it, our hearts melted, and there was no courage left in any of us because of you. The LORD your God is indeed God in heaven above and on earth below. 12 Now then, since I have dealt kindly with you,

heaven above, and in earth beneath.

12 Now therefore, I pray you, swear unto me by the LORD, since I have shewed you kindness, that ye will also shew kindness unto my father's house, and give me a true token:

13 And *that* ye will save alive my father, and my mother, and my brethren, and my sisters, and all that they have, and deliver our lives from death.

14 And the men answered her, Our life for yours, if ye utter not this our business. And it shall be, when the LORD hath given us the land, that we will deal kindly and truly with thee.

....

22 And they went, and came unto the mountain, and abode there three days, until the pursuers were returned: and the pursuers sought *them* throughout all the way, but found *them* not.

23 So the two men returned, and descended from the mountain, and passed over, and came to Joshua the son of Nun, and told him all things that befell them:

24 And they said unto Joshua, Truly the LORD hath delivered into our hands all the land; for even all the inhabitants of the country do faint because of us.

Key Verse: **And they said unto Joshua, Truly the LORD hath delivered into our hands all the land; for even all the inhabitants of the country do faint because of us.**

swear to me by the LORD that you in turn will deal kindly with my family. Give me a sign of good faith 13 that you will spare my father and mother, my brothers and sisters, and all who belong to them, and deliver our lives from death." 14 The men said to her, "Our life for yours! If you do not tell this business of ours, then we will deal kindly and faithfully with you when the LORD gives us the land."

....

22 They departed and went into the hill country and stayed there three days, until the pursuers returned. The pursuers had searched all along the way and found nothing. 23 Then the two men came down again from the hill country. They crossed over, came to Joshua son of Nun, and told him all that had happened to them. 24 They said to Joshua, "Truly the LORD has given all the land into our hands; moreover all the inhabitants of the land melt in fear before us."

Key Verse: **They said to Joshua, "Truly the LORD has given all the land into our hands; moreover all the inhabitants of the land melt in fear before us."**

As You Read the Scripture

Joshua 2:1. After the death of Moses, God chose Joshua, who is here identified as the son of Nun, to be the new leader of the Hebrew people. Joshua's task was the formidable one of planning and carrying out the conquest of the land of Canaan, which God had promised to them. The Israelites were camping at Shittim on the eastern side of the Jordan River, which was the natural boundary of Canaan. Rather than attacking rashly, Joshua first sent two men to the city of Jericho as spies to gain information on which he could make his plans. The men spent the night in the house of Rahab, a prostitute in the city. Probably they chose that location because they hoped that the presence of strange men there would not attract attention.

Verse 8-9. Despite their precautions, the visit of the spies was reported to the ruler of the city who sent orders to Rahab to surrender them. Instead, she hid the men and tricked their pursuers into searching for them outside the city. After she had guaranteed their safety, Rahab explained to the spies that she was helping them because she knew that the Israelites were going to be victorious in the battle for the city. Indeed, great fear had come upon the people of Canaan because they realized that God had given the land to Israel.

Verses 10-11. The inhabitants of Jericho had heard the stories of God's powerful acts on behalf of God's chosen people—the miraculous opening of the waters of the Sea of Reeds when they were escaping from Egypt (Exod. 14) and the overwhelming victories over the Amorite kings who had tried to defeat them (Deut. 2:24–3:11). They were fearful and dismayed because they understood that the God of heaven and earth was on the side of the Israelites.

Verses 12-14. Rahab beseeched the spies to repay the favor that she had done for them. In return for her actions, which had protected their lives, she asked that she and her whole family might be spared when the Israelites conquered the city. The men agreed to this request on the condition that she not tell the city authorities anything about their visit.

Rahab's house was located on the wall of the city. Jericho was surrounded by double walls that were approximately twelve to fifteen feet apart. Her house would likely have been supported by timbers or walls of brick constructed across this gap. She let the spies down outside the wall by a rope through her window. They warned her to gather all of her family together at the time of the Israelite invasion and to allow none of them to leave the house. A red cord was to be tied in her window so as to identify the location and assure its protection from the attacking forces.

Verses 22-23. The spies left Jericho and, at Rahab's instruction, hid out in the rugged countryside for three days so as to be certain not to encounter those who were pursuing them. Then they crossed back over the river and returned to the Israelite camp to report to Joshua.

Verse 24. Their report was highly encouraging. Based on their conversation with Rahab, they were able to tell Joshua that the people of Canaan were already fear-struck at their approach. The certainty of Israelite success in winning the land that God had given them was known even by their enemies. They could proceed with great confidence.

The Scripture and the Main Question

The Historical Setting

As the book of Joshua opens, the Hebrew people were encamped just over the Jordan River anticipating entrance into the land of Canaan. The promise of this territory as their possession went all the way back to God's call of Abraham long centuries before (Gen. 12:1-3, 15:18-20). The promise had been repeated to Abraham and Sarah's son, Isaac (Gen. 26:2-5), and to Isaac and Rebecca's son, Jacob (Gen. 28:13-15). But after living in the land as nomads for some decades, the Hebrews had been forced by famine to leave it. They had migrated to Egypt where they had been enslaved. After centuries of oppression, God had again acted to free them and allow them to return home (Exod. 3:1-8). Under the leadership of Moses, they escaped from Egypt and journeyed toward the land to repossess it. At Mount Sinai, God entered into a covenant with them, promising to be their God and making clear the divine expectations for them as a people (Exod. 19–20:17, 34:10-11). Lacking the strength of faith needed to fight for their land at this time, the Hebrews endured forty difficult years in the desert wilderness. Moses led them, interceded with God for them, and taught them to better understand the demands of the covenant—how to live as God's chosen people. When Moses died, they were at the borders of Canaan and ready, under the leadership of Moses' successor, Joshua, to fight to claim the homeland that God had given to them.

Even this very abbreviated review of Old Testament history reminds us that the timetable of God may be very different from our own. The writer of 2 Peter expressed his understanding of this truth in 3:8a: "With the Lord one day is like a thousand years, and a thousand years are like one day." Often in our own lives, we yearn for the fulfillment of the divine promises and are frustrated and confused by their delay. God's dealings with the Hebrew people assure us that God is the Lord of history, the keeper of the eternal timeclock, whose purposes will ultimately prevail. The German poet Friedrich von Logau reminds us, "Though the mills of God grind slowly, yet they grind exceeding small" (*Sinngedichte*, III, ii. 24; translated by H.W. Longfellow). In our lessons for this and the next several Sundays, we will witness the mills of God slowly grinding out possession of the land for the Hebrew people.

It is strikingly apparent from the very beginning of the account in Joshua that God is commanding the Israelites to act. They are not simply to wait on God or to sit on the sidelines and observe what divine power will accomplish on their behalf. They are to be active participants in the work of taking possession of the land; they will have to fight; they will have to be faithful: "Be strong and courageous; for you shall put this people in possession of the land that I swore to their ancestors to give them" (1:6). Plainly, Joshua does not presume on the promise of God to excuse himself or his people from exerting their best efforts. The sending out of the spies is an early indication that the plans for conquest will be made with care and executed with diligence according to the guidance that God provides.

The Deuteronomic Understanding of History

The book of Joshua is a portion of a great narrative of Hebrew history that begins with the book of Deuteronomy and continues through the books of Judges, Samuel, and Kings. One of the purposes of the writer or writers of this material was to try to explain the various calamities and defeats that befell Israel from time to time. If they were truly God's people, then why did they experience tragedies and loss? The Deuteronomist historian was convinced that the principle governing historical events was very clear: When the people were faithful to God they prospered and when they were disobedient they suffered. This understanding caused the writer sometimes to present an oversimplified, rather idealized view of what happened in the life of individuals and of the community. In our study of this material, we will need to remember that God chose to use imperfect human beings to record the story of the divine action in history. These humans, like all of us, were conditioned by their own limited understandings and prejudices.

An Unlikely Heroine

The focus of this lesson is on the character of Rahab, a most unlikely heroine. She was a Canaanite—one of the enemy people whom the Israelites had to drive out in order to claim their land, probably a worshipper of the pagan fertility gods. She was a woman—one of an inferior, oppressed group in the culture who were valued only as wives and mothers. She was a prostitute—one whose role in society was viewed with contempt, even though patronized by many with regularity.

It is possible that Rahab's real identity might not have been quite so degraded. The famous Jewish historian Josephus spoke of her as an innkeeper. Her reputation as a harlot could have come from the rather unsavory reputation of inns and taverns in that day. Perhaps the spies went to her establishment to overhear the kind of loose talk of current events that such a place might feature. Jewish rabbinic sources speak of Rahab as one of the four most beautiful women in the world, and cite her as the ancestress of eight prophets and of the prophetess Huldah. Even at best, however, Rahab was certainly not the person we might expect to emerge as God's instrument in this story. She was obviously a woman of independent spirit and autonomous means—sufficient in that society to make her moral standards suspect.

The character of Rahab forces us to consider how our ways of judging other persons may be in conflict with the divine criteria. God often employs those whom we might consider unworthy instruments and seems to evaluate them very differently than we might. As God warns the prophet Samuel, "The LORD does not see as mortals see; they look on the outward appearance, but the LORD looks on the heart" (1 Sam. 16:7*b*). Divine approbation of this unlikely heroine becomes even clearer when we look at the three references to Rahab in the New Testament. In the genealogy in Matthew 1, she is listed (v. 5) as the mother of Boaz—an ancestress of King David and of Jesus Christ. Her efforts in protecting the Israelite spies are cited by James as an example of justification through works (James 2:25) and by the writer of Hebrews as evidence of her faith (Heb. 11:31). Having heard of the mighty works of God, she believed and acted courageously on that faith as an instrument of God's saving purpose.

Helping Adults Become Involved

Preparing to Teach

Today's lesson is the beginning of a unit of four studies on the events recorded in the book of Joshua. It will be very important for you to have a clear understanding of how these accounts relate to the overall story of God's action in the history of the Hebrew people. Many study Bibles include articles that concisely survey these events. In Volume I of the widely used *The Interpreter's Bible* series is a helpful article by Theodore H. Robinson entitled "The History of Israel." This will probably be available in your church or your pastor's personal library. Although somewhat literalistic in his interpretations, John R.W. Stott does an excellent job of making biblical history clear in his book *Understanding the Bible.* Time spent consulting these resources will greatly enhance your comprehension of the historical story and your effectiveness in presenting it. In preparation for this lesson on Joshua, read the brief introduction to the book in a good study Bible, such as the *Oxford Annotated NRSV*.

Read the first two chapters of the book of Joshua. This material relates the story of the Israelites' preparations to enter the promised land at God's command and with God's aid. It is not difficult to follow and is the beginning of an exciting narrative. Pay special attention to the verses printed in the lesson, using the material in "As You Read the Scripture" for help. Have available an adequate supply of Bibles for each class member. You will be aided by the use of sheets of newsprint and markers. Consider preparing a dramatization of the role of Rahab. (See III. in "Developing the Lesson.")

The major emphases of the lesson can be developed as follows:

> I. From Abraham to Joshua
> II. Participation rather than presumption
> III. Rahab, a heroine of faith and works

Introducing the Main Question

The focus of this lesson is on the workings of God with and through human beings who act as instruments for carrying the divine purpose into effect. Use the story and thoughts in "The Main Question" to introduce this idea. Lead a brief discussion about the rather surprising truth that God chooses to operate through persons in spite of their limitations and weaknesses.

Developing the Lesson

I. From Abraham to Joshua

The first eleven chapters of the Bible deal with the story of creation and the origins of humanity. This material makes it clear that existence is the product of the deliberate act of a Creator God who wants to be in loving relationship with human creatures. But sadly, these chapters also record the story of how men and women turned away from God and, by their sinful disobedience, ruined the loving relationships—with God, with themselves, with each other, and with the natural world—that they had been created to enjoy. The rest of the Bible is the long account of God's untiring efforts to overcome the effects of sin and to save humanity from the brokenness and lostness that result from our own unfaithfulness. In the Old Testament, God's efforts are largely through the history of the Hebrew (or Israelite) people. In the New, God takes human form in the person of Jesus Christ whose life, death, and resurrection make human salvation possible.

In Genesis 12, God chooses Abraham to be, with his wife Sarah, the ancestor of a people who will serve as God's special instrument. The story of this people down through the centuries is salvation history for all humankind. A unique covenant relationship is established between God and the Hebrews. (The covenant pledges are often repeated, but Genesis 17 is a good description that you might use.) God's promise included the gift of a land as the possession of Abraham's descendants.

Refer to the material in "The Historical Setting" section. This information, plus what you have gained from your reading as suggested in "Preparing to Teach," will enable you to sketch the major events in the life of the Hebrew people from Abraham to Joshua. This will provide the essential background that your class will need to appreciate the significance of the happenings in this week's lesson and in all of the lessons that will follow in this quarter. Make an outline on sheets of newsprint of the most significant events and persons in this period of Hebrew history. It will be helpful to retain this outline, display it each Sunday, and add to it as the story unfolds through the quarter.

II. Preparation rather than presumption

It was necessary that God take the initiative of acting in history because human beings had become so deeply mired in sin as to be unable to save themselves. It is, however, very clear in the story of the Hebrew people that they were expected, even required, to respond actively to the divine initiative. Abraham, Isaac, Jacob, Joseph, and Moses were commanded by God to go to certain places and to undertake specific ventures. With the establishment of the covenant between Yahweh and the whole nation at Mount Sinai, the requirements for faithful living were made explicit. God's people were commanded to behave in conformity with God's will.

In the first two chapters of Joshua, we find the Hebrews again being called on by God to take action toward the fulfillment of the divine promises. They are not to be passive spectators, but assertive participants. Joshua responded to God's command by having the people prepare themselves to invade the land. He sent out spies to reconnoiter the city of Jericho so that they might gain knowledge of the strength of the opposition that they would face. Rahab, who protected these spies, is a salient example of one who recognizes the call of God, makes appropriate preparations, and responds courageously.

Lead your class in a brief discussion of how we are expected to do our part in working with God. Be sure that this does not encourage a "God helps those who help themselves" understanding. This saying is from Benjamin Franklin, not from the Bible. God helps all of us, otherwise we would be powerless to do anything good for ourselves or anyone else. God does, however, require us to do something in response.

III. Rahab, a heroine of faith and works

Use the material about Rahab in the section "An Unlikely Heroine" to introduce this remarkable woman. Her story can be very powerfully presented by using role playing or a dramatic monologue. You may want to enlist the assistance of class members in advance.

Helping Class Members Act

Ask members to identify this week at least one person whose life appears to them morally questionable, as did that of Rahab. Encourage them to think and pray about how God might value and use that person.

Planning for Next Sunday

Ask the class to think about the "rivers that they have crossed" in their lives and those that they still need to cross.

Acting on Faith

Background Scripture: Joshua 3–4

The Main Question

In the early days of the Roman Empire, Julius Caesar was ordered by the Senate to surrender command of the army with which he had conquered Gaul and to return to Rome. Caesar realized that to obey was not only to relinquish his hopes for leadership, but also to risk his very life. He paused on the bank of the Rubicon, a small river marking the boundary between Gaul and Italy. To cross the river with his army was to defy the Senate and to set off a struggle for control of the Roman government. Caesar had only one legion of troops with him; his rival Pompey had ten legions to deploy against him. Nevertheless, Caesar took the decisive step: He and his army crossed the Rubicon and launched the struggle that was to make him undisputed ruler in Rome. As he crossed the river he is reported to have said, "The die is cast!" There was no opportunity for vacillation or retreat. The expression "crossing the Rubicon" has entered the language as a metaphor for the taking of some risky and irrevocable action.

In our lesson for today, Joshua and the Israelite people stand at the bank of the River Jordan much as Caesar and his army stood at the Rubicon. To cross the river was to invade Canaanite territory and, hence, to commit themselves to the arduous struggle to gain control of the land. The outcome was uncertain; the risks, great; the action, irreversible once taken. But with faith in the promise of God and in obedience to the divine command, they take the momentous step of crossing the Jordan.

What are the rivers in our own lives as people of God that we are called to cross over through faith in God and in obedience to God's will?

Selected Scripture

King James Version	New Revised Standard Version
Joshua 3:7-17 7 And the LORD said unto Joshua, This day will I begin to magnify thee in the sight of all Israel, that they may know that, as I was with Moses, *so* I will be with thee. 8 And thou shalt command the priest that bear the ark of the covenant, saying, When ye are come to the brink of the water of Jordan, ye shall stand still in Jordan. 9 And Joshua said unto the children of Israel, Come hither, and hear the words of the LORD your God.	*Joshua 3:7-17* 7 The LORD said to Joshua, "This day I will begin to exalt you in the sight of all Israel, so that they may know that I will be with you as I was with Moses. 8 You are the one who shall command the priests who bear the ark of the covenant, 'When you come to the edge of the waters of the Jordan, you shall stand still in the Jordan.' " 9 Joshua then said to the Israelites, "Draw near and hear the words of the LORD your God." 10 Joshua said, "By this you shall know that among you is the living God

10 And Joshua said, Hereby ye shall know that the living God *is* among you, and *that* he will without fail drive out from before you the Canaanites, and the Hittites, and the Hivites, and the Perizzites, and the Girgashites, and the Amorites, and the Jebusites.

11 Behold, the ark of the covenant of the Lord of all the earth passeth over before you into Jordan.

12 Now therefore take you twelve men out of the tribes of Israel, out of every tribe a man.

13 And it shall come to pass, as soon as the soles of the feet of the priests that bear the ark of the LORD, the Lord of all the earth, shall rest in the waters of Jordan, *that* the waters of Jordan shall be cut off *from* the waters that come down from above; and they shall stand upon an heap.

14 And it came to pass, when the people removed from their tents, to pass over Jordan, and the priests bearing the ark of the covenant before the people;

15 And as they that bare the ark were come unto Jordan, and the feet of the priests that bare the ark were dipped in the brim of the water, (for Jordan overfloweth all his banks all the time of harvest,)

16 That the waters which came down from above stood *and* rose up upon an heap very far from the city Adam, that *is* beside Zaretan: and those that came down toward the sea of the plain, even the salt sea, failed, and were cut off: and the people passed over right against Jericho.

17 And the priests that bare the ark of the covenant of the LORD stood firm on dry ground in the midst of Jordan, and all the Israelites passed over on dry ground, until all the people were passed clean over Jordan.

who without fail will drive out from before you the Canaanites, Hittites, Hivites, Perizzites, Girgashites, Amorites, and Jebusites: 11 the ark of the covenant of the Lord of all the earth is going to pass before you into the Jordan. 12 So now select twelve men from the tribes of Israel, one from each tribe. 13 When the soles of the feet of the priests who bear the ark of the LORD, the Lord of all the earth, rest in the waters of the Jordan, the waters of the Jordan flowing from above shall be cut off; they shall stand in a single heap."

14 When the people set out from their tents to cross over the Jordan, the priests bearing the ark of the covenant were in front of the people. 15 Now the Jordan overflows all its banks throughout the time of harvest. So when those who bore the ark had come to the Jordan, and the feet of the priests bearing the ark were dipped in the edge of the water, 16 the waters flowing from above stood still, rising up in a single heap far off at Adam, the city that is beside Zarethan, while those flowing toward the sea of the Arabah, the Dead Sea, were wholly cut off. Then the people crossed over opposite Jericho. 17 While all Israel were crossing over on dry ground, the priests who bore the ark of the covenant of the LORD stood on dry ground in the middle of the Jordan, until the entire nation finished crossing over the Jordan.

Key Verse: **And the priests that bare the ark of the covenant of the LORD**

Key Verse: **While all Israel were crossing over on dry ground, the priests**

stood firm on dry ground in the
midst of Jordan, and all the
Israelites passed over on dry
ground, until all the people were
passed clean over Jordan.

who bore the ark of the covenant of
the LORD stood on dry ground in the
middle of the Jordan, until the
entire nation finished crossing over
the Jordan.

As You Read the Scripture

Joshua 3:7. God had chosen Joshua to be the successor to the great Moses
as leader of the Hebrew people. Accustomed for more than forty years to
depending on Moses, it must have been difficult for the people to transfer
their loyalty and confidence to another person. God will use the events of
the crossing of the Jordan to show the Hebrews that God was as surely leading them through Joshua as through Moses. Such acceptance of and trust in
Joshua was essential if they were to be successful in the battles to come.

Verse 8. Joshua was to instruct the priests to carry the ark of the covenant
into the edge of the waters of the river. This sacred symbol of Yahweh's presence with them had accompanied Israel through its years of wandering in
the desert wilderness. As the sanctified religious leaders of the community,
only the priests were able to transport it.

Verses 9-11. Joshua proclaimed to the people the divine promise to give
them the land. The ark of the covenant was the sign, and the crossing of the
river would be the evidence of God's action in their behalf. The listing of
seven different groups in Canaan makes clear the demographic diversity of
the population, no doubt a liability in time of attack. God is identified as the
Lord of both history and nature who will literally dispossess these peoples in
favor of the Israelites.

Verse 12. The number twelve always indicates the whole people of Israel,
understood as descendants of the twelve sons of Jacob.

Verse 13. Joshua announced to the people God's promise that as soon as the
priests with the ark stepped into the river, its waters would be stopped and "shall
stand in a single heap." This is the same expression as was used in the song of
Moses in Exodus 15:8 celebrating the miracle of the Sea of Reeds crossing. The
intention of the writer was to underline the similarity of the two events.

Verse 14. The Hebrew wording in this verse is literally "pulled up their
tent stakes." It is a clear reminder that these people had been living for
decades as desert nomads.

Verses 15-16. The Jordan River begins below sea level and drops sharply
as it flows southward. Indeed, its very name means "downcomer." The precise locations of the places mentioned are difficult to determine, but the
assumption is that this crossing would have occurred opposite Jericho, which
is about six miles north of the Dead Sea. At this point, the river would have
normally been approximately ninety to a hundred yards wide and quite ford-
able. The miracle is heightened by the writer's explanation that these events
occurred when the river was swollen to flood stage. It would likely have been
in late April as a result of a combination of seasonal rains and melting snow
in the mountains. Note that the flow of the river is said to have ceased
abruptly when the priests stepped into the water, that is, when they stepped
into the flooding part of the river that had escaped its usual channel.

Verse 17. The priests with the ark moved on to the middle of the riverbed
and stood there until the whole multitude of the people had crossed over on
the dry ground. Yahweh's promise through Joshua had been fulfilled.

The Scripture and the Main Question

Crossing Flooding Rivers

In spite of numerous repetitions in the text as the result of more than one account being brought together, the main events of the story related in chapters three and four are not difficult to follow. While their miraculous nature defies explanation, the happenings are themselves plain enough: God repeated the miracle of the crossing of the Sea of Reeds and provided the Israelites with safe passage through waters that blocked their way. They were enabled to cross over into the land that God had promised them. Forms of the expression "crossing over" are used more than twenty times in these two chapters. This event of crossing the Jordan River has become a metaphor for a variety of significant passages in human life, especially for the experience of death, through which we cross into a new promised land. Exploring the figurative meaning of various crossings of the rivers of life and death will give this lesson relevance in the personal experience of your class.

The Presence and Power of God

God's deliverance of the Hebrews from their centuries of enslavement in Egypt was effected through the dramatic miracle of the crossing of the Sea of Reeds (often erroneously referred to as the Red Sea). In this event, which is narrated in Exodus 14, God had temporarily held back the waters to create a path of dry ground over which the people were able to escape from the pursuing Egyptians. The Exodus under the leadership of Moses had been followed by a period of nomadic existence in the desert wilderness. In the scripture for today's lesson, a new act in the drama of salvation occurs with another miraculous crossing of a body of water, this time under the leadership of Joshua. In Joshua 4:23, the reference to the Sea of Reeds shows that these two events were closely related in the mind of the Hebrew historian. The Jordan River was the last barrier to the return of God's people to the land promised to them since Abraham.

Our modern scientific mindset causes us to seek for naturalistic explanations for these seemingly supernatural occurrences. The banks of the Jordan are composed in many places of soft limestone, subject to collapse in times of heavy rainfall and rushing currents. History records at least three instances—1267, 1906, and 1927—when the flow of the river was completely cut off by heavy landslides. Such facts neither diminish the divine role, nor explain the providential timing in the biblical accounts. Along with our Jewish brothers and sisters, Christians understand these events as part of God's action for human salvation through the history of the Hebrew people. There is nothing surprising about God the Creator using forces of the natural world as instruments of the divine purpose. The writer of Psalm 114 expressed it poetically by asking, "Why is it, O sea, that you flee? O Jordan, that you turn back?" (v. 5) and going on to answer, "Tremble, O earth, at the presence of the LORD, at the presence of the God of Jacob" (v. 7).

The presence and power of God with the Hebrew people are symbolized by the ark of the covenant, which the priests bore as they stepped into the Jordan's waters. The ark was a wooden chest that contained two stone tablets recording the Ten Commandments. Deuteronomy 10:1-5 says that it was

22

built by Moses at Yahweh's command. The ark had accompanied the people during the wilderness wanderings and was a sacred object of veneration viewed as the throne of God. There are some two hundred references to the ark in the Old Testament.

Authentic Leadership

As I write this lesson, the United States is engaged in the 1992 political campaigns. Radio and television commercials hawk candidates with extravagant praise and attack opponents with distorted charges. One hears much talk about credentials for leadership, but many citizens have become weary and cynical, casting their votes for candidates they perceive as the lesser of the evils. There is a pervasive opinion that we are suffering a crisis in leadership.

In the opening chapters of the book of Joshua, the Israelite people were experiencing a change in their leadership. God used the miraculous crossing of the Jordan River to validate dramatically the role of Joshua as the successor to Moses. Joshua understood himself as possessing authority based on his having been chosen by God and subject to his continuing to act in accord with God's command. We live in a very different situation, but are there things that we as contemporary Americans might learn from this about the kind of leaders that we need, and how they might be chosen?

Teaching the Faith

Many scholars believe that the account in Joshua 3 and 4 was used in an annual celebration on the anniversary of the crossing of the Jordan. The story was doubtless read aloud, and perhaps even reenacted, at the sanctuary at Gilgal, located close to the place where the crossing occurred. Such a celebration functioned as more than a remembrance of the great event, more even than a thanksgiving to God. It served, most importantly, as an opportunity to teach the story to those who were coming into the community either as children or as converts. Only by knowing the story of God's mighty acts in their history could persons be incorporated as authentic members of the community of faith. Each new generation must be enabled to make the story their own.

In the fourth chapter, we read about the erection of two monuments of stones taken from the riverbed. These memorials were to create what we might call teachable moments. They would cause curiosity, motivate the children to ask their meaning, and provide occasions for teaching the story anew. A similar function is described in Exodus 13 for the annual celebration of the Passover to commemorate the escape from Egypt through the sea (see v. 14). Ancient Israel took very seriously the responsibility for passing on the story of what Yahweh had done in their history and for nurturing persons in the faith.

One of the tragic weaknesses in many of our churches today is the failure to teach the story of the community of faith in such a way that persons understand who they are and how they are to live as a part of that community. Such teaching cannot be aimed only at children; all who seek to be people of God must be taught how God works in the lives of nations and individuals. To know how to live as God's people in the present requires an appreciation of what God has done in the past.

Helping Adults Become Involved

Preparing to Teach

Read chapters three and four of Joshua with care, recognizing how they relate to the material in last week's and next week's lessons. The crossing of the Jordan was the next step in the planned invasion of Canaan in preparation for which the spies had come to Rahab's house in Jericho. Having crossed the river into Canaan, the Israelites will go on to begin their conquest by the attack on Jericho. The account in these chapters is a bit confusing in places as a result of the blending of two or more accounts, but the flow of major events is not difficult to determine. Use the material in "As You Read the Scripture" to help you with the selected verses. Read Exodus 14 to remind yourself of the dramatic crossing of the Sea of Reeds in order to appreciate the relationship between these two stories.

You will need Bibles and hymnals for all students. For this and upcoming lessons, you will get great benefit from a series of Old Testament maps that can be displayed on an easel or on walls. If these are not available in your church, utilize the maps in study Bibles such as *The Oxford Annotated NRSV* (see map three). In addition to maps focusing on the specific locations being studied, a larger map of the world and/or of the Mediterranean area and Middle East will provide geographic orientation for your students. Take time to familiarize yourself with the maps in advance.

The lesson can be presented by developing these headings:

I. Significance of crossing the river
   A. Entry into Canaan
   B. Joshua as God's chosen leader
   C. Our personal river crossings
II. Remembering and teaching the story
   A. Knowing ourselves as God's people
   B. Living as God's people

Introducing the Main Question

Share with the class the incident of Julius Caesar's crossing the Rubicon, which is sketched in "The Main Question." Then relate briefly the events of the Israelites' crossing of the Jordan as recorded in these chapters. Encourage the class to think and to talk about significant passages in their own lives that might be likened to these decisive historical events—choices, changes, actions, commitments that determined their personal histories. Be ready to share such experiences in your own life to get the discussion flowing.

Developing the Lesson

I. Significance of crossing the river
A. Entry into Canaan

Utilize maps to illustrate how the Hebrew people had left Egypt, travelled through the desert wilderness and arrived on the east bank of the Jordan River, ready to cross over into Canaan in the area of Jericho. Material in "The Scripture and the Main Question," especially the portion entitled "The Presence and Power of God," will allow you to make clear why this action was so important in the unfolding drama of salvation history.

B. Joshua as God's chosen leader

Use the ideas in "Authentic Leadership" to stimulate the group to a conversation about the qualities of leaders and how they can be assessed. It is usually easy to get people to discuss politics, but take care that this does not become an exchange of criticisms of particular political parties or individuals. Guard against the tendency to equate our nation with biblical Israel. The United States of America is not the covenant people of God; that role belongs today to the Christian church. It is, however, legitimate and important that we wrestle with questions about how Christians assess and select the kind of leadership that our cities, states, and nation need. What qualities, commitments, and goals do we look for in the men and women who will lead our political communities?

C. Our personal river crossings

In the introductory portion of the lesson, you have guided the class in consideration of the pivotal experiences in their lives that can be understood as figurative crossings of rivers. Emphasize here the use of this metaphor to describe the experience of death. A good way to encourage thought and discussion is to utilize some of the many hymns that use this metaphor. Examples include "On Jordan's Stormy Banks I Stand," "Because He Lives" (stanza 3), and "Stand by Me" (stanza 5). Consult your church's hymnal for other examples. Help the class to realize that the enduring appeal of this metaphor is the assurance that the promised land lies across the river separating life and death.

II. Remembering and teaching the Story
A. Knowing ourselves as God's people

The ideas in "Teaching the Faith" can be developed here. The major point to convey is the necessity of incorporating persons into the community of God's people by teaching them the story of God's action for human salvation and how that history gives their own lives new meaning. Consider using material from Deuteronomy 6, which emphasizes the community's responsibility to transmit the story through the generations. This is an appropriate time to evaluate the educational program of your local church in terms of its effectiveness in teaching the story to persons of all ages.

B. Living as God's people

When we know what God has done for God's people in the past and understand ourselves as participants in that ongoing community, we are motivated to act in faith, trusting that the divine promises are real for us. It is significant that the waters of the Jordan did not stop until the priests had actually stepped into the flooding stream. We, too, face occasions in life when we must step out into the water, acting in faith, trusting that God—whose guidance we are seeking to follow—will provide us with secure footing. Have a discussion with the class about applications of this idea in their own lives.

Helping Class Members Act

One of the results to be sought from this lesson is that class members better understand themselves as participants in the great drama of human salvation, which God continues to play out in human history. Challenge them to think and pray earnestly about what it means to be a member of the community of faith and how that identity becomes determinative in the decisions and actions of their lives.

Planning for Next Sunday

Ask the class to read Joshua 6, trying to do so as if they had never heard the story before. What are some outstanding and surprising elements in the account?

LESSON 3   SEPTEMBER 18

Winning the Battle

Background Scripture: Joshua 6

The Main Question

Joshua fit de battle of Jericho, Jericho, Jericho;
Joshua fit de battle of Jericho, an de walls come tumblin' down.
You may talk about the man of Gideon,
You may talk about the man of Saul,
Dere's none like good ole Joshua, an' de battle of Jericho.
Up to the walls of Jericho, he marched with spear in han';
"Go blow dem ram horns," Joshua cried,
"for de battle am in my hand."

Perhaps the most familiar of the traditional Negro spirituals, this spirited song celebrates the famous victory of Joshua, the leader of God's people, over the Canaanite city of Jericho. According to the biblical record, this event occurred within months of the miraculous crossing of the Jordan River, which we discussed last Sunday. The Israelites were encamped at Gilgal, a location on the edge of the oasis of Jericho that would later became a religious sanctuary. Following Yahweh's command, they moved out from there to attack the city of Jericho and win a marvelous victory through quite unorthodox means.

The victory at Jericho was a stunning manifestation of the power of God to defeat enemies and to place victory in the hand of God's chosen. It challenges us to consider our frequent failure to appreciate and utilize the power of God that is available to demolish the walls and help us win our own battles in life. But there are troubling aspects to this account, which force us to reexamine our confident assumptions that we understand the will and ways of God and that they are synonymous with our own desires.

Selected Scripture

King James Version	New Revised Standard Version

Joshua 6:1-5, 15-20

1 Now Jericho was straitly shut up because of the children of Israel: none went out, and none came in.

2 And the LORD said unto Joshua, See, I have given into thine hand Jericho, and the king thereof, *and* the mighty men of valour.

3 And ye shall compass the city, all ye men of war, and go round about the city once. Thus shalt thou do six days.

4 And seven priests shall bear before the ark seven trumpets of rams' horns; and the seventh day ye shall compass the city seven times, and the priests shall blow with the trumpets.

5 And it shall come to pass, that when they make a long blast with the ram's horn, and when ye hear the sound of the trumpet, all the people shall shout with a great shout; and the wall of the city shall fall down flat, and the people shall ascend up every man straight before him.

....

15 And it came to pass on the seventh day, that they rose early about the dawning of the day, and compassed the city after the same manner seven times: only on that day they compassed the city seven times.

16 And it came to pass at the seventh time, when the priests blew with the trumpets, Joshua said unto the people, Shout; for the LORD hath given you the city.

17 And the city shall be accursed, *even* it, and all that *are* therein, to the LORD: only Rahab the harlot shall live, she and all that *are* with her in the house, because she hid the messengers that we sent.

18 And ye, in any wise keep *yourselves* from the accursed thing, lest ye make *yourselves* accursed, when ye

Joshua 6:1-5, 15-20

1 Now Jericho was shut up inside and out because of the Israelites; no one came out and no one went in. 2 The LORD said to Joshua, "See, I have handed Jericho over to you, along with its king and soldiers. 3 You shall march around the city, all the warriors circling the city once. Thus you shall do for six days, 4 with seven priests bearing seven trumpets of rams' horns before the ark. On the seventh day you shall march around the city seven times, the priests blowing the trumpets. 5 When they make a long blast with the ram's horn, as soon as you hear the sound of the trumpet, then all the people shall shout with a great shout; and the wall of the city will fall down flat, and all the people shall charge straight ahead."

....

15 On the seventh day they rose early, at dawn, and marched around the city in the same manner seven times. It was only on that day that they marched around the city seven times. 16 And at the seventh time, when the priests had blown the trumpets, Joshua said to the people, "Shout! For the LORD has given you the city. 17 The city and all that is in it shall be devoted to the LORD for destruction. Only Rahab the prostitute and all who are with her in her house shall live because she hid the messengers we sent. 18 As for you, keep away from the things devoted to destruction, so as not to covet and take any of the devoted things and make the camp of Israel an object for destruction, bringing trouble

take of the accursed thing, and make the camp of Israel a curse, and trouble it.

19 But all the silver, and gold, and vessels of brass and iron, *are* consecrated unto the LORD: they shall come into the treasury of the LORD.

20 So the people shouted when the priests blew with the trumpets: and it came to pass, when the people heard the sound of the trumpet, and the people shouted with a great shout, that the wall fell down flat, so that the people went up into the city, every man straight before him, and they took the city.

upon it. 19 But all silver and gold, and vessels of bronze and iron, are sacred to the LORD; they shall go into the treasury of the LORD." 20 So the people shouted, and the trumpets were blown. As soon as the people heard the sound of the trumpets, they raised a great shout, and the wall fell down flat; so the people charged straight ahead into the city and captured it.

Key Verse: **And it came to pass at the seventh time, when the priests blew with the trumpets, Joshua said unto the people, Shout; for the LORD hath given you the city.**

Key Verse: **And at the seventh time, when the priests had blown the trumpets, Joshua said to the people, "Shout! For the LORD has given you the city."**

As You Read the Scripture

Joshua 6:1. In the first lesson of this unit, Rahab had told the spies of the terror that her fellow citizens of Jericho were feeling as they watched the approach of the Israelites and saw God enabling them to triumph over their enemies. This verse indicates that the gates of the city were locked and no traffic in or out was being allowed. The Israelites would clearly not be able to surprise their foes.

Verse 2. Again, as in the earlier chapters of the book, God spoke to Joshua and assured him that the victory was already his as God's gift.

Verse 3-5. God gave explicit instructions as to how the conquest of the city was to be effected. An advance guard of warriors would precede the priests, who were to carry the ark of the covenant. They would be followed by a rear guard of soldiers and, assumedly, by the multitude of the men of Israel. The procession was to march around the city once a day on six consecutive days, with seven priests blowing the *shophar,* or rams' horns. Otherwise, the company was to remain silent. Then on the seventh day, the same procession was to march around the city seven times and conclude their march with a great shout from all the people, at which point the walls of Jericho would fall and the victory would be won. Seven was a sacred number, not only for the Hebrews, but also for other peoples of the day. The number occurs repeatedly in this account and heightens the sense of the supernatural. The ritual actions being described here must have had the effect of psychological warfare on the already frightened inhabitants of Jericho.

Verses 15-16. At Joshua's instruction, the people of Israel followed the strange plans for battle that the Lord had ordered. In commanding them to shout, Joshua reminded them that the victory was already theirs because God had given them the city.

Verses 17-19. All of the people of Jericho are to be slaughtered and all of its property destroyed as *cherem,* or "devoted to the Lord." Only Rahab and her family are to be spared in fulfillment of the pledge made to her by the spies whom she had protected and helped (see Josh. 2). Assumedly, the red cord in Rahab's window enabled the attackers to identify her house and rescue her household. The people of Israel are solemnly warned by God not to allow themselves to be tempted by any of the spoils of the battle lest they bring great trouble on Israel. (The terrible consequences of such disobedience are revealed in Joshua 7 in the account of the sin of Achan, which caused death and defeat in the battle to take the city of Ai.) The concept of *cherem* is not easy for modern Christians to grasp. It meant that all inhabitants and all possessions of a defeated city were to be "placed under the ban" and destroyed because they belonged to God rather than to the human victors. Objects made of metal that could not be burned were to be placed in the sacred treasury as the property of Yahweh.

Verse 20. The people of Israel obeyed the unusual commands that God gave for the conquest of the city. When the trumpets blew and they raised a great shout on the seventh march of the seventh day, the walls of Jericho fell down flat and the Israelites rushed into the defenseless city to claim their victory and to carry out the total destruction that God had ordered (see v. 21).

The Scripture and the Main Question

The account of the battle of Jericho is problematic for biblical scholars. Archaeological evidence uncovered by expeditions in the 1930s appeared to confirm the description of the collapse of the walls and destruction of the city by fire. Later excavations using more advanced methods have revealed a different situation. In the period when the Israelites under Joshua's command are believed to have moved into the area—during the early decades of the thirteenth century before Christ—the city of Jericho was apparently an uninhabited ruin. Certainly it was not a fortified city; it had been destroyed by unidentified enemies at least a century earlier. A variety of efforts have been made to explain these seeming contradictions. It is most likely that earlier tales of the dramatic destruction of the city, perhaps aided by the effects of an earthquake that leveled the walls, were employed by the authors of the biblical material to dramatize the story of victory and to magnify the role of Joshua. Since we are much more interested in the meaning of this account in salvation history than we are in historical or scientific specificities, we need not be troubled by these unresolved questions. We can focus on what the scripture is seeking to reveal to us about God and the divine dealings with humankind.

The land of Canaan had no central government, but was populated by a number of independent city-states. Each of these, through its own ruler, exercised control over the city itself and the surrounding agricultural area. These city-states were quite numerous in the fertile central area of the land; the hill country was much less organized. The book of Joshua relates a series of three military campaigns by which the Israelites took possession of the land. The description of these victories is overstated in the style of a dramatic storyteller. Other accounts in the same book, and especially in the book of Judges, make it clear that the Israelite victories were much less sweeping. Apparently, a foothold was established in the central hill country, but many Canaanite fortified cities in the fertile plain remained unconquered. The story of the continuing efforts to conquer the land will occupy the remainder of the book of Joshua, Judges, 1 and 2 Samuel, and 1 Kings.

Holy War and Utter Destruction

For most modern Christians it is not the archaeological evidence or the historical questions that are the most troubling aspect of this account of the battle of Jericho. Rather, we are appalled at the description here and elsewhere in the conquest narrative of wholesale slaughter of enemy populations at what the Israelites understood to be the command of Yahweh. Entire cities and peoples who were defeated by the Hebrews were "placed under the ban" or "devoted to God"—*cherem*—meaning that they were to be utterly destroyed. On one level, this action can be understood as a sacrifice to the victorious God of war; on another, it was a recognition that the battle had been won by divine might and the spoils belonged only to God. Further, the Canaanite people, and especially their religion, represented a dangerous threat to the Hebrews. They would be severely tempted by the fertility cults of Canaan (which we will discuss more in another lesson). Totally to destroy the Canaanite people was to strive to retain the purity and covenant faithfulness of Israel. The religious truth that we can glean from these accounts is that of God's awful judgment against the forces of evil. All that opposes the will of God must be exterminated; there can be no compromise with evil.

The realization of the seriousness of evil and the necessity of its obliteration before the holiness of God does not, however, enable us to accept these *cherem* passages without qualms and questions. How could the God who has revealed the divine self to us in the person of Jesus Christ ever command such merciless massacre? I believe that the answer is that God did not so command. As Christians, we believe that our most authentic insight into the nature and will of God comes through Jesus Christ; there is nothing in his life, death, and resurrection to make us believe that such slaughter would be pleasing to him. This raises difficult, but not impossible, questions of biblical interpretation. God chose to have the story of salvation history recorded by human writers who, like all of us, had their weaknesses and limitations. Every individual and every religious community in history has suffered from its own inability fully to comprehend the divine. Stories such as Joshua 3, which attribute cruel actions to the will of God, are the result of limited and erroneous human explanations.

The books of the Bible were written over a period of more than a thousand years by dozens of different authors. The various portions of the Bible record numerous efforts on the part of God to reveal what God is like and to teach how human beings are to live in accordance with the divine will. This process reaches its climax in Jesus Christ, but before it does, there were many mistaken ideas and wrong assumptions. The divine self-revelation was progressive—over the centuries humans learned and understood more and more about God. Therefore, every story in the Bible does not present an equally authentic picture of God and all of them must be evaluated by the unique knowledge of God given to us when God took flesh in the person of Jesus Christ.

God's Power Fulfills God's Promise

One of the salient teachings of all three of the lessons from Joshua that we have studied is that God has and uses the power to fulfill the promises that

God has made. The conquest of Canaan by the Israelites at God's direction was the actualization of the promise that had been made to Abraham centuries before and repeated to his descendants. Responses of faithful obedience on the part of the Hebrews were essential to their receiving the land. Through the experiences of the Exodus and during the wilderness wanderings, Moses had exhorted the people to believe that God could and would take them back to the land. Joshua urged them to obey the Lord's commands with full confidence that the promised victories would be given them by divine power. Even in the face of swollen rivers and fortified walls, they trusted and obeyed God.

Israel understood that they possessed the land only as the gift of Yahweh. Ultimately, it still belonged to Yahweh and their possession of it was contingent on their faithfulness in keeping the obligations of the covenant that had been revealed to them in the law given at Mount Sinai. The land belonged to God and so was holy; the people of God who possessed the land belonged to God and so must be holy as well.

Helping Adults Become Involved

Preparing to Teach

The story told in the scripture lesson for this week is a familiar one. The central problem of the lesson is not so much understanding the events that happened, as it is interpreting them for the modern student in ways that are faithful to the message of God. Try to locate and read some materials that will help you with the questions of interpreting difficult passages. Chapters 5–7 of John R. W. Stott's *Understanding the Bible* are useful, as is the introduction to James M. Efird's *The Old Testament Writings*. It is important that you be prepared to lead the class in consideration of questions about the divine nature and commands that will arise in the course of this lesson.

Read Joshua 6 with care and with the assistance of "As You Read the Scripture." Be certain that you can explain how this incident carries forward the story of God's action in Hebrew history.

Collect articles from newspapers and magazines that show examples of men and women doing things that they justify as being the will of God. Violence between ethnic or religious groups would be particularly instructive illustrations. Be prepared to analyze such actions and motivations.

The presentation of the lesson can follow this plan:

    I.   The capture of Jericho as an act in salvation history
   II.   Progressive revelation as a key to understanding the Bible
 III.   Questions for contemporary Christians

Introducing the Main Question

As an attention-grabbing device, open the lesson without preliminary comments by beginning to sing the spiritual "Joshua Fit the Battle of Jericho." Gesture to the class to join in, but be prepared to carry the song yourself through the less familiar lines. (If you are not comfortable singing alone in public, plan in advance with a class member to open this way.) Lead a brief discussion about the spiritual, exploring especially its meaning for slaves in the United States. The major point to establish here is that the song celebrates the power of God to win victory for God's people.

Developing the Lesson

I. The capture of Jericho as an act in salvation history

The use of the term *salvation history* affirms the belief that God is working out the divine plan of salvation for the world in and through the events of human history. This does not mean that everything that occurs does so at the command—or even with the approval—of God. Human beings have been created with freedom which we misuse; the sin that results causes much to happen in our personal and corporate lives that is not pleasing to God. Beyond the tragedy of human sinfulness is the greater reality of a loving God patiently working out the divine purpose. In the Old Testament period, God chose to do this largely through the life of the Hebrew community.

The capture of the city of Jericho, the first and to us the most famous of the Canaanite cities, is presented in our lesson for today as the indisputable sign that God was giving victory to the Hebrew people. The land that had been promised to them from the time of Abraham was now falling under their control as they fought in obedience to the divine commands. God was faithful and powerful; the promise was becoming reality.

Be sure that your students comprehend how the material of this lesson relates to the larger story of Hebrew history. Return to the outline on newsprint that you began in Lesson 1 and bring it up to date by adding the crossing of the Jordan and the conquest of the land. Review the information presented in Lessons 1 and 2 to make these connections. Use "God's Power Fulfills God's Promise" for other ideas.

II. Progressive revelation as a key to understanding the Bible

Use the material in "The Scripture and the Main Question," plus the insights that you have gained by your reading as suggested in "Preparing the Lesson," to lead a discussion on the difficulties of understanding some biblical material. Be sensitive to the fact that this is an emotion-charged issue with some persons, who may tend to jump to the conclusion that you are saying the Bible is wrong. Make clear your commitment to the authority of the Bible, but explain that for Christians, Jesus Christ is the highest authority. All else that the Bible contains must be assessed in the light of that revelation of God.

III. Questions for contemporary Christians

This section of the lesson can develop easily out of the previous one, since many of the questions that members raise will be related to the issue of biblical interpretation. Allow ample time for this important discussion, but do not feel that you must persuade everyone to share the same opinion. Good teaching always demands real respect for the sincere beliefs of other persons, even when those beliefs are quite different from our own. Good teaching also requires challenging our students with new ideas and stimulating possibilities.

Use the news articles that you have brought to encourage discussion about how easy it sometimes is to attribute our own desires to the guidance of God. This is especially true when we are engaged in conflict with other people, particularly people who differ from us. As I write this lesson, newspaper headlines are telling of horrible civil war in the southern European area that was formerly Yugoslavia. Warring ethnic groups appear to be engaged in deliberate efforts to annihilate each other, to achieve what some are calling ethnic cleansing. One is reminded of the efforts of Nazi Germany to exterminate the Jews during World War II. Utilize this kind of historical and current episode in your conversation. Such a discussion should not only help your students to recognize the dangers of arrogantly presuming that God is on our side, but also provide insight into why the Hebrews might have believed that God was directing them to take certain actions.

Conclude on a positive note by affirming the trust exemplified by the Israelites as they marched around fortified Jericho in obedience to God. Sometimes it is easier to determine what God would have us do than it is to summon the faith and courage to do it.

Helping Class Members Act

Urge class members to devote portions of their prayer and study time to considering the sometimes-thin line between too easily assuming the identification of our wishes with God's will or too reluctantly acting in faith that God will see us to victory.

Planning for Next Sunday

Ask the class to read as much of Joshua 7–13 and 23 as possible so as to have the context for next week's lesson.

Choosing to Serve God

Background Scripture: Joshua 24

The Main Question

In the decades before the outbreak of the American Civil War, New England poet James Russell Lowell was distressed by various attempts to add territory to the southern part of the nation. Lowell realized that such expansion would increase the land available for spread of the institution of human slavery. In 1845 he wrote the words to what became a famous hymn with these opening lines:

> Once to every man and nation
> Comes the moment to decide,
> In the strife of truth with falsehood,
> For the good or evil side.

This hymn has recently been dropped in newer editions of the hymnals of several denominations. Some of the objections to it are related to its origin in a specific historical situation, others are due to its exclusive use of male language, others are based on questions about its theology. While I have no particular affection for this hymn and share some of these objections, I also wonder if contemporary Christians may not be uncomfortable with a hymn that so strongly emphasizes the necessity and urgency of making a life-shaping decision. Many people in our churches today find it very difficult to make decisions, even more challenging to remain faithful to commitments once made, and almost impossible to deal with the consequences of their choices.

In the midst of our indecisiveness and ambivalence, in contradiction of our desire to keep our options open and to hedge our bets, the call of God speaks to us through the voice of Joshua saying, "Choose this day whom you will serve."

Selected Scripture

King James Version

Joshua 24:1-2a, 11-16, 22-25

1 And Joshua gathered all the tribes of Israel to Shechem and called for the elders of Israel, and for their heads, and for their judges, and for their officers; and they presented themselves before God.

2 And Joshua said unto all the people, Thus saith the LORD,

....

11 And ye went over Jordan, and came unto Jericho: and the men of Jericho fought against you, the Amorites, and the Perizzites, and the Canaanites, and the Hittites, and the Girgashites, the Hivites, and the Jebusites; and I delivered them into your hand.

12 And I sent the hornet before you, which drave them out from before you, *even* the two kings of the Amorites; *but* not with thy sword, nor with thy bow.

13 And I have given you a land for which ye did not labour, and cities which ye built not, and ye dwell in them; of the vineyards and olive-yards which ye planted not do ye eat.

14 Now therefore fear the LORD, and serve him in sincerity and in truth: and put away the gods which your fathers served on the other side of the flood, and in Egypt; and serve ye the LORD.

New Revised Standard Version

Joshua 24:1-2a, 11-16, 22-25

1 Then Joshua gathered all the tribes of Israel to Shechem, and summoned the elders, the heads, the judges, and the officers of Israel; and they presented themselves before God. 2 And Joshua said to all the people, "Thus says the LORD,

....

11 When you went over the Jordan and came to Jericho, the citizens of Jericho fought against you, and also the Amorites, the Perizzites, the Canaanites, the Hittites, the Girgashites, the Hivites, and the Jebusites; and I handed them over to you. 12 I sent the hornet ahead of you, which drove out before you the two kings of the Amorites; it was not by your sword or by your bow. 13 I gave you a land on which you had not labored, and towns that you had not built, and you live in them; you eat the fruit of vineyards and olive-yards that you did not plant.

14 "Now therefore revere the LORD, and serve him in sincerity and in faithfulness; put away the gods that your ancestors served beyond the River and in Egypt, and serve the LORD. 15 Now if you are

15 And if it seem evil unto you to serve the LORD, choose you this day whom ye will serve; whether the gods which your fathers served that *were* on the other side of the flood, or the gods of the Amorites, in whose land ye dwell: but as for me and my house, we will serve the LORD.

16 And the people answered and said, God forbid that we should forsake the LORD, to serve other gods.

....

22 And Joshua said unto the people, Ye *are* witnesses against yourselves that ye have chosen you the LORD, to serve him. And they said, *We are* witnesses.

23 Now therefore put away, said *he*, the strange gods which *are* among you, and incline your heart unto the LORD God of Israel.

24 And the people said unto Joshua, The LORD our God will we serve, and his voice will we obey.

25 So Joshua made a covenant with the people that day, and set them a statute and an ordinance in Shechem.

Key Verse: **And if it seem evil unto you to serve the LORD, choose you this day whom ye will serve; whether the gods which your fathers served that *were* on the other side of the flood, or the gods of the Amorites, in whose land ye dwell: but as for me and my house, we will serve the LORD.**

unwilling to serve the LORD, choose this day whom you will serve, whether the gods your ancestors served in the region beyond the River or the gods of the Amorites in whose land you are living; but as for me and my household, we will serve the LORD."

16 Then the people answered, "Far be it from us that we should forsake the LORD to serve other gods."

....

22 Then Joshua said to the people, "You are witnesses against yourselves that you have chosen the LORD, to serve him." And they said, "We are witnesses." 23 He said, "Then put away the foreign gods that are among you, and incline your hearts to the LORD, the God of Israel." 24 The people said to Joshua, "The LORD our God we will serve, and him we will obey." 25 So Joshua made a covenant with the people that day, and made statutes and ordinances for them at Shechem.

Key Verse: **Now if you are unwilling to serve the LORD, choose this day whom you will serve, whether the gods your ancestors served in the region beyond the River or the gods of the Amorites in whose land you are living; but as for me and my household, we will serve the LORD.**

As You Read the Scripture

Joshua 24:1-2a. The book could logically have ended with chapter 23 and, indeed, may have done so originally. The addition of the story in chapter 24 is, however, highly significant, for it recounts the renewal of the covenant relationship between God and Israel and the incorporation of additional groups of people into the covenant community. Shechem, located in the central hill country where the Israelites had established themselves, was an ancient shrine. There is no record of the Hebrews capturing the area, so apparently kindred people had welcomed them. The city became a very important religious and political center for Israel, functioning at times as a kind of capital. The formation of a confederacy of the various tribal groups united by their loyalty to Yahweh is being described here.

Verse 11. Speaking through Joshua, the Lord reminded the people of the major events in their salvation history up to this point. These events included the capture of Jericho and the defeat of various enemy groups here named.

Verses 12-13. The meaning of *the hornet* is uncertain. It may refer to the actual use of stinging insects as a weapon, as by catapulting nests into the enemies' ranks. The allusion may be to the Pharaoh of Egypt, one of whose symbols was a hornet or bee, whose incursions into Canaan had helped to keep the area weakened and, hence, easier for the Hebrews to conquer. Most likely, *the hornet* is figurative language for the fear that had swept their enemies as the Hebrews approached and had demoralized their efforts at resistance (see 2:8, 24 for examples). The emphasis is on the successful conquest of the land as a gift of God rather than as a result of human endeavor.

Verses 14-15. In response to what divine power has done for them, the people are called to sincere reverence and faithful service to Yahweh. They are to renounce the false gods that they had worshipped when they dwelt in the wilderness and in Egypt; they are to resist the temptations of Canaanite religious practices. These verses are reminiscent of Exodus 20:1-3 when, as the first of the Ten Commandments, the people are ordered to "have no other gods before me." Joshua exemplified his authentic leadership by proclaiming that for him and his household the decision had already been made: "We will serve the LORD."

Verse 16. The whole assembled people proclaimed their loyalty to Yahweh and their determination to serve no other deities.

Verse 22-23. Joshua warned the people that the loyalty to Yahweh that they were professing was both a serious and a difficult commitment. They must rid themselves of the idols that they possessed and be loyal to the one true God alone.

Verses 24-25. The people reaffirmed their pledge to serve and obey Yahweh. With that commitment, a covenant was established between the people and God, with Joshua serving as the mediator. He made clear to the people the obligations that they were assuming. The covenant was established at the initiative of God and based on the mighty works that God had done for them. The covenant relationship, however, carried with it stringent demands as to how they were to live. To be Yahweh's covenant people was to live in accordance with the divine law that defined the holiness required of them.

The Scripture and the Main Question

"We Will Serve the Lord"

Joshua 24 has often been described as one of the most significant chapters in the entire Old Testament. The ceremony at Shechem established the foundations of the tribal confederacy that would be the vehicle of Hebrew unity until the beginning of the monarchy many decades later. This confederacy did not only include those families who had been in slavery in Egypt, had followed Moses through the years in the wilderness, and crossed the Jordan under Joshua's command. Joining them at Shechem were apparently at least two other groups. One group was made up of kindred Hebrew persons who were already dwelling in central Canaan when the invaders under Joshua arrived. The other group was apparently persons of Canaanite ancestry who had decided, probably for a variety of reasons, to join with the Hebrew community. Rahab and her family may be an example of such persons. It is in part the diverse nature of the assembled people whom he was addressing that causes Joshua to be so adamant about the necessity for absolute commitment to Yahweh. In the assembly at Shechem the real Israel was emerging as a religious confederacy united by their common loyalty to God as King.

None of the people present at Shechem had experienced the whole story that Joshua recounted. Beginning with the family of Abraham and his descendants, continuing through the events of the Exodus and the conquest of the land of Canaan, Joshua rehearsed the sacred history through which God had brought this people thus far. For some the story was almost new; for others, parts of it were very familiar. The entire story of God's actions in the past was becoming their story; they were being incorporated into the community of God's people; they were claiming the story as their own, identifying and understanding themselves through it. It was somewhat similar to the process through which persons who have come to the United States from other parts of the world become authentic Americans. This does not happen simply through the meeting of legal requirements, but requires a learning and appreciation of the story of this nation that results in an understanding of oneself as a participant in that continuing narrative.

The appropriate response to this recitation of salvation history was recognition that these mighty acts had been the work of God, acknowledgement of Yahweh as Lord, and acceptance of the obligations of the covenant relationship. The covenant relationship is not one that is forced on the people. It is conditional, dependent on their willing response. Above all, it required a commitment of supreme loyalty to Yahweh. Such a commitment carried with it significant consequences in the form of religious and ethical obligations. The people heard the call to covenant faithfulness and affirmed their willingness to accept these obligations. They became Israel—the covenant community of God. It is probable that this occasion at Shechem set a precedent for annual ceremonies of corporate renewal of the covenant.

Choices, Commitments, and Consequences

Like the people of ancient Israel, modern Christians are faced with the necessity of making life-shaping choices. Often we find this to be a difficult and uncomfortable demand. We would prefer to avoid the limits and the risks involved. In "The Road Not Taken," one of the most famous of American poems, Robert Frost beautifully describes this dilemma.

One of the characteristics of our society seems to be the unwillingness to make choices and to live with their consequences. Examples can be seen in the declining rate of marriage as persons fear long-term commitment, the rising rate of divorce, an increased option for childlessness, and the frequency of vocational changes. Certainly we would not contend that all such decisions are bad ones; persons need the opportunity to make changes in the direction of their lives, to correct mistakes, to follow new challenges. It is, however, clear that one of the challenges facing the church is to help Christian people learn to make wise decisions and prudent commitments and to live in faithfulness with the results. A major insurance company has recently run a series of unusually appealing magazine advertisements using the theme "For all the commitments you make." The ads in the series have focused on various situations in life in which we are being counted on by others to honor commitments, in this case financial ones. This might be an appropriate theme for the church: To teach its people how to be faithful "for all the commitments you make."

I believe that there are at least two chief reasons why we have such struggles with the issue of commitments and faithfulness. One is that we have been socialized by our culture to expect, or at least to hope, that we do not really have to make difficult choices. In the words of a television commercial, we are deceived into believing that "you can have it all." In the realities of life, we find that this is simply not true. We are finite beings living finite lives, and we must make hard choices. The second reason for our struggle is, I believe, the failure to ground our lives in the same prior and ultimate commitment to God to which Joshua was calling the Israelites. Our choices must result from our priorities, our commitments from our convictions, our consequences from our faithfulness.

Helping Adults Become Involved

Preparing to Teach

Establish the context for the study of Joshua 24 by reading chapters 7–13 and 23, which describe the continued conquest following the battle of Jericho and the division of the land among the tribal groups. Study Joshua 24 using "As You Read the Scripture." A reading of Deuteronomy 30 will also be helpful in order to see the expression of very similar ideas in the farewell words of Moses to the Hebrews. Plan for the oral reading suggested in "Introducing the Main Question"; this should include clearly marking the parts in your Bible.

Have available copies of your denomination's services of Baptism and Holy Communion. These will probably be printed in your hymnals, though your minister may be able to provide a variety of resources. If possible, acquire from your minister copies of marriage and ordination services, as well as of the Wesley Covenant Service. (For United Methodists, all of these are available in the *Book of Worship*.) Consider making handout copies of "The Road Not Taken" or writing it clearly on newsprint. Have paper and pencils or pens accessible. As usual, each student should have a Bible.

A workable outline for the session is as follows:

     I. Israel as a people in covenant with God
       A. Sacred history as the basis of the covenant
       B. Obligations of the covenant people
       C. Defining the covenant community
    II. Living today as people of covenant faithfulness

Introducing the Main Question

Open the session with an oral reading of Joshua 24:1-28 in parts. Have a narrator read the brief sections that are not dialogue; read the words of Joshua as God's spokesperson yourself (or ask a selected person in advance); ask the class to read the words of the people. Lead a brief discussion of the thoughts and feelings of your group in response.

Developing the Lesson

I. Israel as a people in covenant with God

A fundamental, pervasive theme of the Old Testament is Israel's understanding of itself as a people through whose history God has chosen to act for human salvation. The divine choice is inexplicable and does not mean that Israel is superior or has special privileges. As a community in covenant relationship with God, Israel has responsibilities and obligations.

A. Sacred history as the basis of the covenant

The covenant relationship with Israel had been initiated by God and was evidenced by the mighty acts of God throughout history. Whenever the covenant is reaffirmed, there is a rehearsal of these events through which God brought Israel into being and sustained it. For examples, look at parallels to the summary in Joshua 24 and Deuteronomy 6 and 30. Try to help your class understand that their identity as Christians is grounded in this same story and its culmination in the story of Jesus Christ. Without grasping this, we cannot comprehend truly who we are and how we are to live.

The sacramental rituals of most denominations reflect the centrality of such recollection of the sacred history of which we are now a part. Examine your church's rituals for such emphasis, using copies of the baptismal and eucharistic services. A recent rewriting of the United Methodist baptismal service restores the ancient "Thanksgiving over the Water" prayer, which reminds us of God's actions from the creation of the world to the resurrection of Christ. In the liturgy for the Lord's Supper, the Great Thanksgiving includes a review of many of the divine mighty works. If you can obtain a worship book that offers the minister a choice of readings for this service, you will find the same thing variously expressed. The point is that our response to God is grounded in and made possible by God's historic actions to make salvation available to us.

B. Obligations of the covenant people

Use the material in "The Scripture and the Main Question" to make clear the overarching demands of the covenant relationship. Ask the class to discuss their understanding of the specific obligations of Christians who make up God's covenant community today.

C. Defining the covenant community

The covenant community today, as in the time of ancient Israel, is composed of those who have identified themselves with the story of God's saving activity and who strive to live in faithfulness to that identity. Discuss what this means for you as individuals and as a church community.

II. Living today as people of covenant faithfulness

Have the class peruse "The Road Not Taken" and discuss its implications for the lives of Christians. Encourage the relating of events in their personal lives of which this poem might be a reminder. If your class is large, division into smaller groups will facilitate sharing.

Utilize the materials you have gathered, such as marriage and ordination services and the Wesley Covenant Service, as vehicles for enhancing appreciation of the element of commitment in Christian living. If you have sufficient copies, divide the class into small groups and have each focus on a particular service. Encourage discussion of the meaning and the consequences of such commitment.

Helping Class Members Act

If time allows, have class members begin making written personal lists of the determinative decisions and commitments of their own lives. Urge them to continue the making of this list in their devotional time during the week and to begin prayerfully to examine how they are living out the consequences of these choices. Challenge them to prove honestly the degree to which these commitments are grounded in ultimate loyalty to God and how faithfully they are living this out. The desired outcome of this exercise is not simply greater self-awareness, but an authentic recommitment—perhaps redirection—in specific areas of their lives. Challenge your students to maintain a written record in journal form of developments in these areas of their lives as they hear again God's call to covenant faithfulness.

Planning for Next Sunday

Today's lesson is the last in the series focusing on the events in the book of Joshua. Next Sunday will begin a brief consideration of the book of Judges. In preparation for this study, consider these questions: What are some of the false gods that we are today tempted to worship? What are the results in our lives as individuals and as a church of following other gods?

Spiritual Enrichment Article:
Why Your Adult Class Is Important

Educating Today's Christians

Recently, a national study was done of Christian education in today's church. The National Study of Protestant Congregations highlights the great need, the intense hunger for effective Christian education in our churches. The study suggests that those of us who regularly use the *International Lesson Annual* need a renewed commitment to the teaching task of the church.

Back in 1986, Robert L. Wilson and I were working on a book about renewal in the United Methodist Church. The book eventually became *Rekindling the Flame: Strategies for a Vital United Methodism* (Nashville: Abingdon Press, 1987). As we were talking about possible contents for a book that would enumerate the ten absolutely most important things that United Methodists could do to renew our church, Bob suggested a chapter entitled, "Insist That the Clergy Teach in the Parish." I questioned the priority of this subject. It did not seem to fit in a book that stressed larger, more structural changes in the church. Bob remained steadfast in his advocacy of a chapter on pastors teaching. In his lifetime, Bob had studied hundreds of churches, serving as a national consultant in the areas of church growth and development.

"I can think of few factors more important for congregational growth, particularly growth that is sustained and solid, than the necessity for the pastor to be the chief educator in the congregation," Bob insisted.

Now a number of years later, I see that Bob was absolutely right. The Search Institute's work validates Bob's unscientific but fully informed judgment: Pastors must perform many important acts of ministry for their congregations, but few are more important than the ministry of teaching.

If I had any serious doubts about that contention, those doubts would have been discarded after reading the research results from the study of Protestant congregations. The research shows a vast need for more mature faith among our people. When tested for their levels of mature faith, using the criteria of the study, our people are indeed "like sheep without a shepherd" (Mark 6:34). What is perhaps more disturbing, they have been so little exposed to Christian teaching that they do not even know how much they lack. They do not appear, according to the data, to set a high priority on their own need for Christian growth. Their faith is disturbingly limited to the subjective, the purely personal, and the vague. The need is there.

Equipment of the Saints

"The gifts he gave were that some would be apostles, some prophets, some evangelists, some pastors and teachers, to equip the saints for the work of ministry, for building up the body of Christ, until all of us come to the unity of the faith and of the knowledge of the Son of God, to maturity, to the measure of the full stature of Christ" (Eph. 4:11-13 NRSV).

Where one places the comma in the phrase "some pastors and teachers, to equip the saints for the work of ministry" makes a great deal of difference. There is no comma in the original Greek. Is it only teachers who equip the saints, or is it that all these church offices—such as apostles, prophets, evangelists, pastors, and teachers—have their rationale for being in the vital task of equipment of the saints? Surely it is the latter.

All of the church's leaders, the church's clergy (though that is probably an anachronistic term for the Ephesians) are gifts of Christ so that the saints (i.e., all baptized Christians) might have the gifts they need to do the work of ministry. Pastors and teachers are essential as those who equip God's people to share in Christ's ministry to the world.

I believe that the National Study of Protestant Congregations depicts a sad lack of attention to the task of Christian education because of the American church's erroneous assumption that today's Christians do not need mature faith because they are fortunate enough to live in a basically Christian culture. More positively, the study invites renewed commitment to the adventurous task of creating and equipping Christians to live as mature representatives of Christ's Kingdom within a world that knows not Christ nor his Kingdom.

My parents did not worry about whether or not I would grow up Christian. After all, ours was the only game in town. Everybody we knew was Christian. There was a traffic jam in Greenville, South Carolina, at 9:45 on Sunday mornings as everyone scurried into Sunday school. One became Christian, not by intentional, careful, and caring Christian education but rather by osmosis, by being lucky enough to have been born in Greenville. We went to Sunday school, but not so much to become more mature in our faith, much less to be equipped for battle. We came to uncover our feelings about God, to learn to be nice to other people, to be encouraged to be even nicer than we already were. I am overstating it, but my point is that I doubt any of us thought of equipping the saints because few of us had any fundamental quarrel with the world as it was. It was *our* world.

Of course, it was also a racially segregated world, a world that was preparing to devastate Vietnam, a world busy indoctrinating us and converting us into lifestyles and world views that were not Christian. (For a more complete discussion of these themes, see W. H. Willimon and S. Hauerwas, *Resident Aliens: Life in the Christian Colony* [Nashville: Abingdon, 1990].)

Whether or not we were justified in believing that this was *our* world, whether or not we were right to assume that we need not worry about Christian formation because the church had succeeded in making America safe for Christians, whether or not my parents were correct in thinking that I would grow up Christian by osmosis, *no one believes that today.* The study of congregations depicts a church full of poorly equipped, inept Christians who lack the skills to be able to see the difference between church and world, much less the means to be salt and light. The at-risk behaviors of our youth are not only the sex and drugs, but also the superficial materialism and lonely individualism engendered by our culture.

An alternative view of the church, engendering an alternative view of *Christian education,* is found a bit later in Ephesians:

> Put on the whole armor of God, so that you may be able to stand against the wiles of the devil. For our struggle is not against enemies of blood and flesh, but against the rulers, against the authorities, against the cosmic powers of this present darkness, against the spiritual forces of evil in the heavenly places. Therefore take up the whole armor of God, so that you may be able to withstand. (Eph. 6:11-13)

Only when the American church is again so shocked by the gospel will we rediscover our pressing need for equipment in order to "be able to withstand." It makes a great deal of difference, how we read our present situation. I believe that our situation is more like that of Ephesians 6:11-13 than mainline American Protestants have been willing to admit.

In a situation of social breakdown, dislocation, and the corruption of Christian witness, Christian education becomes life or death for the church. It is tough out there. We dare not send out disciples, young or old, without sufficient equipment.

I agree with my colleague John Westerhoff, who says to contemporary pastors, if we are spending more than ten hours a week in activities outside our parish, we are probably wasting our time. The educational needs of today's congregations are too great, the need for pastoral analysis, interpretation, and leadership are too desperate. Pastors are to minister by equipping the saints. On the other hand, Westerhoff says that if laity are spending more than ten hours a week working within the church they are probably wasting their time. The needs of the world for witness are too great for laity to be merely keeping house at the church. The ministry of the laity is to share in Christ's ministry to the world.

I predict that tomorrow's pastors will expend much more time in prayer, analysis, study, and interpretation. Categories between church and world are so confused, the need for careful biblical discernment too great, the present rule of the principalities and powers so subtle, that we need our pastors to do a great deal of thinking in order to equip us to minister within the present age. I predict that seminaries will cease training us merely to service the present cultural arrangements, and begin equipping pastors to instill in our congregations the creative cognitive dissonance that is the necessary prelude to a new church. Seminaries will have more and better Christian education courses when seminaries at last wake up to the recognition that their graduates are going to serve churches in a very different world.

My last congregation was next door to the synagogue. It was instructive to us, as mainline Protestant Christians, to observe a faith community that had never asked for nor expected the surrounding culture to serve as a prop for their faith, a teacher to their young. These Jews knew, from centuries of bitter experience, that if their children were going to grow up Jewish, they would have to make them that way through careful, intentional education and enculturation by the whole congregation, with the rabbi as their guide. I believe that my church will come more closely to resemble the synagogue in its awareness that (to use Tertullian's words) "Christians are made, not born." I believe pastors will come to understand once again why one of the disciples' favorite designations of Jesus was Rabbi.

I therefore celebrate the congregation in Michigan that formed a Bible study and prayer group for its public school teachers. They meet once a week for breakfast. Sometimes they study the Bible, sometimes they present case studies from their teaching that challenge their Christian fidelity. Here is a congregation struggling to equip its people for difficult Christian service.

Blessings on the group of high-school youth in Tulsa who meet every Sunday night, seeking the insights and skills they need in order to witness to their faith in Christ to their peers at school. They study the Bible, they invite a high-school guidance counselor to talk about the psychology and development of youth, they role play various situations involving Christian witness.

Thank God for the pastor in North Carolina who meets once a month with all of her adult church school teachers and guides them through the upcoming sessions in the International Sunday School Lesson. She highlights difficult biblical passages and discusses various educational strategies for explicating scripture. Above all, the pastor, just by her act of teaching the teachers, demonstrates effective pedagogy in the church and signals to the teachers that their work is essential for the faith of the church.

Grant increase to the number of pastors who, like the young pastor in South Carolina, continually teaches a two-month "Inquirers Class." The only requirement for admission is that the older youth or adult is not a member of any other church school class and is willing to commit to two months of study and exploration with the pastor. At the end of the two-month series, the pastor declares an end to this series and begins another. If members want to continue, they must begin their own class. As a result of this pastor's classes, three new adult classes have been born and the church membership in the congregation as a whole has doubled in three years. Pastoral involvement in the teaching ministry of the church thus has beneficial consequences for evangelism and church growth. As the study of congregations shows, people appear to be grateful to congregations that take their Christian educational needs seriously. They are "like sheep without a shepherd." In a world in which people suffer from confusion, anomie, and dislocation, any church that confidently offers some coherent vision gathers a crowd.

Called for Adventure

Years ago, James Gustafson defined the church as "a community of moral discourse." The church was that place set apart to debate the big questions, to discuss the tough, mysterious issues. While I have never liked the rather intellectualized, heavily cognitive and cool sound of this "community of moral discourse," the study of congregations suggests that people really do long for a church that will foster their ability to discuss, debate, question, and grow in their faith. That can take many forms. For instance, I know an African-American congregation in Atlanta that has probably never thought of itself as a community of moral discourse. They have only two adult classes, one youth class and two children's classes in the whole church. So where's the education? On Sunday, toward the end of their service, after the hymns, the readings, and the sermon, their church prays. They pray by having their pastor stand in their midst and invite them to talk about those matters for which they need to pray as a church. Some of the needs mentioned are deeply personal. These are received by the pastor, perhaps with a comment like "Who will take Sara to the hospital this week for her surgery? Mary? Thanks. Who'll pick her up afterwards? John? Good. Just want to be sure we're doing our part while the Lord does his."

The pastor guides their thoughts. "How about the world beyond us? Jesus wants us to pray for others. Who are the strangers for whom we need to pray?"

See what is happening? With their pastor's guidance, they are not only praying, they are learning to pray, maturing in their own prayer skills, deepening their notions of prayer. Worship has become education for them. Or has their education become their worship, another opportunity for bending their lives toward God?

A church that has no quarrel with the surrounding world, a church at ease in Zion, has little need for its pastors to be teachers, has no reason carefully to examine its Sunday worship, its program of education, its treatment of its children and youth. Here is a church where content does not matter, and growth is unimportant because being a Christian is synonymous with being a good human being. Who needs education for that?

I believe, and I believe that the National Study of Protestant Congregations supports my belief, that congregations and pastors are called for considerably more. The present age and its challenges provide pastors with a marvelous opportunity to rediscover the risky, adventurous, countercultural excitement of being Christian, to join with Christ in creating a new people, by water and the word, who are forerunners of a new world. If we cannot be bold enough to allow Christ to use us in the creating of his new world, then about all we can do is service the old world. That is no fun.

Fortunately, Christ has called us for considerably more and promised us that our gifts can be used in the equipment of his saints.

William H. Willimon

UNIT II: THE RULE OF THE JUDGES

TWO LESSONS   OCTOBER 2–9

The two lessons in this unit follow chronologically after the story told in Unit I. The Israelites, having established themselves in the land of Canaan, struggle with the transition to a sedentary, agricultural style of life. Surrounded by various groups of pagan people whom they are unable to drive out, the people of the covenant fall prey to the temptations of the fertility religions. They cease to worship Yahweh alone or to live in faithful obedience to the divine commands. The writer of the book of Judges interprets this two hundred years of history as a repeated cycle of disloyalty and sin, defeat and oppression, repentance and deliverance, followed by return to sin.

The first lesson attempts to explain the fertility cults of Canaan and the appeal that they had for the Israelites. It describes the role of the judges as leaders raised up by God from time to time during these difficult decades. The next lesson focuses on one of the judges—Gideon—and examines his career as illustrative of how God used these human instruments for the divine purposes.

Like the people of Israel during the time of the judges, American Christians today live in an era of social and moral disorder and religious instability. There are messages from God in this study that are relevant to faithful living in the covenant relationship during these days.

LESSON 5   OCTOBER 2

Israel's Tragic Pattern of Life

Background Scripture: Judges 2:6–3:6

The Main Question

As a child I was deeply stirred by the stories I heard in church about men and women, even children, who had triumphantly given their lives rather than renounce their faith in Christianity. I remember wondering, indeed worrying, about what I might do if I were ever to face such a time of persecution. Of course, in my daydreams I always saw myself as courageously enduring torture and even death while steadfastly maintaining my loyalty to Christ. I am grateful that the events of my life have been less dramatic and that I have not had to face the risk of martyrdom. As I have grown older, however, I have realized that for most of us the greatest danger of unfaithfulness to God comes not in times of acute persecution, but rather in the commonplace events of everyday living. At least for martyrs the choices are sharply defined; the points of pivotal decision are clear; the consequences are undeniable. For most of us in the routine round of our living, the dangers are much more subtle and difficult to recognize; small choices for wrong seem quite innocuous; compromises appear to be benign accommodation. We slide gradually into apostasy rather than leaping precipitously.

As the Hebrew people established themselves in the portions of the land of Canaan that they had conquered, they found themselves faced with powerful temptations. They were not so much tempted blatantly to deny and reject Yahweh as they were subtly to blend alien and idolatrous elements into their religious beliefs and practices. Influenced by the practices of their pagan neighbors, they made compromises and concessions which they could persuade themselves were innocent, even necessary. How like them we are often are!

Selected Scripture

King James Version

Judges 2:11-19

11 And the children of Israel did evil in the sight of the LORD, and served Baalim:

12 And they forsook the LORD God of their fathers, which brought them out of the land of Egypt, and followed other gods, of the gods of the people that were round about them, and bowed themselves unto them, and provoked the LORD to anger.

13 And they forsook the LORD, and served Baal and Ashtaroth.

14 And the anger of the LORD was hot against Israel, and he delivered them into the hands of spoilers that spoiled them, and he sold them into the hands of their enemies round about, so that they could not any longer stand before their enemies.

15 Whithersoever they went out, the hand of the LORD was against them for evil, as the LORD had said, and as the LORD had sworn unto them: and they were greatly distressed.

16 Nevertheless the LORD raised up judges, which delivered them out of the hand of those that spoiled them.

17 And yet they would not hearken unto their judges, but they went a whoring after other gods, and bowed themselves unto them: they turned quickly out of the way which their fathers walked in, obeying the commandments of the LORD; but they did not so.

New Revised Standard Version

Judges 2:11-19

11 Then the Israelites did what was evil in the sight of the LORD and worshiped the Baals; 12 and they abandoned the LORD, the God of their ancestors, who had brought them out of the land of Egypt; they followed other gods, from among the gods of the peoples who were all around them, and bowed down to them; and they provoked the LORD to anger. 13 They abandoned the LORD, and worshiped Baal and the Astartes. 14 So the anger of the LORD was kindled against Israel, and he gave them over to plunderers who plundered them, and he sold them into the power of their enemies all around, so that they could no longer withstand their enemies. 15 Whenever they marched out, the hand of the LORD was against them to bring misfortune, as the LORD had warned them and sworn to them; and they were in great distress.

16 Then the LORD raised up judges, who delivered them out of the power of those who plundered them. 17 Yet they did not listen even to their judges; for they lusted after other gods and bowed down to them. They soon turned aside from the walk in which their ancestors had walked, who had obeyed the commandments of the LORD; they did not follow their example. 18 Whenever the LORD raised up judges

18 And when the LORD raised them up judges, then the LORD was with the judge, and delivered them out of the hand of their enemies all the days of the judge: for it repented the LORD because of their groanings by reason of them that oppressed them and vexed them.

19 And it came to pass, when the judge was dead, that they returned, and corrupted themselves more than their fathers, in following other gods to serve them, and to bow down unto them; they ceased not from their own doings, nor from their stubborn way.

for them, the LORD was with the judge, and he delivered them from the hand of their enemies all the days of the judge; for the LORD would be moved to pity by their groaning because of those who persecuted and oppressed them. 19 But whenever the judge died, they would relapse and behave worse than their ancestors, following other gods, worshiping them and bowing down to them. They would not drop any of their practices or their stubborn ways.

Key Verses: And the children of Israel did evil in the sight of the LORD, and served Baalim: And they forsook the LORD God of their fathers, which brought them out of the land of Egypt, and followed other gods, of the gods of the people that were round about them, and bowed themselves unto them, and provoked the LORD to anger.

Key Verses: Then the Israelites did what was evil in the sight of the LORD and worshiped the Baals; and they abandoned the LORD, the God of their ancestors, who had brought them out of the land of Egypt; they followed other gods, from among the gods of the peoples who were all around them, and bowed down to them; and they provoked the LORD to anger.

As You Read the Scripture

Judges 2:11-19. In the verses preceding these, we read that the people of Israel were faithful to the laws of the covenant during the lifetime of Joshua and the others of his generation. After the death of Joshua and his contemporaries, "another generation grew up after them, who did not know the LORD or the work that he had done for Israel" (2:10*b*). Thus begins the pattern of Hebrew history as interpreted by the Deuteronomistic author—unfaithfulness to the covenant, oppression, repentance, deliverance.

Verses 11-13. The implication is that the new generation who had not themselves experienced the mighty works of salvation that God had done were vulnerable to the temptations of rival religions. They compromised the primary commandment of Yahweh: "You shall have no other gods before [or besides] me . . . for I the LORD your God am a jealous God" (Exod. 20:3, 5*b*). The Baals and the Astartes were deities of the pagan culture of Canaan. Reverence to them not only violated the pledge of loyalty to Yahweh, but also involved Israel in religious practices that were ethically unacceptable. In these verses, we see the first step in the Deuteronomistic pattern—unfaithfulness or apostasy.

Verses 14-15. Such violation of the covenant obligations resulted in oppression. Although able to establish control of much of the central highlands of Canaan, Israel had not been successful in ridding the whole land of enemy people. These foes attacked the Israelite settlements, captured much of their property, and defeated them in battle. Yahweh was no longer fighting for the Israelites, and without divine aid they were powerless before their enemies. As God had warned, unfaithfulness to the covenant resulted in the punishment of oppression.

Verse 16. Ever faithful to the divine side of the covenant, Yahweh sent succor in the form of potent leaders—the judges who were able to rally Israel to victory and freedom from enemy oppression. The judges—twelve of whom are named in the book of Judges—were charismatic leaders. They rose to their positions not by hereditary right or by choice of the people, but through the gifts of wisdom, courage, and leadership that God bestowed on them. Many were local leaders who emerged to become military chieftains in the fights against enemy peoples. They were the instruments through whom the Lord brought about deliverance when Israel recognized and repented of its sin. In more peaceful times, they provided some civil authority as they functioned as arbiters of disputes among the Israelites.

Verse 17. Even God's gift of the judges to provide the leadership necessary for victory over their enemies was not enough to keep Israel faithful. After each episode of deliverance, they soon turned away again into idolatry.

Verses 18-19. These verses recapitulate the cycle of Hebrew history for some two centuries as the Deuteronomistic historian understood it. Apostasy and idolatry would issue in persecution and oppression by their foes. Yahweh, "moved to pity by their groaning," would repeatedly intervene through the judges to rescue them. In spite of Yahweh's graciousness, they almost immediately relapsed into sinful ways. Indeed, in the judgment of the writer, each new generation was worse than its ancestors had been.

The Scripture and the Main Question

Life in Canaan

The book of Judges makes it very clear that the conquest of the land of Canaan by Israel was much less complete than a quick reading of the accounts in Joshua might imply. While battles were won and cities captured, a large portion of the country, especially in the fertile valleys and the coastal plain, remained in the hands of various Canaanite groups. Living alongside the Canaanites raised potent challenges to the faith of Israel. The writer of Judges contended that God had refused to drive out these enemies in order that they might test Israel. Certainly they did that, and Israel was not always equal to the test. In addition to the influence of rival groups, Israel itself now contained a diversity of peoples. Some who had joined the twelve-tribe confederacy at Shechem had not experienced the earlier events of sacred history. Some were people of Canaanite background, former practitioners of the nature religion of Canaan. The influences to which Israel was prey in its new historical situation were a threat to its relationship with Yahweh and its identity as the covenant community.

Prior to their settlement in Canaan, the Hebrews had been a nomadic people who migrated from place to place with their flocks and herds. They were tent dwellers who moved from one encampment to another to find pasture and water for the animals, which were their chief source of sustenance. Even Yahweh had a tent—the tabernacle or tent of meeting that contained the ark of the covenant—and moved with them on their journeys.

When they moved into Canaan, the Hebrews began making a major social and cultural transition as they became a settled, agricultural people. The growing of crops was new to them and very different from the old ways.

These changes in their lifestyle necessitated significant changes in their understanding of God. Was Yahweh, the warrior God who travelled with a nomadic people, able to meet the very different needs of a sedentary, farming culture? The religious practices of the Canaanite cult were specifically aimed toward assuring success in agriculture. It is easy to comprehend their attractiveness to the Israelites as they sought to master the mysteries of growing crops. The desire was not so much to reject Yahweh, as to include other practices to guarantee good results in their farming.

Recent archaeological excavations have revealed to us a great deal about the religion of Canaan that the book of Judges refers to as the worship of the Baals and the Astartes. The chief of the gods was El, a cosmic father deity whose female consort was Asherah. El was rather remote from the activities of human life; much more important was his son Baal. The word *baal* means "lord" or "owner." Baal was the god of weather, especially identified with storm and rain. In the central myth of the cult, Baal was annually murdered by the god of death and sterility and his body dismembered and scattered. The effects of Baal's murder were seen in the ceasing of rains in the month of May. His female companion Ashtart (or Anat) slaughtered the death god and brought Baal back to life. The resumption of their sexual relationship was believed to ensure the fertility of the earth and the productivity of animals and humans for another year. The return of the seasonal rains from October to April was the vehicle of this fruitfulness; agriculture in ancient Canaan was impossible without them. The farmers of the land believed that it was essential for human beings to imitate the actions of the gods in order to ensure magically the gift of fertility. This was done through acts of sacred prostitution in which a man identifying himself with Baal had sexual intercourse with a temple prostitute. Such actions were a kind of sympathetic or imitative magic through which the powers of human and divine sexuality vitalized the processes of fertility in nature. Idols of the various gods in the pantheon were common objects of worship throughout the land.

Even if the religion of Canaan had been of a more admirable kind, it would have conflicted sharply with the demand of monotheism which was fundamental to the Hebrew faith: "Hear, O Israel: The LORD is our God, the LORD alone" (Deut. 6:4). Any attempt to add or blend elements of the fertility cults with the worship of Yahweh—an effort referred to as *syncretism*—had to be totally rejected. To make matters worse, the Canaanite cult was a completely nonethical religion. It featured the practice of special rituals that had no relevance in daily life. Magic rather than morality was its focus.

Remembering "All the Great Work That the Lord Had Done"

As the book of Judges relates the recurring tale of Israel's failures to maintain covenant faithfulness, the author emphasizes that a major source of the problem was failure to remember "all the great work that the LORD had done for Israel" (2:7b). Israel's identity as a chosen people in covenant relationship with God was grounded in the story of God's saving action in their history. Both Moses and Joshua had frequently reminded the people of this story and urged them to be diligent in teaching it to their children and to newcomers in the community. The consequences of their inability to accomplish this should serve as a grave reminder to modern Christians. One of the chief weaknesses in many of our churches is our ineffectiveness in teaching the faith. Not only our children and youth, but also our adults often have little comprehension of the biblical story of God's action for human salvation. Our people in general have a superficial and confused understanding of what Christians are to believe and how Christians are to live. Every congregation should study a recent report entitled *Effective Christian Education* (available from Search Institute, 122 W. Franklin Ave., Suite 525, Minneapolis, MN 55404). This provocative and disturbing study of six major Protestant denominations reveals how poorly the task of teaching the faith is being done in the Christian education programs of most churches.

The Theological Perspective of the Deuteronomistic Writer

The biblical books from Deuteronomy through 2 Kings are heavily influenced by a distinct theological perspective which is encapsulated in Joshua 2:6–3:6. This writer believed that God sent oppression on the people in punishment for their sins. Finding it hard to accept the idea of God as intentionally causing suffering, I would prefer to understand the plight of the Hebrews as the moral consequences of their actions. It has been wisely said that we cannot really break God's commandments, but we can break ourselves against them.

Helping Adults Become Involved

Preparing to Teach

The scripture material for today picks up the story immediately where Joshua 24:28 left it; for our purposes the intervening verses can be skipped. Read carefully Judges 2:6–3:6 with the assistance of the comments in "As You Read the Scripture." Outline for yourself the recurring pattern of this period of history as the writer sees it.

Try to obtain a copy of *Effective Christian Education* from your minister or director of Christian education. If this publication is not available in your church, consider having it ordered for future use in evaluating your entire program. You will need newsprint or a chalkboard, and Bibles.

Here is an outline for the lesson:

I. The historical situation
II. Theological interpretation of events
III. Modern parallels

Introducing the Main Question

Use the ideas suggested in "The Main Question" to introduce the theme of unfaithfulness to one's responsibilities as people of God. Be sure to emphasize that unfaithfulness is usually the product of a series of compromises rather than any one dramatic decision.

Developing the Lesson

I. The historical situation

After the death of Joshua, no one successor arose to take leadership in Israel. For most of the next two centuries, the nation struggled through continuing conflicts with neighboring peoples and the lack of any centralized governing authority. At times of extreme crisis, God would raise up a gifted leader who was able to rally the Israelites to temporary victory over their enemies. When the crisis was over, the people soon lapsed back into their old styles of living, which included participation in the Canaanite fertility cult. This cycle was repeated over and over again.

Use the information in "As You Read the Scripture" and in the "Life in Canaan" section of "The Scripture and the Main Question" to sketch this recurring cycle of events. The dangerous temptation of pagan religious practices is a major theme of the story of the Hebrew people from this point in their history to the end of the Old Testament. Take special care to explain this as clearly as possible. The material in "Life in Canaan" should enable you to do this.

II. Theological interpretation of events

Accurate knowledge of historical happenings in the biblical story is important chiefly because it serves as the basis for comprehending the significance of those events in God's plan. Obviously, events are subject to diverse interpretations, however. The Deuteronomistic writer had a very precise, even simplistic, understanding that caused him to interpret the oppression of Israel as punishment sent from God. See the section "The Theological Perspective of the Deuteronomistic Writer" in "The Scripture and the Main Question." I have no doubt that God uses suffering and hardships to serve the divine purpose, but I am uncomfortable with the idea of God actually inflicting pain. Israel was certainly morally weakened by its lack of faithfulness to the covenant. In ceasing to live as the holy covenant community of God, they forfeited their identity and thwarted the workings of divine purpose through them. The defeat and oppression that resulted from their internal weakness was used by God to make them recognize their sin and seek to return to the covenant relationship.

Utilize these differing theological perspectives on the events of the book of Judges to initiate a discussion of how God works in the world. Especially encourage examination of the relationship between the divine will and human suffering.

III. Modern parallels

There are numerous applications of the scripture in today's lesson to our contemporary situation. I will mention three that you might address with your class and perhaps you and they can think of others. First is the ever-present danger of God's people being drawn away into following false gods. For most of us, these gods are not idols carved of stone, but materialistic values such as wealth, success, and acclaim. In pursuit of those things that are most important to us, we sometimes compromise our loyalty to God and fail to remain faithful to the demands of the covenant. We practice a kind of modern syncretism in which we blend elements of authentic Christianity with alien elements from a culture that is largely pagan.

A second parallel is to be found in the nonethical nature of the Canaanite fertility cult and the characteristics of some modern expressions of religion. We live in an age in which there is great interest in the supernatural and the spiritual. I fear, however, that many contemporary movements under the broad label of spirituality are much less than Christian. If we are to be loyal to the covenant, we must be careful that our faith has at its center the affirmation of Jesus Christ as Savior. These ideas should engender a variety of discussion.

Thirdly, use the section "Remembering 'All the Great Work That the Lord Has Done' " to stimulate an evaluation of the Christian education that your class members have received and that your church is presently offering. If you can acquire *Effective Christian Education,* you will find unlimited possibilities for examination. The major points to make are the essential nature of nurturing persons in the faith and how that might be done more successfully.

Helping Class Members Act

Ask your class to consider undertaking a project that would involve studying the program of Christian education and nurture in the faith that your congregation provides for various age groups. Ask this question: How are we teaching and learning the Christian story and the life of faithfulness in covenant relationship with God? This is an area that, in many churches, is in desperate need of improvement. One of the first steps toward improvement is analysis of the present situation. Such a study would, of course, include the Sunday school program but should not be limited to that. All activities in the corporate life of the church have an educational component. A wide variety of material is available from Cokesbury to assist you. If your church has a Christian educator on staff, he or she will likely be your most valuable asset. Call on your minister for help, especially in considering the central role that she or he plays in education. Assistance can also be gotten from your annual conference council on ministries (or similar structure in your denomination's organization).

Planning for Next Sunday

Read chapters 3, 4, 11 and 13–16 for stories of some of the judges.

LESSON 6   OCTOBER 9

Deliverance by God's Hand

Background Scripture: Judges 6:1–8:21

The Main Question

"Not by might, nor by power, but by my spirit, says the LORD of hosts" (Zech. 4:6*b*). This quotation, from scripture written in a time long after the period of the judges, epitomizes the theme of today's lesson. It was a theme that Israel continually forgot and of which Yahweh repeatedly had to remind them: Their success, even their very existence, as a nation was a gift of divine power, not a product of human strength. In the stories of Gideon in Judges 6–8, we read of the career of one of the outstanding judges in Israel, one whose leadership freed the nation from cruel oppression by a dangerous enemy. Running throughout the account is a clear emphasis on the fact that Gideon was God's chosen instrument through whom God's power was channelled. Gideon did not volunteer for his mission; indeed he undertook it reluctantly and only after much reassuring from Yahweh. The battle against the Midianites was fought with a small group of commando raiders who were heavily outmatched, rather than with the massed forces of Israel at their maximum strength. In these ways, God manifested beyond all doubt that the victory was the Lord's, not Israel's.

The stories of Gideon are among the most popular of the tales in the book of Judges. I remember vividly from my childhood book of biblical stories, pictures of Gideon wringing moisture from the fleece, of the troops drinking water in their varying styles, and of the surprise attack with trumpets blowing while jars shattered and torches flamed. Why do these stories have such enduring appeal to our own day? Do we yearn for such manifestations of divine power; do we need to be reminded that victories in life come through the Lord's spirit?

Selected Scripture

King James Version	New Revised Standard Version

Judges 7:2-7, 19-21

2 And the LORD said unto Gideon, The people that *are* with thee *are* too many for me to give the Midianites into their hands, lest Israel vaunt themselves against me, saying, Mine own hand hath saved me.

3 Now therefore go to, proclaim in the ears of the people, saying, Whosoever *is* fearful and afraid, let him return and depart early from mount Gilead. And there returned of the people twenty and two thousand; and there remained ten thousand.

4 And the LORD said unto Gideon, The people are yet *too* many; bring them down unto the water, and I will try them for thee there: and it shall be, *that* of whom I say unto thee, This shall go with thee, the same shall go with thee; and of whomsoever I say unto thee, This shall not go with thee, the same shall not go.

5 So he brought down the people unto the water: and the LORD said

Judges 7:2-7, 19-21

2 The LORD said to Gideon, "The troops with you are too many for me to give the Midianites into their hand. Israel would only take the credit away from me, saying, 'My own hand has delivered me.' 3 Now therefore proclaim this in the hearing of the troops, 'Whoever is fearful and trembling, let him return home.' " Thus Gideon sifted them out; twenty-two thousand returned, and ten thousand remained.

4 Then the LORD said to Gideon, "The troops are still too many; take them down to the water and I will sift them out for you there. When I say, 'This one shall go with you,' he shall go with you; and when I say, 'This one shall not go with you,' he shall not go." 5 So he brought the troops down to the water; and the LORD said to Gideon, "All those who lap the water with their tongues, as a dog laps, you shall put to one side;

unto Gideon, Every one that lappeth of the water with his tongue, as a dog lappeth, him shalt thou set by himself; likewise every one that boweth down upon his knees to drink.

6 And the number of them that lapped, *putting* their hand to their mouth, were three hundred men: but all the rest of the people bowed down upon their knees to drink water.

7 And the LORD said unto Gideon, By the three hundred men that lapped will I save you, and deliver the Midianites into thine hand: and let all the *other* people go every man unto his place.

....

19 So Gideon, and the hundred men that were with him, came unto the outside of the camp in the beginning of the middle watch; and they had but newly set the watch: and they blew the trumpets, and brake the pitchers that were in their hands.

20 And the three companies blew the trumpets, and brake the pitchers, and held the lamps in their left hands, and the trumpets in their right hands to blow *withal:* and they cried, The sword of the LORD, and of Gideon.

21 And they stood every men in his place round about the camp: and all the host ran, and cried, and fled.

Key Verse: **And it was *so*, when Gideon heard the telling of the dream and the interpretation thereof that he worshipped, and returned into the host of Israel, and said, Arise; for the LORD hath delivered into your hand the host of Midian.**

all those who kneel down to drink, putting their hands to their mouths, you shall put to the other side." 6 The number of those that lapped was three hundred; but all the rest of the troops knelt down to drink water. 7 Then the LORD said to Gideon, "With the three hundred that lapped I will deliver you, and give the Midianites into your hand. Let all the others go to their homes."

....

19 So Gideon and the hundred who were with him came to the outskirts of the camp at the beginning of the middle watch, when they had just set the watch; and they blew the trumpets and smashed the jars that were in their hands. 20 So the three companies blew the trumpets and broke the jars, holding in their left hands the torches, and in their right hands the trumpets to blow; and they cried, "A sword for the LORD and for Gideon!" 21 Every man stood in his place all around the camp, and all the men in the camp ran; they cried out and fled.

Key Verse: **When Gideon heard the telling of the dream and its interpretation, he worshiped; and he returned to the camp of Israel, and said, "Get up; for the LORD has given the army of Midian into your hand."**

As You Read the Scripture

The stories of Gideon begin with an editorial introduction customary in the book of Judges: "The Israelites did what was evil in the sight of the LORD, and the LORD gave them into the hand of Midian seven years" (6:1). The Midianites were a nomadic people from the Arabian Desert who raided the productive areas of the country throughout the time of harvest and deprived the Israelites of most of their crops and livestock. The forces of Midian had a great advantage over Israel because of their use of a new means of transportation and warfare—the domesticated camel. They moved into the area in large numbers "as thick as locusts" and "wasted the land" (6:5). God, heeding the cries of suffering from the people, had come to Gideon and called him to leadership: "Deliver Israel from the hand of Midian; I hereby commission you" (6:14). Gideon was reluctant to undertake this responsibility, but dramatically reassured and empowered by God, he finally assembled an army to march against the enemy.

Judges 7:2-3. Because the forces of Midian were so formidable, Gideon sent out a wide call for troops and gathered an army of thirty-two thousand fighting men. God instructed him to reduce these numbers sharply, saying that if Israel used so vast an army they would be tempted to claim credit for the victory themselves. When Gideon told the army that any who were fearful should feel free to go home, more than two-thirds of them departed, leaving a force of ten thousand.

Verse 4. God was still dissatisfied with the size of the army and ordered Gideon to take them to the water where God would make the final selections. The word translated *sift* is the term used to describe the smelting of metal from ore.

Verses 5-7. The test through which the troops were divided was based on each individual's style of drinking water. This has usually been interpreted as a way of identifying those who were more vigilant—who drank by dipping the water up in their hands so that they might stay on guard. However, those who were chosen by God were those who lay down and lapped the water directly "as a dog laps." Perhaps we should understand that Yahweh was selecting those who were less suitable for combat as a way of reiterating that success in the battle would be won by divine, not human, prowess. Through this process a group of three hundred was retained and the others sent back home.

Verse 19. Gideon organized his warriors into three groups and stealthily approached the Midianite encampment at about 10:30 at night. (The night was divided into three watches of four hours each.) The men were lightly armed, but equipped with trumpets and earthenware jars in which lighted torches were hidden.

Verses 20-21. At Gideon's command, the three companies approaching the camp from different directions simultaneously blew their trumpets, shattered their jars to reveal the flaming torches, and shouted. The astonished and terrified Midianites fled in panic, attacking each other in their confusion. The Israelites stood around the camp and watched the rout. Like the capture of the city of Jericho earlier, the victory was unequivocally the work of Yahweh; no human power could be given the credit. The Lord had again delivered the people of the covenant from the consequences of their own unfaithfulness.

The Scripture and the Main Question

Oppression . . . Again!

The recurring pattern in Israel's history throughout the approximately two centuries known as the period of the judges is portrayed in the account of Gideon that begins in chapter 6. The Israelites had again done evil—ceased to live the holy life of God's covenant people worshipping Yahweh alone. Again they are defeated and oppressed by powerful enemies. Chief among these foes were the Midianites who came in from the Arabian Desert, utilizing their camels to give them great advantage over the Israelites, who as yet had no such swift means of travel and attack. Other neighboring peoples—the Amalekites from southern Judah and other nomads from the Syrian desert—availed themselves of the opportunity to raid weakened Israel. These enemy groups moved into the land during the harvest time in overwhelming numbers, encamped, and helped themselves to the fruits of the Israelite agricultural harvest and to their livestock as well. The extremity of the situation is evidenced by the story of Gideon's hiding the wine press—probably a pit cut into the rocky ground—to thresh out his wheat. Normally this was done with oxen and sledges on a public threshing floor located on some high place where the wind would help to carry away the chaff. The threat of enemy confiscation was so great that Gideon instead worked in a cramped place hoping for secrecy. So desperate was the crisis that "Israel was greatly impoverished because of Midian; and . . . cried out to the LORD for help" (6:6). God sent a prophet to remind them of the mighty acts of their sacred history and their disobedience to the divine commands. In yet another manifestation of God's faithfulness and mercy, another judge was called to prominence.

Gideon, from Frightened Farmer to Confident Commando

The account of the call of Gideon by God contains echoes of earlier stories from the lives of the great Hebrew leaders Moses and Abraham. Like Moses in Exodus 3, Gideon's first response to God's choice of him was to make excuses as to why he was unqualified. Similar to the story of the encounter at the burning bush, God answered these protestations with miraculous signs of divine favor. Like Abraham in Genesis 18, Gideon did not realize until he witnessed an act of supernatural power that he was entertaining the angel of the Lord.

Interestingly, the first order that Gideon received from God was to destroy the idols of the fertility gods whose deep infiltration into the worship practices of Israel is apparent here. Gideon's father Joash was either the owner or custodian of this altar to Baal and sacred pole or tree. Gideon, fearful of his own family and the other townspeople, did his work of destruction by night. He was discovered, but defended by his father, who argued that if Baal were a real god he could take care of himself. Apparently, Gideon's example of obedience to Yahweh was already proving influential and his summons to raise an army was met with massive response.

Gideon, however, was himself still less than fully convinced. He tested the will of God and the promise of victory by laying out a woolen fleece on the threshing floor and asking God to perform miracles. Such stories of determining the will of the deity are common in Eastern culture and the expression "putting out a fleece" has entered our language as a metaphor. One of the dilemmas that we share with Gideon is that of deciding with certainty what God's will is in specific situations. Gideon's careful testing may be a valuable model for us in a day when so many claim so easily and so arrogantly to know the will of God, both for themselves and for others. (An excellent source for further reading on this important subject is Leslie D. Weatherhead's *The Will of God*.)

Gideon was right to seek assurance that he was not undertaking this dangerous venture on his own initiative or by his own strength. The mission would certainly fail if it were not the Lord's work. As in the accounts of

other judges, the scripture tells us that "the spirit of the LORD took possession of Gideon." The literal translation of the Hebrew here is "the Spirit of
God put on Gideon" (6:34). The meaning is that the will and power of Yahweh expressed themselves through the person of Gideon; Gideon became
the vehicle and tool of God's activity. The Spirit of God is understood as a
potent, invasive force that transforms those persons who are its recipients.

The response to Gideon's call for troops had been enthusiastic and an
army of thirty-two thousand was gathered. As described in "As You Read the
Scripture," God reduced the size and strength of this force severely. There
would be no question as to the source of power for the victory. God knew
that if the Israelites were able to convince themselves that they had won
their own deliverance from Midian they would not return to their covenant
fidelity and worship of Yahweh. Prior to launching the attack, God allowed
Gideon and his servant to sneak close enough to the enemy camp to hear
the Midianites in conversation. One man was telling another about a dream
that the hearer interpreted as a prophecy of Israelite victory: The barley
bread—representing the farmers of Israel—destroyed the tent of the
nomadic, tent-dwelling Midianites. As in the accounts of the city of Jericho
and other references in the books of Joshua and Judges, the terror of the
Lord was going before the armies of Israel to prepare the way for victory.

"All the People Did What Was Right in Their Own Eyes"

With the words of the above quotation, the book of Judges comes to an
end, acknowledging the moral decay that afflicted the nation during the
period. The stories of the judges make exciting reading. We have only sam-
pled and have not even mentioned such well-known judges as Deborah and
Samson. One does not have to read much in the book to recognize that
these stories are in general amoral and brutal. We may be uncomfortable
with the view that God used such persons to perform such exploits of violence. The time of the judges was a brutal age of social disorder and religious decline; perhaps the judges were the best instruments that God had
available. It is nothing short of miraculous that the worship of Yahweh sur-
vived at all during this time and that the historic faith of Israel was preserved
and passed on. Even in such a time, God found persons who could be transformed by the divine spirit into instruments of divine purpose. God's choice
of tools and agents is often mystifying to us. Perhaps the greatest mystery is
the power of the steadfast love of God, who has been able throughout history to work out the divine plan in spite of the sinful failures of men and
women.

Helping Adults Become Involved

Preparing to Teach

Read through other chapters of the book of Judges, especially those suggested at the end of last week's lesson. Make a list of the names of the best-
known judges. Study the background scripture carefully so that you will be
able to relate the entire story of Gideon's career. Much of the material in
"The Scripture and the Main Question" is designed to assist you in doing
this. Pay special attention to the printed passages and the information in "As
You Read the Scripture."

FIRST QUARTER

Have available the chart of major events in Hebrew history that was begun during the last unit of study; be ready to bring it up to this point in the story. You will also need more newsprint or a chalkboard. Familiarize yourself with a map of Palestine of this period so that you can point out the places mentioned.

If possible, bring to class a picture of the emblem used by the Gideons International, a group well known for their wide distribution of copies of the Bible. This emblem portrays a two-handled pitcher with a torch such as Gideon might have used.

Presentation of the lesson can follow this outline:

I. The historical situation
II. The story of Gideon
III. Implications for today

Introducing the Main Question

Write on the board or newsprint the quotation from Zechariah that opens the section "The Main Question." Engage the class in a discussion of their responses to this verse. Encourage comments that relate to the stories of judges and that relate those to the personal lives of the class members.

Developing the Lesson

I. The historical situation

Lead the class in a discussion that reviews the historical developments up to this point. Use the chart of events in Hebrew history that you are constructing and maps relevant to the period. Make the chart current by adding the period of the judges and the names of some of the most prominent ones. It may be helpful to have the class glance back through the previous lessons in this quarter. The point is to remind everyone of the flow of the historical story.

Use the material in "Oppression . . . Again!" to present the background to the events of Gideon's life.

II. The story of Gideon

Have various persons in the class read aloud selected portions of the Gideon story and ask the class to respond by saying how they think Gideon might have felt at those moments. Doing this will help make Gideon come alive as a real person and allow the class to identify his experiences with God with some of their own. Suggested passages for this exercise include 6:12-16, 19-22, 25-31, 36, 40, and 7:2-7, 19-21.

Utilize the information in "As You Read the Scripture" and in "Gideon, From Frightened Farmer to Confident Commando" to relate the significant events in the career of Gideon as God's chosen instrument for deliverance of Israel.

III. Implications for today

The implications of this lesson for the lives of modern Christians are numerous. I will suggest five that you and your class might consider; you will likely think of others yourself or they will emerge in the course of your discussions. You may wish to divide into small groups, each of which can focus on a particular issue and later share their thoughts with the class.

58

1) Most human beings share the tendency of Moses and Gideon to make excuses when God calls us to service. Anyone who has had the responsibility of recruiting teachers for Sunday school or vacation church school or of persuading persons to join the choir knows this truth. When we are called to various responsibilities in our church or to other opportunities of fulfilling our ministries as Christians, we are prone to hesitate and offer excuses. Often those excuses take the form of protestations of our inadequacy for the proposed task. Why are we so reluctant? How can the church help persons to recognize themselves as gifted by God with talents to be used in service to others? Are we overly modest or simply lazy?

2) It is the responsibility of every person who seeks to be a disciple of Jesus Christ to seek to know and to follow the will of God. Some ways by which we can do this are studying the Bible, reading other writings by faithful persons through the ages, participating in corporate worship, communing with God in prayer and meditation, listening to God in and through the events of our lives. We need to guard against the tendency to assume that our own desires and opinions are identical with the divine will. What are some legitimate ways of putting out fleeces before the Lord in our day?

3) Often acting as an instrument of God means acting against the values and practices of the culture in which we live. The United States cannot be considered in any real sense a Christian nation. In truth, Christians live as much in the midst of an alien culture with the temptations of pagan gods as did ancient Israel. Discuss examples and meanings of this in our lives.

4) When we read the stories of many of the judges, and of many other biblical and historical characters, we realize that men and women do not have to live exemplary lives for God to make use of them in divine service. How is God able to use us in spite of our weaknesses and failures? Why does God choose to operate in the world in this way? How can we become better instruments of the divine purpose?

5) What would it mean in our lives individually and in the life of the church if we could truly believe that victories are won "not by might, nor by power, but by my spirit"? Clearly, for the people of Israel it did not mean that they were to do nothing except sit back and wait for God. What is the relationship between trusting God and working for our own deliverance?

Helping Class Members Act

Show the emblem of Gideons International, which is based on the scripture for today. Your class will probably be familiar with this organization, which over the period of almost a century has distributed millions of Bibles and today is active in dozens of countries. Use this example to challenge them to find specific ways to act as instruments of God's purpose.

Planning for Next Sunday

Ask the class to think about how different forms of government—democracy, dictatorship, monarchy, theocracy—are expressions of varying understandings of both the nature of God and of human beings.

UNIT III: THE BEGINNING OF THE KINGDOM

THREE LESSONS   **OCTOBER 16–30**

These lessons are taken from the book of 1 Samuel, which is a continuation of the Deuteronomistic history that extends from Joshua through 2 Kings. First Samuel picks up the story of Hebrew history at the point at which the book of Judges ends and continues the account of life in the land of Canaan. The chief characters in the portions of the book covered by these lessons are Samuel—the last judge and first named prophet—and Saul, who will be the first king.

A major transition in the life of Israel occurs in the material of Lesson 7. For approximately two centuries, the Israelite tribes had been organized in a loose confederacy and ruled by judges who were raised to positions of leadership by God in times of emergency. In this lesson, the leading men in the nation approach Samuel and demand that he appoint a king to govern them. Samuel is reluctant and warns of the dangers of monarchy. But with God's permission, if not approval, he acquiesces. In Lesson 8, the young man Saul from the tribe of Benjamin is chosen by God and anointed by Samuel to be the first king. Saul proves to be a tragic failure in the kingship. Lesson 9 tells of his disobedience to God and God's rejection of him and his family as rulers of Israel.

LESSON 7   **OCTOBER 16**

Israel Demands a King

Background Scripture: 1 Samuel 7:15–8:22; 12:19-25

The Main Question

And slowly answer'd Arthur from the barge:
"The old order changeth, yielding place to new,
And God fulfills himself in many ways,
Lest one good custom should corrupt the world."

So wrote Alfred, Lord Tennyson, as he described the death of the great King Arthur in *The Idylls of the King.* Our scripture lesson for today tells of a time of major change in the old order for the people of Israel. After some two centuries of life as a group of twelve tribes bound together as a confederacy, they were becoming a nation. After decades of leadership by judges whom God raised up in time of need, they were choosing to have a king. This transition to monarchy was risky; the controversy over its wisdom is still evident in the biblical record. Some felt that monarchy was essential if the nation was to be strong; others believed that to have a human monarch was to reject Yahweh as the divine king. The decision to become a monarchy was determinative of much of Israel's future. From henceforth, its fortunes would be dominated by the character and actions of the kings.

The issues raised for ancient Israel by this fundamental shift in political structure are very relevant to us in a different historical situation. The questions being wrestled with are perennial ones for civilized society: What is the best form of government for groups of human beings? What political structures provide the best conditions for persons to achieve physical and spiritual fulfillment? Through what type of government can the divine will for humankind best be realized? How can we reform our political structures to be more in accord with the working out of God's purpose?

Selected Scripture

King James Version	New Revised Standard Version

1 Samuel 8:4-9, 19; 12:19-25

4 Then all the elders of Israel gathered themselves together, and came to Samuel unto Ramah,

5 And said unto him, Behold, thou art old, and thy sons walk not in thy ways: now make us a king to judge us like all the nations.

6 But the thing displeased Samuel, when they said, Give us a king to judge us. And Samuel prayed unto the LORD.

7 And the LORD said unto Samuel, Hearken unto the voice of the people in all that they say unto thee: for they have not rejected thee, but they have rejected me, that I should not reign over them.

8 According to all the works which they have done since the day that I brought them up out of Egypt even unto this day, wherewith they have forsaken me, and served other gods, so do they also unto thee.

9 Now therefore hearken unto their voice: howbeit yet protest solemnly unto them, and shew them the manner of the king that shall reign over them.

....

19 Nevertheless the people refused to obey the voice of Samuel; and they said, Nay; but we will have a king over us.

....

19 And all the people said unto

1 Samuel 8:4-9, 19; 12:19-25

4 Then all the elders of Israel gathered together and came to Samuel at Ramah, 5 and said to him, "You are old and your sons do not follow in your ways; appoint for us, then, a king to govern us, like other nations." 6 But the thing displeased Samuel when they said, "Give us a king to govern us." Samuel prayed to the LORD, 7 and the LORD said to Samuel, "Listen to the voice of the people in all that they say to you; for they have not rejected you, but they have rejected me from being king over them. 8 Just as they have done to me, from the day I brought them up out of Egypt to this day, forsaking me and serving other gods, so also they are doing to you. 9 Now then, listen to their voice; only—you shall solemnly warn them, and show them the ways of the king who shall reign over them."

....

19 But the people refused to listen to the voice of Samuel; they said, "No! but we are determined to have a king over us."

....

19 All the people said to Samuel,

Samuel, Pray for thy servants unto the LORD thy God, that we die not: for we have added unto all our sins *this* evil, to ask us a king.

20 And Samuel said unto the people, Fear not: ye have done all this wickedness: yet turn not aside from following the LORD, but serve the LORD with all your heart;

21 And turn ye not aside: for *then should ye* go after vain *things,* which cannot profit nor deliver; for they are vain.

22 For the LORD will not forsake his people for his great name's sake: because it hath pleased the LORD to make you his people.

23 Moreover as for me, God forbid that I should sin against the LORD in ceasing to pray for you: but I will teach you the good and the right way:

24 Only fear the LORD, and serve him in truth with all your heart: for consider how great *things* he hath done for you.

25 But if ye shall still do wickedly, ye shall be consumed, both ye and your king.

Key Verse: **And said unto him, Behold, thou art old, and thy sons walk not in thy ways: now make us a king to judge us like all the nations.**

"Pray to the LORD your God for your servants, so that we may not die, for we have added to all our sins the evil of demanding a king for ourselves."

20 And Samuel said to the people, "Do not be afraid; you have done all this evil, yet do not turn aside from following the LORD, but serve the LORD with all your heart; 21 and do not turn aside after useless things that cannot profit or save, for they are useless. 22 For the LORD will not cast away his people, for his great name's sake, because it has pleased the LORD to make you a people for himself. 23 Moreover as for me, far be it from me that I should sin against the LORD by ceasing to pray for you; and I will instruct you in the good and the right way. 24 Only fear the LORD, and serve him faithfully with all your heart; for consider what great things he has done for you. 25 But if you still do wickedly, you shall be swept away, both you and your king."

Key Verse: **And said to him, "You are old and your sons do not follow in your ways; appoint for us, then, a king to govern us, like other nations."**

As You Read the Scripture

The opening chapters of the book of 1 Samuel relate the story of the birth, childhood, and career of Samuel, who was the last of the judges and presided over the nation's transition to a monarchy. This lesson is set toward the end of Samuel's life. Although the people of Israel had been involved in battles with the Philistines during Samuel's career, he was apparently more of an arbiter than a military leader in the style of earlier judges. He resided in the town of Ramah and traveled a circuit of three sanctuaries, probably settling disputes among the people. When Samuel became elderly, he appointed his two sons as judges in his place, but they proved to be dishonest.

1 Samuel 8:4-5. Concerned about the problem of national leadership, the heads of the Israelite families confronted Samuel and asked him to appoint a king "to govern us, like other nations." This request was probably motivated both by the unsatisfactory situation with Samuel's corrupt sons and by the desire to have the form of government that they observed among neigh-boring people.

Verse 6. Samuel's displeasure was partly the result of his disappointment over the rejection of his sons and partly because of his belief that kingship was contrary to God's plan for Israel.

Verse 7-9. When Samuel brought the matter before God he was assured that the rejection was not really of him and his family, but of Yahweh. It was a continuation of the pattern of disloyalty and disobedience that had charac-terized the life of Israel since the Exodus from Egypt. Nevertheless, God instructed Samuel to cooperate with the request for a king, but first to offer a stern and explicit warning on the evils of monarchy. The following nine verses of the chapter summarize this lecture, which the people refused to heed.

Verse 19. In spite of Samuel's graphic recital of the ways in which a king would exploit them and their families, the leaders of Israel still insisted.

Chapters 9–11, which tell of the selection and proclamation of Saul as the first king, will be the subject of next week's study. This lesson skips to chap-ter 12, in which Samuel delivered his farewell address to Israel in the style of Moses and Joshua before him.

Chapter 12:19. In this verse, the people appeared to recognize already that they had erred in demanding a human king. Perhaps it was their emo-tional response to the end of Samuel's great career and their feeling of guilt for having rejected his advice. The writer of this passage was affirming that God's favor remained with Samuel.

Verses 20-22. Samuel's reply was gracious and encouraging. He acknowl-edged that the decision to seek a king had been wrong, but urged the peo-ple not to allow that mistake to lead them into further unfaithfulness. Even though Yahweh had not approved and had been displeased by the people's demand, the monarchy was established by divine permission. God had not chosen them as the people of the covenant because of any virtues that they possessed, but for God's own purpose. God would not reject them as the chosen people and would continue to work in their history, for such was the divine will.

Verses 23-25. Samuel promised to continue to pray for and guide them as long as he could. Again, he warned of the dangers of apostasy.

The Scripture and the Main Question

The Role of Samuel: Standing between the Two Orders

The character of Samuel is familiar to most people who have learned the stories of the Old Testament as children in Sunday school, but we are usually better informed about his early life than about his adult career. Samuel's mother, Hannah, had previously been barren and had beseeched God to enable her to conceive. Samuel's birth was understood as a sign of divine favor and a portent of an unusual life of service to God. Hannah brought her young son to the shrine at Shiloh and committed him to the care of the priest Eli. Samuel had been called to be God's spokesperson in leadership of Israel.

Samuel is sometimes described as the last judge and first prophet of Israel. While this is an oversimplification, for there had been anonymous prophets earlier, it does convey the truth of Samuel's role as a bridge figure between two eras of Hebrew history. With his career, the period of the judges came to an end; with his anointing of Saul, the period of the monarchy began. During that period the prophets played a major role as the spokespersons of Yahweh.

The story in 1 Samuel is somewhat difficult to follow because it is clearly a composite of at least two traditions. Our lesson for today comes from what may be called the Samuel tradition. In this rather conservative perspective, monarchy was not the form of government that God preferred for Israel, but was reluctantly allowed at the insistence of the people. Samuel is portrayed as the faithful servant of God who tried to dissuade them from the demand for a king. In next week's lesson, we will consider the so-called Saul tradition, in which the monarchy is presented in a more favorable light.

In 1 Samuel 8, God allowed Israel to opt for a king, after warning them through Samuel of the unpleasant consequences that would follow their decision. God does not approve of their choice, but allowed it like a parent might allow children to learn from the results of their own mistakes. Why was there such a negative understanding of the kingship in this tradition? A part of this judgment may be the result of the experiences of Israel later under the reign of King Solomon when many of the dangers of which Samuel had warned did, indeed, become real. There is also a theological perspective here that is important for modern students of the scripture. The chief reason given by the elders for their demand for a king was that Israel might be like other nations. But, in God's plan, Israel was not to be like the other nations. Israel was to be unique—a community in covenant relationship with God providing religious leadership and revelation for all humankind. The demand for a king threatened that special identity and role for the covenant community, which was understood to be ruled by Yahweh directly. In seeking to be like other nations, Israel ran the risk of repeating the sin first committed in the Garden of Eden—exceeding their God-given limitations and attempting to control their own destiny by their own power. Some in Israel believed that the leadership of a monarch was essential if the nation was to survive the threats from its powerful enemies, especially the Philistines. The insistence on a king was the expression of a shift in confidence from God to human leaders, an attempt to find security in political and military might.

After the great victory led by Gideon over the Midianites, which we discussed last week, the people had sought to make Gideon king, but he had refused saying, "I will not rule over you, and my son will not rule over you; the LORD will rule over you" (Judg. 8:23). This refusal reflected the ancient understanding of Israel as a theocracy—a community ruled by God. In today's lesson, Samuel is presented as the voice calling for faithfulness to this covenant relationship and Israel's identity as God's people. The movement of history was, however, toward monarchy. Samuel himself became the instrument of God's choosing and anointing of the first two kings of Israel. New political and cultural forms emerged as settings for the old faith. Israel would struggle to understand its relationship to God in the new order. How was God's will revealed through the monarchy? How was the covenant to be kept by people living under the authority of a king?

Politics and Theology

The writer of the Samuel tradition understood very clearly that there was an inherent and inescapable connection between politics and theology, between the structures of government and the tenets of faith. This connection, although real, has proved extremely difficult to work out in the actual existence of nations. How are the religious convictions of a people to be expressed in their governmental structures? Some persons would contend that no such connection should exist, that government and religion are separate spheres and that one should not impact on the other. I would argue that such a clear separation is actually impossible. The values, convictions, and goals of a people *will* influence their political organization no matter how much they may talk about the separation of church and state. In awareness of this, we can examine our political structures and activities quite consciously in order to evaluate how they express our deepest beliefs.

The example of ancient Israel in our scripture for today is one instance of this expression of theology in politics. History offers many others. Many European countries in past centuries based their government on the theory referred to as the divine right of kings. The belief was that the monarch was put into power by God and that loyalty to him (or her in some countries) was a religious duty. (The parents of John Wesley suffered a temporary marital separation over their differences in applying this theory during a time of change in English monarchs.) In contrast, the leaders of the American Revolutionary War believed that when a king abused the rights of his subjects, they had a religious duty to overthrow and replace him. The Puritan colonists who sailed from England to settle what became Massachusetts set up a government in which authority was in the hands of the religious leaders, who were understood to exercise power according to the will of God.

It would be easy to go on citing examples from history, but the point is simply to make clear that religious beliefs and governmental forms are necessarily related. This becomes especially problematic in a nation like the present United States, which is made up of persons of widely varying faith perspectives.

Helping Adults Become Involved

Preparing to Teach

Consider enlisting the help of two members of the class who will be prepared to tell the stories related in 1 Samuel 1–3. Read this material carefully yourself and be ready to make the connection between Samuel, the earlier judges, and the later kings. Use "As You Read the Scripture" for help.

Spend some time thinking about the various forms of government that have been used in human societies in the past and in the contemporary world. You will be able to use your thoughts to stimulate and guide discussion in the class. Have newsprint or chalkboard available, as well as Bibles.

Organize the presentation of the lesson in this way:

> I. The role of Samuel
> II. Monarchy—a new order in Israel
> III. Forms of government and faith

Introducing the Main Question

Have arranged on a low table several pieces of United States money, both currency and coins. Ask the class what is alike about all of them. Keep hint-ing until you get the answer you want: The motto of the United States—In God We Trust—is stamped on them all. Lead a discussion of what this means in our national life today. How well is our trust in God expressed in our political, economic, military, and social policies? Many persons will be surprised to learn that this phrase, while having appeared on coins from time to time since the Civil War, was not adopted as the official national motto until 1956.

Developing the Lesson

I. The role of Samuel

Ask the persons who have prepared in advance to share with the class the stories in 1 Samuel 1–3. Many will recognize these stories and enjoy responding to them briefly. Move on to explain the role of Samuel as a bridge figure between the two orders of Hebrew history—the periods of the judges and of the monarchy. Show that while Samuel did function as a judge, especially in the modern use of that term, meaning an arbiter, he was also a prophet—one who was God's spokesperson to Israel. During the period of the monarchy, the role of the prophets will be increasingly important. Use the material in "As You Read the Scripture" and in the first part of "The Role of Samuel: Standing between the Two Orders."

II. Monarchy—a new order in Israel

Having established the identity and function of Samuel in the larger story, explain his response to the demand for a king as expressed in the chapters for study today. Make it clear that two traditions are intertwined in 1 Samuel and that the writers had differing opinions about the institution of monarchy. Write on the board or newsprint the third verse of Psalm 146: "Do not put your trust in princes, in mortals, in whom there is no help." Explain that this verse expresses the position that Samuel represents in our scripture for today. The information in "The Role of Samuel: Standing between the Two Orders" can be presented here. Have the class look with you at the warning lecture that Samuel delivered on the evils of kingship in 1 Samuel 8:11-18. Lead a discussion on these dangers as the potential consequences, not only of monarchy, but of human governments in general.

III. Forms of government and faith

Any discussion of politics, and especially the relationship between politics and religion, is likely to be controversial. Rather than something that must always be avoided, controversy can serve as a valuable tool for arousing interest and promoting learning. Of course, such discussions must be conducted sensitively with respect for differing opinions.

Use the material in "Politics and Theology" to present the idea that various forms of government express different religious beliefs. If your class members have followed up on the recommendation at the end of last Sunday's lesson, they should have thoughts to share about how our understandings of the nature of God and of the nature of human beings are expressed in different forms of government. Make a list on newsprint or board of as many diverse forms of political structure as your group can think of. These should include various expressions of autocracy such as monarchy and dictatorship, of oligarchy such as aristocracy, and of democracy both direct and representative. Include forms of totalitarianism such as fascism, nazism, and communism. Mention the ways in which leaders are chosen in these forms of government.

Unless your class is quite small, divide into groups and spend some time discussing these questions: What forms of government are most Christian? Why? What beliefs about God and human beings are they based on? How do they function in God's plan for salvation? Share the ideas that have emerged in each group when the whole class reassembles. Lead an evaluation of the government of the contemporary United States based on these same questions. This should relate back to the conversation at the beginning of the lesson about the national motto. Do not worry about differences of opinion nor strive to find right answers to these questions that have been debated throughout human history. The goal is to get your class thinking and talking about these issues. Too often Christians fail to perceive any connections between their lives as people of faith and their actions as citizens.

Helping Class Members Act

Involve the class in a consideration of how the various levels of government under which they live might be changed so as to be more in accord with God's will and plan. Avoid any implication that God works through the secular government of this nation in the same way that God worked through ancient Israel. The point is that our political structures, actions, and decisions express what we believe about God and our relationship to God as individuals and as members of communities.

Divide the class into three groups (mixing persons differently than in the last groups). Have one group focus on local government, one on state, and the other on the national level. Ask each group to agree on one issue or situation at that political level that needs reform. Challenge the class as a whole and as individuals to get involved actively in addressing this concern. The specifics of how this will work will vary with your situation and people, but try to encourage *doing* something, even if it is as simple as writing a letter to a political official.

Planning for Next Sunday

Plan to ask for reports on actions taken on these political concerns.

Saul's Opportunity as King

Background Scripture: 1 Samuel 9:15–10:1a, 20-24

The Main Question

After having won fame for his success during the American Civil War, General William T. Sherman was strongly urged to seek the presidency of the nation. Finding it difficult to convince his supporters that he had no such interest, General Sherman finally announced flatly, "If nominated, I will not run; if elected, I will not serve." A century later, President Ronald Reagan was wounded in an assassination attempt. Secretary of State Alexander Haig rushed to announce to reporters and the nation that "I'm in charge here," quite overlooking the fact that he had no such authority under the law and, ultimately, causing the end of his political career.

The sharp contrast between the attitudes of these two persons in the face of possibilities for leadership may help us grasp the relevance of our lesson for today. Saul's reluctance to be king of Israel, while not as firm as Sherman's, might have been a warning of the difficulties that would plague his reign. Yet, Saul was clearly understood by Samuel, the Israelite people, and the author of this scripture to be God's choice for the kingship.

In our corporate life in both secular and religious communities, we need good leaders lest we fall into social and moral disorder like Israel in the time of the judges when everyone "did what was right in their own eyes." How are we to select those persons to whom we will grant authority and responsibility in our secular government and in our churches? What qualifications should we look for in our potential leaders? How are we to seek divine guidance as we choose those to whom we will entrust the powers of office?

Selected Scripture

King James Version

1 Samuel 9:15-17; 10:1a, 20-24

15 Now the LORD had told Samuel in his ear a day before Saul came, saying,

16 To morrow about this time I will send thee a man out of the land of Benjamin, and thou shalt anoint him *to be* captain over my people Israel, that he may save my people out of the hand of the Philistines: for I have looked upon my people, because their cry is come unto me.

17 And when Samuel saw Saul, the LORD said unto him, Behold

New Revised Standard Version

1 Samuel 9:15-17; 10:1a, 20-24

15 Now the day before Saul came, the LORD had revealed to Samuel: 16 "Tomorrow about this time I will send to you a man from the land of Benjamin, and you shall anoint him to be ruler over my people Israel. He shall save my people from the hand of the Philistines; for I have seen the suffering of my people, because their outcry has come to me." 17 When Samuel saw Saul, the LORD told him, "Here is the man of whom I spoke to you. He it is who shall rule

the man whom I spake to thee of! this same shall reign over my people.

over my people."

....

1 Then Samuel took a vial of oil, and poured *it* upon his head, and kissed him, and said, *Is it* not because the LORD hath anointed thee *to be* captain over his inheritance?

1 Samuel took a vial of oil and poured it on his head, and kissed him; he said, "The LORD has anointed you ruler over his people Israel. You shall reign over the people of the LORD and you will save them from the hand of their enemies all around."

....

20 And when Samuel had caused all the tribes of Israel to come near, the tribe of Benjamin was taken.

21 When he had caused the tribe of Benjamin to come near by their families, the family of Matri was taken, and Saul the son of Kish was taken: and when they sought him, he could not be found.

22 Therefore they inquired of the LORD further, if the man should yet come thither. And the LORD answered, Behold, he hath hid himself among the stuff.

23 And they ran and fetched him thence: and when he stood among the people, he was higher than any of the people from his shoulders and upward.

24 And Samuel said to all the people, See ye him who the LORD hath chosen, that *there is* none like him among all the people? And all the people shouted, and said, God save the king.

20 Then Samuel brought all the tribes of Israel near, and the tribe of Benjamin was taken by lot. 21 He brought the tribe of Benjamin near by its families, and the family of the Matrites was taken by lot. Finally he brought the family of the Matrites near man by man, and Saul the son of Kish was taken by lot. But when they sought him, he could not be found. 22 So they inquired again of the LORD, "Did the man come here?" and the LORD said, "See, he has hidden himself among the baggage." 23 Then they ran and brought him from there. When he took his stand among the people, he was head and shoulders taller than any of them. 24 Samuel said to all the people, "Do you see the one whom the LORD has chosen? There is no one like him among all the people." And all the people shouted, "Long live the king!"

Key Verse: **Then Samuel took a vial of oil, and poured *it* upon his head, and kissed him, and said, *Is it* not because the LORD hath anointed thee *to be* captain over his inheritance?**

Key Verse: **Samuel took a vial of oil and poured it on his head, and kissed him; he said, "The LORD has anointed you ruler over his people Israel. You shall reign over the people of the LORD and you will save them from the hand of their enemies all around."**

FIRST QUARTER

As You Read the Scripture

1 Samuel 9:15-17; 10:1a, 20-24. In our scripture for today Samuel, the great judge and prophet, is proceeding to grant the demand of the Israelites that he appoint a king to rule over them. God's permission and guidance have been secured. Indeed, although the events of the story are focused on Samuel and Saul, the prime actor is God, who takes the initiative and determines the outcome. In the opening verses of chapter 9, Saul was introduced as a "handsome young man . . . [who] stood head and shoulders above everyone else" (v. 2). Saul had gone into the countryside searching for donkeys that had strayed from his father's farm. On the advice of his servant, Saul decided to go into town and inquire of the local seer where the donkeys might be found.

Chapter 9:15. The seer to whom Saul was coming for help was Samuel. Prior to Saul's arrival, God had spoken to Samuel and revealed the divine plans.

Verses 16-17. Saul was from the tribe of Benjamin, the smallest of the Hebrew tribes, and traditionally considered to be descended from the youngest of Jacob's twelve sons. The Philistines were powerful enemies who had been oppressing Israel and had recently defeated them in battle. God revealed to Samuel that Saul was the chosen instrument to deliver the nation from this enemy. The phrase "my people," used by God four times in these two verses, emphasized the special covenant relationship between God and Israel, in spite of the failures of the people to remain faithful. God's side of the covenant was always upheld.

Chapter 10:1a. In private, Samuel carried out God's command and anointed Saul as ruler or prince by putting oil on his head. This was probably a spiced olive oil (see recipe in Exod. 30:22-25) poured from a clay flask. Among the Israelites, this was a sacramental act that indicated the giving of power and holiness from God to the person being anointed. Priests (see Exod. 29:7) and prophets (see 1 Kings 19:16) were anointed as well as kings, as a sign of their designation for special roles. Anointing was understood to authorize and to empower a person for leadership.

Verses 20-21. Later the secret anointing of Saul to be king was made public. Samuel gathered all of the Israelites together and used the sacred lots to reveal God's choice. While this method of decision making is mentioned in several places in the Bible, we do not know exactly how it worked. Apparently the lot could only indicate yes or no. Therefore, the process of determining first the tribe, then the clan, family, and individual must have been rather lengthy. The casting of the lots with faith and prayer was believed to be controlled by God.

Verse 22. Strangely, Saul had fled from the scene of the casting of lots; surely his earlier anointing by Samuel meant that he knew what the outcome was going to be. When his selection was revealed, he could not be found until God indicated where he was. In the words of the King James Version, Saul was hiding "in the stuff." The Hebrew word here, which the NRSV translates as *baggage,* means supplies, equipment, or gear of various sorts.

Verses 23-24. When Saul was located and brought out, Samuel praised him without indication of any reservation and the people added their acclaim. The era of the monarchy began with optimistic expectation.

The Scripture and the Main Question

"He Shall Save My People"

Several times in these chapters dealing with the accession of Saul to the kingship, God made clear that his function would be to rule and to deliver Israel. In 1 Samuel 9:16, God spoke of hearing and responding to the cry of suffering from the people; Saul was to be the instrument through which Israel would be saved from their plight. It is relevant for us to consider this as we think about the function of leaders in our own day.

There are hazards in any discussion that seeks to explore comparisons between ancient Israel and the lives of present-day Christians in the United States. Our nation does not play the same role in the divine drama of salvation as that assigned to the nation of Israel. Indeed, a closer analogy can be drawn between the role of the Christian church and that of Israel—both are the chosen covenant communities in relationship with God. So, as we consider matters of leadership, we must think separately and somewhat differently about secular government and the church.

The government of the United States was founded on the supposition that its chief role was the protection of the rights of its people by establishing and maintaining a civil order characterized by peace, justice, and freedom. Through the decades since this beginning, Americans have vigorously debated just what this ideal means and how it can best be fulfilled in changing situations. How can we today select the best leaders for our government on national, state, and local levels? Many cultures, like ancient Israel, believed that their rulers were picked by the deity. Others have used methods as diverse as combat, chance, heredity, and election. The Greek philosopher Plato devoted long discussions to the question of how society should be ruled, and concluded that power should be exercised by the very wisest persons, those whom he called the philospher-kings. But, Plato was unable to answer satisfactorily the prior question: How, and by whom, is it to be decided who these wisest persons are?

Could contemporary Americans receive help in our dilemmas of political choices if we reexamined the basic purpose for which human government exists? God's charge to the king of Israel was to deliver the nation from oppression and bring the people out of their suffering. Secular government in America was begun with very similar ideas.

As members of the Christian church, we should be even more deeply concerned about the selection of appropriate leadership for the church, which is the community through which the divine purposes are being worked out. How do we understand leadership and how do we choose those who will be empowered to exercise it? Various denominations answer these questions differently, but United Methodism can serve as an illustration of the issues. In this denomination, the leadership role is referred to as ministry or service. We believe that all baptized Christians make up the general ministry of the church; in other words, all Christians are involved in service in the name of Christ. Ordained and diaconal ministers are referred to as the representative ministry. They are understood to have a special call and specific role in representing Christ to the church and the church to the world. How should such persons be chosen? What gifts and graces should they possess? How can the church determine who is qualified and who is not? Answers to these questions are diverse and controversial. An influential example was the work of Thomas Aquinas in the thirteenth century, who listed the characteristics that he believed disqualified a person for ordained ministry. His list included persons who were of illegitimate birth, who were physically handicapped, or who were women. The debate over women's eligibility continues, especially in some churches, and another pressing question today has to do with homosexual persons. United Methodism has always emphasized that the call to leadership as representative minister is twofold—both an inner and outer call. The inner call is the word of God communicated to an individual so that he or she realizes it with heart and mind and believes him or herself to be called. The outer call is the process by which the official structures of the church examine and test the validity of such calls and prepare persons to fulfill them. Both the inner and the outer calls are essential to authentic authorization for ministry as leaders of the faith community.

"Hiding Among the Stuff"

We know well from both ancient and current history that those persons who are most eager and assertive in their desire to be leaders do not always prove to be the most capable. Yet, there is something disturbing about Saul's hiding himself at the very moment when his designation as king is about to be announced. Was it the result of excess modesty, failure of nerve, effort to be coy? The scripture does not even hint at the reason. Only when we read about the remainder of Saul's career as monarch, as we will next Sunday, do we realize that this reluctance may have been an evil portent, a warning of the weaknesses that would plague his reign. Successful leadership requires confidence in one's abilities, grounded in a realistic assessment of one's strengths and limitations. This is one function of the inner call to ministry—to keep a person from being pushed into a role by the efforts of others in opposition to her or his own inclinations. There is a rather pathetic story told about Warren G. Harding after he was inaugurated president in 1921. Those who visited Harding in his office relate that he almost never sat in the chair behind the presidential desk. When asked by his friends about this, Harding explained that he felt extremely uncomfortable, even frightened, at the thought of sitting where predecessors like Washington, Jefferson, and Lincoln had sat. This might have been viewed as appealing modesty had not the subsequent history of his administration proved Harding quite accurate in his realization that he was neither intellectually nor morally competent to serve as the nation's chief executive.

Leadership ability does, of course, require both cultivation and courage. Reluctance to lead may evince neither commendable modesty nor accurate self-evaluation, but the failure that Emily Dickinson addressed in one of her poems:

> We never know how high we are till we are called to rise,
> And then, if we are true to plan, our statures touch the skies.
> The heroism we recite would be a daily thing
> Did not ourselves the cubits warp for fear to be a king.

Helping Adults Become Involved

Preparing to Teach

As an attention-grabbing device to get your class interested in the subject matter of this lesson, consider a display of pictures of secular and religious leaders. There are a variety of ways to do this. You could collect, from newspapers and magazines, pictures of contemporary leaders from various nations and religious groups. Your church may have photographs of the ministers who have served there. An encyclopedia or history book will have pictures of the presidents of the United States, while denominational publications will have photographs of bishops or other church leaders. Your local or church library will contain resources; your minister should be able to help. The idea is to have displayed a variety of pictures of prominent persons in both secular and religious life in order to stimulate thinking about the importance of and qualifications for leadership.

Read the background scripture in 1 Samuel 9 and 10 using "As You Read the Scripture" for assistance. Keep in mind that two traditions about kingship are present here, as we discussed last Sunday.

Make copies for the class of the first paragraph of the American Declaration of Independence and the preamble to the United States Constitution. These can be found easily in history or reference books.

Consider asking your minister to give your class a brief description of the process by which persons become ordained ministers in your denomination. If this is not feasible, obtain a copy of the *Book of Discipline of the United Methodist Church* (or comparable source for your church) and familiarize yourself with the process as described in chapter 3. Note especially "Section IV. Ordination," which deals with the purpose of and qualifications for ordained leadership; be ready to share this with the class. You may decide to make copies of some of this material for distribution and discussion.

Write the Emily Dickinson poem (found at the end of "The Scripture and the Main Question") on the board or newsprint, or copy it as a part of the handout material.

You will need the newsprint chart of events in the history of Israel that you have been making during the quarter, as well as additional newsprint or chalkboard. Bibles should be available for all.

The following outline will enable you to present the biblical material and relate it to today:

    I. Samuel anoints the first king of Israel.
    II. Saul, the reluctant monarch
    III. Choosing secular and religious leaders today

Introducing the Main Question

Use the anecdotes about General Sherman and Secretary Haig in "The Main Question" to introduce the theme of the lesson. Lead a brief discussion about persons in leadership positions at various levels of government today. Allow class members to express opinions freely without feeling that it is your job to make them agree. Guide the discussion to the question of why highly qualified persons often choose not to seek or even to accept public office. The purpose of this introduction is to stimulate thinking about the processes and the problems of obtaining the most capable leaders.

Developing the Lesson

I. Samuel anoints the first king of Israel.
Remind the class of the difference of opinion in Israel over the advisability of kingship, as we saw in last week's lesson. Ultimately, of course, God not

only allowed the transition to monarchy, but directed the process. Through Samuel, judge and prophet, God choose Saul to be the first king. Use the information in the scripture material and in "As You Read the Scripture" to relate the events of this story. Bring your newsprint chart of Israel's history up to this point.

II. Saul, the reluctant monarch

Emphasize Saul's hiding himself at the very moment when his kingship was being made public. Have the class speculate on what his reasons might have been. Tell them that next Sunday's study will reveal much more about the character of Saul. Share with the class the anecdote about President Warren G. Harding from the section "Hiding Among the Stuff" and discuss whether or not Saul might have felt similarly inadequate for the duties. This conversation can lead naturally into a consideration of how leaders can best be chosen. Harding was selected as his party's candidate at the last moment when the nominating convention could not make a decision. He was the choice of powerful leaders who wanted a president who would be too weak to challenge their control. Be sure not to overlook the differences in the stories of these men: Saul was chosen by God and could have succeeded as king if he had been faithful; Harding was chosen in a smoke-filled room by people who planned for him to fail.

III. Choosing secular and religious leaders today

The discussion above will have provided an easy transition into this section. "The Scripture and the Main Question" suggests a variety of approaches to examining this topic; utilize this material to guide your presentation and to be certain that significant points are included. Beyond that, you may need to select the emphases that you believe to be most relevant for your group.

Distribute and discuss the copies of portions of the Declaration of Independence and the Constitution that you have prepared. The discussion should focus on the purposes of government in human society as these documents present them. Make a list on newsprint as your class examines the documents. Try to answer the question "What are leaders supposed to do?" The displayed pictures of particular leaders may be helpful as you consider how well contemporary persons are fulfilling these responsibilities, and what are the best methods for choosing individuals to be leaders. Are some of our problems the result of using the wrong criteria to make our choices?

Turn to a consideration of leadership in the church, especially the position of ordained ministry. Either through the minister's presentation or your own, describe in outline how your church selects ordained leadership. Use the material in the *Discipline* to lift up the purpose and qualifications of ordained persons, again making a list on newsprint. Are there individuals or groups who are being denied ordination because the church is using inappropriate processes or standards?

Conclude by encouraging the class to share insights and questions that have resulted from these discussions.

Helping Class Members Act

Challenge the students to use the Dickinson poem to examine themselves with this question: Am I being called to some leadership role that I have not yet accepted?

Planning for Next Sunday

Read 1 Samuel 13 and 15 to learn about some of the events in the career of Saul as king.

LESSON 9   OCTOBER 30

King Saul Disobeys God

Background Scripture: 1 Samuel 13

The Main Question

A popular column in our local newspaper is written by a child psychologist who responds to letters that he receives from parents. A recurring problem cited in these inquiries is that of disobedience—how to get children to do what they are asked to do. Although the details of the psychologist's answers differ with the ages of the children, his constant theme is the necessity to make acts of disobedience cost the children rather than the parents. Parents should be unapologetic about teaching their offspring that obedience is essential, even when it goes against the child's wishes or understandings. The consequences of failure to obey must be borne by children who will then learn to modify their behavior.

Opinions about child-raising techniques vary widely, but surely this psychologist is sounding a note that is in harmony with the theological views of the writer of the scripture for today's lesson. Obedience to the command of God is an essential requirement. To disobey is to suffer the consequences of one's actions. Especially for the one who is king, the demand for obedience is paramount. God had made Saul king of Israel, but Saul's subsequent actions disqualified him and his family from that position. Even though Saul believed that he had good reasons for his actions, he was judged to have violated his covenant of loyalty to Yahweh and to have usurped divine authority as represented by the prophet. In chapter 15:22 Samuel reminded Saul, "Surely, to obey is better than sacrifice, and to heed than the fat of rams."

How are we to understand this account of Saul's disobedience and punishment? What is its meaning for our lives as Christians?

Selected Scripture

King James Version	New Revised Standard Version
1 Samuel 13:5-14	*1 Samuel 13:5-14*
5 And the Philistines gathered themselves together to fight with Israel, thirty thousand chariots, and six thousand horsemen, and people	5 The Philistines mustered to fight with Israel, thirty thousand chariots, and six thousand horsemen, and troops like the sand on

as the sand which *is* on the sea shore in multitude: and they came up, and pitched in Michmash, eastward from Bethaven.

6 When the men of Israel saw that they were in a strait, (for the people were distressed,) then the people did hide themselves in caves, and in thickets, and in rocks, and in high places, and in pits.

7 And *some of* the Hebrews went over Jordan to the land of Gad and Gilead. As for Saul, he *was* yet in Gilgal, and all the people followed him trembling.

8 And he tarried seven days, according to the set time that Samuel *had appointed:* but Samuel came not to Gilgal; and the people were scattered from him.

9 And Saul said, Bring hither a burnt offering to me, and peace offerings. And he offered the burnt offering.

10 And it came to pass, that as soon as he had made an end of offering the burnt offering, behold, Samuel came; and Saul went out to meet him, that he might salute him.

11 And Samuel said, What hast thou done? And Saul said, Because I saw that the people were scattered from me, and *that* thou camest not within the days appointed, and *that* the Philistines gathered themselves together at Michmash;

12 Therefore said I, The Philistines will come down now upon me to Gilgal, and I have not made supplication unto the Lord; I forced myself therefore, and offered a burnt offering.

13 And Samuel said to Saul, Thou hast done foolishly: thou hast not kept the commandment of the Lord thy God, which he commanded thee: for now would the Lord have established thy kingdom upon Israel for ever.

14 But now thy kingdom shall not continue: the Lord hath sought a man after his own heart, and the

the seashore in multitude; they came up and encamped at Michmash, to the east of Bethaven. 6 When the Israelites saw that they were in distress (for the troops were hard pressed), the people hid themselves in caves and in holes and in rocks and in tombs and in cisterns. 7 Some Hebrews crossed the Jordan to the land of Gad and Gilead. Saul was still at Gilgal, and all the people followed him trembling.

8 He waited seven days, the time appointed by Samuel; but Samuel did not come to Gilgal, and the people began to slip away from Saul. 9 So Saul said, "Bring the burnt offering here to me, and the offerings of well-being." And he offered the burnt offering. 10 As soon as he had finished offering the burnt offering, Samuel arrived; and Saul went out to meet him and salute him. 11 Samuel said, "What have you done?" Saul replied, "When I saw that the people were slipping away from me, and that you did not come within the days appointed, and that the Philistines were mustering at Michmash, 12 I said, 'Now the Philistines will come down upon me at Gilgal, and I have not entreated the favor of the Lord'; so I forced myself, and offered the burnt offering." 13 Samuel said to Saul, "You have done foolishly; you have not kept the commandment of the Lord your God, which he commanded you. The Lord would have established your kingdom over Israel forever, 14 but now your kingdom will not continue; the Lord has sought out a man after his own heart; and the Lord has appointed him to be ruler over his people, because you have not kept what the Lord commanded you."

LORD hath commanded him *to* be
captain over his people, because
thou hast not kept *that* which the
LORD commanded thee.

Key Verse: **But now thy kingdom
shall not continue: the LORD hath
sought a man after his own heart,
and the LORD hath commanded him
to be captain over his people,
because thou hast not kept *that*
which the LORD commanded thee.**

Key Verse: **But now your kingdom
will not continue; the LORD has
sought out a man after his own
heart; and the LORD has appointed
him to be ruler over his people,
because you have not kept what the
LORD commanded you.**

As You Read the Scripture

1 Samuel 13:5. Chief among the reasons why the Israelites had demanded
a king was the threat from their enemy, the Philistines. These people, who
had come originally from the island of Crete, had settled along the sea coast
of Canaan in five strong city-states. As this verse makes clear, they were tech-
nologically superior to the Israelites, especially in their possession of war
chariots and of weapons and tools made of iron. See verses 19-22 of this
chapter for more details of how the Philistines used their advanced knowledge to oppress Israel, whose weapons at this time were largely made of flint
and copper.

Verses 6-7. The intensity of the oppression that Israel was suffering is
graphically described in these two verses. We are reminded of the situation
during the period of the judges when the people were forced to hide from
the Midianites before God called Gideon to deliver Israel (see Judg. 6).

Verses 8-9. Saul, with his volunteer militia, went to the shrine at Gilgal to
await Samuel, who had promised to come in seven days to invoke Yahweh's
blessings on the military effort against the Philistines. Samuel did not come
at the appointed time and the army began to shrink as men left to return
home. Saul, deciding that he could delay no longer, offered the sacrificial
offerings himself.

Verse 10. Saul apparently had no sense that he had done anything wrong.
When Samuel arrived very soon after the sacrifice, Saul went out to greet
him.

Verses 11-12. Samuel was extremely displeased and demanded an explanation from the king. Saul explained and justified his position as an act of
necessity. Samuel had failed to appear at the appointed time and the army
was melting away. Saul was fearful of an imminent Philistine attack and
unwilling to have to fight without having sought divine help. Note that Saul
contended that "I forced myself." He recognized the questionable nature of
his action in offering the sacrifice, but believed that under the circumstances it was something that he had to do.

Verse 13. Samuel responded by berating Saul severely, arguing that the
king's action was not only foolish, but also a violation of the divine commandment. It is difficult to comprehend just what is meant here. There is
no record in the scripture of a previous command to Saul that addressed
this situation. Apparently, he had transgressed by taking for himself the
function that rightly belonged only to God's prophet-priest. Samuel told

Saul that had he not acted so wrongly God would have perpetuated the rule of his family over Israel. Again, this is new information of which both Saul and the reader were unaware. It may be helpful to remind ourselves of the antomonarchial position that is one of the traditions composing this book and certainly the one that is being expressed in this chapter.

Verse 14. Saul was bluntly informed by Samuel that his act of disobedience to God had cost him the kingdom of Israel. Yahweh had rejected him as king, had turned the divine favor away from Saul and toward another—"a man after his own heart." This man, who the reader will later learn is David, had been appointed to the kingship in Saul's place.

The Scripture and the Main Question

Saul's Disobedience

As we read 1 Samuel 13, it is difficult for us to comprehend just why Saul's actions were so unacceptable. Indeed, I find myself feeling quite sympathetic with him. Saul appears to have tried to make the best of a bad situation—the nation was threatened by powerful enemies; the prophet-priest had not come as he had said he would; the army was dwindling; God's blessings needed to be secured. Saul acted reluctantly in offering the sacrifice, trying to do the right thing. Why did it cost him and his family the kingship?

It is probably impossible for us to understand fully the meaning of this incident, but as we examine it more closely, some insights emerge that we can apply to our own lives. Saul took for himself a role that had not been given to him by God. He acknowledged that he had acted hesitantly—against his own best judgment. His action may not have been wrong in itself, but it was wrong because it violated God's order. Sacrifices were to be offered by the religious leaders, not by the king. One might compare this to the eating of the forbidden fruit in the Garden of Eden. Adam and Eve sinned not because there was something inherently evil about the fruit of a particular tree, but because eating it was contrary to God's will. To oversimplify, we might say that an action is wrong when it is a violation of God's law, regardless of how or why. Saul made his own judgment as to right and wrong, rather than seeking to know what God desired. It has been said that sin is insistence on inventing values, rather than willingness to discover them.

Another incident in which Saul acted contrary to God's command is related in 1 Samuel 15. After his victory over the Amalekites, he did not totally destroy all of the booty nor did he execute Agag, the king. Although to us these actions may appear reasonable, even humane, they represented disobedience to what God had commanded. Saul sinned when he assumed for himself the responsibility of deciding not to obey. John Wesley described one aspect of sin as "an actual voluntary transgression of the law; of the revealed, written law of God; of any commandment of God, acknowledged to be such at the time it is transgressed" (sermon: "Whosoever is born of God cannot sin"). By this definition, Saul's transgression can be perceived more clearly. It is simply a fact of religious life that our own common sense and the revealed will of God do not always correspond. Who of us would have thought it reasonable, or even humane, to save the world through the suffering of Christ on the cross?

Living in Obedience to God

Absolute obedience is a difficult concept for contemporary Christians, living as we do in an age that stresses personal autonomy or the right to do one's own thing. We are reluctant to surrender our wills and to allow other powers to make decisions for us. In many ways, this insistence on self-determination is healthy and even essential. In the aftermath of World War II, there were a series of trials at Nuremberg where German military officers were charged with war crimes. The consistent defense offered by these men was not to deny that they had committed the offenses with which they were charged, but rather that they had committed them in obedience to the command of superior officers. The infamous My Lai incident in the Vietnam conflict offered a similar example. The American soldiers charged with slaughtering innocent civilians argued that they were simply carrying out the command that they had been given. Surely there is a point where one's personal moral responsibility must be fulfilled, even if that involves refusal to follow orders. There is a higher moral law that must be obeyed, and we cannot avoid that duty by blaming our decisions and actions on someone else. Blind obedience to human authority is a dangerous threat to personal and corporate integrity. One is reminded of lines from Alfred, Lord Tennyson's famous poem "The Charge of the Light Brigade":

> Someone had blunder'd.
> Theirs not to make reply,
> Theirs not to reason why,
> Theirs but to do and die:
> Into the valley of Death
> Rode the six hundred.

Although this kind of obedience may be celebrated as heroism in military annals, it is not the kind of exercise of moral responsibility that is expected of God's people.

The fundamental issue for Saul and for Christians today is that of obeying divine rather than human authority. In 1 Samuel 15:1, Samuel told Saul that he had been sent by Yahweh to anoint Saul as king of Israel, "now therefore listen to the words of the LORD." Saul's story ended in tragedy; in 15:35 we read that both Samuel and God grieved. His sin was his failure to listen to God; such listening was the condition on which his authority was grounded. Because he did not listen, he fell into the trap of compromising with evil. There are clues here for the living of our lives in obedience to God. First, we must recognize and accept that there is an ultimate authority in our moral universe and that the will of the authority—God—defines the meaning of right and wrong. Ethical decision making is not a matter of chance or of popular vote, but of ascertaining the divine will. While we are unable to do this alone, God enables us to do it if we live in close relationship to God through Jesus Christ. Our emotions or natural reasoning capacities cannot be relied on to guide us correctly, but God can and does work through them. As the words on a popular Christian poster express it: Jesus came to take away your sin, not your mind. Our hearts and minds, once surrendered to God, do function as instruments through which God communicates to us.

What then does it mean to obey God? Many would argue that it is a matter of not violating any of the Ten Commandments. Others contend that right living means obeying the words of Jesus in what we call the Sermon on the Mount. If we comprehend the profound rather than just the superficial meaning of the Ten Commandments, we will realize that we cannot possibly fulfill them. Who of us has no object of our affection and action that comes before God? And who of us would dare to claim to live in accord with the shocking demands of the Sermon? Living in obedience to God is not a series of acts, but an attitude of heart and mind in which we live in close communion with Christ, listen intently for the divine word, and pattern our lives in response to it.

Helping Adults Become Involved

Preparing to Teach

Study carefully 1 Samuel 13 along with the information in "As You Read the Scripture." Read also chapters 14 and 15 for more about the career of Saul and another account of his disobedience to God and subsequent rejection.

The themes of this lesson are not easy to apply to the lives of modern Christians. The moral issues appear cloudy to us; God's reasons for acting are not clear. Read thoughtfully the material in "The Scripture and the Main Question" and spend some time wrestling with the questions. Your class will be better served by your ability to make the issues of this lesson relevant in their lives than by your seeking to explain precisely what happened to Saul and why.

Do some brief research to remind yourself about the Nuremberg trials in Germany after World War II and the My Lai massacre during the Vietnam conflict. Information can be found in encyclopedias or other reference works. You might consider asking members of the class to be prepared to present short summaries.

Have available Bibles, newsprint or chalkboard, paper, and pencils for each student.

The important issues of the lesson can be presented with this outline:

I. Saul's rejection as king
II. Meanings for the lives of Christians today
  A. Moral responsibility
  B. Obedience to God

Introducing the Main Question

Use the ideas in "The Main Question" about the psychologist and the problems of getting children to obey. Note that we speak of teaching children to obey, which implies that such action is not natural for them. Stimulate a discussion with such questions as these: Why do we want our children to obey us? Why is obedience important when children are young, when they are teenagers? Why is it often so hard to teach them to obey? What about adults—what does obedience mean then? Is it possible to be too obedient as either a child or an adult? What are the differences between obeying human authority figures and obeying God? What are some of the problems or difficulties involved in obedience to God? What may be the consequences of disobedience?

Deliberately cut this discussion short while interest and participation are still high. This is preparatory to returning to the issues later in the session.

Developing the Lesson

I. Saul's rejection as king

Briefly describe the events that occur in 1 Samuel 13. Use the material in "As You Read the Scripture" to help you make clear such things as the Philistine threat, Saul's dilemma and action, God's judgment delivered through Samuel.

Organize a trial of King Saul on the charge of disobedience to the commandment of God. Divide your class in half and have the groups meet separately and plan their arguments using the information in 1 Samuel 13 and 15. The first group is to present the case against Saul as convincingly as possible, from the point of view of Samuel as God's spokesperson. The second is to defend Saul just as vigorously with all of the arguments that they can muster as to why he was not guilty, or at least not sufficiently guilty to forfeit his kingship. After allowing time for planning, have the presentation of the arguments in whatever format you believe will work best with your class. Be creative and venturesome; encourage enthusiastic exchanges, disagreements, and debates. The desired outcome of this exercise is to get the group actively involved in feeling and thinking about the issues. It is unnecessary to come to a consensus or to render a decision on Saul's case. As the discussion develops, utilize the points in the section "Saul's Disobedience."

II. Meanings for the lives of Christians today
A. Moral responsibility

It is not necessary, and indeed probably impossible, to resolve all of the questions relating to Saul. Now is the point at which you need to move the class into an examination of the moral issues of the lesson as they apply to the lives of modern Christians. The free-ranging discussion about obedience at the beginning of the session should have laid a foundation for this.

Share with the class information about the Nuremberg and My Lai war crimes trials. Do not dwell on the details of the events, but use them as springboards for consideration of questions of moral accountability. Utilize the ideas suggested in the first paragraph of "Living in Obedience to God." Many students will be familiar with the Tennyson poem from which the quoted lines are taken. Ask them to consider it in the light of this lesson.

B. Obedience to God

Be certain to allow sufficient time to conclude this lesson with the emphasis on our responsibility to obey the commandments of God and some of the difficulties of living this way. Using the material in the last two paragraphs of "Living in Obedience to God," you should have no problem eliciting considerable discussion. Close by acknowledging that all questions have not been answered and challenging the class members to continue to struggle with them as they seek to be faithful disciples of Christ.

Helping Class Members Act

Encourage your students to devote a part of their personal prayer time this week to examining their own obedience to the commands of God. Ask them to identify specific areas in which they (1) believe that they are living in accordance with the divine will, (2) know or suspect that they are not so living, (3) have experienced the consequences of disobedience to God, (4) find it hard to determine what God's command actually is. Leslie D. Weatherhead's *The Will of God* was mentioned in a previous lesson—this is a good time to recommend it again.

Planning for Next Sunday

This lesson marks the end of the unit focusing on the beginnings of monarchy in Israel. The concluding unit of this quarter will concentrate on the personalities and careers of the most powerful and most famous of the Hebrew monarchs—David and his son, Solomon. Ask your class members to brainstorm from their memories this week and write down every fact or story about either of these kings that they can recall. After testing their recollections, encourage them to read as much as possible of the biblical material that describes the events that occurred between today's lesson and next week's. This will include the remainder of 1 Samuel and the first six chapters of 2 Samuel.

UNIT IV: THE KINGDOM UNDER
DAVID AND SOLOMON

FOUR LESSONS   NOVEMBER 6–27

The lessons of this unit focus on the period of greatest power, prestige, and wealth that the nation of Israel ever enjoyed, and on the careers of its two most famous kings, David and Solomon. The first lesson describes the unique relationship that existed between David and God. Israel understood that the Davidic covenant had promised an ideal ruler from the lineage of David who would come to deliver God's people. The messianic hope became an important part of both Judaism and Christianity. However, as Lesson 11 reveals, David committed serious acts of sin. Even though he repented and was forgiven by God, the consequences of his folly plagued his family and all of Israel. Solomon, David's son, succeeded his father on the throne. As Lesson 12 describes, he was widely renowned for his enormous wealth and impressive wisdom. Profound changes took place in the life of Israel as the nation became a political, military, and economic power for at least this brief period. Tragically, Solomon turned away from God and violated the divine commands of covenant loyalty. In the closing lesson, the depth and the consequences of Solomon's unfaithfulness are made clear. His tolerance of the worship of false gods brought divine punishment. The land was divided into two nations and the united kingdom was no more.

Thoughtful students of the Bible are continually surprised by the stark honesty with which its characters are presented. Because these people are so real in all their accomplishments and failures, they enable us to better understand ourselves and our own struggles to be faithful.

David Claims God's Promise

Background Scripture: 2 Samuel 7

The Main Question

The subject of today's lesson is the covenant established between God and the family of King David. Israel had long understood itself as a community in covenant relationship with God. The covenant with David and his descendants must be seen in that context. It should also be recognized as a unique action of God binding the divine self through a special promise to David and to the kings of his family who would follow him on the throne. It would be difficult to overemphasize the importance of David in the history of the Hebrew people even to the present day. Although a man of known weaknesses and sins, he became for the Hebrew people the exemplar of ideal kingship. During his reign, the nation experienced its time of greatest stability and peace. He was acclaimed, both during and after his lifetime, as God's man, chosen by God to lead Israel to be the nation God meant for it to be. In later years when Israel suffered defeat and oppression, it was the hope that God would raise up another king like David, which gave them strength to survive and persevere. Even after the destruction of the Davidic monarchy in later centuries, Israel remembered the promise of God that this lesson explains, and waited for divine deliverance. Even today, a characteristic tenet of Judaism is the hope for a messiah who will fulfill the divine promises made to and through David. Christians from the first century have understood Jesus Christ as the fulfillment of these Old Testament promises. A major emphasis in the New Testament is on the Davidic descent of Jesus, who is viewed as God's promised Messiah.

How are we to understand the covenant made between Yahweh and the dynasty of David? What is its importance for contemporary Christians?

Selected Scripture

King James Version	New Revised Standard Version
2 Samuel 7:18-29	*2 Samuel 7:18-29*
18 Then went king David in, and sat before the LORD, and he said Who *am* I, O Lord GOD? and what *is* my house, that thou hast brought me hitherto?	18 Then King David went in and sat before the LORD, and said, "Who am I, O Lord GOD, and what is my house, that you have brought me thus far? 19 And yet this was a small thing in your eyes, O Lord GOD; you have spoken also of your servant's house for a great while to come. May this be instruction for the people, O Lord GOD! 20 And what more can David say to you? For you know your servant, O Lord GOD! 21 Because of
19 And this was yet a small thing in my sight, O Lord GOD; but thou hast spoken also of thy servant's house for a great while to come. And *is* this the matter of man, O Lord GOD?	
20 And what can David say more	

83

unto thee? for thou, Lord GOD, knowest thy servant.

21 For thy word's sake, and according to thine own heart, hast thou done all these great things, to make thy servant know *them.*

22 Wherefore thou art great, O LORD God: for *there is* none like thee, neither *is there* any God beside thee, according to all that we have heard with our ears.

23 And what one nation in the earth *is* like thy people, *even* like Israel, whom God went to redeem for a people to himself, and to make him a name, and to do for you great things and terrible, for thy land, before thy people, which thou redeemedst for thee from Egypt, *from* the nations and their gods?

24 For thou hast confirmed to thyself thy people Israel *to* be a people unto thee for ever: and thou, LORD, art become their God.

25 And now, O LORD God, the word that thou hast spoken concerning thy servant and concerning his house, establish *it* for ever, and do as thou hast said.

26 And let thy name be magnified for ever, saying, The LORD of hosts *is* the God over Israel: and let the house of thy servant David be established before thee.

27 For thou, O LORD of hosts, God of Israel, hast revealed to thy servant, saying, I will build thee an house: therefore hath thy servant found in his heart to pray this prayer unto thee.

28 And now, O Lord GOD, thou *art* that God, and thy words be true, and thou hast promised this goodness unto thy servant:

29 Therefore now let it please thee to bless the house of thy servant, that it may continue for ever before thee: for thou, O Lord GOD, hast spoken *it*: and with thy blessing let the house of thy servant be blessed for ever.

your promise, and according to your own heart, you have wrought all this greatness, so that your servant may know it. 22 Therefore you are great, O LORD God; for there is no one like you, and there is no God besides you, according to all that we have heard with our ears. 23 Who is like your people, like Israel? Is there another nation on earth whose God went to redeem it as a people, and to make a name for himself, doing great and awesome things for them, by driving out before his people nations and their gods? 24 And you established your people Israel for yourself to be your people forever; and you, O LORD, became their God. 25 And now, O LORD God, as for the word that you have spoken concerning your servant and concerning his house, confirm it forever; do as you have promised. 26 Thus your name will be magnified forever in the saying, 'The LORD of hosts is God over Israel'; and the house of your servant David will be established before you. 27 For you, O LORD of hosts, the God of Israel, have made this revelation to your servant, saying, 'I will build you a house'; therefore your servant has found courage to pray this prayer to you. 28 And now, O Lord GOD, you are God, and your words are true, and you have promised this good thing to your servant; 29 now therefore may it please you to bless the house of your servant, so that it may continue forever before you; for you, O Lord GOD, have spoken, and with your blessing shall the house of your servant be blessed forever."

Key Verse: **And now, O LORD God, the word that thou hast spoken concerning thy servant and concerning his house, establish *it* for ever, and do as thou hast said.**

Key Verse: **And now, O LORD God, as for the word that you have spoken concerning your servant and concerning his house, confirm it forever; do as you have promised.**

As You Read the Scripture

2 Samuel 7:18-29. Scholars have found it difficult to translate this chapter into clear, smoothly flowing English because the Hebrew source is written in such an awkward and confusing style. Second Samuel 7 is, however, recognized as one of the most important chapters in the entire Old Testament, and has been studied intensively. Verses 18-29 contain David's prayer in response to the word of Yahweh that had come to the king through Nathan, the prophet. In this oracle, presented in the first portion of the chapter, God rejected David's plan to build a temple—a house for God—and instead promised to build a house—a dynasty—for David and his descendants.

Verse 18. David went into the tent where the ark of the covenant was housed and prayed in response to God's promise. The ark was understood to represent the presence of Yahweh with the people. David's posture of prayer was probably the common eastern one of kneeling and sitting back on one's heels with head erect.

Verses 19-21. The theme of David's prayer was acknowledgment of the graciousness of Yahweh to him and to his descendants. David realized that it was not his own qualifications or accomplishments that had won for him this divine favor. Instead, he was the beneficiary of a free act of decision by God, an unmerited gift determined only by the divine prerogative.

Verses 22-24. David praised the greatness and uniqueness of Yahweh. In comparison with the God of Israel, the gods claimed by other nations were revealed as false. Here the fundamental monotheistic assertion of the Hebrew faith is again affirmed. The reference to "all that we have heard with our ears" is a reminder of the great events of Israel's sacred history through which God had revealed the divine nature and will and entered into covenant with these people. In verse 23, the focus shifts from David and his family to the people of Israel whom God had redeemed by "doing great and awesome things." All these divine acts of covenant making and covenant keeping were recognized as undeserved graciousness for which Israel could only be thankful and respond with loyalty and obedience.

Verses 25-29. In these latter verses of the chapter, David seems to be restating the promises of God and attempting to hold God to it. It is as if he had heard such unbelievably wonderful news that he could not quite accept it. He needed to repeat the promise over again and hear God affirm that "Yes, that is right; that is what I said." The word *now* occurs three times in these verses with the meaning *therefore,* as if David was clarifying what he had heard. The first portion of the chapter—the oracle from God to the prophet Nathan—featured an extensive play on at least two meanings of the word *house.* God declined David's offer to build a house—a temple—where the ark symbolizing the divine presence might be permanently placed. God had promised, instead, to build David a house—to establish his family as the ruling dynasty of the nation so that his sons, grandsons, and so on through the generations would rule as kings of Israel. The promise was to be perpetual; the word *forever* occurs five times in these verses. Notice the intimate relationship between David and God that is portrayed here. David claims the promise gratefully and very firmly.

The Scripture and the Main Question

From Saul to David

In last week's lesson, we saw the rejection by God of Israel's first king, Saul, because of his failure to obey the commands of God. Although Saul continued to be the king until his death, his reign was characterized by struggles against the Philistines and his own inner demons. God sent Samuel to anoint a new king-to-be long before Saul's death. This new king was not a relative of Saul's; he was the youngest son of Jesse from the small town of Bethlehem. David was a shepherd when God chose him as king; he later became a musician in Saul's court and the king's armorbearer. David first came to public prominence when he single-handedly killed the Philistine giant, Goliath, who had been humiliating the army of Israel. His reputation grew as he won additional military victories. In the meantime, King Saul was suffering increasingly from pathological depression and jealousy. Deeply hurt by his and his family's rejection by God, Saul made David the target of his anger. Perhaps there were rumors at the court that David had already been anointed as his successor. Certainly, David's popularity with the people exceeded that of the king himself. In spite of the close friendship between his son, Jonathan, and David, Saul tried to murder the man he saw as his rival. Eventually, David found it necessary to leave the court. He lived for some time as a fugitive, gathering about himself an army of mercenaries. During this time, David more than once refused to kill Saul when he had the opportunity; he respected the position of God's anointed ruler even though Saul was his mortal enemy. Finally, Saul and some of his sons, including Jonathan, were killed fighting the Philistines. David became the king of Judah—the area of the southern tribes—and seven years later he was recognized as king of all Israel. He was able finally to defeat the Philistines who had plagued Israel for so long. Wisely seeking a capital that was not associated with any portion of his newly unified kingdom, David captured the Canaanite city of Jerusalem and established the seat of his government there. Soon he had the ark of the covenant brought to Jerusalem and placed in a special tent. Thus, the city that was known as "the city of David" became both the political and religious center of Israel. This is a summary of the major events that occurred in the period between last week's and this week's lessons.

"My People Israel"

The phrase *my people Israel* is used repeatedly not only in the first part of 1 Samuel 7, but also throughout the Old Testament. It expresses the special relationship that existed between Yahweh and the Israelite people. In earlier lessons during this quarter, we have discussed the establishment of the covenant between God and the Hebrew people. First to Abraham and his descendants came the divine promise of a people who would be peculiarly God's people and who would receive a land in which to live. In the Exodus event, God acted to bring the Hebrews out of slavery in Egypt. At Mount

Sinai, God gave them—through Moses—the Law, which defined their responsibilities as the covenant people. Under the leadership of Joshua, God had enabled them to conquer and settle in Canaan, the land of promise. Through the judges, God had preserved their existence as a people until the establishment of a centralized monarchy.

The idea of Israel as the chosen people of God is fundamental to the biblical story. God's acts for the salvation of humankind were done through the life of this particular historical group of people. As David acknowledged in today's scripture, and as the later prophets stress, Israel was God's chosen instrument simply because of God's free choice and not because of any virtue or merit. In the New Testament, we find Paul wrestling with the question of the continued role of the chosen people after the event of Jesus Christ as God's work of fullest revelation and salvation. In Romans 11:1a he asserts, "I ask, then, has God rejected his people? By no means!" He argues that Israel is perpetually the elected people of God.

"I Will Establish the Throne of His Kingdom Forever"

In 1 Samuel 7, the idea of election is further refined as the covenant is established not only with the nation, but also in a special way with the ruling family of David and his descendants. A new kind of authority was being set up; henceforth God would rule not through charismatic leaders chosen in particular historical situations, but through a hereditary line of kings. This understanding of the role of David is referred to as the royal theology. This view saw the rise of David as the work of Yahweh who took him from following the sheep to be king. The covenant between God and David's house was unconditional. It would go on into the future with no threat of ultimate rejection such as Saul had suffered. This divine promise is a powerful expression of the profound truth that human salvation comes only through the unconditional love of God.

Historically, the dynasty founded by King David lasted until 587 B.C., although only David and his son, Solomon, ruled over the entire nation. The other Davidic kings reigned over Judah after the division into Israel in the north and Judah in the south. After some four hundred years of rule by the descendants of David, Judah was conquered by the Babylonians in 587 B.C. After some decades of exile, the nation was restored, but not the monarchy. The royal theology, however, did not disappear with the end of the Davidic line of kings. The Jewish people (the term *Jew* from "people of Judah" came into use during the Exile period) continued to hope, pray, and look for the coming of an ideal king—a new David—who would deliver them from oppression and restore their nation as in the great days of David's own reign. The writings of the prophets are filled with promises that God would send an Anointed One—a Messiah. Faithful Jews in the 1990s still cling to this hope and expectation.

For the earliest Christians, Jesus was understood as being this promised Messiah. The Greek word *Christ* is equivalent to the Hebrew *Messiah*. (The New Testament was originally written largely in Greek.) When Peter answers Jesus' question, "But who do you say that I am?" by replying, "You are the Messiah," he was affirming this understanding. (See Matt. 16:13-20, Mark 8:27-30, Luke 9:18-20.) The writers of the Synoptic Gospels (Matthew, Mark, and Luke) were very careful to establish a direct genealogical connection between Jesus and David. In this way, and with other references to Jesus as the son of David, they were affirming that he was the promised Messiah—the ideal King who was the heir to David's throne and the fulfillment of the covenant promises.

Helping Adults Become Involved

Preparing to Teach

Read as much as possible of 1 Samuel 16–31 and 2 Samuel 1–6. Using that material and the information in "From Saul to David," outline the major events that occur in the history of Israel in the time period between last week's lesson and this one. Many of these stories will be familiar to you and your class, but it is important to see them as parts of the unfolding account. The lesson for today needs to be seen as a continuation of the larger story.

Read 1 Samuel 7 with care using the explanation in "As You Read the Scripture." It is essential to pay attention to the oracle or message from God in the first part of the chapter in order to appreciate David's prayer, which makes up the printed scripture for this lesson.

Familiarize yourself with the numerous Old and New Testament references that are used later in the lesson, as well as the Advent and Christmas hymns of your denomination's hymnal.

If you think it workable for your group, make arrangements to play portions of Handel's *Messiah* from a record or tape. (You or a musician in your class may see ways to utilize this great oratorio more fully than has been suggested below.) Bibles and hymnals should be available for each student. You will need newsprint or chalkboard.

Today's lesson outline:

I. David, God's chosen king
II. Israel, God's chosen people
III. The covenant with David
IV. The messianic hope

Introducing the Main Question

Ask the class to turn in their Bibles to Isaiah 9:6-7. Play the portion of Handel's *Messiah* that uses this scripture. Alternately, read aloud these two verses. Discuss the use of these verses in the church in the period prior to Christmas. Who is being described in this scripture? What is meant by "the throne of David and his kingdom"? Do not be concerned about correct answers; the point is to encourage thinking and discussion that will arouse interest in the issues to emerge in the lesson.

Developing the Lesson

I. David, God's chosen king

Call on the class to share from their recalling and reading of the events in the lives of Saul and David, as suggested at the end of last week's lesson. Use newsprint or chalkboard to record these at random. Later, use the material in "From Saul to David" to help organize a chronological account. Be sure, however, to make clear to the class that more than one version of the events is included in the books of Samuel. Because of the interweaving of these different sources, it is sometimes difficult to be certain of the exact flow of events. For example, at the end of 1 Samuel 16, David is playing the lyre in Saul's court and serving as his armorbearer. However, in chapter 17:55-58, Saul is completely unacquainted with him until after he has killed Goliath.

The purpose of this part of the lesson is to provide continuity between the time of Saul's rejection and the establishment of the Davidic dynasty.

II. Israel, God's chosen people

Use the material in "'My People Israel'" to reemphasize the centrality in the Old Testament of the concept of Israel as the chosen people of God. This understanding carries over into the New Testament as well. Note the reference in Mary's "Magnificat" in Luke 1:54-55. Look at Paul's struggle in Romans 11 with the role of Israel in the Christian era and his conclusion that "all Israel will be saved" (v. 26a). Share and discuss with the class these words by Ganse Little from *The Interpreter's Bible* (Vol. 2, p. 1087):

> Bereft of all the outward material characteristics by which we commonly judge a nation to be great, political unity, economic security, military power; possessed of no independent sovereignty for thousands of years, much less empire, this 'God-intoxicated people' was the repository and channel for the loftiest revelations of God's nature and purpose, revelations which have utterly changed the course of human history. The very will of the Jewish people to survive is in itself a historical phenomenon without parallel. God must still have a sovereign purpose for this tragically stricken race.

III. The covenant with David

Use the information in the first two paragraphs of "'I Will Establish the Throne of His Kingdom Forever'" to explain the important concept of the covenant between God and David. Emphasize that this divine promise to David and his descendants is a manifestation of the graciousness of God, on which all hope of human salvation depends. Call attention to the attitude of David expressed in his prayer: grateful and deferential, yet determined to lay firm hold on the divine promise.

Psalm 89 provides a good example of how the Davidic covenant functioned in later decades of hardship, as a source of hope for God's deliverance according to the divine purpose. Note especially verses 1-4, 19-37, 49-52.

IV. The messianic hope

Emphasize that this Jewish expectation of the coming of a Messiah from the house of David became a very significant part of the Christian understanding of Jesus Christ. Use the information in the last paragraph of "'I Will Establish the Throne of His Kingdom Forever.'" The best way to make this point is to look at specific scriptures. Begin with the Isaiah 9 passage that you used earlier and Isaiah 11:1-10. Explain that Christians believe that Christ is the fulfillment of the messianic roles described. For New Testament examples of the importance of the understanding of Jesus as a descendant of David, see Matthew 1:1-6, 20; 21:9, 15; Luke 1:26-27, 32-33, 69; and 2:4, 11; Acts 2:29-36.

Have the class, either as a whole or in smaller groups, go through the Advent and Christmas hymns in your church's hymnal (numbers 196-251 in *The United Methodist Hymnal*), listing references to Jesus' relationship to David. This exercise will enable you to conclude the lesson with a strong emphasis on the importance of the Davidic covenant for understanding the role of Jesus the Christ.

Helping Class Members Act

Encourage the class to do something that will increase their understanding and appreciation of Judaism—attend a synagogue service, talk with a Jewish friend, read about the Jewish faith.

Planning for Next Sunday

Ask your students to read 2 Samuel 11:1–12:24 and Psalm 51.

LESSON 11   NOVEMBER 13

David Sins Against God

Background Scripture: 2 Samuel 11:1–12:19

The Main Question

Have mercy on me, O God,
according to your steadfast love;
according to your abundant mercy
blot out my transgressions.
Wash me thoroughly from my iniquity,
and cleanse me from my sin. . . .
The sacrifice acceptable to God is a broken spirit;
a broken and contrite heart, O God, you will not despise.

These lines from Psalm 51 (v. 1-2, 17) convey poignantly the theme of today's lesson. In most translations of the Bible, there is a note to the song-leader explaining that this psalm was composed by David after he was confronted by the prophet Nathan with the sinfulness of his actions with Bathsheba.

In last week's lesson, we studied the graciousness of God in giving the kingdom to David and establishing his dynasty to rule over it forever. There we saw David at perhaps his best—grateful and reverential before God, yet strong and confident about his destiny. In today's scripture there is an abrupt shift. We are presented with the dark and sinful side of David's nature—his lust, greed, and utter selfishness. And yet, David is not so far gone into evil that he cannot recognize his sin when he is confronted with it, accept his responsibility and his punishment, repent, and receive God's forgiveness.

What can we learn from this ugly incident in the life of Israel's greatest king? What does it reveal not only about David, but also about us? How does God deal with the sin in the lives of each of us?

Selected Scripture

King James Version	New Revised Standard Version

2 Samuel 12:1-10, 13

1 And the LORD sent Nathan unto David. And he came unto him, and said unto him, There were two men in one city; the one rich, and the other poor.

2 The rich *man* had exceeding many flocks and herds:

3 But the poor *man* had nothing, save one little ewe lamb, which he had bought and nourished up: and it grew up together with him, and with his children; it did eat of his own meat, and drank of his own cup, and lay in his bosom, and was unto him as a daughter.

4 And there came a traveller unto the rich man, and he spared to take of his own flock and of his own herd, to dress for the wayfaring man that was come unto him; but took the poor man's lamb, and dressed it for the man that was come to him.

5 And David's anger was greatly kindled against the man; and he said to Nathan, As the LORD liveth, the man that hath done this *thing* shall surely die:

6 And he shall restore the lamb fourfold, because he did this thing, and because he had no pity.

7 And Nathan said to David, Thou *art* the man. Thus saith the LORD God of Israel, I anointed thee king over Israel, and I delivered thee out of the hand of Saul;

8 And I gave thee thy master's house, and thy master's wives into thy bosom, and gave thee the house of Israel and of Judah; and if *that had been* too little, I would moreover have given unto thee such and such things.

9 Wherefore hast thou despised the commandment of the LORD, to do evil in his sight? thou hast killed Uriah the Hittite with the sword,

2 Samuel 12:1-10, 13

And the LORD sent Nathan to David. He came to him, and said to him, "There were two men in a certain city, the one rich and the other poor. 2 The rich man had very many flocks and herds; 3 but the poor man had nothing but one little ewe lamb, which he had bought. He brought it up, and it grew up with him and with his children; it used to eat of his meager fare, and drink from his cup, and lie in his bosom, and it was like a daughter to him. 4 Now there came a traveler to the rich man, and he was loath to take one of his own flock or herd to prepare for the wayfarer who had come to him, but he took the poor man's lamb, and prepared that for the guest who had come to him." 5 Then David's anger was greatly kindled against the man. He said to Nathan, "As the LORD lives, the man who has done this deserves to die; 6 he shall restore the lamb fourfold, because he did this thing, and because he had no pity."

7 Nathan said to David, "You are the man! Thus says the LORD, the God of Israel: I anointed you king over Israel, and I rescued you from the hand of Saul; 8 I gave you your master's house, and your master's wives into your bosom, and gave you the house of Israel and of Judah; and if that had been too little, I would have added as much more. 9 Why have you despised the word of the LORD, to do what is evil in his sight? You have struck down Uriah the Hittite with the sword, and have taken his wife to be your wife, and have killed him with the sword of

and hast taken his wife *to be* thy wife, and hast slain him with the sword of the children of Ammon.

10 Now therefore the sword shall never depart from thine house; because thou hast despised me, and hast taken the wife of Uriah the Hittite to be thy wife.

....

13 And David said unto Nathan, I have sinned against the LORD. And Nathan said unto David, The LORD also hath put away thy sin; thou shalt not die.

Key Verse: **And David said unto Nathan, I have sinned against the LORD. And Nathan said unto David, The LORD also hath put away thy sin; thou shalt not die.**

the Ammonites. 10 Now therefore the sword shall never depart from your house, for you have despised me, and have taken the wife of Uriah the Hittite to be your wife."

....

13 David said to Nathan, "I have sinned against the LORD." Nathan said to David, "Now the LORD has put away your sin; you shall not die."

Key Verse: **David said to Nathan, "I have sinned against the Lord." Nathan said to David, "Now the LORD has put away your sin; you shall not die."**

As You Read the Scripture

2 Samuel 12:1-10, 13. This scripture is a part of a remarkable document that includes chapters 9–20 of 2 Samuel and chapters 1 and 2 of 1 Kings. This *Succession Narrative,* or *Court History,* tells much of the story of David's forty-year reign. Apparently composed by an eyewitness to the events related, it is one of the finest pieces of historical writing that has come down to us from the ancient world. These chapters provide an astonishingly frank portrayal of the character and actions of Israel's greatest national hero, as well as the domestic tragedies that plagued his kingship.

Chapter 11 told the story of David's sin with Bathsheba. Not only did he take another man's wife apparently against her wishes, but he also conspired to have her husband killed in order to cover up his own wickedness. The chapter contains no indication that David was troubled about what he had done, but the last line states that Yahweh was displeased. In chapter 12, the Lord sent Nathan, who was probably David's court prophet, to speak the divine word to the king. Nathan approached David on the pretext of bringing a case before him for judgment, likely a common practice of appealing to royal authority. Nathan's presentation was a masterpiece in the form of a parable that led David to judge and condemn himself.

Verses 1-3. Little was said about the rich man except to establish the fact of his wealth. The poor man was sketched vividly and sympathetically. The touching intimacy of his love for his lamb was emphasized with romantic, even erotic, overtones ("lie in his bosom"), which facilitate the application of the story to David's sin.

Verse 4. The word *took* in reference to the lamb is the same word used in 11:4 to describe David's action toward Bathsheba. The prophet Samuel had warned against such abuse of power in 1 Samuel 8:11-17 when he lectured the people about the evils that would accompany monarchy.

Verses 5-6. The commentary on this book in the *Anchor Bible* series translates verse 5 with David's calling the rich man a "fiend of hell." The king's emotional response to the act of greed and utter selfishness was preparation for his remorse at realizing his own guilt. He declared the necessity of punishment and reparation.

Verse 7a. Nathan sprang the trap that he had so artfully laid for David by identifying the king as the one guilty of the kind of actions that he had so heatedly denounced.

Verses 7b-8. From this point through the next several verses, God spoke through the prophet. God reminded David of all of the undeserved favor that he had received, how God had given him everything he had, and would have been willing to give even more if David had asked. The emphasis in this review of God's gracious actions in the past was on *giving*, as opposed to the *taking* of which David was guilty.

Verse 9. David had violated at least three of the Ten Commandments by coveting, committing adultery, and killing.

Verse 10. David has been unfaithful to the ethical demands of the covenant relationship. Henceforth, a sword will be on him and his family. This sentence was fulfilled both literally and figuratively. Three of David's sons die by the sword. The sword of discord and defeat will afflict his family and the subsequent life of Israel.

Verse 13. David's moral sensitivity was not totally destroyed; he acknowledged and repented of his sin. God would forgive, but not without cost.

The Scripture and the Main Question

"You Are the Man!"

The whole point of Nathan's story was to confront David with the horrendous reality of his sin. The king had sinned first against God, the author of the moral order that governs the universe. In verse 10, God said, "You have despised me"; in verse 14, Nathan announced that "by this deed you have utterly scorned the LORD." David acknowledged his violation of God's will in Psalm 51: "Against you, you alone, have I sinned, and done what is evil in your sight" (verse 4a). Not only had David as an individual broken the divine commandments, but as the king chosen by God he had proven unfaithful to his responsibilities as leader of God's covenant people. Such an act as David committed would not have been unusual for an ancient monarch, but David had been favored by a very special, intimate covenant relationship that God had promised to continue to his descendants. Of course, in spite of the words in Psalm 51 just quoted (which were no doubt exaggerated to stress the point), David's sin was also a violation of other human beings. Certainly it was an act of sin against Bathsheba, who had been treated as a piece of property, sexually violated for the king's pleasure, and suffered the loss of both husband and child. Uriah, the husband of Bathsheba, was also greatly sinned against. Because of the king's lust and power, Uriah lost not only his wife, but also his very life. Uriah was exploited by David when he was brought home from the battlefront and tempted to break his vow of sexual abstinence. Uriah's faithfulness in the face of David's efforts to induce him to indulgence stands in sharp contrast to David's own actions. Not only had the king not accompanied his troops into battle, but also he obviously felt no need to discipline himself while they were in danger. While Uriah and the other soldiers risked their lives and remained faithful to their vows, their king entertained himself with Uriah's beautiful wife. It is of interest to note that Uriah was no ordinary soldier, but was one of the famous group of valiant warriors called The Thirty (see 2 Sam. 23:18-39). Such a man was sent back into battle bearing his own written death warrant after David had been unsuccessful in luring him into unfaithfulness. David's sin also involved the army commander Joab, who was ordered to do the dirty work of arranging for Uriah's death. Joab was both sinned against and caused to sin himself. The other soldiers who were unnecessarily killed through Joab's strategy to guarantee Uriah's death were certainly victims of the king's sin, as well. The infant son born of the illicit union with Bathsheba was another victim of sin; he died within a few days of his birth. All of David's family and, indeed, all of Israel suffered the consequences of these sins of the king, which included adultery, murder, duplicity, utter ruthlessness, and self-centeredness.

This unpleasant recital of the ramifications of David's actions should help us to grasp the seriousness, not only of his transgression, but also of our own. This scripture, which is so deeply revealing of David, is also uncomfortably telling about us. Sin is rarely a simple action; it has far-reaching implications; its stain spreads like ink spilled on the carpet; its effects are often indelible. Although God will grant forgiveness when David repents, innocence lost cannot be recovered and the results of sins committed cannot be cancelled. All of the consequences of sin are not necessarily suffered by the sinner. The death of the child of David and Bathsheba was understood to be the result of God's transferring the punishment of sin away from David. The subsequent acts of violence, rebellion, and arrogance on the part of David's family were seen as resulting from this intrusion of sin. The Davidic covenant was viable, but blemished.

"The Woman"

Bathsheba is most frequently referred to throughout this account as "the woman." That impersonal phrase provides a significant indication of the writer's lack of concern for her as a person or for her thoughts and feelings. We are never told anything from her point of view about what she experienced. She is identified only in terms of her father and her husband. It is interesting, and somewhat puzzling, that in the genealogy of Jesus in Matthew's Gospel, Bathsheba is still identified as the "wife of Uriah" by whom David became the father of Solomon (v. 6). The scripture does not acknowledge the pain of this woman, who suffered rape and the deaths of her husband and her baby within a period of nine months. The loss of the child was interpreted as punishment for David's sin, but the anguish was borne by Bathsheba. Although David was portrayed as praying and mourning for the child, it should be noted that he had been eager to conceal his paternity if Uriah had cooperated. Bathsheba would have been left to deal alone with the internal and external consequences of bearing the king's illegitimate child while married to one of his faithful soldiers. As the story developed, she experienced the death of her baby and marriage to her rapist.

Popular elaborations of this story through the centuries have tended to portray Bathsheba as a seductive temptress. This is a blatant and unfair effort to mitigate the guilt of David. There is absolutely nothing in the scripture text to indicate impropriety or even immodesty in her behavior. Neither bathing in one's own home nor being strikingly beautiful are character faults or seductive actions. What we have seen in the distortions of this story is another in the long and sad line of attempts to blame the female victim of sexual exploitation.

"Blot Out My Transgressions . . . My Sin Is Ever Before Me"

The celebrated greatness of King David shows in this ugly story only in his humble acknowledgment and repentance of his sin. When confronted dramatically with Nathan's "You are the man!" David immediately recognized himself and was appalled. He did not have to be persuaded that he had sinned; he did not attempt to deny or evade his responsibility. His straightforward response in verse 13, "I have sinned against the LORD," was beautifully and poignantly elaborated in Psalm 51. While we cannot be sure that David actually wrote all of this psalm, its sentiments faithfully represent his remorse and desire for forgiveness and restoration.

It is essential for Christians to recognize themselves in the situation of David. Although justified and born again by the Holy Spirit, we continue to fall into sin and have to seek divine forgiveness. Our confession and repentance are met by God's pardon, and we are restored and enabled to move on in growth toward holiness.

Helping Adults Become Involved

Preparing to Teach

An excellent way to present the major themes of this lesson is by role playing the dramatic confrontation between David and Nathan. Try to enlist two men from your class who will prepare this in advance (or play one of the parts yourself). It is not necessary to use the exact words of the scripture account, except for the crucial "You are the man!" Encourage the person playing Nathan to be able to tell the story in his own words. The David character should react to Nathan's speech with gestures and facial expressions, as well as with words acknowledging guilt at the end. If the role playing approach is unworkable with your group, use a dramatic reading of the scene.

Ask one or more women to be prepared to present Bathsheba as a major character in this story. Encourage them to put themselves into Bathsheba's place as fully as possible and be able to share with the class what might have been her thoughts and feelings. The biblical material on Bathsheba is contained in 2 Samuel 11 and 12, 1 Kings 1 and 2:13-27. It will be helpful if they can read more about Bathsheba in a book that deals with biblical women. One of the best is Janice Nunnally-Cox, *Foremothers: Women of the Bible.* Also helpful is the older classic work, *All the Women of the Bible,* by Edith Deen, in which Bathsheba is rather tellingly discussed under the title "Mother of Solomon."

Your preparation should include a careful reading of 2 Samuel 11:1–12:19 and Psalm 51 with the aid of the information in "As You Read the Scripture."

Newsprint or chalkboard will be helpful, and Bibles should be available for all.

FIRST QUARTER

The lesson may be presented under these headings:

I. David's sin
II. Bathsheba
III. Dealing with our own sin

Introducing the Main Question

Read to the class these two quotations and ask if they can identify their source:

"Stars, hide your fires;
Let not light see my dark and deep desires."

"I am in blood
Stepp'd in so far that, should I wade no more,
Returning were as tedious as go o'er."

Both of the quotations are lines said by the title character Macbeth in the play by Shakespeare, which almost everyone in your class will probably have read, at least in high school. Macbeth became a king who in some ways resembled David; he was driven by dark and deep desires to commit acts that were contrary to his best nature. The second quotation, however, highlights an important contrast between Macbeth and David. Faced with the horrible reality of his sin, Macbeth does not repent; instead he continues in his path of evil, committing more crimes in a futile attempt to triumph.

Although the degree of familiarity that you and your students have with *Macbeth* will shape your discussion, any group will benefit from the comparison between this king and King David as shown in the quotations.

Developing the Lesson

I. David's sin

The remainder of the lesson will be largely meaningless unless you devote sufficient time at the beginning to the events related in 1 Samuel 11. This may be done by your own well-prepared telling of the story or by reading it aloud with frequent breaks for questions and comments. Use the material in "'You Are the Man!'" to emphasize points that are essential to comprehending the seriousness of David's sin.

Present the role play or dramatic reading of the events of chapter 12:1-13. Encourage the class to respond with their own ideas and questions. The portion of "'You Are the Man!'" that deals with the consequences of the sin will be helpful here, as will be some of the material in "'Blot Out My Transgressions . . . My Sin Is Ever Before Me.'"

II. Bathsheba

It is essential to recognize and acknowledge that this story, like most of the Old Testament, is written from the perspective of the male characters, and has little interest in the experiences of the woman involved. This biased point of view is one of the ways by which we realize that God used fallible human beings to record the story of sacred history, trusting us through the guidance of the Holy Spirit to hear the divine message in spite of the limitations of the writers. One of the manifestations of human sinfulness has been and continues to be failure to accept the full equality and worth of all persons before God. Recovery of this story from the point of view of Bathsheba is, therefore, crucially important. Call on the woman or women who have studied Bathsheba to share insights in whatever ways they have chosen as most effective. Encourage the class to identify with Bathsheba—to feel the emotions such as fear, powerlessness, guilt, anger, and sorrow that she must have experienced. Use the information in "'The Woman'" to help do this and to raise the issue of current sexual exploitation.

III. Dealing with our own sin

Guide the discussion toward application of this material to the lives of contemporary Christians. The last paragraph of "'You Are the Man!'" and the section "'Blot Out My Transgressions . . . My Sin Is Ever Before Me'" suggest ideas about our sinfulness and its consequences. Read and discuss Psalm 51 and 1 John 1:5–2:11 as much as possible, placing the emphasis on our sin, rather than David's.

Helping Class Members Act

Encourage your class to continue their study of the material in Psalm 51 and 1 John at home in an attempt to come to understand better our own sinfulness and how we are to allow God to deal with it. Remind them that even sins that are forgiven by God often lead to painful consequences for the sinner her/himself and for others who may be innocent. Ask them to analyze their own lives with this truth in mind.

Challenge your people to be newly sensitive to the current abuses and exploitation of women in our society. Encourage them to take actions to combat this evil. Such actions might range from refusing to laugh at sexist jokes, to using inclusive language, to working for justice for victims of rape and other sexual violence.

Planning for Next Week

Indulge yourself in a childhood fantasy about being a king or queen. What joys would you experience? What temptations?

Solomon's Glorious Reign

Background Scripture: 1 Kings 9:1-9; 10:1-24

The Main Question

"Even Solomon in all his glory was not clothed like one of these" (Matt. 6:29). Jesus' reference to Solomon was intended to emphasize the beauty of the wildflowers with which God has adorned the countryside. It reveals, however, that the glory of King Solomon was a legend in the time of Jesus nine centuries later. Even in our own time, the mysterious riches of "King Solomon's Mines" continue to stimulate myths and movies. Solomon's wisdom has also become proverbial; even very young Sunday school students can relate the story of his decision in the case of the disputed baby (1 Kings 3:16-28). Immense wealth and impressive wisdom—these are the attributes that we associate with Solomon, as did the biblical writer: "King Solomon excelled all the kings of the earth in riches and in wisdom" (1 Kings 10:23). Next Sunday we will see that the glittering gold of Solomon's possessions concealed some deep problems within his kingdom, but for today our attention is on the grandeur of his reign.

Why was Solomon reputed to be so wise? What does wisdom mean in ruling an empire or in living a life? How did he get to be so enormously wealthy? What did he do with this vast wealth? Is there a relationship between Solomon's wisdom and his wealth?

When Jesus sent the disciples out on a mission, he instructed them to "be wise as serpents and innocent as doves" (Matt. 10:16*b*). What does it mean for us as Christians to be wise? In the Sermon on the Mount, Jesus warned, "Do not store up for yourselves treasures on earth" (Matt. 6:19*a*). What does it mean for us as Christians to be rich? What is the appropriate relationship between wisdom and wealth?

Selected Scripture

King James Version

New Revised Standard Version

1 Kings 9:1-3; 10:1-7, 23-24

1 And it came to pass, when Solomon had finished the building of the house of the LORD, and the king's house, and all Solomon's desire which he was pleased to do,

2 That the LORD appeared to Solomon the second time, as he had appeared unto him at Gibeon.

3 And the LORD said unto him, I have heard thy prayer and thy supplication, that thou hast made before me: I have hallowed this house, which thou hast built, to put my name there for ever; and mine eyes and mine heart shall be there perpetually.

....

1 And when the queen of Sheba heard of the fame of Solomon concerning the name of the LORD, she came to prove him with hard questions.

2 And she came to Jerusalem with a very great train, with camels that

1 Kings 9:1-3; 10:1-7, 23-24

1 When Solomon had finished building the house of the LORD and the king's house and all that Solomon desired to build, 2 the LORD appeared to Solomon a second time, as he had appeared to him at Gibeon. 3 The LORD said to him, "I have heard your prayer and your plea, which you made before me; I have consecrated this house that you have built, and put my name there forever; my eyes and my heart will be there for all time."

....

1 When the queen of Sheba heard of the fame of Solomon, (fame due to the name of the LORD), she came to test him with hard questions. 2 She came to Jerusalem with a very great retinue, with camels bearing spices, and very much gold, and pre-

bare spices, and very much gold, and precious stones: and when she was come to Solomon, she communed with him of all that was in her heart.

3 And Solomon told her all her questions: there was not *any* thing hid from the king, which he told her not.

4 And when the queen of Sheba had seen all Solomon's wisdom, and the house that he had built,

5 And the meat of his table, and the sitting of his servants, and the attendance of his ministers, and their apparel, and his cupbearers, and his ascent by which he went up unto the house of the LORD; there was no more spirit in her.

6 And she said to the king, It was a true report that I heard in mine own land of thy acts and of thy wisdom.

7 Howbeit I believed not the words, until I came, and mine eyes had seen *it;* and, behold, the half was not told me: thy wisdom and prosperity exceedeth the fame which I heard.

···

23 So king Solomon exceeded all the kings of the earth for riches and for wisdom.

24 And all the earth sought to Solomon, to hear his wisdom, which God had put in his heart.

Key Verse: **So king Solomon exceeded all the kings of the earth for riches and for wisdom.**

cious stones; and when she came to Solomon, she told him all that was on her mind. 3 Solomon answered all her questions; there was nothing hidden from the king that he could not explain to her. 4 When the queen of Sheba had observed all the wisdom of Solomon, the house that he had built, 5 the food of his table, the seating of his officials, and the attendance of his servants, their clothing, his valets, and his burnt offerings that he offered at the house of the LORD, there was no more spirit in her.

6 So she said to the king, "The report was true that I heard in my own land of your accomplishments and of your wisdom, 7 but I did not believe the reports until I came and my own eyes had seen it. Not even half had been told me; your wisdom and prosperity far surpass the report that I had heard."

···

23 Thus King Solomon excelled all the kings of the earth in riches and in wisdom. 24 The whole earth sought the presence of Solomon to hear his wisdom, which God had put into his mind.

Key Verse: **Thus King Solomon excelled all the kings of the earth in riches and in wisdom.**

As You Read the Scripture

1 Kings 9:1-3. Solomon was enamored of great construction projects. Thirteen years of labor had been expended in building a magnificent palace for the king, and seven years in building a temple for God. The temple had been completed, the ark placed in the central holiest area, and a service of dedication held. Solomon experienced another vision of God similar to the one he had had soon after his accession to the throne. God approved the temple and promised Solomon that the divine presence would always remain there.

Chapter 10:1. The reputation of Solomon, the greatness that God had given him, had spread widely throughout that part of the world. He was visited by the famous Queen of Sheba. Sheba was probably in the southwestern part of Arabia, in the location that is the modern nation of Yemen. The Queen of Sheba, whose given name is unknown, is a prominent figure in many legends of eastern countries. She travelled a long distance by camel caravan to meet Solomon, apparently to engage in a contest of wits, although probably with more practical motives as well. Solomon's far-reaching trade contacts may have been competing with the commercial interests of Sheba. If the queen wanted to negotiate a pact with Solomon, she was successful (see v. 13).

Verses 2-3. The queen, who was obviously a monarch of great wealth herself, conversed with Solomon as an equal in a manner unusual for a woman in that day. Apparently they exchanged proverbs, stories, and riddles—all of which were considered to represent wisdom. Solomon was able to answer the queen's questions in a way that she found most impressive, although we do not know the subjects of those queries.

Verses 4-5. In addition to his wisdom, the queen was amazed at the magnificence of Solomon's buildings, the splendor of his court, and the generosity of his religious observances. She was left breathless by such spectacle.

Verses 6-7. The queen praised Solomon extravagantly and gave him rich gifts, which he reciprocated. The extent of their further interaction is unclear and remains the subject of legend. (The royal dynasty of the African nation of Ethiopia has long claimed descent from a child of Solomon and this queen, although there is no scriptural record of such intimacy.) The entire episode was told by the biblical writer to magnify the greatness of Solomon and the glory of his reign.

The Queen of Sheba was mentioned by Jesus, who called her "the queen of the South." In Matthew 12:42 and Luke 11:31, Jesus said that she will rise up at the judgment to condemn the people of Jesus' day for their unwillingness to recognize who he is, in contrast to her recognition of lesser greatness in the person of Solomon.

Verses 23-24. This is a summary of the elevated status of Solomon. His immense wealth was made clear in previous verses, which described all of his drinking vessels and the vessels of his palace as made of pure gold rather than of silver, which was "not considered as anything in the days of Solomon" (v. 21). His astonishing wisdom was probably of a practical, administrative nature, as well as part of an intellectual movement of the age that prized riddles and proverbs.

The Scripture and the Main Question

From David to Solomon

The grandeur of Solomon's reign, which is the focus of this lesson, can best be appreciated by reviewing the events that occurred in the historical period following last week's lesson. David's sin set off a chain of tragic consequences in his family. His daughter, Tamar, was raped by his son, her half-brother Amnon. Another son, Absalom, Tamar's brother, vowed vengeance on Amnon and eventually had him killed. Later, Absalom was himself killed while engaged in a treasonous effort to overthrow David's rule. During this civil war, David and his court were forced to flee from Jerusalem in fear.

More violence followed—further revolts and war with the Philistines. The book of Samuel ends at this point and 1 Kings opens with David as an old man. The struggle for the throne continued. Finally, through the influence of Nathan and Bathsheba, David acted to resolve the question by designating Bathsheba's son, Solomon, as his successor. Solomon was enthroned and consolidated his power by having his rivals killed.

The accession of Solomon to the throne in this manner marked a major change in the understanding of leadership for the nation of Israel. From at least the time of the Exodus, God had raised up leaders for the chosen people. Moses had brought them out of Egypt and through the desert wilderness; Joshua had led the conquest and settlement of the land of Canaan; a series of at least a dozen judges were empowered by God to act in times of need. Even in the change to a monarchical form of government, God chose who would be the leader. Samuel had been directed by God to anoint first Saul and later David as the first kings. With the accession of Solomon, factors such as hereditary claim, political intrigue, and ruthless violence became the determinants of who would rule. Solomon was born to royalty; he knew nothing of the common life of the people of Israel. He did not even seek public acceptance by the people, as his father David had carefully done. He was a king of fabled wealth and wisdom, much admired, but little loved. He enjoyed the blessing of the divine covenant with his father's family, but his policies resulted in the division of the nation.

Israel's Time of National Power

The reigns of David and Solomon lasted about forty years each. These years represent the highest point of political, military, and economic power that the nation of Israel ever enjoyed. Prior to the rule of David, Israel was a confederacy of tribal groups striving for unity and victory over the enemies in their land. After the rule of Solomon, the nation split into two parts, each with its own king and neither with significant power. For the Israelite people, the time of David and Solomon is the period of glorious achievement and prominence to which they look back in pride and from which they look ahead in hope.

One reason for the success of the Israelite nation during this period was the relative weakness of neighboring peoples. Israel formed an important land bridge of the ancient world. It was situated literally on the highway between the great empires of Egypt in the south and those of Mesopotamia (the Fertile Crescent area) in the north. When the great powers of the era struggled with each other for control, Israel found itself inevitably embroiled—a mouse caught between fighting elephants. In the period of David and Solomon—approximately nine centuries before the birth of Christ—there was a power vacuum in the area. In the absence of other contenders, Israel was able to enjoy some decades of ascendancy.

"Solomon in All His Glory"

It must be remembered that the biblical account was written from Israel's perspective and, like all historical accounts, cannot be expected to be totally objective. The descriptions of the glory of Solomon surely have their exaggerated and legendary aspects. They might be compared to the stories told by Americans about George Washington's honesty in confessing to having cut down the cherry tree, or about Abraham Lincoln's walking miles to return a few pennies to a customer. These stories are all true in the deepest sense of accurately portraying the character of the hero, even if the facts are embellished with fiction. Solomon was a typical eastern monarch of the ancient era. He possessed power and wealth, enjoyed them sumptuously, and exercised them with little regard for the common people over whom he ruled.

Solomon was not a great military leader like his father, but fortunately for him, David had finally defeated Israel's perennial enemy, the Philistines, and little military action was needed. He had fortifications constructed at the borders of the empire and poured huge resources into a private army of fourteen hundred chariots and twelve thousand men and horses. His building program was extensive and extravagant; its major projects were the king's palace, the temple, and a palace for one of his wives who was the daughter of the Egyptian pharaoh. Solomon seems to have had a real gift for building and for administration. He divided the nation into twelve regions, disregarding the old tribal identities, in order to have it governed more efficiently.

Trade with surrounding peoples provided part of the enormous wealth that was necessary to support these programs and the luxurious lifestyle of the royal court. Solomon must have been a master businessman, able to make money in almost all of his dealings. His role as middleman in the trade of horses between Egypt and nations to the north was especially lucrative. With the aid of the Phoenicians, Israel became a seafaring nation for the first time. From the seaport he had built at Ezion-geber, Solomon's ships sailed forth on long trading voyages that earned great riches. The natural resources of the land were utilized as never before when the smelting and manufacturing of copper and iron were greatly expanded.

Solomon's reign was also a time of literary and cultural achievement. Much of the history of Israel was put into written form with the production of the great Yahwist history (J source), which constitutes a major part of the Old Testament from Genesis through Numbers, as well as the Court History of David's reign. Solomon was a major figure in the wisdom tradition, as the visit of the Queen of Sheba evidenced. He was credited with the authorship of 3000 proverbs and 1002 songs; he has traditionally been associated with the books of Proverbs, Ecclesiastes, Song of Solomon, and the Wisdom of Solomon in the Apocrypha. Clearly, his reign was, in diverse ways, a period of unparalleled splendor for Israel.

Helping Adults Become Involved

Preparing to Teach

Assemble a variety of pictures and articles featuring wealthy persons and describing their lifestyles. Good sources for this kind of material are popular magazines and supermarket tabloid newspapers. You might also utilize historical materials. Reference and travel books will offer pictures of royalty, palaces and castles, tombs, jewels, and so on. These can all be used to make a display that will be both eye-catching and discussion-prompting.

Read as much as possible from the latter part of 2 Samuel and the first chapters of 1 Kings in order to get a grasp on the events that occur between last week's lesson and this week's. Use this with the earlier section entitled "From David to Solomon." Make an outline of the major events and personalities in this period.

Read the scripture for this lesson with the help of "As You Read the Scripture." Prepare to update the chart of historical events that you have been making throughout the quarter.

Plan for the use of maps of the Hebrew kingdom, either from a set of wall or easel maps or by using those available in Bibles, such as maps four and six in *The New Oxford Annotated NRSV*. Although map six is from a later period of history, it shows the larger area of the Hebrew empire, including the seaport at Ezion-geber. Familiarize yourself in advance with the various locations mentioned in this and earlier lessons. Bibles, pencils, and paper should be available for all.

Today's lesson outline:

I. Solomon becomes king
II. Israel as an empire
III. Solomon's wealth and fame
IV. Being wealthy and wise

Introducing the Main Question

In his book *All Sad Young Men* (1926), F. Scott Fitzgerald wrote: "Let me tell you about the very rich. They are different from you and me." Ernest Hemingway later replied, "Yes, they have more money." With which of these writers do you agree? Are very wealthy persons different from the rest of us in ways that go beyond the balances in their bank accounts? What are the effects of wealth in a person's life? How are riches and wisdom related? Engage the class in a discussion of these questions using these quotations and the pictures that you have displayed.

Developing the Lesson

I. Solomon becomes king

Full appreciation of the uniqueness of Solomon's reign is dependent on a sense of the events that preceded it. Use your reading of the latter chapters of 2 Samuel and first chapters of 1 Kings, plus the survey in "From David to Solomon" to sketch an outline of these major events and personalities. Return to the chart of Hebrew history that you have been developing during the quarter and add to it the pertinent points through Solomon's kingship.

Discuss with the class the change that had taken place in the understanding of leadership in Israel when the throne passed to Solomon, the son of David's favorite, or at least most influential, wife. Compare this to the leadership in earlier centuries as seen in Moses, Joshua, the judges, Saul, and David himself. What potential dangers are to be found here?

II. Israel as an empire

Use maps of the extended area of Israel during the reigns of David and Solomon. Point out the locations of Jerusalem, Phoenicia, Egypt, Mesopotamia, and various places mentioned in the scripture. Also very helpful will be maps covering larger geographic areas on which you can show other locations, such as the routes of Solomon's trading expeditions and the home country of the Queen of Sheba.

Present the material in "Israel's Time of National Power" to explain the uniquely favorable position—at least by worldly standards—that the nation found itself in at this point in history. What were some possible disadvantages, even risks, in such a situation, especially for a people with Israel's unique understanding of its identity and role?

III. Solomon's wealth and fame

The information in "Solomon in All His Glory" will enable you to portray this magnificent monarch and the grandeur of his reign in Israel. Utilize other scripture passages, in addition to those cited in this lesson, to emphasize your points. Examples include 1 Kings 3, which presents Solomon very positively as praying for and receiving wisdom from God, chapters 5 through 7, which describe the elaborate building of the temple, and the additional verses in chapter 10 that detail the extreme wealth of the king. Select in advance portions of this scripture material to read or have read in the class.

IV. Being wealthy and wise

America's best-known wise man or practical philosopher, Benjamin Franklin, wrote, "Early to bed, early to rise, makes a man healthy, wealthy, and wise." Use this much-quoted proverb to stimulate a discussion that will relate to the introduction of the lesson and enable the class to consider issues in the light of what they have learned about the reign of Solomon. Focus the conversation on questions such as these: What does it mean to be truly and holistically healthy? How can such health of body, mind, and spirit be achieved? Was Solomon an example of a healthy person? In similar form, examine issues of wisdom and wealth; urge the class to define these terms thoughtfully and to evaluate both the reign of Solomon and their own lives according to these definitions.

Distribute paper and pencils and ask the class to divide their sheets into two parallel columns. In the first column, ask them to write all of the words or phrases that they believe could accurately be inscribed on their gravestones should they die very soon. In the second, ask them to write those words and phrases that describe how they would want to be remembered after their deaths. This exercise can be ended with discussion or each person's work can be kept private; you and the class can decide in terms of what seems best for you.

Helping Class Members Act

Encourage each student to take his or her list of gravestone descriptions home with them and continue to think about it. Challenge them to take another sheet of paper and reflect in writing about how they might strive to bring the two lists into greater harmony. In other words, what changes need to be made in their lives in order to become the persons they want to be remembered as being?

Planning for Next Sunday

Sample some sections of the book of Proverbs that contain the kind of wisdom traditionally associated with Solomon.

Solomon Turns from God

Background Scripture: 1 Kings 11

The Main Question

"Hear, O Israel: The LORD is our God, the LORD alone. You shall love the LORD your God with all your heart, and with all your soul, and with all your might. . . . Do not follow other gods, any of the gods of the peoples who are all around you, because the LORD your God, who is present with you, is a jealous God" (Deut. 6:4-5, 14-15a). These commandments summarize the highest duty of the people who are in covenant relationship with God. Jesus referred to the first of these verses as "the greatest and first commandment" (Matt. 22:37). In both Judaism and Christianity, God commands supreme allegiance and uncompromising loyalty.

Martin Luther, the great German reformer of the sixteenth century, defined God as that for which a person would be willing to kill or to die. Twentieth-century theologian Paul Tillich expressed a similar idea when he described God as the ultimate reality in a person's life, the object of one's ultimate concern. These emphases on the unquestioned centrality and primacy of the deity help us to understand the biblical judgment that Solomon turned away from God. It was not that Solomon ceased to worship God or that he renounced Yahweh to serve other deities instead. It was rather that he allowed himself to be adversely influenced by those close to him—in this case his foreign wives. He compromised his commitment and divided his loyalty.

How are our beliefs and actions influenced by persons around us? How are we to live faithfully as Christians in the midst of a culture that is at best post-Christian and often more accurately described as unchristian? What may be the results of our turning from God?

Selected Scripture

King James Version	New Revised Standard Version

1 Kings 11:1-13

1 But king Solomon loved many strange women, together with the daughter of Pharaoh, women of the Moabites, Ammonites, Edomites, Zidonians, *and* Hittites;

2 Of the nations *concerning* which the LORD said unto the children of Israel, Ye shall not go in to them, neither shall they come in unto you: *for* surely they will turn away your heart after their gods: Solomon clave unto these in love.

3 And he had seven hundred wives, princesses, and three hundred concubines: and his wives turned

1 Kings 11:1-13

1 King Solomon loved many foreign women along with the daughter of Pharaoh: Moabite, Ammonite, Edomite, Sidonian, and Hittite women, 2 from the nations concerning which the LORD had said to the Israelites, "You shall not enter into marriage with them, neither shall they with you; for they will surely incline your heart to follow their gods"; Solomon clung to these in love. 3 Among his wives were seven hundred princesses and three hundred concubines; and his wives turned away his heart. 4 For when

away his heart.

4 For it came to pass, when Solomon was old, that his wives turned away his heart after other gods; and his heart was not perfect with the LORD his God, as was the heart of David his father.

5 For Solomon went after Ashtoreth the goddess of the Zidonians, and after Milcom the abomination of the Ammonites.

6 And Solomon did evil in the sight of the LORD, and went not fully after the LORD, as did David his father.

7 Then did Solomon build an high place for Chemosh, the abomination of Moab, in the hill that is before Jerusalem, and for Molech, the abomination of the children of Ammon.

8 And likewise did he for all his strange wives, which burnt incense and sacrificed unto their gods.

9 And the LORD was angry with Solomon, because his heart was turned from the LORD God of Israel, which had appeared unto him twice,

10 And had commanded him concerning this thing, that he should not go after other gods: but he kept not that which the LORD commanded.

11 Wherefore the LORD said unto Solomon, Forasmuch as this is done of thee, and thou hast not kept my covenant and my statutes, which I have commanded thee, I will surely rend the kingdom from thee, and will give it to thy servant.

12 Notwithstanding in thy days I will not do it for David thy father's sake: *but* I will rend it out of the hand of thy son.

13 Howbeit I will not rend away all the kingdom; *but* will give one tribe to thy son for David my servant's sake, and for Jerusalem's sake which I have chosen.

***Key Verse:* And Solomon did evil in the sight of the LORD, and went not fully after the LORD, as did David his father.**

Solomon was old, his wives turned away his heart after other gods; and his heart was not true to the LORD his God, as was the heart of his father David. 5 For Solomon followed Astarte the goddess of the Sidonians, and Milcom the abomination of the Ammonites. 6 So Solomon did what was evil in the sight of the LORD, and did not completely follow the LORD, as his father David had done. 7 Then Solomon built a high place for Chemosh the abomination of Moab, and for Molech the abomination of the Ammonites, on the mountain east of Jerusalem. 8 He did the same for all his foreign wives, who offered incense and sacrificed to their gods.

9 Then the LORD was angry with Solomon, because his heart had turned away from the LORD, the God of Israel, who had appeared to him twice, 10 and had commanded him concerning this matter, that he should not follow other gods; but he did not observe what the LORD commanded. 11 Therefore the LORD said to Solomon, "Since this has been your mind and you have not kept my covenant and my statutes that I have commanded you, I will surely tear the kingdom from you and give it to your servant. 12 Yet for the sake of your father David I will not do it in your lifetime; I will tear it out of the hand of your son. 13 I will not, however, tear away the entire kingdom; I will give one tribe to your son, for the sake of my servant David and for the sake of Jerusalem, which I have chosen."

***Key Verse:* So Solomon did what was evil in the sight of the LORD, and did not completely follow the LORD, as his father David had done.**

As You Read the Scripture

1 Kings 11:1-13. The scripture for today picks up the story immediately after the fantastic descriptions of the wealth and splendor of Solomon's court and of the monarch's wisdom and fame. An abrupt shift in tone is evidenced, however, by the very first verse. Prior to this point, the biblical account had been almost uniformly laudatory of Solomon; suddenly there is criticism—severe, even damning criticism—as this chapter continues. The order in which the Solomon stories are arranged might lead readers to believe that all was well during the early decades of the king's reign, and that trouble appeared only toward the end. Careful study reveals, however, that this is not the case. The crucial marriage to the daughter of Pharaoh, for example, had occurred just a few years after Solomon took the throne. Even in the glowing accounts of the king's exploits, there are references to excessive taxation and forced labor. Clearly there were throughout two sides to Solomon's rule—the glory and the apostasy.

Verse 1. Solomon's marriages were instruments of political diplomacy and economic expansion. His most important wife was a princess of Egypt. Other wives came from the neighboring peoples, including many former enemies of Israel.

Verse 2. The writer quotes Deuteronomy 7:3-4 in which Yahweh ordered the Israelites not to intermarry with these peoples because of the threat of being tempted to follow their gods. Solomon had ignored this command. Interestingly, the passage attributes Solomon's action to his love for his wives, rather than to motives of ambition or power.

Verses 3-4. The number of Solomon's marriage partners was certainly excessive, although probably exaggerated in the style of the other Solomon stories. The problem that they caused was not so much that of number, however, but of negative influence. Concubines were wives who had secondary status and whose children usually did not enjoy the same inheritance rights as the offspring of the princesses. In this case, they were probably women from less prestigious and powerful backgrounds. All of these wives are blamed for the king's sin—especially in his old age, he failed to remain loyal to Yahweh. Note that Solomon's unfaithfulness was compared unfavorably to that of David, who despite his great sins, retained a heart that was true to God.

Verses 5-8. Solomon was accused of worshipping the fertility deities of the various Canaanite cults (which were discussed in a previous lesson). He had shrines to these gods built on hilltops that were considered sacred locations. His various wives were allowed to worship their divinities in places that the king had provided for them. Notice that the writer does not accuse Solomon himself of worshiping these gods, but of tolerating and enabling his wives to do so.

Verses 9-10. God was angry about Solomon's disobedience. His transgressions could not be excused as ignorance because God had twice appeared to him (see 1 Kings 3:5-14 and 9:1-9) and given clear commands.

Verses 11-12. God pronounced judgment on Solomon for his apostasy. Because the king had violated the covenant and broken the divine law, the kingdom would be taken away and given to another. In honor of the divine covenant with David, God delayed this tragedy until the reign of Solomon's son and allowed the Davidic dynasty to retain rule over one tribe.

The Scripture and the Main Question

"All That Glitters Is Not Gold"

At the end of chapter 2 of 1 Kings, Solomon's accession to absolute power in Israel was acknowledged: "So the kingdom was established in the hand of Solomon" (v. 46). For the next eight chapters, the scripture presented elaborate stories of the wisdom and wealth that characterized this third king of Israel. Without doubt, this period was the epitome of power, riches, and prestige in the nation's entire history. Clearly, Israel took great pride in the exploits and reputation of Solomon. Reading the account in these chapters might lead one to assume that all was wonderful for both monarch and people. But, in truth, there was another and darker side of Solomon's character that impacted on his nation for evil rather than for good. In the judgment of the Deuteronomistic historian whose interpretation we are reading, there was a fatal weakness in Solomon's heart—a malignant corruption that would eventually taint his fame, contradict his vaunted wisdom, and expose his nation to violence and division.

Decades earlier when the people of Israel were demanding a king like other nations, the prophet Samuel had warned them of the evils of kingship (see 1 Sam. 8:11-18). This denunciation was probably actually written after the time of Solomon in response to and reflection on his reign. The king is attacked for his policies of excessive taxation and of requiring forced labor. First Kings 4:22-23 describes the lavish provisions consumed by the court. Such luxurious indulgence combined with the grandiose building projects and expensive military forces resulted in an enormous need for money. Unable to earn enough to cover such extravagance even from his lucrative commercial enterprises, Solomon exploited his own people. The nation was divided into twelve administrative districts to facilitate the collection of the heavy taxes that the king imposed. Thirty thousand Israelites were sent to Lebanon as laborers and one-hundred-fifty thousand were put to forced labor at home, working one month for the king out of every three.

Playing the Harlot

In the prophetic books of the Old Testament, the nation of Israel is often imaged as being in a marriage relationship with Yahweh—an analogy for the covenant relationship (see Jer. 31:32, for example). When the people are unfaithful to their obligations and disobedience to divine law, they are sometimes said to be playing the harlot. In other words, they are being unfaithful to their covenant partner, committing adultery by indulging their attraction to other gods (see Deut. 31:6). This association of sexual misconduct with the worship of foreign gods helps to explain the condemnation of Solomon, who allowed the religions of his many wives to seduce him away from absolute loyalty to Yahweh. By having places of worship built that were devoted to pagan gods, Solomon violated the fundamental demand of the covenant—"you shall have no other gods besides me."

It is interesting that sexual conduct ensnared Solomon in sin as it did his father David. But note that while David's sin with Bathsheba might appear much more heinous, the scripture records a much harsher judgment on Solomon. David sinned out of selfish lust. Solomon's sin was that of superficial commitment, which made it possible for him to compromise, to try to have it both ways—to worship Yahweh and tolerate other gods. I am reminded of the judgment of God on the Laodicean church recorded in Revelation 3:16: "So, because you are lukewarm, and neither cold nor hot, I am about to spit you out of my mouth."

Ironically, even the very temple of Yahweh provided evidence of Solomon's failure to remain faithful to Yahweh alone. The temple that he had built in Jerusalem was designed and constructed by Phoenician crafts-men. Its design was identical to that of many temples to Baal, the fertility god of the Canaanites, who was the chief rival for the allegiance of the Israelite people. For example, the twelve oxen mentioned in 1 Kings 7:25 were bulls that were the symbol of Baal and of the reproductive powers of nature.

Under Solomon's rule, Israel had become a cosmopolitan nation influ-enced by many other cultures. The caravans and trading ships that sailed to other parts of the world brought back cargos of ideas as well as of products. Just as wealth and power were novel experiences for Israel, so the reign of an oriental monarch was a new kind of political authority. The days of being led by God through miraculously opened waters, of being guided through the desert wilderness, of being empowered directly by God's spirit seemed long ago. It was a new and different age for Israel. Unfortunately, Solomon's reign brought not only new ways of life, but also desertion of the religious values of Israel's past.

"I Will Surely Tear the Kingdom Away from You"

The God of the Bible is a God who works out the divine will in the his-torical events of nations and people. The punishment for Solomon's unfaithfulness was made clear in 11:11-13. The kingdom will be torn away from Solomon's family. Later in the chapter, the prophet Ahijah per-formed the symbolic act of tearing his own new garment into twelve pieces and giving ten of the pieces to Jeroboam, who will rebel against Solomon and his son Rehoboam. (The reader is reminded of Saul's tearing the gar-ment of Samuel when he was confronted with his loss of the kingdom; see 1 Sam. 15:27-28.) Such an action by a prophet was understood to cause an event to happen, as well as signifying it. God promised Solomon that the division of the kingdom would not occur during his reign, but during his son's, and that one tribe would remain under the rule of the heirs of David. The confusion in numbers (ten plus one do not equal twelve) prob-ably can be explained either (1) by assuming that David's tribe of Judah would remain under the rule of his family and counting the tribe of Ben-jamin as the one that God would give to Solomon's son, or (2) not count-ing the tribe of Benjamin at all, since at this time it was quite small and insignificant.

Even during Solomon's reign, the empire was beginning to shrink as por-tions of the border lands of Israel were captured by enemies (see 1 Kings 11:14-25). Jeroboam led a revolt against the king and, unsuccessful, fled to Egypt to await a better opportunity. When Rehoboam, Solomon's son, fol-lowed his father to the throne, Jeroboam returned and rallied the ten north-ern tribes to reject the new king's authority. The unity of Israel so carefully crafted by David was destroyed and the nation divided into the two king-doms of Israel in the north and Judah in the south.

FIRST QUARTER

Helping Adults Become Involved

Preparing to Teach

Begin your preparation by reading the account in 1 Kings 11 of what the footnote in the *Oxford Annotated NRSV* calls "the dark side of Solomon's reign." Evaluate the actions of the king as the Deuteronomistic historian did by comparing them to descriptions of the dangers of monarchy as recorded in 1 Samuel 8:11-17 and Deuteronomy 7:1-4 and 17:14-17. Remember that while these passages appear in the biblical text as parts of the story of Israel before Solomon, they were actually written during or after his reign as condemnations of his policies. Make a list of specific actions that the writer believed were contrary to covenant faithfulness.

Reread chapters 3–10 of 1 Kings. Instead of focusing on the grandeur described, observe the profound changes in the life of the nation that it depicts. Make a list of ways in which life in Israel was sharply different in the days of Solomon from the earlier periods of the tribal confederacy and the early monarchy.

Have available appropriate maps, especially one showing the nation divided into Israel and Judah; the historical chart that you have been developing; additional newsprint or board; paper, pencils, and Bibles for all.

Present the material of the lesson by this outline:

    I. Cosmopolitan influences change Israel
   II. Solomon compromises his faithfulness
  III. God's judgment
  IV. From the conquest of Canaan to the division of the kingdom
   V. Faith and culture

Introducing the Main Question

Distribute sheets of paper and pencils and ask the students to draw pictures that, in their minds, best portray the reign of Solomon. (Dispel concerns about artistic ability by suggesting the use of stick figures and explanatory labels if needed.) Allow a period for discussion of these drawings when they are finished. Lead the class to notice what features are most frequently represented and whether any of the drawings picture the dark side of Solomon's reign.

Move into a consideration of this dark side by utilizing the ideas in "The Main Question." The comments of Martin Luther and Paul Tillich about who one's god really is should be provocative.

Developing the Lesson

I. Cosmopolitan influences change Israel
Your consideration of this topic can follow easily from the discussion of the pictures drawn by the class. Ask them to compare these images of Solomon's reign with the mental pictures that they have of life in earlier periods. Be sure that they recognize not only the differences in economic wealth and political prestige, but also how these impacted on the faith of Israel. The ideas in the last paragraph of "Playing the Harlot" can be developed here along with the results of your own reading and listing as suggested in "Preparing to Teach."

The essential points to emphasize include extreme wealth, urbanization (Jerusalem at this period became a great city in which a large percentage of the nation's population lived), lucrative trade with distant parts of the world, international prestige, the influx of new ideas and customs, the political shift to an absolute monarch with an extravagant court life.

II. Solomon compromises his faithfulness

The sections above—"'All That Glitters Is Not Gold'" and "Playing the Harlot"—summarize the information that needs to be presented here. Utilize that material along with the insights that you gained in your reading and evaluation of the passages suggested in "Preparing to Teach." Be careful that you do not allow the impression that the unfaithfulness of Solomon was the fault of his wives. These women who had been taken from their distant homes to the huge harem of the king were not the villains in the story. They were simply trying to retain the religious customs and values that they had learned among their own people. It was Solomon who knew better, but still was willing to compromise his faithfulness. There is no record that he attempted to win his wives to the worship of Yahweh. Instead, he allowed their faithfulness to their gods to cause him to turn away from his God. Explore with the class reasons why this happened. What were Solomon's motives? Why was it apparently so easy for him to violate God's commandments of absolute loyalty?

III. God's judgment

The information in "'I Will Surely Tear the Kingdom Away From You'" summarizes the action of God in punishment for Solomon's sin. Point out that not only does his family suffer loss, but also the whole nation was racked by violence and division. Use a map to show the two kingdoms into which the united nation split when Rehoboam came to the throne.

IV. From the conquest of Canaan to the division of the nation

Since this is the concluding lesson of this quarter, it is important to spend some time in drawing the material of the thirteen lessons into an unfolding story. Without using your historical chart, get the class to reconstruct together as much as they can of the major events and personalities that have been presented, and then arrange them into chronological order. After doing this from memory, display the chart that you have been developing throughout the quarter, add to it the division of the kingdom, and compare the recollections of the class.

V. Faith and culture

In order to show the relevance of this lesson in the lives of your students, use the verses from Deuteronomy and Jesus' words in Matthew that are quoted in "The Main Question." Emphasize that the divine command for supreme allegiance and uncompromised loyalty is still the greatest and first commandment for Christians today. Talk together about what this means in our daily lives, especially as we live in the midst of a culture that powerfully tempts us to unfaithfulness. Consider the influences on us of other persons whose values and commitments are different from our own. How can we turn them toward God in Jesus Christ rather than being influenced by them to accept foreign gods? What are some of the false gods whose attractiveness threatens our covenant faithfulness?

FIRST QUARTER

Helping Class Members Act

Challenge persons to examine their personal compromises with the values and practices of society, to confront signs of weakened commitment, and to rededicate themselves in loyalty to Christ.

Planning for Next Sunday

Reflect on the meanings of these ancient stories and their relevance to our study of the New Testament and our own lives.

JESUS THE FULFILLMENT

William H. Willimon

UNIT I: JESUS AND JOHN: SETTING THE SCENE

TWO LESSONS   DECEMBER 4–11

Fulfillment. Is there a more wonderful word in our language? Graduation day is the fulfillment of years of dedicated work in a school. A birth in a family is the fulfillment of young parents' dreams for a child. Christmas is the fulfillment of weeks of waiting and expectation.

Matthew, the first of the Gospels in our New Testament, is big on fulfillment. As Matthew presents the story of Jesus, he excitedly depicts Jesus as the fulfillment of the promises of God made centuries before to Israel. Jesus did not arrive on the scene out of nowhere. His presence among us is a vivid, in-the-flesh fulfillment of God's gracious love to Israel.

God's people, Israel, had spent centuries waiting, believing, and suffering because of their belief. Through persecution, famine, war, and national distress, Israel had steadfastly believed that God was faithful, that God would indeed make good on his promises, that they would be delivered and redeemed from their bondage.

Jesus, says Matthew, is the fulfillment of those beliefs and faithful expectations.

What are you waiting for? What star are you looking for in dark December skies? What would it take to make your life full, rich, and meaningful? When the expected is present, when our hopes become reality, when our longing is met, then there is fulfillment. Through this unit of study, your class will have the opportunity to experience anew Jesus as the fulfillment of our deepest desires, our highest hopes.

We have looked into the heavens and seen a great light. We have sensed the near presence of someone standing beside us who loves us. We have met fulfillment. His name is Jesus, God With Us.

LESSON 1   DECEMBER 4

Prepare for a New Life

Background Scripture: Matthew 3

The Main Question

Most of us, for most of our lives, plod along the same path. Rarely do we make major moves; even minor moves frighten us. We are all creatures of habit, old dogs who cannot be taught new tricks. Change is rare.

I have a friend, a pastoral counselor, who has been listening to people's problems for nearly twenty years. The other day I asked him what he had learned from his years of counseling. He replied: "People never change." When I questioned him on his rather dogmatic assertion he said, "Oh, sometimes we encounter modest adjustments in behavior, but fundamental, major personality change is rare."

Does that sound rather bleak to you? It does to me. Even the most self-satisfied among us are not completely at peace with our present selves. We hope that it might be possible for us to become better people—more loving, more caring, more adequate to the demands of living. Is this only wishful thinking, a fantasy that is not to be fulfilled?

John the Baptist came into the world preaching that the long-awaited Messiah was coming and that the world was in the process of major, fundamental, far-reaching change. Furthermore, John the Baptist called on his hearers to change, to repent, to reverse the direction of their lives, to show that they had truly repented by the way in which they now lived.

Is such fundamental, basic change possible? How does new life come to a person? These are the major questions that lie behind today's lesson, our first in this quarter from the Gospel of Matthew.

Selected Scripture

King James Version

Matthew 3:1-15

1 In those days came John the Baptist, preaching in the wilderness of Judea,

2 And saying, Repent ye: for the kingdom of heaven is at hand.

3 For this is he that was spoken of by the prophet Esaias, saying, The voice of one crying in the wilderness, Prepare ye the way of the Lord, make his paths straight.

4 And the same John had his raiment of camel's hair, and a leathern girdle about his loins; and his meat was locusts and wild honey.

5 Then went out to him Jerusalem, and all Judea, and all the region round about Jordan,

6 And were baptized of him in Jordan, confessing their sins.

7 But when he saw many of the Pharisees and Sadducees come to his baptism, he said unto them, O generation of vipers, who hath warned you to flee from the wrath to come?

8 Bring forth therefore fruits meet for repentance:

New Revised Standard Version

Matthew 3:1-15

1 In those days John the Baptist appeared in the wilderness of Judea, proclaiming, 2 "Repent, for the kingdom of heaven has come near."

3 This is the one of whom the prophet Isaiah spoke when he said,

"The voice of one crying out in the wilderness:

'Prepare the way of the Lord, make his paths straight.' "

4 Now John wore clothing of camel's hair with a leather belt around his waist, and his food was locusts and wild honey. 5 Then the people of Jerusalem and all Judea were going out to him, and all the region along the Jordan, 6 and they were baptized by him in the river Jordan, confessing their sins.

7 But when he saw many Pharisees and Sadducees coming for baptism, he said to them, "You brood of vipers! Who warned you to flee from the wrath to come? 8 Bear fruit worthy of repentance. 9 Do not presume to say to yourselves, 'We have Abraham as our ancestor'; for I tell

9 And think not to say within yourselves, We have Abraham to *our* father: for I say unto you, that God is able of these stones to raise up children unto Abraham.

10 And now also the axe is laid unto the root of the trees: therefore every tree which bringeth not forth good fruit is hewn down, and cast into the fire.

11 I indeed baptize you with water unto repentance: but he that cometh after me is mightier than I, whose shoes I am not worthy to bear: he shall baptize you with the Holy Ghost, and *with* fire:

12 Whose fan *is* in his hand, and he will thoroughly purge his floor, and gather his wheat into the garner; but he will burn up the chaff with unquenchable fire.

13 Then cometh Jesus from Galilee to Jordan unto John, to be baptized of him.

14 But John forbad him, saying, I have need to be baptized of thee, and comest thou to me?

15 And Jesus answering said unto him, Suffer *it to be so* now; for thus it becometh us to fulfill all righteousness. Then he suffered him.

Key Verse: **I indeed baptize you with water unto repentance: but he that cometh after me is mightier than I, whose shoes I am not worthy to bear: he shall baptize you with the Holy Ghost, and *with* fire.**

you, God is able from these stones to raise up children to Abraham. 10 Even now the ax is lying at the root of the trees; every tree therefore that does not bear good fruit is cut down and thrown into the fire.

11 "I baptize you with water for repentance, but one who is more powerful than I is coming after me; I am not worthy to carry his sandals. He will baptize you with the Holy Spirit and fire. 12 His winnowing fork is in his hand, and he will clear his threshing floor and will gather his wheat into the granary; but the chaff he will burn with unquenchable fire."

13 Then Jesus came from Galilee to John at the Jordan, to be baptized by him. 14 John would have prevented him, saying, "I need to be baptized by you, and do you come to me?" 15 But Jesus answered him, "Let it be so now; for it is proper for us in this way to fulfill all righteousness." Then he consented.

Key Verse: **I baptize you with water for repentance, but one who is more powerful than I is coming after me; I am not worthy to carry his sandals. He will baptize you with the Holy Spirit and fire.**

As You Read the Scripture

Matthew 3. The strange figure of John the Baptist appears in all four of the Gospels, but as is characteristic of Matthew, this account carries Matthew's unique perspective. We believe that Matthew has taken source material from Mark (3:1-6) and material shared with Luke (3:7-12) and freely adapted this to communicate clearly Matthew's own understanding of John.

Verse 1. Note that John the Baptist is "in the wilderness," far from the established centers of power, suggesting that he is a marginal, anti-establishment figure.

Verse 2 (see also Matt. 4:17). *Repent* means literally "to turn around," or "to change direction." The Greek more literally means "the kingdom of the heavens has drawn near" or "has come near." Marcan and Lucan parallels employ "the kingdom of God" to point to the same reality.

Verses 3-6. John is portrayed in the tradition of the Old Testament prophets. His sermons begin by quoting Isaiah. He also stands in the prophetic tradition as someone who is an outcast, a forerunner who announces dramatic events that are to occur in the history of Israel. His strange clothing also represents someone who is an outsider, someone whose message is so strange and challenging that it cannot be delivered through conventional means.

Verses 7-8. The Pharisees and Saduccees were members of two rival parties in Judaism of that day. Their presence at John's gatherings suggests that all the important people gathered to hear him. Unfortunately for all the important people, John is no respecter of social class. He speaks harshly to them, demanding that *they* repent. This call to repentance undoubtedly struck them as strange, since they considered themselves to be the religious and moral leaders of the day.

Verses 9-10. "Bear fruit that befits repentance." The Greek for *bear* also means *do* and is elsewhere translated as *produce*, as well. For Matthew *fruit* clearly equals *deeds*. Confession and repentance must lead to something more than contrition, that is, to works that embody that radical returning to God.

Verses 11-15. If John the Baptist's hearers thought that his words were harsh and his demands were tough, John assures them that there is one coming after him who is even more demanding. In verse 12, John uses the image of refining wheat, separating the hulls from the kernels of the wheat, to depict the cleansing, refining work of the Messiah.

The Scripture and the Main Question

I Baptize You

Matthew, like the other Gospel writers, depicts John as a transition figure. John the Baptist stands between the Old and New Testaments. He dresses like a prophet of old, his sermons sound like those of the prophets, he quotes the prophets. Like the prophets before him, John preached the coming wrath of God and a call to repentance. John issued the proclamation that "the kingdom of heaven has come near" (3:2). These words also sound the basic theme of Jesus' ministry (compare with Matt. 4:17, 10:7; Mark 1:15) and yet take on new meaning in light of the Cross.

John makes clear that no one is exempt from the need to repent and to prepare to make straight the paths of God. Clearly, Jewish lineage was not enough to guarantee entrance into the kingdom (Matt. 3:9). Only those who bore the fruits of repentance would be spared from God's righteous axe and the fire of judgment (Matt. 3:10, 7:19, 12:33; Isa. 10:34).

So John the Baptist is a prophet, a prophet in the tradition of the Old Testament prophets in that John the Baptist joins the long line of prophets who announced the intrusion of God into our world to love us and, by his love, to change us.

Matthew portrays John as lashing out at the Jewish leadership (the Pharisees and Sadducees) as faithless and sinful: "You brood of vipers! Who warned you to flee from the wrath to come?" (Matt. 3:7), an invective that

Luke addresses to the multitudes (Luke 3:7). For Matthew, the Jewish authorities are those who have willfully forsaken the true Law of God, and are responsible for the people rejecting the Messiah.

John the Baptist Came Preaching

Who is your favorite preacher? Who would you rather hear on a Sunday morning, more than anybody? I would love to hear Carlyle Marney. Great big booming voice, prophet. When I was a student, Marney came to our college and preached. Made me proud to be a Christian. Marney presented the Christian faith in an intellectually demanding way. I loved to hear Marney preach.

I suppose, if we had to isolate what makes a preacher worth hearing, we would say that in some way or the other, that preacher preached *good news*. That is what the word *gospel* means—good news. Not that a good preacher's good news sounds like good news from the very first. When Carlyle Marney preached, his sermons were complicated, tough to comprehend. I heard Marney preach the same sermon on three different occasions. Nobody complained. There was so much, you needed to hear it three times. His was a large, demanding word.

It is strange to hear who was Jesus' favorite preacher. "Jesus, if you invited the preacher, whom would you choose?" The answer may surprise you. Jesus' favorite preacher was *John the Baptist*. No other person exercised so strong an influence over Jesus. All of the Gospels begin their story of Jesus in the same manner as today's lesson from Matthew: by first telling about John. It is as if they want to say, "You can't hear Jesus unless you first hear John."

It is as if the Gospels say, "In order to comprehend Jesus' message, you've got to put it in context." Jesus learned how to preach the good news by hearing John speak it before him.

Mark calls John "the beginning of the gospel of Jesus Christ," the beginning of the good news. Luke says that John and Jesus were first cousins. When John begins his Gospel, he begins not by talk of the preaching of Jesus, but rather by a description of the preaching of John. "Now there was a man sent from God whose name was John."

When Jesus began preaching, he sounded so much like John, that when Herod Antipas heard Jesus preaching, he said, "Oh no, it's John again." Jesus sounded so much like John, old Herod thought that it was John come back from the dead. Jesus' voice sounded just like John's.

John baptized Jesus. And when Jesus finally started preaching, his sermon sounded exactly like John's. We preachers often copy those whom we admire. So when Jesus preached, somebody in the pew said, "Haven't we heard this sermon before?"

"Repent, the Kingdom of heaven is at hand!" Well, he was a new preacher. Young preachers often try to sound like the preachers they admire.

Later Jesus would say, "There has never been anybody born of a woman who was greater than John the Baptist."

The Kingdom of Heaven Is at Hand

Did we not agree that one of the things that make preacher great is that that preacher is able to communicate *good news? Gospel* means "good news." *So why didn't John's preaching sound more like good news?* Does this sound like good news to you? "You brood of vipers! Who warned you to flee from the wrath to come? . . . I tell you, God is able from these stones to raise up children to Abraham. Even now the ax is lying at the root of the trees; every tree therefore that does not bear good fruit is cut down and thrown into the fire" (Matt. 3:7-10).

John told people that, if they thought he was rough on them, just wait until his graduate student got hold of them. "I baptize you with water . . . but one who is more powerful than I is coming. . . . He will baptize you with . . . fire. His winnowing fork is in his hand, and he will clear his threshing floor and will gather his wheat into the granary; but the chaff he will burn with unquenchable fire" (Matt. 3:11-12). Repent!

Fire, winnowing forks, chaff, burned in the fire. Does that sound like good news? When John preached, he hurled grenades. He shouted, raved. No respecter of social class, when people appeared before John in all of their Sunday finery, their minks and fake furs, the told them to rip off those coats and give them away to the poor. He attacked the Pentagon, the White House, Wall Street. John did not care. He looked at all the substantial, important heavyweights of the world and told them that they were chaff blown by the wind into the fire. Strip down. Dive into the Jordan. Be baptized.

Repent!

The images, the strong images John used in his sermons, may not at first sound like good news. In my sermons, I use images of the butterfly emerging from the cocoon; the return of the robin in the spring; "He ain't heavy, he's my brother"; "Tie a yellow ribbon round the oak tree." Not John. John talked about an ax, slicing into the root of the tree. God turning away from all of the good hereditary believers and raising children out of the stones in the muddy Jordan River. He said that there was a winnowing fork in Messiah's hand, separating wheat and chaff! Why would people have clamored to hear that?

They came out into the wilderness to hear this strange preacher named John. When they came, he confronted them with an ax, stones, a winnowing fork separating the wheat from the chaff, fire. Why would people come out to hear that? I will tell you. The ax, the winnowing fork, children from stone, the refiner's fire, these are all *images of change.* Weird John had a simple message. It was a message that everybody wanted to hear, yet nobody wanted to hear. Here was the message: *You can change.* That is what *repentance* means—*change.* Where there is wilderness, the ax is laid to the tree to make a straight path. From nothing but stones in the muddy Jordan, children come forth. Chaff is burned away so that the good wheat is left. Dusty, ugly ore is refined, until there is pure gold. Herod hated John and had him killed, because Herod did not want to hear about change. Those who are in power, those up at the top, the establishment does not want to hear change. Why change? They like things as they are. Sitting atop the good old status quo, the status quo is good enough for them.

But multitudes came to hear John. The majority of us, though we are part of the status quo, are not content with it. When John preached, even his fierce preaching sounded like good news, because *he dared to speak of change.* A friend of mine, a counselor, told me that after twenty years of counselling, he has learned one thing. People rarely change. Oh, there can be some modest movement. But fundamental, drastic change in personality is rare. Change is so rare that most wise counselors do not aim for it. They content themselves with small moves, minor adjustments in behavior.

For most of our days, this is enough. When asked to comment on the state of affairs, we make witty, cynical comments. Contort the voice into a whine. Pick up the paper in the morning, no news there. See? I told you so. Nothing new under the sun. People are always the same.

But occasionally, there may be a voice, a word, an image, which radically reorients us. Before there can be change, there must be promise of change. The Messiah is coming. The Kingdom of God is right now. Not everything is fixed and tied down. You can change. When God's Messiah walks in, stands at the door and knocks, calls your name, is born among us, we can change. The fierce grip of our economic, sociological, and psychological determinism is relaxed. With ax, winnowing fork, and fire, the world begins to shift. Good news.

Here is some of the best news we will ever hear, though it may not at first sound like good news: Repent. You *can* change.

Helping Adults Become Involved

Preparing to Teach

Carefully read the material found in "The Main Question," "The Scripture and the Main Question," and "As You Read the Scripture." As you read, ask yourself, "What are some of the most difficult areas of our lives to change?" Addiction? Old habits? Deep prejudices against others?

Today's lesson can be presented as follows:

I. John the Baptist called on everyone to change in preparation for the arrival of Messiah.
II. Change is very difficult for most adults.
III. The good news of Jesus Christ is the promise that we can change.

While there are a number of possible emphases related to the ministry of John, this lesson focuses on John as the prophet of new life. In your presentation in class, focus on the fact that change is tough for most adults. However, in the light of the gospel, change is possible.

Introducing the Main Question

Using the material in "The Main Question," as well as your own thoughts on those areas in life where change is difficult, lead your class in a discussion of the difficulty of real change in our lives.

Developing the Lesson

I. John the Baptist called on everyone to change in preparation for the arrival of Messiah.

Have someone read today's scripture, Matthew 3:1-15. Using the material found in "As You Read the Scripture," as well as the opening comments in "The Scripture and the Main Question," lead your class in a study of this text, filling in the background information on John and his message.

II. Change is very difficult for most adults.

Using the material in "The Scripture and the Main Question," lead your class in a discussion of the good news of Jesus Christ. In what way does

119

John's preaching not sound like good news when we first hear it? What do the members of your class look for in a preacher's message? Do they agree that effective preachers preach good news? Ask your class: Do people come to church looking for change or do they expect to hear what they have always believed?

III. The good news of Jesus Christ is the promise that we can change.

How can the preaching of change help to accomplish change? Have any members of your group had experiences in which they have personally been changed through the words of a sermon? Can your class think of examples from the Bible in which people changed after meeting Jesus?

Stress to your class that John's call to repent is much more than a pious declaration of our sins, or a vague feeling of contrition. Repentance is nothing less than a radical turning, returning to God, beginning again in a new relationship with God. This word drives home the total demand of repentance in both the Old Testament and the New. The Hebrew root for *repent (sub)* is closely connected to the notion of God's covenant with Israel and implies a returning to that relationship God has established between God and God's people, despite the faithless breaking of that covenant again and again. That sense of radical conversion that puts us back in right relationship with our God clearly lies at the heart of the Baptist's message, reminding us that God has continually searched us out and refused to leave us alone.

Helping Class Members Act

Remind your class that this Sunday begins the Christian season of Advent in the church. Advent is a season of repentance, new possibility, and hope. Advent is an invitation to participate with God in "creating all things new." This is therefore a good time for Christians to recognize that serious personal preparation and intentional outward action must be woven together to make ourselves the very pathways of God. Few of us can be pathways of God in our present state. We must change.

In an Advent essay entitled "Recapturing Lost Visions," my colleague at Duke, John Westerhoff, defines repentance as a change in our perception, the recognition that the reign of God is at hand, that life in the world to come has indeed begun (*A Pilgrim People*, New York: Seabury Press, 1982, p. 46). Advent, says Westerhoff, "is a season of paradoxes: longing anticipation and patient watching; transforming the way we envision life and yet living prepared; living out a wait for what never seems to come and continuing in hopeful trust; desiring to give up control and opening ourselves to new possibilities for life" (*A Pilgrim People*, p. 43).

Ask each person in the class silently to think about his or her own life and one area that needs changing this Advent. Close with a prayer for God to help us to change to be the people God calls us to be.

Preparing for Next Sunday

Having been introduced to the relationship between John and Jesus in this Sunday's lesson, next Sunday we shall continue to study Jesus and John, focusing on a rather disturbing episode from their later lives. Ask everyone to read Matthew 11:2-15 before next Sunday.

Hold On to Your Faith

Background Scripture: Matthew 11:2-15

The Main Question

The other day, I was talking to a young woman who told me that she was having difficulty finding a church that suits her in the town where she was living.

"What are you looking for in a church?" I asked.

"I have a very demanding job," she said. "I work hard, six days a week. So when I go to church on Sunday, I don't want to be bombarded with a bunch of new stuff. I want to go, get a spiritual lift, feel better about my problems, be glad that I came."

She confessed that she had yet to find the church that suited her, even though she had visited more than a dozen congregations.

I think that young woman is similar to many of us. As far as the church is concerned, we live in a buyer's market. We look for a church the same way we might shop for a compatible supermarket or hairdresser. We begin with our wants, our attitudes, our values, then we shop for a church that conforms to us as we presently are—a church that suits *me*.

Do we also shop for a Savior? Now, here at the Second Sunday of Advent, we are preparing for the birth of the Messiah, the Savior of the world. Will the coming Savior meet our expectations? What will we do if we find that the Savior comes, not to fulfill our needs, but rather to make demands on us? What if he tells us things we do not want to hear? Not every savior of the world is named Jesus.

For whom are you waiting as you await the birth of the Messiah? What will happen to our faith in God's Messiah if God sends us a Messiah who fails to meet our present expectations? These are the questions that lie behind Matthew's account of the questions put to Jesus by John the Baptist in Matthew 11.

Today's passage from Matthew reminds us that, from the beginning, Jesus did not fulfill everyone's expectations. We can only receive him, not by having him change to fit our wishes, but rather by having our wishes reformed in his image and likeness.

Christmas means that the Messiah is coming. Is the Messiah for whom we are waiting Jesus? That is the Advent question.

Selected Scripture

King James Version

Matthew 11:2-15

2 Now when John had heard in the prison the works of Christ, he sent two of his disciples,

3 And said unto him, Art thou he that should come, or do we look for another?

New Revised Standard Version

Matthew 11:2-15

2 When John heard in prison what the Messiah was doing, he sent word by his disciples 3 and said to him, "Are you the one who is to come, or are we to wait for another?" 4 Jesus answered them, "Go and tell John

4 Jesus answered and said unto them, Go and shew John again those things which ye do hear and see:

5 The blind receive their sight, and the lame walk, the lepers are cleansed, and the deaf hear, the dead are raised up, and the poor have the gospel preached to them.

6 And blessed is *he*, whosoever shall not be offended in me.

7 And as they departed, Jesus began to say unto the multitudes concerning John, What went ye out into the wilderness to see? A reed shaken with the wind?

8 But what went ye out for to see? A man clothed in soft raiment? behold, they that wear soft *clothing* are in kings' houses.

9 But what went ye out for to see? A prophet? yea, I say unto you, and more than a prophet.

10 For this is *he,* of whom it is written, Behold, I send my messenger before thy face, which shall prepare thy way before thee.

11 Verily I say unto you, Among them that are born of women there hath not risen a greater than John the Baptist: notwithstanding he that is least in the kingdom of heaven is greater than he.

12 And from the days of John the Baptist until now the kingdom of heaven suffereth violence, and the violent take it by force.

13 For all the prophets and the law prophesied until John.

14 And if ye will receive *it,* this is Elias, which was for to come.

15 He that hath ears to hear, let him hear.

Key Verse: **For this *he*, of whom it is written, Behold, I send my messenger before thy face, which shall prepare thy way before thee.**

what you hear and see: 5 the blind receive their sight, the lame walk, the lepers are cleansed, the deaf hear, the dead are raised, and the poor have good news brought to them. 6 And blessed is anyone who takes no offense at me."

7 As they went away, Jesus began to speak to the crowds about John: "What did you go out into the wilderness to look at? A reed shaken by the wind? 8 What then did you go out to see? Someone dressed in soft robes? Look, those who wear soft robes are in royal palaces. 9 What then did you go out to see? A prophet? Yes, I tell you, and more than a prophet. 10 This is the one about whom it is written,

'See, I am sending my
    messenger ahead of you,
who will prepare your way
    before you.'

11 Truly I tell you, among those born of women no one has arisen greater than John the Baptist; yet the least in the kingdom of heaven is greater than he. 12 From the days of John the Baptist until now the kingdom of heaven has suffered violence, and the violent take it by force. 13 For all the prophets and the law prophesied until John came; 14 and if you are willing to accept it, he is Elijah who is to come. 15 Let anyone with ears listen!"

Key Verse: **This is the one about whom it is written, "See, I am sending my messenger ahead of you, who will prepare your way before you."**

As You Read the Scripture

Matthew 11:2-15. This chapter represents a break in Matthew's account of Jesus. Opposition to Jesus is growing. Chapters 11 and 12 deal with questions about Jesus' authority and Jesus' response to those who challenge him. In reading these chapters, we learn about Jesus' own justification for his teaching and work.

Verse 2. "When John was in prison." How things have changed since last week's scripture (Matt. 3:1-15) where John is portrayed as a popular, though controversial, preacher to the multitudes. Is it any wonder that John's fierce preaching (Matt. 3:7-10) has landed him in prison, a *persona non grata* with the authorities? One can easily imagine the disappointment and depression that John must have been suffering in prison at the sad state of events.

Verse 3. The "one who is to come" was spoken of by the prophet Malachi in chapter 3:1 and is a phrase picked up in the New Testament a number of times (Matt. 3:11; John 1:15, 27; 6:14; Acts 19:4; Heb. 10:37; Rev. 1:4, 8). The prophet Malachi was addressing the priesthood of his day, but his strong imagery of purification and cleansing with fire may well have appealed to John the Baptist. It is difficult to tell if the question we have in Matthew's text comes from an actual encounter between Jesus and the disciples of John, but this exchange in Matthew shows that there must have been tensions between the message of John and the message of Jesus that had surfaced in the early church.

Verse 5. "The blind receive their sight, the lame walk, the lepers are cleansed, the deaf hear, the dead are raised, and the poor have good news brought to them" is a list of miracles that constitutes Jesus' answer to the disciples of John. The work of Jesus goes far beyond the traditional expectations of the Messiah (healing miracles), yet does not fulfill the expectations of those who expected the Messiah to come and destroy the unrepentant (John the Baptist's predictions), cleanse the priesthood (Malachi's prophecy), or punish the nations (Isaiah). Unique to the ministry of Jesus is the way in which he finds a place in the community for those who have been exiled for one reason or another. He eliminates the barriers to fellowship—even preaching good news to the poor.

Verse 6. One of Malachi's particular charges against the priests of his day was that their instructions had become a stumbling block (Mal. 2:8). Matthew has Jesus blessing those who have made the difficult decision to become disciples. In this verse, Jesus invites John to find an answer to his own question based on the evidence provided by Jesus' activities. Compare with Luke 4:17-21.

Verse 10. This is quoted from Malachi 3:1. John has value in the gospel, but his value is mainly that of the preparer of the way. There is irony here in that the preparer of the way is apparently not able to recognize the one for whom he has been preparing the way!

Verse 11. The earthly kingdom is here, as contrasted with the heavenly kingdom, which is only a future expectation. John the Baptist receives the highest praise possible here on earth, yet God has even greater things in store as depicted in the message of Jesus.

Verses 12-15. Jesus reminds his examiners that opposition to the prophets of God is not new. God's people have found God's prophetic intrusions to be surprising before; why should they not be surprised now?

SECOND QUARTER

The Scripture and the Main Question

Are You the One?

John the Baptist poses the crucial question to Jesus in today's lesson from Matthew, chapter 11: "Are you the one who is to come, or are we to look for another?" (v. 3). Contained in these few words are the hopes and expectations of John for the prophetic ministry of Jesus. In asking this question, John speaks for the faithful in every generation who must make a decision. Is faith in Jesus the answer to life's pressing problems, to the world's search for new life? Matthew places Jesus in the center of these questions as he tells the story of the encounter between the messengers of John the Baptist and the Christ. Luke shares this story with few changes (see Luke 7:18-35), but Matthew places particular emphasis on John's imprisonment, and so sets the stage for a major turning point in his Gospel.

At this point in his account of the ministry of Jesus, Matthew begins to describe the ways in which hostility to Jesus' message grew so that some who heard the message of the Kingdom became followers willing to give up their lives and others began to plot for Jesus' death. In chapter 11:2-12 there is growing opposition. John the Baptist's imprisonment is the first sign of the price that Jesus and his followers will have to pay.

John the Baptist's ministry did not dovetail so neatly with Jesus' ministry as we might be led to believe from a superficial reading of Matthew's Gospel. In last week's lesson, we studied the excited announcement by John the Baptist that the long-awaited Messiah was at last on his way to save the people. John called on everyone to prepare themselves for his arrival. Today, our lesson deals with a far different reality. The Advent of the Messiah has occurred. Jesus has been born. At last God is moving to save his people, moving within the words and work of this man named Jesus. Yet what had changed? John is languishing in prison. Jesus is encountering not willing acceptance, but growing, fierce opposition.

This particular Advent text, Matthew 11, does not place John the Baptist at center stage, confidently announcing the new Kingdom as we heard him announce it in last week's lesson. Instead, we hear John and his disciples question if Jesus is really who they thought he was. Many biblical scholars, reading this passage, believe that this points back to a time in the early church when people knew disciples of John who had not become Christians. Perhaps, at a very early date, there were followers of John the Baptist competing for converts with the disciples of Jesus. In the opinions of John's disciples, Jesus did not fulfill every expectation for the Messiah. Perhaps for that reason, Jesus caused offense.

For what are you and I waiting during this season of Advent preparation for Christmas? In what ways does Jesus fulfill or fail to fulfill our expectations for how God is supposed to act toward us? The significance of the Advent season is that there is one who is to come, but it is not Santa Claus. You and I are studying Matthew's Gospel in mid-December, mid-Advent. By this time, the expectations for Christmas have reached a fever pitch. Unfortunately, the hopes for Christmas that we now see expressed in television commercials and radio shopping jingles bear almost no relation to the reality of the Kingdom that Jesus proclaimed. Christmas is a holiday that should be enjoyed, but the coming of Christ has much, much more to offer—though not necessarily on our terms. It is truly possible for the modern Christian to take offense at the proclamation of Jesus, even as we supposedly prepare for the coming of the Christ Child.

Are We to Wait for Another?

I know a person who says that he has simply given up on belief in God. He grew up in a loving, Christian home. From the time he could walk, his parents faithfully took him to church. He absorbed willingly the message of the church, learned his Bible stories, believed with an open and trusting heart. As he grew into adulthood, he was secure and confident in his faith.

In his mid-twenties, life began to change for him. He was engaged to be married to a beautiful young woman. They had planned to give their lives to teaching others. But a horrible, painful, and disfiguring disease struck him down. She broke off their engagement. He was not only in great physical pain, but also now he was in mental anguish. His friends deserted him. He became lonely and depressed. To ease some of his pain and anguish, he began to take pain-killing drugs. They dulled some of the pain, but they also made him dependent on the drugs. Now, in his early fifties, my friend is a broken, dependent, horribly disillusioned man.

"I trusted God," he says. "I believed all that stuff about the love of God and how, if you try to do right, God will do right to you. But I no longer believe that. What God has allowed to happen to me in life has totally destroyed any faith I ever had in God as a good and loving God. All that is over for me."

While I have tried to console him, even to argue and debate with him, I must admit that I can see his point. It is as if he is saying, "I played God's game, but God refused to play by the rules of the game." It is as if he were in a class in school in which the teacher told the class, on the first day of class, what the expectations were for fulfillment of the requirements of the course, then, on the last day of class, changed all of the requirements and he flunked the class.

What do we do when God fails to meet our expectations? That is the question, the rather frightening question, behind today's lesson. It was the question put to Jesus by John the Baptist: We have waited for you. I have tried to prepare people for you. Now look at us. I am here in jail awaiting execution and you are encountering nothing but failure and opposition. Are *you* the long-awaited Messiah, or should we expect someone else?

Go Tell What You Hear and See

One might have expected Jesus to take some offense at the questions of John. John is daring to question the authority, the validity of Jesus' ministry. Jesus appears to take no offense at the inquiry of John; rather, he responds, pointing to the visible, tangible work that he has done. Perhaps Jesus has compassion on our doubts. Perhaps Jesus knows how difficult faith can be. At any rate, rather than rebuke John for his questions, Jesus points to the results of his work, visible results that people can "see and hear" (Matt. 11:4). The sick and the maimed are being healed. Those who have had nothing but bad news in life are, for the first time, receiving good news. The poor—those on the outside, those who have been excluded from life's opportunities and joys—at last have "good news brought to them" (11:5).

Perhaps John was confused by Jesus because he expected Jesus to go up to

Jerusalem and confront the powerful. Some believe that John may have expected Jesus to raise an army and to begin a revolution in which the oppressive Romans would be driven out of Judea. To John's consternation, Jesus did none of this. Rather, he went to the poor and the outcast. He spent his time preaching to the lowly and the oppressed. Was this any way for a messiah to act?

From the beginning, Jesus reversed people's expectations for how a messiah should behave. In nearly every parable, in nearly every act, he assaulted conventional religious expectations. He is doing the same here even for one so knowledgeable as John the Baptist. Jesus praises the ministry of John (11:7-11), yet even John, for all his insight, fails to grasp the significance of what God is doing in Jesus of Nazareth.

You and I, in our own struggles to comprehend and to understand Jesus, should take heart from this episode in chapter 11 of Matthew's Gospel. Just as John the Baptist was forced to grow, required to rearrange his expectations in the light of the reality of Jesus' words and deeds, so must we expect to grow and change in our relationship with Jesus. Will our faith grow as he reveals more of himself to us, or will we become disillusioned and embittered because Jesus refuses to fit our mold for how he is supposed to deal with us?

Imagine that you are in a conversation with the friend of mine that I mentioned earlier, the friend who has lost his faith in the goodness of God because of the terrible things that have happened to him in life. What would you say to this man to bolster his faith in Jesus? What evidence of the love and power of God would you point him to in our world today?

Helping Adults Become Involved

Preparing to Teach

The main question behind today's lesson concerns the gap between our religious expectations and the reality of who Jesus really is and what the gospel really demands of us. Keep that question before you as you read through the material in "As You Read the Scripture" and "The Scripture and the Main Question."

The gap between expectation and reality will be different for different people. As you read, jot down your own experiences and impressions that relate to the material in today's lesson.

Organize today's lesson on the basis of this outline:

I. It is natural and normal to be confused or to doubt certain aspects of our faith.
II. John the Baptist had doubts about the identity and work of Jesus.
III. Jesus pointed John to evidence from his compassionate work in the world.
IV. Jesus also helps us during our times of doubt.

Introducing the Main Question

Today's lesson implies that everyone has times of doubt, just as John the Baptist was confused and doubted the mission of Jesus. Begin today's lesson by sharing with your class some experience from your own life in which you felt doubtful or confused about your faith.

I. It is natural and normal to be confused or to doubt certain aspects of our faith.

Retell for your class the account of the person in "The Scripture and the Main Question." Ask your class to respond to this person's attitudes about the church. Have they felt as she has felt about the church? In what ways have people in your class found the church to be a demanding and challenging place for their faith?

II. John the Baptist had doubts about the identity and work of Jesus.

Retell or have someone read aloud the episode in today's scripture, Matthew 11:2-15. Can anyone in your class relate to John's confusion about Jesus and his work? Use the material in "The Scripture and the Main Question" to augment your class' knowledge of this passage from Matthew.

Have any members of your class had disillusioning experiences with religious leaders in which they were confused by the behavior of someone they admired?

III. Jesus pointed John to evidence from his compassionate work in the world.

Note that today's scripture does not leave John in confusion and doubt. Jesus points John to evidence that can help to heal his doubts. Ask your class to imagine that they are talking to someone with doubts about the Christian faith. To what evidence would they point this person in order to convince them that Jesus really was the savior of the world?

In what ways is the church itself evidence for the lordship of Christ? Urge your class to think of specific examples, in much the same way that Jesus pointed John to specifics.

IV. Jesus also helps us during our times of doubt.

Ask class members to share times when they believe that God has helped them during their periods of doubt or confusion. You might have some examples of your own. Today's scripture from Matthew is meant to provide us encouragement to hold on to our faith even during times of doubt.

Helping Class Members Act

In "The Scripture and the Main Question" we note that this is the season of Advent. Advent is a time of preparation for the Messiah. Ask the class to discuss ways in which some of our preparation during this time of year (e.g., our commercialism, sentimentality, etc.) is not really preparation for the arrival of Jesus, but rather for the arrival of false saviors.

Close the class with a prayer, preferably an Advent prayer or hymn such as "O Come, O Come Emmanuel."

Planning for Next Sunday

Next Sunday we will join Matthew in focusing on an often-overlooked star of the Christmas story—Joseph. Ask class members to come to class prepared to tell what they know of this silent witness to the nativity of Christ.

Spiritual Enrichment Article:
The First Christmas Pageant

And he came to her and said, "Hail, O favored one, the Lord is with you! (LUKE 1:28).

There is a little book that has become the major part of our family's Christmas reading-aloud repertoire—Barbara Robinson's delightful *Best Christmas Pageant Ever*. It is the uproarious, irreverent, deeply moving account of an unforgettable Christmas pageant at Second Presbyterian Church in which the chief culprits were "the Horrible Herdmans," who were

> absolutely the worst kids in the history of the world. They lied and stole and smoked cigars (even the girls) and talked dirty and hit little kids and cursed their teachers and took the name of the Lord in vain and set fire to Fred Shoemaker's old broken-down toolhouse.

What the Herdmans—Claude, Leroy, Ralph, Imogene, Ollie, and Gladys—do to the Nativity is a story that you must read for yourself.

Now, I confess that I have always shared Bill Muehl's sentiments about children's Christmas pageants. In *All the Damned Angels*, Muehl writes: "I feel about Christmas pageants the way rats are reputed to feel about sinking ships." Like Muehl, I too have lamented that these theatrical travesties have become as much a part of Yuletide as indigestion. At scores of Christian churches this year, eight-year-old shepherds in their fathers' altered bathrobes, their mothers' sandals, and shoepolish beards will call at cardboard mangers to be greeted by sullen eleven-year-old Josephs and besheeted Marys watched over by tinsel-and-glitter-glued blonde angels adorned in twin-bed sheets. When *your* child is in such a pageant, I consider it a theatrical scandal and a theological sacrilege. When *my* child is in such a pageant, it is strangely the most inspiring thing I ever saw and the highlight of my Christmas!

* * *

But lately, with the help of *The Best Christmas Pageant Ever* and the children at my church, I have come to hold a different opinion of these childhood theatricals. My theory is this: you may never understand the Christmas story until you have seen it done (or undone) as only the kindergarten-through-sixth-grade church school classes can do it.

You know how we usually conceive of the Nativity. In our hands, the people in the first Christmas come out looking as religious and inspired as the participants in the annual Perry Como Christmas Show. Elizabeth, Mary, Joseph, and the shepherds seem so sure of what they are doing and the parts they are to play in the coming of Christ. Mary and Joseph, as if carefully rehearsed for two thousand years, make their entrances on cue, meet Gabriel, confidently go through the birth experience, receive a few shepherds and wise men, then exit majestically for Egypt.

We have heard it and read it so many times that neither we nor Mary is surprised when the angel tells her she is expecting and tells Joseph not to fear. Mary believes she is "blessed." Joseph is not confused. Knowing how the story will end, everyone is in complete control, and it all goes off without a hitch.

But the disarming thing about children's Christmas pageants is that they seem to work that way. No matter how fine the bathrobes or how professional the makeup, or how great the quantity of hay upon the stage, something invariably goes wrong. Mary, Joseph, and the rest of the cast never seem to look as dignified, as pious, or as sure of themselves as they do on Christmas greeting cards. The shepherds usually act as confused and dumbfounded as the sheep they are supposed to be watching over. The wise men may look overdressed but rarely do they look overwise.

Eleven-year-old Joseph is always embarrassed to be standing that close to Mary (or to any other girl, for that matter), and Mary, despite her efforts to look like one who is "blessed among women," always looks like one who is confused, bewildered, about to giggle, and who has not the slightest notion of what to do with a baby, much less what her next line is supposed to be. And so Christmas pageants are usually cute, often comic, sometimes ridiculous, but rarely are they what we envision as the way the Nativity really looked.

* * *

Or are they? Last year, as I watched the children at my church giggle and stumble their way through the incarnation, it occurred to me that this was exactly how Matthew and Luke were trying to tell us that it happened on that very first Christmas.

It was not as tied down and religious and neat as we like to tell it. Whatever that Advent was, it all must have been a little confusing, and unnerving, and even a little ridiculous. For it had to do with God: Lord of Lords, King of Kings, Suffering Servant, Prince of Peace, becoming flesh and dwelling among us. There has got to be something unnerving about that.

I venture that Mary did not look much like the queen of heaven that night in Bethlehem. I venture, with Luther, that she looked more like a rather confused, bewildered teen-ager from your church youth group who was about to giggle in her nervousness and had not the slightest notion of what to do with a baby or what her next line was supposed to be. And Joseph, if he had any feelings at all, must have felt embarrassed. After all, he was in an embarrassing situation. The shepherds, despite all that talk about "fear not," were as scared as you or I would be if a similar thing happened to us while we were at work. They were all in over their heads, wondering what people like themselves were doing on stage in a drama like this.

There was no time to rehearse, or to try to strike a sufficiently religious pose, or to act as if they knew what they were doing or how the play would end. It all came upon them and overwhelmed them and swept them along to Egypt, and Jerusalem, and on and on.

* * *

This is how God is always with us. This is Emmanuel. We—like Mary, like Joseph, like the others—are busy at home minding our own business, falling in love, getting engaged, making plans, paying taxes, complaining about the government, entertaining strange relatives from the East bearing perfume, plodding through the everdayness of our lives in backwater towns; and then God chooses us to reveal something of himself to the world, to run some errand, perform some act of love through us. And we, whether we really like it or not, or have the experience or ability or understanding, get pushed onto the stage of history to act out our parts, with stage fright, filling roles that are too big for us, wondering what the next line will be, doing our best to do what he wants us to do even when we are not sure why he wants us to play the part.

This is Emmanuel.

If by chance some winged angelic messenger from God should appear to us this season, whether it be the angel Gabriel or an angel like most of the ones we see this time of year, with a median age of eight years, wearing an old bedsheet over tennis shoes and Levis, topped with tinseled halo and cardboard wings, I thing that angel's word from the Lord would be the same as those first words that the angel spoke to Mary: "Hail, O favored one, the Lord is with you."

And with you, and you, and you . . .

William H. Willimon

UNIT II: EMMANUEL: GOD WITH US

TWO LESSONS   DECEMBER 18–25

What do you think about when you hear the word *God?* The majority of persons who recently responded to that question said something like, "An old man in the sky with a long beard." Others said that they really had no image, more of a feeling than an image, a feeling about a mysterious, strange, but nevertheless real force in their lives.

Whatever they thought about God, most of the people agreed that God is mysterious, distant, difficult to imagine. God is high and lifted up, remote. How could the Creator of the universe, the one who set the stars in place and pushed the planets into their courses, be otherwise? Here we are down here, tied to the earth, limited, creaturely, and there is God up there, high, lifted up, unlimited, omniscient, omnipotent. "God is that beyond which nothing greater can be imagined," said Anselm.

Yet Matthew's Gospel says that when this great, big, distant, powerful God of the universe chose to come among us, to come stand beside us, God chose to come among us as a baby. As someone so small, fragile, and vulnerable as an infant, the great God came to be with us.

I know of no other religion that makes so bold, so scandalous a claim. No other religion knows of a God who comes so close to humanity. In many other world religions, religion is mostly a matter of how humans can become more like God. Christianity is a religion that is based on a story about a God who became like us.

In the next two lessons, led by Matthew, we shall ponder together the great mystery of the Incarnation, the God who became a human being named Jesus, Emmanuel, God with us. Because, down through the ages, we could not come to God, God came to us.

LESSON 3   DECEMBER 18

Jesus Is Born

Background Scripture: Matthew 1

The Main Question

"I was raised in a good Christian home." How often have you heard someone claim that for themselves? We are right to take some pride that we have been nurtured by loving parents in a Christian environment.

"My mother and father were both very educated people," I heard someone say the other day. "I was taught to value learning from my earliest years."

We are correct in assuming that we can tell a great deal about someone by learning about their roots, their parentage. What can we tell about Jesus by learning about his parents?

The story that Matthew has to tell us about the birth of Jesus is no conventional tale, for Jesus was born in a most unconventional way. His parents were not important people. No one had ever heard of them before. They were poor, unmarried, members of an occupied nation, living in an out-of-the-way town.

Already, right at the first, Matthew is subtly rearranging our preconceptions about how God enters our lives. We may think that God comes to us through the thoughts and lives of the high and the mighty, that God is best approached through those who are learned and wise, mighty and powerful. No, when God came among us as Jesus, he came among us through a poor Jewish peasant couple, Mary and Joseph. Furthermore, his arrival was, at least at first, a great embarrassment. His father did not know what to do with the news that his betrothed wife was pregnant. He was confused.

At times Jesus still confuses us, still even embarrasses us. We come to the manger at Bethlehem with certain preconceptions, certain expectations for how God is supposed to come among us. As we get to know Jesus better, as our relationship to him changes and matures, we are surprised by him, led by him down new paths that we would not have walked had he not led us. What can we learn about the entry of Jesus into your life and mine by studying how Jesus entered the lives of Mary and Joseph long ago? That is the question.

Selected Scripture

King James Version

Matthew 1:18-25

18 Now the birth of Jesus Christ was on this wise: When as his mother Mary was espoused to Joseph, before they came together, she was found with child of the Holy Ghost.

19 Then Joseph her husband, being a just *man,* and not willing to make her a publick example, was minded to put her away privily.

20 But while he thought on these things, behold, the angel of the Lord appeared unto him in a dream, saying, Joseph, thou son of David, fear not to take unto thee Mary thy wife: for that which is conceived in her is of the Holy Ghost.

21 And she shall bring forth a son, and thou shalt call his name JESUS: for he shall save his people from their sins.

22 Now all this was done, that it might be fulfilled which was spoken of the Lord by the prophet, saying,

23 Behold, a virgin shall be with child, and shall bring forth a son, and they shall call his name Emmanuel, which being interpreted is, God with us.

24 Then Joseph being raised from

New Revised Standard Version

Matthew 1:18-25

18 Now the birth of Jesus the Messiah took place in this way. When his mother Mary had been engaged to Joseph, but before they lived together, she was found to be with child from the Holy Spirit. 19 Her husband Joseph, being a righteous man and unwilling to expose her to public disgrace, planned to dismiss her quietly. 20 But just when he had resolved to do this, an angel of the Lord appeared to him in a dream and said, "Joseph, son of David, do not be afraid to take Mary as your wife, for the child conceived in her is from the Holy Spirit. 21 She will bear a son, and you are to name him Jesus, for he will save his people from their sins." 22 All this took place to fulfill what had been spoken by the Lord through the prophet:

23 "Look, the virgin shall conceive
and bear a son,
and they shall name him
Emmanuel,"

which means, "God is with us." 24 When Joseph awoke from sleep, he sleep did as the angel of the Lord had bidden him, and took unto him his wife:

25 And knew her not till she had brought forth her firstborn son: and he called his name JESUS.

did as the angel of the Lord commanded him; he took her as his wife, 25 but had no marital relations with her until she had borne a son; and he named him Jesus.

Key Verse: **Behold, a virgin shall be with child, and shall bring forth a son, and they shall call his name Emmanuel, which being interpreted is, God with us.**

Key Verse: "Look, the virgin shall conceive and bear a son, and they shall name him Emmanuel," which means, "God is with us."

As You Read the Scripture

Matthew 1:18-25. The name *Jesus* may mean *He will save.* Note that Matthew, right here at the very beginning of the story of Jesus, shows that Jesus will save, but he will save in a very peculiar way. Already, right from the first, even before he is born, Jesus causes confusion, consternation, and embarrassment. Obviously, if he will save, he will save in ways which women and men may not expect.

Verse 18. Matthew uses the word for betrothal *(mnesteutheises)*, which indicates the two-stage process in the typical marriage of that day. Betrothal was more formal than our engagement period, and some parts of Israel (Judah) even allowed the man marital rights with the woman. According to Matthew, Joseph and Mary were somewhere in the middle of the stages between the public promise to marry and cohabitation or living together as husband and wife.

Verse 19. Joseph's uprightness *(dikaios)* is shown in that, although the law indicated that a man in his position should press charges of adultery, Joseph chose not to make a display of Mary. Joseph took time to ponder his responsibility to the law, but tempered it with mercy. Thus, Joseph is depicted as a faithful Jewish man who is concerned about the demands of the law; however, he is a man who also believes in lovingkindness. Thus, Joseph represents two cardinal Jewish virtues. Divorce is perhaps too strong a translation for some modern ears. In Today's English Translation of the Bible, "break the engagement" is used or, as the New Revised Standard Version puts it, "planned to dismiss her quietly." There is no exact modern equivalent in our vocabulary.

Verse 23. "Look, the virgin shall conceive and bear a son, and they shall name him Emmanuel." Matthew follows the Septuagint (the Greek translation of the Hebrew scriptures) as he quotes Isaiah 7:14, but his wording for conception is unique and agrees with his earlier mention in 1:18. The earlier Masoretic text of Isaiah uses the word *alma,* which means *young girl,* and Matthew follows the more narrow rendering of the Greek in the Septuagint in calling Mary a *virgin (parthenos).* In other words, Matthew appears to adopt the original wording of Isaiah's prophecy about a young woman bearing a child in Isaiah's day to apply it to the circumstances of Jesus' birth. Matthew is known for his tireless citation of earlier texts in order to show that everything that occurs in Jesus' life has been foretold in the Hebrew scriptures. This is the first instance of four in which Matthew uses a prophecy/fulfillment formula as an introductory formula. "All this took place to fulfill what had been spoken by the Lord through the prophet" (v. 22), is characteristic of all four quotations in the infancy narrative. Usually Matthew chooses to use these quotations to end a particular segment of the narrative.

Verse 25. The words from Isaiah are inserted in the middle of the story. This enables Matthew to conclude the narration of Jesus' birth with the naming of Jesus from the lips of Joseph, "and he [Joseph] named the child Jesus" (v. 1:25b). This established Jesus as Joseph's legal son and ensured his place in the genealogical table as a Son of David.

The Scripture and the Main Question

The Birth of Jesus the Messiah Took Place This Way

"Tell me again about when I was a baby," said my daughter. Once again I told of the months of expectant waiting, the excitement at the prospect of the arrival of a second child, the days of preparation for a new nursery, the excited rush to the hospital, the wonderful birth of a baby girl, the decision to name her Harriet. We got out the book full of baby pictures, turned the pages, relived the memories.

I am glad that we have the pictures. I am glad that we have kept the memories alive. We really do not know someone very well until we know from whence that person came, how that person got here, the earliest days of that person's life. So it is also with Jesus: We really do not know Jesus very well until we know how he got here. Today's lesson concerns the birth of Jesus. In the first events of his earthly life, there was much to be learned about Jesus, much that would illuminate his later activities.

Matthew's infancy narrative is uniquely his own. With consummate care, Matthew has forged a narrative that, scholars believe, addressed a mixed community of Gentile and Jewish Christians and set the stage for a Gospel that had a pluralistic church in mind. This Gospel was directed to a converted community with exhortation and direction for the Christian life. Matthew assumes some familiarity with the Old Testament in his audience. Throughout his Gospel, Matthew makes good use of a prophecy/fulfillment scheme as he tells his story.

Matthew's particular theme in today's lesson is to introduce Jesus and to answer the question, "Who is He?" Matthew's answer is that Jesus is both Son of David and Son of God while at the same time son of Mary and Joseph. To answer these questions Matthew tells the story of Jesus' birth from Joseph's perspective.

In today's key text, Matthew 1:18-25, Joseph's reception of information through his dreams is reminiscent of the Old Testament Joseph who was famous for interpretation of dreams. Recall how in Genesis 40–41 Joseph receives valuable information from God through dreams. Once again, God's interventions into history are so unexpected, so out of the range of human imagination, that they must be announced through the medium of dreams.

Matthew's audience would not be overly concerned about the historicity of the virgin birth. They were well-accustomed to similar claims of divinely initiated birth. Modern readers bring different questions to the text such as, "How could something like this happen?" Matthew's original hearers would have more likely asked, "*Why* did these strange things happen?" or "What is God trying to tell us through these strange and wonderful events?"

It is no longer enough to ask "What happened?" when one studies the birth stories in the Gospels. Even though many feel that the truth is found only in the historical kernel underneath the husk of narrative embellishment, there is a truth beyond the merely historical. These stories are a witness to God's majestic act in coming to the people of every generation, and God does not depend on historians alone to get that message across.

This lesson's focus on Joseph as a parent for Jesus is in keeping with Matthew's intention in this text. Joseph plays the role of believing Jewish witness to the events. He is the one in this story who worries about fulfilling the demands of biblical law. Joseph is also the bearer of the Davidic line. His acknowledgement/naming of Jesus as his legitimate son shows that Joseph represents the very best of the Jewish ideal of faithful obedience to God's will.

Because Joseph was a righteous man, we can imagine the struggle that he had with his own religious scruples in making his decision. We should also give Joseph credit for playing his fatherly role such an upright, faithful, and merciful way. It is perhaps a great shortcoming of the church's tradition that Joseph plays such a cameo role.

Joseph, Being a Righteous Man

We often speak eloquently of Mary, the mother of Jesus. This Sunday, as we stand on the edge of Christmas, let us say a simple word for her quiet husband, Joseph. God, unable to bless Joseph with immaculate conception, settled for simple embarrassment.

Our story takes place in Galilee. Out there, in the hinterland, way out in Galilee, safe sex meant an engaged man and woman did not make love until marriage. If they did, folks in Nazareth called it fornication, no matter what more-sophisticated people in Jerusalem called it. Mary, the woman engaged to Joseph, was pregnant. As a "just man" (Matt. 1:19), a righteous observer of God's law, Joseph could not tolerate adultery. The Law gave him two options: (1) public divorce of Mary (with its public humiliation) in which Joseph's righteous name would be kept clean, or (2) private divorce in which he quietly "put her away." Mary may have been blessed among women. Righteous Joseph was embarrassed among men.

When most of us hear *annunciation,* we think of the announcement to Mary, not to Joseph. We automatically think of the Fra Angelico's angel whispering to Luke's serenely beautiful Virgin. Few painters tried their hands with Matthew's annunciation: Joseph bolting upright in bed, awaking in a cold sweat after the nightmare of being told that his fiancee is pregnant, and not by him, and that he should go ahead and marry her anyway. Here is an embarrassing version of the Nativity.

Joseph, Matthew tells us, was a righteous man. As a righteous person, he found what happened to be offensive. Who are righteous people if not those who are offended by unrighteousness? There are people for whom adultery is but a quaint term used to describe behavior that is modernly called just fooling around. There are people for whom hungry children in Africa are just something that happens. There are those who are not angered by injustice, not offended by war, not embarrassed by oppression. When these people hear *law,* they hear *legalism.* Joseph was not one of these people. He was righteous. Caught in a bind between the rock of loving Torah and the hard place of loving Mary, what was Joseph to do?

Even as God intervened with Mary, God intervened with Joseph. Just like God appeared to an earlier Joseph, God appears to this one in a dream, leading him by a dream to make the scandalous decision to marry Mary.

"This child is part of my plan to bless the world," says the vision. In believing that Mary's child was divinely given, Joseph set out on a lonely, uncharted path of marrying a pregnant fiancee and naming—and thus claiming—her child as his own, assuming the responsibility for the child who, when called, answered not to the name of Joseph, Jr., but to Emmanuel (God With Us).

Joseph, Patron Saint of Uncertain Disciples

Have you ever walked that lonely, poorly illuminated path with Joseph? Taken a road that you thought was right, you hoped was right, but with no signs to tell you for sure?

We would not spend so much of our lives in quandary, in restless, tortured uncertainty if God's will for us were merely to walk the same path as our parents, if being righteous were simply to flip open the Bible and then go by the book, if God would speak to us through crystal-clear messages in neon across the evening sky, rather than dreams that could be from God or just as easily from an evening of Mexican food.

Joseph, silently stumbling along behind Mary to Bethlehem, you remind us of ourselves and our stumblings that we hope will be called faithfulness. We look at Joseph and his silent, dumbfounded discipleship and are reminded of our own. Perhaps that is why, very early on, the church named him *Saint* Joseph.

Joseph reminds us: People who follow Jesus are not always sure of where he is leading them, what he may be requiring them to do. Being sure is not the point. The point is faithfully to follow, to do our best, in our own way, to be faithful to the visions God gives us.

In other words, Joseph is everyone's patron saint.

Helping Adults Become Involved

Preparing to Teach

This lesson ought to be a wonderful way of helping your class to prepare for Christmas, and to deepen their understanding of the Incarnation and its relevance for their lives by this lesson's focus on Joseph.

Use this outline as you present today's lesson:

    I. There were two annunciations of Jesus' birth—one to Mary and one to Joseph. Joseph's annunication depicts the surprise and embarrassment of the manner of Jesus' birth.

   II. Contemporary disciples of Jesus are often confused and uncertain about the demands and commands of God on their lives.

  III. In discipleship, certainty is not always the point. The point is to try to be faithful, to follow Jesus each in our own way.

  IV. The story of Joseph gives each of us hope in our times of uncertainty about what God wants us to do with our lives.

Read carefully "The Scripture and the Main Question" as well as the information found in "As You Read the Scripture." This material will form the heart of today's lesson. "The Main Question" sets forth the question through which you will relate the biblical material from Matthew to the daily lives of people in your class.

As you read this material, think about illustrations from your life or from the lives of friends, when they were confused or embarrassed over what God wanted them to do with their lives. Jot down these ideas in the margins as you read through today's lesson.

Introducing the Main Question

Begin by retelling the story of the annunciation to Joseph as it is told in Matthew 1:18-25. Ask the members of your class to try to imagine the feelings that Joseph must have felt on being told that Mary was going to have a baby. List the words describing those feelings on chalkboard or newsprint. Ask them to share their impressions of the sort of man Joseph must have been, after hearing Matthew's story of Joseph.

Developing the Lesson

I. There were two annunciations of Jesus' birth—one to Mary and one to Joseph. Joseph's annunciation depicts the surprise and embarrassment of the manner of Jesus' birth.

Using the material found in "The Scripture and the Main Question," augmented by the more detailed study of individual verses in "As You Read the Scripture," lead you class in a thorough study of Matthew 1:18-25. Your class may enjoy hearing you discuss the significance of betrothal in Joseph's day.

Give your class the information related to Joseph's dilemma regarding righteousness. On the one hand, Joseph felt that he must follow Jewish law. On the other hand, Joseph did not want to embarrass Mary in public by sending her away. Note how Joseph is thus an image of the conflict that often arises between righteousness and mercy.

Later on, in the Gospel of Matthew, Jesus urged his disciples to "exceed in righteousness" (5:20). Today's lesson suggests that Joseph may be the first example in Matthew's Gospel of this new righteousness. Joseph's righteousness was excessive in that it was righteousness blended with mercy.

There is another thing that you might note to your class concerning Joseph. Joseph's righteousness was also excessive in that it was so quiet. He did not show off his righteousness at Mary's expense. How different the image of righteous Joseph, wanting to do the right thing but wanting not to harm Mary, from our image of the righteous prophet, nostrils flared, teeth exposed, denouncing, pronouncing, publicly pointing to everyone else's racism, materialism, sexism, sin.

Joseph the carpenter left us no poetry to sing, no dramatic monologues or dialogues, no eloquent scenes to depict on Christmas cards, no moving speeches about liberation of captives or "light to those in darkness." The carpenter was not good at speeches and could not carry a tune. His witness is in what he *does* more than what he *says*. He obeys the divine summons to marry, then to flee to Egypt with his family, later to return and settle in Nazareth. All this without a word. Without a single word. His witness is not in speech but in active response to the will of God.

II. Contemporary disciples of Jesus are often confused and uncertain about the demands and commands of God on their lives.

Through Joseph and Mary, Matthew says: From the moment this Emmanuel was conceived he had a way of causing righteous people to rethink what was righteous. When this baby was born, all values were turned upside down, everything had to be reconsidered. For every righteous person such as Simeon or Anna, Zechariah or Elizabeth, for whom baby Jesus was an answer to their prayers and a cause for lots of singing, there had to be about as many righteous people such as Joseph for whom his advent was a tongue-tying embarrassment, a befuddling shock that required a quiet rethinking of everything on which life is based.

Ask your class if they have encountered times in their lives when they felt conflict between the righteous demands of God and the circumstances of a particular situation. It may help if you have some example in mind to share with the class before you ask them for examples. For instance, take an issue like abortion. Many people feel that life is sacred. Yet, they also can envision circumstances when even human life might be sacrificed due to conflicts between one good and another. How does this dilemma remind them of that faced by Joseph?

III. In discipleship, certainty is not always the point. The point is to try to be faithful, to follow Jesus each in our own way.

When today's story of Joseph ends, we do not know how his story will turn out. Will Joseph find that he has been correct in going against tradition and scripture in staying betrothed to Mary? The uncertainty within this story is possibly meant to encourage us in our times of uncertainty regarding God's will.

Ask the class, how do they respond when they are faced with two difficult alternatives? Can they think of instances from scripture when people were forced to venture out, trusting God, even though they did not know how the story was going to end for them?

Perhaps you or some member of your class could share a personal experience in which God was trusted, even though the person was not sure that things were going to work out for the best.

IV. The story of Joseph gives each of us hope in our times of uncertainty about what God wants us to do with our lives.

We really know very little about Joseph after Matthew 1:18-25. What we do know is that, without Joseph's quiet faithfulness, the story of Jesus could not have been continued. There would have been no babe at Bethlehem, there would have been no salvation for the world through the Christ.

Quiet, ordinary people, trying to be obedient to God in quiet, ordinary, unspectacular but very important ways, are the ways that God often touches the world. Ask your class to share their memories of people such as Joseph who touched their lives and became instruments of God's work in the world—ordinary, quiet, faithful people.

Helping Class Members Act

Ask the class to take a moment and think of some situation in their own lives in which they are facing a conflict between one good and another. End with a prayer that God will give us all the encouragement we need to be faithful, like Joseph, in our own time and place, even if we do not yet clearly see the results of our faithfulness.

Planning for Next Sunday

Next Sunday is Christmas day—a day in which we celebrate the gift of the Christ. Ask class members to come to class prepared to share with the rest of the class the name of the best gift they received during this past year.

God's Great Gift

Background Scripture: Matthew 2

The Main Question

Pity me at this time of the year. Not only must I come up with a Christmas present for my wife, but also think of an appropriate birthday present. You see, my wife's birthday is December 26. I manage to think of about one good present every six months, but two major gifts within a twenty-four-hour period? Who can be that creative? Pity me on December 25 and December 26, Christmas and birthday together. Two gifts.

Gift giving is an art. The person who is able to give just the right gift is not only the person who knows us well enough to give us what we want, but also the person who is able to give us what we really need. Sometimes, a person has refined the art of gift giving to the point of not only being able to give us what we need, but also to give us a gift that we would never have given ourselves—perhaps a gift that we would never even have imagined for ourselves, but one that is exactly what we need, what we *really* need.

Rarely do I succeed in being that good a giver. But last Christmas I succeeded. I bought my wife a suit for her birthday (after giving her books and perfume the day before for Christmas). When she unwrapped her birthday gift, I could tell from the look on her face that she was disappointed, or at least confused. Although she tried to be kind about it, she really did not like the suit that I had bought her.

"Don't you think it's just a little young for someone my age?" she asked me. "The colors are a bit too colorful for me."

But we insisted that she try it on. She did and, when she appeared in the suit, we all agreed that it was perfect. The more she wore it that day, the more she grew to like it.

That evening she confessed, "At first I did not like my birthday gift. It just seemed too young for me. However, the longer I tried it, the more I liked that suit. It's not too young for me. It's just right and I appreciate your giving it to me, pushing me to wear something that I might not have chosen for myself. It's perfect."

Isn't that the best of the art of giving? Giving someone something that person might not have chosen for himself, but that is just the perfect, needed gift—*really* needed even though the recipient did not at first recognize the need.

If God were giving each of us a gift, the perfect gift, the gift that each of us *really* needed, what would that gift be?

Selected Scripture

King James Version	New Revised Standard Version
Matthew 2:1-12	*Matthew 2:1-12*
1 Now when Jesus was born in Bethlehem of Judea in the days of	1 In the time of King Herod, after Jesus was born in Bethlehem of

139

Herod the king, behold, there came wise men from the east to Jerusalem,

2 Saying, Where is he that is born King of the Jews? for we have seen his star in the east, and are come to worship him.

3 When Herod the king had heard *these things,* he was troubled, and all Jerusalem with him.

4 And when he had gathered all the chief priests and scribes of the people together, he demanded of them where Christ should be born.

5 And they said unto him, In Bethlehem of Judea: for thus it is written by the prophet,

6 And thou Bethlehem, *in* the land of Juda, art not the least among the princes of Juda: for out of thee shall come a Governor, that shall rule my people Israel.

7 Then Herod, when he had privily called the wise men, inquired of them diligently what time the star appeared.

8 And he sent them to Bethlehem, and said, Go and search diligently for the young child; and when ye have found *him,* bring me word again, that I may come and worship him also.

9 When they had heard the king, they departed; and, lo, the star, which they saw in the east, went before them, till it came and stood over where the young child was.

10 When they saw the star, they rejoiced with exceeding great joy.

11 And when they were come into the house, they saw the young child with Mary his mother, and fell down, and worshipped him: and when they had opened their treasures, they presented unto him gifts; gold, and frankincense, and myrrh.

12 And being warned of God in a dream that they should not return to Herod, they departed into their own country another way.

Judea, wise men from the East came to Jerusalem, 2 asking, "Where is the child who has been born king of the Jews? For we observed his star at its rising, and have come to pay him homage." 3 When King Herod heard this, he was frightened, and all Jerusalem with him; 4 and calling together all the chief priests and scribes of the people, he inquired of them where the Messiah was to be born. 5 They told him, "In Bethlehem of Judea; for so it has been written by the prophet:

6 'And you, Bethlehem, in the land
  of Judah,
    are by no means least among the
      rulers of Judah;
  for from you shall come a ruler
    who is to shepherd my people
      Israel.' "

7 Then Herod secretly called for the wise men and learned from them the exact time when the star had appeared. 8 Then he sent them to Bethlehem, saying, "Go and search diligently for the child; and when you have found him, bring me word so that I may also go and pay him homage." 9 When they had heard the king, they set out; and there, ahead of them, went the star that they had seen at its rising, until it stopped over the place where the child was. 10 When they saw that the star had stopped, they were overwhelmed with joy. 11 On entering the house, they saw the child with Mary his mother; and they knelt down and paid him homage. Then, opening their treasure chests, they offered him gifts of gold, frankincense, and myrrh. 12 And having been warned in a dream not to return to Herod, they left for their own country by another road.

Key Verse: And when they were come into the house, they saw the young child with Mary his mother, and fell down, and worshipped him: and when they had opened their treasures, they presented unto him gifts; gold, and frankincense, and myrrh.

Key Verse: On entering the house, they saw the child with Mary his mother; and they knelt down and paid him homage. Then, opening their treasure chests, they offered him gifts of gold, frankincense, and myrrh.

As You Read the Scripture

Matthew 2. Note that Matthew has no report of the nativity of Jesus. The story of the babe in the manger belongs exclusively to Luke. Matthew chooses to tell of the birth of Jesus by reflecting the significance of that birth in the lives of people who witnessed the event rather than focusing on the event itself. In last week's lesson we met Joseph, the confused fiance of Mary. This week we encounter strange visitors from the east who are mysteriously led to the baby at Bethlehem.

Verse 1. These visitors are not really wise men. The word for them is *magi*, the same word from which we get our *magician*. These visitors are those who dabble in magic and the esoteric arts. Perhaps they are astrologers, those who study the stars in the hope of discerning important events. Perhaps they are alchemists, those who devise various magic potions. The practice of magic is condemned in the Old Testament. In Acts 8:9-24, the apostles have an encounter with a magus named Simon. This episode illustrates the Jews' negative attitude toward the magi. These magi are religious outsiders.

Verse 2. The magi are led to Jesus by a star, a natural sign rather than, as would be the case for devout Jews, the testimony of the scriptures. They have come "to pay homage to him," to worship this newly-revealed king.

Verses 3-6. Herod immediately perceives this child who has been born king of the Jews as a political threat. He is troubled, fearing that his heirs will not be able to inherit his throne. What is more surprising, all Jerusalem is troubled with him. The religious and political establishment perceives the arrival of the long-awaited Messiah as a threat more than as a gift—an irony Matthew would not want us to miss. The prophecy in verse 6 is from Micah 5:2.

Verses 7-9. Herod is deceitful with the magi. From the very beginning, this child provokes trouble with the governmental authorities.

Verses 10-11. The magi are filled with joy when they find the baby. They kneel in worshipful adoration and offer gifts. The gold, frankincense, and myrrh were costly spices from the east. Perhaps they were elements used in the magic potions of the magi—a sign that they have forsaken their foolish magic and offer the tricks of their trade to the child as homage. Some have suggested that these gifts have deeper symbolic significance. Gold for a king. Frankincense and myrrh were often used to prepare a body for embalming and burial. Do these gifts foreshadow events in Jesus' life?

Verse 12. God intervenes through a dream to warn the magi. Even though they are pagans, those who share neither the Jewish faith nor the scriptures of Israel, God speaks to these pagan visitors through the stars and through dreams. Even foreigners, even those who have no part in the promises of God made to Israel, can be used by God for his purposes.

SECOND QUARTER

The Scripture and the Main Question

Wise Men from the East Came to Jerusalem

Many of you, when you present today's lesson from the Gospel of Matthew to your class, will be teaching the lesson to those who have been exchanging Christmas gifts with their families and friends on Christmas morning. Christmas is the season of giving. From earliest times, the custom of giving and getting gifts on Christmas was related by Christians to the story of these mysterious visitors from the east, the magi, who offered their gifts of gold, frankincense, and myrrh to the child at Bethlehem.

Today's lesson therefore suggests an opportunity for us to think about the significance of our gift giving and a wonderful occasion for us to ponder the greatest gift of all—the gift of God's own son, Jesus the Christ.

The gifts we give often tell more about the giver than the receiver. Every parent has had the experience of receiving a gift from a child—a baseball glove, a pocket knife, a book—that says more about the child's idea of the perfect gift than the parent's needs. Our gifts are reflections of our own values. Gifts are not always what the *receiver* wants, but rather what the *giver* feels that the receiver ought to have.

A family in our church has for many years made all of the gifts that they give at Christmas. Some years ago, they became concerned about the commercialism of Christmas, the way they were spending too much money at Christmas, and the way in which the real meaning of the season was being endangered by the buying, getting, and giving. Now they plan for Christmas many months in advance. Last year, they gave everyone on their Christmas list beautiful bluebird houses. The whole family helped to put the houses together. The year before they made everyone a gingerbread house. Each one of their gifts not only testifies to the family's creativity, but also to their love. Each gift is a treasured part of the family's time expended in behalf of and care for other people.

Matthew says that, when Jesus was born, he was born to two poor, Jewish peasant parents in an out-of-the-way little place named Bethlehem. When God got ready to bless the world, note the way God chose to come to the world. Now what does that tell you about God, the giver of the wonderful gift of the Messiah?

He came, not to the learned and the powerful, but to the poor and the outcast. Among those outcasts who clustered around to see the new baby Jesus were these magi from the east whom Matthew describes in the second chapter of his Gospel. Herod the king missed the news. The scholars up at the temple, poring over the scriptures, missed the news. These magi, people who did not have the scriptures, people of another land and race, got the news. What does that tell you about God, the giver of the gift of the Messiah?

We Have Come to Pay Homage

We must attempt this Sunday to recover some of the shock at beginning a gospel like Matthew's with an account of these magi who have come to Bethlehem. I remind you that Matthew has been called the most Jewish of all the Gospels. We have found, already, with these four weeks of lessons from Matthew, how Matthew loves to quote the Hebrew scriptures, how Matthew is concerned to show that Jesus was the fulfillment of Jewish hopes for a Messiah. Most scholars believe that Matthew was definitely writing his Gospel for a Jewish audience, perhaps Jews who had just become, or who were in the process of becoming, Christians.

Can you sense what a shock it must have been for Matthew's audience to hear that the first to come to worship the baby Jesus were not faithful Jews, but these anything-but-faithful Gentile magi? The first people, after Mary and Joseph, to see and to receive the gift of the baby Jesus were those to whom the Messiah had not been promised—Gentiles. That had to be a shock for Matthew's first hearers.

In a way, it is still a shock.

I was visiting a congregation where, during the Sunday service, the preacher indulged in a practice not dear to my heart—a children's sermon. The boys and girls were called down front. Squatting in the chancel, the preacher began, "Boys and girls, today is Epiphany. Can you say, Epiphany? Epiphany falls on January 6, but today it falls on Sunday. Isn't that great, boys and girls? Epiphany means 'revelation,' 'manifestation.' A favorite Epiphany story is found at the beginning of Matthew's Gospel. You know the story. It's the story of the Wise Men who came to Bethlehem to see the baby Jesus. But they weren't really Wise Men or even Three Kings as we call them in the Christmas carol. The Bible calls them magi. Magi. That's where we get our word *magic*. They were magicians, astrologers.

"Matthew tells us that they came 'from the East.' Some people think they came from Persia. Boys and girls, where is Persia?" [Silence. One child ventures, "Iran?"]

"Yes. Iran. Good. That was Persia, but it wasn't all of Persia. What other countries are located in what was Persia?"

[One child says, "Iraq?"]

"Iraq! Good! Iraq. In fact, some people think these magi came from Baghdad, capital of Iraq. There were lots of these magi in Iraq. . . . And Matthew says, these magi, these Iraqis, were the first to get an Epiphany, the first to see and to worship the baby Jesus. A lot of people who had the Bible, a lot of people who thought they were close to God missed it, and these strange people from Iraq saw it."

You tell a story like that, Sunday, 11:15 a.m., it is hard to tell where we will be headed by noon.

That sermon was preached on January 6, 1991. As the bombs were beginning to fall on Iraq, the story being told in church was a story about how the insiders missed the great gift of God and the outsiders worshiped the gift that was supposed to go to someone else.

The story of the magi is an outrageous way to begin a gospel.

They Offered Him Gifts

As we said, the nature of the gift tells a great deal about the giver. If we have come together in church this Christmas morning to celebrate the gift of a savior who has come just for us, just for us insiders, today's scripture from Matthew challenges us. The first to bend the knee at Bethlehem and worship, the first to give him all they had were outsiders, Gentile magi.

What does that tell you about the giver of the gift?

SECOND QUARTER

Helping Adults Become Involved

Preparing to Teach

It is a happy coincidence that today's lesson falls on the very day of Christmas. Historically, the church has celebrated the story of the magi on Epiphany, January 6, but today we are reading it as a Christmas story.

Today's lesson focuses on Matthew's story of the magi, using this story as a means of focusing on the gift of God in Jesus Christ—a gift that is both wonderful and unexpected.

Keep "The Main Question" in your mind as you read through today's lesson. The lesson may be outlined as follows:

    I. The gift tells a great deal about the giver.
    II. We are surprised that the magi were the very first to offer gifts to the child at Bethlehem.
    III. God's gift of Jesus the Messiah is a gift that challenges our preconceptions about God and God's salvation.
    IV. One of the greatest of Christ's gifts is the gift of inclusive love for all people.

Read through "As You Read the Scripture" and "The Scripture and the Main Question." Note the ways in which this material challenges your own preconceptions about the magi and their meaning in the story of Jesus' birth.

Introducing the Main Question

Retell in your own words "The Main Question" as a way of introducing today's lesson. Because everyone in your class has been actively participating in giving and getting gifts, the material you are introducing will have immediate relevance to them.

Today's main question encourages each person to ask what gift we really need from God. Sometimes the gifts we get from God are not the ones we expected. By beginning his story of Christ with the story of the magi, Matthew reveals to us a God whose love and mercy are inclusive and universal, a love for all people. Is that the gift we expected from God?

Developing the Lesson

I. The gift tells a great deal about the giver.

Using the material in both "The Main Question" and the first part of "The Scripture and the Main Question," introduce the idea of how our gifts disclose the nature and the values of the giver. Ask the class for examples of how they have experienced this truth in everyday life in the gifts they have received from others. Is it wrong for our gifts to be expressions of our values?

II. We are surprised that the magi were the very first to offer gifts to the child at Bethlehem.

· Have someone in the class read the story of the magi as told in Matthew 2:1-12. Using the material found in "As You Read the Scripture" and "The Scripture and the Main Question," tell the class about the magi and their

144

significance. Some of this may be new information for members of your class. Stress that the magi were definitely outsiders in the scheme of things for Matthew's first hearers. Note how surprising it was in this Jewish Gospel to begin with the magi.

III. God's gift of Jesus the Messiah is a gift that challenges our preconceptions about God and God's salvation.

Retell the story about the Epiphany children's sermon that is told in the second half of "The Scripture and the Main Question." Ask your class: How does this story capture some of the shock and scandal of the magi appearing first at Bethlehem? Can they think of other biblical stories in which outsiders seem to know more of God than us insiders? Can they think of contemporary parallels to the magi? For instance, sometimes people who are not members of churches seem more Christian in their dealings with others than Christians!

IV. One of the greatest of Christ's gifts is the gift of inclusive love for all people.

Recall that our main question today asks, what is the gift that we really need God to give us? The story of the magi reminds us that Christ came to us as a gift, but many failed to recognize the babe of Bethlehem as their gift. Perhaps they failed to recognize Jesus because his advent challenged their notions of who the Messiah was supposed to be.

We separate the world into the insiders and the outsiders, drawing lines between people. Today's lesson from Matthew suggests that God does not divide the world as we do. In the love of Christ, those whom we treat as outsiders may be the most perceptive of the real nature of God.

Ask your class to discuss ways in which the story of the magi challenges the church today. Retell the story of the arrival of the magi at Bethlehem, substituting some contemporary outcast group.

Helping Class Members Act

Has anyone in your class experienced Christ's inclusive gift of love towards outsiders? Ask class members to identify ways in which your church offers gifts to Christ through its offering of gifts to those whom Christ loves—the poor, the outcast, the sick, and the lonely. Has your congregation offered any such gifts this Christmas season? Having been blessed by the gift of Christ, how can we give to others in the manner in which he has given to us?

Planning for Next Sunday

We will continue our study of Matthew's Gospel next Sunday by studying one of Jesus' healing miracles. Ask class members to think about ways in which people today need deliverance. Next Sunday the class will be asked to list the major sources of bondage at work in our world from which people need deliverance.

UNIT III: JESUS, THE SON OF DAVID

FIVE LESSONS   JANUARY 1–29

Jesus did not simply go about the earth speaking kind and loving words to people. He reached out and touched people. He put his words of love into action. Talk is cheap. Actions do speak louder than words. Through his loving actions, Jesus confronted human need, and thereby showed people the presence of God in their midst.

Performing acts of love to those in need may sound like a worthy thing to do. Yet, as Matthew shows, Jesus' actions provoked controversy. Why would anyone be against helping hurting people? Why was there so much resistance to the ministry of Jesus?

This unit of lessons confronts some of those questions. In the next five lessons, we will see how Jesus, in reaching out to forgotten and marginalized people, upset many of the religious and political conventions of his day. We will watch as storm clouds gather over his ministry, clouds that will break in terrible wrath at a place called Golgotha.

Confrontation with human need and suffering tends to provoke the same response from the establishment and the keepers of the status quo today. Wherever good is served, evil is threatened and, when evil is threatened, evil often responds in violence.

Matthew thus tells a story that is very old, a story that is also as relevant as this morning's newspaper. This is the story that you will be leading your class through during these five lessons from Matthew.

Through your study of Matthew's Gospel, may 1995 truly be for you and your class The Year of Our Lord, 1995.

LESSON 5   JANUARY 1

Deliverance and Forgiveness

Background Scripture: Matthew 8:1–9:8

The Main Question

I know a family with two daughters. As far as I know, both of the daughters were raised in exactly the same way by their parents. Their parents were loving, kind, Christian parents. They provided both of the young women with a caring and affirming home environment.

The older of the two daughters was born with a spinal problem. She was able to walk when she was young, but as she grew older, she spent her life confined to a wheelchair. However, she was a good student, particularly in mathematics. She eventually became an accountant and secured herself a good job. Her friends know her now as an energetic, cheerful, and compassionate adult.

The younger of the daughters was born with no physical infirmity. As far as I know, she was as intelligent as her older sister. Yet she had nothing but problems in school. Her parents tried to help her, but she was angry, unresponsive, sullen, and difficult. Her parents tried her at a variety of schools. She eventually dropped out of school, left home, and began living with a variety of men. Her parents have now paid for a succession of drug treatment programs for her problem with addiction. She is now seriously ill with physical complications brought on by her drug abuse.

How do you explain the difference between these two sisters? What an irony that two so radically different people could come from the same home. Even more ironic is the nature of their different problems and the way they have responded to those problems. It is ironic that the sister who is crippled, unable to walk, seems much more independent, much healthier and happier than her sister who had no physical problem. The one who was born gifted and free is now chained to her self-destructive behavior. Isn't it ironic that we who are privileged to live in a nation that promises so much freedom are often people who feel anything but free? Sometimes, our loudly proclaimed freedom is but the rattling of our chains.

Matthew says that Jesus has come to deliver us. The chains that bind us may be physical. They may also be spiritual. If a savior is coming to save us, the savior must be able to deal with the multiple sources of our enslavement.

When we look at the chains that bind us, the multiple reasons why we are denied abundant life, the main question we ask is, Who can set us free?

Selected Scripture

King James Version

Matthew 8:28–9:8

28 And when he was come to the other side into the country of the Gergesenes, there met him two possessed with devils, coming out of the tombs, exceeding fierce, so that no man might pass by that way.

29 And, behold, they cried out, saying, What have we to do with thee, Jesus, thou Son of God? art thou come hither to torment us before the time?

30 And there was a good way off from them an herd of many swine feeding.

31 So the devils besought him, saying, If thou cast us out, suffer us to go away into the herd of swine.

32 And he said unto them, Go. And when they were come out, they went into the herd of swine: and, behold, the whole herd of swine ran violently down a steep place into the sea, and perished in the waters.

33 And they that kept them fled, and went their ways into the city,

New Revised Standard Version

Matthew 8:28–9:8

28 When he came to the other side, to the country of the Gadarenes, two demoniacs coming out of the tombs met him. They were so fierce that no one could pass that way. 29 Suddenly they shouted, "What have you to do with us, Son of God? Have you come here to torment us before the time?" 30 Now a large herd of swine was feeding at some distance from them. 31 The demons begged him, "If you cast us out, send us into the herd of swine." 32 And he said to them, "Go!" So they came out and entered the swine; and suddenly, the whole herd rushed down the steep bank into the sea and perished in the water. 33 The swineherds ran off, and on going into the town, they told the whole story about what had happened to the demoniacs. 34 Then the whole town came out to meet Jesus; and when they saw him, they

and told every thing, and what was befallen to the possessed of the devils.

34 And, behold, the whole city came out to meet Jesus: and when they saw him, they besought *him* that he would depart out of their coasts.

....

1 And he entered into a ship, and passed over, and came into his own city.

2 And, behold, they brought to him a man sick of the palsy, lying on a bed: and Jesus seeing their faith said unto the sick of the palsy; Son, be of good cheer; thy sins be forgiven thee.

3 And, behold, certain of the scribes said within themselves, This *man* blasphemeth.

4 And Jesus knowing their thoughts said, Wherefore think ye evil in your hearts?

5 For whether is easier, to say, *Thy* sins be forgiven thee; or to say, Arise, and walk?

6 But that ye may know that the Son of man hath power on earth to forgive sins, (then saith he to the sick of the palsy,) Arise, take up thy bed, and go unto thine house.

7 And he arose, and departed to his house.

8 But when the multitudes saw *it,* they marvelled, and glorified God, which had given such power unto men.

begged him to leave their neighborhood.

....

1 And after getting into a boat he crossed the sea and came to his own town.

2 And just then some people were carrying a paralyzed man lying on a bed. When Jesus saw their faith, he said to the paralytic, "Take heart, son; your sins are forgiven." 3 Then some of the scribes said to themselves, "This man is blaspheming." 4 But Jesus, perceiving their thoughts, said, "Why do you think evil in your hearts? 5 For which is easier, to say, 'Your sins are forgiven,' or to say, 'Stand up and walk'? 6 But so that you may know that the Son of Man has authority on earth to forgive sins"—he then said to the paralytic—"Stand up, take your bed and go to your home." 7 And he stood up and went to his home. 8 When the crowds saw it, they were filled with awe, and they glorified God, who had given such authority to human beings.

Key Verse: **And, behold, they brought to him a man sick of the palsy, lying on a bed: and Jesus seeing their faith said unto the sick of the palsy; Son, be of good cheer; thy sins be forgiven thee.**

Key Verse: **And just then some people were carrying a paralyzed man lying on a bed. When Jesus saw their faith, he said to the paralytic, "Take heart, son; your sins are forgiven."**

As You Read the Scripture

Matthew 8:28–9:1. Mental illness was thought to result from possession by demons. Perhaps these demoniacs were afflicted with some sort of personality disorder whereby they were split into multiple personalities.

Swine were considered to be unclean, therefore these swine were fit subjects for possession by the unclean spirits. Because pork is forbidden for consumption by Jews, we wonder who was keeping these swine and for what purpose. Perhaps they were being raised for Gentile consumption. At any rate, the raising of swine would be considered an unclean, prohibited activity.

Even though these demons are hostile to God, and produce states in human beings that are contrary to God's will, they are still considered to be under the rule of God. The demons recognize Jesus and the deeper significance of his work, for even evil power can recognize power in good.

Jesus is portrayed as an exorcist, a victor over demons, in texts such as Mark 5:1-20, Matthew 12:22-32, and Luke 11:14-23.

Verse 28. Gadarenes is a district of Gadara, capital of Pera.

Verse 31. Compare this with the Mark 5:13.

Verse 32. Why would the inhabitants wish for Jesus to leave? Perhaps he upset their commerce in swine. Perhaps they were frightened by his supernatural powers.

Matthew 9:2–9:8. Matthew moves from an episode in which mental illness is cured to one in which he cures paralysis. Compare with Mark 2:1-12 and Luke 5:17-26.

Verses 2-7. Illness was thought to be the result of sin in that day. The dispute between Jesus and the scribes is over his claim of authority to forgive sins. Matthew appears to be more interested in Jesus' ability to forgive sins than in his ability to heal. The healing is done by Jesus "so that you may know that the Son of Man has authority on earth to forgive sins" (v. 6). To forgive sins is an exclusively divine prerogative; therefore, if Jesus forgives, he must be linked to the divine.

Verse 8. Note that the crowd in this story has a different reaction than the preceding crowd in Matthew 8:32. They respond in gratitude to God for giving such authority to a human being. Taken together, both of these episodes show the often ambivalent human response to the intrusion of divine power. Some are threatened by Jesus' healing work; others see it as a gracious gift of God.

The Scripture and the Main Question

What Have You to Do with Us?

As I write today, the news is full of developments in Eastern Europe. Nations that once languished under the heel of cruel Communist dictators are now at last free to determine their own destiny. They are talking about free, democratic elections, and market reforms.

Those of us in the Western world can celebrate this new birth of freedom in our world. Yet, forgive some of us if we have our misgivings about the arrival of freedom for these people. We live in a society that values its freedom. Yet, we also live in a society in which great numbers of our fellow citizens choose to kill themselves slowly through drug and alcohol abuse. Last year, two thousand New Yorkers were murdered by their fellow New Yorkers. Our nation's capital was recently named, "The Murder Capital of the World" because of the many homicides that have taken place there. Does this sound like a people who are free?

Yesterday a person who works with the homeless in California was being interviewed by a television reporter. In speaking about the terrible problem of homelessness in our country, she said, "Our country values freedom, freedom above anything else. That's fine for people who can cope with the demands of freedom, the competition and the struggle. Many homeless people cannot cope. They do not have the educational skills, or they suffer from various forms of mental illness. Unfortunately, for these people, what we call 'freedom' is only the source of their terrible bondage."

Isn't it ironic that our supposedly most free nation in the world has so much evidence that we are a people in dire need of deliverance? Therefore, the gap between our modern world and the ancient world of Matthew's Gospel is not as great as we like to think. In Matthew's world, one could not imagine a more tragic plight than illness—physical or emotional illness. There were no drugs, no doctors, no means of overcoming your illness other than through patience and prayer.

Undoubtedly, there were many who urged simple resignation in the face of illness. Centuries of religious tradition told people that illness was due to a person's sin. Are you sick? Well, then you must have done something terribly wrong that has led to the punishment of your sickness.

Sickness was also attributed to the malevolent deeds of demons. Since the origins of illness were a great mystery, people thought that mysterious forces must be behind illness. Demons entered a person's body and mind, causing that person to think and to feel strange things.

What hope was there in such a world of mysterious, sinister forces that played havoc with people's lives? What hope was there for deliverance?

This was the sort of world to which Jesus came. When confronted by human misery, Jesus did not stand back and offer philosophical observations. He boldly reached out and healed people. He confronted the sinister powers that gripped people's lives and overcame those powers. This is Jesus the healer, Jesus the exorcist that we meet in today's scripture from Matthew.

There were many who, when they witnessed the healing, powerful work of Jesus, said to themselves, "What sort of man is this, that even the winds and the sea obey him?" (Matt. 8:27). For some, like the man who was delivered from his crippling infirmity (Matt. 9:2-8), the presence and work of Jesus was pure good news. For others, such as those who witnessed the demons being driven out of the possessed man into the swine (Matt. 8:28-34), Jesus' power was perceived as a threat.

Why was Jesus a threat to them? Why would they have seen his healing work and cried out, "What have you to do with us, Son of God?" (Matt. 8:29).

Take Heart . . . Your Sins Are Forgiven

While you and I would probably not want to link a person's sin and a person's physical illness in the way that such a linkage is at least implied in Matthew 9:2-8, you and I can readily admit that many of the illnesses that plague us do have moral, spiritual roots.

What is the first question you ask when you hear that someone has lung cancer? "Does he or she smoke?"

A doctor once told me, "It has been estimated that one-third to one-half of all hospital beds are occupied by those who suffer from the results of alcohol abuse."

Modern medicine has documented how a number of illnesses are definitely psychosomatic—physical illnesses that are related to emotional or mental states. All of this suggests that Matthew's linkage of the man's paralysis with sin (Matt. 9:2-8) is not so incredible. Certainly Jesus assumes such a linkage. He heals the man of his sin (9:2) *before* he cures him of his paralysis.

The scribes, keepers of religious traditions, ignore the miracle that has taken place before their very eyes. They launch into a theological debate with Jesus concerning his authority to forgive sins (9:3-6). How often do present day religious authorities often overlook people's pain, showing more loyalty to certain theological convictions than to showing the compassionate power of God?

Jesus performs a number of healing acts in Matthew 9:2-8. He forgives the paralyzed man of his sin; he heals him of his paralysis; he (attempts) to heal the scribes of their disbelief and scorn. Jesus is a healer who works on multiple illnesses.

They Were Filled with Awe

The second crowd (9:8) (unlike the first crowd in 8:34) recognizes Jesus' power. Isn't it interesting that his healing work evokes differing responses in these two groups? Perhaps the healing of physical illness is less controversial than mental illness. Perhaps Jesus was right to note how it is more miraculous to heal us of our sin than to heal us of our paralysis. When you think about it, sin *is* paralysis.

He had been addicted to alcohol as long as anyone could remember. His alcohol dependency had cost him his marriage, his family, his job, and much of his health. When I first met him, when he visited our church, someone who knew him said, "If he gets over his drinking, it will be a miracle."

Six months later, he stood before the church, seeking baptism. He said that his restoration, his new sobriety and recovery, was due to his life having been changed by God through the church.

We called it a miracle. The day he was baptized, it could be said of us as it was said of them of old, "When the crowds saw it, they were filled with awe, and they glorified God, who had given such authority to human beings" (9:8).

Helping Adults Become Involved

Preparing to Teach

This lesson investigates the relationship between our various sources of bondage—physical, emotional, and spiritual—and the ways in which Jesus helps to deliver us from our enslavement. Prepare by reading through the material in "The Main Question" and "As You Read the Scripture." As you read, imagine the questions that might emerge in the minds of your class as they study today's scripture from Matthew.

Today's lesson can be organized as follows:

I. Contemporary people suffer from various forms of enslavement, both physical and emotional.

II. Many of our physical problems have emotional and spiritual origins.

III. Jesus reached out in compassion to deliver those who suffered both emotional distress and physical disability.

IV. Jesus continues to deliver and to forgive people, offering them abundant life.

SECOND QUARTER

Begin organizing the lesson in your mind as you read through "The Scripture and the Main Question." Today's lesson is rich in material that relates to the everyday life concerns of members of your class. Obtain a newspaper to use in the opening section of today's class.

Introducing the Main Question

Retell in your own words the illustration of the two sisters in "The Main Question." Then ask your class to discuss ways in which contemporary people are in bondage today. List on a chalkboard or newsprint what your class believes to be some of the major sources of physical and emotional enslavement today (alcoholism, drug abuse, violence, poverty, etc.).

Developing the Lesson

I. Contemporary people suffer from various forms of enslavement, both physical and emotional.

You have already initiated thought on this point in your introduction to today's lesson. Continue the discussion, using material found in "The Scripture and the Main Question." Bring this morning's newspaper to your class. With a crayon or felt-tipped marker, circle all those stories that, in your mind, depict contemporary personal and social problems that are evidence of our bondage to sin and evil.

II. Many of our physical problems have emotional and spiritual origins.

Have someone read aloud today's scripture, Matthew 8:28–9:8. Using the material in "As You Read the Scripture," provide necessary background information on the scripture for your class.

Ask your class: What do you think of the idea that illness is caused by demons, supernatural forces? Is this idea completely foreign to modern understanding? Some modern illnesses, such as the HIV virus (AIDS), have a demonic character in many people's minds.

Ask your class: How might it be said that our sin relates to some of our illnesses? This is discussed in "The Scripture and the Main Question." While your class may be hesitant to ascribe specific illnesses to an individual's sin, they may be willing to note that many modern maladies do have moral roots. This can be a difficult subject and should be discussed with compassion and sensitivity. Currently, many are saying that those who suffer from the HIV virus, "have no one to blame for their situation but themselves." Is this true? Might sometimes our sin be demonstrated in the way that we so callously accuse sick people of suffering because they have sinned?

III. Jesus reached out in compassion to deliver those who suffered both emotional distress and physical disability.

Note that, in today's scripture, Jesus does not have an abstract theological discussion—Jesus heals. Has your class, in its discussion of the idea of the linkage of sin and sickness, been guilty of responding to human pain in the way the scribes responded in Matthew 9:2-8? Perhaps our best response as Christians is not blaming or arguing, but that of the crowd in Matthew 9:8. We should note the ways in which God in Christ is compassionate toward us and celebrate that compassion.

152

IV. Jesus continues to deliver and to forgive people, offering them abundant life.

Is miraculous healing a thing of the past? Or are we so accustomed to the miracle of healing through modern medicine that we have lost the awe that thrilled the crowd (9:8)?

Ask your class to discuss the possibility of divine deliverance today. Have any in your class experienced such divine healing? Can your class cite instances of divine compassion worked through the church today, such as the one cited at the end of "The Scripture and the Main Question"?

Helping Class Members Act

The church is a major means through which Jesus delivers people today. Have your class list examples of the ways in which God continues to deliver and heal people through the work of your church. In how many of these acts of healing and deliverance are members of your class personally involved?

Ask the class, "Where would we be as Jesus goes about healing people: in the first crowd who wanted Jesus to leave them alone (8:34), or with those who praised God for Jesus' compassion in the second crowd (9:8)?"

Preparing for Next Sunday

Have your class members ask themselves, in preparation for next Sunday's lesson, "What are the characteristics of a good leader?" Next Sunday's class will look at leadership from the perspective of the life of Jesus as presented in Matthew.

Spiritual Enrichment Article:
The Bible as the Church's Book

Jesus returns to his hometown synagogue in Nazareth (Luke 4:16-20). What does Israel do on its holiest of days? Luke gives us a picture of the People of God gathered.

When he came to Nazareth, where he had been brought up, he went to the synagogue on the sabbath day, as was his custom. He stood up to read, and the scroll of the prophet Isaiah was given to him. He unrolled the scroll and found the place where it was written:
"The Spirit of the Lord is upon me,
because he has anointed me
to bring good news to the poor.
He has sent me to proclaim
release to the captives
and recovery of sight to the blind,
to let the oppressed go free,
to proclaim the year of the
Lord's favor."

And he rolled up the scroll, gave it back to the attendant, and sat down. The eyes of all in the synagogue were fixed on him. Then he began to say to them, "Today this scripture has been fulfilled in your hearing." All spoke well of him and were amazed at the gracious words that came from his mouth. They said, "Is not this Joseph's son?" He said to them, "Doubtless you will quote to me this proverb, 'Doctor, cure yourself!' And you will say, 'Do here also in your hometown the things that we have heard you did at Capernaum.' " And he said, "Truly I tell you, no prophet is accepted in the prophet's hometown. But the truth is, there were many widows in Israel in the time of Elijah, when the heaven was shut up three years and six months, and there was a severe famine over all the land; yet Elijah was sent to none of them except to a widow at Zarephath in Sidon. There were also many lepers in Israel in the time of the prophet Elisha, and none of them was cleansed except Naaman the Syrian." When they heard this, all in the synagogue were filled with rage. They got up, drove him out of the town, and led him to the brow of the hill on which their town was built, so that they might hurl him off the cliff. But he passed through the midst of them and went on his way.

Jesus returns to his hometown synagogue. And what do they do? They hand him the scroll, the scriptures of Israel. They do no ask Jesus, "Tell us how it is for you." They do not ask him to report on his days at college or to share his feelings with them. They hand him the scroll and ask him to read. *Then* he interprets, *then* he preaches. Watch closely as they hand him the scroll. In that action, we see a movement which is at the very heart of the faith of Israel.

There may be religions which begin with long walks in the woods, communing with nature, getting close to trees. There may be religions which begin by delving into the recesses of a person's ego, rummaging around in the psyche. However, Christianity is not one of those.

Christianity is a people who begin with the action of taking up the scroll and being confronted with stories of God. These stories insert themselves into our accustomed ways of doing buisness and challenge us to change or else be out-of-step with the way things are now that God has entered human history.

They hand Jesus the scroll. He reads from the prophet Isaiah, speaking of that day when God would again act to set things right, to come for Israel, to lift up the downtrodden and push down the mighty. The Spirit of the Lord is upon me to announce God's advent.

After reading, Jesus begins to interpret. Note that the interprets by setting other biblical stories next to Isaiah's announcement of God's advent. "God is coming among us. And the last time God came among us, during the days of the great prophet Elijah, many of our own people were hungry. But God's prophet fed none of them. Only a widow from Sidon, a foreigner, was nourished."

The congregation grows silent. The young preacher continues. "And were not there many sick people in Israel during the time of the prophet Elisha? Yes. But Elisha healed none of them. Only Naaman, a Syrian, a Syrian army officer."

And the once adoring congregation became an angry mob. As they led the young preacher out, he said to them, "I said nothing new. It's all in the book! It's all in *your* book!"

A distinctive community is being formed here by this reading and listening. A peculiar community is being criticized here as well. What sort of people are being called into being by such stories?

SPIRITUAL ENRICHMENT ARTICLE

The Politics of the Bible

The church was called into being, as if out of nothing, as a people in dialogue with scripture. Unlike conventional means of human organization, the church had no ethnic, gender, or national basis for unity. All it had were these stories called scripture. These scriptures rendered a person, a personality, Jesus. For this new and distinctive community called the church, Jesus of Nazareth, as the Messiah, became the interpretive framework for all reality, the organizing principle for all of life. Thus the function of scripture was political, constitutive. By "political" I do not mean politics as it has degenerated in our own time—the aggressive securing of individual rights, the maximum number of personal desires elevated to the level of needs which are then pursued at all cost. The Bible is "political" in the classic sense of the word politics—the formation of a *polis*, the constitution of a people through a discussion of what needs are worth having, what goals are good.

Thus the Bible must be read "politically," that is, it must be read from the awareness of its desire to form a new people. We would not read Shakespeare's *King Lear* as history or as science. It is a drama. So we should not read the Bible as merely science, history, philology, or personal help. The Bible seeks to engender a people, a *polis*.

In defiance of sociological laws, without conventional cultural, or ethnic support, this new community conquered the Roman Empire in one of the most amazing cultural shifts ever seen in Western history. For instance, there was no value more dear to classical Romans than the family. All of Roman society was organized around the family headed by the *Pater Familias*, the father of the family. Marriage, political power, economic advancement, civil rights were all based upon the family. Family name and status determined a person's situation throughout life. Indeed, the military was virtually the only means of social advancement for someone born into a poor Roman family.

From the beginning, the church was, in complete contrast to Roman society, ambivalent or even hostile to the family. Early Christian leaders like Paul advised against marriage and familial attachments. Christian baptism had as its goal nothing less than the disruption of one's family since one was "reborn" in baptism. The prior natural birth into a human family was overcome through the new birth of baptism so that the family name was changed and one was given a new Christian name, a new identity. This identity was based upon the new standards of adoption into a new family—the church. In baptism, the old distinctions by which the world lives were washed away.

> As many of you as were baptized into Christ have clothed yourself with Christ. There is no longer Jew or Greek, there is no longer slave or free, there is no longer male and female; for all of you are one in Christ Jesus.
>
> (Galatians 3:27-28)

In other words, *the Bible had reality-defining power over the church.* Through scripture we were taught to view and review the world through new categories. Among Christians there could be no deference to family name, gender, race, or economic position. All of those old, dated distinctions had become washed in the waters of baptism.

Scripture gave us a new story, a new narrative account of the way the world was put together, new direction for history, new purpose for being on earth. The world of Rome had many other stories which gave meaning to peoples' lives: eroticism, pantheism, polytheism, cynicism. To be a Christian was to be someone who had been initiated, by baptism, into this alternative story of the world.

It was not the case that ancient Romans felt some inner need in their lives, some vague feeling of emptiness and then went shopping about for a faith that would fill it, found Christianity and then embraced it. Rather, it was that the church incorporated ancient Romans into their story of reality called scripture. The church gave them a different story through which to make sense out of their lives.

When you read scripture, you will note that narrative, or story, is the Bible's primary means of dealing with truth. Occasionally, but only rarely, will the Bible attempt to define the essence of something. Socrates was interested in discovering a good working definition of big words like "truth," and "beauty," but that is not the Bible's way of working. In the Bible, a Jewish carpenter's son comes forward and says, "I am the way, the truth, the life." We must follow his story if we are to know truth.

Occasionally, but only rarely, will the Bible describe some inner, personal experience. Our time is an age in which people are greatly infatuated with themselves, their own feelings, their personal stories. The longest journey most of us venture is the rather short trip deep into the recesses of our own egos. This is not the Bible's path to truth.

Rather, the Bible seeks to catch our lives up in a grand adventure, a great saga of God's dealings with humanity—a saga begun in God's journey with Israel, continued in the surprising call of God even unto the Gentiles. The church is the product of that story.

LESSON 6   JANUARY 8

A Leader Who Serves

Background Scripture: Matthew 12

The Main Question

The political commentator was asked, "What difference does the end of the Cold War, along with its threat of nuclear weapons, mean for the future of American domestic politics?"

To my surprise, he answered, "It means that a woman will now have a much better chance of being elected President."

I wondered why. Fortunately, he explained. "American voters have been reluctant to vote for a woman up until now. The crucial question has always been, 'Maybe she's a good leader, but will she be able to push the nuclear missile button if she needs to?' "

I was shocked to hear that. According to this commentator, the crucial test for presidential leadership is the president's potential to order nuclear annihilation.

I recalled an earlier presidential election in which it was charged that George Bush was a wimp. Leaders must be made of sterner stuff.

We witness Matthew's rearrangement of many of our preconceptions and prejudices about how God's Messiah should act. In today's lesson, Jesus works on our idea of leadership. What are the characteristics of a good leader? If a leader shows compassion and sensitivity to the needs of others, does that make the leader an ineffective wimp?

Once again Jesus challenges our notions of right and good by challenging our presuppositions about leadership. We know what *we* expect of a leader. What does *God* expect of leadership?

Selected Scripture

King James Version

Matthew 12:9-23

9 And when he was departed thence, he went into their synagogue:

10 And, behold, there was a man which had his hand withered. And they asked him, saying, Is it lawful to heal on the sabbath days? that they might accuse him.

11 And he said unto them, What man shall there be among you, that shall have one sheep, and if it fall into a pit on the sabbath day, will he not lay hold on it, and lift it out?

12 How much then is a man better than a sheep? Wherefore it is lawful to do well on the sabbath days.

13 Then said he to the man, Stretch forth thine hand. And he stretched *it* forth; and it was restored whole, like as the other.

14 Then the Pharisees went out, and held a council against him, how they might destroy him.

15 But when Jesus knew *it,* he withdrew himself from thence: and great multitudes followed him, and he healed them all;

16 And charged them that they should not make him known:

17 That it might be fulfilled which was spoken by Esaias the prophet, saying,

18 Behold my servant, whom I have chosen; my beloved, in whom my soul is well pleased: I will put my

New Revised Standard Version

Matthew 12:9-23

9 He left that place and entered their synagogue; 10 a man was there with a withered hand, and they asked him, "Is it lawful to cure on the sabbath?" so that they might accuse him. 11 He said to them, "Suppose one of you has only one sheep and it falls into a pit on the sabbath; will you not lay hold of it and lift it out? 12 How much more valuable is a human being than a sheep! So it is lawful to do good on the sabbath." 13 Then he said to the man, "Stretch out your hand." He stretched it out, and it was restored, as sound as the other. 14 But the Pharisees went out and conspired against him, how to destroy him.

15 When Jesus became aware of this, he departed. Many crowds followed him, and he cured all of them, 16 and he ordered them not to make him known. 17 This was to fulfill what had been spoken through the prophet Isaiah:

18 "Here is my servant, whom I have chosen,
   my beloved, with whom my soul is well pleased.
I will put my Spirit upon him,

spirit upon him, and he shall shew judgment to the Gentiles.

19 He shall not strive, nor cry; neither shall any man hear his voice in the streets.

20 A bruised reed shall he not break, and smoking flax shall he not quench, till he send forth judgment unto victory.

21 And in his name shall the Gentiles trust.

22 Then was brought unto him one possessed with a devil, blind, and dumb: and he healed him, insomuch that the blind and dumb both spake and saw.

23 And all the people were amazed, and said, Is not this the son of David?

Key Verse: **How much then is a man better than a sheep? Wherefore it is lawful to do well on the sabbath days.**

and he will proclaim justice to the Gentiles.

19 He will not wrangle or cry aloud, nor will anyone hear his voice in the streets.

20 He will not break a bruised reed, or quench a smoldering wick until he brings justice to victory.

21 And in his name the Gentiles will hope."

22 Then they brought to him a demoniac who was blind and mute; and he cured him, so that the one who had been mute could speak and see. 23 All the crowds were amazed and said, "Can this be the Son of David?"

Key Verse: **How much more valuable is a human being than a sheep! So it is lawful to do good on the sabbath.**

As You Read the Scripture

Matthew 12:9-14. Opposition to Jesus has been building. In this passage his critics attack Jesus' attitude on the Sabbath. First, he is criticized for plucking grain on the Sabbath (Matt. 12:1-8). Now they confront him with a man with a physical infirmity and ask Jesus if it is lawful to help the man on the Sabbath. In asking them if it is lawful to do good on the Sabbath, Jesus reveals the sad perversion of their Sabbath regulations. In effect Jesus is saying, "I know that it is not right to do work on the Sabbath, but is it right to do *good* work?" Their silence is revealing.

Verses 9-13. The setting is the synagogue, the place where God's law is studied—a fitting place to debate obedience to the law. Matthew, with his strong emphasis on Jesus as the fulfillment of the hopes of Israel, does not mean by this story that the Sabbath laws are unimportant. Rather, he means to show that Jesus has authority, even over the Sabbath. That is, Jesus has the authority correctly to interpret the true meaning and purpose of the Sabbath laws.

In verses 11-12, Jesus uses a kind of parable, noting how his hearers seem more compassionate to a sheep than to the needs of a human being! Without waiting for their debate or reply, Jesus heals the man.

Chapter 12:15-23. Compare Matthew's account of this incident with Mark's earlier account in Mark 3:7-12. Through Jesus' healing work, Matthew portrays Jesus as a compassionate healer, someone who is deeply moved by the suffering of others.

Verses 18-21. We have noted before Matthew's penchant for quoting long passages from the Old Testament to link the work of Jesus with messianic expectations of the Jewish people. This quote is from Isaiah 42:1-4.

In performing his healing work, Jesus is a true servant of God. The images that are used in this quote from Isaiah are images of meekness and gentleness. We are told that God's servant "will not wrangle or cry aloud." The servant will not be a loud mouth. He will not "quench a smoldering wick"—he is so gentle that even a lamp wick whose flame is almost extinguished will not be harmed by him. Note the interesting contrast of images of gentleness with promise of justice and victory. Here is a leader who accomplishes powerful things without the traditional heavy-handed exercise of power.

Verse 23. The concluding question of the crowds is meant to be our question as we end this section of Matthew. Who is this strange leader whose power is manifested in his gentleness and compassion?

The Scripture and the Main Question

Here Is My Servant

My friend, Stanley Hauerwas, teaches Christian ethics at Duke. Stanley does a wonderful job of challenging us, of reminding us of the high demands of being a Christian. Recently, during a discussion about Christianity and politics, someone must have been impressed with Stanley's presentation of the great demands placed on people by the gospel, because this person asked, "Can a Christian be elected to political office?"

Stanley responded, "Of course a Christian can be elected to political office—*once.*"

That may be overstating the matter, but there is truth in what he says. The gospel's vision of how human life ought to be organized is considerably higher than most of our notions for political action. We must not overlook the conflict between the way we judge things and the way God in Christ judges things. For instance, there is a gap between the way we look at leaders and the way Jesus modeled leadership.

I have great admiration for President Jimmy Carter. I really do not remember much about him as president. But Carter has surely conducted himself in retirement about as honorably as any president before or since. He has given his retirement to volunteer work with Habitat for Humanity (the Christian organization that builds houses for the poor) and to teaching about world peace at his Carter Institute at Emory University.

The irony is that President Carter may be better remembered for his work after he was president than while he was president. One of the frequent criticisms of Carter as a president was that he was indecisive, too slow to act, too unwilling to use military muscle to settle international conflict.

Jimmy Carter was a lifelong active Baptist. I do not know precisely how his Christian faith influenced his actions as president, but his career as president illustrates the problem that we may have with leaders who attempt to put their Christianity into practice in their leadership.

Today's scripture from Matthew portrays the peculiar quality of Jesus' leadership. Jesus was certainly no pushover, no wimp, when it came to confronting the established powers. Matthew shows that he was the center of constant conflict with the religious and political authorities of his day. Yet, the conflict was not over his personal power, but rather over his works of compassion and healing. Jesus definitely put human need—particularly need expressed in the lives of the poor and the outcast—above social and religious convention.

Rather than base his work on the latest public opinion poll, Jesus bases his actions on obedience to the love of God. He heals the man with a withered hand (12:9-14). In both of the episodes from today's scripture, Jesus shows himself to be in control of the situation, independent of human praise or criticism, free to act despite social disapproval. Is it not interesting that Jesus, the very model of the true servant of God, is—by the fact of his servant-hood—free and powerful? Perhaps there is a lesson here for each of us.

We say that we want strong, independent leaders. And yet, when a leader steps out ahead of us, attempting to lead us down a path other than the one we would normally take, we resent that leader, even as Jesus' critics in today's scripture resented him. The result is leadership by public opinion polls, elected officials whose ideas for good government are no better than what nine out of ten average Americans think. Good leadership is often a function of the leader's own self-understanding. What matters most in the value system of the leader? Which voices mean the most to the leader? What are the leader's goals?

I Will Put My Spirit upon Him

When the bishop of Stockholm died in the nineteenth century, the philosopher Søren Kierkegaard attended the bishop's funeral. The funeral was a grand social occasion. All of Stockholm was in attendance. Many speakers eulogized the greatness of the bishop. The principal speaker called the bishop a true servant of God.

Later, Kierkegaard wrote a treatise entitled, "Was the Bishop a Servant of God?" He noted that the bishop was renowned mostly for his presence at fashionable Stockholm social events. No one remembered the bishop speaking out on any controversial issue. He was a master at adjusting the demands of the gospel to suit the limitations of the rich and the powerful. If the bishop served anyone, it was society's upper crust.

I remember the Old Testament scholar, Walter Brueggemann, saying, "It is great freedom to know who owns you. If you do not know to whom you belong, you are apt to be the pawn of anyone whose identity is strong enough to overwhelm your own sense of inadequacy." In today's scripture, Jesus shows that he is a true servant of God. His critics have perverted the Sabbath, turning the Sabbath into a means of putting down others. Jesus, as the true spokesperson of God, shows that the Sabbath laws were meant to help order and bless human life rather than to destroy and burden life.

How does the old hymn put it? "Make me a captive, Lord, then shall I be truly free."

He Brings Justice to Victory

We wonder where we would have found ourselves if we had been partici-pants in Matthew's accounts of Jesus in the grainfield and in the synagogue. Perhaps, if we are suffering, we would be the grateful recipients of Jesus' compassionate acts of healing. More than likely, we would find ourselves in the ranks of his critics, troubled that Jesus should dare to step over our reli-gious and cultural boundaries. After all, *we* are the religious experts, we are studying the scripture in our adult class this morning!

Let these stories from Matthew be a reminder to us of how we can know the scriptures and yet, in light of Jesus, not really *know* the scriptures. We can follow the letter of God's law without really fulfilling the purpose for which God's law is intended. Jesus therefore leads us not only to reach out to others, but also to take a good, honest look at ourselves.

Jesus is both the true obedient servant of God and the true leader in the way toward life. While today's passages from Matthew's Gospel are meant to point us toward the significance of Jesus as the Messiah, demonstrating his authority over his critics, showing why he was a threat to the religious and political establishment, they also have a message for how we ought to live our lives. Jesus leads us by demonstrating that we can only be free as our lives are yoked to him and his way. His way is not always an easy, pleasant way, as today's passages demonstrate. Yet, it is the way that leads to life. Truly this is God's servant, the one who bears forth the spirit of God into our world. Let us follow him down his narrow way, a way that leads to life.

Helping Adults Become Involved

Preparing to Teach

Today's lesson focuses on Jesus as a leader and the implications of his leadership for our expectations of our leaders and of ourselves. Read carefully "The Main Question" and "The Scripture and the Main Question." After reading through today's assigned scripture, Matthew 12:9-23, use the background information found in "As You Read the Scripture" to increase your understanding of the biblical material for today's lesson.

Your lesson plan can be outlined as follows:

I. Strong leaders are those show freedom of thought and action.
II. Even though we say we want leaders to be strong, we sometimes resist leaders who act independently of our expectations.
III. Jesus showed the virtues of strong leadership in his interpretation of scripture and in his compassion toward those who were in need.
IV. Jesus demonstrates that the truly independent and free person is the person who serves God.

As you read through the material in today's lesson, jot down illustrations from your own experiences that can help your class better to understand the scripture. Be sure to prepare the imaginary encounter with Jesus that is suggested below in "Helping Class Members Act" before coming to class.

Introducing the Main Question

Use the material in "The Main Question" to introduce your class to the question: What do we expect of our leaders? Or use your own ideas and experiences that will focus on today's main question.

On chalkboard or newsprint, have your class list "Characteristics of Good Leaders." This list will be helpful as you move through the lesson.

Developing the Lesson

I. Strong leaders are those who show freedom of thought and action.

Look over the list that your class has made of the characteristics of good leaders. How many of them illustrate the first point of today's lesson: Strong leaders are those who show freedom of thought and action? Ask the class which contemporary leader demonstrates the sort of leadership that they admire. Is there disagreement in your class over who is a good leader?

II. Even though we say we want leaders to be strong, we sometimes resist leaders who act independently of our expectations.

In "The Scripture and the Main Question" there is a discussion of President Carter and the reactions of the American public to his administration. This material might be used by you to demonstrate the problems of a leader's Christian values clashing with the public's expectations.

Can your group think of examples of leaders whose actions distanced them from the very people who elected them? Ask your group if our present-day leaders are too concerned merely to follow the public's current opinions?

III. Jesus showed the virtues of strong leadership in his interpretation of scripture and in his compassion toward those who were in need.

Your class has been discussing the nature of good leadership in order to prepare you to lead them through today's scripture from Matthew 12:9-23. Have someone read aloud this passage. Then, using the background material in "As You Read the Scripture," highlight aspects of this passage that deal with Jesus as a leader who served God rather than human opinions and traditions.

Can your group think of contemporary parallels to the conflict with Jesus over healing on the Sabbath? For instance, I know a pastor who is having conflict with her church over a proposed ministry to victims of AIDS. She believes that the church ought to be reaching out to persons infected with this virus. Many of the church leaders are disturbed by the lifestyles of those who have the virus. Can your group think of other examples of conflict between majority opinion and the demands of a loving and compassionate God?

IV. Jesus demonstrates that the truly independent and free person is the person who serves God.

Refer your class back to today's scripture. Using the material in "As You Read the Scripture" and "The Scripture and the Main Question," note how these two episodes show the connection between Jesus' obedience to the true purpose of the Sabbath laws and his freedom from the need for human approval or disapproval. Discuss with your class the idea, discussed in "The Scripture and the Main Question," that "it is great freedom to know who owns you." Can members of your class think of examples from their own lives that illustrate this truth?

Imagine that Jesus walked into your congregation this Sunday morning. What conflicts might result from Jesus's challenge to our prejudices and traditions? Would he find us as insensitive and calloused to human need as the scribes whom he confronted in the synagogue?

Helping Class Members Act

As always, the challenge before us is not only to understand the scripture, but also to put it into practice. In "The Scripture and the Main Question," we noted how we can know the scripture but not really *know* it, that is, we can affirm the truth of the text without putting the text into action in our lives.

Before coming to class, rewrite Matthew 12:9-23 in your own words, imagining that Jesus has come to your church and confronted your church on some pressing contemporary issue. "He left that place and entered St. John's Church on Sunday morning. A man was there who suffered from chronic alcoholism. They asked him, 'Do you think that a person with this problem ought to be here on Sunday morning in church?' Jesus said to the good church members at St. John's . . ." Use your own imagination to help today's scripture come alive for your class.

An implication of today's lesson is not only that Jesus is a leader, but also that he calls us to help lead people to God. Ask each person to think about specific ways he or she can be more courageous and caring in reaching out to lead others to God in Christ.

Planning for Next Sunday

Ask your class, Who are the outsiders in today's world? Ask everyone to bring one newspaper clipping of someone or some group whom we consider to be outsiders. These clippings will be used in next Sunday's class.

LESSON 7   JANUARY 15

Persistent Faith

Background Scripture: Matthew 15:1-31

The Main Question

The pastor looked over the assemblage for his Thursday afternoon confirmation class. Only one teenager was there for the class that should have been filled with fifteen youths. Only one teenager was there for the study of the Bible. Only she was there to benefit from the pastor's knowledge and preparation. Only she had prepared her assignment from the week before.

The lone member of the class was a thirteen-year-old girl. Her mother had left her job as a waitress in order to pick her up at school and have her at the class on time. Her mother had told the pastor at the beginning of the series of confirmation classes, "I did not have the benefit of a church when I was growing up. I am determined that things will go better for my daughter than they went for me."

Her mother was definitely determined. Determination was her middle name. She would move any mountain in order to insure that her daughter participated in all church activities.

At first the pastor considered canceling the class. After all, only one student was present. But the determination and dedication of the mother and her daughter moved him. He went ahead with the class. After all, the mother's dedication ought to be rewarded with at least this much response from the church.

Ten years later, when the pastor returned to that church, a beautiful young woman came up and introduced herself to him. She was a new teacher, specializing in children with learning disabilities. She was also an officer in the congregation, a leader of the church's young adults group.

Then the pastor remembered: She was the lone little girl in the confirmation class that Thursday afternoon ten years ago. She was the fruit of her mother's determination that her daughter would receive a blessing from the church.

That mother's persistence and its results led me to ask: Why is it that sometimes, those whom we regard as outsiders, those who know less about the Christian faith than we do, show much more persistence and determination in their faith than we?

Selected Scripture

King James Version

Matthew 15:21-31

21 Then Jesus went thence, and departed into the coasts of Tyre and Sidon.

22 And, behold, a woman of Canaan came out of the same coasts, and cried unto him, saying, Have mercy on me, O Lord, *thou* Son of David; my daughter is grievously vexed with a devil.

23 But he answered her not a word. And his disciples came and besought him, saying, Send her away; for she crieth after us.

24 But he answered and said, I am not sent but unto the lost sheep of the house of Israel.

25 Then came she and worshipped him, saying, Lord, help me.

26 But he answered and said, It is not meet to take the children's bread, and to cast *it* to dogs.

27 And she said, Truth, Lord: yet the dogs eat of the crumbs which fall from their masters' table.

28 Then Jesus answered and said unto her, O woman, great *is* thy faith: be it unto thee even as thou wilt. And her daughter was made whole from that very hour.

29 And Jesus departed from thence, and came nigh unto the sea

New Revised Standard Version

Matthew 15:21-31

21 Jesus left that place and went away to the district of Tyre and Sidon. 22 Just then a Canaanite woman from that region came out and started shouting, "Have mercy on me, Lord, Son of David; my daughter is tormented by a demon." 23 But he did not answer her at all. And his disciples came and urged him, saying, "Send her away, for she keeps shouting after us." 24 He answered, "I was sent only to the lost sheep of the house of Israel." 25 But she came and knelt before him, saying, "Lord, help me." 26 He answered, "It is not fair to take the children's food and throw it to the dogs." 27 She said, "Yes, Lord, yet even the dogs eat the crumbs that fall from their masters' table." 28 Then Jesus answered her, "Woman, great is your faith! Let it be done for you as you wish." And her daughter was healed instantly.

29 After Jesus had left that place, he passed along the Sea of Galilee,

of Galilee; and went up into a mountain, and sat down there.

30 And great multitudes came unto him, having with them *those that were* lame, blind, dumb, maimed, and many others, and cast them down at Jesus' feet; and he healed them:

31 Insomuch that the multitude wondered, when they saw the dumb to speak, the maimed to be whole, the lame to walk, and the blind to see: and they glorified the God of Israel.

Key Verse: **Then Jesus answered and said unto her, O woman, great *is* thy faith: be it unto thee even as thou wilt. And her daughter was made whole from that very hour.**

and he went up the mountain, where he sat down. 30 Great crowds came to him, bringing with them the lame, the maimed, the blind, the mute, and many others. They put them at his feet, and he cured them, 31 so that the crowd was amazed when they saw the mute speaking, the maimed whole, the lame walking, and the blind seeing. And they praised the God of Israel.

Key Verse: **Then Jesus answered her, "Woman, great is your faith! Let it be done for you as you wish." And her daughter was healed instantly.**

As You Read the Scripture

Matthew 15:1-31. Most scholars believe that this is an adaptation by Matthew of Mark's earlier account (7:24-30). Through a process of deletion and rearrangement, Mark's miracle story becomes in Matthew a theological statement about the nature of the church and its mission. Note that the account of Jesus and the woman immediately follows a discourse Jesus had with the Jewish leaders on ritual rules in which he redefines what is clean and unclean (15:10-20). Now his own words are tested by an unclean Canaanite woman who asks that her demon-possessed daughter be healed.

Verse 21. Jesus withdraws from Gennasaret (14:34) to Tyre and Sidon, a pagan territory to the north of Palestine on the Mediterranean coast, now Lebanon. Since it is the woman who "came out," we can conclude that Jesus did not cross the border, nor enter a house as in Mark 7:24. Earlier, Jesus had ordered his disciples to "go nowhere among the Gentiles" (10:5).

Verse 22. Matthew uses the older term *Canaanite* rather than Mark's (7:26) *Syro-Phoenician.* This is the only place in the New Testament where this Gentile name, synonymous with sin in the Old Testament, is used. This familiar petition, "Have mercy on me, O Lord," is here coupled with another title, "Son of David." Used frequently in Matthew as a designation for the Christ, it goes back to the passages in the Old Testament where God promises a son to David (2 Sam. 7:17), and is consistent with Matthew's genealogy in 1:17. Jesus' power to heal the demon-possessed is already established in Matthew, and the Canaanite woman seems well-rehearsed in her address of Jesus. The title Son of David is used almost exclusively in reference to Jesus' earthly ministry, especially his healing ministry. This strengthens the Matthean position that Jesus is the promised Messiah from the line of David.

Verse 23. Interpreters debate how to translate this verse. It seems cruel and out of character for Jesus. Is Jesus' silence an outright contradiction of his earlier teaching in Matthew 15:20*b*? Does God put people to such a hard test in their hard times? Is Jesus testing the disciples? The answer is not certain, but it appears that this interpolation has been added to the miracle story to reinforce the theme that the mission of Jesus was first to Israel—the "harassed and helpless," who are "like sheep without a shepherd" (Matt. 9:36). This is supported by verse 24. In Mark's account, the woman begs Jesus for healing for her daughter, while in Matthew, the disciples beg Jesus to send the woman away. No questions are asked about whether a healing should or should not take place. The disciples want her sent away.

Verse 25. The mother's spontaneous worship of the Lord, and her persistent petitioning, are the springboard for a surprising exchange between Jesus and the Canaanite. He begins by addressing his disciples (15:26). Although the words have a ring of finality, the woman will not be turned away. The Jews frequently compared dogs and Gentiles, since both were considered unclean. Here the epithet is found in the diminutive form, making it a reference to a house pet.

Verse 28. The request for healing is granted. Her faith is in contrast to the lack of faith in the hometown folk who rejected Jesus (Matt. 13:58). It is the stranger, the outcast who receives mercy (compare with Matt. 28:19)!

The Scripture and the Main Question

Send Her Away

I teach a freshman seminar at Duke. Last semester, I had two students who sat next to each other. One student had every possible advantage a young person can have. He had been born in an affluent family, attended exclusive private schools, special camps each summer. The other student had been born into an economically-disadvantaged home. Her father had died when she was very young. Her mother had difficulty keeping the family together on her modest salary as a cleaning woman.

One student, the one with every advantage, spent the entire semester acting as uninterested as possible in class, turning in assignments late and poorly done. The other student, the one who had come up the hard way, was eager, energetic, and determined. Naturally, she did well in the class.

Isn't it interesting how those who ought to excel because of their gifts and advantages often fail, whereas those who have so many obstacles placed in their way do well? Of course, those who have things handed to them on a silver platter often take their advantages for granted. Those who learn early that life is difficult often work more and are more determined. "History," someone has said, "is a long story of silk slippers going down stairs and wooden shoes coming up."

You and I love stories of the little guy who does well, makes good. Perhaps that is one appeal of this delightful story that Matthew tells of Jesus and the Canaanite woman (Matt. 15:21-31). We love this woman who pushes forward, demanding health and opportunity for her little daughter. The disciples want to send her away. After all, she is an outsider, someone who has no part of the promises of God made to Israel. But Jesus reaches out to her and gives her what she asks. "Great is your faith!" Jesus tells her.

There is irony in this story. The disciples, the crowds around Jesus, ought to be the ones who had great faith. After all, they are members of the house of Israel. They know the scriptures. They are supposed to be the ones who have the inside line on the purposes of God. How ironic that this woman who has probably never been inside a synagogue, never read a word of the Bible, never heard a sermon, is the one whom Jesus praises as having great faith! We can imagine how shocked the disciples were to hear Jesus praise this woman whom they considered to be a wretched and ignorant outcast. It is so easy, when one is on the inside to forget what it was like to be on the outside. How ironic that these disciples of Jesus who, only a few months before were busy fishing or collecting taxes, have forgotten what it was like not to know Jesus. They are now insiders who have little empathy for this poor woman and her suffering child. Jesus is the one who reaches over our boundaries, whose love is so great, it makes all of us appear to be outsiders.

Lord, Help Me

The story of Jesus and the Canaanite woman reminds us of St. Paul's conflict with Peter in Galatians (see Galatians 2–3). From the beginning, the early church struggled with the universal reach of Jesus' love. Was salvation based on faith in Jesus Christ or on one's membership in a given national or ethnic group? Today, the church still struggles with how to assimilate the teaching of Matthew 15:21-31. How do we treat the no-good stranger, the foreigner . . . the sinner? Is our response one of openness, forgiveness, and merciful love toward all who are different, or do we, as did the disciples, plead with Jesus for deliverance from such nuisances?

The Canaanite woman is significant for us as individuals and as the church. She is not only a Gentile coming into the midst of Jews, but also a woman who violated traditional customs by daring to come into the presence of males. She is a wonderfully pushy woman who would not be sent away empty-handed.

Even more alienating, she was the mother of a daughter who was ill with demon-possession—a sure indication to others of the presence of sin. As an outcast she embodies each of us in our isolation, alienation, and ungodliness. In her boldness, she challenges us to risk pushing forward in the crowd and attempting to align our lives to God. She is there for all those who are victims of prejudice and injustice. She is there that we all might hear, individually and corporately, the blessed words of Jesus: "Oh, woman, how great is your faith."

Have Mercy on Me, Lord

I am sure that it is no accident that this passage, demonstrating Jesus' compassion for this poor woman, is immediately followed by the "Feeding of the Four Thousand" (15:32ff.) in which Jesus shows compassion for the multitudes. This outcast woman encourages each of us to come, to kneel before Jesus crying, "Lord, help me!" knowing that the good news of her story is that Jesus will help.

Perhaps each of us ought to pray that we might be as importunate as she, to let nothing and no one stand between us and the mercy of God. Unfortunately, one of the worst barriers between us and God is our tendency to divide up the world between the insiders and the outsiders, the saved and the damned. We like to think that, because we are Christians, we have no spiritual needs. We are superior to those on the outside of the church. As

Luther said of our presumption, "When we were right, God laughed at us in our rightness." We are no more spiritually needy than when we claim to have no need. There is more linking us to the outsider than we like to admit. Therefore, this text from Matthew's Gospel invites us to ponder anew the familiar words of the apostle Paul that "there is no longer Jew or Greek, there is no longer slave or free, there is no longer male and female; for all of you are one in Christ Jesus" (Gal. 3:28).

This Canaanite woman reminds each of us that, as far as our relationship to God is concerned, we are all outsiders, that is, we all need God to do for us what we cannot do for ourselves. Our salvation is always God's gift, not our achievement. Therefore, no matter how spiritually adept we become, our best prayer never gets beyond that of the Canaanite woman, Have mercy on me, Lord, Son of David!

Helping Adults Become Involved

Preparing to Teach

You will find helpful material in "The Main Question" and "The Scripture and the Main Question." Use "As You Read the Scripture" to provide essential background information that you can use with your class in helping them better to understand today's lesson from Matthew 15. As you read, jot down ideas and questions in the margins. Some of the best teaching illustrations and ideas will come from your own experiences that you note and then share with your class.

Today's class may be organized on the basis of this outline:

I. We tend to divide our world into insiders (people like us) and outsiders (people who are not like us).
II. Jesus reached out to those whom we tend to exclude, showing merciful love to all people.
III. Sometimes, those whom we consider to be outsiders show greater faith in God than us insiders.
IV. Remembrance of the mercy that God has shown to us can make us more compassionate to all people.

Last week, members of the class were asked to bring clippings of individuals or groups in our society who might be regarded as outsiders by our church. Be sure to collect clippings in case members have forgotten to bring theirs. If you plan to do the role play that is suggested below in the second step of "Developing the Lesson," carefully plan how you will assign roles in the class.

Introducing the Main Question

Using the clippings of stories about outsiders that you have brought to class, as well as those stories brought by members of your class, ask the class to identify various individuals and groups who are outsiders to people like us. There may be disagreement in your class as to just who outsiders are. Ask your group, What makes us think of another person or group as an outsider? Factors such as dissimilar values, different races, religions, economic class are often means of dividing the world between them and us.

Tell the class that today's lesson is about an outsider who came to Jesus looking for help.

Developing the Lesson

I. We tend to divide our world into insiders (people like us) and outsiders (people who are not like us).

Now that your class has begun to think about the relationships between insiders and outsiders, retell in your own words the story about the pastor and the little girl in the confirmation class that is found in "The Main Question." Ask class members to tell how they think the pastor may have pre-judged (the word *prejudice* means pre-judgement) the girl and her mother. Can they cite other instances in which the church deals with certain people as if they were outsiders and we were insiders? Has anyone in your group had an experience, perhaps an experience related to their life in the church, in which an outsider had persistence that put some of us insiders to shame? With whom do members in your class identify in the story of the little girl, her mother, and the pastor?

II. Jesus reached out to those whom we tend to exclude, showing merciful love to all people.

Read aloud to your group, or retell in your own words, today's scripture, Matthew 15:21 31. The material found in "As You Read the Scripture" will be helpful in enabling your class to deepen their understanding of this passage.

You might ask members of the class to do an imaginary role play of this scripture. Assign the parts of Jesus, the mother, the little girl, and a couple of disciples. Have people imagine that this situation is occurring today. What might be their objections? After class members have done this role play, ask other members of the class to tell what they learned in observing the play.

Matthew has been called the most Jewish of the Gospels because of Matthew's constant insistence that Jesus has come "only to the lost sheep of the house of Israel" (Matt. 15:24). How does this story challenge that notion? Can members of your class recall other beloved stories in which Jesus reached out to those whom we would regard as outsiders?

III. Sometimes, those whom we consider to be outsiders show greater faith in God than us insiders.

Refer your class back to the story that you read or retold from "The Main Question." How is that story a contemporary parallel to the story of Jesus and the woman in Matthew 15:21-31? Retell the story that is told in "The Scripture and the Main Question" about the young woman in the college seminar.

"The Scripture and the Main Question," particularly the last paragraphs, have an extended discussion of the various tensions present in the story of Jesus and the Canaanite woman. Retell some of this material to your class in your own words. It will help them better to understand the controversy behind today's scripture and to apply it to their situation today. Note that, in today's lesson and scripture, faith is linked to persistence.

IV. Remembrance of the mercy that God has shown to us can make us more compassionate to all people.

One night, in a church board meeting, we were discussing how much money our church was spending each month to help feed hungry people in our neighborhood. The board was concerned that we were paying out more money for food than our little congregation could afford. After the meeting, a member of the board came up to me and said softly, "Preacher. I know what it is like to go hungry. When I was growing up, I often went to bed without enough to eat. If anybody comes to this church needing food, you see that they get it. I'll pay for it. I've been there."

In the last paragraphs of "The Scripture and the Main Question," it is noted how easily we come to think of ourselves as insiders in our relationship to God and to forget that we all were once outsiders. God had to save us and to take us in, even though we did not deserve such grace. Remembrance of the way we are all utterly dependent on God to love us and to do for us what we cannot do for ourselves should keep each of us open to the needs and requests of others.

Discuss these ideas with your class, using the illustrations provided here.

Helping Class Members Act

Remind your class that, when Jesus was confronted by the need of this Canaanite woman and her daughter, he reached out in compassion. Refer the class back to the list of outsiders that we spoke of at the beginning of this class. Ask your class, In what ways can our church emulate Jesus' example of active, responsive compassion to those who are in need, even if they are not like us?

Ask your class to take a moment as you end today's lesson. Look over the list of needs, and think of one way you could be more actively involved in reaching out to those who make demands on us like that persistent Canaanite woman who sought help from Jesus.

After a few moments of silence, end today's lesson with a prayer.

Planning for Next Sunday

Has God ever spoken directly to you? Wouldn't believing be easier if God would address us directly, in words loud and clear? Ask your class to ponder those questions in preparation for next Sunday's class.

LESSON 8   JANUARY 22

Challenged to Hear

Background Scripture: Matthew 17:1-23

The Main Question

At the chapel where I preach on Sundays, we have this terrible problem with hearing. Our building is a beautiful, stone, neo-Gothic edifice. Its soaring arches, inspiring arcades and vaults, are wonders to behold. The only problem is, all that stone produces a huge amount of reverberation. Music sounds great in the building. Choirs and organists love the lively, resonant sound. Preachers hate it. Every word in the sermon echoes back and forth between the stone walls, floor, and ceiling, making it tough to hear the spoken word.

We have installed an expensive new sound system, have hired talented technicians to run the system; still, it is tough to hear in our chapel.

"Great sermon," a visitor said to me on the way out the door a couple of Sundays ago, "at least what I heard of it." It is tough to hear in our chapel.

Of course, when it comes to hearing the gospel, hearing the words of Jesus, it is tough to hear no matter where you are sitting. The problem with hearing Jesus has nothing to do with the echo. It has to do with the nature of the gospel, with the nature of the way you and I tend to hear what we want to hear, and avoid listening to words that challenge, confront, or confuse. Jesus once complained about people who, seeing, do not see, and listening, do not hear (Mark 8:18).

Last summer, I was speaking to a group of church school teachers in the midwest. As I began my speech, I could see them grimace. I could hear my voice echoing around the rafters in the auditorium.

"Am I talking too loud?" I asked. They nodded, yes, I was talking too loud.

"Excuse me," I said. "I am accustomed to talking to eighteen- and nineteen-year-olds. I tend to talk loudly because most of them appear to be hard of hearing."

When it comes to matters of the divine, the voice of God intruding into our lives, all of us are a bit hearing impaired, all of us struggle to listen and to hear. Many modern people complain that God never says anything to them that they can hear. Is the problem in God's speaking or in our hearing?

Today's lesson explores the question: How is it possible for us to hear, really hear, God when he speaks to us through Jesus?

Selected Scripture

King James Version

New Revised Standard Version

Matthew 17:1-13

1 And after six days Jesus taketh Peter, James, and John his brother, and bringeth them up into an high mountain apart,

2 And was transfigured before them: and his face did shine as the sun, and his raiment was white as the light.

3 And, behold, there appeared unto them Moses and Elias talking with him.

4 Then answered Peter, and said unto Jesus, Lord, it is good for us to be here: if thou wilt, let us make here three tabernacles; one for thee, and one for Moses, and one for Elias.

5 While he yet spake, behold, a

Matthew 17:1-13

1 Six days later, Jesus took with him Peter and James and his brother John and led them up a high mountain, by themselves. 2 And he was transfigured before them, and his face shone like the sun, and his clothes became dazzling white. 3 Suddenly there appeared to them Moses and Elijah, talking with him. 4 Then Peter said to Jesus, "Lord, it is good for us to be here; if you wish, I will make three dwellings here, one for you, one for Moses, and one for Elijah." 5 While he was still speaking, suddenly a bright cloud overshadowed them, and from the cloud a voice said, "This is my Son, the Beloved; with

bright cloud overshadowed them: and behold a voice out of the cloud, which said, This is my beloved Son, in whom I am well pleased; hear ye him.

6 And when the disciples heard *it*, they fell on their face, and were sore afraid.

7 And Jesus came and touched them, and said, Arise, and be not afraid.

8 And when they had lifted up their eyes, they saw no man, save Jesus only.

9 And as they came down from the mountain, Jesus charged them, saying, Tell the vision to no man, until the Son of man be risen again from the dead.

10 And his disciples asked him, saying, Why then say the scribes that Elias must first come?

11 And Jesus answered and said unto them, Elias truly shall first come, and restore all things.

12 But I say unto you, That Elias is come already, and they knew him not, but have done unto him whatsoever they listed. Likewise shall also the Son of man suffer of them.

13 Then the disciples understood that he spake unto them of John the Baptist.

him I am well pleased; listen to him!" 6 When the disciples heard this, they fell to the ground and were overcome by fear. 7 But Jesus came and touched them, saying, "Get up and do not be afraid." 8 And when they looked up, they saw no one except Jesus himself alone.

9 As they were coming down the mountain, Jesus ordered them, "Tell no one about the vision until after the Son of Man has been raised from the dead." 10 And the disciples asked him, "Why, then, do the scribes say that Elijah must come first?" 11 He replied, "Elijah is indeed coming and will restore all things; 12 but I tell you that Elijah has already come, and they did not recognize him, but they did to him whatever they pleased. So also the Son of Man is about to suffer at their hands." 13 Then the disciples understood that he was speaking to them about John the Baptist.

Key Verse: **While he yet spake, behold, a bright cloud overshadowed them: and behold a voice out of the cloud, which said, This is my beloved Son, in whom I am well pleased; hear ye him.**

Key Verse: **While he was still speaking, suddenly a bright cloud overshadowed them, and from the cloud a voice said, "This is my Son, the Beloved; with him I am well pleased; listen to him!"**

As You Read the Scripture

Matthew 17:1-23. The Transfiguration is an event in Jesus' life in which he was transfigured, Moses and Elijah appeared to him, and a voice spoke from heaven. (See Mark 9:2-8, Matt. 17:1-8, Luke 9:28-36.) Note the context of this story within Matthew's Gospel. The Transfiguration story follows Peter's profession of faith at Caesarea Philippi, Jesus' first prediction of his impending suffering and death, and his teaching on the way of the cross. The story precedes the healing of the epileptic boy. Matthew's account mainly follows that of Mark (Mark 9:2-8), and carries to a higher stage the opening of the disciples' eyes that began with Peter's confession.

Verses 1-2. The place where this took place is described as a high mountain. The traditional site is Mt. Tabor, but Mt. Tabor is not a high mountain.
The lack of specificity for the exact site indicates that what was important for
the church was not *where* but *what* occurred. Peter, James, and John are elsewhere portrayed as a select, inner group of disciples (4:18-22; Mark 5:37,
13:3). A mountain is an important place for revelation in Matthew (see 5:1;
28:16). *Metemorphothe* ("transfigured") is used elsewhere in the New Testament, such as in 2 Corinthians 3:18 and Romans 12:2, for the transforma-
tion of Christians at the end of the age.

Verse 3. This strange and wonderful story is rich with allusions to other
divine appearances in the Old Testament. Jesus' shining face reminds us of
the shining of Moses' face (Exod. 34:29-35), a motif that Paul applies to
Jesus in 2 Corinthians 3:17-18. The cloud (Matt. 17:5) also recalls Moses on
Mt. Sinai (Exod. 24:15-18). Jewish lore of that day believed that Moses and
Elijah ascended into heaven. The cloud, the mountain, the shining face are
all meant to show that we are dealing here with a manifestation, a revelation
of God.

Verse 4. Peter's desire to make three tents or booths suggests some connection with the Jewish Feast of Tabernacles. This was a festival of the Jewish
year in which tabernacles are built in remembrance of the Exodus. It was
also associated with certain prophecies about the end of the age (see Zech.
14:16-19). Some of the ceremonies of the Feast of Tabernacles (the
Hosanna and the waving of leafy branches) appear at Jesus' triumphal entry
into Jerusalem.

Verse 5. Matthew adds "with him I am well pleased" to Mark's earlier version, which makes this a parallel to the voice at Jesus' baptism (Matt. 3:17).
The words "listen to him" recall Peter's unwillingness to accept Jesus' prediction of his suffering and death (Matt. 16:22). This suggests to some that the
purpose of the Transfiguration is primarily for the three disciples. This
interpretation is suggested by the voice, which is directed to them, and the
frequent use of the pronoun *them*. What the voice was for Jesus at his baptism, "Thou art" (Matt. 3:13-17), the voice at the Transfiguration was for
Peter, James, and John, "This is." In the baptism of Jesus, the voice of God
speaks to Jesus. Here, the voice addresses his disciples.

Verses 6-7. Matthew in these two verses heightens the emphasis on the
fear of the disciples and adds Jesus' reassurance.

The Scripture and the Main Question

And He Was Transfigured Before Them

What actually happened in Jesus' Transfiguration has been understood
primarily in two ways by biblical interpreters. The first group understands
the Transfiguration as a breaking through Jesus' earthly appearance and his
humanity of the true form of the Son of God (see John 1:14). The second
group of interpreters see this event as a glimpse of the glory of the Son of
God at Christ's Parousia [his second coming] (see 2 Peter 1:6-18). Perhaps
both are involved. Compare Philippians 2:6-11, where both the pre-existent
glory of the Son and the glory resulting from his resurrection/exaltation are
mentioned.

In other words, in this strange and mysterious story, three of Jesus' disciples are coming face-to-face with God. The curtains of heaven are being opened for human beings to see the hidden mysteries of God. That which was once secret is being revealed for ordinary people to see. The voice of God, so often inaudible in most of our lives, speaks with clarity and undeniable certainty. The Transfiguration is a story about revelation. How does the voice of God come to us?

At the beginning of *Remembrance of Things Past,* Marcel Proust remembers his childhood, not through conscious effort, but through revelation. As an adult, one day he casually bites into a madeleine, the little French cookie. And out of nowhere, the taste, the smell of the madeleine evokes memory: "The old grey house upon the street, . . . rose up like a stage set, . . . and with the house the town, . . . the Square where I used to be sent before lunch, the streets along which I used to run errands. . . . The whole of Combray and its surroundings, taking shape and solidity, sprung into being, town and gardens alike, from my cup of tea."

Proust's writing is obsessed with time and its effects. "Time, like an ever rolling stream, bears all its sons away," says the hymn that we sing in church. "They fly forgotten as a dream dies at the opening day." Usually we do not experience time except in bits, fragments, wisps of memory, and recognition. Only rarely are we aware that time is passing, except when some event, some revelation calls it to our attention. Proust specializes in such momentary evocation of remembrance.

Proust remembers, as a child, calling his mother to his bed one night. She comforted him, held him in her arms until he was at peace. But not too much at peace because, he recalls, even in his childhood, time robbed him of his best moments. He was aware, even in his few years of life, that the best moments never last. Time sweeps it all away. "I knew," he recalls, "that such a night could not be repeated; that the strongest desire I had in the world, namely, to keep my mother in my room through the sad hours of darkness, ran too much counter to the general requirements and to wishes of others . . ." (p. 46).

Here, as a child, Proust is not so much remembering what is past, but recognizing what is to come, the future. The sweetness of the moment sours with the recognition that it will not last; the boy must become a man and men do not have mothers to comfort them when the night is dark. As the madeleine evoked in the man a glimpse of his past, so too did his mother, beside his bed on that night, evoke in the child a glimpse of his future.

A few years ago, right after Christmas, I was driving through the countryside with my own mother after a visit to my sister's. As I drove, I happened to glance over at her and she was sleeping. My mother was a dignified woman who carried herself with the consciously genteel air of a lady. But she was now sleeping as I drove and I caught a glimpse of her in sleep as an old woman, mouth open, head to the side. And for the first time, even though she was seventy-eight, for the first time I actually realized, I felt, I knew, that she was old. In less than three weeks, she had died.

I am talking about those sporadic moments that come to us quite unexpectedly, when we experience time in ways unlike our normal encounters, when the curtain between the present and the future is pulled back and we know the future as if it were now.

I am talking about those moments when, in the midst of a confusing cacophony of conflicting voices, we hear one clear, undeniable voice that cuts through all the confusion and we hear, we *hear* down to the very depths of our souls.

The Disciples Heard

The Transfiguration of Jesus is one such revelatory moment. The event occurs right after Peter's great confession of faith. The location within Matthew's Gospel is important to understanding this strange episode. One day Jesus asked, "Who do people say that the Son of Man is?" (Matt. 16:33).

Some of the disciples reply, "Nine out of ten Americans, when asked, say that you are John the Baptist, come back from the dead. Those with incomes of over fifty thousand a year say perhaps you are Elijah. Others think that. . . ."

Then Jesus puts it to them. "But who do *you* say that I am?"

Peter is the first to speak up. "You are the Messiah, the Son of the living God" (Matt. 16:16). Here, standing before them in the flesh, is the living, long-awaited Messiah, sent from God.

But then Jesus shocks them by telling his disciples that he "must go to Jerusalem and undergo great suffering at the hands of the elders and chief priests and scribes, and be killed, and on the third day be raised" (Matt. 16:21). It came as a great, confusing blow to the disciples to hear those words. How can it be that the Messiah should be so weak and ineffective as to suffer and be killed? Is this any way for God's anointed to be treated?

What is perhaps even more troubling, Jesus tells them that suffering and death may be in the cards for them as well. "If any want to become my followers, let them deny themselves and take up their cross and follow me" (Matt. 16:24). Is this any way for Jesus' disciples to be treated?

It was all very confusing to the disciples. How can it be that suffering and rejection are the fate both of God's anointed one and of his disciples? It was in the thick of these troubling, threatening questions that the Transfiguration on the mountain occurred.

From the Cloud a Voice Said

In a dazzling moment of recognition, a voice from the cloud stated, in words clear and true, who Jesus was. It was a wonderful moment for the disciples who had been following Jesus, but who had, up to that point, heard no clear statement of his lordship. Peter blurts out, "Lord, it is good for us to be here; . . . I will make three dwellings here, one for you, one for Moses, and one for Elijah" (17:4).

Peter wanted to make this dazzling moment last forever. But it was not to be. The Transfiguration was a glimpse into the future, but their future was not yet here. The disciples had to go back down the mountain where there were the sick to be healed (Matt. 17:14-21), where there was suffering and death. There was no way to freeze the action on the mountaintop forever, to somehow capture the voice.

I take this to be a kind of parable for the way revelation occurs: undeniable, unforgettable, life-changing, but momentary, mysterious, uncontrolled. The voice speaks. In a moment we hear. Everything comes into focus. Then we must move on.

Have you ever had such an experience? Researcher Morton Kelsey interviewed hundreds of Americans concerning their religious experiences and reported that the *majority* interviewed claimed to have had at least one strange, life-changing, mystical experience. Furthermore, the majority of those having such an experience also reported that they had never told anybody else about their experience, even their pastor or priest. When Kelsey asked why, most of them replied, "Because he would think I was crazy."

It is enough to make you ask, Has God stopped speaking to us in our daily lives or have we stopped listening?

Helping Adults Become Involved

Preparing to Teach

The Transfiguration is a watershed mark in Matthew. As you prepare for today's lesson, you might recall the lessons from the past few weeks. Tension has been building in this Gospel as Jesus comes into increasing conflict with the authorities. Undoubtedly, the Transfiguration is meant as a reassurance of the disciples on the way to the cross.

The theme of revelation and how we receive it is rich, so you ought to prepare for much discussion in your class today. "The Main Question" sets up the issue of how we hear God speaking to us. Think, as you prepare, of those moments in your life when you felt that God was speaking to you. Jot these images, memories, and ideas down as you read through the lesson.

"As You Read the Scripture" and "The Scripture and the Main Question" provide helpful background and interpretive information on Matthew 17. As you read, think of the Transfiguration as a kind of parable of how God's voice gets through to us in our daily lives.

Before you begin working through the details of this material, take a moment and read today's scripture, Matthew 17:1-23. Jot down your first impressions, questions, and images as you read. These first impressions and questions will be helpful before you begin more detailed preparation. It is a wonderful story and you do not want to lose the wonder in your presentation of the story.

Use this outline as you present the lesson:

    I. It is difficult to hear the voice of God in today's world.
    II. On the mountaintop, through the Transfiguration of Jesus, the disciples heard the voice of God.
    III. The Transfiguration reveals to us the nature of revelation to us from God.

A good way to encourage discussion of revelatory moments by members of your class is to remember your own moments of revelation as you read today's lesson.

Introducing the Main Question

Rephrase the opening material in "The Scripture and the Main Question" as a way of introducing the problem of revelation from God in today's world. Ask the class: In what ways can it be said of us that, when confronted with the claims of Jesus, we "hear, but do not hear"?

Developing the Lesson

I. It is difficult to hear the voice of God in today's world.

Ask your class to list on chalkboard or newsprint, all those factors in our lives that make it tough for us to hear the voice of God speaking to us, factors such as pride, prejudice, and our desire to do more talking than listening to God. Does your class believe that it is more difficult to hear God in the modern world than it may have been in the ancient world? Why? For instance, does our modern, scientific world view lead us to exclude certain data, certain signs and signals that do not fit into our scientific world view?

II. On the mountaintop, through the Transfiguration of Jesus, the disciples heard the voice of God.

Using the material in "As You Read the Scripture," and also the discussion of today's passage in "The Scripture and the Main Question," in your own words, discuss Matthew 17:1-23. Walk the class through the passage in much the same way as the last half of "The Scripture and the Main Question." Try to move your class beyond questions such as "How did this happen?" to the more important "*Why* did this happen?" What is being revealed to us about the nature of revelation through this mysterious story?

III. The Transfiguration reveals to us the nature of revelation to us from God.

Relate to your class the observations of Morton Kelsey (toward the end of "The Scripture and the Main Question"). Do they agree with Kelsey's ideas about modern skepticism of revelation? In what ways do we resemble Peter and the other disciples' response to this stunning, though mysterious revelation of God in Matthew 17?

The biblical scholar Gail R. O'Day has written:

In our time, perhaps in every time, there is a yearning for revelation. We long for a word that will come to us from outside ourselves and create the possibility of life in a world that is closed. Only a revelation from God can break open our closed world and give this offer of life against death. We are convinced that God can and does offer such a life-giving and revealing word, but the problem of revelation for us is that we do not know how the revelatory word has access to us. (Gail R. O'Day, *Revelation in the Fourth Gospel* [Philadelphia: Fortress Press, 1986], p. 1)

Read O'Day's quote to your class. In what ways have they found revelation from God to be a problem in their own lives? What is there about us, as modern people, that makes revelation from God difficult for us to comprehend?

Helping Class Members Act

During today's discussion, you have explored the ways in which revelation from God is a problem for us. Today's scripture suggests that our problem in hearing and acting on God's revelation is not new. God's revelation often comes to us unexpectedly, mysteriously, ambiguously, momentarily. Ask members of the class to discuss ways in which we can be more open to the voice of God in our daily lives. Periodic Bible study, times of quiet reflection, curiosity and expectation, might be some of the habits that we ought to cultivate in order to be more open to the voice of God. List these ideas on a chalkboard or newsprint.

Planning for Next Sunday

This Sunday we have discussed the nature of revelation and our resistance to God's intrusions. Next Sunday we will be studying one of the most memorable of divine intrusions, Jesus' entry into Jerusalem on Palm Sunday. Ask your class to read Matthew 21 during this coming week. Also ask them: Have you ever been to a parade in which some dignitary visited your town? Recall your feelings and reactions to that parade. Next week, Jesus parades through our town. How shall we greet him?

LESSON 9   JANUARY 29

Welcome the Savior

Background Scripture: Matthew 20:17–21:17

The Main Question

The crowd began to stir with excited anticipation. Some in the crowd had been standing along the street for many hours. Then, a voice down the street shouted, "Here he comes!"

All eyes strained forward. Looking over the heads of the assembled people along the streets, you could at last see him coming into view, bouncing on the back of a donkey. He was small, barely to be seen over the heads of his admirers. Young children waved palm branches as his procession moved forward. When he and his people passed close by, you could see that they were all common people. Nothing in their outward appearance indicated the crowd's shouts of "Hosanna!" They called him "prophet," and "Son of David!"

Frankly, it was all a bit disappointing. Jesus and his disciples were much less impressive in person than they were alleged to have been. Why all this fuss over this young man from Galilee?

The saviors who march in our parades tend to ride war horses, not donkeys. They are preceded by marching bands with drums and trumpets, not by ragged children waving palm branches. Those whom we stand in line to see ride in long limousines, protected by police motorcades. They are given the key to the city when they arrive in town.

The movement, begun by Jesus out in the hinterland, has at last made it to the capital city of Jerusalem. All of Jerusalem has come out to see what all the fuss is about. Are they pleased or disappointed by what they see in Jesus?

You and I have come to church this morning, looking for a savior, someone come among us to set things right between us and God. With the Palm Sunday crowds, we stand along the roadside, each trying to get a glimpse of Jesus. What do we see when we see him? How does what we see in Jesus challenge our expectations for our saviors?

Selected Scripture

King James Version

New Revised Standard Version

Matthew 21:1-11, 14-16

1 And when they drew nigh unto Jerusalem, and were come to Bethphage, unto the mount of Olives, then sent Jesus two disciples,

2 Saying unto them, Go into the village over against you, and straightway ye shall find an ass tied, and a colt with her: loose *them*, and bring *them* unto me.

3 And if any *man* say ought unto you, ye shall say, The Lord hath need of them; and straightway he will send them.

4 All this was done, that it might be fulfilled which was spoken by the prophet, saying,

5 Tell ye the daughter of Sion, Behold, thy King cometh unto thee, meek, and sitting upon an ass, and a colt the foal of an ass.

6 And the disciples went, and did as Jesus commanded them,

7 And brought the ass, and the colt, and put on them their clothes, and they set *him* thereon.

8 And a very great multitude spread their garments in the way; others cut down branches from the trees, and strawed *them* in the way.

9 And the multitudes that went before, and that followed, cried, saying, Hosanna to the Son of David: Blessed *is* he that cometh in the name of the Lord; Hosanna in the highest.

10 And when he was come into Jerusalem, all the city was moved, saying, Who is this?

11 And the multitude said, This is Jesus the prophet of Nazareth of Galilee.

....

14 And the blind and the lame came to him in the temple; and he healed them.

15 And when the chief priests and scribes saw the wonderful things that

Matthew 21:1-11, 14-16

1 When they had come near Jerusalem and had reached Bethphage, at the Mount of Olives, Jesus sent two disciples, 2 saying to them, "Go into the village ahead of you, and immediately you will find a donkey tied, and colt with her; untie them and bring them to me. 3 If anyone says anything to you, just say this, 'The Lord needs them.' And he will send them immediately." 4 This took place to fulfill what had been spoken through the prophet, saying,

5 "Tell the daughter of Zion,
Look, your king is coming to you,
    humble, and mounted on a donkey,
    and on a colt, the foal of a donkey."

6 The disciples went and did as Jesus had directed them; 7 they brought the donkey and the colt, and put their cloaks on them, and he sat on them. 8 A very large crowd spread their cloaks on the road, and others cut branches from the trees and spread them on the road. 9 The crowds that went ahead of him and that followed were shouting,
"Hosanna to the Son of David!
Blessed is the one who comes in the name of the Lord!
Hosanna in the highest heaven!"
10 When he entered Jerusalem, the whole city was in turmoil, asking, "Who is this?" 11 The crowds were saying, "This is the prophet Jesus from Nazareth in Galilee."

....

14 The blind and the lame came to him in the temple, and he cured them. 15 But when the chief priests and the scribes saw the amazing things that he did, and heard the

he did, and the children crying in the temple, and saying, Hosanna to the Son of David; they were sore displeased,

16 And said unto him, Hearest thou what these say? And Jesus saith unto them, Yea; have ye never read, Out of the mouth of babes and sucklings thou hast perfected praise?

children crying out in the temple, "Hosanna to the Son of David," they became angry 16 and said to him, "Do you hear what these are saying?" Jesus said to them, "Yes; have you never read,
'Out of the mouths of infants and nursing babies
you have prepared praise for yourself'?"

Key Verse: **And the multitudes that went before, and that followed, cried, saying, Hosanna to the Son of David: Blessed *is* he that cometh in the name of the Lord; Hosanna in the highest.**

Key Verse: **The crowds that went ahead of him and that followed were shouting, "Hosanna to the Son of David! Blessed is the one who comes in the name of the Lord! Hosanna in the highest heaven!"**

As You Read the Scripture

Matthew 21:1-11, 14-16. Most of the remainder of Matthew's Gospel will be concerned with those events surrounding the trial and death of Jesus. Note that Matthew portrays Jesus' ministry as beginning out in the countryside, in small towns and villages, far from the centers of military, economic, and cultural power. While he is initially welcomed into Jerusalem by great crowds, his actions—such as the cleansing of the temple (Matt. 21:12-17)—bring him into great conflict, first with the authorities and then with the people.

Verses 1-5. We have seen that Matthew constantly links the events of Jesus with quotations from the Hebrew scriptures. He wants to show that Jesus is the legitimate fulfillment of the hopes of Israel. Matthew's citation of Isaiah 62:11 and Zechariah 9:9 in verse 5 is a bit confused since the Hebrew text refers to one animal, not two. Perhaps he has taken a poetic expression ("a colt, the foal of an ass") to mean two animals. By riding this donkey, Jesus demonstrates his humility, which is counter to many popular expectations for the Messiah.

Verses 6-8. Palm branches were a sign of honor and celebration (see 2 Kings 9:13).

Verses 9-11. *Hosanna* is a word that originally meant something like "Save us!" or "God save the king." It became a shout of joyous acclamation. Many in the crowd obviously link Jesus to the messianic expectations of Israel in calling him "Son of David," while others speak of him as the prophet Jesus.

Verses 14-16. Jesus marches into the temple, the center of national and religious prestige and power. Here he immediately runs afoul of the authorities. The children acclaim Jesus. Matthew thereby shows how the so-called wise and powerful fail to recognize Jesus' authority while the little children, the sick, and the lowly acclaim him. Behind Jesus' actions in the temple is a struggle over power. Who will have control of divine power? Those who dispense power from the temple (the chief priests and scribes) or Jesus, who brings healing power to the blind and the lame?

180

The Scripture and the Main Question

The One Who Comes in the Name of the Lord

It is one thing for us to welcome into our city a famous personality and his entourage. It is another thing to welcome Jesus. When Jesus comes to town, to the capital city of Jerusalem or anywhere else, things begin to happen, there is trouble, those in power become uneasy, the little and the lowly lift up their heads and the turmoil begins. That is what happens when Jesus parades into town.

Those who waved palm branches in Jerusalem that day to welcome the prophet from Nazareth may have remembered the story of another grand procession with palms into Jerusalem that occurred some two hundred years earlier.

Judas Maccabeus became the leader of the Jews during the horrible and brutal rule of Antiochus Epiphanes. In 167 B.C., when Antiochus prohibited Judaism from being practiced, under the penalty of death, there was a revolt among the people. Antiochus hoped to make Judea into a docile, peaceful Roman colony. He moved the holy vessels out of the temple in Jerusalem and set up an altar to the Roman god, Zeus. In order to insult the Jews even further, he offered pig's flesh upon the altar in the temple. In the Old Testament Apocrypha, those books that are not contained in most of our Protestant Bibles, 1 Maccabees describes how Antiochus "put to death the women who had their children circumcised, and their families and those who circumcised them; and they hung the infants from their mothers' necks" (1:60-61).

An old man named Mattathias, along with his sons who included Judas Maccabeus (Judas the Hammer), began a guerrilla campaign against Antiochus' soldiers. Judas Maccabeus and his followers were able, within three years, to cleanse and rededicate the spoiled temple. They established what would be a full century of Jewish rule over Judea before the Romans again put an end to their hopes, about one hundred years before the birth of Jesus.

First Maccabees describes the glorious entry into Jerusalem by the victorious Maccabeean freedom fighters when they had at last overthrown Antiochus. "On the twenty-third day of the second month, in the one hundred seventy-first year, the Jews entered it [Jerusalem] with praise and palm branches, and with harps and cymbals and stringed instruments, and with hymns and songs, because a great enemy had been crushed and removed from Israel" (1 Macc. 13:51).

The entry of Maccabeus into Jerusalem was indelibly etched in the collective memory of Israel as a beloved moment in Israel's history when, in the bravery and leadership of one man, Israel saw her path clear to victory over those who had oppressed her. Israel prayed, while under the heavy heel of Rome, for a new Maccabeus who would come and triumph over Israel's enemies.

Hosanna!

I tell you this ancient story of the entry of Maccabeus in order to set Matthew's account of Palm Sunday and Jesus' entry into Jerusalem in context. When Jesus arrived, the people shouted and waved palm branches. They rushed out to meet Jesus, hoping that this new hero had come to remove from Israel its present enemy, to run out the Romans the same way that Maccabeus removed Antiochus.

Imagine their shock, their confusion when Jesus rode into Jerusalem, not on a war horse, but on a donkey, not leading a mighty army of liberation, but leading twelve ordinary disciples, greeted not by the mayor with the key to the city, but by children waving palm branches.

The palm wavers saw the coming triumph of God in Jesus. But they failed to understand the sort of savior they were welcoming into their town. He did not act as they had planned for him to act. Rather than running out the Romans, Jesus went straight to their temple and ran out the money changers (Matt. 21:12-17). It was the religious authorities, the leaders of Israel, the keepers of the faith who bore his most fierce wrath, not the Romans. What a shock to national expectations!

This Is the Prophet Jesus

As a child, some of my fondest memories relate to the annual Christmas parade in Greenville. It always occurred during the first week of December (yes, in those days we actually waited until December to prepare for Christmas!). We children were dismissed early from school. We went downtown and waited in the cold for what seemed like hours. At last, we heard the notes of the high school band coming down the street, announcing the beginning of the parade. The highlight of the parade was the arrival of Santa, seated on his own float, throwing candy to excited children. This jolly old man, bearded, throwing free candy, signified the beginning of the Christmas season, the season that would be culminated on December 25 with all of us receiving lots of gifts.

In a sense, Santa, as the highlight of the Christmas parade, symbolized everything we were—he made no demands on us, gave us everything we wanted, and then left town as quickly as he came.

On Palm Sunday, someone very different from Santa came to town. He offered us gifts, yes—the gift of salvation, of truth, of hope and healing. But he also made rigorous demands on us, called on us to leave everything and follow him. He did more than give us all that our hearts desire, rather he transformed our hearts and rearranged our desires. So, in a way, the crowds who hailed Jesus as "the prophet Jesus from Nazareth in Galilee" (Matt. 21:11) were right. He came to us as the prophets of old, challenging our present arrangements, speaking the truth even when the truth hurts, calling for obedience to God.

Will we welcome him? What must you and I do to join that joyous Palm Sunday procession, not merely to be spectators of the parade but to join the parade and follow him?

Helping Adults Become Involved

Preparing to Teach

Your challenge as a teacher of this lesson will be to help your adults find new meaning in a rather familiar old story—the story of Jesus' entry into Jerusalem on Palm Sunday. Using the central image of a parade, the lesson attempts to uncover new significance in an old story.

The following outline should help you organize today's lesson:

I. While crowds welcomed Jesus into Jerusalem on Palm Sunday, many in the crowd misunderstood Jesus' mission.

II. Many may have misunderstood Jesus because they attempted to fit him into their preconceptions of a messiah rather than to have their preconceptions changed by him.

III. The demands and the actions of Jesus sometimes confuse contemporary disciples. He doesn't always act as we expect a savior to act.

IV. We must welcome Jesus into our lives with trust and openness, expecting to be surprised by his words and deeds.

Read "The Scripture and the Main Question" as well as the biblical material found in "As You Read the Scripture." You may wish to obtain a Bible that contains the Apocrypha (those books between the Old and New Testaments that are not contained in all Bibles in use by Protestant Christians) and read for yourself the story of Judas Maccabeus.

Today's lesson builds on the human experience of expectancy and anticipation for the arrival of a dignitary in a parade. As you read the material in preparation for your class, recall your own experiences of parades and the arrival of famous people. When were your expectations disappointed or changed by the arrival of the person? Make notes in the margins of the *Annual* as you read for use in our class.

Introducing the Main Question

Begin by reading today's scripture from Matthew 21 to your class, or by retelling it in your own words. Ask class members to imagine that they are standing in the crowd on Palm Sunday welcoming Jesus. What would be their feelings? Apprehension? Amazement? Joy? What do they think would most startle or confuse them in their first glimpse of Jesus? Use the material in "The Main Question" to enrich this first part of your lesson.

Developing the Lesson

I. While crowds welcomed Jesus into Jerusalem on Palm Sunday, many in the crowd misunderstood Jesus' mission.

Using the discussion of Maccabeus in "The Scripture and the Main Question," put in context Jesus' entry into Jerusalem on Palm Sunday. Note to your class the ways in which many in the crowd expected Jesus to be a military leader who would rectify the injustice of the Roman rule of Judea. Retell the material on Maccabeus in your own words rather than simply reading it to your class. Ask your class how the people in the joyous crowd might have responded when Jesus moved to cleanse the temple (Matt. 12–13).

II. Many may have misunderstood Jesus because they attempted to fit him into their preconceptions of a messiah rather than to have their preconceptions changed by him.

Continuing your discussion of the misunderstanding of Jesus, related to contemporary messianic expectations, ask your class to recall the ways in which Jesus acted counter to people's expectations for him. For instance, he attacked influential and powerful people rather than flattered them. Rather than attempt to influence influential people, most of his work was among the poor and the sick (see Matt. 21:14-17).

Martin Luther King, Jr., frustrated many people by his insistence on nonviolent protest. Some thought that King should have advocated violence as a means of the victimized defending themselves. King refused to advocate violence, even in behalf of the oppressed. Was King's collision with people's expectations a contemporary parallel to Jesus on Palm Sunday?

When I was a boy, during the national Boy Scout Jamboree, we were all visited by President Dwight D. Eisenhower. We stood along his parade route for hours, anxiously awaiting the presidential motorcade. When the President finally drove by, amid our cheering, I heard someone say, "He is old! I didn't think a president would be that old." He did not fit our youthful image of a president.

Did anyone in the Palm Sunday crowd feel that way about Jesus?

III. The demands and the actions of Jesus sometimes confuse contemporary disciples. He does not always act as we expect a savior to act.

Relate these observations to the experiences of people in your class. In what ways have they found, in their own relationship with Jesus, that he does not always act as we expect? You might begin this discussion by citing some instance from your own life. For instance, I remember thinking that, if a person was really dedicated to Jesus, and really sincere in trying to do his will, that person would always meet with success. Very quickly I learned that dedication to Jesus and his way often leads to failure (at least failure in the world's eyes) rather than success. I did not expect that.

Thumbing back through the Gospel of Matthew, you might find specific episodes in which Jesus caused confusion and consternation among those who heard him. Share these examples with your class.

IV. We must welcome Jesus into our lives with trust and openness, expecting to be surprised by his words and deeds.

Following Jesus is always an adventure. He continually surprises us, even as he surprised people who welcomed him to Jerusalem on Palm Sunday. Using the illustration of the Christmas Parade that is told toward the end of "The Scripture and the Main Question," ask your group in what ways can it be said, in their own relationship to Jesus, that to welcome Jesus means to be ready to be surprised.

Helping Class Members Act

You began this class by asking members to imagine themselves standing along Jesus' parade route on Palm Sunday. Close the class by asking members again to imagine themselves standing there as Jesus comes into town. But now, ask them to close their eyes and imagine themselves coming forward to follow Jesus, not just to cheer his arrival, but actually to leave the crowd and join the parade. What do they think he would demand of them in their life right now? In what ways would he challenge them, even as he went and cleansed the temple? They do not have to discuss this with the whole class, just think about it in silence.

Planning for Next Sunday

Next Sunday we are going to study Jesus' Last Supper with his disciples. In preparation for that lesson, ask your class members: What is the most memorable meal you have had in your life? Though they may be surprised by the question, their response will form the basis for next Sunday's lesson on the Last Supper.

UNIT IV: JESUS CHRIST: VICTOR OVER SIN AND DEATH

FOUR LESSONS   **FEBRUARY 5–26**

I have just finished talking on the telephone to a young man who has had a terrible jolt. His mother has just died quite unexpectedly. She had been in good health, in her early fifties. He is very upset and in great grief.

Of course the expression "died unexpectedly" is a bit inaccurate. Is death ever totally unexpected? Is there any other way for human beings to live than in a terminal condition? "Only two things are certain," goes the old saying, "death and taxes." Death is certainly, well, *certain*.

Earlier today I spoke with a parent about the recent conviction of a friend's child for drug abuse. The teenager has been sentenced to many years in prison for his crime.

"Although he was deserving of the punishment," said my friend, "I still feel very sad about it. His mother was every bit as conscientious a parent as am I. She tried to be a good mother and yet, look how all this has turned out. That young man could just as well have been my son."

And she was right. I once heard a famous philosopher say that, "the only difference between us and the people who sit on death row is lack of opportunity." We all know, in our more honest moments, that we are guilty, given the right circumstances, of almost any sin.

Until someone can do something about death and sin and their effect upon human life, then little has been done for the betterment of the human condition. Sin and death, the two great human problems, are *the* problem.

In this unit's lessons Matthew shall witness to the ways in which Jesus is victor over our sin and our death, thus showing each of us the way to forgiveness and eternal life.

LESSON 10   **FEBRUARY 5**

Celebrating the Covenant

Background Scripture: Matthew 26:17-35

The Main Question

When your daughter says to you, "There is someone that I would like to bring home after church for Sunday dinner. His name is Tom," you have the good sense to know that something serious may be occurring in your family. To invite a stranger to the family dinner table is to welcome someone into the inner sanctum of the family. There is no more intimate, loving, or significant act than a family's sharing food around the dinner table.

When governments sign a major treaty, they always celebrate the signing with a state dinner. The dinner is a sign of a new understanding and cooperation between the two governments.

SECOND QUARTER

Any child knows that to share a candy bar with the new kid on the block is the way of welcoming that new person into the community of children.

Across all cultures, among every people, the sharing of food together is a sign of unity and solidarity. The person who invites you to dinner is the person who will stand beside you through thick and thin. That is why the psalmist in the twenty-third psalm says, "Thou preparest a table before me in the presence of mine enemies." The psalmist knows that the person who invites you to dinner is the person who will stand beside you even in the face of your enemies.

When Jesus came to the end of his ministry, when the forces of evil were closing in on him, he gathered with his disciples in the upper room of a home and shared a meal with them. In what way does that act, at once so ordinary and everyday, and at the same time so mysterious and powerful, signify the meaning of Jesus' work among us? What is the significance of that meal, celebrated so long ago, for the church's continued celebrations of the Lord's Supper?

Selected Scripture

King James Version

Matthew 26:20-30

20 Now when the even was come, he sat down with the twelve.

21 And as they did eat, he said, Verily I say unto you, that one of you shall betray me.

22 And they were exceeding sorrowful, and began every one of them to say unto him, Lord, is it I?

23 And he answered and said, He that dippeth *his* hand with me in the dish, the same shall betray me.

24 The Son of man goeth as it is written of him: but woe unto that man by whom the Son of man is betrayed! it had been good for that man if he had not been born.

25 Then Judas, which betrayed him, answered and said, Master, is it I? He said unto him, Thou hast said.

26 And as they were eating, Jesus took bread, and blessed *it*, and brake *it*, and gave *it* to the disciples, and said, Take, eat; this is my body.

27 And he took the cup, and gave thanks, and gave *it* to them, saying, Drink ye all of it;

28 For this is my blood of the new testament, which is shed for many for the remission of sins.

29 But I say unto you, I will not

New Revised Standard Version

Matthew 26:20-30

20 When it was evening, he took his place with the twelve; 21 and while they were eating, he said, "Truly I tell you, one of you will betray me." 22 And they became greatly distressed and began to say to him one after another, "Surely not I, Lord?" 23 He answered, "The one who has dipped his hand into the bowl with me will betray me. 24 The Son of Man goes as it is written of him, but woe to that one by whom the Son of Man is betrayed! It would have been better for that one not to have been born." 25 Judas, who betrayed him, said, "Surely not I, Rabbi?" He replied, "You have said so."

26 While they were eating, Jesus took a loaf of bread, and after blessing it he broke it, gave it to the disciples, and said, "Take, eat; this is my body." 27 Then he took a cup, and after giving thanks he gave it to them, saying, "Drink from it, all of you; 28 for this is my blood of the covenant, which is poured out for many for the forgiveness of sins. 29 I tell you, I will never again drink of

drink henceforth of this fruit of the vine, until that day when I drink it new with you in my Father's kingdom.

30 And when they had sung an hymn, they went out into the mount of Olives.

Key Verse: **For this is my blood of the new testament, which is shed for many for the remission of sins.**

this fruit of the vine until that day when I drink it new with you in my Father's kingdom."

30 When they had sung the hymn, they went out to the Mount of Olives.

Key Verse: **For this is my blood of the covenant, which is poured out for many for the forgiveness of sins.**

As You Read the Scripture

Matthew 26:17-35. Matthew depicts Jesus gathering with his disciples to eat the Passover meal, that yearly commemoration of Israel's liberation from Egyptian slavery (see Exod. 12:18-27 and Deut. 16:5-8).

Verses 26-27. It was customary, in many Jewish ceremonial meals, to say a blessing at the beginning of the meal, then pass around the bread and the other food to be eaten. After the meal is eaten, a cup of wine is poured and another, concluding prayer of blessing is offered. Matthew here reports on these two prayers, without giving much information on the meal between them. Jesus' words, "This is my body," and "This is my blood" undoubtedly astounded his disciples. We have no parallel to this in Jewish table ritual.

Verse 28. The blood is linked to a new covenant. Just as God rescued Israel by the signifying blood over the doorposts of the Hebrews, so blood signifies a new deliverance by God, this time deliverance from the slavery of sin. This new covenant was promised by Jeremiah (Jer. 31:31-34). Contracts, promises, and covenants are often ratified by the parties at a feast or banquet.

Verse 29. Jews believed that the Messiah would spread a banquet table for all of Israel to feast upon. Jesus implies that the next time his disciples share food with him, "my Father's kingdom" will have come.

Verses 30-35. Ironically, Jesus speaks of his promise to be faithful to his disciples, yet after the meal his disciples desert him and flee into the darkness. Their desertion makes a vivid contrast with the covenant that Jesus is about to make with his disciples.

The Scripture and the Main Question

The Cup of the New Covenant

Jesus was a wonderful teacher. Did anyone ever speak such noble words of truth? Through his preaching and teaching, Jesus spoke to us of the love and purposes of God. And yet, do you not find it interesting that, when the forces of evil conspired against him, when he had just a few more hours of life to live, on his last occasion with the disciples, Jesus chose to minister to them, not through words, but through a meal?

You and I know, from everyday life, that there are many things in this life that are simply too deep to express by mere words. "Don't tell me, show me," pleads a character in the Broadway musical, *My Fair Lady*. Words are fine, as far as words go. But for some of the most important things in life, words are not enough.

A flag, a kiss, a handshake, these are all everyday means through which we symbolize some of the deepest and most significant mysteries of our lives. Eating together is not only essential for life, it is also a revelation of the most important aspects of our lives.

People who live alone tell me that they are never so lonely as at meal times. There is something about food that cries out to be shared with others. Sharing of food is one of the most deeply intimate human acts.

Recently, in a large city, I had a meal in a crowded cafeteria. There were few free places at the tables in the cafeteria and I was forced to share the table with another person. After I arrived at the table, and began eating in silence, another person joined us. As we ate, our eyes exchanged glances. In just a few minutes, the person across the table from me asked me to pass the salt. I did, commenting on how crowded the place was. He said something back to me. The other person commented that she ate here nearly every day and had not seen this big a crowd in many months.

You know what happened. In just a few minutes we were in conversation. Here, three perfect strangers were becoming acquaintances, perhaps even on our way to becoming friends. The sharing of food does that to people. In the act of eating together, we are bound together. It is almost impossible to join someone at a table for the sharing of food and remain a stranger to that person.

Through so many different acts, Jesus bound himself in solidarity with his disciples. However, of all the acts of love that he showed us, none was more vivid than this last meal that he shared with us in the upper room. Throughout the Gospels, Jesus is reported to have been at a succession of meals. Note that, in all the other meals in the Gospel, Jesus was a guest. At this meal, Jesus serves as the host. More than that, he is not only the host, but also the *one who serves*. By his actions, he thus shows us the manner in which we, as his disciples, are to relate to the world. Even as he served others around the table, so we also are to serve.

Above all, at the table, he instituted with us a new covenant. We call our entire Christian scriptures the New Testament. All of these writings describe a new relationship between humanity and God that was instituted through Jesus. That night, in the upper room, as the cup and the bread were passed, this new covenant was made visible for us all to see and experience. God's new relationship to humanity was ratified in bread and wine.

This Is My Body

I believe that one of the great tragedies of modern life is that modern families so rarely eat together. With T.V. dinners, microwave ovens, instant breakfast, and drive-through restaurants, few families take the time to sit down together and eat. What is this doing to the American family?

Some of my most vivid memories involve time around the family dinner table. Some of the most memorable dinners that occurred in our family were on Sunday after church. All of the relatives gathered at my grandmother's house. A great rite of passage in our family was when one was old enough to sit at the big table with all of the adults. A child had to wait until one of the adults went off to the Army or to college before a place was free at the table. The oldest child moved up when a place became vacant at the table. My moving up to the big table meant that I, even though still a child, was now able to listen in on the adult conversations, to hear stories of family exploits of the past, to join in the fun of the retelling of various characters in the family. In fact, if you were to ask me, "Who is your family?" I am sure that I would have answered, "My family are those who gather around my grandmother's dinner table on Sunday." I worry about modern families who never share meals together. How are the young integrated into family life and history? Where is there a time to listen to the lives of the members of the family? How do people know that they are loved and cherished?

Through the sharing of a loaf and a cup, Jesus powerfully symbolized our membership in his new kingdom. There at the table, he taught his disciples through word and action. Even as they passed the loaf, sharing with one another, he showed them that they would have to continue to share with one another in order to survive in an often hostile world. Even as they needed food in order to live, he demonstrated that they needed the fellowship of the table if they were to survive as his people. Even as the very food on the table demonstrates that we live through the sacrifice, work, and creativity of others, so that night in the upper room, Jesus showed his disciples that his sacrifice was going to make their life possible.

Poured Out for Many

Two thousand years later, Jesus' people continue to show forth his love for us in word and deed every time we gather at the Lord's Supper. Things have changed in the church over the centuries. This great act of love and devotion has remained the constant that links us to the life and work of Jesus. When we gather at the table, Christ is mightily present among us. We experience God's love in an intense and communal way.

Do not ask me how. When the great Christian theologian John Calvin was asked to explain the Lord's Supper, how Jesus could be present among his followers today in this meal, he answered, "I would rather experience it than understand it." We do not always know precisely *how* Jesus is present in this meal. Centuries of Christian experience have testified that he is indeed present among us. When the bread is broken in his name, when the cup of wine is poured, he stands among us, even as he did that night in the upper room. Everything that happened to his disciples that night—his vivid signification of his love and sacrifice, their sense of community and union with one another, their experience of the deep mystery of his love—all of that happens to us today.

As a Protestant Christian, someone who greatly values the preaching of the word and reading of scripture, I sometimes wonder if we Protestants have perhaps overemphasized the word. Perhaps in our worship we do far too much speaking and talking and far too little acting.

Actions speak louder than words. Sometimes on Sunday, our worship has a flat, verbose quality. Too much is explained. Too much is discussed when more ought to be experienced.

The church that denies itself the power of the holy meal, the Lord's Supper, is like a family who live in the same house, but never shares meals together. If Jesus—one of the greatest speakers and masters of the word that the world has ever known—could not demonstrate his kingdom through words alone, why should we think that we could?

The prophets of Israel foretold a day when God's covenant with his people, a covenant that had been written in tablets of stone, would be written on their hearts. The Law of God would someday become so much a part of us that it would become second nature, a part of our deepest beings, written on our hearts.

The Lord's Supper, through its engagement of all of our senses, through its probing of the depths of divine mystery and human experience, is our celebration, our living covenant with God, God's writing on our heart through bread and wine, matters far too deep for mere words.

I would rather experience it than understand it.

Thus the priest has traditionally said, when the wine is poured and the bread is broken, when the sacred food on the altar is blessed and offered to the people, "The gifts of God for the people of God."

Helping Adults Become Involved

Preparing to Teach

There are many times in a church when teachers talk to people about experiences they have never had. Fortunately, today's class is different. Everyone in your class has participated, to some extent, in the celebration of the Lord's Supper. Many of them have probably wondered about the significance and longed for a more meaningful experience of this act of worship. Therefore, they will be grateful for your help in today's class. You want to move quickly from a look at Jesus' celebration of his last supper with his disciples to the church's celebration of the Lord's Supper today.

This outline should be helpful as you present today's lesson:

I. At the end of his earthly ministry, when Jesus wished to show his disciples the full significance of his work among them, he gathered them in an upper room and shared a meal.

II. There are many experiences in our lives that are too deep for words, including our experience of God's love in Jesus Christ. Therefore, signs, symbols, and sacraments such as the Lord's Supper help us to experience our relationship with God in a particularly meaningful way.

III. The Lord's Supper is a link between our everyday celebration of meals, and the deep experience of God's love that Jesus and his disciples shared in the upper room.

Read carefully "The Scripture and the Main Question" as well as the helpful information in "As You Read the Scripture." Your overall goal in this lesson is to relate the biblical material found in Matthew's account of the Last Supper to the church's celebration of Holy Communion, and to the Lord's Supper today.

As you read through this material, think about your own experiences of sharing food with other people, particularly the experience of the Lord's Supper. Illustrations from your own life will be helpful as you encourage others to share their experiences in today's class.

Introducing the Main Question

Have someone read the familiar account of the Last Supper as found in Matthew 26:17-35. Using the material in "As You Read the Scripture," give your class necessary background information on these verses, including the biblical idea of covenant and how the meal relates to covenant.

Developing the Lesson

I. At the end of his earthly ministry, when Jesus wished to show his disciples the full significance of his work among them, he gathered them in an upper room and shared a meal.

You have already begun reflection in your class on today's scripture, Matthew's account of the Last Supper. Ask your class if they can recall any other memorable meals in the Gospels. For instance, Jesus was often criticized for eating and drinking with sinners. Why do the Gospels depict Jesus at so many meals?

I have a friend who recruits executives for a major corporation. When he is recruiting a person, he always makes it a point to take that person to dinner. "You can learn more about a person at the dinner table than you can in hours of conversation across the desk."

What have members of your class learned about Jesus, by watching him at the dinner table with other people?

II. There are many experiences in our lives that are too deep for words, including our experience of God's love in Jesus Christ. Therefore, signs, symbols, and sacraments such as the Lord's Supper help us to experience our relationship with God in a particularly meaningful way.

Using the material in "The Scripture and the Main Question," lead the class in a discussion of our daily experiences of meals. In "The Scripture and the Main Question," it was suggested that family meals are some of the most deeply meaningful. Ask your group to recall favorite meals within their family.

Now ask your group: What is the most memorable meal you have ever had?

Allow people some time to think about that; perhaps you can begin by recalling your most memorable meal. For instance, a man told me once about having flunked out of college and coming back home. He wondered if he would be received back home after his failure. His mother met him at the door, saying, "I have made fried chicken for you and your favorite apple pie. We're glad to have you home." He told me that was the most memorable meal he had ever had.

As each person shares the most memorable meal, ask the class what they hear in that description. That is, what aspects of the meal made it especially meaningful? How was the meal being recounted? Was it a revelation of some deep and wonderful mystery?

By exploring the deeper significance of these everyday meals, we will be able to see better the significance of our meal with Jesus, in the Lord's Supper.

III. The Lord's Supper is a link between our everyday celebration of meals, and the deep experience of God's love that Jesus and his disciples shared in the upper room.

Ask your class to discuss their feelings about Holy Communion or the Lord's Supper (in some churches this is called the Eucharist). Is this a meaningful, or a not so meaningful act of worship for them? On a chalkboard or newsprint, list those aspects of the Lord's Supper your class finds particularly meaningful. Are there ways that your congregation's celebration of the Lord's Supper could be improved? Have they ever thought of the Lord's Supper as a meal, or is this a new idea for them?

I have sometimes said to people, when they ask what the Lord's Supper means, that "the Lord's Supper means everything that eating together means, eating together in the name of Jesus." Just as our human meals mean love, intimacy, friendship, and solidarity with one another, so does the Lord's Supper. Ask your class to list all of the meanings that we experience at the dinner table. How do these meanings in our everyday eating together around the family dinner table compare to the meaning that we experience in the Lord's Supper in our churches?

Helping Class Members Act

If your group has thought of ways in which celebrations of the Lord's Supper can be more meaningful in your church, have someone pass these ideas on to your congregation's worship committee or your pastor. End today's class by taking a prayer out of your church's service of the Lord's Supper (probably found in your congregation's hymnal) and read this prayer as a closing prayer in your class.

Planning for Next Sunday

Ask your class, Have you ever experienced rejection? What was your worst experience of rejection? Think about that in preparation for next week's lesson when we will explore Matthew's story of the rejection of Jesus.

LESSON 11   FEBRUARY 12

Experiencing Rejection

Background Scripture: Matthew 26:36-68

The Main Question

One of our most meaningful Sundays of the year at our chapel is Palm/Passion Sunday. We begin the service with the waving of palms and the commemoration of Jesus' entry into Jerusalem on Palm Sunday. But sometime during the service, we move from a celebration of Palm Sunday to a reflection on the last week of Jesus' life. We read the scripture that describes Jesus' arrest and trial, the same scripture that is designated for our lesson today. In the Common Lectionary, this is the longest scripture reading of the year. Much of the service is therefore taken up with simply reading the scripture.

The story speaks for itself. With steadily building drama, the Gospel describes how Jesus was forsaken and betrayed by his best friends, led away to stand in front of Pilate, and submitted to a sham of a trial.

The most dramatic part of this day is when, as we are reading the account of his Passion, we come to the part of the story where Pilate presents Jesus to the crowd. We station some students up in the triforium of our chapel. (We have a big, dark, neo-Gothic chapel that has a triforium, an arcade that runs along the wall of the chapel, just under the ceiling.) The students, at this point in the narrative, begin shouting, "Crucify him! Crucify him!"

Their shouts startle the congregation. However, the voices, coming as they do from within and over the congregation, make a deep impression. Those shouting voices remind us that those who cried, "Crucify Him!" came from among the people. They are *our* voices.

Jesus was rejected by a wide array of opponents. The chief priest, the governmental leaders, people like Pilate and Caiaphas. But let us remember that perhaps the most painful rejection Jesus suffered was rejection by his own people, his own disciples.

What does this mean for us, as we look at the arrest and trial of Jesus, to admit that *we* are those who have rejected Jesus? What does our rejection of Jesus tell us about ourselves in relationship to God? These are among the painful, though utterly essential questions we will be exploring in today's lesson.

Selected Scripture

King James Version	New Revised Standard Version

Matthew 26:57-68

57 And they that had laid hold on Jesus led *him* away to Caiaphas the high priest, where the scribes and the elders were assembled.

58 But Peter followed him afar off unto the high priest's palace, and went in, and sat with the servants, to see the end.

59 Now the chief priests, and elders, and all the council, sought false witness against Jesus, to put him to death;

60 But found none: yea, though many false witnesses came, *yet* found they none. At the last came two false witnesses,

61 And said, This *fellow* said, I am able to destroy the temple of God, and to build it in three days.

62 And the high priest arose, and said unto him, Answerest thou nothing? what *is it which* these witness against thee?

63 But Jesus held his peace. And the high priest answered and said unto him, I adjure thee by the living God, that thou tell us whether thou be the Christ, the Son of God.

64 Jesus saith unto him, Thou

Matthew 26:57-68

57 Those who had arrested Jesus took him to Caiaphas the high priest, in whose house the scribes and the elders had gathered. 58 But Peter was following him at a distance, as far as the courtyard of the high priest; and going inside, he sat with the guards in order to see how this would end. 59 Now the chief priests and the whole council were looking for false testimony against Jesus so that they might put him to death, 60 but they found none, though many false witnesses came forward. At last two came forward 61 and said, "This fellow said, 'I am able to destroy the temple of God and to build it in three days.' " 62 The high priest stood up and said, "Have you no answer? What is it that they testify against you?" 63 But Jesus was silent. Then the high priest said to him, "I put you under oath before the living God, tell us if you are the Messiah, the Son of God." 64 Jesus said to him, "You have said so. But I tell you,
From now on you will see the Son of Man

hast said: nevertheless I say unto you, Hereafter shall ye see the Son of man sitting on the right hand of power, and coming in the clouds of heaven.

65 Then the high priest rent his clothes, saying, He hath spoken blasphemy; what further need have we of witnesses? behold, now ye have heard his blasphemy.

66 What think ye? They answered and said, He is guilty of death.

67 Then did they spit in his face, and buffeted him; and others smote *him* with the palms of their hands,

68 Saying, Prophesy unto us, thou Christ, Who is he that smote thee?

seated at the right hand of Power and coming on the clouds of heaven."

65 Then the high priest tore his clothes and said, "He has blasphemed! Why do we still need witnesses? You have now heard his blasphemy. 66 What is your verdict?" They answered, "He deserves death." 67 Then they spat in his face and struck him; and some slapped him, 68 saying, "Prophesy to us, you Messiah! Who is it that struck you?"

Key Verses: **Then the high priest rent his clothes, saying, He hath spoken blasphemy; what further need have we of witnesses? behold, now ye have heard his blasphemy. What think ye? They answered and said, He is guilty of death.**

Key Verses: **Then the high priest tore his clothes and said, "He has blasphemed! Why do we still need witnesses? You have now heard his blasphemy. What is your verdict?" They answered, "He deserves death."**

As You Read the Scripture

Matthew 26:57-68. Matthew depicts Jesus appearing before the Jewish supreme court (which is the Sanhedrin as discussed in John 11:47f.). The Sanhedrin was made up of seventy priests, scribes, and elders. It was presided over by the high priest and had jurisdiction in all religious and theological disputes. The Roman occupation forces evidently attempted to let the Sanhedrin officiate in what the Romans regarded as strictly religious matters, while the Romans tried persons for secular offenses. Matthew mainly follows Mark's (probably) earlier account of an unusual night meeting of the Sanhedrin. After the appearance before the Sanhedrin, the Jewish officials turned the case over to Pilate, who dealt with Jesus as a political troublemaker.

Verse 58. Peter's following at a distance indicates that, while Peter has not closely identified himself with Jesus, he alone among the disciples has not fully disassociated himself from him. By inserting this comment about Peter here, it is as if Matthew wants to remind us that Jesus is betrayed, not only by some of the leaders of the Jewish people, but also by his own followers who have deserted him (see Matt. 26:56).

Verses 59-64. Matthew depicts the trial of Jesus as a one-sided, rigged jury. Jesus' earlier statements ("I am able to destroy the temple of God," v. 61; compare with Matt. 24:2; 27:40) are used against him. Jesus' statements about the temple and the Son of Man are taken out of context and used by those who do not understand Jesus' meaning. The Son of Man was a Jewish apocalyptic term (see Dan. 7:13). The Son of Man was the heavenly figure who would come to vanquish Israel's enemies.

Verses 65-68. This sham of a trial reaches a crescendo of mocking and violence. Jesus is blindfolded. His persecutors mock his prophetic claims. Jesus is a prophet in that he is obedient to God, not because he can see through the blindfold and perform other magic tricks. Throughout Matthew, Jesus' detractors have not understood who Jesus is. That misunderstanding culminates in the mocking of him at his trial.

The Scripture and the Main Question

They Laid Hands on Jesus and Seized Him

People are quite wrong who have said things such as, "The Jews killed Jesus." Jesus himself was a Jew, as well as were all of his disciples. The Jews were an occupied people and had no power to try or convict anyone. Jesus was crucified because it was said that he was "King of the Jews" (Matt. 27:15-26). As a king, the Romans saw in Jesus a threat to their power. However, it is true that by the time the Gospels were written, there does appear to be a tendency to shift the responsibility of Jesus' death away from the Romans, such as Pilate, and onto the Jews.

According to Roman law, a private accuser would charge someone with a crime. The Roman governor had considerable freedom in deciding how to treat the accused. In accordance with this procedure, Jesus is brought before Pilate's tribunal (Matt. 27:19). Matthew says that Pilate sat on the judgment seat and that among Jesus' accusers were the chief priests and elders. Jesus did not appear to have been charged with breaking a specific law, but rather with seditious activity.

Matthew indicates that Jesus did not try to defend himself. He is portrayed as the Suffering Servant of Isaiah 53. He is silent before his accusers (Isa. 53:7). In a Roman trial, failure to present a defense brought an automatic verdict of guilty.

But perhaps we should not focus so much on the actual trial of Jesus. Matthew depicts a number of somber events preceding this trial. Among the most disturbing is Matthew's account of how the disciples responded to the arrest of Jesus. Jesus gathers his disciples at Gethsemane (Matt. 26:30-56). Jesus earlier predicted to his disciples, "You will all become deserters because of me this night; for it is written, 'I will strike the shepherd, and the sheep of the flock will be scattered'" (Matt. 26:31). We do not have to wait for that prediction to be fulfilled. Not only do all of his disciples fall asleep while he is at prayer in Gethsemane, but also they desert him when the soldiers come.

Sometimes we tell the story of Jesus' death as if Judas were the only one who betrayed him. Judas, it is true, did turn Jesus over to the authorities. But Matthew is quite clear that Judas was not the only betrayer of Jesus. When the soldiers come, Matthew says, "Then all the disciples deserted him and fled" (26:56). *All.*

To my mind, this is one of the most somber and horrifying verses in the entire account of events of this horrible night. We know why some of the religious authorities rejected Jesus. They saw in Jesus a threat to their authority. We can also imagine why the Roman officials rejected Jesus. They saw Jesus as a dangerous revolutionary, a threat to their hold on Judea.

But how do we explain the rejection by his own disciples? Here were the twelve best friends of Jesus. These were the ones who had followed Jesus throughout his ministry, who had heard his word, who had observed his acts of healing, who had known him in the most intimate and personal way. He had loved them, ministered to them, given them a role in his work. And when the going got rough, as Matthew says, "Then all the disciples deserted him and fled" (26:56). *All.*

False Testimony Against Jesus

Need we be so hard on the disciples? Can not each of us understand how easy it is to reject Jesus? We like to say to ourselves, "If I had been there, I would have certainly stuck up for Jesus."

In our better moments, we know that to be a lie. We are no worse, but we are no better than his first disciples. You and I have not had the opportunity to betray Jesus unto death at the hands of the Roman authorities, but we have certainly had other ample opportunities to reject him.

He asks us to be courageous, to speak his words to the world. But when we are confronted by social disapproval, the jeers of others, or even minor discomfort, we quickly become silent.

I know a man who was on his way up in the banking industry. While he was on his way up he discovered, quite by accident, that one of his colleagues was engaging in some unscrupulous, and possibly even illegal, banking practices. He was shocked that this man whom he admired would bend or break the rules. He knew that he should confront him, or at least go and tell someone else. However, he had become personal friends with him. More than that, this man was his superior in the company.

After some agonizing over what he should do, he decided to do nothing. He knew that by blowing the whistle on this man's activities, he could endanger his own position in the bank.

A couple of months later, the man's activities were discovered by others and he was fired. But his silent accuser was left with the sobering realization that, when the time came for him to be honest, to be courageous and moral, he had done and said nothing. It was as if he, like those disciples of Jesus, had fled into the darkness when the going got rough.

I believe that the story of Jesus' betrayal by his own disciples would send a chill down this man's spine. In not speaking up for what was right, and not showing courage in the face of wrong done by others, he showed that he was willing to reject what he knew in his heart to be right.

Have not all of us been in similar positions?

Then All the Disciples Deserted Him and Fled

My colleague at Duke, Dan Via, distinguished New Testament scholar, says that, when we read scripture, it is a bit like looking through the glass of a window. When we first look through the window, we see outside, through the window, to the world at large. The glass in the window enables us to see through the window to what is beyond the window.

However, if we keep looking through the window, we sometimes see the reflection of our own face in the window. The image we see in the glass is ourselves.

Our reading of scripture can be a similar experience. At first we read Matthew's account of the arrest, trial, and crucifixion of Jesus and we see through the story a realistic picture of what often happens in this world. The good suffer and the innocent are made to pay for their innocence. Yet if we keep looking at this story, we may be horrified to discover that, as we look at these betrayers of Jesus, we see ourselves. Their faces are our faces.

In the story of the arrest, trial, and crucifixion of Jesus, we meet many different forms of rejection of Jesus. The stories become for us a kind of mirror, a very painful mirror, for there is no rejection of Jesus that we encounter in this story, which we have not first encountered in our own hearts.

Helping Adults Become Involved

Preparing to Teach

Carefully read the material in "The Main Question" and "The Scripture and the Main Question," noting ideas and illustrations as you read. Remember, as you prepare, that the main question before you is: How does the rejection of Jesus relate to our times of rejection? If you plan to use hymns in your lesson, be sure to have copies of the suggested hymns or enough hymnals for your class.

This outline should be helpful to you as you lead the lesson:

    I. Jesus suffered rejection by both his disciples and the leaders of the people.

   II. Rejection is an expected, though painful, aspect of everyday human life.

  III. In the account of Jesus' trial, we see our own faces. *We* are among the betrayers of Jesus.

  IV. Remembrance of our betrayals of Jesus can lead us to a more honest assessment of our relationship to him.

Keep "The Main Question" in your mind throughout your planning of the lesson.

Introducing the Main Question

From your own experience, or from the experience of someone you know, retell an occasion when rejection occurred. For instance, I once was rejected by a graduate school, even though a number of professors there had told me I was to be accepted. I could not help feeling betrayed and deceived. Ask your class what their feelings are when someone betrays them. Write these feelings on a chalkboard or newsprint.

Developing the Lesson

I. Jesus suffered rejection by both his disciples and the leaders of the people.

Have someone in the class read aloud today's scripture, Matthew 26:57-68, the account of the trial of Jesus before the Sanhedrin. Ask the class to try to put themselves in Jesus' place during these proceedings. What would be their feelings? Before class, you might break up this scripture into various parts, assigning roles to different members of the class to read as a dramatic reading. The voices in this passage are those of a narrator (Matthew), a witness, the high priest, Jesus, and members of the crowd.

II. Rejection is an expected, though painful, aspect of everyday human life.

Ask your class, What were the aspects of Jesus' life and message that led to his rejection by many people? His criticism of the establishment, his espousal of new ideas, and his welcoming of sinners are some of the possible reasons.

What are the aspects of the lives and message of Jesus' followers (disciples like us!) that might also lead to our rejection by others? Should Christians expect to be popular in the world's eyes? Should Christians be surprised when they are mocked or rejected by today's world? Discuss these questions with your group. It will help for you to have done some thinking about these questions before you lead the discussion. Your ideas can be a catalyst to get the conversation going.

III. In the account of Jesus' trial, we see our own faces. We are among the betrayers of Jesus.

As we have noted, Matthew's account of the arrest and trial of Jesus makes clear that not only the religious and governmental officials rejected Jesus. His own disciples also fled into the darkness. Read or tell the opening story in "The Main Question" to your class. In what way can it be said of us that *we* are those who continue to betray Jesus?

IV. Remembrance of our betrayals of Jesus can lead us to a more honest assessment of our relationship to him.

Many of our favorite hymns, many hymns that have been sung in church during this Lenten season, speak of our complicity in the death of Jesus. Sometimes poetry, such as the poetry of these beloved hymns, speaks better to the complexity of our relationship to God than does our prose. Refer your group to hymns such as "Alas! and Did My Savior Bleed"; "O Love Divine, What Hast Thou Done?"; "Were You There?"; "Ah, Holy Jesus"; and "O Sacred Head Now Wounded." Read aloud selections from these hymns that speak to the issue of Jesus' rejection and our continuing rejection of him and his way. What new insights does your group receive by reflection on these hymns?

Helping Class Members Act

If your class has musical accompaniment, sing one of the hymns that we have discussed as a time of self-examination and reflection to end our thoughts on Jesus' rejection and our rejection. Or ask the class to read aloud one of the hymns as a unison prayer.

Planning for Next Sunday

Not only was Jesus rejected, but also he suffered. Ask the class to think about how they would respond to a person who asked them: If God is good and powerful, why do human beings suffer? This question will begin our preparation for next Sunday's class on the suffering of Jesus.

Suffering for Others

Background Scripture: Matthew 27:1-61

The Main Question

No one ever denied that she had suffered terribly. In her mid-thirties, she had given birth to her first and only child. He was a beautiful, healthy son whom she adored completely. She and her husband, though persons of modest financial means, provided a wonderful home and many advantages for their little boy.

However, during his teenage years, as sometimes happens, something terrible happened to the young boy. He became sullen, moody, and unapproachable. When he was fifteen, we learned that he had become involved in drugs. Many of us said that he had become a part of the wrong group, that his drug dependency was the result of hanging around with the wrong crowd.

Of course, that may be true. However, there is no denying the fact that he himself had decided to guide his life in a terribly wrong direction.

She prayed incessantly for his recovery. She spent many hours with her pastor, seeking help for her son's terrible problem. She and her husband paid for expensive therapy and a variety of treatments.

Nothing seemed to work. The boy became more heavily addicted. By the time he was eighteen, he had dropped out of school, and was virtually nonfunctional in life because of the drugs.

In order to finance his heavy drug habit, he became involved in crime—petty burglaries first, followed by armed robbery. After the police arrested him during an armed robbery, he was sent to prison for ten years.

Needless to say, all of this took its toll on the mother. Not only was her emotional health shattered, but also her physical health as well. She looked twice her age. Constant worry about her son's condition had broken her.

Everyone told her that she had done her best, that she should attempt to let go of her son, and go on with her life. Even her pastor told her that she must somehow overcome her grief about her son's decline. And yet, this mother could not let go. She continued to suffer. She wrote him every day when he was in prison and continued constantly to pray for him.

Was her suffering worth it? What good does the suffering of a mother do in the case of such a wayward child?

All I know is that, when I met this man, now middle-aged, released from prison, free of his drug dependency, and now a useful member of society (he is a teacher at a school for delinquent youth), he told me, "I would have never made it without my mother. Greater than any suffering I was going through, was the suffering that I caused her. One day, that fact came through to me and I started on the way back to life. My mother's pain saved me."

Suffering of any kind is usually regarded by us as an unmitigated evil. But is it possible that true good can arise even out of suffering? Do you believe in vicarious suffering? That is, do you believe that the suffering of one person can be the way for another's healing?

Selected Scripture

King James Version

Matthew 27:27-44

27 Then the soldiers of the governor took Jesus into the common hall, and gathered unto him the whole band of *soldiers.*

28 And they stripped him, and put on him a scarlet robe.

29 And when they had platted a crown of thorns, they put *it* upon his head, and a reed in his right hand: and they bowed the knee before him, and mocked him, saying, Hail, King of the Jews!

30 And they spit upon him, and took the reed, and smote him on the head.

31 And after that they had mocked him, they took the robe off from him, and put his own raiment on him, and led him way to crucify *him.*

32 And as they came out, they found a man of Cyrene, Simon by name: him they compelled to bear his cross.

33 And when they were come unto a place called Golgotha, that is to say, a place of a skull,

34 They gave him vinegar to drink mingled with gall: and when he had tasted *thereof,* he would not drink.

35 And they crucified him, and parted his garments, casting lots: that it might be fulfilled which was spoken by the prophet, They parted my garments among them, and upon my vesture did they cast lots.

36 And sitting down they watched him there;

37 And set up over his head his accusation written, THIS IS JESUS THE KING OF THE JEWS.

38 Then were there two thieves crucified with him, one on the right hand, and another on the left.

39 And they that passed by reviled him, wagging their heads,

New Revised Standard Version

Matthew 27:27-44

27 Then the soldiers of the governor took Jesus into the governor's headquarters, and they gathered the whole cohort around him. 28 They stripped him and put a scarlet robe on him, 29 and after twisting some thorns into a crown, they put it on his head. They put a reed in his right hand and knelt before him and mocked him, saying, "Hail, King of the Jews!" 30 They spat on him, and took the reed and struck him on the head. 31 After mocking him, they stripped him of the robe and put his own clothes on him. Then they led him away to crucify him.

32 As they went out, they came upon a man from Cyrene named Simon; they compelled this man to carry his cross. 33 And when they came to a place called Golgotha (which means Place of a Skull), 34 they offered him wine to drink, mixed with gall; but when he tasted it, he would not drink it. 35 And when they had crucified him, they divided his clothes among themselves by casting lots; 36 then they sat down there and kept watch over him. 37 Over his head they put the charge against him, which read, "This is Jesus, the King of the Jews."

38 Then two bandits were crucified with him, one on his right and one on his left. 39 Those who passed by derided him, shaking their heads and saying, "You who would destroy

40 And saying, Thou that destroyest the temple, and buildest *it* in three days, save thyself. If thou be the Son of God, come down from the cross.

41 Likewise also the chief priests mocking *him*, with the scribes and elders, said,

42 He saved others; himself he cannot save. If he be the King of Israel, let him now come down from the cross, and we will believe him.

43 He trusted in God; let him deliver him now, if he will have him: for he said, I am the Son of God.

44 The thieves also, which were crucified with him, cast the same in his teeth.

the temple and build it in three days, save yourself! If you are the Son of God, come down from the cross." 41 In the same way the chief priests also, along with the scribes and elders, were mocking him, saying, 42 "He saved others; he cannot save himself. He is the King of Israel; let him come down from the cross now, and we will believe in him. 43 He trusts in God; let God deliver him now, if he wants to; for he said, 'I am God's Son.'" 44 The bandits who were crucified with him also taunted him in the same way.

Key Verses: **And they that passed by reviled him, wagging their heads, And saying, Thou that destroyest the temple, and buildest *it* in three days, save thyself. If thou be the Son of God, come down from the cross.**

Key Verses: **Those who passed by derided him, shaking their heads and saying, "You who would destroy the temple and build it in three days, save yourself! If you are the Son of God, come down from the cross."**

As You Read the Scripture

Matthew 27:27-44. It appears that Matthew derived his basic narrative from Mark and embellished it to bring out Jesus' true greatness as King of the Jews. To an earlier account of the Crucifixion, Matthew has added details from the Psalms and the Servant Songs of Second Isaiah. Jesus' cry from the Cross (27:46) is not mentioned by Luke or John. Matthew speaks of gall (v. 34; Ps. 69:21) in place of Mark's myrrh. Certainly Matthew has made the narrative more miraculous, such as the dream of Pilate's wife (Matthew speaks elsewhere of revelation through dreams, see 1:20), and the saints risen from their graves. Most important for our lesson today is Matthew's focus on Jesus' obedience to his Father's will, his dignity in facing rejection and torture, and the centurion's confession that he is Son of God. Mark's insight, still visible in Matthew, is that the full meaning of *Son of God* is shown when Jesus has finally suffered (see Matt. 17:21).

Verse 27. A cohort numbered about five hundred soldiers. Pilate alone had the power to condemn Jesus, but the Gospel writers appear to attempt to excuse him so far as possible (Mark 15:14; Luke 23:13-25). John 19:12 suggests that Pilate was threatened with a report to the emperor that he had released a man who had been found guilty of high treason.

Verse 30. Compare with Isaiah 50:6: "I gave my back to those who struck me . . . ; I did not hide my face from insult and spitting."

Verse 32. The actual word for *cross* here does not denote the entire cross, but the crossbeam that was to be nailed to a pole or tree (see "Crucifixion, Method of," in the *Interpreter's Dictionary of the Bible*, Abingdon, p. 199f.).

Verse 34. Gall is perhaps mentioned to remind us of Psalm 69:21, where the Hebrew word for gall means *poison.* Gall is possibly the myrrh of Mark 15:23.

Verse 35. Compare with Psalm 22:18 and John 19:23.

Verse 37. The sign is meant to be an indication of the offense for which Jesus has been crucified. He is crucified because the Romans perceived in Jesus a threat to their power, a pretender to the throne and a revolutionary.

Verse 39. Compare with Psalm 22:7.

Verse 42. Note that he is here called King of Israel (not King of the Jews), a title of honor, suggesting the eschatological (end of history) restoration of the nation. The taunt calls Jesus to come down from the Cross and be victorious. In Matthew's interpretation of Jesus as King, only his death can establish the true Israel.

Verse 43. Compare with Psalm 22:8.

The Scripture and the Main Question

They Led Him Away to Crucify Him

When all is said and done, we actually know very little about the life of Jesus. We know a few facts surrounding his birth, but we know virtually nothing about him until he is in his early thirties. The Gospels describe only a few years of his adult life, those couple of years of active ministry before his death. One would be hard pressed to write a full biography of Jesus.

However, one thing we do know for certain—Jesus suffered. At the beginning of his ministry, he came into conflict with the governing authorities—both the political and the religious authorities. When he preached in his own hometown synagogue in Nazareth, the once adoring congregation was transformed into a murderous mob. For every one who heard him gladly, many more were repulsed by him and his message. In the end, even his own disciples, those who were closest to him, rejected him and fled into the night. After his arrest by the Roman soldiers, he was submitted to a humiliating trial in which they beat him, spit upon him, and mocked him. Finally, he was led away to be crucified. Surely crucifixion is one of the cruelest, most horrendous forms of death ever devised by the evil imagination of humanity.

Even Josephus, a second-century Jewish historian, records the trial and death of Jesus. There is much about Jesus' life and work that Josephus refuses to believe. While Josephus rejects most of the claims made about Jesus by his followers, Josephus reports as an undeniable and fully-established historical fact that Jesus was crucified, suffered, and died.

Here is the way Josephus describes the death and significance of Jesus: "About this time there lived Jesus, a wise man. He was the one who wrought surprising feats and was a teacher of such people as accept the truth gladly. He won over many Jews and Greeks. When Pilate, upon hearing him accused by men of the highest standing amongst us, had condemned him to be crucified, those who had in the first place come to love him did not give up their affection for him. And the tribe of Christians, so called after him, have still to this day not disappeared." (Quoted by John Dominic Crossan, *The Historical Jesus* [New York: Harper, 1991], p. 373.)

The earliest confession of faith in Christ is that made by Paul in First Corinthians. It is even earlier than the text from Matthew that we have been studying: "For I handed on to you as of first importance what I in turn had received: that Christ died for our sins in accordance with the scriptures" (1 Cor. 15:3). All of the early sources agree: *Jesus suffered.*

They Spat upon Him, They Struck Him on the Head

It is important for us to recall that the suffering and death of Jesus appear to be a great embarrassment for many of his early followers. We need not be surprised by their embarrassment. After all, imagine how you would have felt. Here was the man in whom you had put all of your hope, the one whom you believed to be the Messiah. And look how his ministry had ended. He was rejected by all of the important, wise, and powerful people. He suffered a brutal and humiliating trial. And then he was put to death by a form of punishment so horrible that it was reserved for only the worst of common criminals.

In the history of Christian art, it is interesting to note that there are absolutely no depictions of Jesus on the cross until well after the fifth century. For nearly five hundred years, Christian artists refused to portray that scene. In fact, there are very few representations of the cross before that date. It is as if these early Christian artists were embarrassed to show their beloved Jesus in such a humiliating, vulnerable, and lowly position.

I remember as a boy, hearing a sermon in our church in which the preacher said, "We are not like those Catholics. We do not have crucifixes in our church, portrayals of a bloody body of Jesus hanging on the cross. Our crosses are empty! Our Jesus is not continuing to suffer, he has been raised from the dead and reigns in glory!"

While of course we do believe that Jesus has been raised from the dead and does reign in glory, even the risen Christ has nail prints in his hands. Easter did not somehow erase the suffering and tragedy of the Cross. Easter helped put the Cross in perspective, but it did not remove its scandal and offense. Against any who would claim that Jesus did not *really* suffer, that the Cross was only an *apparent* episode of pain, the church has maintained that Jesus really did suffer on the cross.

One of the earliest heresies to be condemned by the church was the heresy of *Docetism.* The word comes from the Greek word meaning *to seem.* This heresy maintains that Jesus, if he was the son of God, could not really have suffered. He must have only *seemed* to suffer. Who could imagine the great, powerful, and wonderful God, stooping so low as to suffer at the hands of evil people?

The church had the good sense to know that, if we remove the pain and suffering from Jesus, we have removed a major linkage of God with our lives. You and I do not live in some ethereal realm. We live here on earth. Each of us is born in pain. Someone must suffer to bring us to birth. Throughout our lives, we are the victims of painful episodes. Not all of the pain that we suffer is physical pain. Sometimes we suffer emotional and spiritual pain that we call anguish.

Nowhere did God promise a world free from pain or lives that could be lived without suffering. However, God does give us a way through suffering. On the cross, God joined us in our suffering and pain. He suffered not only for us, but also with us. That means, whenever we suffer pain or suffering we can look to the Cross. We can look to the Cross and remember that, no matter how terrible our pain is, God has been there with us, in the suffering, in the pain. There is no tragedy that we endure, no humiliation we suffer, no anguish that we bear that he had not borne before us. He has been there.

Suffered Under Pontius Pilate, Crucified, Dead and Buried

Most of the Gospels, Matthew included, spend most of their space describing the arrest, the trial, and crucifixion of Jesus. This is particularly true of Matthew. Note the large number of chapters Matthew devotes to these few days in Jesus' life. It is as if all of the stories and episodes of Jesus' previous life are seen by Matthew as leading up to this moment. We have noted, in our previous weeks' lessons, how the Cross cast a shadow over nearly every event of Jesus' life in Matthew. It is as if, in all of the earlier controversies, you can see the storm clouds gathering, storm clouds that will break in a terrible tempest over a place called Golgotha.

I believe that Matthew wants to make clear the Cross is central to understanding Jesus. The Cross was not merely some unfortunate episode in the life of Jesus that was quickly overcome by Easter. The Cross is the central fact of his life, that horrible event toward which his life was moving every moment of his life. Because Matthew has given so much space to this event, I believe that Matthew wanted to tell us that the cross, and the suffering of Jesus on it, has central, continuing significance for Christians today.

As someone has said, to be near to the heart of God, is to be near to a heart that is breaking. All of the instances of human evil that nailed Jesus on the cross continue to flourish today. Military power, governmental oppression, religious arrogance, insensitivity to the plight of the poor, the hungry, and the homeless—all of these continue today. And these are the factors that caused the suffering of Jesus. If they caused his suffering then, surely they must cause his continued suffering. To be near to the heart of God is surely to be near to the breaking heart.

Wherein is our hope? In our times of suffering, we can remember that suffering and pain are not unexpected, meaningless episodes in life. Suffering and pain are essential parts of life. Whenever we suffer, we can look at the cross, we can recall the story of Jesus' dark hours, and remember—*he has been there.*

Helping Adults Become Involved

Preparing to Teach

This lesson focuses on suffering and what the cross of Jesus, as well as Matthew's story of Jesus' trial and crucifixion, mean for our suffering today. As you lead today's lesson, the following outline should be helpful:

I. Suffering is a predictable, essential aspect of human life.
II. Throughout his life, Jesus suffered. His suffering culminates in the horrible suffering and pain of the Crucifixion.
III. Our times of suffering need not only be endured, but also can be given meaning, when placed within the context of the suffering of Jesus.
IV. Christians must not somehow explain away, or overlook, the significance of the Cross for suffering today.

Read carefully "The Scripture and the Main Question." The material in "As You Read the Scripture" will be helpful for your verse-by-verse study of today's scripture from Matthew. Keep the ideas, insights, and suggestions in these sections in your mind as you plan today's lesson. Follow the lesson outline in organizing your presentation of today's material.

Remember to obtain newspaper and magazine stories of suffering people before coming to class. You may also want to locate a book of Christian art in your church or town library for use in the discussion of point two in the outline.

Introducing the Main Question

Introduce today's lesson by leading your class in an opening discussion of the nature of pain in human life. In "The Scripture and the Main Question" the point is made that there are at least two categories of suffering—we suffer physical pain, but we also suffer emotional and spiritual pain, anguish. Collect newspaper and magazine articles that describe instances of suffering people today. You may find articles about people living through incurable illnesses or stories of lives that have been wrecked through crime or drug dependency. Present these articles in brief form to your class. Many in your class may have read these stories and can relate to them.

Ask your class: Which type of pain is the most difficult for us to bear—(1.) Physical suffering or (2.) emotional and spiritual suffering?

Developing the Lesson

Retell, in your own words, the story of the suffering mother that is found in "The Main Question." Ask your class if they have known parents who have suffered like this. Some may wish to share these memories with the group. This reflection will help you to make the first point in today's lesson:

I. Suffering is a predictable, essential aspect of human life.
Ask the group to try and imagine human life with absolutely no suffering. What sort of life would it be? Does suffering ever have positive benefits? For instance, in a world totally without pain, would humanity ever be prodded to create and to explore or would we be completely passive? Sometimes we learn from suffering, from our pain teaching us to avoid mistakes.

II. Throughout his life, Jesus suffered. His suffering culminates in the horrible suffering and pain of the Crucifixion.
Ask someone to read part of today's scripture from Matthew's account of Jesus' trial and crucifixion. Using the background material that is found in "The Scripture and the Main Question," lead your class in a discussion of the suffering of Jesus. You may want them to discuss Docetism and the heresy that it represents. Is the idea of a Jesus who suffers difficult for modern Christians to believe? Why do we resist the notion that Jesus suffered as we must suffer?

If you can locate a book of Christian art in your church or town library, share with your group paintings that depict the crucifixion of Christ. Ask your group: What feelings or impressions are evoked in your mind as you look at these pictures of the Cross?

Can your group think of occasions in Jesus' life, before his Cross, when Jesus suffered? (When his family and friends misunderstood him, when the religious authorities condemned him, etc.)

SECOND QUARTER

III. Our times of suffering need not only be endured, but also can be given meaning when placed within the context of the suffering of Jesus.

Now explore the meaning of the Cross for the suffering encountered in human life. Ask the class: Have you ever experienced a time of suffering when your knowledge of God's suffering in Jesus was a help to you? Discuss together how the Cross is a comfort to us. The material toward the end of "The Scripture and the Main Question" that asserts "He has been there" should be helpful to you in leading this discussion.

Ask the class: What if Jesus had lived until a ripe old age and had died peacefully in his sleep rather than dying as he did on a cross? What difference would it make to those of us who follow Jesus today?

IV. Christians must not somehow explain away, or overlook, the significance of the Cross for suffering today.

The lesson makes the point that Jesus' suffering was indeed real suffering. How does honesty about the real suffering of Jesus help us to be honest about our times of pain?

Helping Class Members Act

Refer back to the newspaper clippings with which you opened the class. What might you, as a Christian, thinking of the cross of Jesus, say to the people described in these news stories if you were trying to comfort them? Here is where theology of the cross of Christ really makes a difference, as we are trying to be honest about the pain of others and to comfort them in their suffering.

Planning for Next Sunday

The cross of Christ, while central to our faith, is not the last chapter. Easter is the summit of our faith, the fountain from which all our faith flows. Ask people: What difference does it make to you, as you go about this coming week, that God raised Jesus from the dead?

LESSON 13   FEBRUARY 26

Follow the Leader

Background Scripture: Matthew 27:62–28:20

The Main Question

A worse tragedy could hardly have been imagined. She experienced every parent's nightmare. In the middle of the night, there was a dreaded telephone call.

"Mrs. Smith?" the unfamiliar voice said.

"Yes, I am Mrs. Smith," she said to the strange, official-sounding voice.

"Mrs. Smith, I really hate to have to make this phone call, but it is part of my job. Mrs. Smith, do you have a son named John?"

"Yes," she said, fearing the worst.

"Mrs. Smith, your son is dead. He has been killed in a tragic accident. He was at this railroad crossing, it was raining hard, perhaps he didn't see. His car was struck by the train."

Those were the only words she remembered. That telephone call began the worst year of her life. Her beloved son, a senior in high school, returning home from a party, probably with the windows rolled up in his car, probably with the radio on full blast, did not hear the warning from the train horn. He was killed instantly, his young life snuffed out in great tragedy.

Who would have blamed her if that would have been the end of the story? Who would have thought it odd if her life had descended downhill from this point, descending down into the oblivion of despair, anger, hurt, and torment?

Yet, this was not the end of the story. After some days of terrible torment, she began to focus her grief. The railroad crossing, like many in her state, had no electronic warning device. Motorists were totally dependent on being able to hear the warning blast from the approaching locomotive.

She went to work, focusing her anguish and grief into a program to change the laws of her state so that electronic warning signals with flashing lights and ringing bells would be mandatory at all major railway crossings in her state. She contacted other persons who had been similarly victimized. From out of her home, she formed a grass-roots organization that brought together all sorts of people who were concerned about this problem. Within three years, after much hard work, a law was passed in her state making mandatory the warning lights and bells that might have saved her son.

I tell you, this is an Easter story, an account of someone who was able to wrench life out of death, a testimonial to the power of God to work good even in the face of horrible evil.

Christians are those who believe that, not only was Jesus raised from the dead on Easter morning, but we were raised as well. Just as life overcame death in the resurrection of Jesus, so are we promised that, in our own tragedies, life will triumph.

How is it possible for life to come from death, goodness to arise from tragedy? That is the key question behind today's lesson. Today's lesson answers these questions by urging us to follow the leader—following the risen Christ from death into life.

Selected Scripture

King James Version	New Revised Standard Version
Matthew 28:1-10, 16-20	*Matthew 28:1-10, 16-20*
1 In the end of the sabbath, as it began to dawn toward the first *day* of the week, came Mary Magdalene and the other Mary to see the sepulchre.	1 After the sabbath, as the first day of the week was dawning, Mary Magdalene and the other Mary went to see the tomb. 2 And suddenly there was a great earthquake; for an angel of the Lord, descending from
2 And, behold, there was a great	

earthquake: for the angel of the Lord descended from heaven, and came and rolled back the stone from the door, and sat upon it.

3 His countenance was like lightning, and his raiment white as snow:

4 And for fear of him the keepers did shake, and became as dead *men*.

5 And the angel answered and said unto the women, Fear not ye: for I know that ye seek Jesus, which was crucified.

6 He is not here: for he is risen, as he said. Come, see the place where the Lord lay.

7 And go quickly, and tell his disciples that he is risen from the dead; and, behold, he goeth before you into Galilee; there shall ye see him: lo, I have told you.

8 And they departed quickly from the sepulchre with fear and great joy; and did run to bring his disciples word.

9 And as they went to tell his disciples, behold, Jesus met them, saying, All hail. And they came and held him by the feet, and worshipped him.

10 Then said Jesus unto them, Be not afraid: go tell my brethren that they go into Galilee, and there shall they see me.

....

16 Then the eleven disciples went away into Galilee, into a mountain where Jesus had appointed them.

17 And when they saw him, they worshipped him: but some doubted.

18 And Jesus came and spake unto them, saying, All power is given unto me in heaven and in earth.

19 Go ye therefore, and teach all nations, baptizing them in the name of the Father, and of the Son, and of the Holy Ghost:

20 Teaching them to observe all things whatsoever I have commanded you: and, lo, I am with you alway, *even* unto the end of the world. Amen.

heaven, came and rolled back the stone and sat on it. 3 His appearance was like lightning, and his clothing white as snow. 4 For fear of him the guards shook and became like dead men. 5 But the angel said to the women, "Do not be afraid; I know that you are looking for Jesus who was crucified. 6 He is not here; for he has been raised, as he said. Come, see the place where he lay. 7 Then go quickly and tell his disciples, 'He has been raised from the dead, and indeed he is going ahead of you to Galilee; there you will see him.' This is my message for you." 8 So they left the tomb quickly with fear and great joy, and ran to tell his disciples. 9 Suddenly Jesus met them and said, "Greetings!" And they came to him, took hold of his feet, and worshiped him. 10 Then Jesus said to them, "Do not be afraid; go and tell my brothers to go to Galilee; there they will see me."

....

16 Now the eleven disciples went to Galilee, to the mountain to which Jesus had directed them. 17 When they saw him, they worshiped him; but some doubted. 18 And Jesus came and said to them, "All authority in heaven and on earth has been given to me. 19 Go therefore and make disciples of all nations, baptizing them in the name of the Father and of the Son and of the Holy Spirit, 20 and teaching them to obey everything that I have commanded you. And remember, I am with you always, to the end of the age."

Key Verses: Go ye therefore, and teach all nations, baptizing them in the name of the Father, and of the Son, and of the Holy Ghost: Teaching them to observe all things whatsoever I have commanded you: and, lo, I am with you alway, *even* unto the end of the world. Amen.

Key Verses: Go therefore and make disciples of all nations, baptizing them in the name of the Father and of the Son and of the Holy Spirit, and teaching them to obey everything that I have commanded you. And remember, I am with you always, to the end of the age.

As You Read the Scripture

Matthew 28:1-10, 16-20. The story takes place on the first day of the Jewish work week, in other words, the day when everyday, workaday life resumes. We thus have the impression that the disciples are all going back to business as usual, back to the ordinary and the expected, after the violent weekend.

Verse 1. Note that *women* went out to the tomb at dawn. Where were the men? The women are courageous to be out at this hour after the events of the past week.

Verses 2-3. The earthquake, lightning, and angel are all Matthew's way of underscoring the dramatic, shocking, unexpected quality of the events that are occurring.

Verses 4-5. The soldiers, representatives of the political powers-that-be, the forces of evil who have been in control up to this point, now have their turn to shake with fear. When the angel, the representative of God, speaks, the angel speaks not to the soldiers, but to the women. God is taking control of events, speaking to those who previously have been powerless and defeated.

Verses 8-10. The women, the voiceless ones, are now commissioned by the angel to "go and tell" (v. 10). They are thus commissioned to be the first bearers of the good news of Easter.

Verses 16-20. At a mountain (recalling Moses receiving the Commandments on Mt. Sinai), the disciples all see the risen Christ who commissions them as his representatives, giving them authority to go, to tell, and to make other disciples. In other words, the very authority that Jesus had to make disciples, is hereby given to his disciples. As you lead in today's lesson, you might notice that, even after Easter, even after encountering the risen Christ, "some doubted" (v. 17).

The Scripture and the Main Question

What Do We Do with Tragedy?

St. Augustine, in the aftermath of the early barbarian invasions of the city of Rome, pondered the brute question: If Christians serve and worship the true God, why did they suffer during the barbarian invasions? This was a tough question for Augustine because anybody could see that, when the barbarians sacked Rome, raping and pillaging their way through the city, Christians suffered just as much as pagans. Why did their God not protect them?

Augustine, pondering this deep question, came to the conclusion that, "Christians do not differ from pagans in the ills that befall them. Rather, Christians differ in what they do with the ills that befall them."

Life is full of suffering and tragedy. Illness, pain, sickness, and death afflict Christians just as much as any other people. Yet, in the face of life's inevitable pain, Christians do have a very different perspective. We approach the difficulties and tragedies that beset us in life from the perspective of Easter, from the viewpoint of the empty tomb of Jesus. That makes all the difference.

St. Paul spoke of Jesus as the "pioneer and perfecter of our faith" (Heb. 12:2). Jesus really is the pioneer who blazes the trail ahead of us. There is no suffering, no pain or death that we suffer that he did not suffer before us. When we walk through the "valley of the shadow of death" (Ps. 23) we can take comfort in knowing that he has been there before us. He has led the way, been our leader in how to suffer with dignity and fidelity.

Yet there is more. He has not only preceded us into death, but also into life. In rising from the tomb, Jesus demonstrated what God has in store for us. God's purposes may be temporarily hindered, but the resurrection of Jesus is an affirmation that God's purposes will never be utterly defeated. Jesus shows us the way.

Victory of Life over Death

Today's scripture (Matt. 28) tells the story of Jesus' resurrection. But it is clearly not just a story of something that happened to Jesus alone. The story of the Resurrection is the story of how Jesus returned to his disheartened followers, how he comforted them in their grief and how he commissioned them to go into all the world and tell the story of what had happened to them.

A rather remarkable miracle is occurring before our eyes in Matthew 28. These ordinary, ragtag followers are being miraculously transformed into courageous disciples. It is a miracle equal to that of Jesus' rising from the tomb on Easter. Perhaps we ought to say that the real miracle of Easter is not simply the resurrection of Jesus, but rather the raising of the church! Those who once were nobodies now explode into the whole world with the authority of Christ to baptize and to teach, to make disciples of all nations (Matt. 28:18-20).

How do we know the Resurrection to be true? Not only do we know on the basis of Matthew's testimony here in chapter 28. We also know on the basis of the church—that living, breathing, witnessing group of followers who have been called by Jesus from death to life. The church, still exploding into the whole world two thousand years after Jesus' resurrection, is the living, breathing proof that Easter is real, that the living God really does have power to bring forth life from death, victory from defeat.

The church is properly known as "Easter People." Each of us, in our own attempts faithfully to follow Jesus, are persons of Easter. If Christ had not come back to us, if we had not experienced Easter within each of our lives, in the way goodness does arise out of badness, life is able to come from death, then all our talk about resurrection and the power of God would be in vain.

I therefore agree with the Christian writer, Frederick Buechner, when he says of Easter, "The earliest reference to the Resurrection is Saint Paul's, and he makes no mention of an empty tomb at all. But the fact of the matter is that in a way it hardly matters how the body of Jesus came to be missing because in the last analysis what convinced the people that he had risen from the dead was not the absence of his corpse but his living presence. And so it has been ever since." (Frederick Buechner, *Listening to Your Life*, Harper, San Francisco, 1992, p. 94).

This means that, in your daily struggles with the powers of death and evil, *you* become the ultimate proof of the reality of Jesus' resurrection. *You* in the ways in which you allow God to wrench life out of death, victory out of tragedy, become the very embodiment of Christ's victory over death at Easter. Every time you refuse to bow to the forces of death and despair, every time you clench your fist and refuse to knuckle under to the power of evil, you are following the leader, you are "looking to Jesus the pioneer and perfecter of our faith" (Heb. 12:2).

I Know That My Redeemer Liveth

Even Easter does not change our daily experience of death. Even Easter does not insure us against tragedy in this life. Christians suffer as much as anyone, perhaps sometimes even more as we attempt to be faithful to the gospel. Jesus has led the way for us through pain and suffering, but not around or over pain and suffering.

Our gospel claim is that, knowing the truth of the story that is told of Easter in Matthew 28, we are able to endure, even to triumph in our daily dealings with death. Because we have faith that God is a God of love and life, we have confidence, looking to Jesus who has gone before us, who has endured the pain of the cross, has died, and has risen, has returned to us, blessing us, telling us that all is well.

In the Prague demonstration that sparked the Czech revolution on November 18, 1989, students began chanting to the communist party leadership, "You have lost already! You have lost already!"—though the ultimate victory was still in the future. "We know that we can win," said Karel Srp, leader of the demonstrations, "this is unstoppable."

I was with my chapel choir in Prague last year and I can tell you, the demonstrators knew something that the communist leadership did not. Prague today is a living, breathing embodiment of their faith in the ultimate triumph of good over evil, life over death.

Allan Boesak has spent his entire life fighting South African government policies of racial separation. Time and again he has said to the gathered throngs of antiapartheid demonstrators that South Africa's apartheid system *has* fallen. "The battle is won, even though the struggle is not yet over."

Knowing about Easter, we know something decisive about the end of the story. We are able to go on, even amid our struggles, knowing that life will win out over death.

Lutheran theologian, Ted Peters has written:

It is the experienced power of new life in the Easter resurrection that provided the foundation for our faith and trust in God to fulfill his promise to establish a new creation in the future. What does it take to raise the dead? What does it take to consummate history into a new and everlasting kingdom? It takes mastery over the created order. It takes a loving Father who cares but who is also a creator whose power is undisputed and unrivaled. (Quoted by Elizabeth Achtemeier, in *Nature, God & Pulpit* [Grand Rapids: Eerdmans, 1992], p. 61.)

SECOND QUARTER

Helping Adults Become Involved

Preparing to Teach

You are fortunate in that today's lesson deals with matters that are close to everyone's heart: How do we handle tough, despairing times in life? Yet your challenge will be to lead your class in saying something more than, "Things always work out for the best." Your challenge will be to illustrate the ways in which Easter is relevant to our daily struggles with tragedy and death.

As you read "The Main Question" and "As You read the Scripture," jot down situations from your own life experience that illustrate the conviction that Christ's triumph over death on Easter has relevance for the lives of his followers.

Here as an outline for today's lesson:

I. Contemporary people experience death and defeat in their lives.
II. Christians are not immune from the painful effects of suffering and death, tragedy and defeat.
III. The Resurrection of Christ is God's assurance that God is in ultimate care of creation and that God will not allow death completely to defeat us.
IV. Knowledge of the resurrection of Christ is available to us in our daily experiences of the presence of the living Christ, encouraging us, helping us, wrenching life out of death, victory out of defeat.

Introducing the Main Question

George Orwell once said, "If you want a picture of the future, imagine a boot stamping on the human face—forever" (*1984* [New York: Signet Books, 1950], p. 200). Orwell's grim prediction, now over four decades ago, seems fulfilled in today's headlines. Share with your class instances of tragedy and death today from the newspaper or retell in your own words the story found in "The Main Question."

Developing the Lesson

I. Contemporary people experience death and defeat in their lives.

Ask your class, "What images come to your mind when you hear the word *tragedy*?" List these words or images on a chalkboard or newsprint. You have already started their thinking with the opening illustration from "The Main Question."

Recall that Matthew's story of Easter begins in chapter 27 with the story of the crucifixion of Jesus, the ultimate tragedy.

II. Christians are not immune from the painful effects of suffering and death, tragedy and defeat.

"The Scripture and the Main Question" begins with a quote from St. Augustine. Recall that quote to your class and ask how they have seen this quote illustrated in life. Have they experienced similar instances in which good people were afflicted with bad things? Of course, for Christians, the ultimate instance of undeserved, innocent suffering was the crucifixion of Jesus on the cross.

212

III. The Resurrection of Christ is God's assurance that God is in ultimate care of creation and that God will not allow death completely to defeat us.

Retell the events that are recorded in today's selected scripture, the way defeat was transformed into victory in the Resurrection. The discussion in "As You Read the Scripture" should be helpful to you in your understanding of this passage. Ask class members to put themselves in the place of Jesus' first disciples. How would they have felt after the crucifixion? Why were they so surprised by the resurrection on Easter?

Ask members of the class whether they can think of instances in life when Easter happened to people they have known, that is, when life arose from the grip of death. Are there contemporary stories in the news that illustrate the lesson's contention that Easter keeps on happening today? Some of the quotes and the illustrations found in "The Scripture and the Main Question" might be helpful in developing this point in the lesson.

IV. Knowledge of the resurrection of Christ is available to us in our daily experiences of the presence of the living Christ, encouraging us, helping us, wrenching life out of death, victory out of defeat.

Recalling the statements of Alan Bosak and the protestors in Prague, lead your class in discussing the ways in which Christians know that, even though evil and death have not been completely defeated, the victory is assured by the events of Easter.

Helping Class Members Act

The risen Christ led his disciples from expected death to unexpected life. Do we do a better job in believing in the reality of the Cross than we do in believing in the reality of Easter? Ask the class, "In what ways do you and I, like the disciples of Jesus, expect death, rather than life to win?"

Refer back to today's scripture, the story of the first Easter. End today's class with a prayer asking God to help us see Easter when it continues to occur in our lives.

Preparing for Next Sunday

Next Sunday we begin a new quarter of lessons concerned with the challenges of Christians living in community. In preparation for this unit, ask class members to ponder the difficulties of getting along with one another in the Christian church. Sometimes, life in the church is no picnic! Future lessons will deal honestly and biblically with the issues raised by the challenges of living together in the church.

THIRD QUARTER

CHRISTIAN LIVING IN COMMUNITY

Pat McGeachy

UNIT I: RESPONDING TO CHALLENGES OF LIFE IN COMMUNITY

FOUR LESSONS   MARCH 5–26

For the next quarter we will be dealing with the two letters we possess that Paul wrote to his congregation in Corinth. A bustling metropolis of over half a million people, crowded with temples, sports arenas, theaters, schools, and government buildings, Corinth was located at the point where the north-south and east-west Greek trade routes crossed. (The Romans tried to cut a canal across the narrow isthmus there, but it was too much of an engineering job for them, and this was not accomplished until the seventeenth century.) It reminds us a lot of many American cities, struggling to come to some sense in the confusion of the modern world. There, in the midst of this struggle, a diverse group of early Christians gathered for worship and mutual support. Our two letters are among the earliest known descriptions of church life in the first century, and so offer us rare insights into our heritage. From Paul's words to the Corinthians, we can hope better to understand how *our* congregations ought to live and behave.

This unit asks four main questions: How can we know the truth and effectively pass it on? How can we be good leaders, especially during difficult times? How can we keep our worship pure, with the world's idols all around us? How can we deal with the divisions in our midst? Answers to these questions will turn on the nature of the biblical witness, the content of the gospel, and, to a great extent, on the personality of the apostle Paul, a remarkable leader. I did not like Paul very much when I was a youngster. Compared to Jesus, he seemed humorless, nagging, and not much fun to be around. (But then who would come off very well compared to Jesus!) The older I get, the more I see Paul as a remarkable psychologist, in touch with both halves of his brain, and a master at helping people learn to be God's children. I have enjoyed getting reacquainted with him in these lessons.

Speaking Spiritual Truth

Background Scripture: 1 Corinthians 1:18–2:16

The Main Question

Does God make mistakes? Not too long ago, I received a letter from a person who took me rather strongly to task for using, in one of my lesson helps, the phrase, "the foolishness of God." "I don't like the phrase much either," I replied, "but I'm not going to take the blame for it. It comes from the apostle Paul." And so it does (1 Cor. 1:24). But was Paul serious when he spoke of God's foolishness and weakness? As a child, I was taught to think of God as all wise and all powerful. You and I may make mistakes, but God? Never.

And yet, was not Jesus rather a failure in the eyes of the world? As has often been pointed out, he never wrote a book, never traveled more than a few miles from his home town, never mustered an army, never had any money, never had a decent place to live, and, though he lived a life of innocence, was imprisoned, unjustly convicted, and put to the most horrible of deaths. And when he talked, he said all manner of weird things: "Happy are those who mourn." "If you want to find your life, you must lose it." Are those the words of a sensible person?

Could it be that the sensible thing to do is the foolish thing? Have we got it all backward, believing as we do in common sense and security? God's wisdom is secret and hidden (1 Cor. 2:7). Is there any way we mortals can find it out? That is our main question this week: Can you and I know the truth that

> no eye has seen, nor ear heard,
> nor the human heart conceived? (1 Cor. 2:7)

And, if we ever can come to know it, will we ever be able to speak it to one another?

Selected Scripture

King James Version

New Revised Standard Version

1 Corinthians 2:1-13

1 And I, brethren, when I came to you, came not with excellency of speech or of wisdom, declaring unto you the testimony of God.

2 For I determined not to know any thing among you, save Jesus Christ, and him crucified.

3 And I was with you in weakness, and in fear, and in much trembling.

4 And my speech and my preaching was not with enticing words of man's wisdom, but in demonstration of the Spirit and of power:

1 Corinthians 2:1-13

1 When I came to you, brothers and sisters, did I not come proclaiming the mystery of God to you in lofty words or wisdom. 2 For I decided to know nothing among you except Jesus Christ, and him crucified. 3 And I came to you in weakness and in fear and in much trembling. 4 My speech and my proclamation were not with plausible words of wisdom, but with a demonstration of the Spirit and of power, 5 so that your faith might

5 That your faith should not stand in the wisdom of men, but in the power of God.

6 Howbeit we speak wisdom among them that are perfect: yet not the wisdom of this world, nor of the princes of this world, that come to nought:

7 But we speak the wisdom of God in a mystery, even the hidden wisdom, which God ordained before the world unto our glory:

8 Which none of the princes of this world knew: for had they known it, they would not have crucified the Lord of glory.

9 But as it is written, Eye hath not seen, nor ear heard, neither have entered into the heart of man, the things which God hath prepared for them that love him.

10 But God hath revealed them unto us by his Spirit: for the Spirit searcheth all things, yea, the deep things of God.

11 For what man knoweth the things of a man, save the spirit of man which is in him? even so the things of God knoweth no man, but the Spirit of God.

12 Now we have received, not the spirit of the world, but the spirit which is of God; that we might know the things that are freely given to us of God.

13 Which things also we speak, not in the words which man's wisdom teacheth, but which the Holy Ghost teacheth; comparing spiritual things with spiritual.

rest not on human wisdom but on the power of God.

6 Yet among the mature we do speak wisdom, though it is not a wisdom of this age or of the rulers of this age, who are doomed to perish. 7 But we speak God's wisdom, secret and hidden, which God decreed before the ages for our glory. 8 None of the rulers of this age understood this; for if they had, they would not have crucified the Lord of glory. 9 But, as it is written,
"What no eye has seen, nor ear heard,
nor the human heart conceived,
what God has prepared for those who love him"—
10 these things God has revealed to us through the Spirit; for the Spirit searches everything, even the depths of God. 11 For what human being knows what is truly human except the human spirit that is within? So also no one comprehends what is truly God's except the Spirit of God. 12 Now we have received not the spirit of the world, but the Spirit that is from God, so that we may understand the gifts bestowed on us by God. 13 And we speak of these things in words not taught by human wisdom but taught by the Spirit, interpreting spiritual things to those who are spiritual.

Key Verse: **For I determined not to know any thing among you, save Jesus Christ, and him crucified.**

Key Verse: **For I decided to know nothing among you except Jesus Christ, and him crucified.**

As You Read the Scripture

1 Corinthians 1:18-25. The gospel is so incredible that to the eyes of the world it appears as foolishness. Verse 19 is a quote from Isaiah 29:14. Where *is* the source of wisdom in our day? The King James version uses the phrase "the foolishness of preaching." Does the world think the message of the church is silly? Do you?

Jewish law considered anyone crucified to be accursed (Deut. 21:23); Jesus then could not possibly be the Messiah. On the other hand, the Greek philosophers held that the true God must be without parts or passions; Jesus then must not be God, but a superstition. To any of us who look for God to conquer evil using evil's own methods of power, the Cross appears as weakness; to any of us who look for God to win intellectually, the Cross appears as foolishness. But it is the power (Greek *dunamis,* from which *dynamite* comes) and the wisdom (Greek *sophia,* from which *sophisticated* comes) of God.

Verses 26-31. Paul uses the Corinthians themselves as an example of what he is talking about. For a century or two, Christianity was called a vulgar religion. But in our day, many Christians are rich and sophisticated. It is hard for us to remember that the early church was a ragtag rabble crowd. But God used such folk for glory.

Chapter 2:1-5. Here Paul uses himself as an example. He describes himself as not much of a speaker (perhaps like Moses), who comes with fear and trembling. This means that he would never preach the gospel with arrogance, but always offer it in his own earthen vessel so that the glory should be of God, not of Paul (II Cor. 4:7). Paul concentrates entirely on Jesus, not on himself.

Verses 6-9. But there is a wisdom of which we speak; it is God's mysterious wisdom, which this age and its power structures cannot understand. Paul's thinking is much like that of Jesus (Matt. 11:25), who knows that children can understand what the sages miss. No one knows where the quotation in verse 9 comes from. It serves to remind us that, in the presence of God's mystery, we must all be as ignorant little children, and to accept the gospel with faith and wonder.

Verses 10-16. Paul divides the world into ordinary people (those who are physically alive, but not truly aware), and spiritual people (those who have the mind of Christ). Unspiritual people cannot see beyond the narrow confines of our own orbit, and so are primarily concerned with building up our own reputation, or own power and wisdom. But if we become spiritually aware, we receive the mind of Christ, who emptied himself (see Phil. 2:5-8), and so learn to seek not our own glory, but God's. Verse 14 is a reference to Isaiah 40:13, which is part of a passage (Isa. 40:12-31) that describes in detail the ignorance of the unspiritual, who cannot see the wonders that God is bringing about.

This entire lesson can be summed up in the one verse, "For I decided to know nothing among you except Jesus Christ, and him crucified" (2:2). This is what Paul decided, as a spiritual leader. If all of us would make the same determination in our relationships with one another, we would find that we had somehow solved the problem of both theology and ethics.

The Scripture and the Main Question

The Foolishness of God

Of course God is not foolish! This phrase is Paul's dramatic way of getting our attention, of breaking us out of our worldly way of thinking. It is an almost smart-alec way of talking: The dumbest thing that God ever did is better than the smartest thing you and I ever thought of. And, of course, the gospel does have power. Lives of individuals, and even of nations, have been changed by it. But we are so accustomed to thinking with the mind of the world that we must be very careful not to confuse the power of the gospel with human power. Let me make this point with two pictures of evangelism.

First, picture an imposing speaker, clothed in impressive garments, backed by a chorus of thousands and the sound of a mighty organ. Visualize this person speaking with a voice of great authority (perhaps like that of a highly paid radio announcer), and using the most powerful vocabulary. Add to this vision all the paraphernalia of show business: public address system, technicolor setting, effective audio-visuals...the whole shooting match. And think of this speaker as having all the persuasive charisma of a great politician, skilled in the art of moving people.

Now, in contrast, listen to this definition of evangelism by D. T. Niles (*That They May Have Life* [New York: Harper and Bros., 1951], p. 96):

> Evangelism . . . is one beggar telling another beggar where to get food. The Christian does not offer out of his bounty. He has no bounty. He is simply guest at his Master's table and, as evangelist, he calls others too. The evangelistic relation is to be "along-side of" not "over-against." The Christian stands alongside the non-Christian and points to the Gospel, the holy action of God. It is not his knowledge of God that he shares, it is to God himself that he points. The Christian Gospel is the Word become flesh. This is more than and other than the Word become speech.

Of the two images suggested above, which one, in your judgment, best illustrates power and wisdom?

The Corinthians Themselves an Example

The Corinthian church was probably not composed of upper-middle-class people. They certainly were not the cream of Corinthian society. Indeed, many of them may have been slaves. They came together, for mutual support and protection—probably a fairly small group—in a large and bustling city. (From what we know of Corinth during this period, it had over half-a-million people, and was a center for transportation, sports, theater, and religion. Sounds a little like Nashville, Tennessee!) It is doubtful that, by modern standards of sports heroes, popularity, or political clout, that the little congregation would have had much power as the world understands it.

Paul's Own Example

In 1 Corinthians 4:13, Paul describes himself and the other apostles as like rubbish and dregs (both words mean that which is wiped off when you clean a dirty pot). Do you suppose we make too much over well-dressed clergy, fancy church buildings, and polished sermons? Compare Paul's description of himself as preacher (2:3-4) with that of the impressive evangelist that we imagined when we were thinking of God's foolishness. Do you think Paul was more like that, or like the beggar described by D. T. Niles? To help you in answering that question, note the similarity between what Niles says, about the Christian pointing beyond himself to God, and Paul's own words: "For I decided to know nothing among you except Jesus Christ, and him crucified."

Of course, each Christian, both lay and clerical, will present Jesus in a different way, for we carry the good news in different vessels. (That is why there are four Gospels, not one of which we would want to do without.) My preaching style will be different from another's. We won't all simply get up and mumble, "Jesus Christ crucified," in a monotone. We will use eloquence and gesture, and even the aid of public address systems. But we must not think these things are our power; it belongs to another (see 2 Cor. 4:7).

God's Mysterious Wisdom

In spite of all we have had to say about God's foolishness, we must agree that ultimately God is wise. God in Jesus Christ is self-emptying (Phil. 2:5-8), but that results in glory (Phil. 2:9-11). From the human point of view, what God did in Jesus looks foolish, but from God's point of view it was wise. That is, you and I would probably not have sent a tiny baby into the world, to be born of a poor carpenter's wife, in a tiny captive country. We would have sent in a host of chariots and a legion of shining angels. And yet, God's way, foolish as it seems to us, has turned the world upside down (Acts 17:6). God was wiser than we would have been.

You might think of it as a parent stooping to conquer, pretending to be foolish in order to encourage a child to learn to think independently. This is like a school teacher asking a pupil, "What do *you* think?" I knew of a mother who had a game that she liked to play with her children when they reached a certain age. She would drive in a confusing pattern for a while, and then say to the child riding with her, "Help me find the way home. Do you think we should turn left or right here, or go straight?" And she would follow whatever directions the child gave. Eventually, her kids became very well oriented, and rarely got lost.

A Gift through the Spirit

God comes to us with mysteries so astonishing that our minds cannot comprehend them. "No eye has seen, nor ear heard, nor . . . heart conceived." And yet, those who listen to the Spirit of God are able to touch the hem of that garment. Like the fourth dimension, it is something we can almost picture. And, the more we become like little children (see Matt. 11:25), the more we may be able to discern this amazing grace. Could Paul really have meant it when he spoke of God's foolishness? Is it possible that we are *supposed* to be foolish? Maybe, like the prophet Habakkuk, we are to believe, in spite of logic and sensibility. "Though the fig tree does not blossom," he wrote, "and no fruit is on the vines; though the produce of the olive fails and the fields yield no food . . . and there is no herd in the stalls, yet I will rejoice in the LORD" (3:17-18).

Helping Adults Become Involved

Preparing to Teach

It will be important for this lesson that we help the class do a good job of distinguishing between the church in Corinth and the congregation with which they worship. So I would encourage you to do two things. First, get as

accurate a picture as you can of the Corinthian church by reading the introductory material in a good commentary. (William Barclay is pretty good in
The Daily Study Bible Series, the Letters to the Corinthians, Revised Edition,
Philadelphia, Westminster Press, 1974, pp. 1-8, and also 14-15 and 21.) Also
read what the New Testament says about the Corinthians in Acts 18:1-18, and
24-28. Second, take a fresh look at your own congregation. As I write these
words, I preside over two weekly worship services, one that of a fairly typical
upper-middle-class, extended family congregation, and the other an inner-
city mid-week worship and meal, to which the poor of the city are invited. In
both of them there is incredible diversity; sometimes they remind me of the
Corinthian church, and that gives me both pause and hope. Hope, because I
know the church has been like this since its earliest years, and pause, in that
we do not seem to have improved much over the centuries.

After you have thought about Paul's congregation and yours for a while,
think how much they are alike, or different, and prepare to guide your class
into sharing your thinking.

Introducing the Main Question

You may not want to start with my notions about God's foolishness,
because the phrase makes some people uncomfortable. But, to be honest,
that is why I chose it! Since it has the capacity to jar a little, it may help wake
some of your folks up for a good discussion. The title for this lesson given by
our editors is "Speaking Spiritual Truth," which makes me think more of
Ephesians 4:15 than this part of 1 Corinthians. But I think I see why that
name was used. They were making the point that Paul came to Corinth
determined not to depend on wisdom or eloquence, but to preach the plain
truth of Jesus Christ and his crucifixion, and that his ministry there was
marked by the power of God rather than by human wisdom.

I remember once, when I was a confident young preacher (I knew a
good bit more then than I do now), that I had prepared a rather stuffy
address for a certain congregation. I was all prepared to impress them
with my erudition, when, seated behind the pulpit during the early portion of the service, my eye fell on a brass plaque bearing the words, "Sir,
we would see Jesus" (John 12:20). Rather shamefacedly, I set aside my
planned presentation and spoke simply about Jesus as I saw him. Let me
encourage you, in teaching this lesson, to do that same sort of thing. If we
who are teaching really believe this lesson, we much approach our class
not "proclaiming the mystery of God in lofty words or wisdom" but "in
weakness and in fear and in much trembling." (Maybe, as a teacher, you
already feel pretty much that way; if so, take heart. You do not need my
advice at all.)

Developing the Lesson

Here is an outline, and a few questions you might use to start the class
thinking in these areas.

I. The foolishness of God, 1:18-25

Are there ways in which what God does seems silly to the world?
Should the church sometimes look foolish? If so, how do you decide on
the right sort of foolishness?

II. The Corinthians themselves an example, 1:26-31

Does the life-style of your congregation say anything about Jesus? Is that statement positive, negative, or both?

What do you think of the church bulletin board sign that reads, "You may be the only Bible someone will read"?

III. Paul's own example, 2:1-5

Was Paul here being a kind of Caspar Milquetoast, a sort of, "aw shucks, I'm not really worth anything" person? If not, how would you describe him? What does *meek* (Matt. 5:5) really mean?

What does it mean to know nothing except Christ? Is there such a thing as sensible ignorance?

IV. God's mysterious wisdom, 2:6-9

Is your faith profound or simple? Can it be both? Should Christianity be mysterious? Is it?

Are there some things we are not supposed to understand?

Is all inquiry wholesome? (Evaluate this statement: Drive a stake into the truth of the Lordship of Jesus Christ, and, with your line fastened to that, go where you please.)

V. A gift through the Spirit, 2:10-16

It is not a good idea to divide the world into two kinds of people, but sometimes we have to say there is a difference between those who walk by the Spirit and those who do not. See Romans 8:1-17 for another look at this question. What does it mean to be spiritual? Note that Paul is *not* making the Puritan distinction between an evil body and a good spirit. What is meant by the flesh, or the natural world is our human tendency to glorify ourselves. A person may be digging in the dirt of a garden and still be highly spiritual, or praying aloud in a cathedral, and still be very worldly. How can we know when we are being led by the Spirit?

You will not want to spend an equal amount of time on all of these passages. If you have a good bit of discussion, the class will determine for you which parts are of the most interest.

Helping Class Members Act

Why not suggest spending the next week pretending to be the Corinthian congregation, or at least acting as though we had the spirit of the New Testament church? What would that mean? Could we actually be servants to one another in such a way that we could say we are not glorifying ourselves, but simply knowing Christ and him crucified? What sort of changes would that make in our life-style as a congregation? As individuals?

You might suggest to your class that they keep notes on the number of times in the coming week that they have pointed to Christ crucified, either in word or deed.

Planning for Next Sunday

For next week, read 1 Corinthians 4. Reflect on Paul's astonishing statement, "Be imitators of me." Could you say that?

Faithfulness in Difficult Times

Background Scripture: 1 Corinthians 4:1-2, 6-16

The Main Question

Teachers are supposed to know things, aren't they? I think that way because my first teachers in school did know a great deal more than I, and I depended on them to share that knowledge with me. But every great teacher knows that teaching is something far different from opening our heads and pouring in knowledge. It is a process in which the student plays as much a part as the teacher. Teachers are more like farmers and physicians than like carpenters and engineers. The carpenter and engineer take materials, cut and shape them, and build things out of them. But the farmer can only plant and wait for the growth to take place. The physician can offer medication, but the real healing happens because of the miracle of life, which is beyond the doctor's doing. (Paul himself used this metaphor in 1 Cor. 3:6.)

It boils down to this: You and I are not superior dispensers of the gospel; we are fellow beggars who happen to know where the bread is. The world, it has been said, is divided into two kinds of people: those who divide the world into two kinds of people, and those who do not. Today's lesson can help us to be the second sort. Paul's way of relating to his Corinthian friends is a model for the way in which we Christians should relate to each other.

Life is difficult, even when things are doing smoothly. And it is easy to grow weary in well doing. If your question—like mine—is, "How can I keep on keeping on, when times are tough?" then together we can be helped by the discovery that we, like Paul, do not have to know everything. We have only to remember that we are sinners saved by grace. If we can keep that in mind, then we can help each other.

Selected Scripture

King James Version

1 Corinthians 4:1-2, 6-16

1 Let a man so account of us, as of the ministers of Christ, and stewards of the mysteries of God.

2 Moreover it is required in stewards, that a man be found faithful.

....

6 And these things, brethren, I have in a figure transferred to myself and to Apollos for your sakes; that ye might learn in us not to think of men above that which is written, that no one of you be puffed up for one against another.

7 For who maketh thee to differ

New Revised Standard Version

1 Corinthians 4:1-2, 6-16

1 Think of us in this way, as servants of Christ and stewards of God's mysteries. 2 Moreover, it is required of stewards that they be found trustworthy.

....

6 I have applied all this to Apollos and myself for your benefit, brothers and sisters, so that you may learn through us the meaning of the saying, "Nothing beyond what is written," so that none of you will be puffed up in favor of one against another. 7 For who sees anything

from another? and what hast thou that thou didst not receive? now if thou didst receive it, why dost thou glory, as if thou hadst not received it?

8 Now ye are full, now ye are rich, ye have reigned as kings without us: and I would to God ye did reign, that we also might reign with you.

9 For I think that God hath set forth us the apostles last, as it were appointed to death: for we are made a spectacle unto the world, and to angels, and to men.

10 We are fools for Christ's sake, but ye are wise in Christ; we are weak, but ye are strong; ye are honourable, but we are despised.

11 Even unto this present hour we both hunger, and thirst, and are naked, and are buffeted, and have no certain dwellingplace;

12 And labour, working with our own hands: being reviled, we bless; being persecuted, we suffer it:

13 Being defamed, we intreat: we are made as the filth of the world, and are the offscouring of all things unto this day.

14 I write not these things to shame you, but as my beloved sons I warn you.

15 For though we have ten thousand instructors in Christ, yet have ye not many fathers: for in Christ Jesus I have begotten you through the gospel.

16 Wherefore I beseech you, be ye followers of me.

Key Verse: **Moreover it is required in stewards, that a man be found faithful.**

different in you? What do you have that you did not receive? And if you received it, why do you boast as if it were not a gift?

8 Already you have all your want! Already you have become rich! Quite apart from us you have become kings! Indeed, I wish that you had become kings, so that we might be kings with you! 9 For I think that God has exhibited us apostles as last of all, as though sentenced to death, because we have become a spectacle to the world, to angels and to mortals. 10 We are fools for the sake of Christ, but you are wise in Christ. We are weak, but you are strong. You are held in honor, but we in disrepute. 11 To the present hour we are hungry and thirsty, we are poorly clothed and beaten and homeless, 12 and we grow weary from the work of our own hands. When reviled, we bless; when persecuted, we endure; 13 when slandered, we speak kindly. We have become like the rubbish of the world, the dregs of all things, to this very day.

14 I am not writing this to make you ashamed, but to admonish you as my beloved children. 15 For though you might have ten thousand guardians in Christ, you do not have many fathers. Indeed, in Christ Jesus I became your father through the gospel. 16 I appeal to you, then, be imitators of me.

Key Verse: **Moreover, it is required of stewards that they be found trustworthy.**

As You Read the Scripture

1 Corinthians 4:1-21. This chapter is about leadership, and we need to watch carefully, as we read through it, to discern qualities that will enable us to be better teachers and fellow ministers to one another. Do not make the mistake of thinking that our lesson applies only to the publicly-recognized leaders among us; it is good advice for the life-style of us all.

Verses 1-5. Paul describes himself (and Apollos and Timothy, and all proper missionaries) with two terms that mean a trusted functionary, not the final authority. The first is *servant (huperetes)* a word sometimes also translated as *officer* and *minister*. In ancient times, it was used to describe the aide of a Roman consul, who carried his master's insignia, and cleared the way for him at public appearances. The other is *steward (oikonomous)*, literally, a *house ruler*. Our English word *steward* has a similar origin, meaning *sty-ward*, or pig keeper. The word gradually came to mean one who takes care of the master's property, and eventually became the name of the royal house of Britain: Stewart (or Stuart). Paul says he is not being defensive about his office, and expects to be judged ultimately by God, not by human beings, for his faithfulness to his charge. The role of the servant or steward is not as a possessor of superior or magical powers, but as one who knows where the bread is (see the illustration from D. T. Niles in the last lesson).

Verses 6-13. Paul is using himself and Apollos as models, or illustrations of what leadership means, and he makes it clear that the leader has no cause for boasting; all the leader's gifts are just that: gifts. They were not earned. Indeed, from the point of view of the world, this leadership is not very impressive. They are operating from weakness. Wisdom lies not with us, but with God. You might wish to compare this with the majestic put-down that God gives to Job in Job 38–41, beginning with the sarcastic question:

"Where were you when I laid the foundation of the earth?
Tell me, if you have understanding.
Who determined its measurements—surely you know!" (38:4-5).

God is the true Shepherd (Ps. 23, John 10:11-16), the rest of us are undershepherds.

Verses 14-21. This is a personal appeal to the Corinthians to return to their birthright. There is a play on words here that does not quite come through in English. It might be translated like this:

I begat *(egennesa)* you in Christ, so
become *(ginesthe)* imitators of me.

The amazing paradox is that here, as throughout the whole letter, Paul, who does not wish to be put on a pedestal, nevertheless badly wants them to model themselves after him. It is the old paradox: If you demonstrate your humility, they take away your humility badge.

The kingdom of God (a phrase we usually associate with Jesus, not Paul, but he uses it five times in this letter) does have power (v. 20), but it is not earthly power. "Flesh and blood cannot inherit the kingdom of God" (15:50). It is a shining ideal, whose glory belongs to God, and, like the perfect love in chapter 13, shows up all false claims. It is not talk, but dynamics.

The Scripture and the Main Question

The Paradox of Leadership

Sometimes I think that the more religious we become, the further we get away from God. By "becoming religious" I mean trying harder and harder to improve myself, through ritual and righteous acts. But the Christian faith is not about *my* righteous acts, it is about God's righteous act in Jesus Christ, toward me, a sinner. The more I try to prove my own worth, the harder it is for me to remember God's grace. It is because of this paradox that Jesus warned the chief priests and elders, "The tax collectors and the prostitutes are going into the kingdom of God ahead of you" (Matt. 21:31). It is why the elder brother in Jesus' story (Luke 15:11-32) had difficulty in rejoicing in his father's house, while the younger, who had wasted his inheritance in bad behavior, was welcomed with a robe, a ring, and a fatted calf. The religious son was cut off from his father, while the sinful son found his way back home to him.

Well, should I then stop trying to be a good person? Of course not! But I must ever be mindful of the strange fact that my goodness can become a barrier between me and God, and between me and other Christians. This is especially true for those of us who attempt to teach others. Even to *call* yourself a teacher is to come dangerously close to cutting yourself off from grace. That is because we think (wrongly, I believe) of a teacher as one who dispenses knowledge to the ignorant.

In this lesson we find Paul carefully treading the fine line between being an authority from the top down, on the one hand, and an indifferent director on the other. Only Jesus managed this remarkable balancing act better. He of all people was at one and the same time our Lord and our God (John 20:28), and the human who came "not to be served but to serve" (Mark 10:45).

Servants of God's Mystery

Paul's task as leader is to take care of God's mysteries, to open the way for others through the torn curtain of Jesus Christ's flesh (see Heb. 10:19-20), into the Holy of Holies, the true way. This means, paradoxically, that he is proclaiming the incredible secret that is no longer a secret. Christ has opened the living way (remember that Paul was once an enemy of the way; see Acts 9:2) and all are free to walk in it. So Paul must work himself out of a job, as must all honest professionals. (If physicians healed all diseases, they would be out of work; if lawyers solved all disputes, they would; etc.) This is wonderfully described by the psychiatrist, Sheldon Kopp, in his book, *If You Meet the Buddha on the Road, Kill Him* (New York: Science and Behavior, 1972). He tells us that the secret is, "There is no secret." In his own practice, like Paul, he shares his personal ambiguities and pain with his clients, saying, in effect, "We are here to help each other; there are no hidden meanings." Woe to the church leader who plays the role of the possessor of that which the uninitiated cannot comprehend unless they have said the secret word, or crossed the priestly palm with silver. Indeed, maybe the first test of any mysterious new cult is to ask, "How much do they charge for the secret of happiness?" The gospel is free!

It is not easy to be such a leader. If we do not look out, we will always be second-guessing ourselves. But a leader who wishes to set others free must demonstrate freedom. Our self-examination must always be, like that of Paul, an offering of ourselves to God's judgment—not that of ourselves or others. Then, when we act, we are acting not in our own power, but in the power of the one who said, "Without me you can do nothing."

All We Have Is a Gift

A congregation, or a Sunday school class, will become the community of God when they learn to minimize their own glory, and elevate that of their sisters and brothers. "All this time," Paul says to the Corinthians, "I have been talking about myself and Apollos so that you will catch on and apply it to yourselves." He calls them to stand on the saying, "Nothing beyond what is written" (v. 6), which surely means that they are not to depart from the central truth that they have been saved by grace. How can you look at yourself and say, "How great I am!" when you remember that wisdom lies with God, not with us. Indeed, when we seek to attain it by our own efforts, we become judgmental, self-satisfied, and destructive. Even our very best attempts at worship are transformed into sin:

"Come to The House of God—and transgress!
Come to The Place of Sacrifice—and multiply sins!
Bring your sacrifices every morning,
    your tithes every three days;
        for so you love to do, O people of Israel!"
says the Lord God. (Amos 4:4-5, my translation)

But if we recognize that we already reign (in one sense), we can patiently await the glad day when we will truly reign (in the ultimate sense). Then Paul and Apollos can glory in their accomplishments and assume their rightful sovereignty. But, in the meantime, they are to continue in their role as the scum of the earth. (This is literally what verse 13 means.) It is no accident that, in my city, the most exciting church I know is a house church, without steeple or pomp, where class and racial lines intersect. That is not simply a matter of taste but that, as in Corinth, that inner-city church contains persons in a faith encounter—not people in the static condition of many suburban cathedrals.

A Personal Appeal

So Paul, with amazing reverse humility, can exhort the Corinthians to model themselves after his own example, insofar as he follows Christ. They can imitate Paul because he too turns to the same source for his power. The teacher or preacher who does not understand this is still feeling like a performer or dispenser of truth, rather than a facilitator or enabler. Let me make a suggestion out of my own field of leadership, which is worship. I have long held that the liturgist's vestments should not be thought of as a police or military officer's uniform, badges of authority, but more like that of the resplendent hotel doorkeeper, who looks like an admiral, but really is not very important. That functionary does not own the hotel, but simply knows where to tell you to park your car. We who are leaders should make ourselves visible enough to be there as servants, but the glory belongs not to us, but to God.

Helping Adults Become Involved

Preparing to Teach

I often begin my approach to a lesson with word studies. If you are interested in this method, some of the key words come in the first verse, and deserve your attention: servant, steward, and mysteries. I have examined them a bit in these helps, but you may want to go to a Bible dictionary and work further.

Another way of warming up is to review some devotional works that are related to the lesson's theme. I particularly like John Greenleaf Whittier's old hymn, "All Things Are Thine," which he wrote in 1872 for the opening of the Plymouth Church in Minneapolis, Minnesota. It catches the theme of the gospel as freely given, with no virtue on our part:

> All things are thine; no gift have we,
> Lord of all gifts, to offer Thee;
> And hence with grateful hearts today
> Thine own before thy feet we lay.

He even uses Paul's metaphor, and that of Job and Proverbs, of the Master Builder:

> Thy will was in the builder's thought;
> Thy hand unseen amidst us wrought;
> Through mortal motive, scheme and plan,
> Thy wise eternal purpose ran.

We must, if we are to escape the trap of being too religious, keep as a daily, if not hourly, motto before us, Paul's question of "What do you have that you did not receive?" (v. 7).

Introducing the Main Question

I still like my beginning illustration, that of the difference between one who works by cutting and pasting (carpenters, surgeons, cooks, or clock-makers) and those who nurture that which is already there (farmers, family physicians, the best teachers). You can make too much over this, of course, but I believe that Christians ought to err on the side of shaping and molding (such as the potter of Jer. 18) rather than carving and chopping. Perhaps better still is that of planting and watering (See 1 Cor. 3:6).

Or, you might prefer my closing illustration, the one of the doorkeeper versus the admiral—whose uniforms look similar, but whose authority and status are greatly different. (See Ps. 84:10.)

For still another springboard, another description of leadership from the pen of the great Dane, Søren Kierkegaard (*Purity of Heart* [New York: Harper and Bros., 1956], pp. 158-59):

Alas, in regard to things spiritual, the foolishness of many is this, that they in the secular sense look upon the speaker as an actor, and the listeners as theatre-goers who are to pass judgment on the artist. But the speaker is not the actor—not in the remotest sense.

No, the speaker is the prompter. There are no mere theatre-goers present, for each listener will be looking into his own heart. The stage is eternity, and the listeners . . . stands before God during the talk. . . . In the most earnest sense, God is the critical theatre-goer. . . . The listener, if I may say so, is the actor, who in all truth acts before God.

Developing the Lesson

Here is my outline, with suggested discussion questions:

I. *Servants of God's mystery, 4:1-5*

Who is the hardest judge of your behavior? Your peers, your mother, your children, yourself? What kind of judgment does God render (see Rom. 8:1, 33)?

Of what are you and your class the stewards? (Do not forget the planet Earth!)

II. *All we have is a gift, 4:6-13*

It is very hard for us not to say, "Mother, please! I'd rather do it myself." And God does want us to do some things ourselves. But in what sense must we think of all of life as a gift? What, for example, keeps your heart beating?

What do you think Paul means by being a fool? Should Christians act foolishly?

Try filling out a job résumé on Paul's behalf, based on his description of himself in verses 9-13: doomed to die, a spectacle, a fool, weak, disreputable, hungry, thirsty, naked, beaten, homeless, a drudge, reviled, persecuted, slandered, and, finally, the filth that remains on the rag when the world is wiped clean. Would you hire him?

Is it fair to describe Paul as an anti-hero?

Do you think Paul is one who stoops to conquer? Is he really just pretending to be humble so as to win folks, or is he truly coming down to their level? Is there a paradox here, that only the strong can help the weak? (Montaigne became kittenish with his kitten, but she never talked philosophy with him.)

III. *A personal appeal, 4:13-21*

Paul, who is a master with words, cannot use them as a weapon or rod. He must use them in weakness. Jesus taught and lived the same paradox; see specifically the third Beatitude (Matt. 5:5). Would a truly meek person appear meek in most peoples' eyes?

You and I usually say, "Do what I say, not what I do," for we know that our example is flawed. What sort of person would dare to say, "Be imitators of me?" Could you call that person humble?

Helping Class Members Act

I know a preacher who has a serious speech impediment. Strangely, this makes him a very effective speaker. His people struggle with him as he tries to get out his consonants, and so participate in the act of proclamation with energy; they rarely sleep. (Curiously, as with Mel Tillis when he sings, my friend does not stammer when he prays. Further research is needed here.) Ask your class to watch for examples, in the week to come, of persons who win through losing. Perhaps they may discover themselves doing that very thing. (Incidentally, if my class were one that had pretty much the same group every Sunday, I would not hesitate to use part of next week to get feedback for this week's lesson.)

Planning for Next Sunday

Next week's lesson deals with two themes: temptation and the sacraments. Ask your class to be thinking about how these two could possibly go together.

Resisting Temptation

Background Scripture: 1 Corinthians 10:1-17

The Main Question

Do you believe in magic? Of course not, because you are a sophisticated modern; you know that magic is tricks or illusions, performed by a Houdini or a David Copperfield. In real life there is no such thing as magic. Or so we say. But so subtle is the temptation to desire the black arts that we may fall into danger. When I was little I wished for a button I could push that would do my homework for me. Or I wanted the powers of a super hero. (My favorite was The Flash; I thought that, if I could supernaturally speed up my system, I could become the world's greatest pitcher, with a fast-ball of over two hundred miles an hour, with which I could strike out the entire batting order of the St. Louis Cardinals.)

Of course, when I grew older, I discarded these dreams as wishful thinking, but the temptation to want to do magic is still there. I want to wish away the world's ills: poverty, injustice, pollution. I want to wave my wand and make us all love each other. And I cannot do that, any more than I could wish my homework done. But sometimes we Christians do act as though we think the Christian faith is some kind of magic trick. The Corinthians, to whom Paul was writing this week's lesson, were tempted to think that their Communion Meal was a sort of magic potion for making them spiritually well. Indeed it does have healing powers, though not of the magical sort. In order to escape having a superstitious view of Communion, we must have a sound theological view.

Our main question then, for today's lesson, is this: What is the meaning of the cup and loaf that Christians share?

Selected Scripture

King James Version	New Revised Standard Version
1 Corinthians 10:1-17	*1 Corinthians 10:1-17*
1 Moreover, brethren, I would not that ye should be ignorant, how that all our fathers were under the cloud, and all passed through the sea;	1 I do not want you to be unaware, brothers and sisters, that our ancestors were all under the cloud, and all passed through the sea, 2 and all were baptized into Moses in the cloud and in the sea, 3
2 And were all baptized unto Moses in the cloud and in the sea;	and all ate the same spiritual food, 4
3 And did all eat the same spiritual meat;	and all drank the same spiritual drink. For they drank from the spiritual rock that followed them, and
4 And did all drink the same spiritual drink: for they drank of that spiritual Rock that followed them: and that Rock was Christ.	the rock was Christ. 5 Nevertheless, God was not pleased with most of them, and they were struck down in the wilderness.
5 But with many of them God was	

not well pleased: for they were overthrown in the wilderness.

6 Now these things were our examples, to the intent we should not lust after evil things, as they also lusted.

7 Neither be ye idolaters, as were some of them; as it is written, The people sat down to eat and drink, and rose up to play.

8 Neither let us commit fornication, as some of them committed, and fell in one day three and twenty thousand.

9 Neither let us tempt Christ, as some of them also tempted, and were destroyed of serpents.

10 Neither murmur ye, as some of them also murmured, and were destroyed of the destroyer.

11 Now all these things happened unto them for ensamples: and they are written for our admonition, upon whom the ends of the world are come.

12 Wherefore let him that thinketh he standeth take heed lest he fall.

13 There hath no temptation taken you but such as is common to man: but God is faithful, who will not suffer you to be tempted above that ye are able; but will with the temptation also make a way to escape, that ye may be able to bear it.

14 Wherefore, my dearly beloved, flee from idolatry.

15 I speak as to wise men; judge ye what I say.

16 The cup of blessing which we bless, is it not the communion of the blood of Christ? The bread which we break, is it not the communion of the body of Christ?

17 For we being many are one bread, and one body: for we are all partakers of that one bread.

Key Verse: **There hath no temptation taken you but such as is common to man: but God is faithful, who will not suffer you to be tempted above that ye are able; but will with the temptation also make a way to escape, that ye may be able to bear it.**

6 Now these things occurred as examples for us, so that we might not desire evil as they did. 7 Did not become idolaters as some of them did; as it is written, "The people sat down to eat and drink, and they rose up to play." 8 We must not indulge in sexual immorality as some of them did, and twenty-three thousand fell in a single day. 9 We must not put Christ to the test, as some of them did, and were destroyed by serpents. 10 And do not complain as some of them did, and were destroyed by the destroyer. 11 These things happened to them to serve as an example, and they were written down to instruct us, on whom the ends of the ages have come. 12 So if you think you are standing, watch out that you do not fall. 13 No testing has overtaken you that is not common to everyone. God is faithful, and he will not let you be tested beyond your strength, but with the testing he will also provide the way out so that you may be able to endure it.

14 Therefore, my dear friends, flee from the worship of idols. 15 I speak as to sensible people; judge for yourselves what I say. 16 The cup of blessing that we bless, is it not a sharing in the blood of Christ? The bread that we break, is it not a sharing in the body of Christ? 17 Because there is one bread, we who are many are one body, for we all partake of the one bread.

Key Verse: **No testing has overtaken you that is not common to everyone. God is faithful, and he will not let you be tested beyond your strength, but with the testing he will also provide the way out so that you may be able to endure it.**

As You Read the Scripture

1 Corinthians 10:1–11:1. We really need to look at the whole chapter. It is about two themes: temptation and the sacraments. Paul's discussion of them is inextricably woven together throughout this chapter, and indeed through the first verse of chapter 11. (Remember that chapter and verse numbers were an artificial invention of the middle ages. The first printed Bible with chapters did not appear until after Columbus, in 1525, and the first Bible with verses in 1551. So, while they are very useful for reference, they are not sacred.)

Chapter 10:1-13. Paul begins to get pretty tough with the beginning of chapter ten. He had been saying a lot about Christian liberty (over things like food offered to idols) in chapters 8 and 9, but he had warned us there that we must not misuse our freedom (8:9). The strong Corinthians, those who know that they are under grace and not law, are warned to guard carefully against a tendency to idolatry.

Verses 1-5. In discussing the Red Sea crossing (Exod. 13:21–14:31), the giving of the manna (Exod. 16), and the precious water from the rock (Exod. 17 and Num. 20), Paul is clearly referring to the two Sacraments of Baptism and the Lord's Supper. For Paul, Baptism and the Lord's Supper are closely connected: Baptism is our welcome to the table, the Lord's Supper is a continuation of the grace that was poured out on us in baptism. He makes sure we understand his spiritualizing of this ancient story by clearly identifying the rock with Jesus Christ. But, in spite of God's sacramental presence with Israel, most of them were struck down in the wilderness. This is a warning to us all.

Verses 6-10. Verse 7 clearly refers to the experience with the golden calf (see Exod. 32:6). The reference to the twenty-three thousand in verse 8 may be to Numbers 25:9; if so, Paul must have been quoting from memory, because he was a thousand off. The business about the serpents in verse 9 is found in Numbers 21:4-6. And the complainers and the destroyer in verse 10 may refer to the death that came to many after the grumbling revolt of Korah, Dathan, and Abiram in Numbers 16.

Verses 11-13. Though Paul knows we will be tempted, he also knows that God will be faithful, and that it is possible for us to endure.

Chapter 10:14-22. Now Paul comes to the specific matter of the Sacrament of the Lord's Supper. The demons he refers to are those of selfishness and idolatry, of shouting down our neighbors, and refusing to wait for them. They were turning the Lord's Supper into a pagan shambles. But what was fundamentally wrong was their lack of community.

Chapter 10:23–11:1. Paul continues with his strong celebration of liberty ("Eat whatever is sold in the meat market without raising any question on the ground of conscience," v. 25, and "Do everything to the glory of God," v. 31). But he solemnly warns them to be on guard against offending the conscience of others (v. 28) and against offending either Jews or Gentiles (v. 32). We are, in short, to be just like Paul (all things to all people), so that God will be honored, and the integrity of the community maintained. To summarize the chapter: We are not to take the sacrament superstitiously, but to see it for what it is—an expression of the Body of Christ, the fellowship of believers. All our behavior, in our personal moral lives and in our worship, should reflect our ability to discern that body.

The Scripture and the Main Question

A Warning from History

Why does Paul feel it necessary to go all the way back to the Exodus to make his point about the Corinthians at worship? He knows that those who will not study history must repeat it. He agrees with Isaiah, who called us to

Look to the rock from which you were hewn,
and to the quarry from which you were dug. (51:1)

The God of the New Testament is the God of the Hebrew scriptures. We have not abandoned truth because Jesus has come. No, he came "not . . . to abolish the law or the prophets . . . but to fulfill" (Matt. 5:17).

Christ the Rock

Paul often spiritualizes the events of Hebrew history. This is another way of saying that he sees types of Christ present with the children of Israel. Most Christians agree that this is a proper way to read scripture. For instance, we cannot help seeing the crucifixion of Jesus in the lament of Psalm 22, or the sacrificial life of Jesus in the servant passages of Isaiah 52:13–53:12. Jesus saw himself there; look at his interpretation of Isaiah 61:1-2 in Luke 4:16-21. Probably Paul's Jewish readers would have been aware of the rabbinic tradition that the rock from which Moses drew water followed after the people to ease their thirst.

Some Ancient Disasters

As you read verses 6-11, go back and look at the Exodus stories to which Paul is referring. It is not easy to be certain which ones he means, but we can make an educated guess that they are these:

The golden calf, Exodus 32:1-35. Note the last verse.
The zeal of Phineas, Numbers 25:1-9. Note verse nine.
The fiery serpents, Numbers 21:4-9.
Korah's rebellion, Numbers 16:1-50. Note verses 35 and 49.

You might also want to look at Psalm 78, which is a long historical ballad giving account of God's continual punishment of the people.

Not all plagues and deaths are due to human sin; the book of Job was written to make this clear. But it *is* clear that *some* of our ills are due to our faithlessness and immoral behavior. Having our name on the church rolls, and faithfully taking Communion are not magical proofs against calamity.

God Is Faithful

What are we to make of the trials that come on us? Paul believes that they should all be seen in the light of God's faithfulness. For many of us, when things get so bad that we can hardly stand them, it is comforting to remember the promise that God "will not let you be tested beyond your strength, but with the testing he will also provide the way out" (10:13). We must not fall into the trap of believing that God sets traps for us. We do not need to fear some sort of divine sting operation. Remember what James told us: "No one, when tempted, should say, 'I am being tempted by God'; for God cannot be tempted by evil and he himself tempts no one" (1:13).

I prefer to think of God's moral laws as similar to some of the laws of nature, such as gravity. God does not deliberately make us fall, but, if we defy the law, we are likely to be injured. We do not break the law of gravity; rather we break ourselves on it. But there is more than this. God is not a blind force, as in Star Wars. God is a benevolent, loving parent, and when we make mistakes, God remembers that we are dust, and comes to help us. Indeed, the whole story of the gospel is that God entered into our brokenness in the person of Jesus, forgave our sins, and has given us help in overcoming our sinfulness.

The Lord's Supper

The Eucharist is, for Paul, a powerful non-verbal symbol for the unity of the fellowship. I sometimes think it is a mistake to use, as we often do because they are sanitary and convenient, small chalices and bits of bread. In so doing, we miss the clear symbolism of the oneness of the Body. (The Greek word for *communion (koinonia)* is related to the Greek word for *common,* in exactly the same way that the two English words are related.) When Paul says that "all who eat and drink without discerning the body, eat and drink judgment against themselves" (11:29), he is not referring to our understanding of the mystery of how the ordinary bread becomes the body of Christ, but the mystery of how a vastly diverse community of believers becomes the body of Christ. It is dangerous for us to take Communion when we have hatred for each other, just as surely as it was dangerous for the ancient Hebrew to eat the manna without trusting the God who gave it.

The danger for the Corinthians lay in bringing pagan cultic practices and superstitions to the table of the Lord. The two will not mix, for the Lord's table is not a meal of black magic, but an ordinary meal given extraordinary meaning by the presence of Christ. (Just as ordinary people are given sainthood by that presence.) The danger for moderns is practically the opposite: Communion has little relevance for us because it has little or nothing to do with eating and drinking outside the church. We all know what it means when we take somebody to lunch. It is a sign of fellowship, a good time to get to know someone, or do business with them. In our churches, we ought at least to see that our Holy Meal is a time for us to draw closer to one another.

Conscience and Witness

The Corinthians have a saying: "Knowledge liberates" (implied in v. 23). "Yes," replies Paul, "it does, but liberation is a call to responsibility." Verse 25 is good advice to shoppers. We should not have to wonder, "Is this kosher?" No, as is said to Titus, "To the pure, all things are pure," (1:15). Verse 25 was quoted often to me as, "Eat what's set before you, and ask no questions." This meant to our mother, "Don't embarrass your hostess by inquiring about second helpings." But there is more than manners involved here. We have to do with the basic fact that our liberty was given to us for the good of each other. When Paul says, "Whether you eat or drink, or whatever you do, do everything for the glory of God" (v. 31), he is liberating us just as Augustine did, by saying, "Love God and do as you please." But to love God means to love neighbor ("the second is like unto it"), and if we really love God we will want to take care of our neighbors, especially the weak, ignorant superstitious ones. Our Communion was meant to cast out demons, not conjure them up. So imitate Paul, and be good to one another at every meal, certainly at the Table.

Helping Adults Become Involved

Preparing to Teach

This lesson has a lot to do with some Old Testament stories, so we will want to familiarize ourselves with them. Check out the list suggested above so that you will be able to remind your class about them. You might also want to familiarize yourself with the method of celebrating the Eucharist in your congregation.

Introducing the Main Question

This is not an easy chapter to teach because Paul keeps flopping back and forth between temptation, immorality, and punishment, and the Lord's Supper. Remember two things: First, the first letter to the Corinthians was written for a number of reasons, but one of the most important was to straighten out their ways of worshiping. So expect Paul to have the Communion service in the back of his mind at all times. Second, for Paul, the bottom line in the letter is love (which we will get to in its deepest sense in the last lesson of this quarter, on chapter 13), so when he talks about exorcising the demons of immorality and disobedience, he always has in the back of his mind the way the Corinthians relate to one another.

My reason for raising the issue of magic as part of the main question was partly to get people's attention, and partly because what's at stake in this chapter is a kind of superstitious view of the Lord's Supper. You may want to introduce the question in another way. You might consider starting by letting your class read and report on the Old Testament events involved, or you may wish to begin with the Communion service as practiced in your church. List on the blackboard the various things that the Eucharist means to your members; then use that as grist for your mill in the discussion to follow.

Developing the Lesson

Here is the lesson outline and some suggested questions for discussion.

I. A Warning from history, 10:1-13

Why do Christians study the Old Testament? Is it relevant for us? Debate the question: If you could only have one testament on your desert island, would you take the old or the new? (My answer, believe it or not, is the Old Testament, for several reasons. One, I think I can remember the New Testament better. Two, the Old Testament is longer, with more stories in it, and more reading matter. Third, it was enough Bible for Jesus and the Twelve [in fact, the Old Testament in its present form was not completely put together until *after* the time of Christ]. Finally, my devotional life would not be complete without the book of Psalms.)

A. Christ the Rock, 1-5
God is called a Rock in many Old Testament passages, such as Psalm 19:14. What about New Testament references to Jesus as a rock? (See 1 Pet. 2:4-8; Mark 12:10; Acts 4:11; Rom. 9:32-33.)

Into what other Hebrew scriptures do you think it is appropriate to read the presence of Christ? (The story of Melchizedek, Gen. 14:17-20 and Heb. 7; the story of the Passover Lamb, Exodus 12 and 1 Cor. 5:7-8?) Can this practice be carried too far?

B. Some ancient disasters, 6-10
Does God punish with plagues today? This is a tricky question, especially in the light of the AIDS epidemic, because some people use a simplistic answer as an excuse for dismissing all AIDS victims as sinners. Do not get into this without being willing to look at the other side of the question: Many innocent people suffer from AIDS, and many people who do not have AIDS are sinners. There are other diseases that can easily be oversimplified when thought of as punishments: some forms of addiction, mental illness, even ulcers and heart attacks. Do not forget Job, and also John 9:3.

What can we learn from Israel's failures and punishments?

C. God is faithful, 11-13
Verse 11 implies that Paul expected the world to come to an end soon. Would this have colored his thinking? (For each of us the world will probably come to an end within a very few years.)

Have you ever felt that you were tested beyond your strength? If so, what is the problem with Paul's encouraging word in verse 13?

II. The Lord's Supper, 10:14-22
Evaluate this criticism of Protestants at worship: They gather in a common room for private devotions. Do you speak to one another as the elements are served?

What is the relationship between the Lord's Supper and our everyday meals? Here is a list of scriptural accounts of secular meals in the New Testament that have Eucharistic overtones: Matthew 9:10-13; 14:13-21 (and similar accounts in the other Gospels); Mark 1:29-31; 5:43; 16:13-14; Luke 5:29; 7:36-50; 10:38-42; 14:1-6; 19:1-10; 24:13-35, 36-43; John 2:1-11; 21:9-14; Acts 10:41. What about the Old Testament (Exod. 24:9-11, e.g.)?

Are there demons present in our Communion services? I have suggested that our principal demon is the denial of community. Another way to say it: Their demon was that of stuffing their faces while the neighbor went hungry (11:21), the demon of shouting down their neighbors (14:31), or the demon of drunkenness (11:21), while ours is the demon of false reverence.

III. Conscience and witness, 10:23–11:1
The question of whether to serve wine or grape juice at Communion is a good example of how the strong may have to suppress their own liberty for the good of the weak. Can you think of other examples?

Think of some ways that we can glorify God in our eating and drinking

(v. 31). What about in other common things in life: sleeping, making love, working together, raising children, teaching, recreating?

Helping Class Members Act

I think I would pick up on that last question and see if your class can begin to plan ways in which they may be able to live to the glory of God. That is a vertical way of saying it. The horizontal way of saying it is: How can we live daily to the good of our fellow human beings?

Planning for Next Sunday

The next lesson is on conflict in the church. Ask your class members to be on the lookout for examples that they might discuss.

LESSON 4   MARCH 26

Dealing with Differences

Background Scripture: 2 Corinthians 12–13

The Main Question

"In the beginning," said Martin Buber, "was the Relationship." Christians believe that God contains relationship, so we speak of the Godhead as containing three persons. There is something interpersonal going on even before the creation of the world, so that God says in the beginning, "Let *us* make humankind in *our* image" (Gen. 1:26). It turns out (v. 27) that that image contains relationship: both the masculine and the feminine characteristics. You remember the old French cheer: "Vive le differance!"

What would it be like if we were all alike? It would be terribly crowded at the beach (or in the mountains), because we would all want to go there. We would have no one to talk to because we would all know the same things. What a dull and deplorable world it would be. Thank God for our diversity!

Yet diversity makes for pain. The very things that make life interesting also make it difficult. Or is it the other way around? Thus, the primitive male sang with joy over his bride (Gen. 2:23),

> Flesh of my flesh and bone of my bone,
> It's not good to be alone!

236

But shortly after that he must have sung (though the Bible does not record it):

Women, women, women! What can you do about 'em?
You can't get along with 'em, and you can't get along without 'em!

Women need men, liberals need conservatives, romantics need bean-counters, and readers need writers. We are all different because we need to be. But the question is, how can we deal with our diversity?

Selected Scripture

King James Version	New Revised Standard Version

2 Corinthians 12:19-21; 13:5-13

19 Again, think ye that we excuse ourselves unto you? we speak before God in Christ: but we do all things, dearly beloved, for your edifying.

20 For I fear, lest, when I come, I shall not find you such as I would, and that I shall be found unto you such as ye would not: lest there be debates, envyings, wraths, strifes, backbitings, whisperings, swellings, tumults:

21 And lest, when I come again, my God will humble me among you, and that I shall bewail many which have sinned already, and have not repented of the uncleanness and fornication and lasciviousness which they have committed.

....

5 Examine yourselves, whether ye be in the faith; prove your own selves. Know ye not your own selves, how that Jesus Christ is in you, except ye be reprobates?

6 But I trust that ye shall know that we are not reprobates.

7 Now I pray to God that ye do no evil; not that we should appear approved, but that ye should do that which is honest, though we be as reprobates.

8 For we can do nothing against the truth, but for the truth.

9 For we are glad, when we are weak, and ye are strong: and this also we wish, even your perfection.

2 Corinthians 12:19-21; 13:5-13

19 Have you been thinking all along that we have been defending ourselves before you? We are speaking in Christ before God. Everything we do, beloved, is for the sake of building you up. 20 For I fear that when I come, I may find you not as I wish, and that you may find me not as you wish; I fear that there may perhaps be quarreling, jealousy, anger, selfishness, slander, gossip, conceit, and disorder. 21 I fear that when I come again, my God may humble me before you, and that I may have to mourn over many who previously sinned and have not repented of the impurity, sexual immorality, and licentiousness that they have practiced.

....

5 Examine yourselves to see whether you are living in the faith. Test yourselves. Do you not realize that Jesus Christ is in you?—unless, indeed, you fail to meet the test! 6 I hope you will find out that we have not failed. 7 But we pray to God that you may not do anything wrong— not that we may appear to have met the test, but that you may do what is right, though we may seem to have failed. For we cannot do anything against the truth, but only for the truth. 9 For we rejoice when we are weak and you are strong. This is what we pray for, that you may become perfect. 10 So I write these

10 Therefore I write these things being absent, lest being present I should use sharpness, according to the power which the Lord hath given me to edification, and not to destruction.

11 Finally, brethren, farewell. Be perfect, be of good comfort, be of one mind, live in peace; and the God of love and peace shall be with you.

12 Greet one another with an holy kiss.

13 All the saints salute you.

things while I am away from you, so that when I come, I may not have to be severe in using the authority that the Lord has given me for building up and not for tearing down.

11 Finally, brothers and sisters, farewell. Put things in order, listen to my appeal, agree with one another, live in peace; and the God of love and peace will be with you.

12 Greet one another with a holy kiss. All the saints greet you.

13 The grace of the Lord Jesus Christ, the love of God, and the communion of the Holy Spirit be with all of you.

Key Verse: **Finally, brethren, farewell. Be perfect, be of good comfort, be of one mind, live in peace; and the God of love and peace shall be with you.**

Key Verse: **Finally, brothers and sisters, farewell. Put things in order, listen to my appeal, agree with one another, live in peace; and the God of love and peace will be with you.**

As You Read the Scripture

2 Corinthians 12:1-18. We now take a considerable leap, all the way to the last two chapters of 2 Corinthians, to examine intimately the passionate concern of Paul for his congregation, with some incredible insights into the apostle's own spiritual journey.

Verses 1-10. This is one of Paul's most famous passages, and one of the most debated. Two puzzles stand out: What was the "third heaven" (v. 2), and what was the "thorn in the flesh" (v. 7)? The first question is easier, because we know from the beginning that we are not allowed to answer it. Paul is referring to a deep inner spiritual experience, a mystical ecstasy, which cannot be translated into ordinary language and explained to others (v. 4). Although Paul speaks of the one who had this experience in the third person, it is clear that he is talking about himself. Fourteen years ago would place this in Tarsus, just before the beginning of his missionary activity (Acts 11:25-26). The thorn in the flesh may have been a spiritual enemy, though the most common opinion is a recurring physical illness, such as epilepsy or malaria.

Verses 11-13. These verses can be paraphrased as follows: You have forced me to boast like a fool. You should have known that I had apostolic powers without my having to tell you. The only way I have treated you differently from other churches is not charging you anything. Forgive me! (Is this sarcasm?)

Verses 14-18. "It is not your money I want, it's *you*." Apparently the Corinthians simply could not believe that Paul, for all his refusal to accept a salary, was dipping secretly into the offering. He defends himself by pointing out that Titus and other had helped make sure the offerings got where they were supposed to go. The reference may be to the collection raised for the poor of Jerusalem (1 Cor. 16:1-4).

Chapter 12:9–13:13. The rest of the letter deals with the troubled state of the Corinthian church, and Paul's earnest prayer for them to get their act together.

Verses 19-21. All that he has been saying, he tells them, is not for his own defense, but to try to get them to mend their wicked ways. He gives a disturbing list of their un-Christian behavior.

Verses 1-4. Paul warns the Corinthians that he intends to get in touch with them on what will be his third visit to them. (The first visit is mentioned in Acts 18, when the church was founded, and the second may be the painful visit referred to in 2:1).

Verses 5-10. Paul pleads with them to straighten themselves out on their own, so that he will not have to relate to them as a top-down authority, but can continue to be their servant for building them up.

Verses 11-13. He concludes with a charge and benediction. The charge is that they put things in order and become the community of mutual respect that he has been calling for since the first letter. The holy kiss was a common sign of the fellowship (see Rom. 16:16; 1 Cor. 16:20; 1 Thess. 5:26; and 1 Pet. 5:14). Mediterranean people seem to be more comfortable with expressing their affection for one another, while our culture is given to hand-shaking. The final benediction (v. 13, KJV; v. 14, NRSV) is a lovely trinitarian formula that we often use in our churches today.

The Scripture and the Main Question

Personal Paul

The apostle Paul was a vulnerable man. That is, he was so secure in his faith that he could allow himself to be an open book to others. In his letters we are privileged to see into his mind and heart, for he frankly shares his frustrations, hopes, embarrassments, and triumphs with those to whom he writes. In no portion of his writings we are allowed more intimately into Paul's soul than in 2 Corinthians 12.

Ecstasy and Pain

First, we discover that Paul was a mystic. This does not mean that he lived forever in the clouds, for mystics can be very practical people; but that, at least some of the time, he was able to experience something of the presence of God. The very word *mysticism* can be a little frightening to everyday Christians, because it makes us think of someone in a trance, or in another dimension. We picture the French monk, who, according to legend, went for a walk in the forest and stopped, entranced, to listen to a lark singing. When he returned to his monastery, no one recognized him; it seems that he had been caught up into timeless eternity, and that his spiritual moment had actually lasted for a hundred years. I suppose you might say he had been caught up into the third heaven. (By the way, we need not speculate about the number of levels in heaven, because Paul's use of the *third* simply means *very high,* in the same sense we use the word in the phrase the "third degree.")

Most of us are shy about deep emotional experiences. We are more like the small boy who traveled out west with his family. He seemed unimpressed with all the natural wonders, but, on the evening after their visit to the Grand Canyon, his mother noticed that he made an entry in his trip diary. Curious to see how the immense vista had affected him, she peered into the book to find that he had written, "Today, I spit a mile!"

But, somewhere between the transcendent French monk and the blasé young tourist, we ought to find ourselves. We want to keep our feet on the ground of this real world, but there ought to be some deeply moving experiences in our lives that we find it difficult to communicate to others.

Paul had no trouble keeping his feet on the ground because his thorn in the flesh brought him back to earth (v. 7). All of the following have been seriously suggested as being the recurring trouble that kept him humble: sexual desire, persecution by enemies, doubts, pride, shortness of stature, epilepsy, headaches, eye trouble (see Acts 9:9, and Gal. 4:15; 6:11), and malaria. Whatever it was, it caused him great pain and frustration. But, every time he prayed for it to be taken away, God would answer, "My grace is sufficient for you." It is an answer no human being is good enough to give to another who has problems, but, from God, it is enough.

Fool for Christ

Paul has already spoken of himself as a fool in this letter (11:16, 17, 21), always in the context of his struggle to be both humble and wise. He had said in the first letter, "If you think that you are wise in this age, you should become fools so that you may become wise" (3:18). This is the incredible catch that lies at the heart of the gospel (I call it "Catch One"): Those who want to save their lives must lose them.

Utter Unselfishness

One of the best litmus tests for distinguishing false prophets from true is, "How much do they charge?" The grace of God, by definition, is free, and those who charge for it have proven they do not understand it. (Read Acts 8:18-20 and Matthew 7:15-20.) But, so accustomed are we to paying for our blessings that the Corinthians seem to have been insulted that Paul (who made tents for a living) refused to accept a salary from them.

Ministering to a Troubled Church

The Corinthian church was, from its beginnings, terribly divided. Look back at 1 Corinthians 1:11-12. Paul indicates that there were at least four groups in the church. It has been suggested that those who claimed to belong to Paul were those who believed in Christian liberty; those who claimed to be Apollos' disciples were the intellectually inclined; the followers of Cephas (Peter) would have been the Judaizers, or legalists; and those who claimed to be of Christ were the ultra self-righteous folks in the congregation. Whatever the divisions represented, it was clear for Paul that party spirit is contrary to the way of Christ, as is impurity and licentiousness.

Into the Fray

But, into this combat zone Paul fearlessly charges. It has been said that there are three ways to deal with conflict: flee, fight, or face. You flee when it is not the right time to deal with it (Luke 4:29-30), you fight when you must (John 2:15), but when you can, you calmly face it out (Mat. 22:46). (I have cited an example of Jesus' use of each of the three methods.) Paul's methods of dealing with the conflict in the Corinthian church included his personal example (1 Cor. 11:1), his prayers (13:7), his pleading by letter (the two chapters of this lesson in particular), and his presence (13:2).

A Solemn Warning

Paul warns them that he will not be lenient when he comes. He will insist on the use of fair means of proof (13:1), but he will bring all the power of the crucified Christ to bear on their problems. There are some times when you just have to get tough.

A Prayerful Wish

He prays for their perfection, after the manner of our Lord (Matt. 5:48). Maybe, by some miracle, even these Corinthians will have learned to live with each other by the time he gets there.

A Word of Farewell

But probably not. The conflict in Corinth went on long after Paul's time. Ancient Corinth is no more, but the conflict continues. Today there are more than three hundred parties in the church in this country, and within them even more divisions. And Paul still calls to us, across the years: "Put things in order, listen to my appeal, agree with one another, live in peace; and the God of love and peace will be with you." Kiss and make up.

Helping Adults Become Involved

Preparing to Teach

As you will have noticed, I am so interested in Paul's ecstasy and agony that I spend too much time in the first ten verses of chapter 12, so that little time is left for the matter of conflict in the church in the rest of the lesson. So do not follow my advice. As Paul would say, "I have been a fool." All the same, though, I think that, like Paul, you and I will not be able to handle the conflict as we should until we have plumbed our spiritual highs and lows. In order to be a good mediator, or conflict resolutionist, I must have won some sort of victory over the conflicts in myself. If not, I will be in danger of following the old adage: "When in danger, or in doubt, run in circles, scream and shout." A steady hand is needed. So, as you prepare for this lesson, be sure you have worked through your own conflicts. If you have a third heaven, or a little locked garden (that is what the word *paradise* [12:4] means at the root), then go to it and renew yourself. And, if you have a thorn in the flesh, seek the sufficient grace to enable you to accept it. Then you will be a good teacher. I do not want the conflict management expert to experience a loss of temper. (Unless, of course, it is appropriate.)

Introducing the Main Question

You might try the following trick as you begin your class. My brother, who is a pastor, did it once in his own parish and it worked pretty well. He stood in the middle of the room and said, "I represent the middle ground in this church. Everybody line up on either side of me on left or right according to your ecclesiastical politics." There was much shuffling about, and good-humored teasing, "Hey Charlie, you ought to be out in the street!" In the end they decided they would rather think of themselves as one congregation than as people of different parties. That is what Paul wanted for the Corinthians.

You might read the sentence in the section above ("Ministering to a Troubled Church") that describes the four parties of 1 Corinthians 1:11-12. (This is more fully described in William Barclay's commentary, cited in the first lesson, pages 14-15.) See if your people identify with any of those four cliques, or if they are conscious of any such divisions within your church. Then you can start, with some real divisions to deal with.

If either of the above suggestions are too threatening, you can just talk about conflict in the abstract, as I did in "The Main Question." However, remember the cardinal rule of conflict resolution: Conflicts are far better talked out than swept aside.

Developing the Lesson

Use the following outline and discussion questions:

I. Personal Paul, 12:1-18
Does Paul talk too much about himself?

Should a preacher use anecdotes about his personal life? My father, a minister, told me never to mention myself in the pulpit. I disagree with him; my self is the only person I know much about. How can I talk about the faith in the abstract? But there must be a line between good personal story sharing and burdening people with your own personal problems.

A. Ecstasy and pain, 12:1-10
What do you think Paul's mystical experience was like?

Have you ever had one? Even a little one, like a sense of being deeply moved at a lake-side candlelight service at a Junior High camp?

Are Christians who have been to the third heaven superior to other Christians? No, but do we owe them special respect?

What do you think Paul's thorn in the flesh was? Have you got any other ideas besides those listed above? What about a lazy son or daughter or an old sin, committed long ago that comes back to haunt?

Does 12:9 mean that God deliberately hurts us so we will not get the big head? (I say, no, God not capricious, but the fact that life is frustrating does prevent us from pride.)

B. Fool for Christ, 12:11-13
The word *fool* used by Paul here is the same Greek word warned against by Jesus in Matthew 5:22, *moros*, from which our word *moron* comes. Apparently

there is a good kind of fool and a bad kind. What do you think makes the difference?

Have you ever experienced the same sort of struggle Paul is having here? The closest example in my life is when I have tried to feign ignorance on a question so that my children could exercise their strength. I have become a fool so that they can learn from my wisdom.

C. Utter unselfishness, 12:14-18

Do you think that all clergy should be paid the same salary (perhaps with allowances for dependents)? Should we make them support themselves?

II. Ministering to a troubled church, 12:19–13:13
A. Into the fray, 12:19-21

Paul is eager to go back to the church with all the troubles. Is he crazy, or what? Do you think his description of the Corinthians is anything like our churches today?

B. A solemn warning, 13:1-4

Are there times when pastors and missionaries should get tough? What does this do to their image as followers of Christ? Did Paul ever get tough? Was he ever *not* tough?

C. A prayerful wish, 13:5-10

What would (do) you pray for your congregation? Could some miracle happen and it be made perfect?

D. A word of farewell, 13:11-13 (14)

Do the people in your congregation kiss each other? (In mine they are very standoffish.) But the point is not if they kiss, but rather, if they live in harmony.

Helping Class Members Act

Have them read verses 11-13 and make a solemn promise to live according to those verses for at least one week!

Planning for Next Sunday

We are going back to 1 Corinthians 12 next week. Ask each class member to be thinking about what his or her gift is.

UNIT II: NURTURING THE LIFE OF THE COMMUNITY

FOUR LESSONS   APRIL 2–23

In the first two lessons we look at the spiritual gifts that all of us possess, in incredible variety, and examine the ways in which we put these gifts together in the act of worship. First Corinthians is the closest thing we have to a description of the early church at its liturgy, so it is fascinating to look at our own practices in the light of theirs. We have to remember that much of what Paul wrote was criticism of mistakes and excesses of which the Corinthians were guilty, but, behind those corrections, we can begin to build a picture of what the ideal worshiping community might be like: diverse and enthusiastic, and, when its differences are seen as gifts rather than as burdens, the basis for a rich broth for the nourishment of the soul.

In the last two lessons, we experience the risen Christ as the foundation of our community's joy, and the source of our strength in relating to one another. The first of these, which is our Easter lesson, focuses on the place of the good news in our life as a church. The second lesson focuses on a willingness to restrict voluntarily our own freedom, to support one another more effectively, so that we may fulfill our ministry together.

LESSON 5   APRIL 2

Building Up the Body

Background Scripture: 1 Corinthians 12

The Main Question

This is a continuation of last week's lesson. We are still struggling with the wonderfully rich diversity of the Body of Christ, which is the church. Our lesson takes its title, "Building Up the Body," from a very similar passage (Eph. 4;16), and it would be worth your while to read that chapter (especially Eph. 4:1-16) along with today's passage from 1 Corinthians. They are both about Christians living and working together in harmony and peace. Indeed, that is what the two letters, 1 and 2 Corinthians, are mostly about. They have more to say about Christians getting along with each other than they do about witnessing to the rest of the world.

And that is where we have to start. Evangelism means lots of things. It means the words that we speak, it means the deeds of compassion that we do, and it also means the life-style that we live. My friends who are overseas missionaries tell me that there is no room for dominationalism in the foreign fields. It is pretty hard to explain to a new convert from paganism that you have about three hundred different Christian bodies to choose from when you join a church in this country. Indeed, a watchword for our time

244

might well be, "Let's quit fighting each other so we can start fighting the devil!" (See Ephesians 6:12.)

This marvelous chapter (1 Cor. 12) is like a passage from Beethoven's ninth symphony, building powerfully until the chorus bursts forth with the hymn to love in chapter 13. Study it together, asking two main questions (that are really the same): 1.) What is my spiritual gift? 2.) How does it relate to the gifts of others?

Selected Scripture

King James Version

1 Corinthians 12:4-20, 26

4 Now there are diversities of gifts, but the same Spirit.

5 And there are differences of administrations, but the same Lord.

6 And there are diversities of operations, but it is the same God which worketh all in all.

7 But the manifestation of the Spirit is given to every man to profit withal.

8 For to one is given by the Spirit the word of wisdom; to another the word of knowledge by the same Spirit;

9 To another faith by the same Spirit; to another the gifts of healing by the same Spirit;

10 To another the working of miracles; to another prophecy; to another discerning of spirits; to another divers kinds of tongues; to another the interpretation of tongues:

11 But all these worketh that one and the selfsame Spirit, dividing to every man severally as he will.

12 For as the body is one, and hath many members, and all the members of that one body, being many, are one body: so also is Christ.

13 For by one Spirit we are all baptized into one body, whether we be Jews or Gentiles, whether we be bond or free; and have been all made to drink into one Spirit.

14 For the body is not one member, but many.

15 If the foot shall say, Because I am not the hand, I am not of the

New Revised Standard Version

1 Corinthians 12:4-20, 26

4 Now there are varieties of gifts, but the same Spirit; 5 and there are varieties of services, but the same Lord; 6 and there are varieties of activities, but it is the same God who activates all of them in everyone. 7 To each is given the manifestation of the Spirit for the common good. 8 To one is given through the Spirit the utterance of wisdom, and to another the utterance of knowledge according to the same Spirit, 9 to another faith by the same Spirit, to another gifts of healing by the one Spirit, 10 to another the working of miracles, to another prophecy, to another the discernment of spirits, to another various kinds of tongues, to another the interpretation of tongues. 11 All these are activated by one and the same Spirit, who allots to each one individually just as the Spirit chooses.

12 For just as the body is one and has many members, and all the members of the body, though many, are one body, so it is with Christ. 13 For in the one Spirit we were all baptized into one body—Jews or Greek, slaves or free—and we were all made to drink of one Spirit.

14 Indeed, the body does not consist of one member but of many. 15 If the foot would say, "Because I am not a hand, I do not belong to the body," that would not make it any

body; is it therefore not of the body?

16 And if the ear shall say, Because I am not the eye, I am not of the body; is it therefore not of the body?

17 If the whole body were an eye, where were the hearing? If the whole were hearing, where were the smelling?

18 But now hath God set the members every one of them in the body, as it hath pleased him.

19 And if they were all one member, where were the body?

20 But now are they many members, yet but one body.

....

26 And whether one member suffer, all the members suffer with it; or one member be honoured, all the members rejoice with it.

Key Verse: **But the manifestation of the Spirit is given to every man to profit withal.**

less a part of the body. 16 And if the ear would say, "Because I am not an eye, I do not belong to the body," that would not make it any less a part of the body. 17 If the whole body were an eye, where would the hearing be? If the whole body were hearing, where would the sense of smell be? 18 But as it is, God arranged the members in the body, each one of them, as he chose. 19 If all were a single member, where would the body be? 20 As it is, there are many members, yet one body.

....

26 If one member suffers, all suffer together with it; if one member is honored, all rejoice together with it.

Key Verse: **To each is given the manifestation of the Spirit for the common good.**

As You Read the Scripture

1 Corinthians 12:1-3. The first verse could be translated to begin, "Now concerning spirituality . . ." (the word *gifts* does not occur). Not every voice that speaks to you in the night is the Spirit of God; there are evil spirits as well. "Jesus is Lord" is perhaps the oldest, and certainly the briefest, of our confessions. It may have been the formula in worship by which the new convert testified to his faith in Christ before and after baptism. In the Greek, the evil and the good formula stand as parallel opposites: Anathema Jesus vs. Lord Jesus.

Verses 4-6. This is a lovely trinitarian formula, perhaps unconsciously formed by Paul with his natural gift for rhetoric:

Varieties of gifts *(charismata)* . . . same Spirit who gives,
Varieties of service *(diakonia)* . . . same Lord who serves,
Varieties of activity *(energemata)* . . . same God who activates.

Verses 7-11. The list of gifts is instructive. Note that tongues comes at the end (it was a problem for the Corinthians), closely followed by interpretation. The gifts are:

Wisdom *(sophia;* the deep awareness of God)
Knowledge *(gnosis;* common sense in the world)
Faith (not merely intellectual assent, but commitment)
Healing (a gift many people have the hands for)
Miracles *(energemata dunameon;* literally: works of power)
Prophecy (necessary because there was no New Testament!)

Discernment of spirits (note the comments on verse 1)
Tongues *(glossa)*
Interpretation *(hermeneia;* literally "translation")

Verses 12-13. The phrase "the body of Christ" does not originate with Paul, but with Jesus (Mark 14:22). But it is Paul who squeezes from the metaphor its fullest meanings, including this wonderful parable about the simultaneous unity and diversity of the church. Verse 13 is Paul's strongest statement about Christian equality. It is found also in Galatians 3:28, where Paul adds the phrase "male or female." Why do you suppose he left it out here? The Corinthians had welcomed women into participation in their worship, an extraordinary social revolution, especially in the light of Judaism's customs. Paul cautions them in this letter (14:34-36) not to go too far with this, so he may have omitted the sexual distinction as being too sensitive for the Corinthians at this moment. But the point is that in spite of our differences, we are all one in Body and Spirit.

Verses 14-26. Parables are hard to come up with. They sound so simple, as Jesus tells them, but have you ever tried to write one? This is Paul's best parable, approaching the skills of the master Teacher. A child can understand the metaphor of the body. Indeed, one of my very earliest memories is making a church out of my hands, and chanting, "Open the door, and there's all the people." These verses need little comment.

Chapters 12:27–13:1. If I had been the person putting chapter and verse numbers in the Bible, I would have made a chapter division here. Let's say that the orchestra is building up in chapter 12 to the grand hymn in chapter 13. So do not stop here. The whole point of 1 Corinthians is *agape* love, the more excellent way.

The Scripture and the Main Question

Jesus Is Lord

How can you tell whether a spirit is truly the Holy Spirit? There are many tests (e.g., how much money is being asked for?), such as the scriptures, your common sense, by the fruits shown. Once a beggar asked for some money from one of the members of our church at the close of the worship service. When the church member said he was sorry, but he had no silver or gold, the man flew into a rage. "I am an angel of God," he cried, "and I will bring my curse on you, for I am possessed of the Spirit." And he continued to curse the church member for his selfishness. At this, another member began to quote softly from Galatians 5:22-23, "The fruit of the Spirit is love, joy, peace, patience, kindness, generosity, faithfulness, gentleness, and self-control." The beggar ceased his railing and left. Now he may well have been an "angel unawares" (Heb. 13:2), but he did not sound like it. Anyway, one way to tell is by evidence of love for Jesus. On the other side of the coin, when a person *does* affirm that Jesus is Lord, we can be sure that the Spirit is present, in however faint a way, for without the Spirit, no one can say this.

The Gifts of the Spirit

First Corinthians 12:8-10 is one of several Pauline lists of the Spirit's gifts (see also Gal. 5:22-23, Rom. 12:6-8, and Eph. 4:11). The one and the same

Spirit, Paul concludes, works all these things, distributing individually to each. What sort of list would you make? In thinking of worship, for example, you might list the gifts of playing the organ or piano, singing in the choir, taking up the offering, or ushering. But are those really gifts? Most everybody who practices can learn to do those things. Try another list: the gifts of joyful enthusiasm, of making people feel welcome, of reflective listening. Now we are getting warmer. But we have a long way to go to get to the incredible pluralism of first-century Corinth. Paul is opening us to the possibility of radical pluralism within the Body of Christ. He is giving us the unbelievable truth that God sometimes inspires and loves people who seem very crazy or different, and the opposite—and equally valid—truth that we must listen to one another and upbuild the community in love.

The Spirit and the Body

Paul's soaring spirit does not remain in the stratosphere of the third heaven. He comes down to earth, with the most earthy of images (see also Rom. 12:5), the human body. He got this, of course, from Jesus, but has expanded it into a memorable parable. Can you come up with some others? Because I am a three-chord picker, I sometimes like to picture the church as an orchestra, in which each of us plays a different instrument, to create a whole sound. Or, perhaps, a grand choir (this is the metaphor of Rev. 4–5), in which some of us are sopranos, some altos, some tenors, some basses.

I also have one other image by which to express the simultaneous unity and diversity (e pluribus unum?) of the church, and that is to say that God seems to prefer crunchy peanut butter to the creamy smooth kind. Apparently, God wants a few nuts in the church to make it interesting.

The Body of Christ

I cannot improve on Paul's metaphor of the body. Let me just suggest an additional thought. Only one chapter away from Paul's declaration (v. 27), "Now you are the body," we have the wonderful words of the institution of the Holy Supper (11:23-26) in which Jesus calls the bread his body. I am indebted to Henry Nouwen for reminding me of the many times in which this formula is repeated in the Gospels: at the last supper (Matt. 26:26, Mark 14:22, Luke 22:19), at the feeding of the multitude (Matt. 14:19, 15:36, Mark 8:6, Luke 9:16, John 6:11), and at the Emmaeus supper (Luke 24:30). I will quote only this last verse, but you might wish to look at all the others, to see what a hypnotic repetition of the four verbs you find there. I emphasize them here: "When he was at the table with them, he *took* bread, *blessed* and *broke* it, and *gave* it to them" (Luke 24:30).

Because we, the church, are the Body of Christ, these verbs are applied to us, and we can truly say:

> I have been *taken* (chosen) for God's purpose.
> I have been *blessed* in a special way by God.
> I have been *broken* in spirit, that I may learn to serve.
> I have been *given* as a blessing to others.

It is a high calling to which we have all been called.

The Highest Gift

The highest form that calling takes is the gift of *agape* love. Not *storge,* natural affection, though we are a part of God's family. Not *eros,* passion, though we are married to Christ. And not even *philia,* friendship, though we have been called Jesus' friends. No, the highest calling is *agape,* the divine charity, the never-ending mercy and grace of God that the King James version of the Bible calls *charity.*

There is a tendency on the part of Christians to arrange the gifts in order of their worth in God's eyes. (I remember a cartoon in the *New Yorker* some years ago in which one monk is saying to another, "But I *am* holier than thou!") It is hard for us not to rate the virtues. Paul himself does so in verse 28, listing apostleship first and tongue-speaking last. Perhaps he did this deliberately because of the tendency of charismatic (that word means *gifted,* and can be used equally well for one who is a dusty, intellectual, bookish scholar on a head-trip as for one who shouts during worship) folk to feel that somehow, because they have spoken in tongues, that they are superior to other Christians. But the notion of superiority should be completely foreign to Christianity (see Rom. 12:3). We have *different* gifts, not better.

But there is a better gift, a still more excellent way, without which none of the other gifts are more than an empty gong. We will get to that in our last lesson, appropriately saved for the climax of our Corinthian study. For now, let us simply remember that, however gifted we may be, our gifts are for the mutual upbuilding of the community, not for our own glory. This is one of a number of small paradoxes that run throughout the Bible. We are chosen, but for service, not for self-glorification. We are blessed, but for others, not for ourselves. We are broken, not for punishment, but for promise. And we are sent into all the world.

Helping Adults Become Involved

Preparing to Teach

It occurred to me, at lunch today, that I am writing these lesson helps *three years* before they will be used. Who knows what will happen in the world between now and the time you pick this book up. When I did my lessons for 1992, I had no idea that there would be no such things as world communism by then! So I am shy about telling you how to prepare to teach this lesson. But, let me make a suggestion anyway. Look at the world around you. See what divisions there are separating race from race, nation from nation, class from class, and relatives from relatives. Ask yourself what lines of separation are drawn within your own congregation. Then, having listed those, raise the question of how those lines ought to be crossed by the open arms of the church. Should your church be making a conscious effort to reach out to those who are different, beyond your walls? Should you be reaching in to those who are already within your walls, but who are different?

Think about your class. Is *it* diverse? Is there a way you can celebrate the presence of each individual there, with his or her gifts? You see that I am proposing that you prepare for this lesson not so much by immersing yourself in the scripture (though you should do that, too, for it is so familiar that we might overlook something), but immersing yourself into the family that is your class.

THIRD QUARTER

Introducing the Main Question

You might try asking everyone to write on a three-by-five card one of their strong points. (Be warned, most Christians find it easier to think of their sins than their virtues.) Then you could begin your class with a celebration of gifts, by designing a litany somewhat like the following:

Leader (reading from 3-by-5 card): For musical ability, O Lord,
People: We give you thanks and praise.
Leader: For patience with those around me who are slow, O Lord,
People: We give you thanks and praise.

And so on.

Or you might use a litany built around the scriptures themselves. Verses 4-13 make a wonderful litany. Simply read them aloud, instructing your people to call out, "One Spirit," whenever you raise your hand. Then, raise your hand whenever the phrase "the same Spirit," or "the Spirit," or "one Spirit," (etc.) occurs.

Developing the Lesson

Use the following lesson outline and questions.

I. Jesus is Lord, 12:1-3

Do we really worship idols today (v. 2)? If so, what are they called?

Is Jesus really Lord in our lives? How do you feel about this statement: "Most Christians accept Jesus as Savior (one who gives them eternal life) but do not really believe in him as Lord (one who has duties for them to perform here on earth)."

Could a liar proclaim Jesus as Lord? Would that person then be speaking in the Spirit?

II. The gifts of the Spirit, 12:4-11

Were the Corinthians too enthusiastic? (Look up the meaning of that word.) On the day of Pentecost, the early disciples were accused of being drunk. Would that be a likely charge against United Methodists today? Do you wish it were? (Not "Do you wish we would get drunk," but "Do you wish we would be so fired up that people would *think* we were drunk?")

What are some of the gifts of the Spirit in your congregation? In your Sunday school class? In the world around you?

Does the Spirit move amongst those who some might say are not our kind of people? How? And how are we to spot such movement?

III. The Spirit and the body, 12:12-13

Can you come up with another metaphor or parable for the church as both unity and diversity?

How many jobs can you think of that you can get the church to pay you to do? Here are some that I know of: calligrapher, airplane pilot, dentist, certified public accountant, obstetrician. What does this say about a diversity of gifts?

How would you translate Paul's egalitarian phrases: Jew and Greek, slave and free, male and female, into contemporary terms? East and west? Black and white? Protestant and Catholic? Jew and Christian? Is not male and female (I borrowed this from Gal. 3:28, but it fits here) still a valid phrase today?

Think of the person you like least in this world. Does he or she have a gift to give you? What is it?

Think of yourself. What is your greatest gift?

IV. The Body of Christ, 12:14-26

We belong to more than one body. Most of us, for instance, are Americans. This is another way of saying that whatever we do involves everyone else. "No one is an island." Do you believe this?

What are some of the other bodies you belong to?

Can an individual ever act without affecting others?

Are there times when we must all act as a single sword? That phrase is from Chesterton's hymn, "O God of Earth and Altar." Ask it in some other ways. Should the church ever speak with one voice? Should the parts ever act as a whole? What if they should, but cannot agree in how, when, and where?

V. The highest gift, 12:27–13:1

Should chapter 12 end at verse 26? If not, where would you have made the division?

In what sense is love a gift of the Spirit? Why doesn't Paul put it in his list in verses 8-10?

If love is the greatest gift, then is it true that every one of us is capable of rising to the very top?

Helping Class Members Act

The hardest task of a teacher is to enable the class members to believe in themselves, that they are really full of power for good. Send your people forth ready to go to work, if you can. What about asking each of them to make a resolution for the week to come?

Planning for Next Sunday

Ask everyone to bring a bulletin from their next worship service, noting on it places where they see *love* taking place.

Growing Through Worship

Background Scripture: 1 Corinthians 14:1-33*a*

The Main Question

Well, we have skipped chapter 13, but we will get back to it on the last Sunday in the quarter, as the climax to our studies. But chapter 14 is an important one, too. It contains (v. 26) the closest thing we have to a church bulletin from the first century. What do you suppose worship was really like for the earliest Christians?

From what we can glean from 1 Corinthians, its overall impression to an outsider (14:16, 17) must have been one of confusion! Everybody seemed to be talking at once, some of them in strange tongues, almost shouting each other down in their eagerness to testify. As for the meal, they were stuffing their faces without waiting for one another, and even getting drunk (11:21)! When is the last time anybody got drunk at a Communion service in your church?

Whereas the sin of the early church seems to have been one of rowdy carousing, the sin of our churches today seems to be one of lack of enthusiasm. If Paul should show up today, I think he would not warn us to do more decently and orderly (14:40), but to emphasize the gifts of the Spirit (14:39). If we are to grow through our worship, we must all have a chance to take part—children, youth, and adults. We must all be willing to listen and learn from one another (14:31).

The main question for us, then, is, how can contemporary Christians recover the wonderful joy and enthusiasm of the early church at worship, without losing our heads? Some wag has said, "The Pentecostals will get to heaven if they don't overshoot." Well, maybe the rest of us will too, if we do not fall short.

Selected Scripture

King James Version

*1 Corinthians 14:20-33*a

20 Brethren, be not children in understanding: howbeit in malice be ye children, but in understanding be men.

21 In the law it is written, With men of other tongues and other lips will I speak unto this people; and yet for all that will they not hear me, saith the Lord.

22 Wherefore tongues are for a sign, not to them that believe, but to them that believe not: but prophesy-

New Revised Standard Version

*1 Corinthians 14:20-33*a

20 Brothers and sisters, do not be children in your thinking; rather, be infants in evil, but in thinking be adults. 21 In the law it is written,

"By people of strange tongues
    and by the lips of foreigners
I will speak to this people:
    yet even then they will not
        listen to me,"

says the Lord. 22 Tongues, then, are a sign not for believers but for unbelievers, while prophecy is not for ing serveth not for them that believe not, but for them which believe.

23 If therefore the whole church be come together into one place, and all speak with tongues, and there come in those that are unlearned, or unbelievers, will they not say that ye are mad?

24 But if all prophesy, and there come in one that believeth not, or one unlearned, he is convinced of all, he is judged of all:

25 And thus are the secrets of his heart made manifest; and so falling down on his face, he will worship God, and report that God is in you of a truth.

26 How is it then, brethren? when ye come together, every one of you hath a psalm, hath a doctrine, hath a tongue, hath a revelation, hath an interpretation. Let all things be done unto edifying.

27 If any man speak in an unknown tongue, let it be by two, or at the most by three, and that by course; and let one interpret.

28 But if there be no interpreter, let him keep silence in the church; and let him speak to himself, and to God.

29 Let the prophets speak two or three, and let the other judge.

30 If any thing be revealed to another that sitteth by, let the first hold his peace.

31 For ye may all prophesy one by one, that all may learn, and all may be comforted.

32 And the spirits of the prophets are subject to the prophets.

33 For God is not the author of confusion, but of peace, as in all churches of the saints.

Key Verse: **How is it then, brethren? when ye come together, every one of you hath a psalm, hath a doctrine, hath a tongue, hath a revelation, hath an interpretation. Let all things be done unto edifying.**

unbelievers but for believers. 23 If, therefore, the whole church comes together and all speak in tongues, and outsiders or unbelievers enter, will they not say that you are out of your mind? 24 But if all prophesy, an unbeliever or outsider who enters is reproved by all and called to account by all. 25 After the secrets of the unbeliever's heart are disclosed, that person will bow down before God and worship him, declaring, "God is really among you."

26 What should be done then, my friends? When you come together, each one has a hymn, a lesson, a revelation, a tongue, or an interpretation. Let all things be done for building up. 27 If anyone speaks in a tongue, let there be only two or at most three, and each in turn, and let one interpet. 28 But if there is no one to interpet, let them be silent in church and speak to themselves and to God. 29 Let two or three prophets speak, and let the others weight what is said. 30 If a revelation is made to someone else sitting nearby, let the first person be silent. 31 For you can all prophesy one by one, so that all may learn and all be encouraged. 32 And the spirits of prophets are subject to the prophets, 33 for God is a God not of disorder but of peace.

(As in all the churches of the saints.)

Key Verse: **What should be done then, my friends? When you come together, each one has a hymn, a lesson, a revelation, a tongue, or an interpretation. Let all things be done for building up.**

As You Read the Scripture

1 Corinthians 14:1-25. There are two key elements that must be dealt with here, speaking in tongues *(lalon glosson)* and prophecy *(propheteuon)*. They might be easier to understand if we call them *ecstasy* and *preaching*. They both involve emotion and intellect, but tongue-speaking is essentially a non-verbal experience, and prophecy is clearly a matter of the mind. At the risk of over-simplification, call them the visceral (gut feelings) and the cerebral (head thoughts). This is certainly the way Paul sees them. As we see in verse 14, tongues involve the spirit, not the mind.

Verses 1-5. It is to the credit of the Corinthians that their differences on the pentecostal question had not yet resulted in their separating into two meetings. Paul gives credit to both sides, but makes it clear that he considers tongue-speaking to be primarily a personal experience, whereas prophecy (proclaiming the truth, or preaching) is for the building up of the whole congregation.

Verses 6-12. If you like biblical trivia, you will enjoy answering this question: where in the Bible are all four sections of the orchestra mentioned? In the Old Testament, it is Psalm 150, but in 1 Corinthians 13–14 we also find the four major instruments: percussion (13:1), woodwinds and strings (14:7), and the horns (14:8). Paul's point is that the non-verbal language of music is at best uncertain; surely we should strive to use the best means of clear communication possible. He speaks of those who use non-verbal sounds, saying, "the speaker [is] a foreigner to me" (v. 11). The Greek word for foreigner is *barbaros,* from which we get *barbarian.* Believe it or not, the word comes from "ba-ba-ba-ba," a meaningless repetition of sounds.

Verses 13-19. It is clear that "amen" does not mean "ten-four," as some Christians believe, but "Right on!," or, "Let it be so!" If the outsiders are to say yes, they need to understand the words.

Verses 20-25. tongues then are O.K. for those who understand them, but they are confusing to the outsider, and so not a useful tool for evangelism.

Verses 26-40. The guiding principle for understanding Paul's description of the Corinthians at worship is to remember that he was criticizing them, not describing their ideal worship. We have to ask what it would have been like at best.

Verses 26-33*a*. Apparently worship in old Corinth was a hodge-podge of lay participation, people shouting at once, and the presentation of many different gifts. Wouldn't it be wonderful!

Verses 33*b*-36. It is difficult for us to realize how biased in favor of males the world of the first century was. By ancient standards, Corinth was a liberated church, so Paul seems to feel the need to get the women to be quiet, perhaps so as not to endanger their newfound liberty, which was a radical departure from the Jewish custom in which women were not even allowed in the inner court.

Verses 37-40. The chapter concludes with Paul's call for decency and order. But, please take note, decency and order are not the *sine que non* of worship. Read verses 39 and 40, which essentially say, "Do not neglect the gifts of the Spirit, just make sure they are used decently."

The Scripture and the Main Question

Prophecy and Tongues

Prophecy does not so much mean foretelling the future (though it may include that) as it does setting forth the mind of God. It has always been associated with divine inspiration, and sometimes with outward forms of ecstasy. In 1 Samuel 10:5-10, and again in 19:18-24, we encounter bands of prophets who were experiencing a kind of ecstatic frenzy. Such prophets in the Muslim tradition were once called whirling dervishes. To be a prophet means to have a word from God, but it also carries with it the idea of inspiration (note the "spirit" hiding in the middle of that word), of being Spirit-filled. (See 1 Samuel 10:10 and 19:23.)

Tongue-speaking is clearly associated with the outpouring of the Spirit (Acts 2:4), but it also has to do with communicating the word, for, as the Acts account makes clear, though some folks thought the apostles were drunk (Acts 2:13), for many the result was understanding (Acts 2:8). The two gifts, then, do not have a clear line drawn between them. But, for Paul's purposes, and ours, in this chapter they are contrasted. By prophecy, Paul means intellectually inspired preaching, by tongue-speaking he means emotionally inspired ecstasy. To use the language of some psychologists, prophecy is a left-brain experience and tongue-speaking a right-brain experience. I prefer to say that the one is cerebral, the other visceral. Paul does not say that one is bad and the other good; they are merely different and have different functions. But Paul clearly favors prophecy (v. 19), because it edifies.

The Importance of Communication

Both the verbal and the non-verbal are necessary in worship. Protestants have traditionally emphasized the word, which is verbal, whereas Catholics (at least prior to Vatican II) emphasized the Mass, which is nonverbal. I once asked a Catholic priest friend, "Why is it that I see people of all different economic classes in the Catholic church, while we Protestants seem to have a different denomination for every three thousand dollars in per-capita income?" He replied, "It's because you Protestants make worship an intellectual experience, so the level of education matters. The Mass, which is in Latin, does not involve understanding but feeling. It's a drama, with color, incense, and music. But the sermon, which is the centerpiece of your worship, involves the head more than the heart."

Well, I am not saying he is entirely right, but it makes me think. I have noticed that, since Vatican II, there has been much more emphasis on the word in Roman Catholic churches, and much more interest in color, dance, ritual, and drama among Protestants. But the important thing for us is that we recognize the need for both sides of the brain in what we do. At least the Corinthians had the virtue of bringing their disagreement out in the open. Their problem was that of allowing themselves to feel superior because of their particular gifts.

Interpreting Sounds

What we hear is even more important than what we see. If you want to demonstrate that, try watching television without the sound, then listening to it without the picture. In the latter case it will be much more intelligible. My grandmother who went blind, continued to be an active, interested member of society. My other grandmother, who lost her hearing, withdrew into a kind of paranoid state because she missed the point of all the jokes and thought we were laughing at her. At the heart of all social activity lies the necessity that we understand one another. It is not enough that we be spiritually moved; we must be able to communicate this. Otherwise, we remain babbling barbarians to one another. Indeed, we are back to the confusion of the tower of Babel, which Pentecost came to restore to normalcy.

Saying the Amen

High-churchers say, "Amen," when it is written in the book, low-churchers say it whenever they feel like it; the rest of us are afraid to say it. The problem is that we, unlike the Corinthians, have forgotten that we are part of the service; we think it is a performance put on by the clergy and the choir. But "Amen" is the people's word; and if we do not say it, then we are leaving ourselves out. (By the way, either pronunciation, "Ah-men" or "A-men," is correct.)

Sharing the Truth

Isaiah warned Israel (Isa. 28:11-12) that if they would not listen, God would use barbarians (in this case the Assyrians) to make the message clear. Paul uses this passage in verse 21 to support his case that we must listen to one another, and make ourselves clear, in order both to strengthen the community and to reach out to others.

Decency and Order

I know that our passage for today stops in the middle of verse 33, but we have to go on to the end of the chapter, for Paul sums up all that he has been saying there. But decency and order are not the purpose of worship—that is like saying, "The speed limit is the purpose of the highway." The purpose of worship is love and joy; decency and order are the wine-skins that contain it.

Our Earliest Order of Worship

The mimeograph machine was not working in those days, so we do not know exactly how the bulletin looked in those days, but here is a clue. What would worship be like today if we each contributed to it as the Corinthians did? Paul criticizes them for trying to talk all at once, but, behind the criticism we get a picture of a healthy church with an incredible diversity. Wouldn't you love to have been there!

Don't Overdo It

Paul had a long way to go on this issue (as he did on slavery and some others). Given what we know about his openness to women (Gal. 3:28), we can only conclude that he was giving in to the traditional chauvinism for the sake of decency and order. I am not happy with him, but, when I remember how far he had come from his Jewish upbringing, I feel better about him.

Be Both Enthusiastic and Sensible

Do not make the mistake of quoting only verse 40; without verse 39 it is an incomplete sentence. Frankly, I think the church today needs the first half more than the last. I am not for indecency and disorder, but our sin today is lack of enthusiasm. When it gets out of hand, we can send for Paul to come and say, "Cool it." In the meantime, let there be more shouting and singing.

Helping Adults Become Involved

Preparing to Teach

Last week, I suggested that you have your class look over the order of worship for Sunday, searching for places where love could be found. You might want to do the same thing. Love hides very subtly in many places. Since I do not know what order you customarily follow, let me give several illustrations.

If you have a time of Confession of Sin, is it not true to say that love accepts us, even when it does not approve, and allows us to be honest in our confession?

If you have a Declaration of Pardon, you are clearly showing love when you say to one another, "In Jesus Christ we are forgiven," or similar words.

If you say the Apostles' Creed, you are uniting yourself in love with all other Christians who say or have said it through the years.

Of course if you pass the peace, it is obvious that you are showing love. Or is it? Could it be made more loving?

This is a difficult lesson in some ways because, in order to get at the truth of what Paul has to say to us, we must get behind what he was saying to the Corinthians. He was criticizing the way they were doing things. What if he had expressed it in the positive? We have to ask ourselves what would *their* church bulletin have been like. This will require your best pious imagination.

Introducing the Main Question

If it were my class, I would start with verses 39 and 40, and suggest that we ask ourselves, concerning *our* service of worship, which half of Paul's counsel needs to be emphasized:

Do not neglect the gifts of the Spirit (39),

or

All things should be decent and orderly (40).

This may be different for you, but I am a Presbyterian, and we are the most decent, orderly, dead branch in Christendom. We need the first half of the sentence! But maybe your congregation is over-enthusiastic and needs to be calmed down somewhat. If that is true, I would like to come and worship with you for a while.

Developing the Lesson

Use the following outline and questions.

I. Prophecy and tongues, 14:1-25

Do we need both intellect and emotion in our worship? Assuming that we do, what proportion should they be in? There is an old proverb that goes, "One who sings prays twice." Doesn't that mean that a prayer with both words and music uses both halves of the brain? By the way, when I quoted that in a rural church that I was serving, one of the elders said, "Yep. And one who taps his foot prays three times!"

A. *The importance of communion, 1-5*

Do you have anyone in your congregation who has had the experience of speaking in tongues? If so, why not ask them what they think about these verses? If not, what do you think they would say? Please note that Paul does not disapprove of the phenomenon (v. 18). Why does it make us so nervous?

B. *Interpreting sounds, 6-12*

Instrumental music, or any song without words (such as scat singing) is purely abstract. Can intellectual content be conveyed through musical instruments? (I am not talking about imitative sounds, such as bird calls ["The Dawn" from the overture to William Tell], or taxi-cab horns ["Slaughter on Tenth Avenue"], but the simple playing of notes.) Why do we use pianos and organs in our worship?

C. *Saying the Amen, 13-19*

How is "Amen" used in your service? Lots of Christians think it means "ten-four," or "the end," or is a cue for the organist to do something. The word is a Hebrew oath, which belongs to the people, not the priest. We are told that in some ancient Jewish liturgies, such as the saying of the blessing, the people responded with "Amen" after every sentence. *Amen* is one of the few Hebrew words that nearly everyone knows. (*Alleluia* is another.) Do you think we would say it more frequently if we translated it into modern English? If so, how would you translate it? Right on? So mote it be? Me, too? Let me on board? I'm with you? If we are going to bring back the Amen Corner, shouldn't there be an "Oh, yeah?" corner as well? The point is, do we worship as participants or as spectators?

D. *Sharing the truth, 20-25*

How well or how quickly do strangers fit into our worship? Someone has said, "It's unfamiliar hymns that make us feel strange." But aren't we bound not to know the hymns if we are a new kid on the block?

II. *Decency and order, 14:26-40*

You may want to leave off most of this section, because, as we have noted, our lesson omits it. But I think it is important.

A. *Our earliest order of worship, 14:26-33a*

In the Corinthian Church, everyone was talking at once, so Paul had to encourage them to take turns. In our church, nobody much talks except the preacher. Should the rest of us be encouraged to take turns?

B. *Don't overdo it, 33b-36*

Women in church made Paul uneasy; we have come a long way since then. Are there still times when we should be slow to put our new-found liberties into practice? Is this another example of what Paul was talking about in 11:28, in which we should not use our liberty if it causes burdens to others?

C. Be both enthusiastic and sensible, 37-40
The purpose of worship is joy, not decency and order. To say it the other way around would be like saying, "The purpose of money is bank books and ledgers." How can we restore some elements of joy to our worship?

Helping Class Members Act

It is my conviction that most Christians really want to be more enthusiastic participants in worship, but they have been conditioned since childhood to shut up and be still. It is hard to break out of this mode, but at least we can give each other permission. Why not covenant together that in our next worship service we will say amen at least once? (Or chose your own point of attack.)

Planning for Next Sunday

Next Sunday is Easter. Ask, do we *really* believe in the Resurrection?

Becoming a Resurrection People

Background Scripture: Luke 24:1-11; 1 Corinthians 15

The Main Question

Jesus once said, "He is God not of the dead, but of the living" (Mark 12:27). One way to put the question for this week's lesson is to ask whether we are the people of death or of life. Of course, we will quickly reply (with Moses in Deut. 30:19), "Choose life!" Only a fool would choose death.

But is that so? The second most common cause of death among teenagers is suicide. The first, of course, is accidents, but how many of them are related to self-destructive behavior? How many of us adults persist in habits that are clearly not good for us? There was a popular country music song a few years ago with the nihilistic title, "I wanna live fast, love hard, die young, and leave a beautiful memory." Do not many of us rush headlong toward death?

And for those who do not rush toward it, some betray our neurotic fear of it by the way it occupies our minds. We will not mention it, or, if we do, it is with hushed tones, muffled by organ music. We invent euphemisms to pretend it away, such as "passed on" or "bought the farm." An even older country song claims that "Mother's not dead, she's only a-sleepin'."

Healthy tears, part of what some call good grief, are appropriate in the presence of death (remember what made Jesus weep [John 11:35]). But in the midst of our tears, we who belong to Christ should be those who affirm that life, not death, has the last word. That truth is summed up for us in the word *resurrection*. Our question then, not just when there is a death in the family, but in every waking moment, is, "Are we the people of the funeral, or of the Resurrection?"

Selected Scripture

King James Version	New Revised Standard Version
Luke 24:1-11; 1 Corinthians 15:12-17, 56-58	*Luke 24:1-11; 1 Corinthians 15:12-17, 56-58*

King James Version

Luke 24:1-11; 1 Corinthians 15:12-17, 56-58

1 Now upon the first day of the week, very early in the morning, they came unto the sepulchre, bringing the spices which they had prepared, and certain others with them.

2 And they found the stone rolled away from the sepulchre.

3 And they entered in, and found not the body of the Lord Jesus.

4 And it came to pass, as they were much perplexed thereabout, behold, two men stood by them in shining garments:

5 And as they were afraid, and bowed down their faces to the earth, they said unto them, Why seek ye the living among the dead?

6 He is not here, but is risen: remember how he spake unto you when he was yet in Galilee,

7 Saying, The Son of man must be delivered into the hands of sinful men, and be crucified, and the third day rise again.

8 And they remembered his words,

9 And returned from the sepulchre, and told all these things unto the eleven, and to all the rest.

10 It was Mary Magdalene, and Joanna, and Mary the mother of James, and other women that were with them, which told these things unto the apostles.

11 And their words seemed to them as idle tales, and they believed them not.

....

12 Now if Christ be preached that he rose from the dead, how say some among you that there is no resurrection of the dead?

13 But if there be no resurrection of the dead, then is Christ not risen:

New Revised Standard Version

Luke 24:1-11; 1 Corinthians 15:12-17, 56-58

1 But on the first day of the week, at early dawn, they came to the tomb, taking the spices that they had prepared. 2 They found the stone rolled away from the tomb, 3 but when they went in, they did not find the body. 4 While they were perplexed about this, suddenly two men in dazzling clothes stood beside them. 5 The women were terrified and bowed their faces to the ground, but the men said to them, "Why do you look for the living among the dead? He is not here, but has risen. 6 Remember how he told you, while he was still in Galilee, 7 that the Son of Man must be handed over to sinners, and be crucified, and on the third day rise again." 8 Then they remembered his words, 9 and returning from the tomb, they told all this to the eleven and to all the rest. 10 Now it was Mary Magdalene, Joanna, Mary the mother of James, and the other women with them who told this to the apostles. 11 But these words seemed to them an idle tale, and they did not believe them.

....

12 Now if Christ is proclaimed as raised from the dead, how can some of you say there is no resurrection of the dead? 13 If there is no resurrection of the dead, then Christ has not been raised; 14 and if Christ has not

14 And if Christ be not risen, then is our preaching vain, and your faith is also vain.

15 Yea, and we are found false witnesses of God; because we have testified of God that he raised up Christ: whom he raised not up, if so be that the dead rise not.

16 For if the dead rise not, then is not Christ raised:

17 And if Christ be not raised, your faith is vain; ye are yet in your sins.

....

56 The sting of death is sin; and the strength of sin is the law.

57 But thanks be to God, which giveth us the victory through our Lord Jesus Christ.

58 Therefore, my beloved brethren, be ye stedfast, unmoveable, always abounding in the work of the Lord, forasmuch as ye know that your labour is not in vain in the Lord.

Key Verse: **Therefore, my beloved brethren, be ye stedfast, unmoveable, always abounding in the work of the Lord, forasmuch as ye know that your labour is not in vain in the Lord.**

been raised, then our proclamation has been in vain and your faith has been in vain. 15 We are even found to be misrepresenting God, because we testified of God that he raised Christ—whom he did not raise if it is true that the dead are not raised. 16 For if the dead are not raised, then Christ has not been raised. 17 If Christ has not been raised, your faith is futile and you are still in your sins.

....

56 The sting of death is sin, and the power of sin is the law. 57 But thanks be to God, who gives us the victory through our Lord Jesus Christ.

58 Therefore, my beloved, be steadfast, immovable, always excelling in the work of the Lord, because you know that in the Lord your labor is not in vain.

Key Verse: **Therefore, my beloved, be steadfast, immovable, always excelling in the work of the Lord, because you know that in the Lord your labor is not in vain.**

As You Read the Scripture

Luke 24:1-11. This grand and familiar story of the most incredible morning in history needs little explanation or introduction. However, two comments might help. First, note that our selection ends with verse 11, with its note of unbelief. This is really where Mark's whole Gospel ends (look at Mark 16:1-8, which is probably where the original manuscript stopped). But Luke adds some post-Resurrection stories, as do the other three Gospels. Second, note also that, though this passage is listed first, Paul's letter to the Corinthians is many years earlier (at least twenty or so) than Luke's Gospel, so the Corinthian passage precedes this reading. But bear in mind that preceding *both* of these writings was the actual event itself, and the story that was certainly passed on from the women to the eleven to the rest of the disciples, and faithfully preserved as oral tradition. We do not know exactly when it was first written down, but, thanks be to God, it was, and it has been passed on to you and me.

1 Corinthians 15:1-11. Paul summarizes just what we have been saying with regard to the Luke passage, bringing it down to himself. This is the earliest text in the New Testament that speaks of the resurrection of Jesus from the point of view of those who witnessed it. Paul is apparently repeating some early creeds and formulas in worship. Verses 3-5 contain what may have been recited in early services like this:

> Christ died for our sins in accordance with the scriptures.
> Christ was buried.
> Christ was raised on the third day in accordance with the scriptures.
> Christ appeared to Peter and the twelve.

(Characteristically, the male-dominated church forgets to mention Mary Magdalene and the other women.) Paul adds himself at the tag end with a curious self-effacing remark; he calls himself a miscarriage. But, always confident in Christ and his convictions, he is able to affirm, "I am who I am."

Verses 12-34. Now Paul puts to rest the question of the resurrection. His points are:

1.) Either there is no such thing as a resurrection or our preaching is false, and we are all liars (v. 13-14).
2.) There's no point in faith or life without resurrection (v. 17).
3.) Our Christian hope depends upon it (v. 19).
4.) All human activity, from baptism for the dead to courage, is a waste of time, and we might as well be cynics (v. 32).

None of the scholars seem to agree on what the business about baptism for the dead in verse 29 really means. Barclay says it could refer to the fact that some of us are baptized out of respect and affection for those who have gone on before us. I do not know. But the point is, Christ *has* been raised.

Verses 35-58. However the resurrection happened, what we know for sure is that one must die to become truly alive. This had already been said by Jesus (John 12:24). It is the same as self-denial. Because we trust God to raise us, we are free to give ourselves up. Because of this incredible truth, our labor is not in vain in the Lord.

Helping Adults Become Involved

Preparing to Teach

Easter Sunday is a strange day in the modern church. Like so many of our festivals, it borrows much from the ancient pagan rites that it took over and baptized. The fertility symbols are still there: rabbits, eggs, flowers. The modern pagan rites are present, too: parading in new bonnets, making our annual appearance at church. You are going to have a hard time breaking through all that to help people see the main point of this high feast day. It is as though, on the Fourth of July, the firecrackers drown out the Declaration of Independence.

But do not give up, because this may the most important lesson of the quarter. The belief in Christ's resurrection is the very starting point of all our living and thinking as Jesus' disciples. It is the power of the resurrection that gives us the courage, the power, and the insight to keep up our zeal, to trust the gifts of the Spirit, and to love with charity, expecting nothing in return.

In addition to reading your lessons carefully, and studying your commentaries, which I assume you do every week, this time you will want to work yourself into a resurrection mood. Fortunately, the passages chosen for today should help you do just that. I cannot read 1 Corinthians 15:50-58 without a fresh stirring in my soul. You might get up early on Sunday morning, and read those words again, in a quiet place (a garden, if you have one), in that rich, cobwebby time when the world is not yet quite awake. May you, like Magdalene, sense the presence of One who stands with you, in the garden, so that you may run and tell the others.

Introducing the Main Question

Try to get your class thinking about funerals. Everybody has a burial anecdote or two, and they usually like to talk about them. See if you can get them to describe the ways in which the funerals we attend contribute to our sense of gloom and doom. In other words, ask them to distinguish between a good funeral and a bad funeral. I grant you that a lot of it depends on the nature of the death. At the funeral of one who died tragically, or very young, or in great agony, things may be so highly colored as to make celebrating difficult. But, for me, here are some of the positives and negatives I would list:

Good funerals	*Bad funerals*
Strong hymns	Lugubrious music
Good rich earth	Green Astro-turf
Words of hope	Words of judgment
A sense of humor	Long faces
The presence of friends	The faces of strangers

Ask your class, "Are we funeral people or resurrection people?" And if the former, how can we become the latter?

Developing the Lesson

I. Easter morning, Luke 24:1-11

Some of your class members may already have been to a sunrise service this morning; they might like to share some of their feelings. Or you can think back to some you remember from the past. One that stands out in my mind involved a reenactment of Matthew's account, by three or four young ladies in bathrobes, and a young man in a white choir robe. It was all done in pantomime. The women came to the tomb, were confronted by the angels, and then ran breathlessly off, stage left (or actually cemetery left). I saw that scene fifty years ago, but I still remember the pure white of the angel's garment, and the excited running of the maidens. Ask your class to share such experiences, and then discuss the question, "Why can't we feel that way every morning?"

You may be familiar with the following creed, which is based on several passages of scripture, including ours for this week. Your people might like to use it during, or at the end of, today's class:

This is the good news, which we have received, in which we stand, and by which we are saved, if we hold it fast: that Christ died for our sins, according to the scriptures, that he was buried, that he was raised on the third day, and that he appeared, first to the women, then to Peter, and to the Twelve, and then to many faithful witnesses. We believe that Jesus is the Christ, the Son of the living God. Jesus Christ is the first and the last, the beginning and the end; he is our Lord and our God.

II. The Resurrection tradition, 1 Corinthians 15:1-11

Paul calls this section the good news, or the gospel. Do we pass on good news to others by the way we speak, act, and live? Or are we sometimes people of the bad news?

What would have it been like to be one of those to whom the risen Christ appeared?

The James mentioned in verse 7 was probably Jesus' brother. Is there any significance that he was among the last to see the risen Lord?

Paul says he was untimely born. Would you argue with that?

III. The resurrection of the dead, 1 Corinthians 15:12-34

Paul says, in effect, "Either the gospel story is true, or we are all liars." That is a rather strong either/or. Would you agree?

In connection with verses 21-22, look at Romans 5:12-18. In 1 Corinthians 15:45, Jesus is called the second Adam. Remember that in Hebrew, the word *adam* means man. Do you see any universalism in verse 22? (I do, and it makes an optimist out of me.)

IV. The victory, 1 Corinthians 15:35-58

Frankly, Paul does not use the expression of our creed: "the resurrection of the body." He speaks, rather, of "the resurrection of the dead." Do not be a fool, Paul is saying, by thinking of the new body as anything like your old one. But, at the risk of being fools, what *do* you think it will be like?

Immortality (v. 53) is not something we automatically have, but something we must put on. Do you support this is part of what is meant by the white robes in Revelation 6:11?

Helping Class Members Act

How do you live as though you believed in resurrection? With a song in your heart? A spring in your step? Make plans to do it!

Planning for Next Sunday

Next week we are going back to chapter 8. Ask your class to be thinking of ways in which we should deliberately give up our freedom for the sake of others.

Exercising Christian Freedom

Background Scripture: 1 Corinthians 8

The Main Question

The main point of 1 Corinthians is that there is room in the church for a great variety of people. But if we each insist on our own way, claiming that those who see things differently are foolish, wrong, or even immoral, the community will be destroyed. This leads Paul to say succinctly: "Knowledge puffs up, but love builds up" (8:1). This may be the most important sentence in the letter, because it raises both the difficulty and the importance of our Christian liberty. We must preserve our freedom, but not at the expense of those around us.

I suppose this is most clearly seen by those of us who are married, or who live intimately with another person (I know two sisters who argue and fuss almost as well as a married couple). Husbands and wives know well how difficult it is to preserve your integrity as an individual, and, at the same time, make space for the individuality of your mate. But we also know how wonderful this balancing act can be when it is successfully achieved.

In the church, we have two apparently conflicting maxims, both of which deserve our allegiance:

1.) Christians must be free (Gal. 5:1).
2.) Christians must serve one another (Gal. 6:2).

The main question for us this week is, how shall we carry out both of these commissions? There is a wonderful line in one of the collects in the 1928 *Book of Common Prayer* that speaks of God, "whose service is perfect freedom." How can this be? Is not *free servant* an oxymoron, like *honest government* or *fresh-frozen*? The main task of this lesson will be to bring these two terms into harmony.

Selected Scripture

King James Version

1 Corinthians 8

1 Now as touching things offered unto idols, we know that we all have knowledge. Knowledge puffeth up, but charity edifieth.

2 And if any man think that he knoweth any thing, he knoweth nothing yet as he ought to know.

3 But if any man love God, the same is known of him.

4 As concerning therefore the eating of those things that are offered in

New Revised Standard Version

1 Corinthians 8

1 Now concerning food sacrificed to idols: we know that "all of us possess knowledge." Knowledge puffs up, but love builds up. 2 Anyone who claims to know something does not yet have the necessary knowledge; 3 but anyone who loves God is known by him.

4 Hence, as to the eating of food offered to idols, we know that "no

sacrifice unto idols, we know that an idol is nothing in the world, and that there is none other God but one.

5 For though there be that are called gods, whether in heaven or in earth, (as there be gods many, and lords many,)

6 But to us there is but one God, the Father, of whom are all things, and we in him; and one Lord Jesus Christ, by whom are all things, and we by him.

7 Howbeit there is not in every man that knowledge: for some with conscience of the idol unto this hour eat it as a thing offered unto an idol; and their conscience being weak is defiled.

8 But meat commendeth us not to God: for neither, if we eat, are we the better; neither, if we eat not, are we the worse.

9 But take heed lest by any means this liberty of yours become a stumblingblock to them that are weak.

10 For if any man see thee which hast knowledge sit at meat in the idol's temple, shall not the conscience of him which is weak be emboldened to eat those things which are offered to idols;

11 And through thy knowledge shall the weak brother perish, for whom Christ died?

12 But when ye sin so against the brethren, and wound their weak conscience, ye sin against Christ.

13 Wherefore, if meat make my brother to offend, I will eat no flesh while the world standeth, lest I make my brother to offend.

Key Verse: **But take heed lest by any means this liberty of yours become a stumblingblock to them that are weak.**

idol in the world really exists," and that "there is no God but one." 5 Indeed, even though there may be so-called gods in heaven or on earth—as in fact there are many gods and many lords—6 yet for us there is one God, the Father, from whom are all things and for whom we exist, and one Lord, Jesus Christ, through whom are all things and through whom we exist.

7 It is not everyone, however, who has this knowledge. Since some have become so accustomed to idols until now, they still think of the food they eat as food offered to an idol; and their conscience, being weak, is defiled. 8 "Food will not bring us close to God." We are no worse off if we do not eat, and no better off if we do. 9 But take care that this liberty of yours does not somehow become a stumbling block to the weak. 10 For if others see you, who possess knowledge, eating in the temple of an idol, might they not, since their conscience is weak, be encouraged to the point of eating food sacrificed to idols? 11 So by your knowledge those weak believers for whom Christ died are destroyed. 12 But when you thus sin against members of your family, and wound their conscience when it is weak, you sin against Christ. 13 Therefore, if food is a cause of their falling, I will never eat meat, so that I may not cause one of them to fall.

Key Verse: **But take care that this liberty of yours does not somehow become a stumbling block to the weak.**

As You Read the Scripture

1 Corinthians 8. Paul changes the subject here. He had been discussing matters of sex and slavery, but turns now to matters specifically relating to worship: the question of false gods and how to relate to them. Sometimes I get the feeling that reading Paul's letters is like listening to someone talk on the telephone when you cannot hear what the other party is saying. You have to infer from the replies what the real issues are. But in this chapter we get some pretty good ideas as to what the person on the other end of the line is saying. Some of these appear to be:

> "All of us possess knowledge" (v. 1).
> "No idol in the world really exists" (v. 4).
> "There are many gods and many lords" (v. 5).
> "Food will not bring us close to God" (v. 8).

Yes, says Paul to all of these comments, you are right. But that is not all there is to it. Let us look at these things in relationship to others.

Verses 1-3. Yes, Paul agrees, you do have knowledge. He agrees with the Corinthians that in Christ they have insights that some of the less sophisticated folks in the congregation may not fully understand. But do not let that go to your head. It can be summed up with this antithetical proverb:

> Knowledge *(gnosis)* puffs up, but
> Love *(agape)* builds up.

The problem is that we think the knowledge belongs to us; it does not. What knowledge means at bottom is not that we know all about God, but that God knows all about us! And that is a major difference; we must not let our knowledge give us the big head.

Verses 4-6. In their new-found freedom, the Corinthians have retired into a kind of private religion, the same sort that caused them to stuff their faces at family-night supper without regard for those around them (see 11:21). Paul is clearly on the side of those who claim to have knowledge. Yes, it is true, the so-called idols do not really exist. You are spiritually mature when you recognize this. But you are *not* spiritually mature if this leads you to forget the one God, from whom all things come, and for whom we exist. We must obey him alone, and that means we should be in a state of constant concern for our sisters and brothers, especially those whose knowledge has not quite caught up to ours.

Verses 7-13. With this compassionate approach, Paul appeals to the strengths of the strong. Come now, he is saying, I need you to help me with these folks lest they be led astray. You will want to look at the more detailed discussion of this same matter in Romans 14:1–15:6, which Paul concludes with this gracious prayer: "May the God of steadfastness and encouragement grant you to live in harmony with one another, in accordance with Christ Jesus, so that together you may with one voice glorify the God and Father of our Lord Jesus Christ." The key verse in this section affirms the same wish: "Take care that this liberty of yours does not somehow become a stumbling block to the weak" (v. 9). And the last verse says it all. If my freedom is a stumbling block to others, then I must be strong enough to let my freedom go.

The Scripture and the Main Question

Love Builds Up

It must have been a liberating thing to belong to the church in Corinth. In the language of today's dependency groups, many of the Corinthians were recovering legalists. They had spent their whole lives trying to get themselves right with God through all sorts of rituals and ethics. During the period known as Hellenism (the three hundred or so years after Alexander the Great conquered the known world and the coming of Christ) an incredible cultural phenomenon swept the whole (known) world. All the strange religions of Asia Minor, Babylon, and Egypt (to say nothing of the pantheons of Roman and Greek deities) became known to everyone. Through astrology, fertility cults, emperor worship, and every sort of bizarre cult, people were seeking peace of mind and a sense of having control over their own destiny. (It sounds a lot like the world we live in, with television and jet travel making the world all one, so that our children know about all sorts of cults and nostrums that you and I had only heard of!)

But, with the coming of the good news in Jesus Christ, folks were beginning to learn that salvation was a gift from God, not something you earn by pulling the strings of the gods, or living on certain diets and rituals. As Paul had emphasized to the Galatians, "For freedom Christ has set us free" (5:1). And this new-found freedom was a breath of fresh air in the pagan city of Corinth, which stood at the crossroads of traffic throughout the empire, a town of many temples, theaters, sports complexes, and commercial undertakings. If I had been a new convert to Christianity back then, I might have felt so wonderful after being liberated from all those superstitions that I would be, as the Corinthians were, in danger of becoming a libertine.

But we must not! Paul never understood that freedom to be a license for evil. He meant it to bear fruit, "love, joy, peace, patience, kindness, generosity, faithfulness, gentleness, and self-control" (Gal. 5:22-23), and to bring an end to the longer list of selfish and unbridled destructive behavior that he gives in Galatians 5:19-21. We *are* free, but not libertines. Freedom calls for responsibility. Our knowledge does not take the form of "I know God, but you don't," which is spiritual arrogance, but rather the form of the 139th Psalm: "O Lord, you have searched me and known me."

There Is No God but One

Paul agrees with the knowledgeable Corinthians. They are right in claiming that the false gods do not exist. But it is not enough to sweep the false gods away; they must be replaced with the one true God (see Luke 11:24-26). Verse 6 may be a fragment of an early Christian worship service, and is surely related to the famous creed in Deuteronomy 6:4. So this creed is directed both to Jews and Greeks in the congregation:

> There is One God, the Father,
> from whom are all things,
> and for whom we exist.

> And one Lord Jesus Christ,
> through whom are all things,
> and through whom we exist. (v. 6)

This creed is an affirmation that the whole creation is good. (Compare it with Psalm 104, especially verses 14-15). It is an affirmation to the stronger brothers and sisters that they are right not to give a flip about the idols. But the weaker folk have not yet learned to face what Emerson called the terror of life. They are still clinging to some of their superstitions, and we must be gentle with them.

For, in fact, there *are* lesser gods out there, as you and I well know. They have the power to destroy us (but not the power to save). Some of them are Bacchus, whose temple is the bar, Mammon, whose temple is the bank, Venus, whose temple is the massage parlor, and, of course, Pride, whose temple is (well, you name it). Not that these things are all bad. It is only when we worship them that they destroy us. But when we worship the one true God, then (and only then) the lesser gods come into their own. (One example: money, when worshiped, is the root of all evil; when put at the disposal of God, it is a powerful force for good.)

The Strong Care for the Weak

Having settled the question of the gods, Paul helps us to understand how we should relate to those who are still to some extent under their influence. (If we are honest, we will admit that *we* are, too—like it or not.) It is not surprising that some of the Corinthians were worried about food offered to idols. Probably most of them were relatively poor, and the meat markets abounded with day-old groceries, foods that had been used as sacrifices to (but of course, not eaten by) the pagan gods. The Christians might find themselves invited to eat with heathen friends, and be confronted with the likelihood that some of what they were being served was possibly tainted (see 10:25). What if there *were* some truth to the notion that this was devil's food? Could a Christian in good conscience eat it? We can understand that they might be nervous. It would be like an orthodox Jew tasting a casserole at a party and wondering, "Could this possibly be pork?" or a Seventh Day Adventist wondering, "Is this only vegetables?" or a recovering alcoholic thinking, "Is this punch spiked?"

The thinking of the strong Corinthian, the one who knows that there is nothing to the superstitions about the idols, is also easy to understand. They might be saying to themselves something like this: "Why should I have my freedom curtailed over nothing, just because these other folks are so uptight? After all, I've come a long way to this freedom in Christ." This argument is O.K. so far as it goes, but it is only half a theology. It has recognized the vertical relationship with God ("You shall love God with your whole being"), but it has neglected the horizontal relationship ("You shall love your neighbor as yourself"). Try thinking of it in terms of a simple but common contemporary problem: You are musically sophisticated, and some simple soul insists on singing an old country song you outgrew long ago. Be very careful that your knowledge does not puff you up. It could be that your weak friend needs the comfort of that old tune. In fact the person might know something that you do not know. Remember that love can build up. It will not hurt you to sing that old favorite. To be truthful, it might do you some good!

Helping Adults Become Involved

Preparing to Teach

This is a rather short chapter, so it should not take too much time to master the biblical material. One thing you should be sure to do is take a good look at Romans 14:1–15:13, where Paul deals with this same concern in somewhat more detail. If nothing else, we need to pick up on Romans 15:1: "We who are strong ought to put up with the failings of the weak, and not to please ourselves," for this is the key.

Since the scripture lesson is short, you ought to have more time to think about your class and their needs. Are there ways the strong among you can help their classmates?

Introducing the Main Question

Let us start with the first verse: "Knowledge puffs up." The first and last great temptation is the temptation to know. The tree of knowledge of Genesis 2:9 was an integral part of the roots of human sin (Gen. 3:6). Paul was greatly tempted to know more than he knew, so he limited himself to the one knowledge that does not puff up, the knowledge of Christ crucified (1 Cor. 2:2). The knowledge that saves, the knowledge of the Resurrection, is not an act of superiority on my part, it is a gift of grace. It is a knowledge that cannot be known (see 2 Cor. 4:18, and Eph. 3:19). The things we can know are temporal, but what we cannot know is eternal.

I think the problem is that we, like some of the Corinthians, tend to confuse *our* knowledge with God's knowledge. Paul is telling us (v. 3) that when one loves God, that one does not so much know God as one is known *by* God. It is true that one "who loves is born of God and knows God" (1 John 4:7), but that knowledge is an act of grace. It is God who initiates it. When we are known by God, that is, when we are elected and engendered by God, we are then free to love each other. We then know that what is important is not so much matters of individual conscience as matters of interpersonal relationships. Which does God prefer: that our hymns have good theology or that we love one another?

Turn to the text and let Paul provide us with the answer. The question is, of course, how do responsible Christians find the necessary balance between our need to be free in the Lord, and our responsibility to take care of each other?

Developing the Lesson

Use the following outline and questions.

I. Knowledge puffs up; love builds up, 1-3

You would think that those who know the most would be the least defensive, but it does not always work that way. What makes some of us lord it over others?

In heaven, perhaps, "I will know fully, even as I have been fully known" (1 Cor. 13:12). Why is it more important to say, "God knows me," than to say, "I know God"? Perhaps it is like Abraham Lincoln's statement, "The important question is not, is God on our side, but, are we on God's side?"

II. There is no God but one, 4-6

We all know that there is no such thing as an idol. Certainly you and I do not worship graven images! But are there more subtle idols in our lives?

What lesser gods and their temples can you think of in your community? Do we sometimes make a god out of the church? The Bible? Our country? What does it mean to say, "The false gods cannot save, but they can destroy"?

The creed that Paul quotes in verse 6 is a binitarian creed, that is, it leaves out the Holy Spirit. Why do you suppose Paul did this? Could it be because the Corinthians were having problems with their understanding of the role of the Spirit (see 12:1-13, and chapter 14)? (Paul has just made an almost sarcastic reference to his own relationship to the Spirit in the last verse of chapter 7.)

III. The strong care for the weak, 7-13

Make a list of ways in which strong members of a Sunday school class can help weaker members. Here are some that I have thought of: (1.) Gate-keep. That is, make sure those that are shy about speaking up get the privileges of the floor from time to time; (2.) Refrain from laughing at somebody's silly suggestion—they will be more likely to come up with a good one next time; (3.) Listen carefully when a weaker sister or brother is speaking—you may learn something, and you certainly will help them develop confidence.

Does it bother you to call some Christians strong and others weak? Is it not rather presumptuous of me to think that I have a superior conscience to someone else's? And is it not the height of arrogance to say, "The rules that ordinary people have to go by don't apply to me"? That cannot be what Paul means. How can we show our strength without making other people feel inferior? But we have to do that. The lifeguard can't say, "I didn't dive in after him because the fact that I'm a better swimmer would have embarrassed him."

Can you think of examples in our day that would be the same sort of thing as the Corinthians' problem of eating meat that had been offered to idols? People usually bring up the problem of alcohol here, but can you think of some others? What areas of knowledge might some Christians possess that they must be careful about pushing off on others? Biblical scholarship? Musical taste? Popularity and self-confidence? What about this one: "I know that the language I use or don't use doesn't make me Christian or unchristian. But I must be careful what kind of language I use around tender ears." You can come up with better ones.

One last question: Are there times when I must go ahead and dare to use my Christian liberty, even though it might cause some problems for others?

Helping Class Members Act

Here are two possible ways you could get your class members thinking about this lesson in the days ahead:

Give each one a card that says on it: "I am a strong person, so I must use my strength to help others"; or give them a card that says, "I will be especially gentle with all people I meet in the week to come, in the light of Isaiah 42:1-3."

Planning for Next Sunday

Next week we will be going on (actually back) to 2 Corinthians. If you can, read chapter 1:1-14, and come to class having thought seriously about the question, "What consolation from God can I give to others?"

UNIT III: MINISTERING AS A CHRISTIAN COMMUNITY

FIVE LESSONS APRIL 30–MAY 28

Here we are invited to live and proclaim the gospel, with each other, and with the world beyond the walls of the church. We learn how, through the leadership and example of the Spirit, we can be comforters and advocates for one another. We explore the basis of Christian motivation, learning from Paul how to achieve both the freedom and the discipline of the missionary task. We discover that the true motivator in our lives is Jesus Christ, and learn from him how to view ourselves and those around us as "new creations." In the end, we discover the meaning of life in the giving away of ourselves, in the true stewardship to which we are called. The crowning glory of the two letters (1 Corinthians 13) is saved for last, and we celebrate the presence of divine love, Christian charity, at the heart of all that we are and do.

In the course of this quarter, we will find that we are not so very different from the early church. We share its fears, its frustrations, its hopes, and its dreams. Above all, we share its saving grace, the gospel of our salvation, which unites us with Christ and with one another, and gives us the power and wisdom to succeed at our task, even in so astonishing a time as that in which we live today.

LESSON 9 APRIL 30

Sharing One Another's Pain

Background Scripture: 2 Corinthians 1:1-14

The Main Question

The opening verses of 2 Corinthians describe a time when Paul had been going through great suffering. We do not know the exact nature of his problems, but they were very nearly fatal (see v. 8). Moreover, Paul was away from his Corinthian friends, probably in Ephesus, and there is good evidence that there was some genuine disagreement between him and the Corinthians. Indeed, this may have been part of the trouble; physical difficulties can be bad, but sometimes our emotional problems are even harder to take. (Which is easier to say: "My tooth is aching," or, "My heart is broken"?) At any rate, these verses have to do with friends who are both separated and hurting.

What can you do when someone you love hurts, and you cannot even get to them? Somehow the physical nearness is important to us. When loved ones are in the hospital, even when they are sealed off from us by the closed-door rules of Intensive Care, or CCU, or some other ominous initials, we want to be close to them. I do not know how many families I have called on, curled up uncomfortably in chairs in the waiting room, when they could just

272

as well have been in their own beds a few miles away. But I have never fussed at them about it, because I understand their need to be as close as possible, even though there is nothing they can do. Even if you could get into the room with them, what could you do?

But is it true that you can do nothing? In this lesson, Paul makes the case that, through Christ, and through our sisters and brothers in the faith, we can reach out across space, through medical barriers, and touch, heal, and help. Our question: Why don't we do it?

Selected Scripture

King James Version

2 Corinthians 1:3-14

3 Blessed be God, even the Father of our Lord Jesus Christ, the Father of mercies, and the God of all comfort;

4 Who comforteth us in all our tribulation, that we may be able to comfort them which are in any trouble, by the comfort wherewith we ourselves are comforted of God.

5 For as the sufferings of Christ abound in us, so our consolation also aboundeth by Christ.

6 And whether we be afflicted, it is for your consolation and salvation, which is effectual in the enduring of the same sufferings which we also suffer: or whether we be comforted, it is for your consolation and salvation.

7 And our hope of you is stedfast, knowing, that as ye are partakers of the sufferings, so shall ye be also of the consolation.

8 For we would not, brethren, have you ignorant of our trouble which came to us in Asia, that we were pressed out of measure, above strength, insomuch that we despaired even of life:

9 But we had the sentence of death in ourselves, that we should not trust in ourselves, but in God which raiseth the dead:

10 Who delivered us from so great a death, and doth deliver: in whom we trust that he will yet deliver us;

11 Ye also helping together by prayer for us, that for the gift

New Revised Standard Version

2 Corinthians 1:3-14

3 Blessed be the God and Father of our Lord Jesus Christ, the Father of mercies and the God of all consolation, 4 who consoles us in all our affliction, so that we may be able to console those who are in any affliction with the consolation with which we ourselves are consoled by God. 5 For just as the sufferings of Christ are abundant for us, so also our consolation is abundant through Christ. 6 If we are being afflicted, it is for your consolation and salvation; if we are being consoled, it is for your consolation, which you experience when you patiently endure the same sufferings that we are also suffering. 7 Our hope for you is unshaken; for we know that as you share in our sufferings, so also you share in our consolation.

8 We do not want you to be unaware, brothers and sisters, of the affliction we experienced in Asia; for we were so utterly, unbearably crushed that we despaired of life itself. 9 Indeed, we felt that we had received the sentence of death so that we would rely not on ourselves but on God who raises the dead. 10 He who rescued us from so deadly a peril will continue to rescue us; on him we have set our hope that he will rescue us again, 11 as you also join in helping us by your prayers, so that many will give thanks on our

bestowed upon us by the means of many persons thanks may be given by many on our behalf.

12 For our rejoicing is this, the testimony of our conscience, that in simplicity and godly sincerity, not with fleshly wisdom, but by the grace of God, we have had our conversation in the world, and more abundantly to you-ward.

13 For we write none other things unto you, than what ye read or acknowledge; and I trust ye shall acknowledge even to the end;

14 As also ye have acknowledged us in part, that we are your rejoicing, even as ye also are ours in the day of the Lord Jesus.

Key Verses: **Blessed be God, even the Father of our Lord Jesus Christ, the Father of mercies, and the God of all comfort; Who comforteth us in all our tribulation, that we may be able to comfort them which are in any trouble, by the comfort wherewith we ourselves are comforted of God.**

behalf for the blessing granted us through the prayers of many.

12 Indeed, this is our boast, the testimony of our conscience: we have behaved in the world with frankness and godly sincerity, not by earthly wisdom but by the grace of God—and all the more toward you. 13 For we write you nothing other than what you can read and also understand; I hope you will understand until the end—14 as you have already understood us in part—that on the day of the Lord Jesus we are your boast even as you are our boast.

Key Verses: **Blessed be the God and Father of our Lord Jesus Christ, the Father of mercies and the God of all consolation, who consoles us in all our affliction, so that we may be able to console those who are in any affliction with the consolation with which we ourselves are consoled by God.**

As You Read the Scripture

2 Corinthians 1:1-2. Paul begins his letter in the usual Greek manner, with his own name and a word of greeting, but he adds two important things: an affirmation of his apostleship (which had been called into question by some of his Corinthian detractors) and a benediction. Contrary to the popular notion, benediction does not mean a prayer at the end. It means, "A good (or well) saying," and is appropriate at the beginning of the service, as well as at the end.

Verses 3-7. Paul customarily begins his letters with a prayer of thanksgiving and does so here, thanking God for consolation. This is the same word (*paraklesis*) that Jesus used to describe the Holy Spirit, in John 14:16 and 25, and it means more than a sympathetic pat on the back. In John, it is translated comforter in the King James, counselor in the RSV, and advocate in the New Revised Standard Version. This last is probably closer to the real meaning; it has legal implications (we call lawyers who plead our case for us, counselors or advocates). It basically means someone who helps us. Paul uses the word ten times in these five verses.

Notice that it is those who have suffered who are able to comfort others in their suffering. This is what makes support groups for those with dependency problems so effective; those who are helping have been through the same thing, and can truly say, "I understand." Paul sees his own sufferings (v. 6) as purposeful in enabling him to console others. He also makes it clear both at the beginning and the end of this paragraph, that with the suffering comes consolation, and that its source is God.

Verses 8-11. Paul now describes his own recent deliverance, using the phrase, "We do not want you to be unaware" (v. 8), which, as Paul uses it, means, "Listen! This is important!" But he does not tell us what happened. My feeling is that it was a recurrence of the illness that he calls his " thorn in the flesh" (12:7), but we do not even know if *that* was an illness, so it is at best only a guess. Perhaps it was the sort of danger as those described in 11:23-27. Whatever it was, it was very, very serious. He says (v. 8) that he was completely crushed by it.

Verses 12-14. Then Paul makes an extraordinary claim for himself, one that I envy. He boasts that his conscience is clear. My conscience is so rarely free from self-doubt that I find it hard to imagine how anybody could say, as Paul does, "We have behaved . . . with frankness and godly sincerity" (v. 12). Verse 14 implies that the Corinthians have begun to come around to appreciate what Paul has been trying to tell them, and, in the light of this he suggests that they can boast about each other.

Verses 15-24. The rest of the chapter is not part of our lesson for this week, but it is important to point out that Paul continues to claim purity of purpose. He explains that the change in his travel plans was not due to his being wishy-washy, but that God sometimes overrules human intentions. He gives them what I think is one of the greatest statements in all Paul's writings: "In him [Christ] every one of God's promises is a 'Yes' " (v. 20). Even in the midst of all his sufferings, and in spite of the problems he has had with the Corinthians, Paul remains the eternal optimist, certain that God will be faithful.

The Scripture and the Main Question

We *can* help each other in our afflictions. Christ's power can be made available to us, and through us to others. The main question of this week's lesson is divided into the following two parts:

Part 1: Do we really believe that one person can suffer for another, that Christ's sufferings help us, and that in our sufferings we can help each other?

Part 2: If we do believe that, how can we put it into practice?

Let me tell you about a dear friend whom I used to visit regularly in her nursing home. She was a victim of Alzheimer's disease, or some form of dementia. In fact, she had not spoken an intelligible word in many years. Usually, when I visited her, I would take someone else with me, so that we could have some conversation, for there was no talking with my friend. But, on this occasion, I was alone, and wondering what I might say to pass our time together pleasantly. On impulse, I picked up my guitar and took it into the room with me, thinking, "She loved the old gospel songs; I'll just sing to her." And I did. A number of the other residents wheeled themselves into the room, a few nurses joined us, and we had a great time for a little while. But the miracle was this: I realized that my friend, who had been completely out of contact with the world, was singing along, in old-fashioned harmony! Across the miles of shattered neuro-circuitry, over the wall that separated us, somehow a spark had leaped, and, at some level, she and I were in communication. We will now look at the ways in which Paul, writing from a distance to the Corinthians, gave them a touch across the miles.

THIRD QUARTER

Paul's Benediction

This letter was probably intended to be read aloud when the Corinthians gathered for word and meal. It begins with a benediction. In some churches, it is customary to begin worship with a benediction:

> Leader: The Lord be with you.
> People: And also with you.

In an even shorter form, we use the same benediction when we sign off at the end of conversations, "Good bye," which originally meant "God be [with you]." The Spanish and the French have exactly the same expression: "Adios" and "Adieu." But what we sometimes forget is that "Hello," is also a benediction. It has at its heart the root meaning of "health" or "wholeness." In the Kasai region of Zaire, in the Tshiluba dialect, the people greet one another with a phrase that means, "Life to you." That is former cannibal country, and it is mighty reassuring when a stranger can say, "I wish you life." Our word means the same, "I wish you to be whole." So it would be an appropriate thing to begin a telephone conversation with goodbye, and end it with hello, but I guess that would confuse us.

So Paul begins by blessing the Corinthians. As mad as he has been at them, he has never ceased to love them, and to long for his relationship with them to be healthy and happy. Note that Paul does not call them, "The First Corinthian Church," but, "the church of God that is in Corinth." If we could all think of our congregations in this way, it might preserve us from denominational pride. The ecumenical movement could be completed overnight, if we would simply all agree to change the signs on the front of our churches to read, "The Church of Jesus Christ, Methodist Section," "The Church of Jesus Christ, Baptist Section," and so on. But we would probably get into an argument over what color the signs should be.

Paul's Prayer

You probably feel pretty inadequate when you go to call on someone who is going through great grief. I remember with the most genuine anguish how helpless I felt, when, on the first day in my first parish, the phone rang at 7:30 in the morning, and a woman cried, "Come quick! My husband has fallen down the stairs, and I think his neck is broken." I got there before the doctor and the ambulance, but it was clear that the man was dead. What on earth was I to say?

What I did say, I do not remember. But that was nearly forty years ago, and I have come to the strong conclusion that it did not really matter what I said. The important thing was that I came. My presence was more important than my words, and, as in the case of the woman with whom I sang the old hymns, that could be understood even by someone to whom words had lost their meaning. But I will go further than that; you do not even have to be there. A letter, a note, a phone call can bring great blessing to a suffering person. I did not realize until this until the death of my father, when the outpouring of messages of sympathy overwhelmed me. I cannot tell you anything that anybody said, only that it helped profoundly to know that someone cared.

But let us go another step still. They do not even need to know you care, provided that you do. It is good to be there, it is good to call or write, but if you can do none of these, you can still pray. It is a first, not a last, resort. We ought not neglect this powerful gift. We can indeed be comforter, counselor, advocate, helper to each other, through the Spirit, who is all those things to us.

Paul's Sufferings

It would be interesting to know what Paul had been going through in Asia (possibly in Ephesus). But the point Paul is making is not that we must realize the seriousness of the suffering, but that we must realize the power of God to help us in such times. Paul does not bore us with the details of his operation, he just reinforces his assurance that the God of the Resurrection (v. 9) can deliver us through anything.

Paul's Boast

Again, his boast is not about his own ability to bear up under suffering, or his superior skills as an apostle. His own life, he says, is an open book, which everyone can read. There is no need to brag here, you can look for yourself. No, the boast is in the power and grace of God, echoed in Isaac Watts' wonderful old hymn "When I Survey the Wondrous Cross":

> Forbid it, Lord, that I should boast,
> Save in the death of Christ, my God.
> All the vain things that charm me most,
> I sacrifice them to his blood.

Whatever calamities you and I may encounter, we have one precious possession that no one can steal from us: the love of God in Jesus Christ our Lord, from which we can never be separated (Rom. 8:38-39).

Helping Adults Become Involved

Preparing to Teach

Paul begins the second letter to the Corinthians by blessing them, praying for them, and then by sharing his sufferings with them. We might think of this as good advice to the teacher. So, let me suggest three ways to get ready for this session, in addition to careful reading and thinking about the scripture itself (which is always necessary).

1.) Think about each member of your class, one at a time if there are not too many of them, and ask God to bless that person.

2.) Think about each member of your class, and in so far as you can, identify the need that person has. Everyone has *some* sort of problem. It could be anything from a serious illness to a shyness that keeps them from being a full participant in class discussions. Try to put yourself in the place of that person, and pray for them, that they may be comforted and relieved from their distress.

3.) Finally, think of your own needs, as a person and as a teacher. Be prepared to express such needs to your class, and ask them to pray for you. Every teacher knows that we learn more from our class than we are able to give to them. Someone stopped a member of a congregation who had lost their famous pastor, and asked, "Can your new pastor fill those shoes?" "Certainly," was the reply. "Our congregation has a tradition of making great preachers." A great class can make a great teacher.

Introducing the Main Question

If you are comfortable with it, you might begin by reflecting with your class on some of the thoughts you had in the preparation exercise above. Suggest that you and your class members can be *paracletes* for one another, enabling, encouraging, consoling and advocating. Together you can draw from Paul motivation and skills for being a part of the community of belonging that we call the church.

Developing the Lesson

Use the following outline and accompanying questions.

I. Paul's benediction, 1-2

When, in worship, the pastor says, "The Lord bless you and keep you," or some other form of benediction, do you believe that does any good? How does benediction help us?

There is a tradition these days, when we part from people, even those we hardly know, such as store clerks, to say something positive, such as "Have a nice day." Is this adequate? Do you sometimes wish we were more deliberately Christian? Would it be better to say, "God bless you"? Jews say, "Shalom," to one another, both on greeting and taking leave. This rich old word means not only "peace," but also more than that. It is a wish for wholeness, blessing, and peace of mind as well as freedom from conflict. Should we not be in the habit of blessing one another in some way? What would you suggest?

II. Paul's prayer, 3-7

Can we do a better job of being mutual comforters? Are there folks in your class or congregation who are in special need? How can we help them? Is someone in your class responsible for checking on those who are not there?

Sometimes we fail to say something because we are shy; we do not want to be nosy or intrusive. The regular sending of cards can get to be a meaningless routine. But turn it around the other way. If you write, or call, or speak, there *is* a possibility that you will be intruding. But if you do or say nothing, there is a certainty that this will be perceived as not caring. Is it not better to err on the side of comfort than on that of indifference?

Can the Spirit help us in our weakness (see Rom. 8:26)? How?

III. Paul's sufferings, 8-11

Paul says (4:11) that "while we live, we are always being given up to death" (4:11). We may not be confronting literal death, as Paul did at Ephesus, but not one of us is free from what Emerson called "the terror of life." Can we comfort one another in this respect? How?

I can think of times in the past when congregations that I have served have literally saved my life. I keep in my personal file some notes that have lifted up my spirits when I was so low I did not know if I would be able to carry on. Can you think of such notes, or touches, or other forms of comfort that have saved your life? How can we do a more effective job of saving one another?

What do you think Paul's near-death experience may have been? Do we have them, too?

IV. Paul's boast, 12-14

Paul claims that there are no hidden meanings in his writing, that he is completely straightforward in his relationships with the Corinthians. This is a remarkable boast; could you or I make the same claim? If not, can we at least determine to aim at this? William Barclay reminds us of the old story about the man who went from door to door saying, "Flee! All is discovered!" and how the most unlikely people fled. Wouldn't it be wonderful if we could live, speak, and act as open books to one another?

There are some things, I suppose, in every one of us, that we would not want to admit to our Sunday school class. But we can at least admit that! There is nothing we cannot tell to God. No matter how down we are, there is a yes from God that can lift our spirits (v. 20) and set us on a fresh path. I am planning a book called, *The Yes Book,* about a mother who never said no to her children. If one asked, "Can I play in the street?" she would answer, "Yes, when you're old enough." If one asked, "Am I big?" she would put him on top of the refrigerator and say, "Yes." Are there ways in which we can say yes more effectively to each other? Will the sun rise tomorrow?

Helping Class Members Act

Send your people forth with a sense of mission, a mission of consolation. Leave them with our key verse for today, "Blessed be the God and Father of our Lord Jesus Christ . . . who consoles us in our affliction, so that we may be able to console those who are in any affliction" (3-4). Encourage them to live as advocates and comforters for one another.

Planning for Next Sunday

Next week's lesson is about motivation. Motivate them to read it!

Committed to Serve

Background Scripture: 1 Corinthians 9

The Main Question

Why do you do what you do? Maybe that sounds like a rather simple question, with an obvious answer, but think about it for a minute, for most of us have reasons for our behavior of which we may not be conscious. Do you remember the old story about the woman who was showing her daughter how to cook a ham? She said, "First you cut a few inches off the end, like this," and her daughter asked, "Why?" "Well, to tell you the truth," she answered, "I don't know. That's the way I've always done it; I learned it from my mother." Curious, she phoned her own mother, who did not know either. Finally they got through to the great-grandmother, who solved the mystery. "Oh, I had to cut off a few inches," she told them. "My pot was too small."

Our behavior may be determined by our subconscious, by what Freud called the *super ego*, that parental voice that speaks to us out of our upbringing. We may act as we do just because "that's the way we've always done it," in ways learned from the television, the tape-player, the schoolyard, or our favorite newspaper columnist. Or, and here it is getting uncomfortably close for me, we may do things because of how we think it will affect those around us. We are programmed to please; we want people to like us, so we do things we know will be accepted.

From the very moment we are born we begin the long task of discovering who we are in relationship, first to mother and daddy, then to siblings, then to other children, then adults, then society, then the universe. God has set us free to be ourselves, but the question is: Who are you? Are you really a self-motivated person, or are you jumping through somebody else's hoop?

Selected Scripture

King James Version	New Revised Standard Version

1 Corinthians 9:1-7, 19-27

1 Am I not an apostle? am I not free? have I not seen Jesus Christ our Lord? are not ye my work in the Lord?

2 If I be not an apostle unto others, yet doubtless I am to you; for the seal of mine apostleship are ye in the Lord.

3 Mine answer to them that do examine me is this,

4 Have we not power to eat and to drink?

5 Have we not power to lead about a sister, a wife, as well as other apostles, and as the brethren of the Lord, and Cephas?

6 Or I only and Barnabas, have not we power to forbear working?

7 Who goeth a warfare any time at his own charges? who planteth a vineyard, and eateth not of the fruit thereof? or who feedeth a flock, and eateth not of the milk of the flock?

....

19 For though I be free from all men, yet have I made myself servant

1 Corinthians 9:1-7, 19-27

1 Am I not free? Am I not an apostle? Have I not seen Jesus our Lord? Are you not my work in the Lord? 2 If I am not an apostle to others, at least I am to you; for you are the seal of my apostleship in the Lord.

3 This is my defense to those who would examine me. 4 Do we not have the right to our food and drink? 5 Do we not have the right to be accompanied by a believing wife, as do the other apostles and the brothers of the Lord and Cephas? 6 Or is it only Barnabas and I who have no right to refrain from working for a living? 7 Who at any time pays the expenses for doing military service? Who plants a vineyard and does not eat any of its fruit? Or who tends a flock and does not get any of its milk?

....

19 For though I am free with respect to all, I have made myself a

unto all, that I might gain the more.

20 And unto the Jews I became as a Jew, that I might gain the Jews; to them that are under the law, as under the law, that I might gain them that are under the law;

21 To them that are without law, as without law, (being not without law to God, but under the law to Christ,) that I might gain them that are without law.

22 To the weak became I as weak, that I might gain the weak: I am made all things to all men, that I might by all means save some.

23 And this I do for the gospel's sake, that I might be partaker thereof with you.

24 Know ye not that they which run in a race run all, but one receiveth the prize? So run, that ye may obtain.

25 And every man that striveth for the mastery is temperate in all things. Now they do it to obtain a corruptible crown; but we an incorruptible.

26 I therefore so run, not as uncertainly; so fight I, not as one that beateth the air:

27 But I keep under my body, and bring it into subjection: lest that by any means, when I have preached to others, I myself should be a castaway.

slave to all, so that I might win more of them. 20 To the Jews I became as a Jew, in order to win Jews. To those under the law I became as one under the law (though I myself am not under the law) so that I might win those under the law. 21 To those outside the law I became as one outside the law (though I am not free from God's law but am under Christ's law) so that I might win those outside the law. 22 To the weak I became weak, so that I might win the weak. I have become all things to all people, that I might by all means save some. 23 I do it all for the sake of the gospel, so that I may share in its blessings.

24 Do you not know that in a race the runners all compete, but only one receives the prize? Run in such a way that you may win it. 25 Athletes exercise self-control in all things; they do it to receive a perishable wreath, but we an imperishable one. 26 So I do not run aimlessly, nor do I box as though beating the air; 27 but I punish my body and enslave it, so that after proclaiming to others I myself should not be disqualified.

Key Verse: **For though I be free from all men, yet have I made myself servant unto all, that I might gain the more.**

Key Verse: **For though I am free with respect to all, I have made myself a slave to all, so that I might win more of them.**

As You Read the Scripture

1 Corinthians 9:1-2. What is an apostle? The word "one who is sent," in other words, an ambassador or messenger. Technically, an apostle had to be one of those who had accompanied the disciples "during all the time that the Lord Jesus went in and out among us" (Acts 1:21). This was one of the conditions set up for the selection of a successor to Judas, who turned out to be Matthias (Acts 1:26). Paul, of course, was not there at the beginning, but he makes the claim for his apostleship here, saying, "Have I not seen Jesus?" He had met the Lord on the Damascus road, and this, he feels, qualified him for the job. He certainly met the second condition: he "must become a witness with us to his resurrection" (Acts 1:22). His ministry among the Corinthians, though, is the real proof (Paul says "seal") of his authority.

Verses 3-14. That authority entitles him, had he chosen it, to be materially rewarded for his work. Apparently others were traveling with their wives on their expense accounts, including James, and some of Jesus' other brothers, as well as Peter (Cephas). Paul uses several illustrations of his right to be paid: the soldier on duty, the steward of a vineyard, the keeper of a flock. This goes way back to the Torah, he says, quoting Deuteronomy 25:4, "You shall not muzzle an ox while it is treading out the grain." All this means that he has every right to benefit materially. But (v. 12), like Barnabas (whom he had mentioned in v. 6), he has not demanded his rights. He cites one more example: the priest who is allowed to eat the meat of sacrifices.

Verses 15-18. But his real reward is not money, it is the freedom to do what he *has* to do. Remember Jeremiah (20:9): "Within me there is something like a burning fire, shut up in my bones; I am weary with holding it in, and I cannot." "Woe to me," says Paul, "if I do not proclaim the gospel!" (Literally: "If I do not evangelize!")

Verses 19-23. But, in keeping with his main message to the Corinthians, Paul makes it clear that he is not going to use his freedom under God to take advantage of others. Rather, he will identify with others, empathize with them, if you will. He will be a Jew if need be—that is, keep kosher; this may have been why he had Timothy circumcised (Acts 16:3), and why he underwent the act of purification (Acts 21:17-26). But he does not mind living as one free from the law with the Gentiles. Is he being wishy-washy here? He does not think so; rather, he says he is doing it "for the sake of the gospel." One of the most important gifts we can give to others is to walk in their moccasins.

Verses 24-27. These brief verses give us a fresh insight into Paul. An American politician said of Boris Yeltsin, the first president of the newly democratic Russia, "I admire him for sticking to his guns." In this sense Paul dares "to be a Daniel." He may become all things to all people, but he will not give up his inner integrity. At heart he is a self-disciplinarian, constantly in training as a good athlete should be. Freedom, in Christ, does not mean freedom to do as you please. It may look like it from the outside, as a good broken-field runner appears to run with abandon on the field. But you can bet he achieved his skill to run free by learning the rules and the disciplines of the game.

The Scripture and the Main Question

Is Paul an Apostle?

If the criteria for apostleship are these:

1. Being with Jesus from the beginning, and
2. Being a witness to the resurrection,

then who, in the New Testament, was the first apostle? I say it was a woman; specifically, Mary Magdalene. She, according to Matthew 28:1, Mark 16:1, Luke 21:10, and John 20:1 (all *four* of the Gospels), was the first person at the tomb, and the first person to see the risen Christ in the flesh (John 20:16). Moreover, it was she who ran and told the twelve. She had surely been with Jesus from the beginning (her earliest mention is Luke 8:2, during his Galilean ministry, as one of his strong supporters). Why do you think Paul didn't mention her in his list of the Resurrection appearances (1 Cor. 15:5-7)? It is just one more example of the fact that people did not really notice women much in those days, and that it made them uncomfortable when they insisted on being noticed (11:2-16 and 14:33-35). Thank goodness, in his heart of hearts, Paul knows that women have every right to be fully included in Christ's body (Gal. 3:28).

But, apart from the gender issue, who is truly an apostle? If we are to accept Paul's defense, the argument goes something like this: In one sense, apostleship belongs to those who were Jesus' historical companions, and who continue to witness to the Resurrection. But, in another sense, no less legitimate, an apostle is *anyone* who has seen Jesus and believes the good news that he has overcome death. In that sense, I am an apostle, and so are you.

Paying the Preacher

I know a lot of preachers who play the "Caspar Milquetoast" game, a kind of hard-to-get, false-humility role. It goes like this: "I'm glad to work for whatever you want to pay me"; or, "Aw shucks" (in the words of Ps. 22:6:), "I am a worm and not human." Paul, fortunately, plays no such passive-aggressive game. He is perfectly straightforward about his rights to munch a little of the grain as he goes around the threshing floor. Don't you like his style? Some years ago, a celebrated football star was hired to coach at a college for a rather remarkable figure. A newspaper reporter, properly skeptical, asked him at a press conference, "Isn't that an unusually high amount for someone as young as you are?" "Maybe so," he replied, "but I'm worth it." May God grant such humility to all of us! How much are you worth?

The True Reward

Of course, money is not the real issue anyway. Someone has said that the simplest doctrine of Christian vocation is to decide what you would rather do than anything else in the world, and then find somebody to pay you to do it! I will go along with that. (Although, when he heard that suggestion, a person I know said, "In that case, I will see if I can persuade *Field and Stream* to hire me to fish every trout stream in America and write an article about each one.")

So Paul is able to make unembarrassed requests of his people, having a ground of boasting that no one can take away. The strange paradox (I have called it "Catch One") is that his ground for boasting is precisely his renunciation! But whether they pay him or not does not really matter; that is not the issue. He is under compulsion. He is going to preach, no matter what. When he says, "Woe to me if I do not proclaim the gospel!" he does not mean, "If I don't evangelize, God's going to get me." He means, rather, "The good news, by its very nature, demands to be passed on. If I don't preach the gospel, I will never experience the power of the gospel." If you are so full of good news that you cannot hold it in, then it must be good news indeed. "Let the redeemed of the Lord say so!" (Ps. 107:2).

THIRD QUARTER

All Things to All People

We said, in outlining the main question, that our behavior may be motivated, not by our own inner calling, but by our desire to please others. Of course, this is not necessarily bad. Those who do not stop to think how our behavior will affect others are irresponsible members of society. As a Christian I care, and care deeply, lest I hurt others, or lead them astray. But there is a danger here. I may try so hard to please others that I forget that my responsibility is, at bottom, to my own truest self, that is, to God.

My wife tells me that she can usually tell who I am talking to on the telephone by the way I speak. (I am not sure I believe all this, but she swears it is true.) She says that when I am talking to a cultured person, I will tend to sound like an Englishman, and that if I am talking to a "good old country boy" tradesperson, I begin to sound like a Tennessee hillbilly. Maybe so; maybe I, like Paul, am trying to become "all things to all people" (v. 22). I am suggesting that this is a good thing in one way, but there is a fine line between being empathetic to others and being a coward who has no personal convictions, who shapes all positions based on how they affect other people. For Paul, this required considerable discipline (see the next paragraph). In the end, he chose to act "neither for fear of reward nor for hope of heaven," but for the sake of truth itself.

The Athletic Christian

Paul literally beat himself "black and blue" (v. 27) to keep in spiritual shape, so as to tread the fine line between being responsible to no one except Christ and himself, and caring deeply for others. Are we that well disciplined? This is the same issue that the whole first letter to the Corinthians is all about: the individual over and against the community. But we need to come at it once more because it is the critical question in life. A good broken-field runner must know the rules of the game, an abstract painter must learn to draw apples and oranges, a musician must know how to play scales before launching out into rhapsody. You cannot jazz up a melody without knowing the tune.

We sometimes think that "marriage should be easy because we're so much in love," or "worship should be easy because we all love the Lord so much." Nonsense! Good marriages, good worship, and good Christian living are all hard work (although well worth it). Jesus Christ himself sweated blood to do it right, and you and I should content ourselves with no less. Paul could not step outside the law to regain the lawless, were he not disciplined under the gospel. Paradoxically, he could not become as one under the law, if he were not under grace.

Helping Adults Become Involved

I do not know how to motivate people! But that is what this lesson is about. I take comfort from whoever it was who said, "You may build the altar, but only God can strike it with fire." (Actually the fire quite often comes down somewhere else!) Another metaphor I sometimes use is, "I can set the sails, but the wind comes from God" (see John 3:8). It is as old as John Heywood's *Proverbs* (1546): "A man may well bring a horse to the water, but he cannot make him drinke without he will." Or, even older, "I planted, Apollos watered, but God gave the growth" (1 Cor. 3:6).

The point is this: There is only one person in the whole world over whose motives I have any control, and that is myself. You cannot make your students learn; you can only make yourself learn. So let us covenant together to take the example of Paul's motivation in this chapter, and scatter it on the ground. If it falls on good ground, takes root and bears fruit, that will say something about the soil, not about the sower.

Preparing to Teach

Start with your own motivation: "Why am I teaching this class this Sunday?" (I started with mine. Why am I writing this lesson plan? Because I enjoy it [writing and the Bible] more than anything I know, and because I get paid a modest amount for doing it. What more could I ask?) Then consider why your class is there. You probably know their motives fairly well. What are they trying to prove?

If you want me to say what I think your approach *ought* to be, I would say it like this: "Woe is you if you do not teach the gospel!" If it is meaningful to you, how can you keep it bottled up inside yourself? If it is not meaningful, then what are you doing preparing to teach it?

Introducing the Main Question

I would lead the class through the very process just described in the preceding section. Ask them why they are here. (Be prepared for surprises; I heard of a speaker who once gave a speech to a group in a mental hospital. "Why are we all here?" he asked. "Because we're not all there," someone replied.) Their reasons may be no more profound. But this is a lesson in which we are going to be asking ourselves about our inner motivation, and the first step is to be honest about it.

Developing the Lesson

Use the following outline and questions:

I. Is Paul an apostle?, 1-2

Is Paul an apostle? What do you think? Are you? What constitutes apostleship? If you decide you are not an apostle, then what are you? What was Paul?

The word *missionary* is like the word *apostle*, only it is Latin. It is from the word meaning "to send," the perfect tense: *mitto, mittere, missus est,* meaning "having been sent." A missionary is one who has been sent. Have you been sent? (See John 20:21.)

How do you decide that you have a gospel message to declare? Martin Buber said, "Prophetic power is the knowledge that the God who speaks to me in my own conscience is the Lord of the universe."

II. Paying the preacher, 3-14

What do you think of the proposal, "We should pay all our pastors the same amount, regardless of the size of their churches" (maybe with some allowance for cost-of-living, number of children, years of experience, etc.; that could get as complicated as the tax laws)?

THIRD QUARTER

Here is an even tougher question: Why pay them anything? Why not let them get jobs (like Paul did, making tents) and support themselves? At one time we actually did not pay them anything. It has been within my lifetime that most clergy lived in a free house, furnished with hand-me-down, clothes out of the missionary barrel, and occasional tips for weddings and funerals. What about 1 Timothy 5:18: "The laborer deserves to be paid"?

Because of the tradition of free housing for clergy, today's preachers get a double tax break: their housing allowance is not considered taxable income, but they get to deduct the interest on their mortgages. Do you think that is fair to the rest of us?

III. The true reward, 15-18

I can testify that you could never pay me enough to do what I do; I do it for other reasons. Why do you do what you do? What is your payoff?

Someone has said that all jobs are partly gathering eggs and partly cleaning out the henhouse. Blessed then is the one whose livelihood is 60 percent gathering and only 40 percent shoveling. For most of us it is 20-80, or worse. But I do know a few happy souls who are 100 percent happy at what they do; a lot of musicians, artists, actors, and writers are people like that. What is your percentage?

What motivates you to do what you do? The wolf at the door? Your parent's nagging? A high sense of calling?

IV. All things to all people, 19-23

Where do you draw the line between trying to empathize with others and sticking to your guns? Can you do both?

There were a couple of songs a few years back with lines like, "I did it my way," or "I've gotta be me." Is that a form of egotism or simply a healthy ego?

V. The athletic Christian, 24-27

Where do you draw the line between living a life of Christian freedom and the hard discipline of discipleship (note the similarity between those two words)? Can you do both?

Helping Class Members Act

I said at the beginning of this lesson that I do not know how to motivate people, and I do not. So I do not know how you can help your class members to act. Why not put it up to them? Suggest that they make a list of intentions based on the following: "Believing that the gospel is good news, I resolve to . . . ," or, "Believing that I am called of God, I resolve to . . . ," or, "Given who I am, I resolve to . . ." (those are really the same question).

Planning for Next Sunday

Next week's lesson will help us on the motivation question. Read 2 Corinthians 5, especially verses 18-20, and see if they help answer this week's questions.

Motivated by Christ's Love

Background Scripture: 2 Corinthians 5

The Main Question

This week's question is like last week's, only now it has become a yes-or-no question. Last week we asked ourselves, why do we do what we do? This week we want to ask it more pointedly: Are we motivated by Jesus Christ? It is impossible, looking at the surface (see 1 Sam. 16:7), to spot the Christians in the world, but, at bottom, one who is a Christian ought to be a different sort of person. That is the promise of this week's lesson: "If anyone is in Christ, there is a new creation: everything old has passed away; see, everything has become new!" (2 Cor. 5:17).

The question for us is, are we new creatures? Are we the same old grungy folks, plodding along through life, getting from breakfast to bedtime and trying to make a buck, or do we have an exciting and empowering purpose in life? According to 2 Corinthians 5:19, something incredible has happened, the most spectacular, unbelievable event in all of history: "In Christ God was reconciling the world to himself, not counting their trespasses against them, and entrusting the message of reconciliation to us." God has given a gift to all the world: to the pious and the pagan, the poor and the rich, to you and to me. It is the gift of salvation.

Incredibly, God has entrusted this astonishing gift to ordinary folks like us. We have the opportunity to be made completely new, into fresh, lively, joyful, creative people, and to share this gift with others. The more I think about it, the more excited I get, and the more I want to be a part of it. So I am asking myself the question, and I hope you are, too: "Is my life motivated by Jesus Christ?"

Selected Scripture

King James Version

2 Corinthians 5:11-21

11 Knowing therefore the terror of the Lord, we persuade men; but we are made manifest unto God; and I trust also are made manifest in your consciences.

12 For we commend not ourselves again unto you, but give you occasion to glory on our behalf, that ye may have somewhat to answer them which glory in appearance, and not in heart.

13 For whether we be beside ourselves, it is to God: or whether we be sober, it is for your cause.

New Revised Standard Version

2 Corinthians 5:11-21

11 Therefore, knowing the fear of the Lord, we try to persuade others; but we ourselves are well known to God, and I hope that we are also well known to your consciences. 12 We are not commending ourselves to you again, but giving you an opportunity to boast about us, so that you may be able to answer those who boast in outward appearance and not in the heart. 13 For if we are beside ourselves, it is for God; if we are in our right mind, it is for you. 14 For the love of Christ urges us

287

14 For the love of Christ constraineth us; because we thus judge, that if one died for all, then were all dead:

15 And that he died for all, that they which live should not henceforth live unto themselves, but unto him which died for them, and rose again.

16 Wherefore henceforth know we no man after the flesh: yea, though we have known Christ after the flesh, yet now henceforth know we him no more.

17 Therefore if any man be in Christ, he is a new creature: old things are passed away; behold, all things are become new.

18 And all things are of God, who hath reconciled us to himself by Jesus Christ, and hath given to us the ministry of reconciliation;

19 To wit, that God was in Christ, reconciling the world unto himself, not imputing their trespasses unto them; and hath committed unto us the word of reconciliation.

20 Now then we are ambassadors for Christ, as though God did beseech you by us: we pray you in Christ's stead, be ye reconciled to God.

21 For he hath made him to be sin for us, who knew no sin; that we might be made the righteousness of God in him.

on, because we are convinced that one has died for all; therefore all have died. 15 And he died for all, so that those who live might live no longer for themselves, but for him who died and was raised for them.

16 From now on, therefore, we regard no one from a human point of view, even though we once knew Christ from a human point of view, we know him no longer in that way. 17 So if anyone is in Christ, there is a new creation: everything old has passed away; see, everything has become new! 18 All this is from God, who reconciled us to himself through Christ, and has given us the ministry of reconciliation; 19 that is, in Christ God was reconciling the world to himself, not counting their trespasses against them, and entrusting the message of reconciliation to us. 20 So we are ambassadors for Christ, since God is making his appeal through us; we entreat you on behalf of Christ, be reconciled to God. 21 For our sake he made him to be sin who knew no sin, so that in him we might become the righteousness of God.

Key Verse: **And all things are of God, who hath reconciled us to himself by Jesus Christ, and hath given to us the ministry of reconciliation.**

Key Verse: **All this is from God, who reconciled us to himself through Christ, and has given us the ministry of reconciliation.**

As You Read the Scripture

2 Corinthians 5:1-5. Paul has been talking about the burdens of this life (4:7-12), but they point beyond themselves to "an eternal weight of glory" (4:17). Now, in our passage, he talks about that glory, an eternal house "not made with hands." Against all human logic, he reaffirms that this life, though it seems solid, is ultimately transient and ephemeral, but heaven is what is truly real. This is guaranteed for us by the presence of the Spirit (see Phil. 1:6).

Verses 6-10. Paul would not mind dying, he says. In fact, he would really rather like to (see Phil. 1:21). That would enable him to see the Lord face to face. Indeed, it would be a homecoming, to use Paul's language. It would involve facing judgment (v. 10). But, as hard as it may be to believe, he looks forward even to that, sure in the confidence that nothing can prevent him from passing safely through that event. (See his optimism in Romans 8:31-38.) In the meantime (v. 6) we are in another home, a temporary one, our "earthen vessel" (4:7), our "tent" (5:1).

Verses 11-15. He begins this paragraph by speaking of "the fear of the Lord," but this does not frighten him. Fear in this case does not mean terror (as in, say, an earthquake) but holy awe, as in Isaiah's experience of a vision of God (Isa. 6:1-9). Terror is too strong, reverence (as we use the word today) is not strong enough. The fear of the Lord is a powerful sense of the wonder, majesty, and greatness of God. (See Job 28:28, Ps. 111:10, Prov. 1:7, Mal. 4:2, and many other references.)

The mysterious phrase "beside ourselves" refers to Paul's numerous ecstatic religious experiences: his Damascus road conversion, of course; his speaking in tongues (1 Cor. 14:18); and his being caught up into "the third heaven" (2 Cor. 12:2-4). These are largely private matters, between himself and God (see 1 Cor. 14:4), whereas, when he is discussing theology rationally, it is for the edification of those around him. He would like to stay in a state of ecstasy, but the love of Christ (v. 14) urges him to continue to minister to others. He is convinced that Christ has died for everyone (see also 1 John 2:2), and that he has a divine commission to make sure everyone knows about it.

Verses 16-17. Incredibly, we (those who have experienced grace) see the world differently, as though through spiritual eyes. Everything has been made new. It not only seems different, it *is* different (see Rev. 21:1 and 5). The way we relate to everyone else in the world has been radically altered. They may not yet know the good news, but we do, and so we have a new relationship with everyone we encounter.

Verses 18-21. The good news is summed up, briefly and profoundly, in the phrase, "In Christ God was reconciling the world" (v. 19), and the apostolic (missionary) task is summed up in the same verse, for God was also "entrusting the message . . . to us." In all this it is God who takes the initiative, but we are invited to participate with God in making it come to full fruit. God is the Creator, but we are the stewards of the creation (Gen. 1:28, 2:15). God has taken on our sin in Christ (v. 21), and we have been radically changed, from sinful human beings, to those clothed in the pure radiance of God.

The Scripture and the Main Question

It is not always easy to identify Christians by their behavior. Some years ago, when an airplane crashed in Washington, D.C., a man dove many times into the icy waters, rescuing people with no thought of his own safety, until he was drowned. Someone said, "That was a mighty Christian thing to do." But a secular humanist was heard to remark, "That's strange; I thought it was a very humanistic thing to do!"

Imagine two grocery stores, right across the street from each other. One is operated by a Christian, who has a sincere commitment to provide a good honest service to his neighbors. The other is run by a non-Christian entrepreneur, who is in it for the money. The Christian finds that he cannot give his groceries away free, or he will go out of business, and cannot pay his employees, so he charges modest prices. The non-Christian finds that if he overcharges people no one will shop there, and he must be fair with his employees or no one will work there. They both are smiling and pleasant to their customers, the one because of love, the other because it pays off. So if you go into either store, you will find a genial atmosphere and sensible prices. The difference must be something internal, having to do with motivation.

Now there may be some tests you could use to discover the inner makeup of those storekeepers. One way would be to live with them for a good while; I suspect the real motivation would begin to reveal itself. Another might be to observe them in an emergency. (Somebody has said, "If you want to know if there are rats in the barn, open the door suddenly.")

Living Inside Our Skin

But, in the meantime, these are the only bodies we have, and we have to live in them. (In fact, it is better not to talk too much about living in our bodies, as though our selves were somehow something apart from them. Remember that [Gen. 2:7] it says that the newly created Adam *became* a human being, not that he *contained* a soul.) Anyway, these are our bodies, and we are stuck with them. Let us "make it our aim to please the Lord" (v. 9), in or out of our bodies.

The Love of Christ Urges Us

We now come to the key verse that has to do with our motivation. Last week we asked, "Why do we do what we do?" This week, we are saying, we ought to follow orders. It ought to be the love of Christ (v. 14) that urges us on. (I learned that in the Elizabethan language of the King James Bible: "The love of Christ constraineth us.") In or out of the body, in or out of our minds, we are to put ourselves under Christ's spell. This sounds a little like the old marriage vows: "in plenty and in want, in joy and in sorrow, in sickness and in health, as long as we . . . shall live." The ideal state for the Christian is utterly swayed by the control of Christ. "But I want to be in charge of my own life!" you cry. Yes, that is the ultimate temptation, but, do you really? Imagine what it would be like if the pilot of a huge jumbo jet called you into the cockpit with its thousands of instruments and said, "Here, you take over!" It would be like that if suddenly you had to handle your automatic nervous system and all its synapses, let alone the myriad destinies that may be about to cross your paths. Better let God be in charge.

The New Creation

The good news is that, in Christ, our way of seeing things is radically altered, and to serve him is to be truly free. Because I am sure of Christ's love, for me and everyone else, then my way of relating to them and myself is brand-new. It is not a puerile optimism that makes me want to sing, "It's a wonderful world." It is a conscious decision to opt for that which is good, and just, and kind, and faithful. From now on, I will treat everyone I encounter as one for whom Christ died. For that is who they are.

Ambassadors for Christ

It is not enough for me to know this; I must tell others. It is not a matter of having a "fire in my bones" like Jeremiah. It is much simpler than that. Here is a humble illustration. Say you are a small child, and you have just seen an elephant walk into your schoolyard, trample on all the band instruments, suck the water out of the fountain in front of the school, and blow it all over the principal. Then, on your way home from school, you meet some of your schoolmates, and they ask you, "What's new?" Would you say, "Oh, nothing"? I rather doubt it. In fact, I will bet this word processor that your next words would be, "You're not going to believe this. . . ." Don't you think some enthusiasm at least that strong is called for when we remember that we have been privileged to behold the greatest event that ever happened?

Helping Adults Become Involved

Preparing to Teach

Begin this lesson by rereading verse 19. (And maybe the last paragraph that I just wrote above.) What a wonderful, joyful, incredible thing it is for you and me to be involved in the business of passing on the good news! If you can carry that enthusiasm into the classroom with you, I do not think it makes too much difference what you say. The truth will shine through in spite of you.

If you are a little (or a lot) discouraged about your task as teacher, go back a chapter and look at 2 Corinthians 4:7-11. Paul knew what it was to have setbacks. His teaching task was not a bed of roses. Or, at any rate, they had plenty of thorns. But somehow he managed to stay spiritually up. He was able to call all these troubles a "slight momentary affliction" (v. 17). He is bribing himself to keep on keeping on, with the promise of eternity. You can do the same.

Introducing the Main Question

Say to your class, "Sisters and brothers, the success of today's lesson is up to you. I can lead you to the water, but I can't make you drink. I don't know much about motivation. But I don't have to. It is not I who motivates, but Christ. So walk with me into 2 Corinthians 5 this morning, anticipating that we will find there something exciting, that will stir us to action. Let's begin by giving away the punch line, and reading our key verse together: 'God . . . reconciled us to himself through Christ, and has given us the ministry of reconciliation' (v. 18)."

Developing the Lesson

Use the following outline and discussion questions:

I. Longing for heaven, 1-5
There are a number of jokes about going to heaven such as:
A. The man who didn't rise when the preacher asked everyone who wanted to go to heaven to stand. On questioned, he said, "Oh I want to go eventually; I thought you were getting up a bus-load for right now."

B. I've got good news and bad news. The good news is they've got golf courses in heaven. The bad news is, your tee time is this morning!

Now, what is wrong with those stories? If we really longed for heaven, why would we not want to go right now? If you were a golfer, why would it not be *good* news to know that in a few hours you would be on the heavenly tee? Do we really long for heaven?

II. Living inside our skin, 6-10

I have heard it said that death is not so bad, it is dying that is frightening. What do you think? Do you look on death as a great terror or a great adventure? Maybe some of both?

I once heard a country music song with the line, "No matter who you lay with, you have to go to sleep alone." I take this to mean that our destiny is our own responsibility, and that our dying cannot be done for us by somebody else. But can it? Did not Jesus walk "this lonesome valley" for us, so that we do not have to walk it by ourselves?

Does the Judgment make you nervous? Should it?

Hamlet said of the possibility that we might be conscious after death, "There's the rub." What do you think?

III. The love of Christ urges us, 11-15

Last week's question was, "Why do we do what we do?" Ask it again now, in the light of this lesson. What keeps us keeping on?

Paul says that Christ died for all. Does that include those who have never even heard of him? Those who lived in the centuries before Christ? Those people whom you encounter every day, their uncaring faces passing you blankly on the street, or sitting in parked cars as your train passes by? That despicable person who is always putting you down and making you feel like a fool, or frightening you? Did Christ really die for my enemies? If so, then what difference does it make in the way I relate to them?

IV. The new creation, 16-17

If you once thought of Christ as simply an historical character like everybody else, how do you think of him now? He is still fully historical and human, but is he not something more (or other) than that?

Do you think that Paul (as he describes himself in v. 17) is looking at the world through rose-colored glasses? Is he right to be optimistic? Is he in fact optimistic? Someone has said, "I am a pessimist about humanity, but an optimist about God." Someone else added, if you are really an optimist about God, you cannot be a pessimist about humanity. The second automatically follows the first.

I remember once looking at a picture on the wall of an architect's office, a picture of distant hills and fluffy clouds. "Not very great art," I thought, "but pleasant enough." Then, to my utter amazement, I saw that I was looking, not at a picture, but at an actual scene. It was a window, framed so that it appeared to be a painting on the wall. Nothing that I was looking at had changed, but it was altogether new. When you look at the world through eyes of faith, it will be the same world. Or will it? If you have changed, will that change what you are looking at?

V. Ambassadors for Christ, 18-21

We have jobs to do, you and I. The Ruler of the Universe has seen fit to put the most important message of all times into our shaking hands: "Here, go, run, tell!" God is always doing things like this. Is it not absurd that God has put the most important task in the world, that of raising children, into the hands of amateurs, folks who have never done it before? (By the time you have finished ruining the oldest child by being too conscientious in practicing on her you spoil the youngest by giving up and being too lax.) But here we are, appointed missionaries, apostles, ambassadors. We represent God to the world. We had better get at it.

Helping Class Members Act

I have said it three times already: I do not know how to motivate other people. You are on your own here. But do not give up. Admit it to them. They have got to motivate themselves. Tell them to ask Christ to help them do this.

Planning for Next Sunday

Ask them to write in one sentence what they believe to be the secret of happiness. Tell them: "We will see if you want to revise it next week after we have looked at chapters 8 and 9."

Ministry Through Giving

Background Scripture: 2 Corinthians 8–9

The Main Question

Jesus sees the world upside down. Or, does it just seem that way to me because I see the world upside down? I am told by medical experts that we all view the world as inverted. The lens of the eye, they say, projects an image on the retina that is upside down, but we learn to reverse it in our brains. Experiments have been conducted with special glasses that make the world look upside down, but, strangely, after people wear them a while, they get used to them and then when they take them *off* things look reversed.

But enough about optical physics. Our main question has to do with spiritual sight. Truly, when you examine the things Jesus says, they appear to be altogether backward from the way the world sees things. Here is a short list:

Jesus: Those who want to save their life will lose it (Luke 9:24).
  The World: You have got to look out for number one.
Jesus: Blessed are you poor, for yours is the kingdom of God (Luke 6:20).
  The World: Them as has, gets.
Jesus: Blessed are you who are hungry now, for you will be filled (Luke 6:21).

293

THIRD QUARTER

The World: Eat, drink and be merry, for tomorrow we die.

Jesus: Blessed are you who weep now, for you will laugh (Luke 6:21).

The World: Follow your bliss.

Jesus: If any want to become my followers, let them deny themselves (Luke 9:23).

Our main question: Are we looking at life upside down?

Selected Scripture

King James Version	New Revised Standard Version

2 Corinthians 9:1-8, 10-15

1 For as touching the ministering to the saints, it is superfluous for me to write to you:

2 For I know the forwardness of your mind, for which I boast of you to them of Macedonia, that Achaia was ready a year ago; and your zeal hath provoked very many.

3 Yea have I sent the brethren, lest our boasting of you should be in vain in this behalf; that, as I said, ye may be ready:

4 Lest haply if they of Macedonia come with me, and find you unprepared, we (that we say not, ye) should be ashamed in this same confident boasting.

5 Therefore I thought it necessary to exhort the brethren, that they would go before unto you, and make up beforehand your bounty, whereof ye had notice before, that the same might be ready, as a matter of bounty, and not as of covetousness.

6 But this I say, He which soweth sparingly shall reap also sparingly; and he which soweth bountifully shall reap also bountifully.

7 Every man according as he purposeth in his heart, so let him give; not grudgingly, or of necessity: for God loveth a cheerful giver.

8 And God is able to make all grace abound toward you; that ye, always having all sufficiency in all things, may abound to every good work:

2 Corinthians 9:1-8, 10-15

1 Now it is not necessary for me to write you about the ministry to the saints, 2 for I know your eagerness, which is the subject of my boasting about you to the people of Macedonia, saying that Achaia has been ready since last year; and your zeal has stirred up most of them. 3 But I am sending the brothers in order that our boasting about you may not prove to have been empty in this case, so that you may be ready, as I said you would be; 4 otherwise, if some Macedonians come with me and find that you are not ready, we would be humiliated—to say nothing of you—in this undertaking. 5 So I thought it necessary to urge the brothers to go on ahead to you, and arrange in advance for this bountiful gift that you have promised, so that it may be ready as a voluntary gift and not as an extortion.

6 The point is this: the one who sows sparingly will also reap sparingly, and the one who sows bountifully will also reap bountifully. 7 Each of you must give as you have made up your mind, not reluctantly or under compulsion, for God loves a cheerful giver. 8 And God is able to provide you with every blessing in abundance, so that by always having enough of everything, you may share abundantly in every good work.

10 (Now he that ministereth seed to the sower both minister bread for your food, and multiply your seed sown, and increase the fruits of your righteousness;)

11 Being enriched in every thing to all bountifulness, which causeth through us thanksgiving to God.

12 For the administration of this service not only supplieth the want of the saints, but is abundant also by many thanksgivings unto God;

13 Whiles by the experiment of this ministration they glorify God for your professed subjection unto the gospel of Christ, and for your liberal distribution unto them, and unto all men;

14 And by their prayer for you, which long after you for the exceeding grace of God in you.

15 Thanks be to God for his unspeakable gift.

10 He who supplies seed to the sower and bread for food will supply and multiply your seed for sowing and increase the harvest of your righteousness. 11 You will be enriched in every way for your great generosity, which will produce thanksgiving to God through us; 12 for the rendering of this ministry not only supplies the needs of the saints but also overflows with many thanksgivings to God. 13 Through the testing of this ministry you glorify God by your obedience to the confession of the gospel of Christ and by the generosity of your sharing with them and with all others, 14 while they long for you and pray for you because of the surpassing grace of God that he has given you. 15 Thanks be to God for his indescribable gift!

Key Verse: **But this I say, He which soweth sparingly shall reap also sparingly; and he which soweth bountifully shall reap also bountifully.**

Key Verse: **The point is this: the one who sows sparingly will also reap sparingly, and the one who sows bountifully will also reap bountifully.**

As You Read the Scripture

2 Corinthians 8:1-6. In saying "We want you to know," Paul marks a clear transition in his letter. It is his way of saying, "Okay, now listen up!" He tells them about the generosity of the Macedonians. (That is the northern part of present-day Greece, which would have included Beroea, Philippi and Thessalonica.) They have evidently been persecuted by the non-Christian (v. 2), but this has not prevented their generosity from overflowing. They gave more (v. 3) than they would have been expected to, and now Paul wants this same magnanimity to infect the Corinthians.

Verses 7-15. Though the example of the Macedonians is important, the true example for our stewardship is Jesus Christ (v. 9). The Corinthians had evidently started a collection earlier (vv. 10-11); perhaps this had been interrupted by their conflict with Paul, but now that that has been settled, it is time to get on with it. He reminds them of their relative affluence. No early Christian church was wealthy by the world's standards, but they are better off than the Macedonians, and certainly than the poor struggling mother church in Jerusalem. Giving should be according to means (v. 12). He concludes with a quote from Exodus 16:18, about the distribution of the manna, to remind them that God's people should not have more than they actually need when others might be hungry. (See Acts 2:44-45.)

Verses 16-24. Paul is sending Titus (who could have been the bearer of this letter) and two others who are not named, though tradition has it that the one who was "famous among the churches" might have been Luke. Second Corinthians is, in part, a letter of recommendation for these three, that they will be accepted and trusted by the Corinthians. The word used for messengers in verse 23 is literally *apostles,* though they were surely not of the Twelve. (You may wish to look back at our discussion of what makes an apostle, in lesson 10.)

Chapter 9:1-5. Paul has bragged on the Corinthians to others, and he does not want them to embarrass him! So he urges them to get on with it. Paul's habit of using one congregation to inspire another is in the best tradition of fund-raisers, and a healthy form of competition. ("Outdo one another!" Rom. 12:10.)

Verses 6-15. Finally he comes to the basic principles of Christian charity:

1.) If you are a giving person, you will receive much. (See also Eccl. 11:1, Gal. 6:7, and Luke 9:24.)
2.) Giving should be joyful. The Greek word for cheerful is *hilaros,* so we could translate this, "God loves a hilarious giver!"
3.) Generosity is more than passing the hat. It is also (vv. 12-13) a form of worship.
4.) Ultimately, giving is *thanks*giving; our generosity is a way of expressing gratitude to God for the unbelievable generosity (v. 15) that God showed to us in giving, while we were yet sinners, Christ to die for us. At the heart of this whole concept is the word *grace.* That is the word translated "generous act" in 8:9, and describes the way God acts toward us, which ought to be the motive, the means, and the method of our own generosity. Paul uses the word ten times in these two chapters; it is the word translated "thanks" in the last sentence.

The Scripture and the Main Question

I have a young friend who wants, more than anything else, to be a successful musician. But doors keep getting closed (take my advice; do not try to make a living as a singer unless you are (a) a child prodigy, (b) incredibly lucky, or (c) have more determination than a bulldog). One day I reminded him about Jesus' saying, "If you want to find your life, you have to lose it." "Are you telling me that if I don't want it, I can have it?" he almost shouted. "That doesn't help me at all." (The fact that I am his father does not help much either.) He is right, of course; it is not logical. But the weird thing about it is that, logical or not, it is true. And it works.

In this lesson, we are going to look at how Paul tries to teach the Corinthians Jesus' upside-down way of looking at the world. This is not the first time he has done this. All the way back in the first chapter of 1 Corinthians Paul has been saying that what looks like foolishness to the world is wisdom and power to God. But, for some reason, this is easier to visualize in terms of money.

An Inspiration from Others

There is a kind of good infection (I think the phrase is from C. S. Lewis) that passes from one Christian to another, and from Christians to the rest of the world. We teach generosity by being generous ourselves. Paul does not hesitate to lift up the Macedonians by way of example. What is remarkable about them is that their outburst of generous giving came during a time of trouble, probably religious persecution. But there is evidence from history that the church is at its most vigorous when its critics are most vocal. We are beginning to discover that behind the iron curtain powerful things were at work in the underground church, and that the people actually grew in faith when times were the hardest.

Paul encouraged financial aid to Jerusalem throughout his ministry (see Acts 11:27-30, Gal. 2:10, and, possibly, Rom. 15:31). He knows that there is more there than simply raising money. If he can convince the mission churches to support the Jerusalem Christians, there will be a bond between them. "Where your treasure is, there your heart will be also" (Matt. 6:21).

Christ's Generosity and Ours

It is the nature of Jesus Christ to give; indeed, this is God's own nature. Think of the creation of the universe as a gift, God's self-outpouring. Of course, there was pleasure in it for God; the giver always gets as much or more pleasure than the giver (Acts 20:35). God kept looking at the creation as it unfolded step by step, and admiring the work, saying, "That's good!" (Gen. 1:4, 12, 18, 21, 25 and, especially, 31). But in such self-giving, as in a good marriage, good parenting, good pastoring, good teaching, and good stewardship, the rewards are greater than that which is given us.

I tell young couples whom I marry this impossible tale: Say you have $200.00. If you are into *need* love, you get into an argument over to whom it belongs (because you each want to buy something special), and it turns out that you each get nothing, because it has been spent on utilities, or getting the brakes fixed. If you practice *shared* love, you split it 50-50, which is better (though you still cannot afford that special something). But if you practice *gift* love, Christian charity, and each gives it to the other, you end up with $400.00. A joy shared is twice the joy. (A sorrow shared is half the sorrow.)

Affirmation of Titus

Titus, Paul's trusted companion, is not mentioned in the book of the Acts, but frequently in the epistles; he even has a letter of his own. He was a Gentile, possibly one of Paul's own converts. He had been to Corinth before, and you can read about it in chapter 7:2-15. Paul thinks of him as a brother (2:13), but he also feels the same way about the two unnamed persons (v. 18 and 22). His going to Corinth this second time is at Paul's request, but also due to enthusiasm of his own. These three make a distinguished team; Paul is setting up the machinery for taking a considerable offering to Jerusalem, so he cannot be too careful.

As I think of Titus and his two comrades, my mind drifts back over the congregations that I have served, and I remember with gratitude how many strong and capable people donated many hours of time, many units of energy, and many hard-earned dollars to the life of the church. Do you know, I do not believe there is a single one of them who would not say, "I have received a great deal more than I have given."

Hurry Up and Give!

There is a way in which we Christians infect one another for good, as we have said. But the infection can work the other way, too. Paul is anxious that the slow movement of the Corinthians might work to dilute the enthusiasm of the Macedonians. He is anxious that the Corinthians not be embarrassed if they do not do as well as predicted. So Paul flagellates them here with a little pep talk. He does not say, "Give till it hurts," rather he exhorts them to "Give till it feels good!"

God Loves a Cheerful Giver

Stewardship and money are a constant preoccupation of the church; we do not like it when the old every-member-canvass time rolls around. But it does not have to be a time for gloom and doom. If we remember that giving of ourselves is a high and holy calling, the request for pledges will be just as spiritual a moment as a call to profession of faith. Notice how in the transition between chapters 15 and 16 of 1 Corinthians Paul goes from his sublime hymn to the resurrection to talking about the offering, without a pause. (There is no space between the sentences in the original manuscript.) It does not insult Christians to talk to them about their pocketbooks. That simply proves that you care about them where it matters!

Every Lord's day, in churches all over the world, ushers lift money in golden plates, and put it on high altars. Not because we worship the money, but because the offering of our money to God is the committing of ourselves. In a small church I once fussed at the women for clicking open their purses during the silent dedication before the offering. I thought it disturbed the mood. One of the ladies advised me, "No, that is a sacramental sound, the sound of people dedicating themselves." So it is. Let there be the unzipping of wallets! There is no holier noise than the noise of Christians giving themselves away.

Helping Adults Become Involved

Preparing to Teach

As in most of these lessons, we will try to draw our teaching style from the text itself. Since our theme today is the giving of ourselves, let us practice teaching as a giving of gifts. I am not here to promote my own scholarship, my own reputation, my own ego, but to give of myself to others. If I do this well, they will call me a scholar, I will have a good reputation, and it will boost my ego, but, deep inside, I will know that I have only done my duty. That is as it should be (Luke 17:10).

What are the gifts you have to give in this week's lesson? Last week it was easy to say, "I have the gospel to share!" But there is gospel this week, too. The word *grace*, meaning "a gift," occurs ten times in these two chapters, translated in different ways. The root meaning is *charis*, from which we get the word *charity* and *charismatic*. If you can use this as a starter, here the verses are, with the key words underlined:

> 8:1   We want you to know . . . about the *grace* of God . . .
> 4   begging us for the *privileges* of sharing in this ministry . . .
> 6   so he should also complete this *generous undertaking* . . .
> 7   we want you to excel also in this *generous undertaking*.
> 9   You know the *generous act* of our Lord Jesus . . .

16   But *thanks* be to God . . .
19   while we are administering this *generous undertaking* . . .
9:8   God is able to provide you with every *blessing* . . .
14   the surpassing *grace* of God that he has given you.
15   *Thanks* be to God for his indescribable gift!

See how many gifts there are here, that we are privileged to share!

Introducing the Main Question

If you have the time, list the nine beatitudes (Matt. 5:4-11) on the board, and ask your class to list opposite them the beatitudes of the secular world. I would start them like this:

Happy are the poor in spirit.	Happy are the well-to-do.
Happy are those who mourn.	Happy are those in a good mood.

Let your class figure them out. The point is to get them all thinking upside down. The world thinks: It is great to get! We want them to come to know the secret: It is more blessed to give!

Developing the Lesson

Use the following outline and questions:

I. An inspiration from others, 8:1-6
Who taught you your giving habits? I know some parents who will not let their children put change in the church offering plate, but insist that they take part in their parents' decision to tithe. Each child takes turns putting in the family check. The children see that their parents give many dollars each week, so they do not grow up to be nickel-and-dime Christians. What do you think of this habit?

Have you ever been shamed into giving by a widow with two mites, or some other struggling generous soul? This may not be much motive, but if it works, is it not better than no motive at all?

Jesus said, "Sound no trumpet when you give alms." Should we publicize the Macedonians' stewardship so as to inspire the Corinthians?

II. Christ's generosity and ours, 8:7-15
Reread Isaiah 12:13–13:12 and Philippians 2:5-11. Do you see a pattern in them? (The same pattern is present in the Apostles' Creed; do you see it there?) What did Christ give up for us? What are we called to do in response?

What were Jesus' rewards in the above passages?

Is it really true that "if you empty your cup it will be filled and running over?" Have you ever tried a life of total giving?

Have you heard the phrase "living is giving"? Do you agree?

III. Affirmation of Titus, 8:16-24
Does it make a difference who the church treasurer is? I know of a church that lost its treasurer. They asked a certain man to serve, and he said he would, but first he confessed that he had once embezzled some money from

his employer. "I spent some time in prison," he said, "and I paid it all back. But I thought you should know that before you offer me the job." Would you have offered it? (They did and he served well.)

IV. *Hurry up and give! 9:1-5*

Do stewardship sermons irritate you? Could we do without them?

What motivates people to give? Duty? Self-satisfaction? Prestige? A sense of guilt? William Barclay says the highest motive is "to give because one can't help giving." Would you agree?

V. *God loves a cheerful giver, 9:6-15*

Can the time of the offering really be a time of worship? My college economics professor taught that money is the symbol of our goods and services. If he is right, then are we not giving ourselves when we put money in the plate? During the offering, should we be thinking of Romans 12:1? Of Isaiah 6:8?

What are the rewards of giving? It may help others; does it help us? Does God need our gifts (see Ps. 50:9-12, and Mic. 6:6-8)?

Jesus said to a certain young man: "Go, sell what you own, and give the money to the poor, and you will have treasure in heaven; then come, follow me" (Mark 10:21). Does this apply to us? Could you really give away everything?

What, actually, do you *own*? Do you not, in fact have only temporary custody of everything in your life? Could you stand to see it go down the drain? What would happen to you then? Would God take care of you? Isaiah 58:6-8 says that if you share with others, the glory of God will be your rear guard. Can you believe that?

Read the parable of the talents, Matthew 25:14-30. Will you bury your riches in the ground?

Helping Class Members Act

We are presently in the spring. Is it too early to ask your class to start thinking about this fall's stewardship campaign? Is there a class project you could start, something like getting up a collection for Jerusalem? Say a mother church in your community that needs your help? What could your class give away that would make you rich?

Planning for Next Sunday

Next week, at last, we get to the greatest chapter in Corinthians. It is so familiar that it might be best to read it in an unfamiliar translation, to shake us into listening.

Serving with Love

Background Scripture: 1 Corinthians 13

The Main Question

First Corinthians 13 is a hymn to love, a powerful poem. (If you have not already done so, you might consider memorizing it.) I have officiated at several hundred weddings, and at almost all of them I have read or sung these magnificent words. But I have always had an uneasy feeling about it, because I suspect that many of the married couples in the congregation are troubled by the utter perfection of unselfishness that is described here. When we speak of love that never gets upset, never tears its shirt, never loses its cool, continues to give and give and give without expecting anything in return, and puts up with everything, most of us must be thinking, "That's not *my* marriage Paul is talking about!" And of course it is not. Paul is not speaking here of marriage, nor indeed of any human institution. He is singing the praises of the unalterable, unutterable, unbelievable love of God.

It is the love of which the psalmist sings (100:1, 5):

> Make a joyful noise to the Lord, all the earth.
> For the Lord is good;
> his steadfast love endures forever,
> and his faithfulness to all generations.

But our human institutions must be modeled after that Divine Charity, and to our chagrin, they never seem to measure up. So our main question is really, "What must I do to be saved?" It is the deepest cry at the heart of everyone, "How can I be what I long to be?" In every one of us there runs a powerful conflict between our dreams and our realities. It is an insurmountable difficulty, and the only thing that can bridge the gap is the never-ending love and mercy of God.

Selected Scripture

King James Version

1 Corinthians 13

1 Though I speak with the tongues of men and of angels, and have not charity, I am become as sounding brass, or a tinkling cymbal.

2 And though I have the gift of prophecy, and understand all mysteries, and all knowledge; and though I have all faith, so that I could remove mountains, and have not charity, I am nothing.

3 And though I bestow all my

New Revised Standard Version

1 Corinthians 13

1 If I speak in the tongues of mortals and of angels, but do not have love, I am a noisy gong or a clanging cymbal. 2 And if I have prophetic powers, and understand all mysteries and all knowledge, and if I have all faith, so as to remove mountains, but do not have love, I am nothing. 3 If I give away all my possessions, and if I hand over my body so that I may boast, but do not have love, I gain nothing.

301

goods to feed the poor, and though I give my body to be burned, and have not charity, it profiteth me nothing.

4 Charity suffereth long, and is kind; charity envieth not; charity vaunteth not itself, is not puffed up,

5 Doth not behave itself unseemly, seeketh not her own, is not easily provoked, thinketh no evil;

6 Rejoiceth not in iniquity, but rejoiceth in the truth;

7 Beareth all things, believeth all things, hopeth all things, endureth all things.

8 Charity never faileth; but whether there be prophecies, they shall fail; whether there be tongues, they shall cease; whether there be knowledge, it shall vanish away.

9 For we know in part, and we prophesy in part.

10 But when that which is perfect is come, then that which is in part shall be done away.

11 When I was a child, I spake as a child, I understood as a child, I thought as a child; but when I became a man, I put away childish things.

12 For now we see through a glass, darkly; but then face to face: now I know in part; but then shall I know even as also I am known.

13 And now abideth faith, hope, charity, these three; but the greatest of these is charity.

Key Verse: **And now abideth faith, hope, charity, these three; but the greatest of these is charity.**

4 Love is patient; love is kind; love is not envious or boastful or arrogant 5 or rude. It does not insist on its own way; it is not irritable or resentful; 6 it does not rejoice in wrongdoing, but rejoices in the truth. 7 It bears all things, believes all things, hopes all things, endures all things.

8 Love never ends. But as for prophecies, they will come to an end; as for tongues, they will cease; as for knowledge, it will come to an end. 9 For we know only in part, and we prophesy only in part; 10 but when the complete comes, the partial will come to an end. 11 When I was a child, I spoke like a child, I thought like a child, I reasoned like a child; when I became an adult, I put an end to childish ways. 12 For now we see in a mirror, dimly, but then we will see face to face. Now I know only in part; then I will know fully, even as I have been fully known. 13 And now faith, hope, and love abide, these three; and the greatest of these is love.

Key Verse: **And now faith, hope, and love abide, these three; and the greatest of these is love.**

As You Read the Scripture

1 Corinthians 12:31–13:3. I have added the last verse of chapter 12 here to drive home the powerful connection between this grand hymn to love and the description of the Spirit and the Body that came before it. (And, indeed, it is also powerfully connected with the chapters that come after.) First Corinthians 13 is the climax of a letter that celebrates love from the very beginning. This love is not *storge,* affection, the natural love of parent for child, of puppies in a litter for each other. It is not *philia,* friendship, love between comrades, those who are like us, or whose differences make us complete. And it is not *eros*, passion, delight in the beloved (which can be the most fickle of all the loves). No, it is *agape*, charity, the Divine Love that is proven because "while we still were sinners Christ died for us" (Rom. 5:8). "In this is love, not that we loved God but that he loved us and sent his Son to be the atoning sacrifice for our sins" (1 John 4:10). (Even if we have the mightiest church organ in town, if we do not have love, it is but a tooting of whistles.)

Verses 4-8a. The love to which Paul sings in 1 Corinthians 13 is the model by which we ought to shape our marriages ("Husbands, love your wives, just as Christ loved the church and gave himself up for her" [Eph. 5:25]). It is the model by which all of our interpersonal relationships should be defined ("Be kind to one another, tenderhearted, forgiving one another, as God in Christ has forgiven you" [Eph. 4:32]). It is the high aim of the Christian ("Be perfect, therefore, as your heavenly Father is perfect" [Matt. 5:48]).

But our track record is not very good. We may give and give for a time, but we get burned out, and we give up. Do not be surprised if your marriage does not sound like 1 Corinthians 13, or your patience with your children does not sound like Ephesians 6:4. You and I are not God, and, though we long for perfection (Matt. 5:6), we are always a long way from it. Like the Sermon on the Mount, this lovely hymn raises such a high standard that we seem forever to be following it, like the donkey after the proverbial carrot, for such wondrous love as this recedes from us. It is "as high as the heavens" and "as far as the east is from the west."

Verses 8b-12. When we learn to be childlike (Mark 10:13-16), we may eventually cease to be childish. When that day comes, the other gifts of the Spirit will be no longer needed. Preaching will be pointless. ("No longer shall they teach one another, or say to each other, 'Know the Lord,' for they shall all know me" [Jer. 31:34], or "I saw no temple in the city, for its temple is the Lord" [Rev. 21:22].) But love will never cease to be needed, for "God is love" (1 John 4:16).

Verse 13. *Faith* will no longer be needed when the things that are hoped for have come to pass, and *hope* will no longer be needed when the things that are not seen have been made visible (Heb. 11:1). But the *love* that is the tie that binds together the church, and even the Trinity itself, will never cease to be needed. I know that scientists think the universe is held together by gravity, magnetism, and atomic force, but I predict that when their research takes them all the way back to the big bang (Gen. 1:3) they will discover that the ultimate glue is *agape*.

The Scripture and the Main Question

In the section called "As You Read the Scripture" I have given you the four Greek words for love. (If you are interested in pursuing them further, you might try C. S. Lewis' *The Four Loves*, Harcourt Brace Jovanovich, New York, 1960.) I love words so much that I have to be careful not to spend too much time writing *about* words rather than writing *with* them! But let me tell you about just one more. It is a Hebrew word and it is the great word of the Old Testament. The word is *chesed*. It rhymes with blessed and the "c" is silent. (Well, actually it is a little clearing of the throat, as in the German *ich*.) It is not easy to translate into English. The King James version usually renders it "mercy" and the Revised Standard Version says "steadfast love." I like to call it both: God's "never-ending mercy and love." It is a kind of combination of love and grace (see what we said about grace in the last session), and it runs like a theme throughout the Hebrew Scriptures. It is the reason we make that joyful noise (see the quote from Ps. 100 above). There is one of the psalms (136) that has the word twenty-six times, once for every verse.

Why introduce it here? Well, mainly to make the point that Paul's hymn is not something really new (see 1 John 2:7), but belongs to the whole of scripture, from Genesis to Revelation. The faithful, merciful, all-giving, never-ending love of God is what the gospel is all about. It was in love that God created the world and made us in the divine image. It was in love that God brought the children of Israel out of the land of Egypt, and gave them the Law. It was in love that God sent the prophets. It was in love that God sent Jesus Christ to die for us (Rom. 5:8), to be the atoning sacrifice for our sins (1 John 4:10). God is love (1 John 4:16), and love never ends (1 Cor. 13:8). In that light, let us look at Paul's hymn.

The More Excellent Way

In chapter 12, Paul has been extolling the gifts of the Spirit, pointing out that they are found in different manifestations in each of us, and that, when they are all working together properly (Eph. 4:16), they build up the body in love. But we must not fall into the trap of claiming that one gift is better than another. Instead, whatever our gifts, we must all strive for the one great gift, which is available to all Christians, and that is love. The King James version translates *agape* as "charity," which in some ways is to be preferred (note that charity has the same root as *charismatic*, meaning "gifted.") The problem with *charity* is that it is loaded with some negative freight in our day. I sometimes hear people say, "Don't give me charity," meaning, I think, "I don't want to live on the church, or on a welfare state. I want to stand on my own feet." But, when you think about it, is not that exactly what we have to do: Accept God's charity? Is not the basic act of the Christian, repentance, a matter of overcoming our pride and accepting the free gift of God's charity? It is a rather biggish step, but one that we must all take. The sin that keeps us from God is always, at bottom, our pride. We might paraphrase verses 1-3 like this:

> If I have the most moving, ecstatic, emotional religious experience, but don't have love, I am just so much noise. If I can preach like Peter on the day of Pentecost, and can understand all the great theologians, and have enough faith to leap tall buildings at a single bound, but don't have love, I'm a nobody. If I do all manner of wonderful works, and even kill myself with good deeds, I am still left sitting at square one.

Without the great gift, all the other gifts are nothing but junk (see Phil. 3:8).

The Nature of Love

This love (*agape*, charity, *chesed*, mercy) is impossible without the grace of God (Mark 10:27). It is perfection (Matt. 5:48). Let me try another paraphrase. (By the way, you might prefer to write your own paraphrase of this chapter; it would be an excellent preparation for teaching.)

A Christian puts up with people's faults. A Christian is gentle and forgiving. A Christian never worries about who gets the credit, or brags about personal accomplishments. A Christian is never pushy, and doesn't lord it over others, or have inflated ideas of self-worth. A Christian stays cool, and is happy when others succeed. A Christian puts up with frustrations, holds on to the faith, looks forward to the future, and quietly maintains an equilibrium when everybody else is running in circles. A Christian never gives up.

Notice that I have substituted "A Christian" for the word *love,* to make the point that love is a way of life. Try rewriting the paragraph using the pronoun *I* in each case. Makes you a little uneasy, doesn't it. Well, remember that Paul is not talking about what a Christian is like, or what you and I do, but about what God is like and does. It is the model toward which we strive, but that, left to our own resources, is an impossible dream.

Our Incompleteness

As long as we live, we will have to be thinking of ourselves, in one sense, as adolescents, trying to become grownups. What a horrible thought! I would not go through adolescence again for anything. Have you noticed how teenagers sometimes have blank expressions on their faces, as though they were fearful of being thought childish? Isaac Newton, the scientific genius, described himself as a child playing on the seashore, unaware of the vast ocean of truth around him. So are we, in comparison with the great mind and heart of God. But God knows us, even though we hardly know God at all. Prophecy, tongues, and knowledge are forever partial; God alone is complete.

These Three

There is nothing wrong with faith; it is the doorway to salvation. But without love it is dead (Jam. 2:26). There is nothing wrong with hope; where there is hope there is life. But without love, hope is cold and grim, and we are its prisoners (Zech. 9:12). When prophecy, tongues, and knowledge have all fallen silent, faith, hope, and love will remain, but the first two do not really matter. When we get to heaven, what will we need faith and hope for? But love is the story that goes on and on, each adventure greater than the last.

Helping Adults Become Involved

Preparing to Teach

We need to take off our shoes this week, for we are standing on holy ground. I am shy about teaching the great passages. Psalm 23, or Isaiah 40, or John 14, or Romans 8 all shine with such brightness that I feel that adding my words is an insult or an intrusion. Surely that goes for 1 Corinthians 13. About all I can suggest is that you immerse yourself in it, as one might soak in a hot tub. Let its powerful themes flow over you, and absorb them as best you can, by osmosis. But that will not help much when you try to share it with others. What you pick up or absorb from a great scripture like this is difficult to pass on. You are like those wise virgins in Jesus' story

THIRD QUARTER

(Matt. 25:1-13). It seems selfish of them not to be willing to share their lamp oil with their foolish sisters, but they could not. How can you share the preparation of a lifetime with another? It would take a lifetime. So how can you share what you have soaked up from 1 Corinthians 13 with your class? I can only suggest you let them soak in it with you, for however long your class time is, and see what seeps through.

Introducing the Main Question

I have said that 1 Corinthians 13 is a hymn, and sometimes when I teach it, I sing it. For a long time I searched for an easy familiar tune for Paul's song, but without success. Every love song (like "Tell Me Why the Stars Do Shine") always seemed cloying and sweet, and would not carry the freight of Divine Charity. But then I heard Patrice Munsel sing "Go 'Way from My Window," an old Appalachian blues song, and I saw that it would do. The blues are about unrequited love, and that is something like *agape*. I do not know where to tell you how to find the tune, but it was discovered by John Jacob Niles, and if you are interested in learning it, you might be able to run it down.

> If I could speak like angels, in every mortal tongue,
> But have no love within my heart, I am a noisy gong,
>   A hollow cymbal's song.
> And if I am a prophet, and understand it all,
> And with my faith make mountains move, and have no love, I fall.
>   I'm nothing then at all.
> Even if I give away everything I own,
> And leave my body to be burned, what profit have I shown?
>   No profit have I known.
> Love is kind and patient, not envious or proud,
> It is not arrogant, or rude, contemptuous of the crowed,
>   Not boastful, not loud.
> Love will stand beside you, when everything goes wrong,
> But when the world goes right for you, then love will sing along.
>   Love is a joyful song.
> Love keeps on believing, whatever life may send.
> Love bears all things, and hopes all things, and love will never
>   end. No, love will never end.
> Three things that last forever, were sent from heaven above:
> Praise God for faith; praise God for hope. But the best of all is
>   love; the best of these is love.

If singing it is not your cup of tea, try reading it as a dramatic reading, or asking the best reader in your class to do it. Or maybe have them spend the whole period trying to write a paraphrase in their own language. I do not know; we are in the presence of mystery here.

Developing the Lesson

Use the following outline and questions.

I. The More Excellent Way, 12:31–13:3

Can one Christian be superior to another? The upside-down logic of 1 Corinthians here comes to its fulfillment: The better lover you become,

306

the less your own superiority matters to you. To use the biblical language: Are you more excellent when you do not try to excel?

Is it really possible to speak in tongues without love, or be a prophet without love, or a theologian who does not love? What about the leaders of the Spanish Inquisition? Have you ever known a person who was good but not kind?

II. The nature of love, 13:4-8a

In human terms, say in a marriage, if one person practices *agape* love, and keeps on giving, while their partner keeps on taking, the giver is bound to burn out. Does God ever burn out?

How long can you keep on being charitable? (See Matt. 18:22.)

This passage has been called the Christian equilibrium. But that makes me think of a sort of steady, middle-of-the-road, not too interesting, blah kind of Christian. Where is the place of verve, enthusiasm, and joyful self-expression in all this humility?

III. Our incompleteness, 13:8a-12

What is the difference between childish and childlike? (See Ps. 8, Mark 10:13-16, Luke 9:48, Isa. 11:6, etc.)

Do you think we ever will really know it all?

Will sermons ever end? (See Jer. 31:34.)

IV. These three, 13:13

I have said that love is the glue that holds the universe together. Let me try one more metaphor, knowing that none can really do the job. How about, love is the rubric of life. In the earliest printed prayer books, the instructions to people and priest, things like, "Then shall a hymn be sung," etc., were printed in red, hence (from *ruby*) they are called rubrics. Faith and hope may be the hymns we sing, and the prayers we pray, but love is what we do and are, and what holds us together as a community. We can have the finest prayers and songs in Christendom, but without love, our worship is empty. On the other hand, *with* love, we can worship around a pot-bellied stove with a musical saw and our prayers will reach heaven itself.

Helping Class Members Act

I am going to leave you now. If your class members have not caught on by now that these lessons were meant to be translated into life beyond the classroom, I do not know what else we can do. It has been good to be visiting with you, on the back pew of the First Corinthian Church. What a time those folks had! And what a time is in store for us, if we can take with us only a small part of the faith, hope, and love that Paul and his friends have shared with us.

Planning for Next Sunday

Next Sunday begins a new unit. Ask your class to read 1 Kings 11 and think about "the price of power."

Spiritual Enrichment Article:
Why the Old Testament Is Necessary for the Church

A Lost Resource

It is fair to say that the Old Testament is largely a lost book in many parts of the U.S. church. The people in our congregations have only the most limited knowledge of its contents. Many preachers rarely, if ever, preach from the Old Testament. Even the Psalter, which has been the treasury of devotion for the people of God for three thousand years, is, in nonliturgical denominations, fading into disuse and unfamiliarity. Our people may know or recognize a few lines from some psalms; they hear a number of prophetic promises at Christmastime; they can recognize the creation story when someone reads it to them. But beyond that, the Old Testament is unknown and unimportant to them, an unopened antique book from the distant past that can safely be left with the other antiques on the curio shelf.

Such an ignorance of the Old Testament has serious consequences. If we in the church do not know the Old Testament and do not teach and preach from it to our people, we leave them with no means for properly understanding and appropriating the Christian faith. When our forebears in the faith finally decided on at least the basic shape of the canon, they prefaced New Testament with Old as an essential part of the gospel. The last third of the Bible cannot be understood, they implied, without those first two-thirds in the Old Testament. We and our people, for all practical purposes, fall into the heresy of Marcionism, and that has the most serious consequences for the church and for everyday Christian living.

The Necessity of the Old Testament

In the first place, apart from the Old Testament, it is almost impossible properly to understand the nature of the world. We twentieth-century moderns see the universe as a closed system of cause and effect, in which everything operates automatically according to natural law, and we are now bending our efforts to harmonize with nature and not to upset its delicate ecological balances. We are spaceship earth, we say, with limited resources and powers, called on to guard what we have in order to preserve life in our float through the galaxies. But sometimes that is a terrifying prospect because we do not know if we have the wisdom to harmonize and guard and thus keep ourselves alive.

It is in the Old Testament traditions of creation, however, that we learn that the earth in its universe is not a closed system, but subject to a God who stands over and above it as its sovereign Lord. He sustains the world's processes of life and guards its order against the forces of chaos, and indeed he remains and takes us into an eternal fellowship with himself, though heaven and earth should pass away. It is that God, that Creator and Sustainer of the universe, whom the New Testament presupposes.

Second, apart from the Old Testament, it is almost impossible properly to understand ourselves as human beings. Many in our culture would like to classify us as nothing more than animals, with instincts and drives that must be met, no matter what the human cost. Others try to dissolve our individual unique personalities into a oneness with some mystical soul or primal matrix or great being of life and nature. Marxists understand us totally in terms of economic forces. Sociologists classify us according to groups and cultures. The government has glibly made us statistics; the military talks about body counts and coolly reckons how many of us are expendable in a nuclear attack. For medicine, we may become nothing more than a liver, a kidney, a collection of cells to be fed from tubes. To advertisers, we are consumers to be manipulated with appeals to our pride or fear or greed. But it is in the Old Testament that we learn that we are fearfully and wonderfully made, like no other creatures in all God's good creation, made uniquely in his image, given dominion over the earth, and told that we were created for fellowship with one another and that it is not good that we be alone. Above all, it is in the Old Testament that we learn that we were created for relationship with God and that we cannot properly be understood apart from that relationship. That view of human nature is presupposed by the New Testament.

Third, apart from the Old Testament, we also cannot properly understand who God is—that he is not identifiable with or found in anything in all creation, but that he is *holy* God, uniquely other than everything he has made. It is in the Old Testament that we learn that God is always personal, that he cannot be identified with an idea or process or emotional experience, and that he must be pictured, to be pictured rightly, in the metaphors of person, as Husband, Father, Savior, King, who loves and weeps and speaks and sends, and whistles and calls and takes. The Judge who grieves, the Warrior who fights, the Redeemer who buys back his family member—such is the God whom we meet through the Old Testament's figures of speech. It is in the Old Testament that we learn we cannot know such a God except as he himself breaks into time and reveals his own person and nature, through the words he speaks and the deeds he does in particular places.

Indeed, it is in the Old Testament that we first learn such a God is working out a purpose in human history, which has a definite beginning in time and which will be brought to a fulfilled end. The New Testament presupposes that kind of God and that historical purpose.

We cannot appropriate the New Testament view of the world and of human beings and of God unless we absorb those views first of all from the Old Testament. In many respects that last third of our canon in the New Testament is simply a final reinterpretation and summing up of the two-thirds that have gone before in the Old Testament.

This is not to say that there is nothing new in the New Testament. There is much that is new. There is something greater than Solomon there, something greater than Jonah and Abraham. The prophets, kings, sages, and psalmists desired to see what the New Testament sees, and did not see it. They desired to hear what the New Testament hears, and did not hear it. But who is this new figure who walks the roads of the New Testament story? Who is Jesus Christ?

The New Testament writers themselves were convinced we could not know him apart from the Old Testament. The first thing that Matthew can think to tell us about Jesus Christ, the first sentence in his Gospel, reads, "The book of the genealogy of Jesus Christ, the son of David, the son of Abraham"—Christ can be understood only in terms of Abraham and David. For Luke, it was the Old Testament scriptures that illumined everything that

Jesus did. After the meeting on the Emmaus road, the risen Christ appears to his disciples in the upper room and says to them: " 'These are my words that I spoke to you while I was still with you—that everything written about me in the law of Moses, the prophets, and the psalms must be fulfilled.' " Then he opened their minds to understand the scriptures (Luke 24:44-45). Christ was understood by the New Testament writers as the fulfillment of the Old.

The Old Testament and Jesus

In fact, as the New Testament writers set forth their testimony to the nature of Jesus Christ, they framed that testimony in terms of the traditions and theologies of the Old Testament. I fully set forth that framing in an earlier book, *The Old Testament and the Proclamation of the Gospel*. Let me give a summary statement of it.

There is a great variety in the witness to Jesus in the New Testament. Some writers emphasize one thing, some emphasize another, but their total testimony gives us the definitive picture of our Lord, and every New Testament writer drew on Old Testament traditions and theology.

Some New Testament writers described Jesus Christ in terms of the royal traditions of the Old Testament. In that description, Jesus was variously the messiah, the long-awaited son of David, the shepherd prince promised by Ezekiel, the high Priest after the order of Melchizedek, who had been designated Son of God and exalted to the right hand of the Father as the Lord over all enemies and powers. Jesus was the one to whom the Old Testament traditions of David and of the royal psalms pointed, the Ruler whose coming inaugurated the beginning of the kingdom of God.

For those New Testament writers who told the story of Jesus' earthly life and death, Jesus was described as a new Moses (Matt.); or as the prophet like Moses, who was to come (John, Acts); or as the Suffering Servant who gave his life as a ransom for many (Mark). He was the one who freed Israel from her final slavery (Gal.); the one who instituted the new Sinai covenant of the prophets in his blood (1 Cor., Heb.); who made the perfect sacrifice for sin once for all (Heb.). He was Psalm 118's stone that the builders rejected, which had become the head of the corner (1 Pet.). He was Isaiah 8's rock of stumbling for the Jews and foolishness for the Gentiles (1 Cor.). He was the ideal righteous man of the Psalms, suffering and praising his Father from the cross (Passion stories). In short, the traditions of the Exodus, Passover, and Sinai, the Hexateuchal and prophetic traditions and the Psalter, and, as we shall see, the Wisdom writings, all found their goal in Jesus Christ. The plan that God began with his first release of his people from Egypt was, according to the New Testament writers, brought to completion in the story of the Crucifixion and Resurrection.

For those New Testament writers who concentrated on the fullness of the Incarnation, Jesus was—in various traditions—the new obedient son of Israel (Matt.), the incarnate temple (John), Isaiah's cornerstone of the new congregation of faith on Zion (I Pet.). He was the incarnate covenant and light and lamb in his role as servant. He was the true vine (cf. Ps. 80; Isa. 5), the true manna, the bread, and drink of life. Jesus was the word of the Old Testament made flesh who gave the light that shone in the darkness (John). In Hebrews, he was even described as the incarnate promised land, that place of rest offered to all who faithfully held fast to him.

In other words, the New Testament writers were convinced that Jesus Christ was not some mysterious figure suddenly dropped from the blue, with no connection to the almost two thousand years of God's activity in history that had preceded him. Rather, Jesus Christ was the completion and fulfillment and final reinterpretation of that lively history, and so he can only be fully understood in terms of it. Unless we preach from the Old Testament, our people really cannot know who their Lord is.

The Old Testament and the Church

In the same manner, unless our people are allowed to appropriate the Old Testament witness, they also cannot know who they are as the church of Jesus Christ. What is the church, according to the New Testament? It is the body of Christ, to be sure. It is the dwelling place of God in the Spirit, the "household of God" (Eph. 2:19). But it is "build upon the foundation of the apostles and prophets," with Christ as Isaiah's foretold cornerstone (Eph. 2:20). In Galatians, Paul calls the followers of Christ "The Israel of God" (6:16), the true children of Abraham (3:7), who have become the inheritors of the promise to the patriarchs (3:8, 29). It is the church now that is "the true circumcision" (Phil. 3:3), the new people of Yahweh envisioned by Hosea, the saved remnant foreseen by Isaiah (Rom. 9:25-27). We wild branches have now been grafted into the root of Israel (Rom. 11:17-20). We have become members of the commonwealth of Israel (Eph. 2:12).

The church is now the new Israel in Christ, according to the New Testament, but we cannot possibly understand what that means unless we know who the old Israel was. What does it mean to be Israel? Who was she? How was she created and ordered? What was she supposed to do? Our people can answer those questions only if we use the Old Testament in our preaching along with the New.

Most of the time we avoid preaching about the church in terms of Israel, because we rightly think that our people do not know anything about Israel and that therefore the use of such terminology would just confuse them. We employ every other metaphor of the church but that of the new Israel in Christ, and thus we foster our people's ignorance of the Old Testament and their feeling that the Old Testament is irrelevant for their Christian lives. We never fully, biblically proclaim to them who they actually are.

The story of Israel, in its long pilgrimage with God, can powerfully set forth the nature of our pilgrimage with him also. Look at the analogies between our life as the church and the life of Israel. Both of us are redeemed out of slavery, apart from any deserving on our part. Both of us have that deliverance as the sole basis of our peoplehood. Both Israel and the church are brought to the table of covenant and enter into an exclusive relationship with God in which we agree to serve him alone as his elected people. Both of us are given a new beginning and a new life as a foretaste of the glorious liberty of the children of God. Both are set under commandments from God that are to be the sole basis of the guiding and ordering of our lives. Both of us are set on a pilgrimage toward a promised place of rest and fulfillment. Both are accompanied on our journey by the presence of God himself. Both are loved as the sons or children of God or as the bride of God. Both are to be a holy nation, set apart for God's special purpose and use. Both are to be a kingdom of priests, mediating the knowledge of God to the world. The history of the church, of the new Israel in Christ, recapitulates the history of the old Israel, as the prophets had promised it would. And how we impoverish our people, and their understanding of themselves as the church, if we do not let them enter into the full story of who they are—that story told over the two thousand years of struggle, temptation, defeat, and redemption given us in the Old Testament! It is no wonder that our forebears included the Old Testament in our canon of scriptures, for the Old Testament is indispensable for understanding the nature of the world and of human beings and of God; and it is indispensable for knowing who Jesus Christ is and who we are as his new covenant people, the church.

Elizabeth Achtemeier

FOURTH QUARTER

A NATION TURNS TO GOD

David Neil Mosser

UNIT I: THE PRICE OF POWER

FOUR LESSONS   JUNE 4–25

In my church there are many baby-boomers. Sometimes they are called yuppies, meaning that they are young, upwardly-mobile professional people. Among this group are lawyers, doctors, and upper-level managers in large corporations. Many of these folk poke fun and tease one another by talking about power lunches and power ties. Most understand they have been given power by virtue of their birth, education, and position in society. The truth is that all people deal in and with power one way or another.

In politics, we often hear about politicians' power plays and power bases. Politics itself mobilizes power and uses influence. In a recent survey on limiting congressional terms in office to no more than twelve years, 63 percent of Americans agreed that this idea was a good one. Limiting politicians' power seems to be a popular idea these days. In fact, one might say power limitation was a guiding rationale behind the checks and balances in our own United States Constitution.

The Bible also has much to say about power. In the Christian scripture, the gift of the Spirit is often linked to power. Luke tells us, "But you will receive power when the Holy Spirit has come upon you" (Acts 1:8). And of Stephen it is said that he was "full of grace and power, did great wonders and signs among the people" (Acts 6:8).

Our lessons from Hebrew scripture in this unit are about power: the power of people and the power of God or Yahweh. The spokespersons for God are prophets and they play a major role by reminding those who misuse power that they are betraying their stewardship of authority that is given them by none other than God Almighty. These lessons are about being faithful as leaders in the Realm of God.

When Power Is Misused

Background Scripture: 1 Kings 11:26–12:24

The Main Question

There is an old familiar adage: "Power corrupts and absolute power corrupts absolutely." "Power comes in strange packages, too. For instance, our two-year-old is fully capable of shutting down restaurants and grocery stores with his blood-curdling screams. That is real power, as any parent will quickly attest.

Also, though people often think of power in negative terms, the truth is, power invariably exists in nature and in human relationships. Power, then, is essentially neutral and can be used for good or ill. Power is much like water. It can be used in the sacrament of baptism, as well as the source of destructive floods. This same phenomenon of power is also true whether it is used in the service of government or used in the decision of a married couple selecting a place to go to eat. The important thing about power, is not whether it exists, but how it is used. As I am typing these words now, lightning struck a transformer near our house. We have no power at all. So the absence of electrical power, in this case, is very disconcerting. But, there is the power of batteries.

The Bible is a realistic testimony to human life and God's search for God's people. There is no topic the Bible is shy about confronting or addressing. The Bible speaks of power in both the divine and human realms and does so without embarrassment. Perhaps there are few places we moderns can look for more graphic examples of power's use than in the stories of the kings of Israel and Judah. Why does this phenomenon of power—its use and misuse—seem to be so universal? Could one say that the essence of faith has to do with whether one subscribes to human or divine power? I think it is safe to say that the answer to this power question holds the key to our faith. To what power do the kings—and we—give ultimate allegiance?

Selected Scripture

King James Version

1 Kings 12:6-11, 16-17

6 And king Rehoboam consulted with the old men, that stood before Solomon his father while he yet lived, and said, How do ye advise that I may answer this people?

7 And they spake unto him, saying, If thou wilt be a servant unto this people this day, and wilt serve them, and answer them, and speak good words to them, then they will be thy servants for ever.

New Revised Standard Version

1 Kings 12:6-11, 16-17

6 Then King Rehoboam took counsel with the older men who had attended his father Solomon while he was still alive, saying, "How do you advise me to answer this people?" 7 They answered him, "If you will be a servant to this people today and serve them, and speak good words to them when you answer them, then they will be your servants forever." 8 But he disregarded the

8 But he forsook the counsel of the old men, which they had given him, and consulted with the young men that were grown up with him, *and* which stood before him:

9 And he said unto them, What counsel give ye that we may answer this people, who have spoken to me, saying, Make the yoke which thy father did put upon us lighter?

10 And the young men that were grown up with him spake unto him, saying, Thus shalt thou speak unto this people that spake unto thee, saying. Thy father made our yoke heavy, but make thou *it* lighter unto us: thus shalt thou say unto them, My little *finger* shall be thicker than my father's loins.

11 And now whereas my father did lade you with a heavy yoke, I will add to your yoke; my father hath chastised you with whips, but I will chastise you with scorpions.

....

16 So when all Israel saw that the king hearkened not unto them, the people answered the king, saying, What portion have we in David? neither *have we* inheritance in the son of Jesse: to your tents, O Israel: now see to thine own house, David. So Israel departed unto their tents.

17 But *as for* the children of Israel which dwelt in the cities of Judah, Rehoboam reigned over them.

Key Verse: **And they spake unto him, saying, If thou wilt be a servant unto this people this day, and wilt serve them, and answer them, and speak good words to them, then they will be thy servants for ever.**

advice that the older men gave him, and consulted with the young men who had grown up with him and now attended him. 9 He said to them, "What do you advise that we answer this people who have said to me, 'Lighten the yoke that your father put on us'?" 10 The young men who had grown up with him said to him, "Thus you should say to this people who spoke to you, 'Your father made our yoke heavy, but you must lighten it for us'; thus you should say to them, 'My little finger is thicker than my father's loins. 11 Now, whereas my father laid on you a heavy yoke, I will add to your yoke. My father disciplined you with whips, but I will discipline you with scorpions.' "

....

16 When all Israel saw that the king would not listen to them, the people answered the king,

"What share do we have in David?

　We have no inheritance in the son
　　of Jesse.

To your tents, O Israel!

　Look now to your own house, O
　　David."

So Israel went away to their tents. 17 But Rehoboam reigned over the Israelites who were living in the towns of Judah.

Key Verse: **They answered him, "If you will be a servant to this people today and serve them, and speak good words to them when you answer them, then they will be your servants forever."**

As You Read the Scripture

1 Kings 12:6-11, 16-17. This opening section of our unit tells the story of the beginning of the unraveling of the united monarchy of Israel previously ruled by David and Solomon. The background scripture tells us about Jeroboam and the death of Solomon (see 1 Kings 11:26–12:24).

Verse 6. Israel had made Rehoboam king at Shechem, a place of national assembly in the northern territory of Israel. During this assembly, Jeroboam on behalf of the people asks Rehoboam to "lighten the hard service of your father and his heavy yoke that he placed on us, and we will serve you" (v. 4). Verse 6 tells us that in response to this request, Rehoboam confers with the elders for part of three days.

Verse 7. This is the key verse, for it reflects the wisdom of the elders. The wise ones suggest that if Rehoboam becomes a servant to the people then they in turn will be his servants and be so forever. This exaggeration suggests that for a leader to survive for any length of time, then the leader would do well to put the needs of the people before the leader's own needs. At any rate, the leader's needs and the people's needs are not mutually exclusive.

Verses 8-9. The critical mistake is made now by Rehoboam. Rather than taking the wise advice of those who had counselled Solomon before him, the new king gathers his younger contemporaries together. Rehoboam asks the young men attending him the question put to him by the national assembly: Should he "lighten the yoke that your father put on us"?

Verses 10-11. The advice given the king by the young men is impetuous and foolish. They suggest a course of intimidation to the king, in essence, to frighten the people into submission. In giving this advice they also suggest to Rehoboam that he emphasize how much stronger he is than his father, Solomon, using whips. The son is willing to use scorpions for disciplining the people. A fearsome image indeed!

Verses 16-17. Our scripture passage today ends with Rehoboam's ill-fated decision to follow the advice of the young men rather than the older. The people of the northern tribes seem to be saying that they now have no share in the nation as presently ruled. "To your tents" indicates a military slogan or rallying cry. The last verse intimates the consolidated kingdom is beginning the process of division with some Israelites left in Judah to be dominated by the policies the new king has unfortunately charted for them.

The Scripture and the Main Question

Understanding Power

Power is the stuff of everyday life. Each time there is a difference of opinion or a decision to be made, power plays a part. A wise political philosopher has said, "Politics is the art of influence." In this case, influence is simply a sophisticated way to speak about power. So, whether your family is trying to decide to watch the evening news, a rerun of "Gone with the Wind," or a baseball game on TBS, some form of power—perhaps subtle influence, perhaps brute strength—will be used to make the decision. Again, it is important to remember in human transactions, power is neither good nor bad in and of itself. It is how that power is exerted that determines whether it is good or bad.

Our biblical text for today focuses on how Rehoboam used the power that was at his disposal as the new king of the unified nation Israel. We learn he had choices about how he ruled the people. The elders, who had been his father Solomon's advisors, told him the people desired to be led by a kinder and gentler ruler. The beginning half of 1 Kings told us Solomon, in his drive to build the temple and increase his stature among other rulers of the day, laid a heavy yoke of labor on the people.

At Solomon's death, the people were given a new hope in a new ruler who might make life better for them. This issue of hard labor is ironically part of the story of the Israelites exodus from Egypt—a story that defined them as a special and unique chosen people. The irony is, of course, now it is one of their own rulers laying this heavy burden on them.

Power Is Yahweh's

One of the basic articles of Hebrew faith was the truth that Yahweh was the ultimate source of power for Israel. The beginning of the Hebrew scriptures makes this unequivocally clear. In the beginning . . . "God said, 'Let there be light'; and there was light. And God saw that the light was good; and God separated the light from the darkness" (Gen. 1:3-4). Thus, from the outset, as Israel told the story about its ongoing relationship with God, God had the power to create by simply saying a word. In fact, the Word.

Later, in this same book of beginnings, Yahweh was powerful enough to make promises to Abraham and Sarah, concerning not only a child and descendants, but also a relationship with this powerful God. This powerful God continues to abide with the people throughout their history. When Yahweh is introduced to Moses on Mount Horeb, the power of the relationship is emphasized. Yahweh, responding to Moses' question about who this God is, simply says: "I AM WHO I AM." Yahweh continues, "Thus you shall say to the Israelites, 'I AM has sent me to you.' " God also said to Moses, "Thus you shall say to the Israelites, 'The LORD, the God of your ancestors, the God of Abraham, the God of Isaac, and the God of Jacob, has sent me to you': This is my name forever, and this my title for all generations."

If we were to carefully examine the theology of the Hebrew scriptures, this theme of God's power used on behalf of the children of Israel would be prominent.

The People Want Power

There came a time in Israel's history, however, when the nation wanted to be like other nations. The surrounding countries all had kings, and because they seemed to prosper, Israel began to clamor for a king. The other day I bought a new car and as I was walking out of the dealership the owner, sensing my anxiety about such a large purchase, said a curious thing, "Don't worry about it, son, this is what you have worked for."

I hate to admit this, but his phrase of reassurance almost made me nix the deal. A new car, or big house, or any other material object is not what we work for. These are not the things of which meaningful lives are constructed. The problem for us humans is we, like teenagers, are driven by peer pressure and a herd mentality. Perhaps we are not precisely like the lemmings who periodically march to the sea, but most of us follow the crowd and value the possessions our friends and neighbors have.

It was into this trap that the people of Israel fell during the time of Samuel, the Judge. They wanted to be like other nations. Yahweh relents and gives the people a king, which proved to be Israel's undoing. The story about Rehoboam's decision is one that goes far beyond one short-sighted despot in 922 B.C.E. It is a lesson that says, left to our own devices, human creatures will invariably make the wrong decisions. The elders of Israel wanted Rehoboam to rule with a gentle hand, but the younger advisors said only naked displays of raw power were in the king's best interest—and the younger advisors, too, no doubt. Rehoboam's folly catches up with him just beyond the scope of our text, but it is worth noting. At 1 Kings 12:18 is this telling statement: "King Rehoboam then hurriedly mounted his chariot to flee to Jerusalem." His strategy of intimidation did not work and even his best interest was not served. There is a lesson on power here for all who lead, especially in God's realm.

Biblical Understandings of Power

Since Rehoboam made the wrong choice in his leadership style, it would be good to look at the other, and missed, alternative posed by our text. The people were tired of the old style of leadership that imposed on them a heavy yoke of servitude. The text also makes clear from the elders' point of view, a leadership style of being a servant is the preferable choice. From what subsequently happens to the nation, this does seem to be the better choice. The elders said, "If you will be a servant to this people today and serve them, and speak good words to them when you answer them, then they will be your servants forever." In other words, if the leader is willing to serve the subjects, then the leader will also be served.

This sounds strangely like the Golden Rule, "do unto others as you would have them do unto you." To be a real leader in God's realm is to be willing to put oneself in the position of servant. In this philosophy of life, conventional wisdom is put on its head. Christ, as the true king, was the epitome of this understanding of life. Christ laid down his life for the sheep and taught that the first will be last and the last shall be first. But if this arrangement is strictly true, it is only because Jesus recognized God as the ultimate power.

To be able to put our egos and insecurities aside as human beings is to acknowledge a greater power than we can ever muster in and of ourselves. It is trust that God alone rules and overrules God's creation. This is why Paul could talk about the wisdom and power of the cross of Christ being a folly and stumbling block to those who did not believe. Paul says it well in 1 Corinthians 1:24, "But to those who are the called, both Jews and Greeks, Christ the power of God and the wisdom of God."

Helping Adults Become Involved

Preparing to Teach

Because people in your class are always in situations of power, because power is one of the basics of human life together, this lesson will be easy to grasp. They may not be familiar with the historic background, but they will understand about ruling heavily or lightly. They do it, or have it done to them, every day. Do not be surprised if Rehoboam's situation and decision elicit a vibrant response from your class members.

This outline will not exhaust your possibilities as a teacher, but will help you get started:

    I. Leaders have a choice about how they use power.
    II. Rehoboam's choices affected many people's lives.
    III. Good leaders put the interests of the group first.
    IV. The strongest leaders are often those who do not appear to be strong.

As you prepare, you will want to consult a study Bible to get a sense of the historic setting of today's lesson. This can be found in a chronological table of rulers. You will also want to review the first part of Kings to understand the death of David and the reign of Solomon, which give us the backdrop for the story of Rehoboam's folly.

As you read and think about the lesson you may want to draw on your own experiences of effective leaders in your life. It could be a parent, scout leader, politician, or a teacher who exemplified the ideals of good leadership. What did they do that made people want to follow them? Conversely, how do people in positions of leadership forfeit their trust of those being led?

Introducing the Main Question

Have a class member read the story of Rehoboam found in 1 Kings. It would probably be helpful to the class to begin at verse 1 and read through verse 17. You might choose to break it up, inserting material from the "As You Read the Scripture" section for clarification. Help the class see the basic decision Rehoboam has before him: following the advice of the elders or the younger advisors.

Developing the Lesson

I. Leaders have a choice about how they use power.

Once you have shared with the class what choices of leadership were available to Rehoboam, discuss how these same kinds of options are available to us in our own lives. Parents and grandparents can usually relate to the leading or influencing of children. What are effective ways of working with children in situations that often become battlegrounds: bedtime, eating their vegetables, doing homework, and cleaning up their messes? These problem areas represent challenges of authority. Do parents command respect because of their power over children? Or do they earn respect because the children sense a deep commitment to them in love? How do these parenting techniques apply to leading adults in the church and community?

II. Rehoboam's choices affected many people's lives.

One of the truisms of leadership is that leadership builds on itself. If one has several small successes in leading people, a trusting relationship is fostered and leadership becomes easier. Since Solomon's leadership style was called into question from the beginning of Rehoboam's reign, why was he so blind in understanding the people's earnest plea?

In leading people there is always a ripple effect. As leaders, nothing done is ever in isolation, but always affects many other people. Help the class explore ways in which leadership decisions either help or hurt people. Obviously, not every person can get their way. How do we judge what is the best course of action, remembering that Rehoboam's stubbornness began the process of dividing the monarchy? Eventually, this led to the fall of both Samaria in the north and Jerusalem in the south.

III. Good leaders put the interests of the group first.

From our vantage point, it may be easy to see that Rehoboam did a very foolish thing when he listened and acted on the advice of the wrong group of people. Why is this so easy for us to do even now?

The key to leadership is offered in several places in our text today. This key is in the realm of God. Good leaders are not despots ruling for their own gain or by their own whim. They are servants of God, given leadership as stewards. Have the class discuss other biblical leaders exercising faithful leadership according to the servant-leader model suggested to Rehoboam by the northern tribes and Jeroboam. How do we see this leadership in Jesus? Do we see it in our own church?

IV. The strongest leaders are often those who do not appear to be strong.

This is really not true. Strong leaders do not need to bully or intimidate people to be effective, might be a better way to say this. In our world today, though, conventional wisdom says leaders need to be dynamic and in a sense overpowering. Discuss with the class the old fable of Aesop's called "The Wind and the Sun."

This story tells of the sun and wind having an argument about which was the strongest. They saw a man with a coat coming down the road, and decided the one who could force the man to remove the coat was the stronger. The wind went first and the harder it blew the tighter the man held on to the coat. The sun went next and shone bright and hot. The man quickly removed his coat.

After talking about this story, have your class break into three or four smaller groups and try and create a modern version of this fable. Being able to apply this story to our more modern lives can help us better visualize the real nature of leadership.

It is too bad for Rehoboam that he did not understand the nature of power that this story tells. Are there other folk stories that illustrate this point of power and leadership?

Helping Class Members Act

Where are areas in our lives where we need better to understand leadership, power, and authority? How would we be better supervisors, teachers, parents, and marriage partners were we to learn what Rehoboam did not? Is it within our grasp to become servant-leaders and understand the principle that Paul spoke of in Corinthians, love "does not insist on its own way"?

Planning for Next Sunday

Ask your class members to read 1 Kings 18:30-39, which is the story about how Elijah broke a long drought with the help of the Lord. What is the price to be paid for faithfulness and what is faith's reward?

Whom Will You Follow?

Background Scripture: 1 Kings 18:30-39

The Main Question

A year or two ago there was a trend in magazines to have articles dealing with people's personality profiles. These were not so much in-depth psychological articles, as much as articles about how ordinary people could apply scientific research to their everyday lives.

One article I remember in particular dealt with what it called the classic type-A personality. Type-A persons, in the face of a decision, would act rather than think out what course of action is best. Their motto, in other words, is that doing anything, even if it turns out badly, is better than doing nothing. Type-A people are so decisive, they would rather go back and correct a mistake than weigh all the alternatives before making a decision.

It is good to analyze, think, and weigh alternatives before one comes to a decision. Type-A personalities spend much time doing work over since often it was not well thought-out in the first place. Swinging too far the other direction, however, is not a good alternative either. People can be caught in the paralysis of analysis, never coming to a moment of decision. When this happens, human beings can become like deer frozen in the oncoming headlights of an automobile. Being frozen in the middle of a road always spells disaster for the deer. People who agonize over decisions, to the point of not deciding, have, in fact, decided; for to not decide is to decide.

After World War II, Harry Truman was getting advice on the condition of the United States' economy. He said at one point, "Economists tell me on the one hand this and on the other hand that. What I need right now is a good one-handed economist." In a crisis, most of us understand that the endless agony over coming to a conclusion is sometimes worse than making a wrong decision.

Elijah calls the people to faith in the one true God. He urges them to see they are in a crisis situation. Therefore, they must decide. He reminds the Israelites of this Lord God who has acted on the people's behalf and has been with their ancestors through history. His implied question is "to whom will you give your ultimate allegiance?" In a way it is Joshua's challenge to a previous generation, long before, "choose this day whom you will serve . . . but as for me and my household, we will serve the Lord" (Josh. 24:15).

All people eventually come to terms with the things valued above all others. To whom or what will we pay our ultimate allegiance? To not decide is to, in fact, decide.

Selected Scripture

King James Version	New Revised Standard Version
1 Kings 18:30-39	*1 Kings 18:30-39*
30 And Elijah said unto all the people, Come near unto me. And all	30 Then Elijah said to all the people, "Come closer to me"; and all

the people came near unto him. And he repaired the altar of the LORD *that was* broken down.

31 And Elijah took twelve stones, according to the number of the tribes of the sons of Jacob, unto whom the word of the LORD came, saying, Israel shall be thy name:

32 And with the stones he built an altar in the name of the LORD: and he made a trench about the altar, as great as would contain two measures of seed.

33 And he put the wood in order, and cut the bullock in pieces, and laid *him* on the wood, and said, Fill four barrels with water, and pour *it* on the burnt sacrifice, and on the wood.

34 And he said, Do *it* the second time. And they did *it* the second time. And he said, Do *it* the third time. And they did *it* the third time.

35 And the water ran round about the altar; and he filled the trench also with water.

36 And it came to pass at *the time of* the offering of the *evening* sacrifice, that Elijah the prophet came near, and said, LORD God of Abraham, Isaac, and of Israel, let it be known this day that thou *art* God in Israel, and *that* I *am* thy servant, and *that* I have done all these things at thy word.

37 Hear me, O LORD, hear me, that this people may know that thou *art* the LORD God, and *that* thou hast turned their heart back again.

38 Then the fire of the LORD fell, and consumed the burnt sacrifice, and the wood, and the stones, and the dust, and licked up the water that *was* in the trench.

39 And when all the people saw *it*, they fell on their faces: and they said, The LORD, he *is* the God; the LORD, he *is* the God.

Key Verse: **And Elijah came unto all the people, and said, How long halt ye between two opinions? If the**

the people came closer to him. First he repaired the altar of the LORD that had been thrown down; 31 Elijah took twelve stones, according to the number of the tribes of the sons of Jacob, to whom the word of the LORD came, saying, "Israel shall be your name"; 32 with the stones he built an alar in the name of the LORD. Then he made a trench around the altar, large enough to contain two measures of seed. 33 Next he put the wood in order, cut the bull in pieces, and laid it on the wood. He said, "Fill four jars with water and pour it on the burnt offering and on the wood." 34 Then he said, "Do it a second time"; and they did it a second time. Again he said, "Do it a third time"; and they did it a third time, 35 so that the water ran all around the altar, and filled the trench also with water.

36 At the time of the offering of the oblation, the prophet Elijah came near and said, "O LORD, God of Abraham, Isaac, and Israel, let it be known this day that you are God in Israel, that I am your servant, and that I have done all these things at your bidding. 37 Answer me, O LORD, answer me, so that this people may know that you, O LORD, are God, and that you have turned their hearts back." 38 Then the fire of the LORD fell and consumed the burnt offering, the wood, the stones, and the dust, and even licked up the water that was in the trench. 39 When all the people saw it, they fell on their faces and said, "The LORD indeed is God; the LORD indeed is God."

Key Verse: **Elijah then came near to all the people, and said, "How long will you go limping with two differ-**

LORD *be* God, follow him: but if
Baal, *then* follow him. And the people answered him not a word.

ent opinions? If the LORD is God,
follow him; but if Baal, then follow
him." The people did not answer
him a word.

As You Read the Scripture

1 Kings 18:30-39. The context of our passage today is in the region of
Samaria, over which Ahab is king. It has been enduring a severe drought
for three years. This drought caused a great famine in the land and pro-
duced great suffering. Elijah is sent by the Lord to king Ahab, bring a word
of prophecy. This prophecy to Ahab is that his faithlessness and worship of
the Baals has brought, among other things, the drought on Israel. Elijah
then proposes a contest. Who can bring rain on the land: The prophets of
Baal or the word of the Lord coming through Elijah? Elijah says, "You call
on the name of your god and I will call on the name of the Lord; the god
who answers by fire is indeed God." Verses 20 to 29 record that the
prophets of Baal and Asherah fail totally. This sets up the verses we are
studying today.

Verse 30. The people of Israel have been observing carefully the incanta-
tions, dancing, and self-mutilation the prophets of Baal had been doing
from morning until the offering of the oblation, which was about 3:00 pm.
No rain or fire had come on the altar, however. Elijah beckons the people to
move closer. They are fearful and Elijah's request heightens the drama of
the moment. He rebuilds the altar carefully, which had been knocked down,
and this rebuilding is for full effect. To worship the true God, the altar must
be built from scratch—it has been dishonored by the worship of false gods.
In this tense moment, all eyes are on Elijah.

Verses 31-32. Next, as an act of remembrance, Elijah seizes twelve stones.
Each stone reminds the people of one of the twelve tribes of Yahweh. To further reinforce his point, he tells all who hear that a new name, Israel, was
given to Jacob, sealing the Lord's relationship with this people. Israel means,
"he who strives with God" or "God strives."

Elijah then carefully reconstructs the altar with these twelve stone representing Israel's tradition as God's people. A trench was dug around the altar.
It was large enough to contain two measures (about twelve bushels) of
seed—a trench of uncertain size, but substantial.

Verses 33-35. Note the care Elijah takes in rebuilding the altar. The
tediousness dramatizes the moment's tension and the pressure builds. The
sacrificial bull is readied, suggesting to the reader a symbol of the Baals.
Wood is laid on the altar, then jars of water are poured over the whole construction. Not once, but three times, four jars of water are poured over the
altar. Thus, twelve stones and twelve jars of water are used on the altar.
There is so much water that it runs into the trench that has been dug. Since
Israel is in the midst of a terrible drought, the emphasis on the prodigal
amounts of water called for by Elijah serves again to heighten the story's tension.

Verses 36-37. The hour of oblation is 3:00 pm. In Acts 3:1 it is called the
hour of prayer when Peter and John go to the temple; the ninth hour. Elijah's prayer is an obvious sacrifice, too. He reminds the people who this
Lord God is to whom he is praying. The Lord is the Lord of these people,
but more, the Lord of their ancestors—recounting their names, Abraham,

Isaac, and Israel. Elijah also makes clear, in his prayer, this sacrificial matter is not at anyone's bidding except the Lord's.

The final part of this dramatic prayer asks the Lord to prosper Elijah in this contest. Not so that Elijah might prove successful, but so that the people might come to a decision about the nature and power of the one true God. In this prayer of Elijah's, everything is at stake. This is a moment of decision and the prophet speaks of it as "turning back their hearts."

Verse 38. This is the dramatic climax in the story. The people have waited since early in the morning to see which god, or the Lord God, would answer by fire. God's response is so complete, so overwhelming, that everything on the altar is absolutely consumed—bull, stones, wood, dust, and all twelve jars of water. There is no question. This is a real fire from heaven.

Verse 39. A minor (or major) miracle now occurs. The people fall on their faces and confess before the God of Elijah and their ancestors. Their confession is a traditional one, found in three Hebrew Psalms: 95, 100, and 105. The people falling on their faces, as the Lord's fire falls from heaven, is a fitting response of true worship. For the moment, the people have decided which to worship.

The Scripture and the Main Question

Elijah's Question

Our unit for today concerns the prophet Elijah's calling down fire from heaven. The people of Israel seem to be limping between two opinions. In fact, the key verse in our study today is 1 Kings 18:21, which precedes our lesson. It says, "Elijah then came near to all the people, and said, 'How long will you go limping with two different opinions? If the LORD is God, follow him; but if Baal, then follow him.' " Elijah is urging the people, in no uncertain terms, to make a decision about who or what it is they will put their ultimate allegiance in. Which God, or gods, will they worship?

On the one hand, they say they are loyal to God Almighty, but as a calculating people, they also hedge their theological bets by lapsing into Baal worship. In this course of action, they are opposite to the type-A personality we spoke about above. The people keep deferring the decision for the Lord until a later time. Perhaps they need a sign or miracle in order to be convinced. Elijah will give them, not only a stupendous miracle, but also he will remind them about the nature of the Lord God acting on behalf of these people's ancestors.

The Historical Situation

Until the time when the children of Israel entered into the promised land, they had been together only as a band of Hebrews. There were no outside influences of note. We remember that for forty years they were sojourning in the wilderness led by Moses and for a time Miriam, until she died in Kadesh (Num. 20:1). After the conquering of the land of promise, however, the Israelites begin to live in a society that was not exclusively Yahweh worshippers.

Beginning in the book of Judges, we begin to see evidences of Baal worship, which was the principal Canaanite god. From the time of their introduction to these foreign gods, there always existed a grave danger for Israel to fall down and worship false gods. The danger of this temptation is shown by the words of Moses in giving the commandments: "You shall have no other gods before me. You shall not make for yourself an idol, whether in the form of anything that is in heaven above, or that is on the earth beneath, or that is in the water under the earth" (Deut. 5:7-8). As long as the people of Yahweh lived with other cultures who were worshiping other gods, this was a critical danger to the people's monotheistic belief in the one true God, the Lord.

Baal and the Prophets

During this period of the kings in Israel's history, each king is measured, from the biblical writer's viewpoint, as either being faithful to Yahweh alone or unfaithful. When Ahab was king, he was brought under the influence of his wife Jezebel, a fervent worshipper of Baal.

Thus, Ahab is constantly judged as an unfaithful king according to texts in 1 Kings. In fact, a scathing parenthetical judgment on Ahab's leadership occurs at 1 Kings 21:25-26, "(Indeed, there was no one like Ahab, who sold himself to do what was evil in the sight of the LORD, urged on by his wife Jezebel. He acted most abominably in going after idols, as the Amorites had done, whom the LORD drove out before the Israelites)." From the Bible's viewpoint, Ahab is a failure as a king, for he is not guided by Yahweh. The truth is, as we read about Ahab, he often seems to be nothing but a hapless figurehead, influenced solely by his wife Jezebel.

It is into this royal situation the Lord calls Elijah to prophesy the Lord's word. The people of Israel, under Ahab's leadership, seem to be limping between two opinions. Limping is a play on words, alluding to the dance that the prophets of Baal did before the altar when they failed in their attempts to call down the fire. Elijah's prayer and careful reconstruction of the altar show the people his deep faith that the God he worships is the one true God. After the fire comes down from heaven and totally obliterates everything that was the altar of the Lord, the people confess that this indeed is the Lord.

The Story's End

The end of this particular battle between Elijah and the prophets of Baal has a bad ending for them. Elijah calls on the people who have just confessed their faith in the Lord to seize the prophets, and Elijah kills them at the brook of Kishon. But there is a happy ending for the people in Samaria. The drought ends. The next chapters tell of Jezebel's efforts to do to Elijah what he has done to her prophets.

Worshipping False Gods Today

Occasionally, when we think of idol worship we are prone to think this only happened long ago in the Bible. Truthfully, idolatry is always something that tempts people of faith and in every age. Idolatry is simply the act of seeking ultimate assurance in something other than the God we profess to worship. It is the act of putting our hope and trust in something beyond or beside the God we confess as Lord.

In the Hebrew scriptures, idolatry is usually seen in Baal worship, but today we see idolatry in other, more sophisticated ways, we think. Whenever our jobs, families, nation, political views, or anything else become the object of our worship, then we have fallen into the temptation of idolatry. When these things give our lives all the meaning and purpose we think necessary to live full abundant lives, then we have slipped into idol worship.

Often people think unwittingly that idol worship is the worship of something evil, but this is not always the case. When Jesus was tempted (Luke 4:1-13), none of the satanic temptations was evil in and of itself. Stones into bread is a good thing in a world of hunger. Jesus proving himself to be the Son of God is not bad, by itself. In fact, he does this at the resurrection. Jesus ruling over the kingdoms of the earth would seem to be the answer to Christian's prayers for centuries. These things are evil temptations only because they attempt to circumvent the process of God's working in the world. God works in human affairs according to God's determination and God's timetable. Jesus knew this and was faithful to God's will, which is why he was called the faithful witness in later Christian traditions.

Our scripture today teaches the lesson to the Hebrew people, via the prophecy of Elijah, that God comes first. It is to the Lord God, the people are to show ultimate allegiance. This is what it is to be a person of faith. Many centuries later Jesus makes this same point when he says, "But strive first for the kingdom of God and his righteousness, and all these things will be given to you as well."

Helping Adults Become Involved

Preparing to Teach

The issue of divided allegiances is one every person in your class will be able to identify in their own lives. Daily we are called on to make decisions. To decide for one thing often means to decide against something else. This may be a Sunday lesson that will elicit a lively class discussion. This outline may help you and your class begin to explore ways in which the decisions every Christian must make are made difficult by the influence our culture exerts on us.

    I. Drought is a life-and-death situation.
    II. Our spiritual preparation shows our faith.
    III. Elijah's prayer puts the matter on the line.
    IV. Elijah's question is our question, too.
    V. The Lord's fire elicits a response of faith from us.

One of the best ways to prepare for this lesson is to think carefully about the ways our culture tries to manipulate the gods, as the prophets of Baal tried to manipulate the gods of nature. It will help you to have a good understanding of 1 Kings 18, as you guide your class in discussion.

Introducing the Main Question

After beginning the class with a prayer, read verses 17 to 29 out loud. Then have someone in the class recount, in their own words, the actions Elijah takes in preparing the altar for the fire from the Lord. You might want to use the material from the section "As You Read the Scripture" to answer and clarify the action in the story for today. Guide the class into a discussion about ultimate allegiance and how we are often put into faith binds by the world in which we live now.

Developing the Lesson

I. Drought is a life-and-death situation.

In our modern United States, we sometimes forget that in agrarian societies (such as Israel during Elijah's time) drought was feared more than any other natural phenomenon. When there was no rain, there was no food. Famine and starvation have always been one of the evils with which humans have had to contend. I like the bumper sticker I often see on farmers' trucks: "If you eat, you're involved in agriculture." What issues do we deal with as twentieth-century people that are similar to the drought predicament the people of Israel faced?

II. Our spiritual preparation shows our faith.

In the whole story of 1 Kings 18, there is a marked contrast between the frantic behavior of the prophets of Baal and the calm, deliberate preparations made by Elijah. The prophets went so far as to cut themselves and bleed to no avail. Elijah is very deliberate and purposeful in his rebuilding of the altar of the Lord. How is our individual faith history a preparation for times of crisis and decision? The class might want to share instances in their own lives when questions of faith were prompted by non-religious people only because they were in the midst of a crisis.

III. Elijah's prayer puts the matter on the line.

When Elijah prays that day, he prays as if the whole sweep of his people's history is at stake. He addresses the God of the Hebrews' ancestors. He prays in the present moment that God may act on his people's behalf. He prays that their hearts might be changed for the future. Thus, Elijah's prayer concerns the past, present, and future. Later, at the end of the Christian scripture in Revelation, the verse occurs: "Grace to you and peace from him who is and who was and who is to come" (Rev. 1:4). The God Elijah worships and the God we worship today not only has the whole world in his hand, but also the whole sweep of history—past, present, future—too!

IV. Elijah's question is our question, too.

Our key verse for today is from 1 Kings 18:21, in which Elijah asks the people, "How long will you go limping with two different opinions? If the Lord is God, follow him; but if Baal, then follow him" (1 Kings 18:21). In a moment of crisis, people are forced to make a decision. What are the moments of crisis for people today, in our community, in our church, and in our world? To not decide is to decide. How does our faith keep us from sitting on the fence indefinitely?

V. The Lord's fire elicits a response of faith from us.

When the Lord God sent fire from heaven and consumed the altar and everything around it, the people responded with a confession of faith. They also fell on their faces as an act of worship. Even though this dramatic scene in the text explains this well by its very intensity, are there things that happen to us that elicit such a response? How does God get the attention of God's people today? Has anything like this ever happened to you?

Helping Class Members Act

We are people who have been trained to think things out. In school we have all been taught the scientific method where trial and error are used to analyze phenomena from a multitude of perspectives. At the same time, many people are coming back to church to find solid answers to life's perplexing problems. How does the church balance its theology between religion as personal and individual, and religion as social, to be experienced in community? Talk about how your church reflects and acts on its faith.

Planning for Next Sunday

As your class is dismissed, ask them to read the story of Naboth's Vineyard in 1 Kings 21. Think about ways in which injustice visits the innocent and how our society at large either stands for or against those who have no voice to protest.

LESSON 3   JUNE 18

Justice Corrupted

Background Scripture: 1 Kings 21:1-4, 15-20

The Main Question

Land speculation has consistently been an avenue to quick wealth. From "Seward's Folly" in purchasing Alaska, to our present problems with banking and bad real estate investments, people have used land as a means to get rich quick.

Real estate exchanges have dotted the history of many countries. The United States is a good case in point. We are familiar with Manhattan's purchase for a few beads and trinkets from the Native Americans, the Louisiana Purchase from Napoleon that doubled our nation's size overnight, and other less honorable land appropriations from the Native Americans in the Dakotas, Florida, and Oklahoma. Many other nations have these stories, as well. Karl Marx built a whole philosophical and economic theory on public ownership of private property.

When I was a much younger person my friends and I would shout "Justice," when anything good and unexpected happened to us. Whether it was a lucky basketball shot, or a good grade on a test that came back better than we had hoped, "Justice" was always our refrain. In truth, we probably should have shouted "Grace" instead, because justice denotes fairness or something people deserve.

All people want to be treated fairly and with equity. Our text today deals with a king who acted very unfairly in taking a piece of property from a righteous man named Naboth. The main question before us is: Does anyone have the right—even a king—to do as he pleases with regard to other people and their property? Can a community ever be whole and healthy, if certain persons have rights and privileges surpassing the ordinary people? When do our personal wants rob the community of its needs?

Selected Scripture

King James Version	New Revised Standard Version

1 Kings 21:1-4, 15-20

1 And it came to pass after these things, *that* Naboth the Jezreelite had a vineyard, which was in Jezreel, hard by the palace of Ahab king of Samaria.

2 And Ahab spake unto Naboth, saying, Give me thy vineyard, that I may have it for a garden of herbs, because it *is* near unto my house: and I will give thee for it a better vineyard than it; *or,* if it seem good to thee, I will give thee the worth of it in money.

3 And Naboth said to Ahab, The LORD forbid it me, that I should give the inheritance of my fathers unto thee.

4 And Ahab came into his house heavy and displeased because of the word which Naboth the Jezreelite had spoken to him: for he had said, I will not give thee the inheritance of my fathers. And he laid him down upon his bed, and turned away his face, and would eat no bread.

....

15 And it came to pass, when Jezebel heard that Naboth was stoned, and was dead, that Jezebel said to Ahab, Arise, take possession of the vineyard of Naboth the Jezreelite, which he refused to give thee for money: for Naboth is not alive, but dead.

16 And it came to pass, when Ahab heard that Naboth was dead, that Ahab rose up to go down to the vineyard of Naboth the Jezreelite, to take possession of it.

1 Kings 21:1-4, 15-21a

1 Later the following events took place: Naboth the Jezreelite had a vineyard in Jezreel, beside the palace of King Ahab of Samaria. 2 And Ahab said to Naboth, "Give me your vineyard, so that I may have it for a vegetable garden, because it is near my house; I will give you a better vineyard for it; or, if it seems good to you, I will give you its value in money." 3 But Naboth said to Ahab, "The LORD forbid that I should give you my ancestral inheritance." 4 Ahab went home resentful and sullen because of what Naboth the Jezreelite had said to him; for he had said, "I will not give you my ancestral inheritance." He lay down on his bed, turned away his face, and would not eat.

....

15 As soon as Jezebel heard that Naboth had been stoned and was dead, Jezebel said to Ahab, "Go, take possession of the vineyard of Naboth the Jezreelite, which he refused to give you for money; for Naboth is not alive, but dead." 16 As soon as Ahab heard that Naboth was dead, Ahab set out to go down to the vineyard of Naboth the Jezreelite, to take possession of it.

17 And the word of the LORD came to Elijah the Tishbite, saying,

18 Arise, go down to meet Ahab king of Israel, which *is* in Samaria: behold, *he is* in the vineyard of Naboth, whither he is gone down to possess it.

19 And thou shalt speak unto him, saying, Thus saith the LORD, Hast thou killed, and also taken possession? And thou shalt speak unto him, saying, Thus saith the LORD, In the place where dogs licked the blood of Naboth shall dogs lick thy blood, even thine.

20 And Ahab said to Elijah, Hast thou found me, O mine enemy? And he answered, I have found *thee*: because thou hast sold thyself to work evil in the sight of the LORD.

Key Verse: **And Ahab said to Elijah, Hast thou found me, O mine enemy? And he answered, I have found *thee*: because thou hast sold thyself to work evil in the sight of the LORD.**

17 Then the word of the LORD came to Elijah the Tishbite, saying:

18 Go down to meet King Ahab of Israel, who rules in Samaria; he is now in the vineyard of Naboth, where he has gone to take possession. 19 You shall say to him, "Thus says the LORD: Have you killed, and also taken possession?" You shall say to him, "Thus says the LORD: In the place where dogs licked up the blood of Naboth, dogs will also lick up your blood."

20 Ahab said to Elijah, "Have you found me, O my enemy?" He answered, "I have found you. Because you have sold yourself to do what is evil in the sight of the LORD, I will bring disaster on you."

Key Verse: **Ahab said to Elijah, "Have you found me, O my enemy?" He answered, "I have found you. Because you have sold yourself to do what is evil in the sight of the LORD, I will bring disaster on you."**

As You Read the Scripture

1 Kings 21:1-4, 15-20. This passage today gives the beginning and end of a fascinating story whose characters are Naboth, King Ahab, Jezebel, Elijah, and offstage, Yahweh. To understand this text, we will need to fill in the missing verses below, for they have a dramatic impact on the story's thrust.

Verses 1-2. These two verses set the stage for the conflict between Ahab and Naboth. They also furnish the reason for Naboth being stoned to death by Jezebel's hench-people. Naboth, as the story tells us, has a vineyard; an ancestral inheritance. Therefore, it would logically be placed in the territory of Jezreel. If this is so, Ahab must have had two royal residences, one in Samaria and one in Jezreel. This is because the text tells us, "Naboth the Jezreelite had a vineyard in Jezreel, beside the palace of King Ahab of Samaria."

The king desired the property of Naboth and offers him either "a better vineyard for it; or, if it seems good to you [Naboth], I [Ahab] will give you its value in money" (v. 2). This seems to be a reasonable and fair business offer.

Verse 3. For reasons not entirely clear in the text, Naboth rejects the king's proposition. The refusal may hinge on an interpretation of keeping inherited ancestral property in the family (see Deut. 25:5-10), but this is not altogether plain. In any event, Naboth seems so certain of his conviction about the sale he swears an oath, "The LORD forbid that I should give you my ancestral inheritance." This astonishing and surprising stance of Naboth's sets in motion events soon spelling his death.

Verse 4. Ahab's reaction to his rejected offer, generous though it seemed to him, was unkingly, to say the least. Like a teenager wrongfully disciplined by a parent, Ahab went to his room, threw himself on the bed, turned toward the wall, and refused to eat.

Verses 5-15. The story continues with verses 5-15, though it is outside the specific passage we are studying. Jezebel is the primary actor, orchestrating events bringing about Naboth's death. In a series of calculated political maneuvers, she engineers a plan to get rid of Naboth. This releases the property's ownership, allowing Ahab to take control. There is no mention of Naboth's legal heirs rightfully inheriting the property at his death. This matter is omitted by the text.

Verse 16. Jezebel informs Ahab that the problem about the property has been resolved because "Naboth is not alive, but dead" (v. 15). Ahab leaps to action and goes to take possession of the property he had lusted after. Did he know what had been done behind the scenes to make this possible? A yes or no to this question still puts Ahab in a very bad light either way as a king.

Verses 17-19. Yahweh's word then comes to the prophet Elijah. A good review of Elijah's previous dealings with Ahab and Jezebel will be helpful to the flow of the plot (see 1 Kings 17–19). Like David's situation, regarding the unprincipled treatment of Uriah the Hittite (see 2 Samuel 11–12), the prophet Elijah, like Nathan before him, condemns the evil use of royal power to steal from the powerless. Elijah does not mince words. Ahab's evil actions will bring disaster on himself and, later, his whole household. "Dogs licking up the blood" is a particularly gruesome touch indicating the prophecy's horror.

Verse 20. The prophet of God, Elijah, concludes the prophecy, indicating that the reason Ahab has been found out and will be punished is "because you have sold yourself to do what is evil in the sight of the Lord."

The Scripture and the Main Question

Surprises in the Vineyard

"Surprises in the Vineyard" might be an excellent title for this marvelous Hebrew story. King Ahab offers Naboth a better piece of property in exchange for his vineyard or, at least, the fair-market value in money.

The story, however, takes an unexpected twist. Naboth refuses the king's offer, invoking Yahweh's name in an oath: "the LORD forbid." It seemed Naboth's refusal involved his ancestors' previous ownership of the vineyard. Perhaps, Naboth understood the passing down of the inherited vineyard as a divine gift. Evidently, the worth of the property seemed too high to consider selling it—even to King Ahab.

Ahab's Big Problem

Ahab's greatest asset as king turns out to be his greatest liability. Does anyone have the right—even a king—to do as he pleases regarding other people or their property? Can a community ever be whole and healthy if certain persons have rights and privileges surpassing the ordinary people? Ahab, if he had been an ordinary citizen, would never have been in a position—nor his wife—to orchestrate the scenario ridding the royal couple of their

Naboth dilemma. It was Ahab and Jezebel's unbridled use of power that eventually spelled their downfall. Like Rehoboam before them, neither partner in the royal household had a concept of servant-leadership. This is the model lifted up in Hebrew scriptures as the prototype for leadership among the people of God. King David, too, was disciplined by Yahweh for overstepping his authority. For the Hebrew people in general, and the Israelite monarchs in particular, all power comes from Yahweh. Hebrew kings never rule at their own behest, but always by the authority granted by Yahweh, Israel's true King.

The Nature of Human Sin

From the cradle to the grave, or better, from the servant's quarters to the throne room, all people are in a condition the Bible calls sin. First John squarely summarizes the unbroken biblical idea of sin when it says, "If we say that we have no sin, we deceive ourselves, and the truth is not in us" (1 John 1:8).

I like to think of sin as not knowing our place, at least as far as the realm of God is concerned. In this condition the Bible calls sin, we are often guilty of overreaching. We attempt to be more, or less, than God created us to be. Pride for position, status, or recognition can drive the best, and worst, of us into doing things we know we ought not to have done. On the other side of the equation is the sin of being less than we were created to be. This is when we lapse into the sin of despair. The sin of despair is when people give up on life before God does. Often people turn their backs on the gifts God has given, and given exclusively to them, over which only they can be stewards. Ahab was guilty of the first type of sin described: the sin of overreaching.

Ahab and, by extension, Jezebel forgot who they were, thinking nothing was beyond their grasp. The Bible is full of this grabbing, overreaching theme: Eve grabs the forbidden fruit, Jacob grabs the heel of his elder brother and his blessing, David grabs the wife of Uriah, and Ahab grabs the land belonging to Naboth. This is one biblical theme with a wealth of illustrations. Perhaps you and your class could identify others?

God's Counterbalance to Human Sin

As our text ends, Ahab has the prophetic word of God delivered to him in explicit terms; he and his household are utterly and completely denounced by Elijah, the spokesperson for Yahweh. The verses beyond our lesson tell the lot of Ahab's household: The birds of the air will eat anyone who belongs to Ahab if they die in the open country. Ahab's kin dying in the city shall be eaten by dogs—this includes Jezebel. The dogs will lick up Ahab's blood, too! The writer of Kings then adds to the indictment an inserted editorial comment: Ahab was as faithless and wicked a king as Israel would ever see. If there was ever a person having no prospect of divine compassion, this individual was Ahab. Verse 25 puts it coldly: "Indeed, there was no one like Ahab, who sold himself to do what was evil in the sight of the LORD, urged on by his wife Jezebel."

This same spirit of God's strong word of judgement and grace is operative in Peter's defense before the council in Jerusalem (Acts 11:1-18). During Peter's visit with Cornelius, Peter broke bread with the Gentiles in Cornelius' household. This breached strict adherence to Jewish ritual law. Peter says persuasively, in response to his antagonists, "If then God gave them [the Gentiles] the same gift that he gave us [the Jews] when we believed in the

Lord Jesus Christ, who was I that I could hinder God?" (Acts 11:17). God can and does show mercy to those we often consider beyond the scope of divine forgiveness. Ahab is a recipient of God's grace, in that the sentence delivered by Elijah is stayed, at least temporarily. A pertinent question for us: Is God's grace large enough to accommodate our theology?

Grace and Human Life Today

Naboth, Ahab, Jezebel, and Elijah all provide surprising twists and turns in this story. None acts as we might anticipate. Naboth refuses to make a quick profit on land he had inherited. Ahab hardly acts like a king, pouting in his room and refusing to eat. Jezebel, a foreign wife, is a surprising power behind the throne. Elijah, just a few chapters before, was wanting to die. Each character is their own person, acting in unconventional and unexpected ways.

The biggest surprise of this story of Naboth's vineyard, however, is the one sprung by Yahweh. Though it is outside the range of our text, it is nonetheless an astonishing end to this startling Hebrew chronicle.

Often, Christians are taught that the God of the Old Testament is a God of justice, while the God of the New Testament is a God of mercy. The surprise for all of us is that God, in this story and in both testaments, is a God who is interested in the salvation of all people. If God can defer judgement against the household of Ahab, if even for a bit, then we can live in the hope that this is a God who is interested in our salvation, too. God is always full of surprises. The greatest surprise of all is that God wants all people to be in fellowship with God.

Helping Adults Become Involved

Preparing to Teach

The issue of justice is an issue that seems to consume people. A few years ago the liberation movement gripped Eastern Europe and the former Soviet Republics. People called for just treatment from the government on political and economic grounds. In recent memory, South Africa and other nations have struggled with these issues, too. Since biblical times, of course remembering this overarching theme in Exodus, the idea of justice and freedom has been a prominent one. Here in the story of Naboth, the issue of justice and fairness is front and center. King Ahab's deportment is a scandal to Israel's concept of covenant community. As a teacher, getting folk from Naboth's vineyard to a twentieth-century world should be our goal. This outline may help you and the class move toward some of this text's major themes:

I.   Naboth's oath is sacred.
II. Ahab's coveting begins a series of events over which he has no control.
III. Jezebel's seizure of power runs against the grain of Israel's understanding of justice.
IV. The word of the Lord is a compelling word.
V.   The Lord defers judgment.

Like David's reaction to Nathan's parable of the ewe lamb, most of us are outraged by the rich stealing from the poor. As you prepare for the lesson, think of situations today in which this same theme of Naboth's vineyard is played out.

Introducing the Main Question

Have your class read dramatically the story of Naboth's vineyard, but not just our assigned text. The class should read 1 Kings 21 in its entirety. Then, assign members the parts of Naboth, Ahab, Jezebel, Elijah, a narrator, and Yahweh. Have your class read with a sense of drama and then discuss their feelings as they moved through the text. Each character's perspective gives this story a variety of entry points for discussion in your class. Letting the class develop a sense of injustice as the class moves along will be more satisfying than simply telling them they should be outraged.

Developing the Lesson

I. Naboth's oath is sacred.

We all remember when a person's word was as much of a pledge as one would ever need. People kept promises. Naboth keeps his promise, perhaps an unspoken one to his ancestors, and refuses to sell his vineyard. In fact, he swears an oath to the Lord, "God forbid." What kinds of issues are important enough to the class members to make them consider an oath? Why do we suppose James reversed this honored practice, at least the way Naboth did it, by saying, "Above all, my beloved, do not swear, either by heaven or by earth or by any other oath, but let your 'Yes' be yes and your 'No' be no, so that you may not fall under condemnation" (Jam. 5:12)?

II. Ahab's coveting begins a series of events over which he has no control.

A good exercise for all of us is not only looking at others' lives to see how coveting has destroyed community, but look at our own lives. Several years ago, the Mazda auto company tried an advertising campaign that had as a theme that their cars would not give people status, but would give them reliable transportation. The campaign failed miserably and advertising executives speculated that cars, like perfume and other commodities, need to be sold not on their merit, but rather on the image of success they offered to those who bought particular products.

The Christian view of life runs against such ideas. How do we avoid being sucked into secular mindsets? What drives people to be so competitive in the acquisition of material wealth far beyond the needs of our daily bread?

III. Jezebel's seizure of power runs against the grain of Israel's understanding of justice.

Have your class contrast Jezebel's words, "Go, take possession of the vineyard of Naboth the Jezreelite, which he refused to give you for money; for Naboth is not alive, but dead," with the words of the father in the parable of two sons: "This brother of yours was dead and has come to life" (Luke 15). How do these statements from our Bible show the focus of faith and the worth of persons that goes far beyond the need for greed?

IV. The word of the Lord is a compelling word.

The word of the Lord came to Elijah in verse 17. How powerful it must have been to compel Elijah to confront Ahab, and also Jezebel, especially when we remember that Jezebel had threatened the prophet's life only a few chapters before. How does the Lord's word come to us to confront the evils in our lives? Are there instances when we, too, have put our lives on the line for truth and justice?

V. The Lord defers judgment.

Perhaps the most surprising feature of this story occurs when Ahab shows signs of repentance and the Lord defers judgement, at least for a time. This is why the verses in 1 Kings 21:21-29 are important, showing divine mercy operating in this narrative account. What does this story tell us about God's willingness to show compassion to even those who appear to be beyond such mercy?

Helping Class Members Act

Power is given to rulers as a sacred trust, at least from the perspective of the Bible. When rulers misuse power they have been wicked stewards of the divine trust given them by God. Do our leaders have this understanding of power? Do we as leaders of the church live by the same standard of justice that we expect from those who lead us? How are power and humility yoked in the biblical understanding of justice?

Planning for Next Sunday

A group of four lepers, outcasts in their own community, provide a surprising gift to alleviate a famine in the city of their own people. Have your class read 2 Kings 6–7.

LESSON 4   JUNE 25

Sharing the Good News

Background Scripture: 2 Kings 7:1-9

The Main Question

Last Sunday, my church was part of a CROP walk. CROP walks are community hikes in which people walk 6.2 miles, or 10 kilometers. The walkers secure pledges from people sponsoring them for so many dollars per mile/kilometer. The money raised (in our town it was over $6,000) goes toward the battle against world hunger. Thus, even in the twentieth century, and in communities where few of the hunger walk's participants have ever seen a hungry person, the concern of hunger is still important. I have a pastor friend who says the one special appeal best received in her church is the one helping people eat. Perhaps it should not be surprising that the central sacramental element of our Christian life together takes place around a common table we call the Lord's.

Our lesson today has to do specifically with a famine that has afflicted Samaria. This famine is caused, not by a drought as we studied in 1 Kings 18, but rather by the siege of the armies of the king of Aram. We are told, "As the siege continued, famine in Samaria became so great that a donkey's head was sold for eighty shekels of silver, and one-fourth of a kab of dove's dung for five shekels of silver" (2 Kings 6:25). Not only were people starving, but also lack of food had created the collapse of a stable economy.

When famine and economic panic strike, there occurs a moment of crisis for the community. In Chinese, the two characters making the word *crisis* consist of *danger* and *opportunity*. This reminds us that crisis is not simply a negative term, but also affords challenge and opportunity to do something of value.

Along with each crisis comes either the dangers or the opportunities of faith. The opportunity of faith is an occasion to witness to God's grace and mercy. Where are the crises of faith in our lives and in the lives of those with whom we live? What dangers or opportunities are presented to your faith?

Selected Scripture

King James Version

2 Kings 7:1-9

1 Then Elisha said, Hear ye the word of the LORD; Thus saith the LORD, To morrow about this time *shall* a measure of fine flour *be sold* for a shekel, and two measures of barley for a shekel, in the gate of Samaria.

2 Then a lord on whose hand the king leaned answered the man of God, and said, Behold, *if* the LORD would make windows in heaven, might this thing be? And he said, Behold, thou shalt see *it* with thine eyes, but shall not eat thereof.

3 And there were four leprous men at the entering in of the gate: and they said one to another, Why sit we here until we die?

4 If we say, We will enter into the city, then the famine *is* in the city, and we shall die there: and if we sit still here, we die also. Now therefore come, and let us fall unto the host of the Syrians: if they save us alive, we shall live; and if they kill us, we shall but die.

5 And they rose up in the twilight, to go unto the camp of the Syrians: and when they were come to the uttermost part of the camp of Syria,

New Revised Standard Version

2 Kings 7:1-9

1 But Elisha said, "Hear the word of the LORD: thus says the LORD, Tomorrow about this time a measure of choice meal shall be sold for a shekel, and two measures of barley for a shekel, at the gate of Samaria." 2 Then the captain on whose hand the king leaned said to the man of God, "Even if the LORD were to make windows in the sky, could such a thing happen?" But he said, "You shall see it with your own eyes, but you shall not eat from it."

3 Now there were four leprous men outside the city gate, who said to one another, "Why should we sit here until we die? 4 If we say, 'Let us enter the city,' the famine is in the city, and we shall die there; but if we sit here, we shall also die. Therefore, let us desert to the Aramean camp; if they spare our lives, we shall live; and if they kill us, we shall but die." 5 So they arose at twilight to go to the Aramean camp; but when they came to the edge of the Aramean camp, there was no one there at all. 6 For the Lord had caused the Aramean army to hear the sound of

behold, *there was* no man there.

6 For the Lord had made the host of the Syrians to hear a noise of chariots, and a noise of horses, *even* the noise of a great host: and they said one to another, Lo, the king of Israel hath hired against us the kings of the Hittites, and the kings of the Egyptians, to come upon us.

7 Wherefore they arose and fled in the twilight, and left their tents, and their horses, and their asses, even the camp as it *was*, and fled for their life.

8 And when these lepers came to the uttermost part of the camp, they went into one tent, and did eat and drink, and carried thence silver, and gold, and raiment, and went and hid *it*; and came again, and entered into another tent, and carried thence *also*, and went and hid *it*,

9 Then they said one to another, We do not well: this day *is* a day of good tidings, and we hold our peace: if we tarry till the morning light, some mischief will come upon us: now therefore come, that we may go and tell the king's household.

Key Verse: **Then they said one to another, We do not well: this day *is* a day of good tidings, and we hold our peace: if we tarry till the morning light, some mischief will come upon us: now therefore come, that we may go and tell the king's household.**

chariots, and of horses, the sound of a great army, so that they said to one another, "The king of Israel has hired the kings of the Hittites and the kings of Egypt to fight against us." 7 So they fled away in the twilight and abandoned their tents, their horses, and their donkeys leaving the camp just as it was, and fled for their lives. 8 When these leprous men had come to the edge of the camp, they went into a tent, ate and drank, carried off silver, gold, and clothing, and went and hid them. Then they came back, entered another tent, carried off things from it, and went and hid them.

9 Then they said to one another, "What we are doing is wrong. This is a day of good news; if we are silent and wait until the morning light, we will be found guilty; therefore let us go and tell the king's household."

Key Verse: **Then they said to one another, "What we are doing is wrong. This is a day of good news; if we are silent and wait until the morning light, we will be found guilty; therefore let us go and tell the king's household."**

As You Read the Scripture

2 Kings 7:1-9. In the previous verse the king asked Elisha, "Why should I hope in the LORD any longer?" Naturally, as the nation's leader, the responsibility for both the siege and the famine fall directly on his shoulders. He now, in turn, tries to ascribe this state of affairs to Elisha and, by implication, to Yahweh.

Verse 1. Elisha, however, meets the king's challenge with a new and unexpected word—and from none other than Yahweh. Elisha's prophecy relates there will be an absolute reversal of Samaria's fortune. "Tomorrow about this time" indicates that the period of Samaria's waiting will be over. No longer should Samaria expect more of the same treatment. That is, the famine and out-of-control inflation will be resolved. Samaria can expect a choice meal for a reasonable price. This greatly altered circumstance will not be hidden. Rather, it will occur out in the open at the city gate, the hub of the community. Everyone will benefit, not simply the privileged. This is the unexpected word of the Lord.

Verse 2. The king's captain is the chief military officer. During a time of war he is a prominent person in the royal household. His opinions are more than simply another voice among many. His is the voice of authority. His statement, "Even if the LORD were to make windows in the sky, could such a thing happen?" looks like a question, but in fact it is a statement of utter disbelief. "Windows in the sky" is an odd phrase, since the famine is a result of the siege, not drought. Elisha informs the captain he will see God's power working, but he will not eat from what is provided.

Verse 3. The scene shifts to four leprous men sitting by the city gate. The gate was a public gathering site. Often business deals were negotiated and secured there, much like today in a restaurant or hotel lobby. Beggars often sat at the city gate because many people would pass through it going in and out of the city. The question, "Why should we sit here?" is a rhetorical one, for in the midst of a famine it mattered little where they were when they starved.

Verse 4. The four lepers devise a plan risking everything and approach the enemy's camp. The risk is two-fold. First, they will be considered traitors by their own people for deserting to the enemy's camp. Second, they risk being killed immediately by the Arameans as enemy spies. They feel as if there is no other alternative. They are desperate. Doing anything will be preferable to sitting and starving. Note the term *leprosy* is a generic description covering a number of skin diseases.

Verse 5. At sundown, the four sneak to the edge of the enemy's encampment. To their absolute astonishment, no one was there.

Verses 6-7. Apparently, the text tells us as an aside, the Lord had caused a great commotion and terrified the enemy occupying force into a complete and total retreat. They left so quickly they took no provisions with them. Indeed, they even left their valuables, along with their livestock. Perhaps they thought the king of Samaria had hired mercenaries from several surrounding nations to fight on his behalf. Whatever the reason, the Arameans left, taking nothing with them.

Verse 8. The leprous men, certainly surprised, but also famished, went into a tent and feasted. After eating their fill, they then plundered the tent, taking all the silver, gold, and clothing they could carry. Then they also did the same to another tent, hiding their booty for future sale. They appeared to be like children turned loose in a candy store—with no adult supervision!

Verse 9. Soon, however, they did as the younger son in Luke's parable, so called the prodigal son, and they came to themselves. They realized that what they were doing was wrong and for two reasons. First, if they were caught by the king when the morning light brought their deeds out in the open, they realized the punishment could be severe. A second and more benevolent reading is they wanted to share the food with those in Samaria suffering from the famine as they had.

The Scripture and the Main Question

The opportunity of faith is an occasion for witnessing to God's grace and mercy. The text before us today tells of a crisis of faith for the people of

Samaria. This crisis is so acute, even the king is prompted to ask, "Why should I hope in the LORD any longer?"

From where the king sits, though, we would be hard pressed to say his question is not logical. Famine and hunger can cause great community problems, even civil disturbances and riots. I heard a story about a lecturer, some years ago, at a symposium on human behavior. This scholar had researched the nature of altruism, or the philosophy that states that there is a basic goodness that slumbers in each person. The scholar remarked that the reason most Americans are benevolent is because they live essentially comfortable lives.

Going further, he described an experiment he had conducted. A group of fine, upstanding Quakers was put into a concentration camp-like environment for a selected period of time. Soon, these mild-mannered Quakers began to contend and scrap for food and water, just like animals do when hungry, trying to survive. This scholar concluded, after his experiment, all people deprived of daily necessities begin to act like animals, having no regard for anyone but themselves. Altruism, he concluded, is only wishful thinking on the part of well-meaning, overly optimistic people.

During the question-and-answer session, I was told, several preachers in the audience went berserk, saying the scholar was dead wrong and had a depraved view of humanity. I was led to believe that, as these preachers acted so belligerently, the scholar's point was nicely illustrated before the group gathered in the lecture hall.

From the perspective of the king, the future looks bleak and his faith in the Lord's benevolence is shaken by the events of the Aramean siege. Things got so bad there is even a hint of cannibalism in 2 Kings 6:28-29. The land's famine has caused not only a theological crisis as the king's question indicates. It has also caused a crisis of economy and justice, as well. Whenever limited resources exist, in this case food, it is the poor, the old, and young who suffer disproportionately.

The Word of Elisha

This story, however, is not primarily about the problems of the king, nor even about the suffering of the people. It is a story about the power of the word of God and the power of the prophet in times of crisis. The story's tension is set up by the exchange between the king's question about remaining hope-filled and Elisha's response. The prophet of God says, "Hear the word of the LORD: thus says the LORD, tomorrow about this time a measure of choice meal shall be sold for a shekel, and two measures of barley for a shekel, at the gate of Samaria" (2 Kings 7:1). This prophecy runs absolutely counter to everything the king is thinking and feeling.

"Tomorrow" indicates that the period of waiting is nearly over. According to the prophet's word, tomorrow will be a new day! This is the hope to which Christians can relate, especially during the high holy times of the church year. At Advent, for instance, many churches rush past the waiting and anticipation of Advent, beginning the singing of Christmas hymns too soon. We are like children who can barely wait until Christmas Day comes. One has to think our children come by this instant gratification need honestly. Even we adults have trouble waiting for the coming of the Lord, though we are more sophisticated about our anxiety.

Why is waiting so difficult? Why are we so anxious about what tomorrow will bring, even when we believe in God's promise for tomorrow at Christmas, or as in this text, the promise of food and end to famine? Is it because to believe in the promise is to believe our own means of self-reliance are bankrupt? For persons of faith, there come times when we know that no more effort, or trying, or hard work will change the particular situation in which we find ourselves. At these moments, it is most difficult to stop and wait in expectation. As faithful people, however, at some moment we must turn our lives and destiny over to God. This is an act of faith and a confession made with our lives.

These questions of trust are questions that we all might do well to spend considerable time with. Remember, later in the Gospels, how Jesus says, "Therefore do not worry, saying, 'What will we eat?' or 'What will we drink?' or 'What will we wear?' . . . So do not worry about tomorrow, for tomorrow will bring worries of its own. Today's trouble is enough for today" (Matt. 6:31, 34). This is the prophet Elisha's word to the king and people of Samaria, as well.

Despair or Confident Expectation

When famine and economic panic strike, there comes with them a moment of crisis for the community. Along with every crisis come either the dangers or the opportunities of faith. The opportunity of faith is a chance to witness to the grace and mercy of God. This story of Elisha and siege of Samaria is a story of contrasting perspectives.

On one side of the matter is the despair of the king, who admits in his own words he has lost hope in God's mercy. After all, he says, "this trouble is from the LORD!" (6:33). His captain of the guard, likewise, reflects the cynical doubt and skepticism of a conventional-thinking person. On the other side of the matter is Elisha's stance. He has absolute hope in the prophecy and reflects this directly to the king's captain. Though Elisha has, perhaps, no idea how the Lord will provide for the people, he nonetheless has a confident hope the Lord will provide—and tomorrow! At the gate, people will get choice meal at a reasonable price. Telling the chief military officer of Samaria he will see this, but not taste it, seems to be nothing more than a bold challenge. His faith in the prophecy is so certain, he stakes his life on it. This is the conviction of those who believe in God's promises.

Outsiders Become Insiders

The last section of our text could be read with a sense of humor, or at least irony. It looks like something out of a Laurel and Hardy movie. Four outcasts from society, by virtue of their disease, come to the rescue. They find a way to provide food for the Samarians and do it without a plan. It looks like an accident. These lepers, despairing and figuring out the best place to die, suddenly discover a stockpile of food and wealth beyond their wildest dreams.

Those who are cut off from society become the bearers of good news and provide the salvation needed by the people. This is the biblical message, par excellence. Abraham, too old to bear children becomes the father of many nations. Moses, arguing with Yahweh for the better part of two chapters in Exodus concerning his lack of leadership skills, becomes the great liberator of his people. David, the youngest son of a sheep-raising family, becomes

Israel's most magnificent king. Jesus, son of a poor carpenter and a young woman named Mary, is God's savior of the world. The point of this story, I want to suggest, is God has a way of doing mighty works through the lives of the most unlikely people.

Where are the crises of faith in our lives and in the lives of those with whom we live? For the lepers, there was great risk in their actions. Their very lives depended on the mercy that was shown by God in the four lepers' precarious actions and in the retreating Arameans. What dangers and opportunities are presented to your faith?

Helping Adults Become Involved

Preparing to Teach

As you read the text, imagine the story unfolding in a place of power—for instance, the war room at the Pentagon. Imagine the intensity of the nation's leadership dealing with a crisis of foreign siege and the possibility of civil riots because of the famine caused by the siege. In such a war room, ultimate seriousness reigns. What would Elisha's words sound like to such people, who feel the whole nation's destiny is in their hands?

Our lesson today is a lesson in which the characters and their perspectives shape the story. This being so, a good approach to this reading will be to explore the point of view of each of the characters. Helping your class identify the feelings and thoughts of the characters will help them get a better grasp of the action. Here is an outline to help guide you:

    I. The king suffers from doubt and despair.
    II. The king's captain speaks a word of common sense.
   III. Elisha's prophecy is a profound word of hope.
   IV. The leprous men are the unlikely bearers of good news.

As you prepare, you may want to reflect on the types of experience that cause a community to undergo crisis. How does the role of faith play a part in each character's actions in our story today?

Introducing the Main Question

As you begin your lesson, review for your class the action of 2 Kings 6:24–7:9. Then break your class into four groups and have them relate the story from the perspective of the king, the king's captain, Elisha, and the four lepers. Have each group take one character's point of view. What response of faith or doubt does the crisis in Samaria provoke from each person's outlook?

Developing the Lesson

I. The king suffers from doubt and despair.

The siege of Samaria has caused a crisis for the people. Not only are they starving, but the available food is so expensive that there is an economic crisis, as well. The king does not doubt so much the power of God, as the goodwill God has for the nation. Where does a king turn when his normal sources to solve problems are ineffective? Where are the places in our lives where we might be likely to ask, "Why should I hope in the Lord any longer?

II. The king's captain speaks a word of common sense.

In the world of the Samarians, and in ours, there is always the voice of practicality and utility. They are often dominating voices. These voices customarily suggest that only common sense should be considered in times of crisis. Ask your class to illustrate places in their own lives when they acted contrary to commonsense advice given in a particular situation. How did the unconventional solution work out to be a blessing in their lives? What powers are at work in our lives that often seem to defy common sense?

III. Elisha's prophecy is a profound word of hope.

Against all apparent odds, Elisha speaks a bold word of prophecy. Can your class name some modern predicaments when a bold word spoken in the midst of general skepticism turned out to be prophetic? Why is a deep faith necessary for those who speak an unusual and often illogical word? Has your church ever followed the lead of a prophetic voice in your congregation to do the thing for Christ that safer persons would not have risked?

IV. The leprous men are the unlikely bearers of good news.

Throughout the scripture, the people of God are led by surprising and unexpected leaders. In our lesson today, four lepers lead the people out of a severe famine. These unlikely ones are the bearers of good news. Isaiah 11:6 says, "The wolf shall live with the lamb, the leopard shall lie down with the kid, the calf and the lion and the fatling together, and a little child shall lead them." This is a picture of the messianic age and a time when God will rule absolutely. Why, in the opinion of your class, will a child lead the people? What did Jesus say about children's place in the realm of God? Are their other prophetic voices we, as a society, squelch because they seem infantile or impractical?

Helping Class Members Act

Faith in the midst of crisis is a spiritual weapon that believers have to live lives befitting the gospel. Where are the crisis points in our community and world that need the word of faith spoken? How can we as individuals and as a church speak and act prophetically in our day as Elisha did in his? What price are we willing to pay to deviate from the common sense, business-as-usual world in which we try to be disciples?

Planning for Next Sunday

Have your class members read next week's lesson, Amos 2:4-8, 3:1-2. Guilt and grace go hand in hand. What is our part in a nation under condemnation? How can we help grace become a gift that operates for the whole people of our country?

UNIT II: THE APPROACHING JUDGMENT

FIVE LESSONS   JULY 2–30

A few years ago a newspaper reported a man in Mishawaka, Indiana, was warming a T.V. dinner in the oven when bullets began to spray. Edwin Styker had hidden his .357 magnum from his children in the broiler below the oven. Indiana liberals will want to ban handguns and conservatives will want to ban men from the kitchen, the newspaper noted. Is not this the way life is? Depending on your point of view, we can cite anything to defend our point of view.

Our unit this month has to do with the theme of God's approaching judgment. Depending on your perspective, this can be seen as either a blessing or as a curse. Each prophet, though in different ways, calls the people back to the foundational doctrine of the Hebrew faith—the sovereignty of God. This doctrine says it is God who rules and overrules. God's rule reaches every part of creation and God will rule creation to completion.

Many theologians argue that the doctrine of God's sovereignty is one from which all other doctrines are derived. If this is so, then the doctrines of creation, redemption, and consummation are derived from the principal doctrine of sovereignty. The approaching judgment then can be seen as a way to discipline, nurture, or encourage people to hold fast to faith in the sovereign God of all creation.

When we think of prophets today, we may think of those iconoclastic human beings who seem to be progressive predictors of the future. In truth, however, the prophets of Israel were conservative, for they called people *back* into faithful covenant relationship with their God Yahweh. Prophets called people back to the faithful relationship that God had initiated with God's chosen people.

When we hear the word *judgment,* it is easy to hear the word as negative; but in truth, judgment to people of faith can be heard also as a word of grace. It is grace because it is a reminder about the God we worship. "I believe in God . . . maker of heaven and earth" is how we say it in the Apostle's Creed. The sovereign God we worship is the creator.

We, as Christians, reflect our relationship to the sovereign God through the crucified and risen Christ, while our Hebrew brothers and sisters reflected their relationship to God through the teachings, or Torah, of God. Either way, the important matter is that there is a way to relate to God. This is a way of redemption.

Last of all, the prophets call the people toward the hope that is held out by the sovereignty of God, and this is in the end of human history. Isaiah 65:17 puts it this way: "For I am about to create new heavens and a new earth; the former things shall not be remembered or come to mind." Our unit lessons this month all deal with faith relationship with the sovereign God.

Condemning for National Wrongs

Background Scripture: Amos 2:4-8; 3:1-2

The Main Question

One of the ways we teach children about God is to speak of God as creator. In my church each year, about one-third of the children's messages are about God, creator of the universe. A passage in Genesis 2 is one to which the children readily respond. God kneels down and fashions a little clay figure, blowing into it the breath of God, which is God's Spirit. This breath of God animates and activates. It gives life. This same Spirit or wind gives birth to the church in Acts 2:1-2: "When the day of Pentecost had come, they were all together in one place. And suddenly from heaven there came a sound like the rush of a violent wind, and it filled the entire house where they were sitting."

For the Hebrews, and for us, this creative power of God's Spirit indicates Yahweh's absolute sovereignty over creation. Amos, as well as other prophets, believed all people in God's creation were accountable to this God called Yahweh. When the people deviated from the will and ways of God they were in a state of sin. Sinning against God was to sin against their fellow human beings. Conversely, to sin against other people was to sin against God. For the Hebrew people, to be accountable to Yahweh was to be accountable to one another, and vice versa.

Today's lesson is Amos's judgment against Judah, and more emphatically against the people of Israel. In the latter part of our text, Amos catalogues the sins that the people commit against their fellow humans. What is our individual part of responsibility for our society? To what extent should we be held accountable by God for the sins of others?

Selected Scripture

King James Version

New Revised Standard Version

Amos 2:4-8, 3:1-2

4 Thus saith the LORD; For three transgressions of Judah and for four, I will not turn away *the punishment* thereof; because they have despised the law of The LORD, and have not kept his commandments, and their lies caused them to err, after the which their fathers have walked:

5 But I will send a fire upon Judah, and it shall devour the palaces of Jerusalem.

6 Thus saith the LORD; For three transgressions of Israel, and for four,

Amos 2:4-8, 3:1-2

4 Thus says the LORD:
For three transgressions of Judah,
    and for four, I will not revoke the
        punishment;
because they have rejected the law
    of the LORD,
    and have not kept his statutes,
but they have been led astray by the
    same lies
after which their ancestors walked.

5 So I will send a fire on Judah,
    and it shall devour the strongholds
        of Jerusalem.
6 Thus says the LORD:
For three transgressions of Israel,

344

I will not turn away *the punishment* thereof; because they sold the righteous for silver, and the poor for a pair of shoes;

7 That pant after the dust of the earth on the head of the poor, and turn aside the way of the meek: and a man and his father will go in unto the *same* maid, to profane my holy name:

8 And they lay *themselves* down upon clothes laid to pledge by every altar, and they drink the wine of the condemned *in* the house of their God.

....

1 Hear this word that The LORD hath spoken against you, O children of Israel, against the whole family which I brought up from the land of Egypt, saying,

2 You only have I known of all the families of the earth: therefore I will punish you for all your iniquities.

Key Verse: **You only have I known of all the families of the earth: therefore I will punish you for all your iniquities.**

and for four, I will not revoke the punishment;

because they sell the righteous for silver,
and the needy for a pair of sandals—

7 they who trample the head of the poor into the dust of the earth,
and push the afflicted out of the way;

father and son go in to the same girl,
so that my holy name is profaned;

8 they lay themselves down beside every altar
on garments taken in pledge;

and in the house of their God they drink
wine bought with fines they imposed.

....

1 Hear this word that the LORD has spoken against you, O people of Israel, against the whole family that I brought up out of the land of Egypt:

2 You only have I known
of all the families of the earth;
therefore I will punish you
for all your iniquities.

Key Verse: **You only have I known of all the families of the earth; therefore I will punish you for all your iniquities.**

As You Read the Scripture

Amos 2:4-8, 3:1-2. Today is the end of the opening prediction of judgment on the nations by Amos. In the first chapter, Amos condemns Damascus, Philistia, Tyre, and other neighbors of Israel. Then, our text follows. It is part of the judgment against Judah and Israel.

Verses 4-5. After Amos has prophesied against other nations, he turns his attention to the covenant community. Using the same prophetic formula, "Thus says the LORD," Judah receives a harsh word of judgment. For Judah, this judgment must have stung.

The judgment is because Judah has rejected the law. Even though, as chosen people, they might be exempt from God's law, this is not valid. These people, like all people, are subject to God. Fire will come to consume the strongholds of Jerusalem.

Verses 6-8. Beginning with the same prophetic formula, Amos, though an outsider to the northern tribes of Israel, nonetheless speaks a word of condemnation. The Lord will not revoke punishment, just as Amos has told the other nations.

Taking a cue from Amos's words, some of the people in Israel are so interested in making money, they sacrifice the righteous and poor. This means in Israel, judges and officials are bribed for decisions. So interested are the unrighteous authorities to gain silver they take advantage of those least likely to afford such treatment. Even the afflicted are pushed out of the way!

Even in sexual relations, there is no limit to the people's appetite. Fathers and sons have sex with the same girl. This indicates a non-Hebrew practice of temple prostitution. Father and son renounce the ethical and sexual mores of their religion, using the pretext of neighbor's worship gratifying their sexual desires. In any event, the Lord's name is profaned.

Garments taken in pledge may refer to Exodus 22:26-27, which said an outer garment taken in pledge must be returned by sundown. It may be a poor person's only protection against the cold night air. To use someone else's property for lusty pursuits, often done at night, indicates a violation of law. The wine is bought with money obtained from the poor's fines, paid to wealthy authorities. Economic inequity rules in Amos's time.

Chapter 3:1-2. Amos commands the people to listen to the Lord's condemnation spoken against them. They are the whole family—the Hebrew nation—whom God has rescued from Egypt. The Exodus story, Amos's reference here, is the story defining the Hebrew people. If they are the chosen people of God, they are accountable before God. Amos tells them this is God's word: "Therefore I will punish you for all your iniquities."

The Scripture and the Main Question

What is our individual part of responsibility for our society? To what extent should we be held accountable by God for the sins of others? These are reasonable questions for all people, but especially for those in Judah and Israel hearing the prophecy of Amos.

A Community of Faith

Judah, no less than Israel, is a people Yahweh has "brought up out of the land of Egypt" (Amos 3:1); this makes them chosen people of God. Deuteronomy, a series of Moses' departing speeches to the wandering Israelite children, emphasizes the unique relationship. Deuteronomy 26 is a ritual response that worshiping Hebrews make before the Lord: "A wandering Aramean was my ancestor; he went down into Egypt and lived there as an alien, few in number, and there he became a great nation, mighty and populous. When the Egyptians treated us harshly and afflicted us, by imposing hard labor on us, we cried to the LORD, the God of our ancestors; the LORD heard our voice and saw our affliction, our toil, and our oppression. The LORD brought us out of Egypt with a mighty hand and an outstretched arm, with a terrifying display of power, and with signs and wonders; and he brought us into this place and gave us this land, a land flowing with milk and honey" (vv. 5-9).

Holding a family together are the stories that it shares. For Israel, the Exodus story is the defining story about who they are. Interestingly, this story happens not to just a few, but to all. It was not just some, nor simply the important persons who escaped bondage, it was everyone—women, children, livestock. Exodus 12:37-38 says, "The Israelites journeyed from Rameses to Succoth, about six hundred thousand men on foot, besides children. A mixed crowd also went up with them, and livestock in great numbers, both flocks and herds." Thus, from the beginning, the Hebrews saw themselves as one people, bound by a particular story of Yahweh's intervention on their behalf.

Responsible for One Another

Today we value individualism, but in ancient times the primary social group of value was community. Today few people have extended family gatherings of more than two generations. In Amos's time, however, it was not uncommon for four generations to live under one roof. Community was as normal to the eighth century as individualism is today.

Because this community idea was prevalent, the question, "Am I my brother's keeper?" would be answered affirmatively. Twentieth-century folks are conditioned to mind our own business and to look out for number one. Illustrating the differences, there are two matters today considered private— death and marriage. "Fewer and fewer people are going to funerals these days," a friend said at the funeral home last week. He concluded, in our mobile society, people are becoming more private about things that used to be shared by everyone. Marriage is much the same. I suggested to a couple in counseling, Christian marriage is a worship rite of the church. I told them the most appropriate time for people to marry is at Sunday worship. I cannot describe the look they gave me.

During Amos's time no one missed a wedding or funeral, unless they had good reason. These were community events. Until only a few years ago, we laughed with our neighbors at a wedding's joy and wept during a funeral's grief. People are responsible for one another. We are community and we are connected.

Shared Guilt

Amos's prophetic assumption was two-fold. First, all creatures were accountable to the creator. Second, the people of Judah and Israel were also accountable for one another because they were part of the community of faith. To be accountable for someone is to be responsible for them. This is the rub of Amos's prophecy: In this community of faith, shared responsibility also means shared guilt. No one in this community of faith—Judah or Israel—can say, "Your end of the lifeboat is sinking." As in the Exodus event, they are in covenant together.

In our day, we are still all in it together. Once white suburbia could say drug problems were only in the inner cities. Now, few communities having fewer than 2,000 people can say they have no concern with drugs. Crime, AIDS, the national debt, the national health crisis, and a multitude of common predicaments show us that few problems are so isolated they do not concern all of us.

I saw a poster on a college professor's door. It quoted Martin Niemoller, a Protestant theologian and pastor in Germany during World War II. His quote summarizes well the idea that all of us are responsible for one another. In a rough paraphrase, it said, when the Nazi came for the Jews, he did nothing. When the Nazi came for the Communists, and the trade unionists, Niemoller did nothing. When they came for him, no one was left to stand up for him.

FOURTH QUARTER

Faith Community as an Alternative Community

What is our individual part of responsibility for our society? To what extent should we be held accountable by God for the sins of others? If these were pertinent questions for Amos's people, then they are for us, as well. A conviction exists within the Christian community that we are united in Christ; responsible for and to one another. In the baptismal liturgy of my denomination, parents and blood relatives make vows on an infant's behalf—but so does the church! In fact, when anyone has a problem with another church member, I occasionally hear, "Since we are joined together by our baptism, what do you think . . . ?"

Amos called a whole people to repentance, not an isolated few. Amos knew, as a community of faith, the people were necessarily responsible for one another. This, for Amos, was what it meant to be a faith community, a covenant community.

Helping Adults Become Involved

Preparing to Teach

This lesson's aim is to understand and to take responsibility for one another as God's children. Israel and Judah both have a distinct relationship to Yahweh. To prepare for the lesson, consult a Bible dictionary to find out about Amos's century, before the fall of Samaria in 721 B.C.E. This simple outline will help you work through the material:

I. God will judge all people.
II. Israel stands in a unique relationship to God.
III. Amos's prophecy has a timeliness ring about it.

There will be instances in current events where many seem to pay the price for a few. Your class will readily respond to these issues, and, perhaps, in emotional ways. None of us ever lives in isolation, however, so Amos's concerns for the community of faith will be our concerns. How can a whole nation be under indictment for the transgressions of a few? Do the righteous, sold for silver, also stand under condemnation from God? These are questions you will want to be prepared either to raise or to address with your class. They are not easy questions, either!

Introducing the Main Question

What is our responsibility for community? Amos prophesied to the whole nation, yet condemned the powerful. To what extent should we be held accountable for the sin of others? These questions can be lifted up as someone from your class reads the text for today: Amos 2:4-8, 3:1-2. How are we accountable for the leaders we elect to local, state, and national governments?

Developing the Lesson

I. God will judge all people.

Judgment has traditionally been a source of anxiety for people, possibly because we are motivated primarily by fear. School teachers tell me that even though the motivational hammer in schools—the grade—is not the force it used to be, it is still better than anything else. Looking at our criminal justice system, one has to wonder if fear of jail is a deterrent to crime. Unfortunately, not many preferable notions have surfaced.

The truth is we are all judged or evaluated daily. This daily evaluation comes in two ways: formal and informal. Formal evaluations (or judgments) are occasions like final grades or sentencing before a judge. Informal evaluations are less anxiety producing, but can be just as serious. Do I like the way a certain product works? Do I respect the way my senator has performed these past six year? Is my pastor faithful to the call to ministry? Whether we like it or not, we all are judged regularly, as we constantly evaluate, too.

Amos's point to the people is this: God judges people based on faithfulness. In Israel's and Judah's cases, we could understand God's judgment as an evaluation of their devotion to covenant with God. Unfortunately, this word *judgment* is typically understood only in its negative connotations. There is, I believe, a gracious side to judgment. Commonly, it is the inadequate and unprepared student who fears grades. Likewise, if the justice system is just, then it is those who transgress society's laws and statutes who have reason to tremble.

The scripture is filled with stories of God's judgment, tempered by God's grace. In Genesis, two stories about Yahweh bear this out. First, after the so-called fall of humankind, divine curses are delivered to the human creatures. God grants the humans death, releasing them from the curses' eternal bondage (Genesis 2–3). Yes, they will have pain in childbirth and will toil to eat; but not forever. They are graciously freed from the curses at death. This is a novel view of death today, but the case can be made from the perspective of faith and the scripture.

Cain's mark, too, is a sign of grace. "Then the LORD said to him, 'Not so! Whoever kills Cain will suffer a sevenfold vengeance.' And the LORD put a mark on Cain, so that no one who came upon him would kill him" (Gen. 4:15).

In the experience of your class, has something happened that was initially experienced as an absolute negative, but, later in retrospect, turned out to be a blessing? Take some time in class to reflect on this question.

II. Israel stands in a unique relationship to God.

What makes Judah and Israel unique? Why does Amos pick these nations for particularly harsh judgment? The answers to these questions hinge on the distinction that Israel is not like other nations. Israel is a special people, a people chosen by God to be, as another eighth-century prophet will say, "a light to the nations." Isaiah 42:6 says, "I am the LORD, I have called you in righteousness, I have taken you by the hand and kept you; I have given you as a covenant to the people, a light to the nations." Thus, Israel's obligation to live as a covenant people of God has to do with her unique status as a chosen people.

There had been times in Israel's history when this status was understood to be solely a privilege. To Amos, however, being the chosen people is rather an assignment and obligation. With the honor also comes responsibility and sacrifice. These are not simply people in the conventional sense of the word—these are the people of God.

In Hebrews 3, a striking contrast is made between Moses and Jesus as the Christ. "Now Moses was faithful in all God's house as a servant, to testify to the things that would be spoken later. Christ, however, was faithful over God's house as a son" (Heb. 3:5-6a). The difference between son and servant is in the relationship. One is the legal heir, the other is not. In the heir's relationship there is a degree of privilege. WIth the privilege, however, comes the matching degree of responsibility.

Ask your class if they have ever used the phrase, "because you're the oldest, that's why," with their children. Or have they ever caught themselves saying, "I don't care if everyone else does it, this is not the kind of thing *we* do?" These phrases, as well as many others, could start a discussion about the privileges and obligations of standing for beliefs setting people apart. This, by the way, is a good definition of being sanctified. The sanctified are those who stand apart.

III. Amos's prophecy has a timeless ring about it.

In Amos's prophetic declaration in chapters 1 and 2, Judah and Israel receive separate judgments unlike other nations. This is because the chosen people are set apart. They are different from other nations. Amos makes explicit reference to the story of these people—the liberation from Egypt. He calls Israel the family brought up out of the land of Egypt. This is the story that makes this clan different. As Amos recalls this distinctive relationship with God, the intent is to tell Israel again of its place in God's scheme of history.

Remembering is a powerful tool in thinking about who we are. Every family has certain rituals setting it apart from other families. It may be a special vacation spot the family visits every summer, a vacation place and time helping the family define who it is. Christmas is another ritual occasion drawing us together as a family. In our family, for instance, we always met at my grandparents' house on Thanksgiving. My first Thanksgiving away from home seemed strange because I missed the ritual that made Thanksgiving, Thanksgiving for me.

The church, too, has rituals reminding us of our roots and traditions. At baptism, the church gathers around the font, making promises for the person baptized and reaffirming promises we have made to God. At Holy Communion, we "do this in remembrance" of Christ. When we forget who we are, we forget God's power. How does a church celebrate the story defining who we are as a people of God? Ask your class to name some rites of remembrance in your own church. How do you assimilate people into your church's continuing story?

Helping Class Members Act

Tagging onto the questions above, ask the newer members of your class what events in the life of this church made them feel as if they belonged. Encourage the class to plan ways making new people welcome. How is being a steward of hospitality both a difficult and a simple thing churches ask of their members?

Planning for Next Sunday

Have your class read the lesson for next Sunday from Amos 4:4-5, 5:18-24. Have them reflect on whether any of us really want to see God's justice.

Working for Justice and Righteousness

Background Scripture: Amos 4:4-5; 5:18-24

The Main Question

Some years ago I was a student-intern, teaching in the Gbarnga School of Theology in Liberia, West Africa. On weekends, the student pastors would invite me to preach in their churches. It was, of course, an honor and I went as I was asked, often in bush churches, far off the motor road. I preached in English, which would then be translated into their indigenous language.

In one remote village, I remember preaching a spirited sermon in English, wondering at the time if anyone really knew what I was saying. After the service an old and animated woman came up to me and said something excitedly in the Pelli language. The translator told me, "She said, 'You really preached a great sermon.'" How did she know that, really? She had not understood a word I said, only hearing through a third-party translator. Could the Spirit be working? I thought to myself.

Acts 2 has this same quality. The Spirit is poured out on the people and they understand others' languages: Parthians, Medes, Elamites, and residents of Mesopotamia, Judea, and Cappadocia, Pontus, and Asia (Acts 2:9). Then, Peter preaches a sermon, and as I read it I wonder what makes the preaching so powerful, for it is only the simple message of the gospel. Nothing particularly awe-inspiring happened, no healings or miracles. Yet, about three thousand were baptized and their souls were added (Acts 2:41).

My experience in Liberia is sometimes duplicated in my church in Texas. After a sermon I have not been terrible satisfied with, someone will later tell me it has been important in their life. Many preachers can share this story, too. There are moments when, not because of us, but in spite of us, the word of God is heard profoundly. Perhaps it is simply a combination of music, prayer, and sacrifice of thanksgiving. Whatever it is, we can point to the Spirit, moving in human worship, and give thanks.

Every worship experience should announce two things. First, what God has done for us, and second, what God is doing for us. Those who wait for the Lord in faithful anticipation, know the God they worship will be merciful and just. This is faithful hope.

In our lesson today, Amos poses an interesting question as he asked the people: "Why do you want the day of the LORD?" To the faithful, it is a strange question, for we expect good things from God. God's day is our day. Amos, however, knows the people have not been faithful. Therefore, the question he asks, though outwardly one of hope, is in reality a statement of judgment.

Do people want the Lord today? Would the Lord now find our worship and discipleship to be faithful? Amos's question for his people is also one for us, too.

FOURTH QUARTER

Selected Scripture

King James Version

Amos 4:4-5; 5:18-24

4 Come to Bethel, and transgress; at Gilgal multiply transgression; and bring your sacrifices every morning, *and* your tithes after three years;

5 And offer a sacrifice of thanksgiving with leaven, and proclaim *and* publish the free offerings: for this liketh you, O ye children of Israel, saith the Lord GOD.

....

18 Woe unto you that desire the day of the LORD! to what end *is* it for you? the day of The LORD *is* darkness, and not light.

19 As if a man did flee from a lion, and a bear met him; or went into the house, and leaned his hand on the wall, and a serpent bit him.

20 *Shall* not the day of the LORD *be* darkness, and not light? even very dark, and no brightness in it?

21 I hate, I despise your feast days, and I will not smell in your solemn assemblies.

22 Though ye offer me burnt offerings and your meat offerings, I will not accept *them*: neither will I regard the peace offerings of your fat beasts.

23 Take thou away from me the noise of thy songs; for I will not hear the melody of thy viols.

24 But let judgment run down as waters, and righteousness as a mighty stream.

Key Verse: **But let judgment run down as waters, and righteousness as a mighty stream.**

New Revised Standard Version

Amos 4:4-5; 5:18-24

4 Come to Bethel—and transgress; to Gilgal—and multiply transgression; bring your sacrifices every morning, your tithes every three days;

5 bring a thank-offering of leavened bread, and proclaim freewill offerings, publish them; for so you love to do, O people of Israel!

says the Lord GOD.

....

18 Alas for you who desire the day of the LORD! Why do you want the day of the LORD? It is darkness, not light;

19 as if someone fled from a lion, and was met by a bear; or went into the house and rested a hand against the wall, and was bitten by a snake.

20 Is not the day of the LORD darkness, not light, and gloom with no brightness in it?

21 I hate, I despise your festivals, and I take no delight in your solemn assemblies.

22 Even though you offer me your burnt offerings and grain offerings, I will not accept them; and the offerings of well-being of your fatted animals I will not look upon.

23 Take away from me the noise of your songs; I will not listen to the melody of your harps.

24 But let justice roll down like waters, and righteousness like an ever-flowing stream.

Key Verse: **But let justice roll down like waters, and righteousness like an everflowing stream.**

As You Read the Scripture

Amos 4:4-5. In this lesson, these two verses set the stage for the denouncing prophecy, because Amos sees the test of true faith in the sanctuary.

Verse 4. "Come to Bethel—and transgress" is a jarring jab at worshipers who have come to the sanctuary. Many scholars believe Amos's prophetic words were delivered at Bethel. It was at Bethel, which in Hebrew means "house of God," where Jacob had his ladder dream, fleeing his brother (Gen. 28). The irony is that at Bethel the people would be called to transgress, rather than the worship invitation they doubtless expected.

Gilgal was another sacred worship center in Amos's time. The terms used in verse 4 are startling in context. The people are invited to come, but then told to "transgress . . . and multiply transgression." These terms are sprinkled among other worship phrases, like "sacrifices" and "tithes every three days," indicating worshipers piously oversubscribe in excessive sacrifice. Amos's intention was to shock the people, declaring the truth of their worship. To Amos, it was not worship.

Verse 5. The denouncement of worship continues. The people bring thank-offerings and proclaim freewill offerings, which are individual acts of ritual worship. From an outside perspective, this looks holy and righteous, but Amos cuts to the people's intention. Worship is for show. The people seem to be interested in the worship's public relations aspect. Amos says coldly: "Publish them; for so you love to do!"

Chapter 5:18-24. These seven verses are Amos's call for justice and righteousness. They delineate the sins of the people in detail.

Verses 18-20. Amos begins with a woe, saying, "Alas for you who desire the day of the LORD!" It will not be what they expect. It will be a day of darkness and fear. He then uses the analogy of the people running from one disaster—a lion—only to be met by something worse—a bear.

The people think they want the day of the Lord, but it will be a day calling their sanctuary motives into account. The people have not worshipped in their hearts, only in their desire to be seen as pious through outward observance of sanctuary ritual. Again he tells them that the Lord's day will be darkness and gloom, not the brightness they complacently await.

Verse 21. Amos tells the people Yahweh "hates and despises" their ritual observances, which are not motivated by a love of God, but rather their own self-seeking standing in the community. "I take no delight" can be literally translated "I do not like the smell of," a reference to the rising sacrificial smoke. Their solemn assemblies stink to God's nose, according to Amos.

Verses 22-23. Yahweh totally rejects the people's offerings, for they are given in bad faith. Yahweh will not regard them. The intensity is seen in the detailed offerings not accepted. In fact, the noise of their songs and the music of their instruments is to be removed from the Lord's presence.

Verse 24. Finally, Amos now suggests what the Lord wants—justice and righteousness. It is for the worshipers, piously in the sanctuary, to be in right relationship with other people. Both righteousness and justice imply relations with persons—and these others may be outside sanctuary worship. They are spoken of explicitly at Amos 8:4, "Hear this, you that trample on the needy, and bring to ruin the poor of the land." Those who do evil to the needy are the ones worshiping with suspect piety.

The Scripture and the Main Question

Amos asks the people of Israel, the Northern Kingdom, "Why do you want the day of the LORD?" (Amos 5:18). Do modern people want the Lord today? Would the Lord find our worship and discipleship faithful? Or would Yahweh find in our worship the attitude of those in the sanctuaries of Bethel and Gilgal?

Parallels with Today

Many scholars believe the book of Amos is in nearly the original words Amos authentically prophesied, these words being either recorded by Amos himself, or by some of his devoted followers. In fact, this book is the oldest book from Hebrew scripture in its present form. Therefore, we can have confidence the words from our lesson were actually the kinds of words Amos delivered to his hearers—bold words indeed!

During the reign of Jeroboam II in Israel, relative prosperity prevailed for the covenant people. For the briefest time, the nation faced threats from neither great power on its borders. Both Assyria and Egypt were dealing with internal problems, hence not eyeing the expansion of territory, as was their wont. Being left alone for a time, Israel spent its energy on domestic policies and on the pursuits peace allowed.

Today in the United States, we can see the same situation. The Cold War, which our nation has been both physically and psychologically preoccupied with for forty years, was brought to an end when the Soviet Union dissolved. This vast nation is now broken into a multitude of smaller independent states. All of Eastern Europe has changed geographically and politically. No longer is our nation's foreign policy tied to defending the world against communism. We now, for the first time in two decades, have the luxury of attending to other matters. With no common enemy, which the USSR and Eastern Europe had provided, we find ourselves ironically at odds with ourselves. Many in our nation, however, are complacent with respect to the plight of our own people.

Several years ago, I saw a cartoon depicting this attitude of complacency, to which Amos's prophecy was directed almost three thousand years ago. The cartoon parodies a view of Los Angeles' riots that began with the acquittal of the police in the Rodney King matter of 1992. In the first frame, Uncle Sam is watching the reports on television and says, "I remember the Watts riot."

In the second and third frames he says, "I saw it the next day on my ten-inch black and white TV. This time I taped on a remote-activated digital VCR, direct from six simulcast live-feeds and watched on a new high-resolution forty-inch split-screen color monitor with surround sound." The last frame has Uncle Sam think, "Talk about progress . . . !" (*New York Times,* Sunday, May 17, 1992, page 4E). This political cartoon articulates, though we may see predicaments differently, that the economic and social problems every society faces are essentially the same. It was to these problems Amos leveled his prophetic dynamite.

A Frenzy of Church Activity

When one thinks of Amos's criticism, it may strike us as odd. The people seemed to be at worship and, after all, they did tithe every third day. I am certain the people of Israel considered themselves pious and righteous people. They attended festivals and frequented the places of worship. What more could they do? No wonder they anticipated the day of the Lord.

Do we want the Lord today? Would the Lord find our worship and discipleship faithful? This is a pertinent question, I suggest, given the types of secular promotion in which many churches engage. A popular book among pastors in the early 1980s was a book that told forty-odd ways to boost church attendance. Of course, boosting attendance is not necessarily bad, but sometimes we stoop so low to appeal to people's interests that we forget what we have to offer foremost is the word of God.

I learned early in my ministry, the church will be asked to sponsor a wide variety of activities, only some of which further the realm of God. I was appalled once, when an insurance agent asked me if he could call all the members of my church and tell them it was my idea because "we" wanted to help them. He was disturbed when I started laughing out loud. What else?

Another area of the church's life that is particularly disgraceful is the fall budget drive. You may know what I am speaking about. Churches appeal to a wide collection of interests, many having nothing to do with Christ's gospel. We give only because God first gave to us. This is at the core of Christian stewardship. Yet, often we are asked to think of the benefits the church provides us an individuals as something like a T.V. advertisement. This is not Christian stewardship: This is twentieth-century consumerism. Do people want the Lord today?

A wise pastor told me to evaluate anything the church does by this question: Does it further the gospel or not? If it does not, then do not attempt it. God will not be with you. Thus, when thinking of any program in our church, be it music, education, counseling, or youth, we always ask this question: Does it further the gospel of Jesus Christ?

Focus on God—Not Us

Amos seems to hit the prophetic nail on the head when he says, "Bring a thank-offering of leavened bread, and proclaim freewill offerings, publish them; for so you love to do, O people of Israel!" In other words, these sacrifices and offerings are not given out of love, but for self-congratulations. They say, to Amos's thinking, look how faithful and generous *we* are! Worship done in this attitude is an abomination. When one loves the act done in God's name more than God, then it is not done in good faith. It is what we can call good old-fashioned hypocrisy.

Jesus had something to say about good deeds as acts of faith. He says, "Beware of practicing your piety before others in order to be seen by them . . . whenever you give alms, do not sound a trumpet before you, as the hypocrites do in the synagogues and in the streets, so that they may be praised by others. Truly I tell you, they have received their reward. But when you give alms, do not let your left hand know what your right hand is doing" (Matt. 6:1-3). These are true acts of charity, for they are done out of love for God.

The problem for the people of Israel was not that their worship was not in proper liturgical form, because from the text in Amos it is obvious that it was. The problem was the perspective the people brought with them to worship, the same attitude carried from worship, as well. Our unfaithful worship on Sunday can lead to unfaithful living on Monday.

No Substitute for Justice

Amos asks the pointed question: Why do you want the day of the Lord? The day of the Lord is to be anticipated as a day of light and joy for the people of God. Yet, Amos guarantees them that as they run from a ferocious lion they will encounter a bear. As the people rest their hand on a wall they will be bitten by a snake. The day of the Lord will be a day of gloom, with no brightness. This reversal of expectation is Amos's intent. In reading this prophecy, one is not sure whether it is too late for the people. Do they still have time to repent?

If this alternative is still open, then the last verse will prove instructive. Amos 5:24 says, "But let justice roll down like waters, and righteousness like an everflowing stream." This may mean God's justice and righteousness will soon descend upon these faithless people of Israel. But an alternative understanding can be, if Israel repents, then they can do justice and righteousness toward the needy.

This is where true God-centered worship plays its most important role. True worship shapes worshipers to be the people of God—respecting all persons and their inherent worth in God's eyes. I have a doctor friend who told me a story about his life in the church. He had a long-haired brother who was an acolyte in the Lutheran church. Some of the people on the church's altar guild thought the young man should not be allowed to participate in worship until he cut his hair. This caused quite a stir.

But the pastor interceded saying, "Folks, there is a picture of another long-haired fellow out there in the hall and we call him Savior. I think the boy's heart is right with the Lord and that's all that matters to God, regardless of how bad his haircut looks to us." The doctor concluded, "That pastor's integrity sold me on church. Because he was willing to put up then with a lot of torment for my brother, I love the church today."

Helping Adults Become Involved

Preparing to Teach

Human worship is always a response to the word God has first given us. As you prepare for the lesson, which is about true worship of God, think about different responses worship calls believers to make. Many of our people will be surprised to consider Amos, this most incendiary prophet, as one who understands worship as foundational to right living before God. Many of our people understand worship as something of an alternative to the Christian life. You might address why worship was so vital to Amos and his prophecy. You may find this outline helpful:

I. People can rebel—even in worship.
II. Sabbath is a faithful key to the believer's week.
III. God does not want people's sacrifices as much as their hearts.
IV. Faithful relationship with God is paramount.

Since Amos's prophecy is only nine chapters long, read the whole prophecy. It will be time well spent.

Introducing the Main Question

Begin your class with a prayer. Then, read the whole lesson, picking out questions Amos asks the people of Israel for emphasis. You might ask these same questions, but cast them in a twentieth-century light. Do we want the Lord today? Do we anticipate the day of the Lord, or do we fear it?

Developing the Lesson

I. People can rebel—even in worship.

I often hear people make assessments of worship on the basis of whether one likes something or not. This is typical of our culture, which evaluates everything on the grounds of whether it suits our tastes or not. Our whole society is one of shoppers. Regularly I visit people who are church-shopping and hear this question, "What can your church do for me?" I have visited few people who said, "What can we do for our Lord in your church?"

Should worship be entertainment or not? Are there elements of worship that are so important in your church, it does not matter whether they are entertaining or not? Spend some class time discussing why and how people in your church rebel against worship.

II. Sabbath is a faithful key to the believer's week.

Amos believed one's worship experience should equip them to live godly lives the rest of the week—in the marketplace or among the poor. Just going through the motions of ritual worship was not enough for Amos. The people's hearts must be changed by the Sabbath worship experience. How does your church change lives through its ministry of worship? What Sabbath worship elements speak best to class members in their discipleship? Ask them how they prepare for Sabbath worship. Make a list on your chalkboard of the most meaningful aspects of worship and the least meaningful. Why do you think some parts of worship speak to us profoundly, and not to others? Is your Sabbath holy?

III. God does not want people's sacrifices as much as their hearts.

Amos's prophecy makes quite clear it is not the outward form God is as concerned with, as much as the inward hearts of the people. In every worship service there are several places we are asked to respond with our lives to God. Let your class name some of these, discussing why they are particularly important to them. Also talk about why baptism is a community event. Why is it so important to celebrate baptism within the context of Christian worship? What does the class think? Does your pastor ever celebrate private baptisms—why or why not?

IV. Faithful relationship with God is paramount.

Over and over again in scripture, we see the principle that God wants to be in relationship with God's people. The creation story makes this abundantly clear, as does the whole Exodus story of Israel. Ask your class to think about this idea from Amos's perspective. How does worship continue to bind God's people to God? Also, how is right living, that is, being just toward others and being righteous toward God, reflected in our worship? Do we want the day of the Lord? Do we worship God as if we did?

Helping Class Members Act

After you have shared, as a class, these questions about worship and working for justice and righteousness, ask them to take these questions with them to worship. Encourage them to jot down any thoughts or feelings they have while in your church's worship services. Is worship a central act of faith in your church?

Planning for Next Sunday

The lesson for next week comes from the prophecy of Hosea. Ask your class to read the lesson from Hosea 1:2-9 and 3:1-5, and reflect on how they would respond if Yahweh asked them to take a spouse out of harlotry.

LESSON 7   JULY 16

Demonstrating Undeserved Love

Background Scripture: Hosea 1:2-9; 3:1-5

The Main Question

Fifty percent of first marriages fail in the United States today. Worse yet, 60 percent of second marriages fail and 70 percent of third trips to the matrimonial altar end in failure. Fourth marriages have little statistical chance to survive at all. Some have even given up on marriage altogether, so the statistics seem to indicate. A few years ago 5 percent of our adult population never married, today the figure is close to 10 percent.

Numbers do not tell everything about human life, but they do give indications about how people behave in certain circumstances. Another disturbing trend in the figures about marriage is that over half of marriage breakdowns are caused by one of the marriage partners getting involved sexually with someone other than their spouse. This behavior in twentieth-century marriage is in marked contrast to the teaching of scripture, at least as interpreted by the church's tradition. A text often quoted as God's blessing on the marriage covenant says, "So God created humankind in his image . . . male and female he created them. God blessed them, and God said to them, 'Be fruitful and multiply, and fill the earth' " (Gen. 1:27-28).

The church has always, perhaps naively, assumed the vows taken in marriage were vows for life. The Roman Catholic Church, for instance, observes holy matrimony as one of seven sacraments. Though most Protestants do not elevate marriage to sacramental status, one could say with confidence that the failure in marriage today is a grave concern for all churches. The detrimental effects of failed marriages have been felt among children, families, and our entire society.

In our lesson today, Hosea's troubled marriage covenant is a living illustration of the troubled covenant relationship between Yahweh and the people of Israel. This illustration, nearly three-thousand years old, is a mirror to the troubles people today have in keeping not only their covenant promises to one another, but also their covenant promises before God.

Why do we have trouble with the commitments we make to other persons? How do these human failures indicate our failure to keep the promises we make to God? Since many of us suffer from broken relationships, why is it so difficult to remain faithful, particularly when we know the pain of broken covenantal promises? Can we learn to forgive in Christian love? What, if anything, can we learn today from Hosea's life and prophecy?

Selected Scripture

King James Version

New Revised Standard Version

Hosea 1:2-9; 3:1-5

2 The beginning of the word of the LORD by Hosea. And the LORD said to Hosea, Go, take unto thee a wife of whoredoms and children of whoredoms: for the land hath committed great whoredom, *departing* from the LORD.

3 So he went and took Gomer the daughter of Diblaim; which conceived, and bare him a son.

4 And the LORD said unto him, Call his name Jezreel; for yet a little *while,* and I will avenge the blood of Jezreel upon the house of Jehu, and will cause to cease the kingdom of the house of Israel.

5 And it shall come to pass at that day, that I will break the bow of Israel in the valley of Jezreel.

6 And she conceived again, and bare a daughter. And *God* said unto him, Call her name Loruhamah: for I will no more have mercy upon the house of Israel; but I will utterly take them away.

7 But I will have mercy upon the house of Judah, and will save them by the LORD their God, and will not save them by bow, nor by sword, nor by battle, by horses, nor by horsemen.

8 Now when she had weaned Loruhamah, she conceived, and bare a son.

9 Then said *God,* Call his name Loammi: for ye *are* not my people, and I will not be your *God.*

....

1 Then said the LORD unto me, Go yet, love a woman beloved of *her* friend, yet an adulteress, according to the love of the LORD toward the

Hosea 1:2-9; 3:1-5

2 When the LORD first spoke through Hosea, the LORD said to Hosea, "Go, take for yourself a wife of whoredom and have children of whoredom, for the land commits great whoredom by forsaking the LORD." 3 So he went and took Gomer daughter of Diblaim, and she conceived and bore him a son.

4 And the LORD said to him, "Name him Jezreel; for in a little while I will punish the house of Jehu for the blood of Jezreel, and I will put an end to the kingdom of the house of Israel. 5 On that day I will break the bow of Israel in the valley of Jezreel."

6 She conceived again and bore a daughter. Then the LORD said to him, "Name her Loruhamah, for I will no longer have pity on the house of Israel or forgive them. 7 But I will have pity on the house of Judah, and I will save them by the LORD their God; I will not save them by bow, or by sword, or by war, or by horses, or by horsemen."

8 When she had weaned Loruhamah, she conceived and bore a son. 9 Then the LORD said, "Name him Loammi, for you are not my people and I am not your God."

....

1 The LORD said to me again, "Go, love a woman who has a lover and is an adulteress, just as the LORD loves the people of Israel, though they

children of Israel, who look to other gods, and love flagons of wine.

2 So I bought her to me for fifteen *pieces* of silver, and *for* an homer of barley, and an half homer of barley:

3 And I said unto her, Thou shalt abide for me many days; thou shalt not play the harlot, and thou shalt not be for *another* man: so *will* I also *be* for thee.

4 For the children of Israel shall abide many days without a king, and without a prince, and without a sacrifice, and without an image, and without an ephod, and *without* teraphim:

5 Afterward shall the children of Israel return, and seek the LORD their God, and David their king; and shall fear the LORD and his goodness in the latter days.

turn to other gods and love raisin cakes." 2 So I bought her for fifteen shekels of silver and a homer of barley and a measure of wine. 3 And I said to her, "You must remain as mine for many days; you shall not play the whore, you shall not have intercourse with a man, nor I with you." 4 For the Israelites shall remain many days without king or prince, without sacrifice or pillar, without ephod or teraphim. 5 Afterward the Israelites shall return and seek the LORD their God, and David their king; they shall come in awe to the LORD and to his goodness in the latter days.

Key Verse (Hosea 2:19): **And I will betroth thee unto me for ever; yea, I will betroth thee unto me in righteousness, and in judgment, and in lovingkindness, and in mercies.**

Key Verse (Hosea 2:19): **And I will take you for my wife forever; I will take you for my wife in righteousness and in justice, in steadfast love, and in mercy.**

As You Read the Scripture

Hosea 1:2-9. This section of our lesson today states the main theme of Hosea's whole prophecy: Israel has been unfaithful to God as if Israel were a wayward spouse. The prophecy also will make plain, through Hosea's words, what God proposes to do about this state of Israel's faithlessness.

Verse 2. The first phrase, "when the LORD first spoke through Hosea," can be literally translated, "the beginning of the word of Yahweh through Hosea." The prophecy will be enacted through the life and words of the prophet, showing Yahweh's complete claim on Hosea. Most scholars see this relationship with "a wife of whoredom" as not literal, but allegorical. However the phrase is understood, it is a total indictment of Israel, "for the land commits great whoredom by forsaking the LORD."

Verse 3. The text indicates no questions from Hosea. He simply "took Gomer daughter of Diblaim." Our questions abound: Was she a Canaanite cult prostitute or a common street-walker? In either case, she was to portray Israel's harlotry against Yahweh.

Verses 4-5. Israelite children's naming was a sacred act and occasionally names were given by Yahweh (see Gen. 17:19; Isa. 8:3; and Matt. 1:21). Jezreel, in Hebrew means, "God sows or plants." The beauty of this garden-like spot called Jezreel contrasts with the bloodshed occurring there. Was this another garden of perfection (Eden) trashed by human failure? (See 2 Kings 9–10.)

Verses 6-7. The children's names get progressively worse as a daughter is born, to be called Lo-ruhamah, meaning "no pity." In other words, this name with the negative Hebrew prefix *lo,* intimates Yahweh will no longer have compassion, for *ruhamah* means mercy or compassion. Judah is, at this time at least, not under the judgment. But notice Judah will not be saved by bow, sword, or horsemen—only, as Yahweh says, "I will save them by the LORD their God." The relationship with God saves.

Verses 8-9. The last child will be a son named Lo-ammi, meaning "not my people." Not only are the people chastened by the first two names of Hosea's children. The people have been cut off from God in a final double statement. First, they are not God's people. Second, Yahweh is no longer their God. The naming of the children represents a terrible progression: no pleasant land, no compassion or mercy from God, and last, no God whatsoever.

Chapter 3:1-5. On the heels of this obviously devastating prophecy, chapter 3 begins on a more hope-filled note, with yet another word from the Lord. This word is the reforming or redemption of Gomer—and thus, for the whole people.

Verse 1. Again, Yahweh commands Hosea to love a woman. Given the consistency of the prophecy, this woman is in all likelihood Gomer. Hosea is to love her as Yahweh loves Israel, which is totally and unconditionally, in spite of continual deceit.

Verses 2-3. He buys her back for a price, "fifteen shekels of silver and a homer of barley and a measure of wine." Was she bought as a prostitute or as a slave? The text is silent, though Hosea chastises her severely, setting new boundaries for the new relationship between them. These are the conditions of the restoration of the marriage covenant.

Verses 4-5. These last verses are commentary about Israel's conditions on reentering the covenant with Yahweh. Israel will be deprived of kings, sacrifices, and other Baal worship elements that had crept into Yahweh worship. This deprivation would be for a time, then afterward presumably, the people would return to full status "in awe to the LORD."

The Scripture and the Main Question

Marriage as a Model of Faith

The analogy of the marriage relationship to Israel's relationship with God is one having a long history. One reason for this analogy is that marriage is a pervasive human relationship, transcending cultures with a rare tenacity among human institutions. Though human sexuality is strong, so too are stable family relations.

George Whitefield and John Wesley struggled with the demands of their ministries over and against the demand of marriage. In both cases, their marriages suffered, though their ministries thrived. Peter had a wife, but Paul, knowing the time was short and the demands of itineracy potent, chose singleness. Many pastors today struggle with this conflict between family at home and family at church. The self-revealing deliberations of these saints of the church, Whitefield, Wesley, Peter, and Paul, stand in marked contrast to many modern people's approach to marriage. I have often heard in premarital counseling phrases such as, "We'll try it awhile and see how it works out. Don't worry about us, Pastor. We know what we are doing." Unfortunately, those harboring these attitudes typically stop by an attorney's office later. Did they really know what they were doing? Do any of us?

Why do the commitments we make to other persons give us such grief? How do our failures with other people indicate our failure with respect to the promises we make to God? Since many of us suffer from broken relationships, why is it so difficult to remain faithful, especially when we know the pain of broken covenantal promises? Can we learn to forgive in Christian love? What, if anything, can Hosea's life and prophecy teach us?

Hosea's Prophecy to Israel

During the time of Hosea's ministry, four kings were assassinated in fourteen years. Hosea prophesied for twenty-five years, beginning in Jeroboam II's prosperous reign. During Israel's history, people relied on combining Yahweh worship with Baal worship. This was a continuing problem, seen in the prophets' messages between Solomon's death and Samaria's fall. Hosea's message concerns this covenant breakdown with Yahweh.

Hosea 4:2-6 puts the situation graphically, "Swearing, lying, and murder, and stealing and adultery break out; bloodshed follows bloodshed . . . with you is my contention, O priest. You shall stumble by day; the prophet also shall stumble with you by night. . . . My people are destroyed for lack of knowledge; because you have rejected knowledge, I reject you from being a priest to me. And since you have forgotten the law of your God, I also will forget your children." The people forgot Yahweh—even the religious leaders—the priests and prophets!

Marriage Covenant: Faith Covenant

I cherish celebrating a service of marriage—and the marriage service *is* worship. I relish watching the bride and groom's families and friends gather in the sanctuary. Most of them have known either the bride or groom longer than the bride and groom have known each other. During the vows, I often survey the family and friends as the couple says, "for better, for worse; for richer, for poorer; in sickness and in health, till death us do part." I do not always hear snickers, but I usually see smirks. Family and friends know these making the sacred vows. Many are skeptical these holy promises will be faithfully kept. Those gathered certainly do not always act as though the couple knows what they are doing. Such is our society's jaded attitude toward long-term promises. We have all been disappointed too often. Perhaps the reason is closer at hand: We remember in pain our own broken promises.

I recall my bishop, McFerrin Stowe, asking me the traditional Wesleyan ministerial question, with no sense of irony whatsoever, "Do you expect to be made perfect in love in this life?" I replied, with awkward irony, "Yes, sir!" We know the tenuous nature of human vows, whether before God in ordination or not. Whether at confirmation, accepting our vows as adults, or at baptism promises made for us as infants, or whether our vows are membership promises, pledging loyalty to the church with presence, prayers, gifts, and service, we know too well these promises are much too big for any of us to assume without fear and trembling. I want to suggest God knows this, as well. These sacred promises are ones taking us a lifetime to grow into, not fitting now, but maybe later. Only by grace we can grow into them. This is the hope with which one makes such holy promises.

The Church as the Bride of Christ

The church's scripture has employed the symbol of the church as bride of Christ. One place in Hebrew scripture connecting God and his people symbolically in marriage is Jeremiah 2:2. "Go and proclaim in the hearing of Jerusalem, Thus says the LORD: I remember the devotion of your youth, your love as a bride, how you followed me in the wilderness." The faithful people's early devotion was that of a new bride, brimming with love and devotion. They were willing to go through the desert as a sign of this reverence. Of course, in Jeremiah's time, as in Hosea's, the people have fallen far short of their former loving commitment.

Hosea's prophetic theme, in New Testament garb, is a powerful picturing of a heavenly wedding banquet—symbolizing a consummation of history. One of Jesus' parables about the realm of God, "The Ten Bridesmaids," begins, "Then the kingdom of heaven will be like this. Ten bridesmaids took their lamps and went to meet the bridegroom" (Matt. 25:1). The coming Christ is the bridegroom.

Revelation uses the wedding image saying, "And I saw the holy city, the new Jerusalem, coming down out of heaven from God, prepared as a bride adorned for her husband" (Rev. 21:2). The church is depicted as Christ's bride, "Come, I will show you the bride, the wife of the Lamb" (Rev. 21:9). Last, as this divine wedding between earthly church and heavenly Christ is completed, the people worship God: "The marriage of the Lamb has come, and his bride has made herself ready" (Rev. 19:7). This is the image of the marriage between God and God's people.

Hosea's Vision for Us

What can we learn from Hosea's prophetic life? In order to love unconditionally, as Hosea did, then pride in community status must take a secondary role to the task God sets before us. Can we imagine what the neighbors thought and said about Hosea? Was he pitied, or did most people think he got what he deserved? Surely, the neighbors thought Hosea knew what kind of woman Gomer was when he married. To his credit, however, Hosea stayed on the course God had chosen. He did as Yahweh commanded and spoke the prophetic word Yahweh gave him to speak. It was a humiliating human experience. Yet, he did not waver.

Why do we have trouble with our commitments to other persons? Perhaps the reason is it takes great grace on God's part and great faith on our part to keep the human commitments made in the divine presence. Marriage is not a once-and-for-all declaration of love. It is a process of saying a thousand times and in a thousand ways, "I am still growing in loving commitment." No human being can make ordination, confirmation, baptism, or matrimonial vows in our own strength of will. We confess our weakness in character and in ability to keep these promises by ourselves. We need God's help. This is why we make these promises in the most sacred place we know: The church of Jesus Christ. The sanctuary is the ultimate place of grace. Grace is what makes our puny vows powerful.

FOURTH QUARTER

Helping Adults Become Involved

Preparing to Teach

Unless you are the teacher of a singles class, many members will likely be married or have been married. Even if your class is one of single persons, remember that one of the primary topics for singles is marriage. We all have a stake in good marriages. Thus, marriage will help you lead the class toward territory familiar to everyone. Since this and next week's lessons are from Hosea, read all fourteen chapters. It should take you thirty to forty-five minutes, giving you a good overall grasp of Hosea's prophecy. You may want to use this outline:

I. Hosea's faith is in itself a prophetic act.
II. Naming children is a startling means of prophecy.
III. Yahweh loves the people unconditionally.
IV. Hosea chastens Gomer as the Lord chastens Israel.

As you prepare the lesson, you will want to reflect on the many promises we make in our lives and particularly at church—the core of the faith community. Allow your class time to share moments when they felt betrayed by broken promises. Be prepared to draw similarities between our disappointments and the disappointments God feels when we break our promises. Also, reflect on the promises that people keep. There are surely many. This will allow people to accentuate the positive experiences of promise keeping.

Introducing the Main Question

Use the questions at the end of "The Main Question" section, then read today's text, Hosea 1:2-9 and 3:1-5. Share emotionally, Hosea's pain, faced in light of Yahweh's extraordinary demands of prophecy placed on him. Are we called to put ourselves at the mercy of public opinion as Hosea was? Why is our community standing so important to us? When does it become an idol? How do public opinion polls help or hinder the political process in America today? Does the church face similar pressures?

Developing the Lesson

I. Hosea's faith is in itself a prophetic act.

Hosea was not only called to speak a difficult word, but also to enact a difficult style of life. One could hardly imagine a more emotionally demanding challenge than to keep house with an unfaithful person. It is a betrayal of trust that erodes our concept of self-worth. Ask your class to discuss Hosea's sacrifice of self-respect.

Often we are our own worst enemies, struggling with what it means to be a human, but also attempting to be respected by those living around us. To deal with our own emotions of self-worth when things are intact is hard enough. Yet, imagine living with a person who broke marriage vows with impunity. It was, however, to this task that God called Hosea, and Hosea was faithful to the calling. Can we identify people in our own time who have this kind of commitment to causes they speak for? Does the church put itself in this position often in our time? Ask your class, why or why not?

364

II. Naming children is a startling means of prophecy.

Not only does Hosea live his exemplary life on behalf of Yahweh's word to Israel, but also names his children in a prophetic way, too. This gives his prophecy teeth, in that, those hearing the prophetic word also see it lived absolutely in the household of Hosea. His total commitment to Yahweh's word is evidenced in a graphic way—naming his children in this bizarre fashion underlines the desperate situation with which Israel is faced. Let your class discuss places where their personal sacrifices have caused their families to sacrifice, too. To what extent is your pastor's call also a call to the pastor's family?

III. Yahweh loves the people unconditionally.

Hosea shows total commitment to Gomer as a living form of Yahweh's love for Yahweh's people. There are no bounds. When one thinks of the pride Hosea forgoes, one is struck correspondingly by God's pride that has been shamelessly presumed on by Israel. Whatever the people think of Hosea and the management of his household, they must apply these to God and the house of Israel. It is not a flattering picture. Do we live in times of the passion Hosea demonstrates? Are there places in your community where the voice of the church is often the only prophetic voice? Spend some time addressing your church's concrete prophetic role in your community in which the church does what it believes is faithful to God, despite community public opinion.

IV. Hosea chastens Gomer as the Lord chastens Israel.

In Hosea 3:3-4, Hosea disciplines his wife Gomer, giving her the new boundaries within which their relationship may resume. God, too, makes these claims on the people of Israel. Israel will be called on to forfeit its many comfortable idolatrous institutions. Over time, Israel has begun to drift away from exclusive worship of Yahweh. The nation has begun to synthesize its once pure worship with other gods and idols. The nation, led by its kings, puts its trust in military alliances and treaties. Where are the idols in which modern Christians put their trust? Can your class list on the chalkboard a number of modern god-substitutes with which the church must contend? How is worship's song, praise, and proclamation prophetic in your church, reminding us of God's will for our lives?

Helping Class Members Act

Using 3:1-5, have your class identify with the feelings of Hosea, Gomer, the people of Israel, and Yahweh. If we can understand the emotions of this nation under judgment, perhaps we can better understand the urgency of their situation, and thereby ours. Does Hosea speak to our needs today? How?

Planning for Next Sunday

The lesson for next week is about God's love for Israel. Ask your class to read Hosea 11:1-9 and consider how being a parent of a rebellious child might be a reliable model of Yahweh's relationship to rebellious Israel.

Experiencing Undeserved Love

Background Scripture: Hosea 11:1-9

The Main Question

Oscar Wilde once said, "Children begin by loving their parents; after a time they judge them; rarely, if ever, do they forgive them." To some extent, all parents know the truth of Wilde's observation. For instance, when the weather is bad outside, and my daughter cannot ride her horse, she blames me. This happened today and prompted me to say to my wife, "Only a parent could be blamed for the weather." She replied, "Finally, I got a word out of you I can agree with—the perfect quote!"

Mr. Wilde's aphorism also indicates that from birth parents and children have a bond never broken; they are bound together for eternity. In my church, there is a constant request from people ages twenty to fifty for classes helping them raise children. They tell me that, of all the pressures they face in life, the most constant and difficult challenge is how to be a good parent. I agree. I have three children of my own. In fact, probably the greatest source of tension in most marriages is what to do about the children. Is discipline correct or not? Do people buy too many things for them, or not enough? What about their schooling—too much or too little? And so on!

Perhaps the maddening thing about parenting is no one can predict which parents will have good children and vice versa. We all know good, long-suffering parents who have horrid children. The reverse is also true, horrid parents sometimes have children who turn out wonderfully. One never knows.

Our lesson today is shot through and through with images of God as loving parent. Another image prominent in Hosea's prophecy is Israel as wayward child. Why is parenting so difficult and why is the parenting image of God so universal throughout the Bible? Why is the love people give their children so rewarding, and yet, at times, also so frustrating?

God is, in addition, seen in images throughout scripture as Judge. How are God's judging and God's parenting similar? It is to these questions we now turn.

Selected Scripture

King James Version	New Revised Standard Version
Hosea 11:1-9	*Hosea 11:1-9*
1 When Israel *was* a child, then I loved him, and called my son out of Egypt.	1 When Israel was a child, I loved him, and out of Egypt I called my son.
2 *As* they called them, so they went from them: they sacrificed unto Baalim, and burned incense to graven images.	2 The more I called them, the more they went from me; they kept sacrificing to the Baals, and offering incense to idols.

3 I taught Ephraim also to go, taking them by their arms; but they knew not that I healed them.

4 I drew them with cords of a man, with bands of love: and I was to them as they that take off the yoke on their jaws, and I laid meat unto them.

5 He shall not return into the land of Egypt, but the Assyrian shall be his king, because they refused to return.

6 And the sword shall abide on his cities, and shall consume his branches, and devour *them,* because of their own counsels.

7 And my people are bent to backsliding from me: though they called them to the most High, none at all would exalt *him.*

8 How shall I give thee up, Ephraim? *how* shall I deliver thee, Israel? how shall I make thee as Admah? *how* shall I set thee as Zeboim? mine heart is turned within me, my repentings are kindled together.

9 I will not execute the fierceness of mine anger, I will not return to destroy Ephraim: for I *am* God, and not man; the Holy One in the midst of thee: and I will not enter into the city.

Key Verse: **Hosea 14:4 I will heal their backsliding, I will love them freely: for mine anger is turned away from him.**

3 Yet it was I who taught Ephraim to walk,
I took them up in my arms;
but they did not know that I healed them.

4 I led them with cords of human kindness,
with bands of love.
I was to them like those
who lift infants to their cheeks.
I bent down to them and fed them.

5 They shall return to the land of Egypt,
and Assyria shall be their king,
because they have refused to return to me.

6 The sword rages in their cities,
it consumes their oracle-priests,
and devours because of their schemes.

7 My people are bent on turning away from me.
To the Most High they call,
but he does not raise them up at all.

8 How can I give you up, Ephraim?
How can I hand you over, O Israel?
How can I make you like Admah?
How can I treat you like Zeboiim?
My heart recoils within me;
my compassion grows warm and tender.

9 I will not execute my fierce anger;
I will not again destroy Ephraim;
for I am God and no mortal,
the Holy One in your midst,
and I will not come in wrath.

Key Verse: **Hosea 14:4 I will heal their disloyalty; I will love them freely, for my anger has turned from them.**

As You Read the Scripture

Hosea 11:1-2. This part of Hosea's prophecy is probably his best known. This is because the language is beautiful. There a unique tenderness with which God speaks of God's people.

Verse 1. Speaking of the whole nation as one child, God confesses love for Israel. This refers to Exodus 4:22, "Then you shall say to Pharaoh, 'Thus says the LORD: Israel is my firstborn son.'" Matthew 2:15, speaking of the Holy Family's Egyptians sojourn says, "Out of Egypt I have called my son." Israel's destiny is tied to God, as a child's destiny is tied to a parent.

Verse 2. God the parent calls the child, but the child rebels, refusing to heed the parental call, apparently finding other more satisfying substitutes—the idols of the Baals—the gods that competed with the God of Israel for affection and worship. Incense to idols refers to specific acts of Baal worship.

Verse 3. As children often forget who changed their diapers and taught them to walk, so too does Israel forget. Referred to as Ephraim, Israel has forgotten Yahweh, who has provided everything. God holding a sick child is a powerful image and one that parents remember vividly from tending their children's late-night fevers.

Verse 4. This picture of God's concern is one of tenderness. Engulfing them with "cords of human kindness, with bands of love," Yahweh cares for God's own children. Note how the Lord bends down, reminiscent of Yahweh bending down at creation to make a clay figure that becomes the man/woman. This is divine condescension, as pictured later in the incarnation of Christ.

Verse 5. This is an ominous prophecy against the people. God has brought them out of the land of Egypt; now they shall return to bondage. The Assyrians shall become their rulers, for the people have not honored the genuine king of Israel—Yahweh.

Verse 6. Soon war will rage when the Assyrians trigger Samaria's fall, ending Israel/Ephraim's nationhood. *Oracle-priests* refers to religious leaders who have not stopped Israel's idol worship—their primary obligation.

Verse 7. This verse may be translated several ways, but it is an indication of Israel's religious rebellion. Israel turns away from Yahweh to other gods. This is in direct opposition to the Torah's commandment of one God—Yahweh. Calling God Most High, they also call to other gods; there is no single-mindedness in Israel.

Verses 8-9. Yahweh asks a series of rhetorical questions, as though thinking out loud. Could Yahweh be changing decisions outlined in previous verses? This is reminiscent of Abraham's question, "Shall not the Judge of all the earth do what is just?" (Gen. 18:25). Yahweh then says, "I will not again destroy Ephraim," as if Yahweh is answering the rhetorical question in the affirmative. How deeply God loves God's people.

The Scripture and the Main Question

Yahweh, Parents, and Judgment

God is regarded throughout scripture as Judge. When a dispute arose between Sarai and Hagar, Sarai said, "May the wrong done to me be on you! . . . May the Lord judge between you and me!" (Gen. 16:5). Sarai understands Yahweh as ultimate judge in all human affairs, even in her own household.

Another example of God as Judge is when the Israelite supervisors, returning from an audience with Pharaoh, say boldly to Moses and Aaron, "The LORD look upon you and judge! You have brought us into bad odor with Pharaoh and his officials, and have put a sword in their hand to kill us" (Exod. 5:21). Another example is "The LORD will judge the ends of the earth" (1 Sam. 2:10). Images of Yahweh as Judge are images of a God who gave the sacred Torah, the law. In the early days of Israel, judges—representing Yahweh—were prophet-like people, who not only decided Torah disputes, but also were military and spiritual leaders. Moses, Barak, and Deborah are good examples of biblical judges.

How are judging and parenting similar? Parents are often called on to settle disputes among children. When children are young, parents have virtually absolute authority over children. Though this may change, parents generally judge their households. Parenting manuals advise parents to let children settle their own conflicts, but with the crowded American court dockets, one can understand why this is so practically difficult—at any age.

Lenient Judges

Recently, a man in my church went through an exasperating period regarding a judgment he made. He was on our state's parole board. Someone he had voted to parole had allegedly committed another murder, a few months after serving a twenty-two-year prison term. As expected, an unyielding angry public outcry followed! My friend was caught in the dilemma of who should be paroled and when, after committing a heinous crime. His career is threatened and he has suffered public humiliation and ridicule. With his responsibility for making these judgments came accountability when the authorized judgment went sour. Obviously, there will never be enough prisons to lock all offenders up forever, so there are practical, as well as moral, implications to my friend's decision to parole.

The truth is, no one likes a lenient judge. All we have to do is listen to a murderer's mother tell us her son or daughter was "really good, deep down," and our eyes roll upward. When a judge believes such a mother's story, or a convicted felon is released on parole, we hear complaints about it in the newspapers and in the state legislature. We are all interested in justice.

A Story of Unpopular Grace

My Presbyterian minister friend, John Poling, tells an uncommonly prophetic story about his minister grandfather. When the seventy-three-year-old preacher retired, his former congregations hosted a retirement party. The same week, there was to be nearby the execution of a murderer on death row. He had exhausted all his appeals over several years. At the close of the retirement party, the old man stood up saying, "Thank you for your generosity toward me. I don't deserve it, but most of the things in life worth having are more than any of us deserve."

He went on to describe how he had tried his best, preaching and pastoring for fifty years, to proclaim God's grace to all people. He closed the program saying, "Grace is the ultimate love of God and is the only hope we have. . . . It is the salvation of the world. . . . It is available and offered to you and me without price. . . . God's love is for you and me and our children . . . *and our brother on death row.*" Then he told those gathered he was leaving the party to stand by the prison gate and visit the man to be executed, as a sign of God's grace for all people. He would await the man's death and pray for his soul.

As he left, he invited everyone to come with him. No one went with the old preacher. In fact, as he walked out the door alone, everyone felt disappointed. Their gracious party had ended on a sour note. How far should grace be extended? What does Yahweh attempt to tell Yahweh's people through the ministry of Hosea?

God's Judgment Is to Chasten God's People

At the beginning of Hosea's prophecy there is a strong word of judgment for Ephraim/Israel. This is reflected in Hosea's naming of two of his children: Lo-ruhamah and Lo-ammi (Hos. 1:6, 9). These names mean "not pitied" and "not my people," respectively. Thus, Yahweh's judgment falls on the people. Though there is a strong judgment against the people at the prophecy's beginning, our lesson speaks also of God's mercy.

When human judges bring forth a verdict, they declare the person accused either guilty or innocent. There is no other alternative. Perhaps this is why our legal system is such a vexation: Life is rarely so cut and dry. Human circumstances are complex and varied. When we stand before God, we are declared guilty or innocent. When declared innocent by God's salvation, we are *justified* or made righteous by grace.

There is another act, however, which cannot be duplicated by human judges. This is the act of *making* us righteous or justified. In theology, this is called *sanctification*. John Wesley described sanctification as the perfecting love of God. By this he meant that after God *declares* us instantly justified, God then uses our lives as a process to make us grow in love—until the day we die. This is the sanctifying love of God. Thus, God both *declares* us righteous in justification and *makes* us righteous in sanctification.

God is willing to go this far with God's people "for I am God and no mortal" (v. 9). God has the power, not just to declare our outward standing regarding justice to be mended. God also has the power to make us just, and thereby reclaim the righteousness that is creation's most precious gift. The parable of the prodigal son, or as Helmut Thielicke names it, perhaps more appropriately, the parable of the waiting father, is a good narrative illustration of Hosea's prophetic poetry in chapter 11.

Pondering the main question and the scripture, we are left with this question: Which is best, justice or mercy? In a family, siblings are interested in justice involving brothers and sisters. When the eye of justice is pointed in their direction, however, most youngsters are interested in mercy for themselves. This is true regarding people before the judgment bench of God, too. People are interested in justice for others, but mercy for themselves. As God's children, we often ask the same from God.

Helping Adults Become Involved

Preparing to Teach

Today's lesson revolves around the heart-rending issue of Yahweh, Ephraim/Israel's parent. Everyone in your class is either a parent or an expert on parenting. Rather than concentrating on parenting techniques, such as using physical punishment or not, concentrate on parenting responsibilities. In addition, employ the feelings of love and frustration, which all parents have, indicating how God feels for God's people.

To best prepare, reread the book of Hosea. It will take thirty to forty-five minutes and will supply the emotive passions of this prophecy so explicit in Hosea. Help your class relate to the feeling level of the book, not just the content. This outline will relate the lesson to the class members' life experience:

I. Yahweh's relationship with Israel is parent to child.
II. Israel is a rebel without a God.
III. Punishment hurts God more than the people.
IV. Yahweh has a change of heart.
V. Yahweh's love is a love that will not let go.

Most people in your class have experienced disappointing times in which their own children, or a close friend's children, have rebelled. Let your class explore these concerns, for they go to the heart of Hosea's message about God's relationship to us.

Introducing the Main Question

Use the questions found in "The Main Question." Read to your class for their reflection. Then, have someone read aloud our lesson from Hosea 11:1-9. Many people advocate tough love for children today. How is this part of Yahweh's plan for Ephraim/Israel? Are people helped when all forms of accountability are dismissed? How do grace and judgment go hand in hand?

Developing the Lesson

I. Yahweh's relationship with Israel is parent to child.
Hosea's prophecy begins with a troubled marriage. Our modern service of marriage has a statement saying, "No other human ties are more tender, no other vows are more sacred than those you now assume." Marriage vows are often implicitly extended to one's children. Conceivably, if Hosea had marriage difficulties with Gomer, then he may have had difficulty with his children.

From our text, Hosea paints images of God and the people of Israel as parent-child. Hosea understood, from his own painful human experience, what Yahweh was experiencing with the rebellious people of Israel. Just as human parents know the risks of raising children, so too does Hosea relate the risks God runs by being a parent to God's child, Israel.

Where are places God acts as our heavenly parent? List on your class's chalkboard similarities God has with human parents.

II. Israel is a rebel without a God.
This theme of Israel's rebellion against God does not need documentation here; the whole biblical story is about God's faithfulness and the people's rebellion. Note, though, Israel's idolatry is both *for* other gods and *against* Yahweh. Another example is when Israel puts its trust somewhere other than in Yahweh, such as in ill-fated military alliances. Lesson 13 will describe in detail this circumstance, another illustration of Israel's rebellion. Second Kings 17:4, describing the double-dealing king Hoshea, tells us, "The king of Assyria found treachery in Hoshea; for he had sent messengers to King So of Egypt, and offered no tribute to the king of Assyria, as he had done year by year; therefore the king of Assyria confined him and imprisoned him." This is the last vain attempt by Hoshea to provide security for the people that only comes from Yahweh.

III. Punishment hurts God more than the people.

Beginning Hosea's prophecy is the statement, "She did not know that it was I who gave her the grain, the wine, and the oil, and who lavished upon her silver and gold that they used for Baal" (Hos. 2:8). This she refers to Israel and the I is Yahweh. Israel either did not know, or at least refused to acknowledge, that everything she had was given by Yahweh. Israel acted as a rebellious child.

Children can never see the future. Experience gives parents a glimpse into their children's future, but this is where parents and children often become adversaries. Thus, parents can regularly use the phrase "I told you so." What lies ahead for Israel is bondage: "They shall return to the land of Egypt." Given the ink spilled cataloguing Yahweh's many warnings, this outcome grieves God immeasurably.

IV. Yahweh has a change of heart.

This is no ordinary god, however, for Yahweh still retains relationship with the people, not so much because of them, but rather, despite them. In the last two verses of our lesson, the personal pronouns *me, mine,* and *I* overpower, being used twelve times. This indicates Yahweh's personal nature. These verses pose a troubling theological question: *Can God change?* We speak about an unchanging, eternal God. But here the Lord has second thoughts about the judgment God has rendered against Israel.

Two instances, for example, show the idea of God changing from scripture. "And the LORD changed his mind about the disaster that he planned to bring on his people" (Exod. 32:14). Another instance is, to the prophet Jonah's chagrin, "When God saw what they did, how they turned from their evil ways, God changed his mind about the calamity that he had said he would bring upon them; and he did not do it" (Jon. 3:10). Thus, in light of human repentance, God does change the divine mind. The two verses following today's lesson give the impression God may indeed bring God's people to their homes (Hos. 11:11).

When people change their minds about something, often they "eat crow." Could this be applied to God when God changes a course already set? Share in your class when this happened to you. If it is difficult to admit we are wrong, then how hard would it be for God to change God's mind? Was God wrong or merciful? What do you think?

V. Yahweh's love is a love that will not let go.

George Matheson wrote a hymn titled "O Love That Wilt Not Let Me Go." It describes the love that God has for God's people and, perhaps, the exuberant love parents have for their children. It is a trustworthy hymn, describing what Hosea is trying to relate through his prophecy. Divide your class into small groups, letting people share from scripture and the church's tradition illustrations of Hosea's message about a God who refuses to give up on or let go of God's people.

Helping Class Members Act

All people need to hear a harsh word of truth from time to time. Let some members of your class recount moments in their lives when a friend gave an unwelcome word of judgment, but later, it turned out to be a word of blessing. Is the pain of the moment redeemed when the painful judgment keeps us from doing something foolish or harmful? How do modern people speak a word of grace-filled judgment in Christian love today?

Planning for Next Sunday

Our lesson next week is designated as "Beware of Greed." Few people will take long to warm up to this lesson's topic. Have your class read Micah 3:5-12, but remind them, as Christians they are leaders in Christ. Does this put a different twist on the prophecy of Micah?

Beware of Greed

Background Scripture: Micah 3:5-12

The Main Question

A main question for every season is: *Why are human beings so greedy?* In Eden's garden of perfection, the man and the woman curse themselves by taking the forbidden fruit. Thus, we have what theologians for centuries have called original sin. Jacob's name means "he who supplants," or in modern idiom "he who grabs." In our lesson of June 18, "Justice Corrupted," we read the story of Naboth's vineyard. Recall that King Ahab's wife Jezebel had Naboth killed because the king wanted Naboth's vineyard, and Naboth refused to sell it. Earlier, in the biblical story, David stole the wife of Uriah the Hittite, and so goes the Bible's long story about people who could never get enough. We all grab.

We could dismiss these stories as being just stories, except they are repeated over and over, even in our own lives. When I was an adolescent, a family friend named Riley Wheaton gave me a completed penny collection, with the exception of just a few years' pennies. He told me to finish the set, then it would be mine. I was very proud of my gift.

One day after school, I realized my penny collection had disappeared. My brother cashed them in at a local convenience store, buying candy for himself and his friends with the proceeds. I was furious; so were my parents. When they asked why he did such a thing he said, "I wanted them." This phrase explains much about human behavior. We want. We want. We want!

A pastor friend told me another story of greed, though with a different twist. In her church, a man came into the church office every Sunday after worship to cash a $100 check, saying he needed cash to take his wife to lunch. Since a different group counted money each Sunday, no one paid much attention to his regular request. Later the I.R.S. investigated whether this man had actually given the church $5,000 he had reported the past three years. Another case of greed; in reality he had not given anything.

Micah calls down judgment from God on leaders who use their position to gain wealth. The sacred trust that has been given them as a godly privilege is now openly sold to the highest bidder. Micah speaks clearly: Jerusalem will become a ruin, all because Judah's leadership perverts justice.

Why are people so greedy and why do leaders steal from those whom they are called to serve? Does this greed have consequences in our lives? What makes this sin of greed or coveting wrong?

Selected Scripture

King James Version	New Revised Standard Version

Micah 3:5-12

5 Thus saith the LORD concerning the prophets that make my people err, that bite with their teeth, and cry, Peace; and he that putteth not into their mouths, they even prepare war against him.

6 Therefore night *shall be* unto you, that ye shall not have a vision; and it shall be dark unto you, that ye shall not divine; and the sun shall go down over the prophet, and the day shall be dark over them.

7 Then shall the seers be ashamed, and the diviners confounded: yea, they shall all cover their lips; for *there is* no answer of God.

8 But truly I am full of power by the spirit of the LORD, and of judgment, and of might, to declare unto Jacob his transgression, and to Israel his sin.

9 Hear this, I pray you, ye heads of the house of Jacob, and princes of the house of Israel, that abhor judgment, and pervert all equity.

10 They build up Zion with blood, and Jerusalem with iniquity.

11 The heads thereof judge for reward, and the priests thereof teach for hire, and the prophets thereof divine for money: yet will they lean upon the LORD, and say, *Is* not the LORD among us? none evil can come upon us.

12 Therefore shall Zion for your

Micah 3:5-12

5 Thus says the LORD concerning
the prophets
who lead my people astray,
who cry "Peace"
when they have something to eat,
but declare war against those
who put nothing into their mouths.

6 Therefore it shall be night to you,
without vision,
and darkness to you, without revelation.
The sun shall go down upon the
prophets,
and the day shall be black over
them;

7 the seers shall be disgraced,
and the diviners put to shame;
they shall all cover their lips,
for there is no answer from God.

8 But as for me, I am filled with
power,
with the spirit of the LORD,
and with justice and might,
to declare to Jacob his transgression
and to Israel his sin.

9 Hear this, you rulers of the house
of Jacob
and chiefs of the house of Israel,
who abhor justice
and pervert all equity,

10 who build Zion with blood
and Jerusalem with wrong!

11 Its rulers give judgment for a
bribe,
its priests teach for a price,
its prophets give oracles for money;
yet they lean upon the LORD and say,
"Surely the LORD is with us!
No harm shall come upon us."

12 Therefore because of you

sake be plowed *as* a field; and Jerusalem shall become heaps, and the mountain of the house as the high places of the forest.

Zion shall be plowed as a field; Jerusalem shall become a heap of ruins, and the mountain of the house a wooded height.

Key Verse (Micah 3:4): **Then shall they cry unto the LORD, but he will not hear them: he will even hide his face from them at that time, as they have behaved themselves ill in their doings.**

Key Verse (Micah 3:4): **Then they will cry to the LORD, but he will not answer them; he will hide his face from them at that time, because they have acted wickedly.**

As You Read the Scripture

Micah 3:5-12. This section of Micah's prophecy dooms Judah and Jerusalem. The secular leaders and the religious leaders have been more interested in their own well-being than in the truth with which God entrusted them. Micah denounces the leaders of the nation, predicting bleak days for Jerusalem.

Verse 5. Following verse 4, a statement pertaining to God's silence in response to the "heads of Jacob's" cries, Micah speaks the word of the Lord concerning the prophets. They lead the people astray, thus are false prophets. They give good words to those who feed them, that is, "when they have something to eat." To those, however, "who put nothing into their mouths," they declare war. The meaning is clear: These prophets that Micah addresses tailor their message to suit their own purposes. Yahweh's truth, however, does not vary with the audience.

Verse 6. Therefore, says Micah to these false prophets, you will have no vision and will live (and work/prophesy) in darkness. The light of God's revelation, the necessary component of true prophecy, will be beyond their reach. Their days of prophecy will be black and their visions barren.

Israel's light has gone out. When the world was without God, "the earth was a formless void and darkness covered the face of the deep" (Gen. 1:2). Another day in biblical history that illustrates darkness as a sign of the divine absence is Jesus' death on the cross. "From noon on, darkness came over the whole land until three in the afternoon" (Matt. 27:45). Micah's prophecy should have devastated the prophets.

Verse 7. Without judging the methods of receiving the divine word, several are singled out for bankruptcy. The religious practitioners have forfeited their right to Yahweh's truth. The seers will be disgraced, for their esteem comes from the ability to see. Diviners, too, will be shamed. Each will have to stop their operations, for no word will be revealed. God is silent.

As darkness is a sign of divine displeasure, so, too, is the silence of Yahweh. Yahweh creates by the divine word, now there will be silence. People should be rightly terrified by the silence of Yahweh, though Micah thinks Yahweh has already been silenced by the false prophets.

Verse 8. Micah now speaks about himself in contrast to the false prophets, seers, and diviners. Unlike them, he has the Spirit of Yahweh giving him power. This power enables him to fear no one. He is free in justice and might to declare the sin and transgression of Jacob and Israel.

Verses 9-11. "Hear this," the prophet says to those who care not about the justice of religion, only its profitability. The reference to "build Zion with blood and Jerusalem with wrong!" may have to do with the forced labor of the people, or at least labor at reduced wages. The common people and their labor are always used by those in power, Micah says.

Then Micah singles out rulers, priests, and prophets for censure. They pervert justice for money. False leaders give false hope saying, "Surely the LORD is with us! No harm shall come upon us." In their thirst for more money, power, and bribes, they sell the word of Yahweh.

Verse 12. The final judgment-statement says that Zion will be plowed under; Jerusalem destroyed. This results from its leaders' flagrant misuse of Yahweh's trust. It will prove a high price, indeed.

The Scripture and the Main Question

Yahweh's Representatives

As Yahweh worshipers, the seers, prophets, leaders, diviners, priests, and rulers have one thing in common: They have been entrusted as God's representatives and, therefore, stewards of Yahweh. No one in Israel or Judah has a leadership role not derived by Yahweh's will. Yahweh chooses Yahweh's people, they do not choose Yahweh. In fact, God gives these persons a sacred trust. They are stewards of divine trust, managing the Creator's property. This is Jesus' theme in several parables (see the parable of the faithful and unfaithful servants, Matt. 24:45-51; the parable of the talents, Matt. 25:14-30; the parable of the wicked tenants, Mark 12:1-12). To be called as a prophet, seer, or priest is to be called into the Lord's stewardship.

Yahweh always calls people to be divine representatives. Abram was in Ur when his call came. Likewise, Moses, tending Jethro's herd, received the call. Throughout Israel's history, judges, kings, and prophets were called by God. Today, as people enter ordained ministry, they are asked to articulate their calls. We need church leaders with a sense of call.

The people to whom Micah speaks prophetically, however, have forfeited their call from God. They turned their backs on the Torah teachings of Yahweh. As Yahweh's representatives, they shirked responsibility for following and teaching Torah, being cut off from the word of Yahweh. They no longer fulfill their vocation of being tied directly to the Lord's word. When Micah says, "There is no answer from God," this is a crushing word.

The Sheol of Silence

In our culture today, there are cute images of the devil in a red suit, carrying a pitchfork. Neither this image, nor the image of burning hell, exhausts biblical images of hell. It does speak of lakes of fire, but this is not the Bible's only image.

The *silence of God* is another image by which the Bible speaks of hell or, in Hebrew scripture, *sheol*. Sheol is where people are separated from God and where God is silent. For example, in Psalms we see pictures of this notion of Sheol. "If the Lord had not been my help, my soul would soon have lived in the land of silence" (Psalm 94:17). Sheol is a land of silence because there is no word from the Lord.

Another Sheol-image is that no one worships Yahweh. "The dead do not praise the LORD, nor do any that go down into silence" (Ps. 115:17). To be cut off from hearing and praising Yahweh is what Hebrews feared most about death. Micah suggests that those turning from Yahweh's Torah commit faith-suicide, for they have chosen to live without the word of Yahweh.

Trust or Comfort?

The choice has been made. Those responsible for the word of Yahweh's truth have instead sold it for profit. Why are they so cursed? They betrayed their sacred trust as stewards. Betrayal is a biblical sign of the end times. It is an apocalyptic sign, for when betrayal occurs, the end is near. When Judas betrays Jesus, the events of the crucifixion are set into motion.

When Jesus speaks of end times he also speaks of betrayal. Matthew 10:21 says prophetically, "Brother will betray brother to death, and a father his child, and children will rise against parents and have them put to death." When the end comes, the people will know: "Many will fall away, and they will betray one another and hate one another" (Matt. 24:10).

Why are people so greedy and why do leaders steal from those whom they are called to serve? They are seeking their own comfort and security. This is counter to God's word, which in many ways is the same: "I will be with you." These are Jesus' words to his disciples as he leaves them. They are also God's words to Israel, now relegated, like so many sheep and goats sold in the markets. Does this greed have consequences in our lives? This is a question each of us must answer.

What makes the sin of greed so wrong? Greed and materialism put our security in things other than God. The prophets name this over and over as *idolatry*. It breaks Yahweh's covenant command to "have no other gods before me." God only gives security. "Trust in the LORD, and do good; so you will live in the land, and enjoy security" (Ps. 37:3). Micah says the prophets, rulers, and priests have been judged by Yahweh, precisely because they have not trusted God and not done good.

Micah's prophecy is summarized in Hebrew wisdom: "No one finds security by wickedness, but the root of the righteous will never be moved" (Prov. 12:3). When false prophets say, "Surely, the Lord is with us," surely they whistle in the dark.

Integrity of Leadership

One reason Jerusalem is to be destroyed and Zion plowed under is the institutional response to false prophets and priests. There were likely people who could have spoken against the abuses taking place. Yet, no one, save Micah, had the courage to speak against the status quo. When the truth of God is tied to economic standing, then the justice of God is perverted and compromised. This is precisely Micah's point. Jacob's transgression and Israel's sin are not fastened exclusively to failures of individual leaders. It is an indication that the whole nation's hands have blood on them.

This is an important lesson: People are more important than institutions—whether the institutions are religious, medical, or governmental. The eminent leaders in American history have always been servant-leaders. One of the most endearing qualities of Harry S. Truman was that he always saw himself as an ordinary citizen and not a dignitary. Church leaders might well take note of Mr. Truman's philosophy. The prophetic church is the servant-church, existing to be broken for the world, like the Savior it professes to follow. If the prophets in Micah's time had attended to their leadership as servants, then Micah's prophecy would have been unnecessary.

Echoing Micah's words, Timothy outlines qualities for bishops. "Now a bishop must be above reproach, married only once, temperate, sensible, respectable, hospitable, an apt teacher, not a drunkard, not violent but gentle, not quarrelsome, and *not a lover of money*" (1 Tim. 3:2). These qualities befit any church leader, for all Christians are spiritual leaders.

Helping Adults Become Involved

Preparing to Teach

Our lesson involves stewardship of call and the claim of Christ on our lives. It is individual; we each hear Christ's call in different ways. It is communal; the church is faith's household. Micah denounces those using religion to profit, an issue to which many in the church can relate. Where does one cross the line between fairness to church workers and prostituting the message of God, benefitting the self rather than God's truth?

To prepare, read the seven chapters of Micah's prophecy. Also read 2 Kings 15–17, giving Micah's text its historical and political background. Maps and tables of rulers will also help. This outline will aid you in covering topics Micah deals with:

I. God's judgment, like God's grace, comes in unexpected ways.
II. People often judge themselves in their faith decisions.
III. The silence of God is deafening.
IV. The relationship with God is faith's crucial element.

Since Micah's prophecy has not held the prominence in the church it should have, your class members may be unfamiliar with his prophecy. You can help them by giving the prophecy a general overview. *The Interpreter's One Volume Commentary,* or other comparable resource, will serve this purpose, and good study Bibles provide introductions to the Bible's individual books such as Micah.

Introducing the Main Question

Share the questions from "The Main Question" section: Why are people so greedy and why do leaders steal from those they are called to serve? Does this greed have consequences in our lives? What makes this sin of greed or coveting wrong? Have a class member read Micah 3:5-12, keeping these questions in mind.

Developing the Lesson

I. God's judgment, like God's grace, comes in unexpected ways.
For many people, the judgment of God is a fearsome thing. Images of heaven and hell have developed not only in our church experience, but also within our culture. The judgment of God, however, has both positive and negative elements.

Positively, one aspect of judgment is the promise of heaven. While this image is often childlike—harps, clouds, St. Peter, and so on—it can be further developed in a mature faith. I like other images in the New Testament for God's realm, which is Matthew's kingdom of heaven. Ask your class to reflect and share some of the images. Revelation has several: new Jerusalem, new earth, water of life, heavenly wedding. Heaven's biblical images often focus on *relationship with God,* praising and praying, for instance, in the presence of the living Creator.

Negatively, images of New Testament hell, are like those in the Hebrew image *sheol.* This is a cursed place, both dark and silent. The light of God's revelatory word is absent. Though images of the lake of burning fire and the outer darkness are used, a more practical image of hell is as *a place where God is neither seen nor does God speak.* Hell is eternal silence/darkness, without God. Let your class converse about these images, which move beyond our childlike understanding of hell and heaven.

II. People often judge themselves in their faith decisions.

Perhaps an obstacle to understanding judgment is that it occurs at the end of history. Often we call this consummation or final judgment. Micah's truth was: In the prophets, seers, and priest's daily activities, *God's judgment had already taken place.*

This is true for faith today. It is in the nickels and dimes of daily life where faith's decisions are made. Each day we are called to be just and righteous in the Lord. Human sin occurs when we separate from God, either in self-security or in self-despair. Israel's leaders tried securing their future by selling God's word for a price, a bribe, and for money. In so doing, they put themselves in God's place. This is idolatrous.

God's judgment can, therefore, be understood as God's separation from people. This image is of a people lost from God, placed where no word from God is heard or seen. This is hell: A situation without God. Allow your class to talk about how in relationships we cut one another off—parents from children, husbands from wives, and friends from friends. This is God's judgment: We are alone. How does this make sense to your class?

III. The silence of God is deafening.

Have your class imagine writing their religious autobiography. Give them time to do this. Let them share verbally their moments of silence, helping them feel closer to God. In Habakkuk, another minor prophet, are these words: "The Lord is in his holy temple; let all the earth keep silence before him!" (Hab. 2:20). We value silence, positive moments where the world's noisy competition for our attention is overcome, if only for a time. Before the last seal is broken in Revelation, uncovering the mystery of God, "there was silence in heaven for about half an hour" (Rev. 8:1), a holy moment for God's word. Silence is the appropriate mode for prayer. Paraphrasing Martin Luther, prayer is more listening than talk.

Unfortunately, the silence of God can also be a curse, as the seers and diviners of Micah's prophecy heard from Micah; "there is no answer from God." This is different from silence *before* God, as one waits in anticipation of a word. This is silence *of* God, indicating starkly that one is cut off from God. The verbal relationship with God, creating by the word and talking to the ancestors, is over. For Hebrews, this is Sheol—the land of silence. I spend time with families having experienced unbelievable trauma. Words cannot substitute for silence in these moments. Is it heaven or hell? Let your class talk about their times when God's silence was deafening.

IV. The relationship with God is faith's crucial element.

Our lesson has primarily focused on the trust betrayed by Israel's political and religious leaders. In greed for power or money, they trust their ability to secure their own future. In so doing, they disgrace the stewardship of leadership, which betrays Yahweh and Yahweh's people. Relationship with God is in trust, not given to manipulation or false hope. Relationship with Yahweh is grounded in God's judgment of accountability and mercy. Ask your class how God shows mercy, while holding us accountable in relationships with both God and each other.

Helping Class Members Act

Even though no person in your class would ever think that money brings happiness, many in our society (and churches) live as though this were true. How can we develop a trust in God that understands our material possessions as gifts from God, rather than tokens of our own security and success? Is money the greatest idol we face in the twentieth century? Have things changed much since Micah's day? What do you think?

Planning for Next Sunday

Ask your class to prepare for next week by reading Isaiah 6:1-8 and 1:14-17. How does worship and a sense of call help people today respond to the word of God?

UNIT III: THE JUDGMENT ARRIVES

FOUR LESSONS   **AUGUST 6–27**

H. Rap Brown said in the 1960s that violence was as American as apple pie. What he meant was, though many might say, "Peace, peace," there is no peace. This reflects Ezekiel's words denouncing the false prophets of Israel, when he said, many centuries earlier, "In truth, because they have misled my people, saying, 'peace,' when there is no peace; and because, when the people build a wall, these prophets smear whitewash on it" (Ezek. 13:10).

I grew up in a violent time in American history. A president was assassinated when I was in the fifth grade. Civil rights leaders Medgar Evers and Martin Luther King, Jr., were also murdered. Riots in Chicago, Detroit, Newark, Los Angeles, and a multitude of other American cities portrayed the sick spirit in our society three decades ago. Yet, at the time, I remember many of the nation's leaders saying there was something wrong only with those who took to the streets in protest. To their way of thinking, it was all right to bomb innocent civilians in North Vietnam, but violence at home was done exclusively by malcontents and hooligans. Most of us today, no matter our personal philosophy or politics, can say confidently that there was plenty of blame to go around then. No one group need accept all responsibility. In retrospect, we all must take responsibility for the state of our nation.

Our unit this month is entitled "The Judgment Arrives." In many ways, the messages to Israel and Judah parallel the message God speaks uniformly through history. When people turn their backs on problems, preferring false peace, rather than facing the problems, then there will be a price to be paid. The message of the prophets, especially Isaiah, is clear: Either the nation finds its moral focus again, or the consequences will be dire.

In my high school, reflecting the danger of the times, there was a popular saying: "Mess around, mess around, pretty soon, you won't be around." In a real sense, this is also the message of the prophets to Israel. When a nation departs from the ways of Yahweh, its people may find themselves not around.

Responding to God's Call

Background: Isaiah 6:1-8; 1:14-17

The Main Question

A recent and surprising shift in the life of the church is the laity's desire for hands-on ministry. Until recently, there was an attitude in the church that clergy did the real ministry. Lay people's role was supporting and sustaining. This is no longer the case. Many youths and adults see themselves as missionaries for Christ. Mission trips for laity now fill as quickly as they are organized.

One church's motto is "Every member in ministry." In fact, in our church, we rarely speak of church jobs anymore; they are ministries of teaching, evangelism, and administration. Many churches are finding a new understanding of stewardship.

My denomination currently makes a distinction between the general ministry of all Christian believers and the representative ministry of the clergy. To the degree Christ's church moves in this direction, the stronger it becomes.

Though there are as many theories about this new spirit whistling through the church today as there are those who put theories forward, I think it has to do with call. A revival of baptismal understanding has driven many to rethink their place in the realm of God. To experience authentic relationships with God and other people is what people want, causing believers to welcome their call to discipleship with new hearts.

It is not enough simply to know we are saved by faith through grace: We need to experience it. It is this simple. After a generation or two of relative wealth and comfort, Americans now realize life is more than what we eat, drink, and wear. We crave encountering God in everyday life.

FOURTH QUARTER

How do modern people hear and feel the call to faith and the ministry based on God's grace? Where are the places one might encounter the word of salvation? Do we hear God's voice and see God's presence, high and lifted up, as Isaiah did? Or are there other means God uses to speak words of grace? These are the questions before us as we look at the call of Isaiah.

Selected Scripture

King James Version

Isaiah 6:1-8; 1:14-17

1 In the year that king Uzziah died I saw also the Lord sitting upon a throne, high and lifted up, and his train filled the temple.

2 Above it stood the seraphims: each one had six wings; with twain he covered his face, and with twain he covered his feet, and with twain he did fly.

3 And one cried unto another, and said, Holy, holy, holy, *is* the LORD of hosts: the whole earth *is* full of his glory.

4 And the posts of the door moved at the voice of him that cried, and the house was filled with smoke.

5 Then said I, Woe *is* me! for I am undone; because I *am* a man of unclean lips, and I dwell in the midst of a people of unclean lips: for mine eyes have seen the King, the LORD of hosts.

6 Then flew one of the seraphims unto me, having a live coal in his hand, *which* he had taken with the tongs from off the altar:

7 And he laid *it* upon my mouth, and said, Lo, this hath touched thy lips; and thine iniquity is taken away, and thy sin purged.

8 Also I heard the voice of the Lord, saying, Whom shall I send, and who will go for us? Then said I, Here *am* I; send me.

···

14 Your new moons and your appointed feasts my soul hateth: they are a trouble unto me; I am weary to bear *them*.

15 And when ye spread forth your hands, I will hide mine eyes from

New Revised Standard Version

Isaiah 6:1-8; 1:14-17

1 In the year that King Uzziah died, I saw the Lord sitting on a throne, high and lofty; and the hem of his robe filled the temple. 2 Seraphs were in attendance above him; each had six wings: with two they covered their faces, and with two they covered their feet, and with two they flew. 3 And one called to another and said:
"Holy, holy, holy is the LORD of hosts;
the whole earth is full of his glory."
4 The pivots on the thresholds shook at the voices of those who called, and the house filled with smoke. 5 And I said: "Woe is me! I am lost, and for I am a man of unclean lips; and I live among a people of unclean lips; yet my eyes have seen the King, the LORD of hosts!"

6 Then one of the seraphs flew to me, holding a live coal that had been taken from the altar with a pair of tongs. 7 The seraph touched my mouth with it and said: "Now that this has touched your lips, your guilt has departed and your sin is blotted out." 8 Then I heard the voice of the Lord saying, "Whom shall I send, and who will go for us?" And I said, "Here am I; send me!"

···

14 Your new moons and your appointed festivals
my soul hates;
they have become a burden to me.
I am weary of bearing them.
15 When you stretch out your hands,

you: yea, when ye make many
prayers, I will not hear: your hands
are full of blood.

16 Wash you, make you clean; put
way the evil of your doings from
before mine eyes; cease to do evil;

17 Learn to do well; seek judgment, relieve the oppressed, judge
the fatherless, plead for the widow.

I will hide my eyes from you;
even though you make many prayers,
I will not listen;
your hands are full of blood.
16 Wash yourselves; make yourselves
clean;
remove the evil of your doings
from before my eyes;
cease to do evil,
17   learn to do good;
seek justice,
rescue the oppressed,
defend the orphan,
plead for the widow.

Key Verse: **Also I heard the voice
of the Lord, saying, Whom shall I
send, and who will go for us? Then
said I, Here *am* I; send me.**

Key Verse: **Then I heard the voice
of the Lord saying, "Whom shall I
send, and who will go for us?" And I
said, "Here am I; send me!"**

As You Read the Scripture

Isaiah 6:1-8; 1:14-17. These two passages at first glance may seem to be
placed together in an odd ordering. As we read the text, however, the first
part of our lesson, Isaiah 6:1-8, will be Isaiah's call into the service of Yahweh
as prophet. The concluding part of our lesson, Isaiah 1:14-17, will form the
word of Isaiah's prophecy to the people of Judah.

Chapter 6:1. The year that Uzziah died, sometimes also called Azariah, is
usually calculated as being 742 B.C.E. The particular date given for this vision
in the Jerusalem temple perhaps gives the experience more historical credi-
bility. Since Isaiah is apparently in the temple, he may have had a priestly
function. Note the experience is a visual one.

Verses 2-3. The seraphs were some sort of angelic beasts attending the
Lord in the temple, though there is no descriptive material in the Bible
about them beyond this passage. They are described as having wings, and
are spatially above the Lord, already high and lifted up. They call to one
another a threefold ascription of glory: "Holy, holy, holy is the LORD of
hosts; the whole earth is full of his glory." As with the creatures around the
throne of God in Revelation, these seraphs' chief role is to worship and
glory God Almighty. Note Isaiah's experience is both visual and authority.

Verse 4. As the seraphs call to one another in praise, the whole temple
shakes as if an earthquake occurs. In addition to the shaking of the foundations or pivots, the whole temple fills with smoke. One can hardly imagine
that this smoke was only the incense that may have been burning during
temple worship. The whole experience—sight, sound, smell, being physically shaken, and perhaps even taste—will set the stage for Isaiah's confes-
sional response.

Verse 5. Speaking in first person, Isaiah makes his confession, both for
himself and also for his people. In the midst of this confession, however, he
also notes the grace received: "Yet my eyes have seen the King, the LORD of
hosts!" The Hebrews knew that to see Yahweh face to face meant certain

death, yet Isaiah is spared. We recall Yahweh telling Moses, "You cannot see my face; for no one shall see me and live" (Exod. 33:20).

Verses 6-7. One of the seraphs then takes a burning coal from the altar's fire and touches the previously mentioned unclean lips of Isaiah's. This is a sign and symbol of purification—an act of penance done for Isaiah.

It has been suggested this was not a live coal, but likely a heated flat stone, often used in household baking. "He looked, and there at his head was a cake based on hot stones" (1 Kings 19:6). In any event, Isaiah is told his sin is blotted out by this act of divine grace.

Verse 8. After this act of purification, Isaiah hears the voice of the Lord. This is the prophet's call to ministry on God's behalf, hence the phrase "who will go?" Isaiah responds to the call by the familiar words: "Here am I; send me!"

Chapter 1:14-17. These verses are the prophet's words spoken on Yahweh's behalf. They are a ringing denunciation of Judah's worship and moral practices. Outwardly the people are going through the motions of liturgical worship by praying with outstretched hands and observing feast and festival days. Inwardly, though, their hearts are not right. According to the prophecy, true righteousness is reflected in just dealings with other people in the faith community.

The people have apparently turned their backs on the poor, orphans, widows, and other oppressed groups in Jerusalem. This censure of Isaiah's reminds us of Jesus' words when he said, "Now you Pharisees clean the outside of the cup and of the dish, but inside you are full of greed and wickedness" (Luke 11:39).

The Scripture and the Main Question

Human Hunger for the Divine

We live in a time that has been described as one hungry for the word of God and an experience of the holy. Major magazines write full-length features on religion. *Time* and *Newsweek* have both featured cover stories on prayer and the church in the past year. Around the world there is a revival of interest in religion, whether it be Christianity, Judaism, or Islam.

Sociologists of religion suggest two powers are at work in today's world of religion. The first is that religion performs a hope-filled function for people on the brink of despair. This is why religion has such potency in third-world countries. These poverty-stricken people, often caught in war's conflict, deprived of the food and necessities siphoned off to wage war, hold to the promises of religion.

On the other side of the economic ledger, many affluent folk, at least by the rest of the world's standards, have found that more money and riches do not meet all their desires. Prosperous people, many of them in our country, are turning to religion, hoping to find a deeper meaning and purpose for life than the accumulation of wealth provides. This is today's religion's second power at work.

How do modern people hear and feel the call to faith and the ministry based on God's grace? Where are the places we encounter salvation? Do we hear God's voice and see God's presence high and lifted up, as Isaiah did? Or are there other means God uses to speak words of grace?

Isaiah's Judah

From what we can gather about Isaiah's ministry, it took place in Jerusalem during the reigns of kings Uzziah, Ahaz, and Hezekiah. From the context of Isaiah's prophecy, we believe he was from the ruling class and had access to power. He also had the privilege of saying what he wanted when he wanted. For instance, later in the prophecy we are told: "When the servants of King Hezekiah came to Isaiah, Isaiah said to them, 'Say to your master, "Thus says the LORD: Do not be afraid because of the words that you have heard, with which the servants of the king of Assyria have reviled me" (Isa. 37:5-6). This shows the kings of Judah sent for Isaiah, willing to hear what he had to say.

During Isaiah's long prophetic career, a number of distressing political incidents absorbed Judah. One was the Syro-Ephraimite War. Other alliances and even international political realignments took place within his lifetime. Perhaps this is why his prophecy dwells not only on the religious themes we might expect, but also on the themes of politics.

Isaiah's Call

Our text today speaks about the prophet's call to ministry, although there is much discussion about whether it is rather, in fact, a charge to ministry. The idea that this is a story of call or charge comes about for two reasons. First, some scholars suggest Isaiah was probably already a priest, explaining his presence in the temple when the vision occurs. This, then, suggests Isaiah is already converted to faith in Yahweh. Second, in its particularity, "Whom shall I send, and who will go for us?" we find a specific task for Isaiah. This is not a call to conversion, rather it is *the charge to do something distinctive*—a charge to do the work of the Lord in a new way.

Whether one understands this experience as call or charge, however, one thing is noteworthy. The vision comes during *worship*. When we ask the question today, "Where do we encounter the word of salvation?" worship is probably not a site jumping to mind. Perhaps many of us think worship too ritualistic, formal, or institutionalized for the word of the Lord to be heard with the power that Isaiah heard it. In earlier times, one might hear someone saying that a call to ministry came in a local church service. In my experience, though, I hear people announcing that their call to ministry occurred at church camp or in the mountains, as if the sanctuary encumbered the word of God.

This is one of the strengths of this lesson for people today. Worship has been a customary time and place where people are most likely to encounter the word of God. As Jesus gathered people on a hillside or a plain to teach, so too do we hear the Word as people are gathered in community, hearing the church's teaching and preaching. In Acts, again and again, the people are gathered together in the household of faith hearing Peter or Paul preach. Worship is one of the means of grace for God's people. Isaiah's experience is that the word can be powerfully heard in communal worship.

In the 1700s, George Whitefield accomplished the great revival in America, England, and Scotland, preaching outdoors. This field-preaching of Whitefield's took advantage of crowds hungry to hear the word of the Lord. Today many people are coming to a new understanding and appreciation for worship. Church attendance has climbed steadily the last two decades.

Modern folk are discovering what the people of Judah and Israel had known all along: God works in the community of faith, not only in individual lives.

The Sensory Nature of Isaiah's Call

I have a friend who is something of a specialist in worship for children. This subject, frankly, did not have much interest for me initially. Then, as I watched our congregation and other congregations perk up during that liturgically suspect moment of children's time, I began to rethink my former position. One of the questions that came to me as I watched the adults was, what interests adults and commands their attention during the children's time? So I asked her.

My friend's response was as simple as it was disarming: People do not all think like we presume adults think. That is, the typical worship service in many of our old-line Protestant denominations makes worship abstract and verbal. During children's time, at least for a moment, worship becomes an interval of story and imagination. We allow people creativity in worship, rather than simply explicating a series of doctrines.

In Isaiah's worship experience from our lesson, all five senses are utilized. Isaiah hears the voice of God and the praises of the seraphs. He also feels the shaking of the temple in its pivots and the live coal on his lips. Perhaps he also tastes the coal, as well as smells the acrid smoke that filled the temple. In addition, he sees the Lord high and lifted up. One could certainly use the imagination in conjuring up all the sensory experiences packed into these few verses.

The point is this: Worship is more than getting our theological ducks and doctrines lined up in some consistent and systematic way. Worship, at its heart, is an experience of the awesome and holy God we profess as Lord. Only from such a lively occasion can one surrender to the call of God on our lives.

This in no way demeans a fully thought-out theology, but godly ideas alone cannot provide the passion to sustain faith in any and all of life's circumstances. Our faith calls us to unite heart and mind in pursuit of faithful living. Jesus said, quoting his own scriptures, "You shall love the Lord your God with all your heart, and with all your soul, and with all your mind, and with all your strength" (Mark 12:30, see Deut. 6:4).

Where are places we encounter God's word of salvation? Do we hear God's voice and see God's presence high and lifted up, as Isaiah did? One answer for today that leaps from our lesson is *worship*. Worship and experience of the holy sustained Isaiah's prophetic ministry throughout difficult circumstances. Would that we might be grasped by the Holy One of Israel, too.

Helping Adults Become Involved

Preparing to Teach

Many of us have a call story we can relate, that moment in our lives when God spoke words of forgiveness and grace to us. Not everyone in your class will be comfortable telling their story, or testimony as it is sometimes called, but there will be those willing to share with the class. As a teacher, you may want to refer to moments in your life, pivotal in your decision to follow Christ and even to teach others about Christ.

Another interesting exercise you may want to use involving your class is by taking a copy of your church's hymnal and using the order of worship in the front or a copy of your church's Sunday bulletin. Can your class design an "order of worship" from elements in today's lesson from Isaiah?

To further explore our passage, this outline may prove useful:

     I. Isaiah's call occurs while he is at worship.
    II. Isaiah's individual call is extended to the nation.
    III. Isaiah calls a nation to repentance.
    IV. True worship reflects true repentance.

In your preparation, you may also want to think about the special worship rites of our church: baptism, confirmation, and the Lord's Supper. How do these rites relate God's grace and forgiveness in our daily twentieth-century lives? How do these rites also call for congregational repentance?

Introducing the Main Question

Ask your class members to imagine they are sitting in the back of the sanctuary one Sunday morning. Have them think about how they prepare for the worship service. Then read the passage from Isaiah.

Ask for reactions. Do any of them come to worship with a sense that anything like this could happen in your church? Why or why not? Then read the section titled "The Main Question." This idea of worship and call will be an issue to which most class members will be able to relate.

Developing the Lesson

I. Isaiah's call occurs while he is at worship.

Moses was tending his father-in-law's flocks and David was watching his father's sheep when the word of God came. Paul was traveling the road to Damascus, and Peter and his brother Andrew were casting nets into the sea when they were called by Jesus. St. John, who wrote the apocalypse we call Revelation, relates, "I was in the spirit on the Lord's day, and I heard behind me a loud voice like a trumpet saying, 'write in a book what you see and send it to the seven churches'" (Rev. 1:10-11). The call of God to God's tasks comes in many and various ways.

For Isaiah, the call to go perform a work for the Lord came while he was in the temple. One might speculate if something unusual had happened to Isaiah that day, or if it was simply God's will that in the year King Uzziah died, Isaiah would see the Lord high and lifted up. Do we today expect to hear God's voice and see God's presence high and lifted up, as Isaiah did? What keeps today's people in a state of expectation to hear the word of God?

II. Isaiah's individual call is extended to the nation.

You may have noticed the unusual ordering of today's lesson. First, we have the account given of Isaiah's call or charge to ministry. Second, we have Isaiah's words from chapter 1 that are spoken to the people of Jerusalem, and presumably all of Judah. It appears the people are keeping the worship calendar, but their hearts and actions do not befit true faith.

Thus, the Lord says, "Your new moons and your appointed festivals my soul hates; they have become a burden to me, I am weary of bearing them" (1:14). Though the people's worship may conform outwardly to proper liturgy, there is something missing in their devotion. How are we guilty today of taking worship for granted and simply going through the motions? Does being at church really make us better simply by attending?

III. Isaiah calls a nation to repentance.

Notice in Isaiah's call to repentance the action verbs he uses: wash, make, remove, cease, learn, seek, rescue, defend, and plead. Out of Isaiah's worship experience and call, is a command to the nation of Judah to action. They are to hear the word of God in a new way that will convict their lives and hearts to performance on behalf of others. Worship is to form and make Christians. It also is where we get our direction for lives of faith and the works that follow. Good works only follow a faith informed by the true worship of God. How does our worship inspire us to be disciples of Christ? Can you think of other ways God makes us holy people?

IV. True worship reflects true repentance.

In Isaiah's call, more than the conviction of unclean lips is at stake. There is the matter of forgiveness. In his temple experience, Isaiah is reassured that his sins have been blotted out. Thus, if it is trustworthy that true worship reflects true repentance, then the converse is also surely true. True repentance reflects true worship. Our action, both in worship and in the faith our worship represents, go hand in hand. Our service to God is in our service to God's people—those so outlined in our lesson today. How do we serve God and others? Does worship sustain us in this difficult human activity?

Helping Class Members Act

As a class, look at your church's usual order of worship. List the ways we can make worship come alive for our people by using their senses in the worship experience.

Planning for Next Sunday

The nation is in danger. Have your class continue thinking about Isaiah and his prophecy by reading and studying Isaiah 7:2-6, 10-17.

Only God Can Protect

Background Scripture: Isaiah 7:2-6, 10-17

The Main Question

Next Sunday will be a red-letter day in the life of our church. This is because we are going to baptize twins. The mother has called, in her anxious state, at least six times to make certain everything will be just right. Since her father is a United Methodist pastor and has served faithfully for over forty years, this is an especially grand time for their family, too.

The young woman has helped me plan the order of service and even requested four hymns, although she said we could choose three out of the four, since we typically sing three. She has been adamant about one part of the service, however, and that is the announcement "At the Birth of a Child." Here are the words from *The United Methodist Hymnal:*

Hail the day on which a child, (name), was born. Rejoice! Let us all sing and her that gave birth to a (son/daughter) for whom she longed. Greet this day with joy. Our hearts are glad! (The Masai people, Kenya and Tanzania, *The United Methodist Hymnal,* 1989, 146)

Few moments in the life of the church stir emotions as do the holy times when we celebrate the baptism of a child—or in our case this week, the baptisms of two children into the community of faith. It is a powerful reminder that we are indeed saved by God's grace. I like the quote I once heard about the birth of children: "Every time a child is born, God gives the world another chance."

Hope and faith go hand in hand. This will be the essence of our lesson today. What is it that can give faithful people hope? How can believers take the hope that is within them and share it with a world of despair?

Selected Scripture

King James Version	New Revised Standard Version
Isaiah 7:2-6, 10-17	*Isaiah 7:2-6, 10-17*
2 And it was told the house of David, saying, Syria is confederate with Ephraim. And his heart was moved, and the heart of his people, as the trees of the wood are moved with the wind.	2 When the house of David heard that Aram had allied itself with Ephraim, the heart of Ahaz and the heart of his people shook as the trees of the forest shake before the wind.
3 Then said the LORD unto Isaiah, Go forth now to meet Ahaz, thou, and Shearjashub thy son, at the end of the conduit of the upper pool in the highway of the fuller's field;	3 Then the LORD said to Isaiah, Go out to meet Ahaz, you and your son Shear-jashub, at the end of the conduit of the upper pool on the highway to the Fuller's Field, 4 and say to him, Take heed, be quiet, do
4 And say unto him, Take heed,	

389

and be quiet; fear not, neither be fainthearted for the two tails of these smoking firebrands, for the fierce anger of Rezin with Syria, and of the son of Remaliah.

5 Because Syria, Ephraim, and the son of Remaliah, have taken evil counsel against thee, saying,

6 Let us go up against Judah, and vex it, and let us make a breach therein for us, and set a king in the midst of it, *even* the son of Tabeal;

....

10 Moreover the LORD spake again unto Ahaz, saying,

11 Ask thee a sign of the LORD thy God; ask it either in the depth, or in the height above.

12 But Ahaz said, I will not ask, neither will I tempt the LORD.

13 And he said, Hear ye now, O house of David; *Is it* a small thing for you to weary men, but will ye weary my God also?

14 Therefore the Lord himself shall give you a sign; Behold, a virgin shall conceive, and bear a son, and shall call his name Immanuel.

15 Butter and honey shall he eat, that he may know to refuse the evil, and choose the good.

16 For before the child shall know to refuse the evil, and choose the good, the land that thou abhorest shall be forsaken of both her kings.

17 The LORD shall bring upon thee, and upon thy people, and upon thy father's house, days that have not come, from the day that Ephraim departed from Judah; *even* the king of Assyria.

Key Verse: **And say unto him, Take heed, and be quiet; fear not, neither be fainthearted for the two tails of these smoking firebrands, for the fierce anger of Rezin with Syria, and of the son of Remaliah.**

not fear, and do not let your heart be faint because of these two smoldering stumps of firebrands, because of the fierce anger of Rezin and Aram and the son of Remaliah.

5 Because Aram—with Ephraim and the son of Remaliah—has plotted evil against you, saying, 6 Let us go up against Judah and cut off Jerusalem and conquer it for ourselves and make the son of Tabeel king in it.

....

10 Again the LORD spoke to Ahaz, saying, 11 Ask a sign of the LORD your God; let it be deep as Sheol or high as heaven. 12 But Ahaz said, I will not ask, and I will not put the LORD to the test. 13 Then Isaiah said: "Hear then, O house of David! Is it too little for you to weary mortals, that you weary my God also? 14 Therefore the Lord himself will give you a sign. Look, the young woman is with child and shall bear a son, and shall name him Immanuel. 15 He shall eat curds and honey by the time he knows how to refuse the evil and choose the good. 16 For before the child knows how to refuse the evil and choose the good, the land before whose two kings you are in dread will be deserted. 17 The LORD will bring on you and on your people and on your ancestral house such days as have not come since the day that Ephraim departed from Judah—the king of Assyria."

Key Verse: **And say to him, Take heed, be quiet, do not fear, and do not let your heart be faint because of these two smoldering stumps of firebrands, because of the fierce anger of Rezin and Aram and the son of Remaliah.**

As You Read the Scripture

Isaiah 7:2-6, 10-17. Our lesson's context is the Syro-Ephraimite War (734-733 B.C.E.). King Uzziah has died and the mantle of leadership has fallen on his grandson Ahaz. The text falls into three parts. Verse 2 gives account of the political situation. Verses 3-6 record Isaiah's warning to Ahaz commanded by God. Verses 10-17 provide a word of salvation to the king, via the sign of Immanuel. In a world of desperation, these are hope-filled words.

Verse 2. The phrase "house of David" refers to the monarchy of Judah. Aram is Syria, joining forces with Ephraim, or Israel. Judah is shaken with fear, since the forces against it are considerable.

Verses 3-6. These verses give the word that the Lord commands Isaiah to speak. Isaiah is to take his son, having the ghastly name Shear-jashub—meaning "only a remnant will return"—and meet the king. The place specified, at the end of the conduit of the upper pool on the highway to the Fuller's Field, is a public place. Evidently, more than the king is to hear Isaiah's words.

The words are to be of comfort and hope. The king and his nation are visibly shaken, for in view of the armies that could march against them, the odds are against Judah surviving this onslaught. The Syro-Ephraimites plotted against Judah, planning a puppet government with "the son of Tabeel king in it." Second Kings 16:1-20 gives another version of Judah's political predicament.

Verses 10-12. The Lord speaks again to the reluctant Ahaz, notorious for his idolatry and shrewd ability to form beneficial military alliances protecting himself. Isaiah invites him to seek a sign of the Lord "deep as Sheol or high as heaven." Such is Isaiah's faith in Yahweh.

The king says, "I will not ask, and I will not put the Lord to the test." Hebrew religious culture forbids putting God to the test. For examples of God putting people to the test see Exodus 20:20 and Genesis 22:1. Given what we know about Ahaz's fidelity, his profession is a self-serving dodge, at best.

Verse 13. Isaiah's response shows prophetic irritation with Ahaz. Isaiah begins by saying, "Hear then, O house of David!" suggesting Ahaz wearies mortals and God. Isaiah proposes even ever-patient God is fatigued by Ahaz's lack of conviction.

Verses 14-17. Often these verses are picked up in Christian theology foreshadowing the Messiah's birth. It is important here, though, to let Hebrew scripture speak its own word. The original intended meaning may be closer to either a promise or a threat to the king, and therefore, to the nation.

Either way, the mater is Yahweh's, not the king in power at the moment. The Lord will give a sign and will determine the time. The promise is that no matter what happens in the short term, God will be with the faithful in the long term.

The Scripture and the Main Question

What is it that can give faithful people hope? How can believers take the hope within them and share it with a world of despair? How do the promises of God guide and direct our lives, informing decisions we must make?

FOURTH QUARTER

A Despairing King

In times of crisis, a leader has the opportunity to be hero or goat, depending on the crisis' outcome. Aram, which was Syria, had entered into an alliance with Ephraim or the Northern Kingdom. This news could spell military torment for Judah. When Ahaz and his court heard about the alliance, they—and the whole nation of Judah—"shook as trees of the forest shake before the wind." Thus, the story tells us the people had reason to despair; Judah was obviously in danger!

Each of us experience times when life is going smoothly and suddenly a change of circumstance occurs and life dramatically changes. When I was a student-intern in West Africa, our supervisor died, leaving no one to issue our stipends. This could have caused us despair had it not been for missionaries and Africans who helped make arrangements for our daily bread.

In light of Judah's predicament, Ahaz is forced, perhaps by those inside Judah, to enter into an alliance against Syria and Israel. Because panic reigned, the king made an expedient decision, but one that was not in Judah's long-term self-interest. Biblical history tells us in 721 B.C.E. the Northern Kingdom disappears from history. King Ahaz and his desperate nation needed a word of hope.

The Word of the Prophet

Isaiah knows what Ahaz seems to have forgotten in his terror: Judah is a people of faith. Isaiah knows when humans put trust in human beings, neglecting Yahweh, they will be disappointed. Humans tend to protect their self-interest.

Yahweh calls Isaiah to deliver a hope-filled word to the king, and thereby, to the whole nation. Isaiah takes his son to a specific place and delivers the prophecy. The prophecy is symbolically tied to the child's name, Shear-jashub, which means "a remnant shall return" or "only a remnant shall return." However the prophecy is interpreted, it is one of judgment and hope. Judgment, for a remnant indicates for the majority there will be tragic consequences for the nation's actions. The prophecy is hopeful, in that, the faithful return to the land of promise. Seeing Isaiah's ominously named son, as the people hear the prophecy, reinforces Isaiah's word at the conduit of the upper pool. This is the prophecy's vivid, living illustration.

Isaiah's word contains both the terror of judgment and the hope of judgment. Isaiah is neither an uncritical lover of the chosen people, but neither is he simply an unloving critic. His prophecy has elements of both verdict and promise. The verdict comes upon a people who have been warned again and again about the repercussions of living life apart from God. There will be an element of judgment on the people: Life will change dramatically, and in unforeseen ways. In the midst of this contrary judgment there will also be mercy because some will return.

We tend to hold onto the negative and the horrifying aspects of life. Ordinary events are rarely discussed at the family meal. Usually, it is the novel that is noticed among us. The 10:00 p.m. news is an example. How often do we see customary events on our local news? Rather, we see a steady stream of rapes, murders, and robberies. What sustains people in the midst of negative reports about people living around us?

A twentieth-century German philosopher, Ludwig Wittgenstein, said only creatures having language are capable of thoughts or beliefs. Because human beings are self-conscious and have a language, they look beyond the moment for future redemptive hope. Hope comforts people of faith in moments of despair. Isaiah suggests, to the people and the king, that hope lies beyond expedient military alliances. This realistic hope is properly centered in Yahweh. Paul in his hymn to love says much the same thing: "And now faith, hope, and love abide, these three; and the greatest of these is love" (1 Cor. 13:13). I like the twist Harrell Beck once put on these words while preaching, "If love is the cake, then surely hope is the icing on the cake." Hope is a deep and abiding trust, helping us face uncertain futures, ousting our own natural despair.

Isaiah's Ancient Word for Us

What is it that can give faithful people hope? This is a question just beneath the surface of much glib talk of faith. When life goes as expected, we rarely question life's goodness. The moment, however, when death or any other unplanned and uninvited event invades our life, this question rears its head.

A close friend pastored a rural church in Red Oak, Texas, for four years. After two years, he noticed each time he celebrated a funeral, three older community women would attend. In fact, his curiosity was prodded when they attended a funeral of an elderly man, nearly a hundred years old, who had not lived in the community for many years. So my friend asked them, "Why do you three attend every funeral in the Red Oak Funeral Home?"

They replied: "We never hear preachers talk about hope, except at funerals and we are old now. We need hope every week and that is why we come."

If we were better at describing the common lives we lead, we might say something similar. Life, even in its most ordinary guises, is difficult. To live life abundantly, we need words of hope. This is especially true when life disappoints and crushes. We know too well, if we live long enough, moments come when our decision toward life wavers between hope and despair.

Despair proceeds from a number of sources. Teen suicide rates for our twentieth century tell us that living as a teen today is not devoid of burden. Teens grapple with many issues other generations have missed, or at least had ways with which to cope. Contemplating suicide gives up on future's hope. To have such a view of life, especially in one's early years, indicates how uncharitable life can be to today's young people. Isaiah's word is no matter how bleak the future looks, there is always hope, for God never gives upon God's people.

In marriage, too, people can simply surrender. I remember one writer saying people often commit psychological suicide within marriage. He said, even though people do not legally divorce each other, they go their separate ways, never formally ending the marriage, but never passing beyond a silent truce, each minding his or her own affairs independently. Is this marriage in the Christian sense? Isaiah's word again speaks to the modern faithful: Relationship with God is a relationship of trust with the future in God's hand.

Placing Our Trust in God's Promise

God's word to Ahaz is an appropriate word today. People of faith put their trust neither in themselves nor in other people. People of faith do not put their trust in their own strength, intelligence, or ability to cope with life. People of faith, however, put their trust in God, for God is our hope.

The rite of infant baptism is an explicit expression of hope in any congregation's worship life. In the midst of a group of God's people, parents and other believers make vows for an infant, who obviously has no remote idea of what is happening. The infant also has none of the religious feelings normally associated with coming into salvation through Christ. Infant baptism is a fair illustration of John Wesley's prevenient grace—grace that runs before us meeting us at life's need.

The gospel world is a world of children. Jesus shocked his original hearers when he said, "Let the little children come to me; do not stop them; for it is to such as these that the kingdom of God belongs" (Mark 10:14). Infant baptism confirms the God who takes care of those who cannot care for themselves and from the Christian's and Isaiah's perspective, this is all of us!

Later in the prophecy, Isaiah endorses this perspective of childlike faith by saying, "For a child has been born for us, a son given to us; authority rests upon his shoulders; and he is named Wonderful Counselor, Mighty God, Everlasting Father, Prince of Peace" (Isa. 9:6). And again, Isaiah says, "and a little child shall lead them" (Isa. 11:6). Is it any wonder our text today ends with yet another picture of this kind of kingdom, not of flesh and blood, but rather of a God who gives a sign like this: a "young woman is with child and shall bear a son, and shall name him Immanuel." This is the hope the people of God can envision when in the bowels of despair.

Helping Adults Become Involved

Preparing to Teach

The issue for today's class is, how does hope become an article of faith in a world that seems to be crumbling around us? The historical situation in Judah in the eighth century B.C.E. will give us insight into situations we face today. To prepare to teach this lesson, a good understanding of the precise historical situation in Judah will be essential. For background, you will want to read both the lesson for today, Isaiah 7, and another historical perspective in 2 Kings 16. Each chapter will help round out the telling and understanding the other.

This outline will help present the material to the class:

    I. Life's circumstances often seem to conspire against us.
    II. God gives God's promise throughout scripture.
    III. People often hide behind religious cliches.
    IV. The sign God gives is relationship.

As you prepare this lesson you will want to use all the research materials at your disposal: Bible dictionaries, chronological lists of Israel's rulers, and maps. You will also want to consult a biblical commentary. It will put the characters and historical circumstances in a more orderly fashion than you will get by simply studying the lesson by itself.

Introducing the Main Question

After beginning your class with a prayer, have a member read Isaiah 7:2-6. Then help the class put these verses into historical context. Then read Isaiah

7:10-17. Discuss the element of hope found in each part of the prophecy. Divide your class into two parts; one taking the side of Ahaz and his practical, political approach, the other the hope-filled, prophetic word of Isaiah. Think of this division in today's world.

Developing the Lesson

I. Life's circumstances often seem to conspire against us.

The case could be made, at least by those in Judah, that the political events surrounding their lives and country had little to do with them. They are caught by circumstances beyond their control. What part of the responsibility should fall on Judah and on the king for the nation's predicament? What part of our nation's present woes could be laid at our own feet? How does our faith help us cope when it seems as though life's circumstances are unfair? Do you find it easier to give words of comfort or receive words of comfort?

II. God gives God's promise throughout scripture.

An old bumper sticker says, "When God seems far away, ask yourself, who moved?" Isaiah throughout his prophecy calls the people back to justice and righteousness. The nation has been enjoying relative prosperity, but some in Judah—the young, old, and poor—have suffered greatly. No one seems to have noticed. For a nation on the brink of despair, however, Isaiah reminds them the God of promise, their God, is still willing to show mercy to a remnant, even though many of them will suffer. These are still God's people, however, and God has promised to be merciful. How, in today's world, does God show mercy? Can your class identify some places in our Bible where God has promised deliverance to God's people, when all apparently *looked* lost?

III. People often hide behind religious cliches.

King Ahaz says he will not put the Lord to the test, but the context of our lesson implies this is an insincere evasion of the matter before him. Talk about ways in which we sidestep our religious obligations by using one pious phrase or another. When tragedy strikes, how do you respond when someone says, "Well, it must be God's will"? Can you cite any Bible texts where it is God's will that innocent people suffer? Talk about how pious religious phrases sometimes subvert the comfort that real faith offers.

IV. The sign God gives is relationship.

Throughout Hebrew history, whenever a community crisis developed, God raised up leaders. Without Moses there would have been no liberation from Egypt, without Samuel, no monarchy, and perhaps, without David, no golden age of Israel. How does God intend for the Word to be incarnate within the faith community?

Why would Isaiah's two signs to the king be wrapped in the persons of two children—his son and the child of the young woman? What kind of God is it who gives us people and relationship, rather than pat answers that seem to be easier to understand? Is this true for Jesus, who becomes messiah and savior, fully human and fully divine? What do you think?

FOURTH QUARTER

Helping Class Members Act

Discuss how your church gives hope to your immediate community—both inside and outside your congregation. How does the church give hope to a world that often looks hopeless? Why do you think the good news of the gospel is really good news? How can we share this good news with a skeptical world?

Planning for Next Sunday

Have your class read the lesson for next week from Isaiah 5:8-12, 18-23. What constitutes a fair warning? How many times should people be warned before they suffer the consequences of their actions and decisions? Do you think God's patience is infinite?

LESSON 12   AUGUST 20

Fair Warning

Background Scripture: Isaiah 5:8-12, 18-23

The Main Question

This past week I had an opportunity to talk with someone whose job it is to put fear into high school students. What kind of job is this, you might well ask. It is the job of counseling students about the effects of misusing sex, drugs, and alcohol.

As a registered nurse and a public health worker, my friend is much too sophisticated to call what she does an attempt to scare some sense into unsuspecting students. Rather, she calls it education. However we label her task, it is nonetheless to warn young people of the dangers inherent in experimenting with treacherous activities teens often look at as privileges of adulthood.

Our youth group presented her with a problem last Sunday night. Our good nurse was sharing with the senior high UMYF the resulting probabilities of premarital sex. After going through the laundry list of possible disasters when youth experiment with sex—broken marriages, teen pregnancy, AIDS, psychological trauma, and suicide—one of the young women raised her hand and asked, "Isn't it true that sometimes people can really be in love at our age? My parents married when they were teenagers and they have a wonderful marriage."

Given teen marriage statistics, this young woman's parents had beaten the odds. To have a successful marriage from the teens onward through life is a long shot, at best. Much like quitting school to play professional sports, most of us know chances for success are slim, but it is this unlikely prospect that many young people cling to, often for several disappointing years.

396

Experience is the best teacher, has been a standing cliche for the older generation for, well, generations. How can one warn the inexperienced about behavior that will almost certainly put them at risk? When is fear a good thing? "The fear of the LORD is the beginning of wisdom; all those who practice it have a good understanding. His praise endures forever" (Ps. 111:10). How and why does Isaiah use holy fear to warn his people, indeed to give them fair warning?

Selected Scripture

King James Version	New Revised Standard Version

Isaiah 5:8-12, 18-23

8 Woe unto them that join house to house, *that* lay field to field, till *there be* no place, that they may be placed alone in the midst of the earth!

9 In mine ears *said* the LORD of hosts, Of a truth many houses shall be desolate, *even* great and fair, without inhabitant.

10 Yea, ten acres of vineyard shall yield one bath, and the seed of an homer shall yield an ephah.

11 Woe unto them that rise up early in the morning, *that* they may follow strong drink; that continue until night, *till* wine inflame them!

12 And the harp, and the viol, the tabret, and pipe, and wine, are in their feasts: but they regard not the work of the LORD, neither consider the operation of his hands.

....

18 Woe unto them that draw iniquity with cords of vanity, and sin as it were with a cart rope:

19 That say, Let him make speed, *and* hasten his work, that we may see *it*: and let the counsel of the Holy One of Israel draw nigh and come, that we may know *it*!

20 Woe unto them that call evil good, and good evil; that put darkness for light, and light for darkness; that put bitter for sweet, and sweet for bitter!

Isaiah 5:8-12, 18-23

8 Ah, you who join house to house,
    who add field to field,
until there is room for no one but you
    and you are left to live alone
    in the midst of the land!

9 The LORD of hosts has sworn in my
        hearing:
Surely many houses shall be desolate,
    large and beautiful houses, without inhabitant.

10 For ten acres of vineyard shall
        yield but one bath,
    and a homer of seed shall yield a
        mere ephah.

11 Ah, you who rise early in the
        morning
    in pursuit of strong drink,
who linger in the evening
    to be inflamed by wine,

12 whose feasts consist of lyre and
        harp,
    tambourine and flute and wine,
but who do not regard the deeds of
        the LORD,
    or see the work of his hands!

....

18 Ah, you who drag iniquity along
        with cords of falsehood,
    who drag sin along a with cart
ropes,

19 who say, "Let him make haste,
    let him speed his work
        that we may see it;
let the plan of the Holy One of
        Israel hasten to fulfillment,
    that we may know it!"

20 Ah, you who call evil good and
        good evil,
    who put darkness for light

and light for darkness,
who put bitter for sweet
and sweet for bitter!

21 Woe unto *them that* are wise in their own eyes, and prudent in their own sight!

21 Ah, you who are wise in your own eyes,
and shrewd in your own sight!

22 Woe unto *them that are* mighty to drink wine, and men of strength to mingle strong drink:

22 Ah, you who are heroes in drinking wine
and valiant at mixing drink,

23 Which justify the wicked for reward, and take away the righteousness of the righteous from him!

23 who acquit the guilty for a bribe,
and deprive the innocent of their rights!

Key Verses (Isa. 1:16-17): Wash you, make you clean; put away the evil of your doings from before mine eyes; cease to do evil; Learn to do well; seek judgment, relieve the oppressed, judge the fatherless, plead for the widow.

Key Verses (Isa. 1:16-17): Wash yourselves; make yourselves clean; remove the evil of your doings from before my eyes; cease to do evil, learn to do good; seek justice, rescue the oppressed, defend the orphan, plead for the widow.

As You Read the Scripture

Isaiah 5:8-12, 18-23. Our lesson today consists of two sections of Isaiah 5, which we might characterize as a list of woes. You will, as always, want to consult several translations of this text. It is especially important today, because the text comes to us in poetic form. Different translations will help flesh out the fuller meaning of the text than any one version can.

Verses 8-10. These woes are directed toward land owners with large holdings. The issue here is economic justice. It seems that they bought property that, in turn, displaced the land's former tenants. Those who did not have the resources to purchase either land, nor put up houses, were thrown into a crisis for shelter and livelihood.

During King Uzziah's time, a monetary economy became more and more dominant. Small farmers and landowners were forced by economic realities to sell their property. When one remembers the sacredness of the land (see Lev. 25:23) to the Hebrews, then the intensity of Isaiah's prophecy is more easily understood. Also, the land will be devoid of people—a curse in terms of the Hebrew understanding of community.

The resulting prophecy is that: "For ten acres of vineyard shall yield but one bath, and a homer of seed shall yield a mere ephah" (v. 10). This is to say, as divine punishment the yield from the land will be negligible, perhaps as little as one-tenth the normally expected yield.

Verses 11-12. This part of the prophecy has to do with the luxury of the rich that allows them outward signs of success, but has warped their inner sense of righteousness and equity. Only a wealthy person could afford, in Isaiah's time, the luxury of pursuing strong drink early in the morning, when most people go to work. Poor people have to go to work. The implication here is the rich are rich because of their economic abuse of the middle class, now poor because they have been displaced from the land.

Moral laxity comes directly from those who should be faithful, but are not. They play at religion and worship, and Isaiah catalogs their worship instruments.

But these persons, celebrating the (sacred?) feasts, "do not regard the deeds of the LORD, or see the work of his hands!" In other words, their perception of who God is and what God does has been clouded by their own ease of life.

Verses 18-23. These concluding verses are woes against the various guilty ones in Judah. One group makes light of God's power saying, "Let him speed his work that we may see it," not realizing that they will soon see what they least expect—the total collapse of their comfortable lives.

Another group in Judah has reversed evil and goodness, while another has become wise in its own eyes, apart from the ways of Yahweh. Some have become "heroes in drinking wine and valiant at mixing drink," selling the innocent for money to buy drink. Not only this, but those who have been given authority to administer law in Jerusalem and Judah are being bought off by the guilty.

The picture of Jerusalem and Judah painted by Isaiah in this prophecy is not a faithful one. As the people will soon see, there will be a dear price to be paid for their indiscretion.

The Scripture and the Main Question

How can warning about conduct that will almost certainly put people at risk be given? When is fear a good thing? How does Isaiah employ holy fear to warn his people?

Fair Warning's Context

It is important to understand the context of our lesson today, because context often determines a particular set of words' meaning. For instance, we all know the tenderness usually associated with the words "I love you." Imagine, if you will for a moment, the many and various ways these three words could be spoken, altering their meaning. Spoken by a couple celebrating a sixtieth wedding anniversary, these words may be radically different than spoken between two persons who are "looking for love in all the wrong places," as an old country-and-western song puts it.

The other day, as I was passing through our church office, I heard one of the secretaries say over the phone, "I love you, too." I was shocked, because I was unaccustomed to hearing that intimate phrase used over the phone in our church office. Seeing my surprise, I was told that it was Mrs. Sharkey on the phone, a resident at the Wesleyan Retirement Home across the street from our church. That put a whole different twist on the conversation I was imagining. I only wish we had more people calling our church office like Mrs. Sharkey!

The first seven verses in Isaiah 5 are called the song of the unfruitful vineyard. In a nutshell, it could be described as God's love song to a sinful people—the people of God called the southern kingdom. In a manner much like Hosea, these seven verses speak about God's fidelity to the people and the people's infidelity to God. It is, in every measure, a very sad song telling about God's broken heart at having God's love for his people scorned.

Luke 20:9-18 tells Jesus' parable of the wicked tenants. A certain landowner planted a vineyard and leased it to some tenants, going away for a time to another country. In due course, he sent three servants to collect the rent due him. Each time the servants were treated with contempt, beaten, insulted, and sent away empty-handed. Finally the owner said, "I will send my beloved son; perhaps they will respect him."

Rather than treat the son any better than his servants, the wicked tenants "threw him out of the vineyard and killed him." Jesus' point is that, since the tenants had reneged on their agreement with the owner of the vineyard, then they should be thrown off the land. One might even expect stern legal action against the tenants even to the point of death for murder.

Isaiah is making much the same point with his prophecy that will follow. The people have been given a beautiful vineyard, or garden (using Genesis terminology) in which to live—the promised land of milk and honey. In exchange for this gracious arrangement, they have only been asked to return their faithfulness to Yahweh. Isaiah says instead, "For the vineyard of the LORD of hosts is the house of Israel, and the people of Judah are his pleasant planting; he expected justice, but saw bloodshed; righteousness, but heard a cry!" (Isa. 5:7).

The People's Attitude Denounced

After Isaiah speaks about the disappointment in the people's attitude from God's perspective, the prophecy hits full stride. In the NRSV translation it begins, "Ah, you who . . . ." Other translations are helpful here, saying "Woe to those who . . ." (Revised Standard Version) and "Woe unto them that . . ." (King James Version). The Revised English Bible says, "Woe betide those who . . . ." In fact, much of the remainder of chapter 5 is a series of woes against the people of Jerusalem and Judah. It is as if the people have asked, "What is it that we have done to make God feel as though we have scorned God's love?"

The first condemnation is a denouncement about how the land is shared. In the time of Uzziah, Judah was enjoying economic prosperity. There was wealth enough for all to live in relative comfort. Rather than share the wealth, however, the prosperous have devised means of consolidating the land's ownership, placing title in the hands of a few. This economic strategy displaced persons who, heretofore, had lived on and worked the land for their daily bread. Midwestern farmers, in the 1980s and 1990s, can well identify with the plight of those who have been bought out by large agricultural corporations. This is much the same situation in eighth-century Judah.

The prophecy says, however, this attitude of the prosperous toward those who had lived on the land for years will play out in this way: "Ten acres of vineyard shall yield but one bath, and a homer of seed shall yield a mere ephah." In other words, the riches that those who had seized the land had hoped to gain will be withheld by Yahweh. Why is this utilitarian way of doing agribusiness so deplored by the prophet speaking God's word?

There are two primary reasons. First, the land represents, in a most tangible way, Yahweh's covenant with the Hebrew people. Yahweh, making a covenant promise to Abram, says, "Go from your country and your kindred and your father's house to the land that I will show you" (Gen. 12:1-2). The land, thus, has had more than simply a purely economic meaning for the people of God. *It is a sign of the covenant with Yahweh.* To play fast and loose with the land is to do the same with the covenantal relationship with Yahweh.

The second reason Isaiah deplores this misuse of the land is Judah is not simply a group of independent individuals in economic competition with one another. They are the community of faith—*the people of God.* They worship, live, and survive together, just as they were liberated together from their mutual bondage in Egypt. What has happened now, at least in Isaiah's estimation, is the new land-wealthy Hebrews are becoming like Pharaohs to their brother and sister Hebrews. Preservation of the faith community is Isaiah's plea and warning.

From verses 11-12, we might well see why Judah has lost its way. It still celebrates [sacred?] feasts with instruments of worship, but those who enjoy the feasts "do not regard the deeds of the LORD, or see the work of his hands!" They celebrate themselves and their alleged accomplishments. The people of God seem to have lost their focus. This can be particularly seen in the verses that follow, for the people now call goodness evil and evil goodness. They think it heroic to drink all night, yet forget to do justice to those who most assuredly need justice: the innocent.

The Coming Fulfillment

The last part of chapter 5 is beyond the scope of our lesson, but is important in terms of the fulfillment that is prophesied by Isaiah. From Isaiah 5:24 onward, the details of Isaiah's prediction of a foreign invasion loom. Just as the Assyrians had ravaged Samaria in 721 B.C.E., so too will a nation far away be an instrument of the Lord's judgment. Since the people have rejected the instructions of the Lord of hosts, they too will meet a fate similar to their northern counterparts. This is Isaiah's fair warning.

Today many of us take our circumstances for granted, especially the good things that make life easier for us, or so we think. Just yesterday, I was counseling with a couple who cannot pledge to our church, due to their present financial circumstances, but want to very much. They are disturbed about this. I tried to reassure them that when they got back on sounder financial ground, the church would still be here and in need of good stewards. It became clear why they were having trouble managing their money, in the course of our conversation, however. Both of them had been tempted by the debt binge, buying several large and unnecessary items. They used credit cards for instant gratification, living beyond their means. I thought about the people in Judah, living good lives, but lulled to sleep by a false sense of security that everything would always be this way. For Judah, and the young couple in my church, there always comes a time to pay the piper. Isaiah was only trying to give fair warning.

Helping Adults Become Involved

Preparing to Teach

To teach this lesson it will be important to let your class develop links between Isaiah's time and ours. This class outline will let you make this eighth-century text one that speaks to us, nearly three thousand years later. Here are the five subtopics:

    I. Human goals often backfire.
    II. People are blinded by their perceptions.
    III. Our perceptions often confuse idolatry with worship.
    IV. What goes around, comes around.
    V. Woe to all those who lose the ability to discern sweet and bitter.

To effectively teach this lesson, you as a teacher will want to help bridge the thousands of years between today's world and the one in which Isaiah lived. It is good to remember: Though outwardly cultures may change, our inner human nature is relatively constant. We are more like Judah than we like to admit.

Introducing the Main Question

Begin your class with a prayer, then introduce the song of the unfruitful vineyard (Isa. 5:1-7). Next ask your class to consider these questions: How can warning about conduct putting people at risk be given? When is fear a *good* thing? How does Isaiah employ holy fear to warn his people? Have a class member read Isaiah 5:8-12, 18-23. Explore with your class the poetic imagery used. Why is poetry so rich in its possible interpretation and why does Isaiah write this section in poetic form, rather than prose?

Developing the Lesson

I. Human goals often backfire.

Using the first three verses, have your class discuss how goals in their lives, once idealistic, were often subverted in the real world. We have all had that experience, too.

Once I met a bank president who had abruptly resigned from a lucrative position. He faced an uncertain future with no other job in sight. He simply walked into the bank one day and resigned. He told me, "I had been forced by my position and the 'powers that be' to foreclose on just one too many persons having nothing to fall back on. I had become part of a system I could not tolerate anymore. Looking in the mirror, I told myself, 'no job is worth this to my sense of decency.' "

When have any of us felt that strongly about our lives and integrity?

II. People are blinded by their perceptions.

We live in a world where we are told and shaped by what others expect and want from us. From the cars we drive to the houses we live in, someone tells us it is what we have that defines us, rather than who we are. How is it possible in our Madison Avenue world to come to a better and more balanced understanding of who we are in God's world? How do we define ourselves as the people of God today? What price is paid to be a disciple of Jesus Christ in your town or city today?

III. Our perceptions often confuse idolatry with worship.

Micah and Amos both denounce the people's worship practices in the eighth century B.C.E. "I hate, I despise your festivals, and I take no delight in your solemn assemblies. Even though you offer me your burnt offerings and grain offerings, I will not accept them; and the offerings of well-being of your fatted animals I will not look upon. Take away from me the noise of your songs; I will not listen to the melody of your harps" (Amos 5:21-23). How could we interpret Isaiah 5:12 as saying something similar? How do each of your class members examine themselves to make certain, in their worship, they do not merely go through the motions?

IV. What goes around, comes around.

Our lesson today consists of Isaiah's fair warning to the people of Jerusalem and Judah. Ask your class to explore this idea together: on descending the ladder of success, we pass those coming down we stepped on going up. How does Jesus' Golden Rule apply to relations between the haves and the have nots, especially in economic terms? Did Jerusalem and Judah get what they deserved when the Babylonians eventually carried them into exile?

V. Woe to all those who lose the ability to discern sweet and bitter.

Our self-perception is tied to our perspective on who God is. When we forget that we worship a God who rules and overrules, then we lose our place in the creation as people of faith. How does worship today help us keep our faith perspective? Why was regular worship so essential to the Hebrew's identity? How can worship remain vital in our secular world today? What does your class think?

Helping Class Members Act

Have your class members reflect on times when they have tried to warn their friends or family members about behavior that could prove dangerous. When have others tried to issue similar warnings to us? How much fair warning do any of us really deserve?

Planning for Next Sunday

Next Sunday the lesson is about the fall of Samaria, the northern kingdom. Have your class read and pray over the text in 2 Kings 17:6-14.

Disobedience Brings Destruction

Background Scripture: 2 Kings 17:6-14

The Main Question

There is a saying that goes, "Those who live by the sword, die by the sword." Our lesson from 2 Kings 17:6-14 is about a people who have spurned the words of God for several generations. In this biblical history there is a cycle that seems to repeat itself. It goes something like this: the people are blessed, the people reject the blessing, divine warnings are issued, often by spokespeople for God, and then punishment is exacted after multiple warnings.

This issue of multiple warnings reminds me of a story I tell my six-year-old dare-devil son who likes to do dangerous bicycle tricks. Once there was a little boy, appropriately about six years of age, who rode his bike by his parents as they were sitting out in their front yard. The first time he rode by, he shouted, "Look mom, no hands!" The second time he rode by, he shouted, "Look dad, no feet!" The third time he rode by, he shouted, "Look mom and dad, no teeth!" As the little boy's parents repeatedly warned him about doing dangerous tricks, because the tricks would hurt him, so too, do the people of Israel learn their hard lesson: Disobedience brings destruction.

As religious people, many of us have been warned in church for years about the day of reckoning, or the judgment day. A day of judgment is when life's accounts, so to speak, all come due. There is something about people, however, which makes us want to live dangerously, whether we are six or sixty. Though we know better, no number of cautions or warnings will compel us to change our courses of action. Why are human beings this way? Is there something in our character that makes us so stubborn as to be dangerous to ourselves?

Looking back over the history of the Northern Kingdom in our lesson today, can we in the twentieth century learn from others' mistakes? Judah, only 140 years later, apparently did not learn from their northern counterpart's errors. The Southern Kingdom fell to Babylon, not learning much from the experience of Israel. Are we any different these many centuries later? Can modern people understand God's judgment as a tool of God's discipline?

Selected Scripture

King James Version	New Revised Standard Version

2 Kings 17:6-14

6 In the ninth year of Hoshea the king of Assyria took Samaria, and carried Israel away into Assyria, and placed them in Halah and in Habor *by* the river of Gozan, and in the cities of the Medes.

7 For *so* it was, that the children of Israel had sinned against the LORD their God, which had brought them up out of the land of Egypt, from under the hand of Pharaoh king of Egypt, and had feared other gods.

8 And walked in the statues of the heathen, whom the LORD cast out from before the children of Israel, and of the kings of Israel, which they had made.

9 And the children of Israel did secretly *those* things that *were* not right against the LORD their God, and they built them high places in all their cities, from the tower of the watchman to the fenced city.

10 And they set them up images and groves in every high hill, and under every green tree:

11 And there they burnt incense in all the high places, as *did* the hea-

2 Kings 17:6-14

6 In the ninth year of Hoshea the king of Assyria captured Samaria; he carried the Israelites away to Assyria. He placed them in Halah, on the Habor, the river of Gozan, and in the cities of the Medes.

7 This occurred because the people of Israel had sinned against the LORD their God, who had brought them up out of the land of Egypt from under the hand of Pharaoh king of Egypt. They had worshiped other gods 8 and walked in the customs of the nations whom the LORD drove out before the people of Israel, and in the customs that the kings of Israel had introduced. 9 The people of Israel secretly did things that were not right against the LORD their God. They built for themselves high places at all their towns, from watchtower to fortified city; 10 they set up for themselves pillars and sacred poles on every high hill and under every green tree; 11 there they made offerings on all the high places, as the nations did whom the LORD carried away

then whom the LORD carried away before them; and wrought wicked things to provoke the LORD to anger:

12 For they served idols, whereof the LORD had said unto them, Ye shall not do this thing.

13 Yet the LORD testified against Israel, and against Judah, by all the prophets, *and by* all the seers, saying, Turn ye from your evil ways, and keep my commandments *and* my statutes, according to all the law which I commanded your fathers, and which I sent to you by my servants the prophets.

14 Notwithstanding they would not hear, but hardened their necks, like to the neck of their fathers, that did not believe in the LORD their God.

Key Verse: **Yet the LORD testified against Israel, and against Judah, by all the prophets, *and by* all the seers, saying, Turn ye from your evil ways, and keep my commandments *and* my statutes, according to all the law which I commanded your fathers, and which I sent to you by my servants the prophets.**

before them. They did wicked things, provoking the LORD to anger; 12 they served idols, of which the LORD had said to them, "You shall not do this." 13 Yet the LORD warned Israel and Judah by every prophet and every seer, saying, "Turn from your evil ways and keep my commandments and my statutes, in accordance with all the law that I commanded your ancestors and that I sent to you by my servants the prophets." 14 They would not listen but were stubborn, as their ancestors had been, who did not believe in the LORD their God.

Key Verse: **Yet the LORD warned Israel and Judah by every prophet and every seer, saying, "Turn from your evil ways and keep my commandments and my statutes, in accordance with all the law that I commanded your ancestors and that I sent to you by my servants the prophets."**

As You Read the Scripture

2 Kings 17:6-14. Our lesson today narrates the final death notice of the Northern Kingdom of Israel, under its last king, Hoshea. Verses 1-6 set the historical context, while verses 7-14 give us the theological conclusion for this peculiar judgment coming to pass.

Verse 6. The approximate date of Assyria's conquest of Samaria, or the Northern Kingdom of Israel, is given as "in the ninth year of Hoshea." It is at this point in Israel's history that her ten tribes vanish from history, being carried into exile, never returning to the land of promise. Probably 10 percent of the population, that is, the most influential and well-educated, were in fact carried away. This cream of the crop portion consisted of the nation's leadership. This was an Assyrian technique of domination, effectively crippling Israel.

Verses 7-8. These verses begin a retrospective theological explanation regarding the momentous events that the historical books of Kings have described. Many scholars call this the Deuteronomic interpretation of history. Our passage makes explicit theologically what the narrative has suggested in its storytelling. Theological history is disclosed from the faith perspective rather than from the factual point of view we normally associate with objective history. It is history written to make a statement of faith more than to relate dates and places. Luke and Acts are both types of theological history with which most of us are familiar.

The chosen people in 2 Kings have turned their collective backs on Yahweh "who had brought them up out of the land of Egypt from under the hand of Pharaoh king of Egypt." These people had forgotten the God of their forebears and worshiped other gods, no doubt encouraged by Israel's long sequence of unfaithful kings.

Verses 9-12. The writer gives a list, in these verses, of specific deeds of the people's unrighteousness against their God. Thee things were done in secret, a tongue-in-cheek metaphor, as if anything could be hidden from the all-seeing Yahweh. Their offenses centered around worshiping idols set up against the divine prohibition of Yahweh in the Torah or teaching of the Hebrew people: "Thou shalt have no other gods before me." (See Exodus 20 and Deuteronomy 5 for other prohibitions in the Ten Commandments.)

The impetus for idol worship comes from other nations and Israel's desire to be like them. Whenever Israel wants to be like other nations they forget who they are as a distinctive people of God—the chosen people! It was this longing to be like other nations that gave Israel the gift of the monarchy, which, from one part of the biblical perspective, was the beginning of Israel's problems with self-identity and nationhood in the first place (see 1 Sam. 8:6-22).

Verses 12-14. Described here, as in most of the prophetic writings, is the warning to the people that was issued repeatedly by God. There was no lack of warning for the people. Yahweh had sent the Lord's servants, prophet after prophet, to warn the people, yet "they would not listen but were stubborn." The conclusion is that essentially, much like those who had gone before them, the people now would not believe in the promises of Yahweh. The result was the end of a nation. Their disobedience had brought about their destruction. This message is clear.

The Scripture and the Main Question

Looking back over the history of the Northern Kingdom, in our lesson today, can twentieth-century people learn from Israel's mistakes? Are we really any different, these many centuries later? How can people begin to understand judgment as a tool of God's discipline? Does this text bring to mind any idolatrous sacred poles or pillars that we set up and worship today?

Today's Decisions

Perhaps one of the greatest myths Christians must overcome is that faith is simply future oriented. However we understand faith, and it does have a future thrust to be sure, faith is also a condition of the *here* and *now*. Both the present and future are tied together in a person's faith. Faith active and alive today will shape the future to which people are all aimed. The writer of 2 Kings also binds the past to both the future and present thrust of faith, reminding the Israelites they had sinned against the Lord "who had brought them up out of the land of Egypt from under the hand of Pharaoh king of Egypt. They had worshiped other gods" (v. 7). Thus, one can well say, from the biblical perspective, the faith decisions made yesterday and today will determine tomorrow's future.

I remember reading with interest a story some years ago about a preacher's wife who had bought a number of lottery tickets. This was not a problem for the preacher, until she hit a big jackpot of over a million dollars. As the couple won the lottery, they also lost their ministry. His church, from a small independent denomination, forced him to resign his pastorate because of his gambling. There are many decisions we make today affecting life tomorrow. For this pastor and his wife, conceivably the million dollars helped ease the pain of resignation, but how many times do we make seemingly innocent decisions that will later have grave consequences for our lives? This pastor's life changed dramatically with the pick of a number. How many of us play the lottery game with God? One could easily make the case from our text today that Israel certainly did and lost.

Israel's Idol Lottery

The first six verses of 2 Kings 17 describe the political lottery in which the king of Israel was investing heavily. Hoshea, son of Elah, had entered into a political alliance with Assyria's King Shalmaneser. Hoshea was to pay tribute to him annually in return for political protection. This arrangement worked for a season. Israel paid tribute and Israel was protected. Over time, though, the text says Hoshea tried to strike a deal with Egypt, failing to pay the annual tribute due Assyria. It seems as though King Hoshea is playing the two political powers off against one another. Hoshea will learn the dear price to be paid by playing one superpower off against another. This is also an indication of Israel's religious and covenantal problem, as well.

As the strategy of playing two ends against the middle in the political arena proved disastrous, so does this strategy prove the undoing of Israel in its sacred life. In fact, our text from verse 7 forward details the failure of Samaria, or Israel, in its national worship life. It is stated in the text, "This occurred because . . ." so no one misses the point being made. Israel worships other gods, as if to hedge a bet, just in case more protection is needed than Yahweh could provide. By doing so, the people lapse into idolatry, one of the principal prohibitions of Israel's Torah. They were called to pay for this decision, for like all people, the decisions made by them yesterday and today will determine tomorrow's future. For Israel, this text spells out the disastrous future in bold, bleak strokes.

Jesus Issues Warnings

For some illogical reason, many people think judgment day or a day of reckoning is perpetually out in a future beyond us. Those who genuinely understand the biblical faith, however, know that judgment is with us always. Now. An example of this is in Matthew 25, when Jesus tells a story called the ten maidens. It begins, "Then the kingdom of heaven will be like this. Ten bridesmaids took their lamps and went to meet the bridegroom. Five of them were foolish, and five were wise. When the foolish took their lamps, they took no oil with them; but the wise took flasks of oil with their lamps" (Matt. 25:1-4).

A foremost point of Jesus' parable, among several, is that some are prepared and some are not prepared for the coming of the Lord. Our preparations for God's coming are not made at the last moment, but are made in our prudent anticipation because no one knows the day nor the hour when the Lord's coming will occur. It is in the daily and hourly faith decisions that faithful people prepare for the future.

According to our text, the people of Samaria have been warned time and again by the servants of God, the prophets. Yet, the people disregarded these warnings as frequently as they were discharged. In a sense, the people have no one to blame but themselves. True devotion does not consist of last-minute arrangements. True devotion consists in the steady and habitual attendance to the holy things of God.

Devotion for Today

Several years ago, believe it or not, there was a refreshingly honest and frank television commercial. It was for an oil filter company whose message was, take care of the little things on your automobile today, or later you would have to take care of big things. The tag line was: "You can pay me now, or you can pay me later." The implication was that an ounce of prevention is worth a pound of cure. In a sense, the judgment on Samaria was they had not attended to the things of God. They had been furnished plenty of warning from the prophets, but the people had not heeded the word of caution. Their disobedience spells their destruction.

One of the unsettling prospects for our nation today and tomorrow is how we are going to deal with our national debt. Any politician who wants to deal directly to solve the debt problem seems unable to get elected. Those elected do not seem willing to make the hard decisions necessary to resolve the national debt dilemma. Sooner or later, however, we will have to face up to the financial quandary in which we have been mired now for some two decades. We can pay now or we can pay later.

Our religious lives are similar in terms of the hard decisions we are called to make regularly. Many of the resolutions we make in light of our faith are not easy, nor are they comfortable, but they must be made nonetheless. Are we any different these many centuries later from the people in King Hoshea's time? How can we begin to understand judgment as a tool of God's correction? The religious and faith decisions we make today and yesterday will determine tomorrow's future. Judgment occurs in the past, present, and future—but not simply and exclusively in the future!

Helping Adults Become Involved

Preparing to Teach

As the teacher, you will want to be familiar with 2 Kings 17:1-14, for both the historical and theological basis for the Samarians' exile. A helpful exercise would be finding maps of Assyria and Samaria during the time of King Hoshea, about 732–721 B.C.E. Be prepared to show where the exiles went when leaving the Northern Kingdom and transported to Assyria. Also, can you imagine some of today current events as judgments on nations unfaithful in decisions made by their leaders on behalf of a whole country?

This outline will help you move through today's lesson:

    I. The people of Israel sinned against God.
    II. Idolatry bypasses the living God.
    III. The Lord had constantly warned the people of Israel.
    IV. Belief in God is a willingness to listen.

Idolatry is alive and well in today's world. Reflect on your personal experiences. When have you been tempted to search for God in the wrong places or in the wrong things? How can Americans view ourselves as a chosen nation? Can you think of instances when loyalty to our nation became idolatrous? Since this issue of idolatry and judgment is an issue for each and every generation of Christians, you will want to let your class explore this issue in distinctive personal ways.

Introducing the Main Question

Ask someone in your class to read today's text and its historic introductory verses, 2 Kings 17:1-14. Lift up these phrases and ideas for the class's consideration: walking in the customs of other nations, secretly doing things not right, sacred poles, making offerings on all the high places, and serving idols. Try to stimulate your class into comparing and contrasting these idolatries of the eighth century B.C.E. to our own idolatries of late twentieth-century America.

Developing the Lesson

I. The people of Israel sinned against God.

The writer of today's lesson from 2 Kings, states up front and in unmistakable language that the people of Israel were directly responsible for the Assyrian exile inflicted on them. In fact, in other Hebrew prophecies, Assyria is looked on as a tool in the hand of Yahweh. In both the political double-dealings of King Hoshea, and in the general lack of faithful worship, Israel comes up short in the devotion expected and demanded by Yahweh. In the end, they pay a dear price for trying to deceive the Assyrians and their own all-knowing, all-powerful God. They end up without the land given to them generations before, a sign of God's promise and favor. The people end, at the close of this text, homeless and landless. They are displaced people and displaced forever. If Israel's forfeiture of the land was the worst imaginable punishment for the people, what would be analogous for us today? Are any in your class willing to share where a misjudgment on their part cost them dearly?

II. Idolatry bypasses the living God.

The people's idolatry has cut off their relationship with Yahweh—the life-giver and covenant partner of Israel. In Deuteronomy 5 (and Exodus 20), the sacred law of the people has said, "I am the LORD your God, who brought you out of the land of Egypt, out of the house of slavery; you shall have no other gods before me. You shall not make for yourself an idol, whether in the form of anything that is in heaven above, or that is on the earth beneath, or that is in the water under the earth. You shall not bow down to them or worship them; for I the LORD your God am a jealous God, punishing children for the iniquity of parents, to the third and fourth generation of those who reject me, but showing steadfast love to the thousandth generation of those who love me and keep my commandments" (Deut. 5:6-10).

They have replaced their sacred relationship with God, substituting imitation, false gods for the genuine creator and liberator God. Since this is a foundational article of faith for the Hebrew people, this is not a sin done in ignorance. From the greatest to the least in Israel, idolatry is to be spurned above all other trespasses against God. Make a list on the chalkboard in your classroom of the idolatries with which members of your class must daily contend. Is the temptation to supersede God with other little gods greater or lesser today than it was in the days of Hoshea?

III. The Lord had constantly warned the people of Israel.

Two points in the text show us that Israel had received ample warnings about their sin. First, the text reminds us the Lord God, to whom they owe exclusive worship, was the one who brought them out of the land of Egypt. Second, they have been warned time and time again by God's servants, the prophets, about their infidelity to God. How many warnings are needed to serve warning?

How are people reminded today of the great things God has done for them? Does the preaching of the church today call people back to remembrance of the greatness of God? Also, as a class, think about modern prophets who issue warning to us as individuals and as a society. Are these persons seen to be eccentrics or crackpots? Do you think the prophets were seen much differently in the time of the Hebrews?

IV. Belief in God is a willingness to listen.

Our last verse in the lesson today says explicitly, "They would not listen but were stubborn, as their ancestors had been, who did not believe in the Lord their God." Thus, we might assume those who listen are those who are counted as faithful. Discuss with the class why listening to the myriad of voices, many suggesting that they alone are speaking the word of the Lord, is so difficult? How can modern people comprehend which voices are true and trustworthy?

For those with spiritual discernment, the task of listening informs all they do and are. Why is listening such a difficult gift to practice? Have you ever had someone give you the gift of listening? Does God expect us to listen to the Lord's word?

Helping Class Members Act

For many of us, our own idolatries are so close to us they are difficult to see. Encourage your class to examine the things tending to replace God as the center of their lives as they move toward next Sunday. Ask them to make a list of potential idols in their lives. Perhaps all of us will be surprised.

Planning for Next Sunday

Next Sunday we begin a new school year and a new study. The first quarter moves into the New Testament with "The Story of Christian Beginnings," lessons from the book of Acts. Ask class members to prepare by thinking about all of their beliefs about the Holy Spirit. Instruct them to be prepared to discuss their beliefs in the light of the first chapter of Acts.